THE STUDENT'S
LIFE OF WASHINGTON

LECTOR HOUSE PUBLIC DOMAIN WORKS

This book is a result of an effort made by Lector House towards making a contribution to the preservation and repair of original classic literature. The original text is in the public domain in the United States of America, and possibly other countries depending upon their specific copyright laws.

In an attempt to preserve, improve and recreate the original content, certain conventional norms with regard to typographical mistakes, hyphenations, punctuations and/or other related subject matters, have been corrected upon our consideration. However, few such imperfections might not have been rectified as they were inherited and preserved from the original content to maintain the authenticity and construct, relevant to the work. The work might contain a few prior copyright references as well as page references which have been retained, wherever considered relevant to the part of the construct. We believe that this work holds historical, cultural and/or intellectual importance in the literary works community, therefore despite the oddities, we accounted the work for print as a part of our continuing effort towards preservation of literary work and our contribution towards the development of the society as a whole, driven by our beliefs.

We are grateful to our readers for putting their faith in us and accepting our imperfections with regard to preservation of the historical content. We shall strive hard to meet up to the expectations to improve further to provide an enriching reading experience.

Though, we conduct extensive research in ascertaining the status of copyright before redeveloping a version of the content, in rare cases, a classic work might be incorrectly marked as not-in-copyright. In such cases, if you are the copyright holder, then kindly contact us or write to us, and we shall get back to you with an immediate course of action.

HAPPY READING!

THE STUDENT'S LIFE OF WASHINGTON

WASHINGTON IRVING

ISBN: 978-93-89614-73-2

Published: 1876

© 2020
LECTOR HOUSE LLP

LECTOR HOUSE LLP
E-MAIL: lectorpublishing@gmail.com

WASHINGTON AS A SURVEYOR

THE STUDENT'S
LIFE OF WASHINGTON;

CONDENSED FROM THE LARGER WORK OF

WASHINGTON IRVING.

FOR YOUNG PERSONS AND FOR THE USE OF SCHOOLS.

WITH ILLUSTRATIONS.

1876.

PUBLISHER'S NOTE.

In condensing into one compact volume Mr. Irving's elaborate Life of Washington, care has been taken to retain, not only all the important facts connected with Washington's career, but also those circumstances and incidents which may be supposed to contribute to a full estimate of his character in all its aspects. Nor have any portion of the great events connected with the era in which he filled so grand and controlling a part been unduly neglected or subordinated. The work, in its present abbreviated form, still presents a continuous and complete record of American history during the period of Washington's official life. Mr. Irving's language, as a rule, has been retained; but in cases where a variation from his sentences has been necessary, in order to secure the requisite brevity, the paragraphs are enclosed in brackets.

CONTENTS

WASHINGTON AND THE AMERICAN REVOLUTION.

CHAPTER I.

BIRTH OF WASHINGTON.—HIS BOYHOOD.

The Washington family is of an ancient English stock, the genealogy of which has been traced up to the century immediately succeeding the Conquest. Among the knights and barons who served under the Count Palatine, Bishop of Durham, to whom William the Conqueror had granted that important See, was WILLIAM DE HERTBURN. At that period surnames were commonly derived from castles or estates; and de Hertburn, in 1183, in exchanging the village of Hertburn for the manor of Wessyngton, assumed the name of DE WESSYNGTON. From this period the family has been traced through successive generations, until the name, first dropping the *de,* varied from Wessyngton to Wassington, Wasshington, and finally to Washington. The head of the family to which our Washington immediately belongs sprang from Lawrence Washington, Esq., of Gray's Inn. He was mayor of Northampton, and received a grant of the manor of Sulgrave from Henry VIII. [Sir William Washington of Packington, was his direct descendant. The Washingtons were attached to the Stuart dynasty. Lieut.-Col. James Washington perished in defence of that cause. Sir Henry Washington, son of Sir William, distinguished himself under Prince Rupert, in 1643, at the storming of Bristol; and still more, in 1646, in the defence of Worcester against the arms of Fairfax. We hear little of the Washingtons after the death of Charles I. England, during the protectorate, was an uncomfortable residence for those who had adhered to the Stuarts, and many sought refuge in other lands. Among many who emigrated to the western wilds were John and Andrew Washington, great-grandsons of the grantee of Sulgrave.]

The brothers arrived in Virginia in 1657, and purchased lands in Westmoreland County, on the northern neck, between the Potomac and Rappahannock rivers. John married a Miss Anna Pope, of the same county, and took up his residence on Bridges Creek, near where it falls into the Potomac. He became an extensive planter, and, in process of time, a magistrate and member of the House of Burgesses. Having a spark of the old military fire of the family, we find him, as Colonel Washington, leading the Virginia forces, in co-operation with those of Maryland, against a band of Seneca Indians, who were ravaging the settlements along the Potomac.

The estate continued in the family. His grandson Augustine, the father of our Washington, was born there in 1694. He was twice married; first (April 20th, 1715), to Jane, daughter of Caleb Butler, Esq., of Westmoreland County, by whom he had four children, of whom only two, Lawrence and Augustine, survived the years of childhood; their mother died November 24th, 1728, and was buried in the family vault. On the 6th of March, 1730, he married in second nuptials, Mary, the daughter of Colonel Ball, a young and beautiful girl, said to be the belle of the northern neck. By her he had four sons, George, Samuel, John Augustine, and Charles; and two daughters, Elizabeth, or Betty, as she was commonly called, and Mildred, who died in infancy.

George, the eldest, the subject of this biography, was born on the 22d of February (11th, O. S.), 1732, in the homestead on Bridges Creek. This house commanded a view over many miles of the Potomac, and the opposite shore of Maryland. Not a vestige of it remains. Two or three decayed fig trees, with shrubs and vines, linger about the place, and here and there a flower grown wild serves "to mark where a garden has been." Such at least, was the case a few years since; but these may have likewise passed away. A stone marks the site of the house, and an inscription denotes its being the birthplace of Washington.

Not long after the birth of George, his father removed to an estate in Stafford County, opposite Fredericksburg. The house stood on a rising ground overlooking a meadow which bordered the Rappahannock. This was the home of George's boyhood; but this, like that in which he was born, has disappeared.

In those days the means of instruction in Virginia were limited, and it was the custom among the wealthy planters to send their sons to England to complete their education. This was done by Augustine Washington with his eldest son Lawrence. George, as his intellect dawned, received the rudiments of education in the best establishment for the purpose that the neighborhood afforded. It was what was called, in popular parlance, an "old field school-house;" humble enough in its pretensions, and kept by one of his father's tenants named Hobby. The instruction doled out by him must have been the simplest kind, reading, writing, and ciphering, perhaps; but George had the benefit of mental and moral culture at home, from an excellent father. When he was about seven or eight years old his brother Lawrence returned from England, a well-educated and accomplished youth. There was a difference of fourteen years in their ages, which may have been one cause of the strong attachment which took place between them. Lawrence looked down with a protecting eye upon the boy whose dawning intelligence and perfect rectitude won his regard; while George looked up to his manly and cultivated brother as a model in mind and manners.

Lawrence Washington had something of the old military spirit of the family, and circumstances soon called it into action. Spanish depredations on British commerce had recently provoked reprisals. Admiral Vernon, commander-in-chief in the West Indies, had accordingly captured Porto Bello, on the Isthmus of Darien. The Spaniards were preparing to revenge the blow; the French were fitting out ships to aid them. Troops were embarked in England for another campaign in the West Indies; a regiment of four battalions was to be raised in the colonies and sent to join them at Jamaica. There was a sudden outbreak of military ardor in the province. Lawrence Washington, now twenty-two years of age, caught the infection. He obtained a captain's commission in the newly-raised regiment, and embarked with it for the West Indies in 1740. He served in the joint expeditions of Admiral Vernon and General Wentworth, and acquired the friendship and confidence of both of those officers. We have here the secret of that martial spirit so often cited of George in his boyish days. He had seen his brother fitted out for the wars. He had heard by letter and otherwise of the warlike scenes in which he was mingling. All his amusements took a military turn. He made soldiers of his school-mates; they had their mimic parades, reviews, and sham fights.

Lawrence Washington returned home in the autumn of 1742. He formed an attachment to Anne, the eldest daughter of the Honorable William Fairfax, of Fairfax Comity; his addresses were well received, and they became engaged. Their nuptials were delayed by the sudden and untimely death of his father, which took place on the 12th of April, 1743, after a short but severe attack of gout in the stomach, and when but forty-nine years of age. George had been absent from home on a visit during his father's illness, and just returned in time to receive a parting look of affection.

Augustine Washington left large possessions, distributed by will among his children. To Lawrence, the estate on the banks of the Potomac, with other real property, and several shares in iron-works. To Augustine, the second son by the first marriage, the old homestead and estate in Westmoreland. The children by the second marriage were severally well provided for, and George, when he became of age, was to have the house and lands on the Rappahannock.

In the month of July the marriage of Lawrence with Miss Fairfax took place. He now settled himself on his estate on the banks of the Potomac, to which he gave the name of MOUNT VERNON, in honor of the admiral. Augustine took up his abode at the homestead on Bridges Creek, and married Anne, daughter and co-heiress of William Aylett, Esq., of Westmoreland County.

George, now eleven years of age, and the other children of the second marriage, had been left under the guardianship of their mother, to whom was intrusted the proceeds of all their property until they should severally come of age. She proved herself worthy of the trust. Endowed with plain, direct good sense, thorough conscientiousness, and prompt decision, she governed her family strictly, but kindly, exacting deference while she inspired affection. George being her eldest son, was thought to be her favorite, yet she never gave him undue preference, and the implicit deference exacted from him in childhood continued to be habitually observed by him to the day of her death. He inherited from her a high temper and a spirit of command, but her early precepts and example taught him to restrain and govern that temper, and to square his conduct on the exact principles of equity and justice.

Having no longer the benefit of a father's instructions at home, and the scope of tuition of Hobby being too limited for the growing wants of his pupil, George was now sent to reside with Augustine Washington, at Bridges Creek, and enjoy the benefit of a superior school in that neighborhood, kept by a Mr. Williams. His education, however, was plain and practical. He never attempted the learned languages, nor manifested any inclination for rhetoric or belles-lettres. His object, or the object of his friends, seems to have been confined to fitting him for ordinary business. His manuscript school-books still exist, and are models of neatness and accuracy. Before he was thirteen years of age he had copied into a volume forms for all kinds of mercantile and legal papers; bills of exchange, notes of hand, deeds, bonds, and the like. This early self-tuition gave him throughout life a lawyer's skill in drafting documents, and a merchant's exactness in keeping accounts. He was a self-disciplinarian in physical as well as mental matters, and practised himself in all kinds of athletic exercises, such as running, leaping, wrestling, pitching quoits, and tossing bars. His frame, even in infancy, had been large and powerful, and he now excelled most of his playmates in contests of agility and strength. Above all, his inherent probity and the principles of justice on which he regulated all his conduct, even at this early period of life, were soon appreciated by his school-mates; he was referred to as an umpire in their disputes, and his decisions were never reversed. As he had formerly been military chieftain, he was now legislator of the school; thus displaying in boyhood a type of the future man.

CHAPTER II.

WASHINGTON'S YOUTH.—FIRST SURVEYING EXPEDITION.

The attachment of Lawrence Washington to his brother George seems to have acquired additional strength and tenderness on their father's death; he now took a truly paternal interest in his concerns, and had him as frequently as possible a guest at Mount Vernon. Lawrence had deservedly become a popular and leading personage in the country. He was a member of the House of Burgesses, and adjutant-general of the district, with the rank of major, and a regular salary. A frequent sojourn with him brought George into familiar intercourse with the family of his father-in-law, the Hon. William Fairfax, who resided at a beautiful seat called Belvoir, a few miles below Mount Vernon, and on the same woody ridge bordering the Potomac.

William Fairfax was a man of liberal education and intrinsic worth. Of an ancient English family in Yorkshire, he had entered the army at the age of twenty-one; had served with honor both in the East and West Indies, and officiated as governor of New Providence, after having aided in rescuing it from pirates. For some years past he had resided in Virginia, to manage the immense landed estates of his cousin, Lord Fairfax, and lived at Belvoir, in the style of an English country gentleman, surrounded by an intelligent and cultivated family of sons and daughters. An intimacy with a family like this, in which the frankness and simplicity of rural and colonial life were united with European refinement, could not but have a beneficial effect in moulding the character and manners of a somewhat home-bred school-boy.

Other influences were brought to bear on George during his visit at Mount Vernon. His brother Lawrence still retained some of his military inclinations, fostered, no doubt, by his post of adjutant-general. William Fairfax, as we have shown, had been a soldier, and in many trying scenes. Some of Lawrence's comrades of the provincial regiment, who had served with him in the West Indies, were occasional visitors at Mount Vernon; or a ship of war, possibly one of Vernon's old fleet, would anchor in the Potomac, and its officers be welcome guests at the tables of Lawrence and his father-in-law. Thus military scenes on sea and shore would become the topics of conversation. We can picture to ourselves George, a grave and earnest boy, with an expanding intellect, and a deep-seated passion for enterprise, listening to such conversations with a kindling spirit and a growing desire for military life. In this way most probably was produced that desire to enter the navy which he evinced when about fourteen years of age. The great difficulty was to procure the assent of his mother. She was brought, however, to acquiesce; a midshipman's warrant was obtained; but at the eleventh hour the mother's heart faltered. This was her eldest born. A son, whose strong and steadfast character promised to be a support to herself and a protection to her other children. The thought of his being completely severed from her, and exposed to the hardships and perils of a boisterous profession, overcame even her resolute mind, and at her urgent remonstrances the nautical scheme was given up.

To school, therefore, George returned, and continued his studies for nearly two years longer, devoting himself especially to mathematics, and accomplishing himself in those branches calculated to fit him either for civil or military service. Among these, one of the most important in the actual state of the country was land surveying. In this he schooled himself thoroughly, using the highest processes of the art; making surveys about the neighborhood, and keeping regular field books, some of which we have examined, in which the boundaries and measurements of the fields surveyed were carefully entered, and diagrams made, with a neatness and exactness as if the whole related to important land transactions instead of being mere school exercises. Thus, in his earliest days, there was perseverance and completeness in all his undertakings. Nothing was left half done, or done in a hurried and slovenly manner. The habit of mind thus cultivated continued throughout life. He took a final leave of school in the autumn of 1747, and went to reside with his brother Lawrence at Mount Vernon. Here he continued his mathematical studies and his practice in surveying. Being a favorite of Sir William Fairfax, he was now an occasional inmate of Belvoir. Among the persons at present residing there was Thomas, Lord Fairfax, cousin of William Fairfax, and of whose immense landed property the latter was the agent. Another inmate was George William Fairfax, about twenty-two years of age, the eldest son of the proprietor. He had been educated in England, and since his return had married a daughter of Colonel Carey, of Hampton, on James River. He had recently brought home his bride and her sister to his father's house.

The merits of Washington were known and appreciated by the Fairfax family. Though not quite sixteen years of age, he no longer seemed a boy, nor was he treated as such. Tall, athletic, and manly for his years, his early self-training, and the code of conduct he had devised, gave a gravity and decision to his conduct; his frankness and modesty inspired cordial regard. Lord Fairfax was a staunch fox-hunter, and kept horses and hounds in the English style. The hunting season had arrived. The neighborhood abounded with sport; but fox-hunting in Virginia required bold and skilful horsemanship. He found Washington as bold as himself in the saddle, and as eager to follow the hounds. He forthwith took him into peculiar favor; made him his hunting companion; and it was probably under the tuition of this hard-riding old nobleman that the youth imbibed that fondness for the chase for which he was afterwards remarked.

This fox-hunting intercourse was attended with important results. His lordship's possessions beyond the Blue Ridge had never been regularly settled nor surveyed. Lawless intruders—squatters, as they were called—were planting themselves along the finest streams and in the richest valleys, and virtually taking possession of the country. It was the anxious desire of Lord Fairfax to have these lands examined, surveyed, and portioned out into lots, preparatory to ejecting these interlopers or bringing them to reasonable terms. In Washington, notwithstanding his youth, he beheld one fit for the task. The proposition had only to be offered to Washington to be eagerly accepted. It was the very kind of occupation for which he had been diligently training himself. All the preparations required by one of his simple habits were soon made, and in the month of March, 1748, just after he had completed his sixteenth year, Washington set out on horseback, in company with George William Fairfax.

Their route lay by Ashley's Gap, a pass through the Blue Ridge, that beautiful line of mountains which, as yet, almost formed the western frontier of inhabited Virginia. They entered the great valley of Virginia, where it is about twenty-five miles wide; a lovely and temperate region, diversified by gentle swells and slopes, admirably adapted to cultivation. The Blue Ridge bounds it on one side, the North Mountain, a ridge of the Alleghanies, on the other; while through it flows that bright and abounding river, which, on account of its surpassing beauty, was named by the Indians the Shenandoah — that is to say, "the daughter of the stars."

The first station of the travellers was at a kind of lodge in the wilderness, where the steward or land-bailiff of Lord Halifax resided, with such negroes as were required for farming purposes, and which Washington terms "his lordship's quarter." It was situated not far from the Shenandoah, and about twelve miles from the site of the present town of Winchester. In a diary kept with his usual minuteness, Washington speaks with delight of the beauty of the trees and the richness of the land in the neighborhood, and of his riding through a noble grove of sugar maples on the banks of the Shenandoah; and, at the present day, the magnificence of the forests which still exist in this favored region justifies his eulogium.

His surveys commenced in the lower part of the valley some distance above the junction of the Shenandoah with the Potomac, and extended for many miles along the former river. Here and there partial "clearings" had been made by squatters and hardy pioneers, and their rude husbandry had produced abundant crops of grain, hemp, and tobacco. More than two weeks were passed by them in the wild mountainous regions of Frederick County, and about the south branch of the Potomac, surveying lands and laying out lots, camped out the greater part of the time, and subsisting on wild turkeys and other game. Having completed his surveys, Washington set forth from the south branch of the Potomac on his return homeward; crossed the mountains to the great Cacapehon; traversed the Shenandoah valley; passed through the Blue Ridge, and on the 12th of April found himself once more at Mount Vernon. For his services he received, according to his note-book, a doubloon per day when actively employed.

The manner in which he had acquitted himself in this arduous expedition, and his accounts of the country surveyed, gave great satisfaction to Lord Fairfax, who shortly afterwards moved across the Blue Ridge, and took up his residence at the place heretofore noted as his "quarters." Here he laid out a manor, containing ten thousand acres of arable grazing lands, vast meadows, and noble forests, and projected a spacious manor house, giving to the place the name of Greenway Court.

It was probably through the influence of Lord Fairfax that Washington received the appointment of public surveyor. This conferred authority on his surveys, and entitled them to be recorded in the county offices, and so invariably correct have these surveys been found that to this day, wherever any of them stand on record, they receive implicit credit. For three years he continued in this occupation, which proved extremely profitable, from the vast extent of country to be surveyed and the very limited number of public surveyors. It made him acquainted, also, with the country, the nature of the soil in various parts, and the value of localities; all which proved advantageous to him in his purchases in after years.

While thus employed for months at a time surveying the lands beyond the Blue Ridge, he was often an inmate of Greenway Court. The projected manor house was never even commenced. On a green knoll overshadowed by trees was a long stone building one story in height, with dormer-windows, two wooden belfries, chimneys studded with swallow and martin coops, and a roof sloping down in the old Virginia fashion, into low projecting eaves that formed a verandah the whole length of the house. It was probably the house originally occupied by his steward or land agent, but was now devoted to hospitable purposes and the reception of guests.

Here Washington had full opportunity, in the proper seasons, of indulging his fondness for field sports, and once more accompanying his lordship in the chase. The conversation of Lord Fairfax, too, was full of interest and instruction to an inexperienced youth, from his cultivated talents, his literary taste, and his past intercourse with the best society of Europe, and its most distinguished authors. He had brought books, too, with him into the wilderness, and from Washington's diary we find that during his sojourn here he was diligently reading the history of England, and the essays of the "Spectator." Three or four years were thus passed by Washington, the greater part of the time beyond the Blue Ridge, but occasionally with his brother Lawrence at Mount Vernon.

CHAPTER III.

RIVAL CLAIMS OF THE ENGLISH AND THE FRENCH.—PREPARATIONS FOR HOSTILITIES.

During the time of Washington's surveying campaigns among the mountains, a grand colonizing scheme had been set on foot, destined to enlist him in hardy enterprises, and in some degree to shape the course of his future fortunes. The treaty of peace concluded at Aix-la-Chapelle, which had put an end to the general war of Europe, had left undefined the boundaries between the British and French possessions in America. Immense regions were still claimed by both nations, and each was now eager to forestall the other by getting possession of them, and strengthening its claim by occupancy.

The most desirable of these regions lay west of the Alleghany Mountains, extending from the lakes to the Ohio, and embracing the valley of that river and its tributary streams. The French claimed all this country quite to the Alleghany Mountains by the right of discovery. In 1673, Padre Marquette, with his companion, Joliet, of Quebec, both subjects of the crown of France, had passed down the Mississippi in a canoe quite to the Arkansas, thereby, according to an alleged maxim in the law of nations, establishing the right of their sovereign, not merely to the river so discovered and its adjacent lands, but to all the country drained by its tributary streams, of which the Ohio was one; a claim, the ramifications of which might be spread, like the meshes of a web, over half the continent.

To this illimitable claim the English opposed a right derived, at second hand, from a traditionary Indian conquest. A treaty, they said, had been made at Lancaster, in 1744, between commissioners from Pennsylvania, Maryland and Virginia, and the Iroquois, or Six Nations, whereby the latter, for four hundred pounds, gave up all right and title to the land west of the Alleghany Mountains, even to the Mississippi, which land, *according to their traditions*, had been conquered by their forefathers. It is undoubtedly true that such a treaty was made, and such a pretended transfer of title did take place, under the influence of spirituous liquors; but it is equally true that the Indians in question did not, at the time, possess an acre of the land conveyed; and that the tribes actually in possession scoffed at their pretensions, and claimed the country as their own from time immemorial.

Such were the shadowy foundations of claims which the two nations were determined to maintain to the uttermost, and which ripened into a series of wars, ending in a loss to England of a great part of her American possessions, and to France of the whole.

As yet in the region in question there was not a single white settlement. Mixed Iroquois tribes of Delawares, Shawnees, and Mingoes, had migrated into it early in the century from the French settlements in Canada, and taken up their abodes about the Ohio and its branches. The French pretended to hold them under their protection; but their allegiance, if ever acknowledged, had been sapped of late years by the influx of fur traders from Pennsylvania. These were often rough, lawless men, generally in the employ of some trader, who, at the head of his retainers and a string of pack-horses, would make his way over mountains and through forests to the banks of the Ohio, establish his head-quarters in some Indian town, and disperse his followers to traffic among the hamlets, hunting-camps, and wigwams, exchanging blankets, gaudy colored cloth, trinketry, powder, shot, and rum, for valuable furs and peltry. In this way a lucrative trade with these western tribes was springing up and becoming monopolized by the Pennsylvanians.

To secure a participation in this trade, and to gain a foothold in this desirable region, became now the wish of some of the most intelligent and enterprising men of Virginia and Maryland, among whom were Lawrence and Augustine Washington. With these views they projected a scheme, in connection with John Hanbury, a wealthy London merchant, to obtain a grant of land from the British government, for the purpose of forming settlements or colonies beyond the Alleghanies. Government readily countenanced a scheme by which French encroachments might be forestalled, and prompt and quiet possession secured of the great Ohio valley. An association was accordingly chartered in 1749, by the name of "the Ohio Company," and five hundred thousand acres of land was granted to it west of the Alleghanies; between the Monongahela and Kanawha rivers; though part of the land might be taken up north of the Ohio, should it be deemed expedient. The company were to pay no quit-rent for ten years; but they were to select two-fifths of their lands immediately; to settle one hundred families upon them within seven years; to build a fort at their own expense, and maintain a sufficient garrison in it for defence against the Indians. Mr. Thomas Lee, president of the council of Virginia, took the lead in the concerns of the company at the outset, and by many has been considered its founder. On his death, which soon took place, Lawrence Washington had the chief management. His enlightened mind and liberal spirit shone forth in his earliest arrangements.

Before the company had received its charter, the French were in the field. Early in 1749, the Marquis de la Galisionniere, governor of Canada, despatched Celeron de Bienville, an intelligent officer, at the head of three hundred men, to the banks of the Ohio, to make peace, as he said, between the tribes that had become embroiled with each other during the late war, and to renew the French possession of the country. Celeron de Bienville distributed presents among the Indians, made speeches reminding them of former friendship, and warned them not to trade with the English. He furthermore nailed leaden plates to trees, and buried others in the earth, at the confluence of the Ohio and its tributaries, bearing inscriptions purporting that all the lands on both sides of the rivers to their sources appertained, as in foregone times, to the crown of France. The Indians gazed at these mysterious plates with wondering eyes, but surmised their purport. "They mean to steal our country from us," murmured they; and they determined to seek protection from the English.

Celeron finding some traders from Pennsylvania trafficking among the Indians, he summoned them to depart, and wrote by them to James Hamilton, governor of Pennsylvania, telling him the object of his errand to those parts, and his surprise at meeting with English traders in a country to which England had no pretensions; intimating that, in future, any intruders of the kind would be rigorously dealt with. His letter, and a report of his proceedings on the Ohio, roused the solicitude of the governor and council of Pennsylvania, for the protection of their Indian trade. Shortly afterwards, one Hugh Crawford, who had been trading with the Miami tribes on the Wabash, brought a message from them, speaking of the promises and threats with which the French were endeavoring to shake their faith, but assuring the governor that their friendship for the English "would last while the sun and moon ran round the world."

Governor Hamilton knew the value of Indian friendship, and suggested to the assembly that it would be better to clinch it with presents, and that as soon as possible. An envoy accordingly was sent off early in October, who was supposed to have great influence among the western tribes. This was one George Croghan, a veteran trader, shrewd and sagacious, who had been frequently to the Ohio country with pack-horses and followers, and made himself popular among the Indians by dispensing presents with a lavish hand. He was accompanied by Andrew Montour, a Canadian of half Indian descent, who was to act as interpreter. They were provided with a small present for the emergency; but were to convoke a meeting of all the tribes at Logstown, on the Ohio, early in the ensuing spring, to receive an ample present which would be provided by the assembly.

It was some time later in the same autumn that the Ohio company brought their plans into operation, and despatched an agent to explore the lands upon the Ohio and its branches as low as the Great Falls. The man chosen for the purpose was Christopher Gist, a hardy pioneer, experienced in woodcraft and Indian life. He was allowed a woodsman or two for the service of the expedition. He set out on the 31st of October, crossed the ridges of the Alleghany, arrived at Shannopin, a Delaware village on the Alleghany, swam his horses across that river, and descending along its valley arrived at Logstown, an important Indian village a little below the site of the present city of Pittsburg. Here usually resided Tanacharisson, a Seneca chief of great note, being head sachem of the mixed tribes which had migrated to the Ohio and its branches. He was generally surnamed the half-king, being subordinate to the Iroquois confederacy. The chief was absent at this time, as were most of his people, it being the hunting season. George Croghan, the envoy from Pennsylvania, with Montour his interpreter, had passed through Logstown a week previously, on his way to the Twightwees and other tribes, on the Miami branch of the Ohio. Scarce any one was to be seen about the village but some of Croghan's rough people, whom he had left behind—"reprobate Indian traders," as Gist terms them. He took his departure from Logstown, and at Beaver Creek, a few miles below the village, he left the river and struck into the interior of the present State of Ohio. Here he overtook George Croghan at Muskingum, a town of Wyandots and Mingoes. He had ordered all the traders in his employ who were scattered among the Indian villages, to rally at this town, where he had hoisted the English flag over his residence, and over that of the sachem. This was in consequence of the hostility of the French, who had recently captured, in the neighborhood, three white men in the employ of Frazier, an Indian trader, and had carried them away prisoners to Canada.

Gist was well received by the people of Muskingum. They were indignant at the French violation of their territories, and the capture of their "English brothers." They had not forgotten the conduct of Celeron de Bienville in the previous year, and the mysterious plates which he had nailed against trees and sunk in the ground. A council of the nation was now held, in which Gist invited them, in the name of the governor of Virginia, to visit that province, where a large present of goods awaited them, sent by their father, the great king, over the water to his Ohio children. The invitation was graciously received, but no answer could be given until a grand council of the western tribes had been held, which was to take place at Logstown in the ensuing spring.

Similar results attended visits made by Gist and Croghan to the Delawares and the Shawnees at their villages about the Scioto River; all promised to be at the gathering at Logstown. From the Shawnee village, near the mouth of the Scioto, the two emissaries shaped their course north two hundred miles, crossed the Great Moneami, or Miami River, on a raft, swimming their horses; and, on the 17th of February, arrived at Piqua, the principal town of the Twightwees or Miamis; the most powerful confederacy of the West, combining four tribes, and extending its influence even beyond the Mississippi. A king or sachem of one or other of the different tribes presided over the whole. The head chief at present was the king of the Piankeshas. At this town Croghan formed a treaty of alliance in the name of the governor of Pennsylvania with two of the Miami tribes. And Gist was promised by the king of the Piankeshas that the chiefs of the various tribes would attend the meeting at Logstown to make a treaty with Virginia. [In the height of these demonstrations of friendship, two envoys from the French governor of Canada entered the council-house and sought a renewal of the ancient alliance. But the Piankesha chief turned his back upon the ambassadors, and left the council-house.]

When Gist returned to the Shawnee town, near the mouth of the Scioto, and reported to his Indian friends there the alliance he had formed with the Miami confederacy, there was great feasting and speech-making, and firing of guns. He had now happily accomplished the chief object of his mission—nothing remained but to descend the Ohio to the Great Falls. This, however, he was cautioned not to do. A large party of Indians, allies of the French, were hunting in that neighborhood, who might kill or capture him. He crossed the river attended only by a lad as a travelling companion and aide, and proceeded cautiously down the east side until within fifteen miles of the Falls. Here he came upon traps newly set, and Indian footprints not a day old; and heard the distant report of guns. The story of Indian hunters then was true. Abandoning all idea, therefore, of visiting the Falls, and contenting himself with the information concerning them which he had received from others, he shaped his course homeward.

While Gist had been making his painful way homeward, the two Ottawa ambassadors had returned to Fort Sandusky, bringing word to the French that their friendship had been rejected and their hostility defied by the Miamis. They informed them also of the gathering of the western tribes that was to take place at Logstown, to conclude a treaty with the Virginians.

It was a great object with the French to prevent this treaty, and to spirit up the Ohio Indians against the English. This they hoped to effect through the agency of one Captain Joncaire, a veteran of the wilderness, who had grown gray in Indian diplomacy, and was now sent to maintain French sovereignty over the valley of the Ohio. He appeared at Logstown accompanied by another Frenchman, and forty Iroquois warriors. He found an assemblage of the western tribes, feasting and rejoicing, and firing off guns, for George Croghan, and Montour, the interpreter, were there, and had been distributing presents on behalf of the governor of Pennsylvania.

Joncaire was said to have the wit of a Frenchman, and the eloquence of an Iroquois. He made an animated speech to the chiefs in their own tongue, the gist of which was that their father Onontio (that is to say, the governor of Canada) desired his children of the Ohio to turn away the Indian traders, and never to deal with them again on pain of his displeasure; so saying, he laid down a wampum belt of uncommon size, by way of emphasis to his message. For once his eloquence was of no avail; a chief rose indignantly, shook his finger in his face, and stamping on the ground, "This is our land," said he. "What right has Onontio here? The English are our brothers. They shall live among us as long as one of us is alive. We will trade with them, and not with you;" and, so saying, he rejected the belt of wampum.

Joncaire returned to an advanced post recently established on the upper part of the river, whence he wrote to the governor of Pennsylvania: "The Marquis de la Jonquiere, governor of New France, having ordered me to watch that the English make no treaty in the Ohio country, I have signified to the traders of your government to retire. You are not ignorant that all these lands belong to the King of France, and that the English have no right to trade in them." He concluded by reiterating the threat made two years previously by Celeron de Bienville against all intruding fur traders. In the meantime, in the face of all these protests and menaces, Mr. Gist, under sanction of the Virginia Legislature, proceeded in the same year to survey the lands within the grant of the Ohio company, lying on the south side of the Ohio river, as far down as the great Kanawha.

The French now prepared for hostile contingencies. They launched an armed vessel of unusual size on Lake Ontario; fortified their trading-house at Niagara; strengthened their outposts, and advanced others on the upper waters of the Ohio. A stir of warlike preparation was likewise to be observed among the British colonies. It was evident that the adverse claims to the disputed territories, if pushed home, could only be settled by the stern arbitrament of the sword.

In Virginia, especially, the war spirit was manifest. The province was divided into military districts, each having an adjutant-general, with the rank of major, and the pay of one hundred and fifty pounds a year, whose duty was to attend to the organization and equipment of the militia. Such an appointment was sought by Lawrence Washington for his brother George, who set about preparing himself, with his usual method and assiduity, for his new duties. Virginia had among its floating population some military relics of the late Spanish war. Among these was a certain Adjutant Muse, a Westmoreland volunteer, who had served with Lawrence Washington in the campaigns in the West Indies. He now undertook to instruct his brother George in the art of war; lent him treatises on military tactics; put him through the manual exercise, and gave him some idea of evolutions in the field. Another of Lawrence's campaigning comrades was Jacob Van Braam, a Dutchman by birth, who had been in the British army, but was now out of service, and, professing to be a complete master of fence, recruited his slender purse in this time of military excitement, by giving the Virginian youth lessons in the sword exercise. Under the instructions of these veterans Mount Vernon, from being a quiet rural retreat, was suddenly transformed into a school of arms.

Washington's martial studies, however, were interrupted for a time by the critical state of his brother's health. The constitution of Lawrence had always been delicate, and he had been obliged repeatedly to travel for a change of air. There were now pulmonary symptoms of a threatening nature, and, by advice of his physicians, he determined to pass a winter in the West Indies, taking with him his favorite brother George as a companion. They accordingly sailed for Barbadoes on the 28th of September, 1751. George kept a journal of the voyage with log-book brevity, recording the wind and weather, but no events worth citation. They landed at Barbadoes on the 3d of November. The resident physician of the place gave a favorable report of Lawrence's case, and held out hopes of a cure.

The brothers had scarcely been a fortnight at the island when George was taken down by a severe attack of small-pox. Skilful medical treatment, with the kind attentions of friends, and especially of his brother, restored him to health in about three weeks; but his face always remained slightly marked.

The residence at Barbadoes failed to have the anticipated effect on the health of Lawrence, and he determined to seek the sweet climate of Bermuda in the spring. He felt the absence from his wife, and it was arranged that George should return to Virginia, and bring her out to meet him at that island. Accordingly, on the 22d of December, George set sail in the "Industry," bound to Virginia, where he arrived on the 1st of February, 1752, after five weeks of stormy winter seafaring.

Lawrence remained through the winter at Barbadoes; but the very mildness of the climate relaxed and enervated him. He felt the want of the bracing winter weather to which he had been accustomed. Even the invariable beauty of the climate, the perpetual summer, wearied the restless invalid. Still some of the worst symptoms of his disorder had disappeared, and he seemed to be slowly recovering; but the nervous restlessness and desire of change, often incidental to his malady, had taken hold of him, and early in March he hastened to Bermuda. He had come too soon. The keen air of early spring brought on an aggravated return of his worst symptoms. He was now afflicted with painful indecision, and his letters perplexed his family, leaving them uncertain as to his movements, and at a loss how to act. At one time he talked of remaining at Bermuda, the next letter, written shortly afterwards, in a moment of despondency, talks of the possibility of "hurrying home to his grave!" The last was no empty foreboding. He did indeed hasten back, and just reached Mount Vernon in time to die under his own roof. His death took place on the 26th of July, 1752, when but thirty-four years of age.

Lawrence left a wife and an infant daughter to inherit his ample estates. In case his daughter should die without issue, the estate of Mount Vernon, and other lands specified in his will, were to be enjoyed by her mother during her lifetime, and at her death to be inherited by his brother George. The latter was appointed one of the executors of the will; but such was the implicit confidence reposed in his judgment and integrity, that, although he was but twenty years of age, the management of the affairs of the deceased was soon devolved upon him almost entirely.

CHAPTER IV.

WASHINGTON'S MISSION TO THE FRENCH COMMANDER.

The meeting of the Ohio tribes, Delawares, Shawnees, and Mingoes, to form a treaty of alliance with Virginia, took place at Logstown, at the appointed time. The chiefs of the Six Nations declined to attend. Colonel Fry and two other commissioners from Virginia concluded a treaty with the tribes above named; by which the latter engaged not to molest any English settlers south of the Ohio. Tanacharisson, the half-king, now advised that his brothers of Virginia should build a strong house at the fork of the Monongahela, to resist the designs of the French. Mr. Gist was accordingly instructed to lay out a town and build a fort at Chartier's Creek, on the east side of the Ohio, a little below the site of the present city of Pittsburg. He commenced a settlement, also, in a valley just beyond Laurel Hill, not far from the Youghiogeny, and prevailed on eleven families to join him. The Ohio Company, about the same time, established a trading-post, well stocked with English goods, at Wills' Creek (now the town of Cumberland).

The Ohio tribes were greatly incensed at the aggressions of the French, who were erecting posts within their territories, and sent deputations to remonstrate, but without effect. There were reports that the French were ascending the Mississippi from Louisiana. France, it was said, intended to connect Louisiana and Canada by a chain of military posts, and hem the English within the Alleghany Mountains.

The Ohio company complained loudly to the lieutenant-governor of Virginia, the Hon. Robert Dinwiddie, of the hostile conduct of the French and their Indian allies. They found in Dinwiddie a ready listener; he was a stockholder in the company. A commissioner, Captain William Trent, was sent to expostulate with the French commander on the Ohio for his aggressions on the territory of his Brittanic majesty; he bore presents also of guns, powder, shot, and clothing for the friendly Indians. Trent was not a man of the true spirit for a mission to the frontier. He stopped a short time at Logstown, though the French were one hundred and fifty miles further up the river, and directed his course to Piqua, the great town of the Twightwees, where Gist and Croghan had been so well received by the Miamis. All now was reversed. The place had been attacked by the French and Indians; the Miamis defeated with great loss; the English traders taken prisoners; the Piankesha chief, who had so proudly turned his back upon the Ottawa ambassadors, had been sacrificed by the hostile savages, and the French flag hoisted in triumph on the ruins of the town. The whole aspect of affairs was so threatening on the frontier that Trent lost heart, and returned home without accomplishing his errand.

Governor Dinwiddie now looked round for a person more fitted to fulfil a mission which required physical strength and moral energy; a courage to cope with savages, and a sagacity to negotiate with white men. Washington was pointed out as possessed of those requisites. It is true he was not yet twenty-two years of age, but public confidence in his judgment and abilities had been manifested, by renewing his appointment of adjutant-general, and assigning him the northern division. He was accordingly chosen for the expedition.

By his letter of instructions he was directed to repair to Logstown, and hold a communication with Tanacharisson, Monacatoocha, alias Scarooyadi, the next in command, and the other sachems of the mixed tribes friendly to the English; inform them of the purport of his errand, and request an escort to the head-quarters of the French commander. To that commander he was to deliver his credentials, and the letter of Governor Dinwiddie, and demand an answer in the name of his Brittanic majesty; but not to wait for it beyond a week. On receiving it, he was to request a sufficient escort to protect him on his return. He was, moreover, to acquaint himself with the numbers and force of the French stationed on the Ohio and in its vicinity; their capability of being reinforced from Canada; the forts they had erected; where situated, how garrisoned; the object of their advancing into those parts, and how they were likely to be supported. Washington set off from Williamsburg on the 30th of October, 1753, the very day on which he received his credentials. At Fredericksburg he engaged his old "master of fence," Jacob Van Braam, to accompany him as interpreter.

Having provided himself at Alexandria with necessaries for the journey, he proceeded to Winchester, then on the frontier, where he procured horses, tents, and other travelling equipments, and then pushed on by a road newly opened to Wills' Creek, where he arrived on the 14th of November. Here he met with Mr. Gist, the intrepid pioneer, whom he engaged to accompany and pilot him in the present expedition. He secured the services also of one John Davidson as Indian interpreter, and of four frontiersmen. With this little band, he set forth on the 15th of November through a wild country, rendered almost impassable by recent storms of rain and snow.

As the rivers were all swollen so that the horses had to swim them, Washington sent all the baggage down the Monongahela in a canoe under care of two of the men, who had orders to meet him at the confluence of that river with the Alleghany, where their united waters form the Ohio. "As I got down before the canoe," writes he in his journal, "I spent some time in viewing the rivers, and the land at the fork, which I think extremely well situated for a fort, as it has the absolute command of both rivers." The Ohio company had intended to build a fort about two miles from this place, on the south-east side of the river; but Washington gave the fork the decided preference. French engineers of experience proved the accuracy of his military eye, by subsequently choosing it for the site of Fort Duquesne, noted in frontier history.

In this neighborhood lived Shingiss, the king, or chief sachem, of the Delawares. Washington visited him at his village, to invite him to the council at Logstown. He was one of the greatest warriors of his tribe, and subsequently took up the hatchet at various times against the English, though now he seemed favorably disposed, and readily accepted the invitation.

They arrived at Logstown after sunset on the 24th of November. The half-king was absent at his hunting-lodge on Beaver Creek, about fifteen miles distant; but Washington had runners sent out to invite him and all the other chiefs to a grand talk on the following day. About three o'clock the half-king arrived. Washington had a private conversation with him in his tent, through Davidson, the interpreter. He found him intelligent, patriotic, and proudly tenacious of his territorial rights. He stated that the French had built two forts, differing in size, but on the same model, a plan of which he gave, of his own drawing. The largest was on Lake Erie, the other on French Creek, fifteen miles apart, with a wagon road between them. The nearest and levellest way to them was now impassable, lying through large and miry savannas; they would have, therefore, to go by Venango, and it would take five or six sleeps (or days) of good travelling to reach the nearest fort.

On the following morning at nine o'clock, the chiefs assembled at the council-house; where Washington, according to his instructions, informed them that he was sent by their brother, the governor of Virginia, to deliver to the French commandant a letter of great importance, both to their brothers, the English, and to themselves; and that he was to ask their advice and assistance, and some of their young men to accompany and provide for him on the way, and be his safeguard against the "French Indians" who had taken up the hatchet. He concluded by presenting the indispensable document in Indian diplomacy, a string of wampum.

The chiefs according to etiquette, sat for some moments silent after he had concluded, as if ruminating on what had been said, or to give him time for further remark. The half-king then rose and spoke in behalf of the tribes, assuring him that they considered the English and themselves brothers, and one people; and that they intended to return the French the "speech-belts," or wampums, which the latter had sent them. This, in Indian diplomacy, is a renunciation of all friendly relations. An escort would be furnished to Washington composed of Mingoes, Shannoahs, and Delawares, in token of the love and loyalty of those several tribes; but three days would be required to prepare for the journey.

Washington remonstrated against such delay; but was informed that an affair of such moment, where three speech-belts were to be given up, was not to be entered into without due consideration. Besides, the young men who were to form the escort were absent hunting, and the half-king could not suffer the party to go without sufficient protection. His own French speech-belt, also, was at his hunting-lodge, whither he must go in quest of it. Moreover, the Shannoah chiefs were yet absent and must be waited for. Washington soon found that to urge a more speedy departure would be offensive to Indian dignity and decorum so he was fain to await the gathering together of the different chiefs with their speech-belts.

In fact there was some reason for all this caution. Tidings had reached the sachems that Captain Joncaire had called a meeting at Venango, of the Mingoes, Delawares, and other tribes, and made them a speech, informing them that the French, for the present, had gone into winter-quarters, but intended to descend the river in great force, and fight the English in the spring. He had advised them, therefore, to stand aloof, for should they interfere, the French and English would join, cut them all off, and divide their land between them.

With these rumors preying on their minds, the half-king and three other chiefs waited on Washington in his tent in the evening, and after representing that they had complied with all the requisitions of the governor of Virginia, endeavored to draw from the youthful ambassador the true purport of his mission to the French commandant. Washington had anticipated an inquiry of the kind, knowing how natural it was that these poor people should regard with anxiety and distrust every movement of two formidable powers thus pressing upon them from opposite sides; he managed, however, to answer them in such a manner as to allay their solicitude without transcending the bounds of diplomatic secrecy.

After a day or two more of delay and further consultations in the council-house, the chiefs determined that but three of their number should accompany the mission, as a greater number might awaken the suspicions of the French. Accordingly, on the 30th of November, Washington set out for the French post, having his usual party augmented by an Indian hunter, and being accompanied by the half-king, an old Shannoah sachem named Jeskakake, and another chief, sometimes called Belt of Wampum, from being the keeper of the speech-belts, but generally bearing the sounding appellation of White Thunder.

Although the distance to Venango, by the route taken, was not above seventy miles, yet such was the inclemency of the weather and the difficulty of travelling, that Washington and his party did not arrive there until the 4th of December. The French colors were flying at a house to which Washington repaired, and inquired of three French officers whom he saw there where the commandant resided. One of them promptly replied that he "had the command of the Ohio." It was, in fact, the redoubtable Captain Joncaire, the veteran intriguer of the frontier. On being apprised, however, of the nature of Washington's errand, he informed him that there was a general officer at the next fort, where he advised him to apply for an answer to the letter of which he was the bearer.

In the meantime, he invited Washington and his party to a supper at head-quarters. It proved a jovial one. Joncaire and his brother officers pushed the bottle briskly. "The wine," says Washington, "as they dosed themselves pretty plentifully with it, soon banished the restraint which at first appeared in their conversation, and gave a license to their tongues to reveal their sentiments more freely." Washington retained his sobriety and his composure throughout the bacchanalian outbreak. He took careful note, however, of all their revelations, and collected a variety of information concerning the French forces; how and where they were distributed; the situations and distances of their forts, and their means and mode of obtaining supplies. If the veteran diplomatist of the wilderness had intended this revel for a snare, he was completely foiled by his youthful competitor.

On the following day there was no travelling on account of excessive rain. Joncaire, in the meantime, having discovered that the half-king was with the mission, expressed his surprise that he had not accompanied it to his quarters on the preceding day. Washington, in truth, had feared to trust the sachem within the reach of the politic Frenchman. Nothing would do now but Joncaire must have the sachems at head-quarters. Here his diplomacy was triumphant. He received them with open arms. He was enraptured to see them. His Indian brothers! How could they be so near without coming to visit him? He made them presents; but, above all, plied them so potently with liquor, that the poor half-king, Jeskakake, and White Thunder forgot all about their wrongs, their speeches, their speech-belts, and all the business they had come upon; paid no heed to the repeated cautions of their English friends, and were soon in a complete state of frantic extravagance or drunken oblivion.

All that day and the next was the party kept at Venango by the stratagems of Joncaire and his emissaries to detain and seduce the sachems. It was not until twelve o'clock on the 7th of December, that Washington was able to extricate them out of their clutches and commence his journey. A French commissary by the name of La Force, and three soldiers, set off in company with him. La Force went as if on ordinary business, but he proved one of the most active, daring, and mischief-making of those anomalous agents employed by the French among the Indian tribes. It is probable that he was at the bottom of many of the perplexities experienced by Washington at Venango, and now travelled with him for the prosecution of his wiles. He will be found, hereafter, acting a more prominent part, and ultimately reaping the fruit of his evil doings.

After four days of weary travel the party reached the fort. It was situated on a kind of island on the west fork of French Creek, about fifteen miles south of Lake Erie. On the death of the late general, the fort had remained in charge of one Captain Reparti until within a week past, when the Chevalier Legardeur de St. Pierre had arrived, and taken command.

The reception of Washington at the fort was very different from the unceremonious one experienced at the outpost of Joncaire and his convivial messmates. When he presented himself at the gate, accompanied by his interpreter, Van Braam, he was met by the officer second in command and conducted in due military form to his superior — an ancient and silver-haired chevalier of the military order of St. Louis, courteous but ceremonious, mingling the polish of the French gentleman of the old school with the precision of the soldier. Having announced his errand, Washington offered his credentials and the letter of Governor Dinwiddie, and was disposed to proceed at once to business with the prompt frankness of a young man unhackneyed in diplomacy. The chevalier, however, politely requested him to retain the documents in his possession until his predecessor, Captain Reparti, should arrive, who was hourly expected from the next post.

At two o'clock the captain arrived. The letter and its accompanying documents were then offered again, and received in due form, and the chevalier and his officers retired with them into a private apartment. In this letter Dinwiddie complained of the intrusion of French forces into the Ohio country, erecting forts and making settlements in the western parts of the colony of Virginia, so notoriously known to be the property of the crown of Great Britain. He inquired by whose authority and instructions the French commander-general had marched this force from Canada, and made this invasion; intimating that his own action would be regulated by the answer he should receive, and the tenor of the commission with which he was honored. At the same time he required of the commandant his peaceable departure.

The two following days were consumed in councils of the chevalier and his officers over the letter and the necessary reply. Washington occupied himself in the meantime in observing and taking notes of the plan, dimensions, and strength of the fort, and of every thing about it. He gave orders to his people, also, to take an exact account of the canoes in readiness, and others in the process of construction, for the conveyance of troops down the river in the ensuing spring. As the weather continued stormy, with much snow, and the horses were daily losing strength, he sent them down, unladen, to Venango, to await his return by water. In the meantime, he discovered that busy intrigues were going on to induce the half-king and the other sachems to abandon him, and renounce all friendship with the English. Upon learning this, he urged the chiefs to deliver up their "speech-belts" immediately, as they had promised, thereby shaking off all dependence upon the French. They accordingly pressed for an audience that very evening. A private one was at length granted them by the commander, in presence of one or two of his officers. The half-king reported the result of it to Washington. The venerable but astute chevalier cautiously evaded the acceptance of the proffered wampum; made many professions of love and friendship, and said he wished to live in peace and trade amicably with the tribes of the Ohio, in proof of which he would send down some goods immediately for them to Logstown.

On the evening of the 14th, the chevalier delivered to Washington his sealed reply to the letter of Governor Dinwiddie. The purport of previous conversations with the chevalier, and the whole complexion of affairs on the frontier, left no doubt of the nature of that reply. The business of his mission being accomplished, Washington prepared on the 15th to return by water to Venango; but a secret influence was at work which retarded every movement. "The commandant," writes he, "ordered a plentiful store of liquor and provisions to be put on board our canoes, and appeared to be extremely complaisant, though he was exerting every artifice which he could invent to set our Indians at variance with us, to prevent their going until after our departure; presents, rewards, and every thing which could be suggested by him or his officers.... He had promised them a present of guns if they would wait until the morning. As I was very much pressed by the Indians to wait this day for them, I consented, on the promise that nothing should hinder them in the morning."

The next morning (16th) the French, in fulfilment of their promise, had to give the present of guns. They then endeavored to detain the sachems with liquor, but Washington reminded the half-king that his royal word was pledged to depart, and urged it upon him so closely that, exerting unwonted resolution and self-denial, he turned his back upon the liquor and embarked.

It was rough and laborious navigation. French Creek was swollen and turbulent, and full of floating ice. The frail canoes were several times in danger of being staved to pieces against rocks. It was not until the 22d that they reached Venango. Here Washington was obliged, most unwillingly, to part company with the sachems. White Thunder had hurt himself and was ill and unable to walk, and the others determined to remain at Venango for a day or two and convey him down the river in a canoe.

On the 25th of December Washington and his little party set out by land from Venango on their route homeward. They had a long, winter's journey before them, through a wilderness beset with dangers and difficulties. The pack-horses, laden with tents, baggage, and provisions, were completely jaded; it was feared they would give out. Washington dismounted, gave up his saddle-horse to aid in transporting the baggage, and requested his companions to do the same. None but the drivers remained in the saddle.

The cold increased. There was deep snow that froze as it fell. The horses grew less and less capable of travelling. For three days they toiled on slowly and wearily. Washington was impatient to accomplish his journey, and make his report to the governor; he determined, therefore, to hasten some distance in advance of the party, and then strike for the fork of the Ohio by the nearest course directly through the woods. He accordingly put the cavalcade under the command of Van Braam, then disencumbering himself of all superfluous clothing, buckling himself up in a watch-coat, strapping his pack on his shoulders, containing his papers and provisions, and taking gun in hand struck manfully ahead, accompanied only by Mr. Gist, who had equipped himself in like manner.

At night they lit a fire, and "camped" by it in the woods. At two o'clock in the morning they were again on foot, and pressed forward until they struck the southeast fork of Beaver Creek, at a place bearing the sinister name of Murdering Town. Here Washington, in planning his route, had intended to leave the regular path, and strike through the woods for Shannopins Town, two or three miles above the fork of the Ohio, where he hoped to be able to cross the Alleghany River on the ice.

At Murdering Town he found a party of Indians, who appeared to have known of his coming, and to have been waiting for him. One of them accosted Mr. Gist, and expressed great joy at seeing him. The wary woodsman regarded him narrowly, and thought he had seen him at Joncaire's. If so, he and his comrades were in the French interest, and their lying in wait boded no good. The Indian was very curious in his inquiries as to when they had left Venango; how they came to be travelling on foot, etc., these questions increased the distrust of Gist, and rendered him extremely cautious in reply.

The route hence to Shannopins Town lay through a trackless wild, of which the travellers knew nothing; it was deemed, therefore, expedient to engage one of the Indians as a guide. He entered upon his duties with alacrity, took Washington's pack upon his back, and led the way by what he said was the most direct course. After travelling briskly for eight or ten miles, Washington became fatigued, and his feet were chafed; he thought, too, they were taking a direction too much to the north-east; he came to a halt, therefore, and determined to light a fire, make a shelter of the bark and branches of trees, and encamp there for the night. The Indian demurred; he offered, as Washington was fatigued, to carry his gun, but the latter was too wary to part with his weapon. The Indian now grew churlish. Mr. Gist's suspicions increased but he said nothing. Washington's also were awakened. They proceeded some distance further: the guide paused and listened. He had heard, he said, the report of a gun towards the north; must be from his cabin; he accordingly turned his steps in that direction.

They went on two miles farther, when Washington signified his determination to encamp at the first water they should find. The guide said nothing, but kept doggedly on. After a little while they arrived at an opening in the woods, when the Indian, who was about fifteen paces ahead, suddenly turned, levelled his gun, and fired. Washington was startled for an instant, but, feeling that he was not wounded, demanded quickly of Mr. Gist if he was shot. The latter answered in the negative. The Indian in the meantime had run forward, and screened himself behind a large white oak, where he was re-loading his gun. They overtook, and seized him. Gist would have put him to death on the spot, but Washington humanely prevented him.

Arriving at a small stream they ordered the Indian to make a fire, and took turns to watch over the guns. While he was thus occupied, Gist observed to Washington that, since he would not suffer the Indian to be killed, they must manage to get him out of the way, and then decamp with all speed, and travel all night to leave this perfidious neighborhood behind them; but first it was necessary to blind the guide as to their intentions. He accordingly addressed him in a friendly tone, and adverting to the late circumstance, pretended to suppose he had lost his way, and fired his gun merely as a signal. The Indian, whether deceived or not, readily chimed in with the explanation. He said he now knew the way to his cabin, which was at no great distance.

"Well then," replied Gist, "you can go home, and as we are tired we will remain here for the night and follow your track at daylight."

Whatever might have been the original designs of the savage, he was evidently glad to get off. Gist followed him cautiously for a distance, and listened until the sound of his footsteps died away; returning then to Washington, they proceeded about half a mile, made another fire, set their compass and fixed their course by the light of it, then leaving it burning, pushed forward, and travelled as fast as possible all night. Continuing on the next day they never relaxed their speed until nightfall, when they arrived on the banks of the Alleghany River, about two miles above Shannopins Town.

Washington had expected to find the river frozen completely over; it was so only for about fifty yards from each shore, while great quantities of broken ice were driving down the main channel. Trusting that he had out-travelled pursuit, he encamped on the border of the river; still it was an anxious night, and he was up at daybreak to devise some means of reaching the opposite bank. No other mode presented itself than by a raft, and to construct this they had but one poor hatchet.

With this they set resolutely to work and labored all day, but the sun went down before their raft was finished. They launched it, however, and getting on board, endeavored to propel it across with setting poles. Before they were half way over the raft became jammed between cakes of ice, and they were in imminent peril. Washington planted his pole on the bottom of the stream, and leaned against it with all his might, to stay the raft until the ice should pass by. The rapid current forced the ice against the pole with such violence that he was jerked into the water, where it was at least ten feet deep, and only saved himself from being swept away and drowned by catching hold of one of the raft logs.

It was now impossible with all their exertions to get to either shore; abandoning the raft therefore, they got upon an island, near which they were drifting. Here they passed the night exposed to intense cold, by which the hands and feet of Mr. Gist were frozen. In the morning they found the drift ice wedged so closely together, that they succeeded in getting from the island to the opposite side of the river; and before night were in comfortable quarters at the house of Frazier, an Indian trader, at the mouth of Turtle Creek, on the Monongahela.

Leaving Frazier's on the 1st of January, where they had been detained two or three days endeavoring to procure horses, they arrived on the 2d at Gist's residence, sixteen miles from the Monongahela. Here they separated, and Washington, having purchased a horse, continued his homeward course. He reached Williamsburg on the 16th of January, where he delivered to Governor Dinwiddie the letter of the French commandant, and made him a full report of the events of his mission.

We have been minute in our account of this expedition as it was an early test and development of the various talents and characteristics of Washington. The prudence, sagacity, resolution, firmness, and self-devotion manifested by him throughout, pointed him out, not merely to the governor, but to the public at large, as one eminently fitted, notwithstanding his youth, for important trusts involving civil as well as military duties. It is an expedition that may be considered the foundation of his fortunes. From that moment he was the rising hope of Virginia.

CHAPTER V.
MILITARY EXPEDITION TO THE FRONTIER.

The reply of the Chevalier de St. Pierre was such as might have been expected from that courteous, but wary commander. He should transmit, he said, the letter of Governor Dinwiddie to his general, the Marquis du Quesne, "to whom," observed he, "it better belongs than to me to set forth the evidence and reality of the rights of the king, my master, upon the lands situated along the river Ohio, and to contest the pretensions of the King of Great Britain thereto. His answer shall be a law to me."

This was considered evasive, and only intended to gain time. The information given by Washington of what he had observed on the frontier convinced Governor Dinwiddie and his council that the French were preparing to descend the Ohio in the spring, and take military possession of the country. Washington's journal was printed, and widely promulgated throughout the colonies and England, and awakened the nation to a sense of the impending danger and the necessity of prompt measures to anticipate the French movements.

Captain Trent was dispatched to the frontier, commissioned to raise a company of one hundred men, march with all speed to the fork of the Ohio, and finish as soon as possible the fort commenced there by the Ohio Company. He was enjoined to act only on the defensive, but to capture or destroy whoever should oppose the construction of the works, or disturb the settlements. The choice of Captain Trent for this service, notwithstanding his late inefficient expedition, was probably owing to his being brother-in-law to George Croghan, who had grown to be quite a personage of consequence on the frontier, where he had an establishment, or trading-house, and was supposed to have great influence among the western tribes, so as to be able at any time to persuade many of them to take up the hatchet. Washington was empowered to raise a company of like force at Alexandria; to procure and forward munitions and supplies for the projected fort at the fork, and ultimately to have command of both companies.

Governor Dinwiddie in the meantime called upon the governors of the other provinces to make common cause against the foe; he endeavored, also, to effect alliances with the Indian tribes of the south, the Catawbas and Cherokees, by way of counter-balancing the Chippewas and Ottawas, who were devoted to the French. The colonies, however, felt as yet too much like isolated territories; the spirit of union was wanting. Some pleaded a want of military funds; some questioned the justice of the cause; some declined taking any hostile step that might involve them in a war, unless they should have direct orders from the crown.

Dinwiddie convened the House of Burgesses to devise measures for the public security. Here his high idea of prerogative and of gubernatorial dignity met with a grievous countercheck from the dawning spirit of independence. When he propounded his scheme of operations on the Ohio, some of the burgesses had the hardihood to doubt the claims of the king to the disputed territory; a doubt which the governor reprobated as savoring strongly of a most disloyal French spirit. Others demurred to any grant of means for military purposes which might be construed into an act of hostility. To meet this scruple it was suggested that the grant might be made for the purpose of encouraging and protecting all settlers on the waters of the Mississippi. And under this specious plea ten thousand pounds were grudgingly voted.

Ways and means being provided, Governor Dinwiddie augmented the number of troops to be enlisted to three hundred, divided into six companies. The command of the whole, as before, was offered to Washington, but he shrank from it, as a charge too great for his youth and inexperience. It was given, therefore, to Colonel Joshua Fry, an English gentleman of worth and education, and Washington was made second in command, with the rank of lieutenant-colonel. The recruiting, at first, went on slowly. Governor Dinwiddie proclaimed a bounty of two hundred thousand acres of land on the Ohio River, to be divided among the officers and soldiers who should engage in this expedition; one thousand to be laid off contiguous to the fort at the fork, for the use of the garrison. This was a tempting bait to the sons of farmers, who readily enlisted in the hope of having, at the end of a short campaign, a snug farm of their own in this land of promise.

It was a more difficult matter to get officers than soldiers. Very few of those appointed made their appearance; one of the captains had been promoted; two declined; Washington found himself left, almost alone, to manage a number of self-willed, undisciplined recruits. Happily he had with him, in the rank of lieutenant, that soldier of fortune, Jacob Van Braam, his old "master of fence," and travelling interpreter. In his emergency he forthwith nominated him captain, and wrote to the governor to confirm the appointment. On the 2d of April Washington set off from Alexandria for the new fort, at the fork of the Ohio. He had but two companies with him, amounting to about one hundred and fifty men; the remainder of the regiment was to follow under Colonel Fry with the artillery, which was to be conveyed up the Potomac. While on the march he was joined by a detachment under Captain Adam Stephen, an officer destined to serve with him at distant periods of his military career. At Winchester he found it impossible to obtain conveyances by gentle means, and was obliged reluctantly to avail himself of the militia law of Virginia, and impress horses and wagons for service; giving the owners orders on government for their appraised value. Even then, out of a great number impressed, he obtained but ten, after waiting a week. Thus slenderly fitted out, Washington and his little force made their way toilfully across the mountains, having to prepare the roads as they went for the transportation of the cannon, which were to follow on with the other division under Colonel Fry. They cheered themselves with the thoughts that this hard work would cease when they should arrive at the company's trading-post and store-house at Wills' Creek, where Captain Trent was to have pack-horses in readiness, with which they might make the rest of the way by light stages. Before arriving there they were startled by a rumor that Trent and all his men had been captured by the French. With regard to Trent the news soon proved to be false, for they found him at Wills' Creek on the 20th of April. With regard to his men there was still an uncertainty. He had recently left them at the fork of the Ohio, busily at work on the fort, under the command of his lieutenant, Frazier. Washington was eager to press forward and ascertain the truth, but it was impossible. Trent, inefficient as usual, had failed to provide pack-horses. It was necessary to send to Winchester, sixty miles distant, for baggage wagons, and await their arrival. All uncertainty as to the fate of the men, however, was brought to a close by their arrival, on the 25th, conducted by an ensign, and bringing with them their working implements. The French might well boast that they had again been too quick for the English. Captain Contrecoeur, an alert officer, had embarked about a thousand men with field-pieces, in a fleet of sixty bateaux and three hundred canoes, dropped down the river from Venango, and suddenly made his appearance before the fort, on which the men were working, and which was not half completed. Landing, drawing up his men, and planting his artillery, he summoned the fort to surrender, allowing one hour for a written reply. All that the ensign could obtain was permission to depart with his men, taking with them their working tools.

Such was the ensign's story. He was accompanied by two Indian warriors, sent by the half-king to ascertain where the detachment was, what was its strength, and when it might be expected at the Ohio. They bore a speech from that sachem to Washington, and another, with a belt of wampum for the governor of Virginia. In these he plighted his steadfast faith to the English, and claimed assistance from his brothers of Virginia and Pennsylvania. One of these warriors Washington forwarded on with the speech and wampum to Governor Dinwiddie. The other he prevailed on to return to the half-king bearing a speech from him, addressed to the "Sachems, warriors of the Six United Nations, Shannoahs and Delawares, our friends and brethren." In this he informed them that he was on the advance with a part of the army, to clear the road for a greater force coming with guns, ammunition, and provisions; and he invited the half-king and another sachem to meet him on the road, as soon as possible, to hold a council.

In fact, his situation was arduous in the extreme. Regarding the conduct of the French in the recent occurrence an overt act of war, he found himself thrown with a handful of raw recruits far on a hostile frontier, in the midst of a wilderness, with an enemy at hand greatly superior in number and discipline; provided with artillery, and all the munitions of war, and within reach of constant supplies and reinforcements. Besides the French that had come from Venango, he had received credible accounts of another party ascending the Ohio; and of six hundred Chippewas and Ottawas marching down Scioto Creek to join the hostile camp. Still, notwithstanding the accumulating danger, it would not do to fall back, nor show signs of apprehension. His Indian allies in such case might desert him. The soldiery, too, might grow restless and dissatisfied.

In this dilemma he called a council of war, in which it was determined to proceed to the Ohio Company store-house, at the mouth of Redstone Creek; fortify themselves there, and wait for reinforcements. Here they might keep up a vigilant watch upon the enemy, and get notice of any hostile movement in time for defence, or retreat; and should they be reinforced sufficiently to enable them to attack the fort, they could easily drop down the river with their artillery.

With these alternatives in view, Washington detached sixty men in advance to make a road; and at the same time wrote to Governor Dinwiddie for mortars and grenadoes, and cannon of heavy metal. Aware that the Assembly of Pennsylvania was in session and that the Maryland Assembly would also meet in the course of a few days, he wrote directly to the governors of those provinces, acquainting them with the hostile acts of the French, and with his perilous situation; and endeavoring to rouse them to co-operation in the common cause.

Before setting off for Redstone Creek, he discharged Trent's men [who, having enlisted as volunteers, considered themselves exempt from the rigor of martial law, and had become refractory] from his detachment, ordering them to await Colonel Fry's commands; they, however, in the true spirit of volunteers from the backwoods, dispersed to their homes.

On the 29th of April Washington set out from Wills' Creek at the head of one hundred and sixty men. He soon overtook those sent in advance to work the road; they had made but little progress. It was a difficult task to break a road through the wilderness sufficient for the artillery coming on with Colonel Fry's division. All hands were now set to work, but with all their labor they could not accomplish more than four miles a day. On the 9th of May they were not further than twenty miles from Wills' Creek, at a place called the Little Meadows.

Every day came gloomy accounts from the Ohio; brought chiefly by traders, who, with pack-horses bearing their effects, were retreating to the more settled parts of the country. Some exaggerated the number of the French, as if strongly reinforced. All represented them as diligently at work constructing a fort. By their account Washington perceived the French had chosen the very place which he had noted in his journal as best fitted for the purpose. One of the traders gave information concerning La Force, the French emissary, who had beset Washington when on his mission to the frontier, and acted, as he thought, the part of a spy. He had been at Gist's new settlement beyond Laurel Hill, and was prowling about the country with four soldiers at his heels on a pretended hunt after deserters. Washington suspected him to be on a reconnoitering expedition. It was reported, moreover, that the French were lavishing presents on the Indians about the lower part of the river, to draw them to their standard. Among all these flying reports and alarms Washington was gratified to learn that the half-king was on his way to meet him at the head of fifty warriors.

After infinite toil through swamps and forests, and over rugged mountains, the detachment arrived at the Youghiogeny River, where they were detained some days constructing a bridge to cross it. This gave Washington leisure to correspond with Governor Dinwiddie concerning matters which had deeply annoyed him. By an ill-judged economy of the Virginia government at this critical juncture, its provincial officers received less pay than that allowed in the regular army. It is true, the regular officers were obliged to furnish their own table, but their superior pay enabled them to do it luxuriously; whereas the provincials were obliged to do hard duty on salt provisions and water. The provincial officers resented this inferiority of pay as an indignity, and declared that nothing prevented them from throwing up their commissions but unwillingness to recede from approaching danger.

Other instances of false economy were pointed out by Washington, forming so many drags upon the expedition that he quite despaired of success. "Be the consequence what it will, however," adds he, "I am determined not to leave the regiment, but to be among the last men that leave the Ohio; even if I serve as a private volunteer, which I greatly prefer to the establishment we are upon.... I have a constitution hardy enough to encounter and undergo the most severe trials, and I flatter myself resolution to face what any man dares, as shall be proved when it comes to the test."

While the bridge over the Youghiogeny was in the course of construction, the Indians assured Washington he would never be able to open a wagon-road across the mountain to Redstone Creek; he embarked therefore in a canoe with a lieutenant, three soldiers, and an Indian guide, to try whether it was possible to descend the river. The river was bordered by mountains and obstructed by rocks and rapids. Indians might thread such a labyrinth in their light canoes, but it would never admit the transportation of troops and military stores. Washington kept on for thirty miles, until he came to a place where the river fell nearly forty feet in the space of fifty yards. There he ceased to explore, and returned to camp, resolving to continue forward by land.

On the 23d Indian scouts brought word that the French were not above eight hundred strong, and that about half their number had been detached at night on a secret expedition. Close upon this report came a message from the half-king. "It is reported," said he, "that the French army is coming to meet Major Washington. Be on your guard against them, my brethren, for they intend to strike the first English they shall see."

In the evening Washington was told that the French were crossing the ford of the Youghiogeny about eighteen miles distant. He now hastened to take a position in a place called the Great Meadows, where he caused the bushes to be cleared away, made an intrenchment, and prepared what he termed, "a charming field for an encounter." A party of scouts were mounted on wagon-horses, and sent out to reconnoitre. They returned without having seen an enemy.

On the 25th Mr. Gist arrived from his place, about fifteen miles distant. La Force had been there at noon on the previous day, with a detachment of fifty men, and Gist had since come upon their track within five miles of the camp. Washington detached seventy-five men in pursuit of him and his prowling band. About nine o'clock at night came an Indian messenger from the half-king, who was encamped with several of his people about six miles off. The chief had seen tracks of two Frenchmen, and was convinced their whole body must be in ambush near by. Washington considered this the force which had been hovering about him for several days, and determined to forestall their hostile designs. Leaving a guard with the baggage and ammunition, he set out before ten o'clock, with forty men, to join his Indian ally. They groped their way in single file, by footpaths through the woods, in a heavy rain and murky darkness. It was near sunrise when they reached the camp of the half-king.

The chieftain received the youthful commander with great demonstrations of friendship, and engaged to go hand in hand with him against the lurking enemy. He set out accordingly, accompanied by a few of his warriors and his associate sachem Scarooyadi or Monacatoocha, and conducted Washington to the tracks which he had discovered. Upon these he put two of his Indians. They followed them up like hounds, and brought back word that they had traced them to a low bottom surrounded by rocks and trees, where the French were encamped, having built a few cabins for shelter from the rain.

A plan was now concerted to come upon them by surprise; Washington with his men on the right; the half-king with his warriors on the left; all as silently as possible. Washington was the first upon the ground. As he advanced from among the rocks and trees at the head of his men, the French caught sight of him and ran to their arms. A sharp firing instantly took place, and was kept up on both sides for about fifteen minutes. Washington and his party were most exposed and received all the enemy's fire. The French at length, having lost several of their number, gave way and ran. They were soon overtaken; twenty-one were captured, and but one escaped, a Canadian, who carried the tidings of the affair to the fort on the Ohio. The Indians would have massacred the prisoners had not Washington prevented them. Ten of the French had fallen in the skirmish, and one been wounded. Washington's loss was one killed and three wounded. He had been in the hottest fire, and, having for the first time heard balls whistle about him, considered his escape miraculous. Jumonville, the French leader, had been shot through the head at the first fire.

Of the twenty-one prisoners the two most important were an officer of some consequence named Drouillon, and the subtle and redoubtable La Force. As Washington considered the latter an arch mischief-maker, he was rejoiced to have him is his power. The prisoners were conducted to the camp at the Great Meadows, and sent on the following day (29th), under a strong escort to Governor Dinwiddie, then at Winchester. Washington had treated them with great courtesy; had furnished Drouillon and La Force with clothing from his own scanty stock, and, at their request, given them letters to the governor, bespeaking for them "the respect and favor due to their character and personal merit."

The situation of Washington was now extremely perilous. Contrecoeur, it was said, had nearly a thousand men with him at the fort, beside Indian allies; and reinforcements were on the way to join him. The messengers sent by Jumonville, previous to the late affair, must have apprised him of the weakness of the encampment on the Great Meadows. Washington hastened to strengthen it. He wrote by express also to Colonel Fry, who lay ill at Wills' Creek, urging instant reinforcements.

The half-king was full of fight. He sent the scalps of the Frenchmen slain in the late skirmish, accompanied by black wampum and hatchets, to all his allies, summoning them to take up arms and join him at Redstone Creek, "for their brothers, the English, had now begun in earnest." He went off for his home, promising to send down the river for all the Mingoes and Shawnees, and to be back at the camp on the 30th, with thirty or forty warriors, accompanied by their wives and children. To assist him in the transportation of his people and their effects thirty men were detached and twenty horses.

"I shall expect every hour to be attacked," writes Washington to Governor Dinwiddie, on the 26th, "and by unequal numbers, which I must withstand, if there are five to one, for I fear the consequence will be that we shall lose the Indians if we suffer ourselves to be driven back. Your honor may depend I will not be surprised, let them come at what hour they will, and this is as much as I can promise; but my best endeavors shall not be wanting to effect more."

CHAPTER VI.

MISFORTUNES.—CAPITULATION OF FORT NE-CESSITY.

Scarcity began to prevail in the camp. Contracts had been made with George Croghan for flour, of which he had large quantities at his frontier establishment; for he was now trading with the army as well as with the Indians. None, however, made its appearance. At one time the troops were six days without flour. In this time of scarcity the half-king, his fellow sachem, Scarooyadi, and thirty or forty warriors, arrived, bringing with them their wives and children—so many more hungry mouths to be supplied.

News came of the death of Colonel Fry at Wills' Creek, and that he was to be succeeded in the command of the expedition by Colonel Innes of North Carolina, who was actually at Winchester with three hundred and fifty North Carolina troops. The colonel, however, never came to the camp, nor did the North Carolina troops render any service in the campaign—the fortunes of which might otherwise have been very different. By the death of Fry, the command of the regiment devolved on Washington.

The palisaded fort was now completed, and was named Fort Necessity, from the pinching famine that had prevailed during its construction. The scanty force in camp was augmented to three hundred by the arrival from Wills' Creek of the men who had been under Colonel Fry. With them came the surgeon of the regiment, Dr. James Craik, a Scotchman by birth, and one destined to become a faithful and confidential friend of Washington for the remainder of his life.

A letter from Governor Dinwiddie announced, however, that Captain Mackay would soon arrive with an independent company of one hundred men, from South Carolina. The title of independent company had a sound ominous of trouble. Troops of the kind, raised in the colonies, under direction of the governors, were paid by the crown, and the officers had king's commissions; such, doubtless, had Captain Mackay. "I should have been particularly obliged," writes Washington to Governor Dinwiddie, "if you had declared whether he was under my command or independent of it. I hope he will have more sense than to insist upon any unreasonable distinction, because he and his officers have commissions from his majesty."

On the 9th arrived Washington's early instructor in military tactics, Adjutant Muse, recently appointed a major in the regiment. He was accompanied by Montour, the Indian interpreter, now a provincial captain, and brought with him nine swivels, and a small supply of powder and ball. Fifty or sixty horses were forthwith sent to Wills' Creek, to bring on further supplies, and Mr. Gist was urged to hasten forward the artillery. Major Muse was likewise the bearer of a belt of wampum and a speech, from Governor Dinwiddie to the half-king; with medals for the chiefs, and goods for presents among the friendly Indians, a measure which had been suggested by Washington. They were distributed with that grand ceremonial so dear to the red man.

On the 10th there was agitation in the camp. Scouts hurried in with word, as Washington understood them, that a party of ninety Frenchmen were approaching. The report of the scouts had been either exaggerated or misunderstood. The ninety Frenchmen in military array dwindled down into nine French deserters. According to their account, the fort at the fork was completed, and named Duquesne, in honor of the governor of Canada. It was proof against all attack, excepting with bombs, on the land side. The garrison did not exceed five hundred, but two hundred more were hourly expected, and nine hundred in the course of a fortnight.

On the same day Captain Mackay arrived, with his independent company of South Carolinians. The cross purposes which Washington had apprehended, soon manifested themselves. The captain was civil and well disposed, but full of formalities and points of etiquette. Holding a commission direct from the king, he could not bring himself to acknowledge a provincial officer as his superior. He encamped separately, kept separate guards, would not agree that Washington should assign any rallying place for his men in case of alarm, and objected to receive from him the parole and countersign, though necessary for their common safety. Washington conducted himself with circumspection, avoiding everything that might call up a question of command, and reasoning calmly whenever such question occurred; but he urged the governor by letter, to prescribe their relative rank and authority.

On the 11th of June, Washington resumed the laborious march for Redstone Creek. As Captain Mackay could not oblige his men to work on the road unless they were allowed a shilling sterling a day; and as Washington did not choose to pay this, nor to suffer them to march at their ease while his own faithful soldiers were laboriously employed; he left the captain and his independent company as a guard at Fort Necessity, and undertook to complete the military road with his own men. Accordingly, he and his Virginia troops toiled forward through the narrow defiles of the mountains, working on the road as they went.

At Gist's establishment, about thirteen miles from Fort Necessity, Washington received certain intelligence that ample reinforcements had arrived at Fort Duquesne, and a large force would instantly be detached against him. Coming to a halt, he began to throw up intrenchments, calling in two foraging parties, and sending word to Captain Mackay to join him with all speed. The captain and his company arrived in the evening; the foraging parties the next morning. A council of war was held, in which the idea of awaiting the enemy at this place was unanimously abandoned.

A rapid and toilsome retreat ensued. There was a deficiency of horses. Washington gave up his own to aid in transporting the military munitions, leaving his baggage to be brought on by soldiers, whom he paid liberally. The other officers followed his example. The weather was sultry; the roads were rough; provisions were scanty, and the men dispirited by hunger. On the 1st of July they reached the Great Meadows. Here the Virginians, exhausted by fatigue, hunger, and vexation, declared they would carry the baggage and drag the swivels no further. Contrary to his original intentions, therefore, Washington determined to halt here for the present, and fortify, sending off expresses to hasten supplies and reinforcements from Wills' Creek, where he had reason to believe that two independent companies from New York were by this time arrived.

The retreat to the Great Meadows had not been in the least too precipitate. Captain de Villiers, a brother-in-law of Jumonville, had actually sallied forth from Fort Duquesne at the head of upwards of five hundred French, and several hundred Indians, eager to avenge the death of his relative. Arriving about dawn of day at Gist's plantation, he surrounded the works which Washington had hastily thrown up there, and fired into them. Finding them deserted, he concluded that those of whom he came in search had made good their retreat to the settlements, and it was too late to pursue them. He was on the point of returning to Fort Duquesne, when a deserter arrived, who gave word that Washington had come to a halt in the Great Meadows, where his troops were in a starving condition. De Villiers ordered the fellow into confinement; to be rewarded if his words proved true, otherwise to be hanged. He then pushed forward for the Great Meadows.

In the meantime Washington had exerted himself to enlarge and strengthen Fort Necessity, nothing of which had been done by Captain Mackay and his men, while encamped there. The fort was about a hundred feet square, protected by trenches and palisades. It stood on the margin of a small stream, nearly in the centre of the Great Meadows, which is a grassy plain, perfectly level, surrounded by wooded hills of a moderate height, and at that place about two hundred and fifty yards wide. Washington asked no assistance from the South Carolina troops, but set to work with his Virginians, animating them by word and example; sharing in the labor of felling trees, hewing off the branches, and rolling up the trunks to form a breastwork.

At this critical juncture he was deserted by his Indian allies. They were disheartened at the scanty preparations for defence against a superior force, and offended at being subjected to military command. The half-king thought he had not been sufficiently consulted, and that his advice had not been sufficiently followed; such, at least, were some of the reasons which he subsequently gave for abandoning the youthful commander on the approach of danger. Most of his warriors followed his example.

Early in the morning of the 3d, while Washington and his men were working on the fort, a sentinel came in wounded and bleeding, having been fired upon. Scouts brought word shortly afterwards that the French were in force about four miles off. Washington drew up his men on level ground outside of the works to await their attack. About eleven o'clock there was a firing of musketry from among trees on rising ground, but so distant as to do no harm; suspecting this to be a stratagem designed to draw his men into the woods, he ordered them to keep quiet, and refrain from firing until the foe should show themselves, and draw near. The firing was kept up, but still under cover. He now fell back with his men into the trenches, ordering them to fire whenever they could get sight of an enemy. In this way there was skirmishing throughout the day; the French and Indians advancing as near as the covert of the woods would permit. In the meantime the rain fell in torrents; the harassed and jaded troops were half drowned in their trenches and many of their muskets were rendered unfit for use.

About eight at night the French requested a parley. Washington hesitated. It might be a stratagem to gain admittance for a spy into the fort. The request was repeated, with the addition that an officer might be sent to treat with them, under their parole for his safety. Unfortunately the Chevalier de Peyrouney, engineer of the regiment, and the only one that could speak French correctly, was wounded and disabled. Washington had to send, therefore, his ancient swordsman and interpreter, Jacob Van Braam. The captain returned twice with separate terms, in which the garrison was required to surrender; both were rejected. He returned a third time, with written articles of capitulation. They were in French. As no implements for writing were at hand, Van Braam undertook to translate them by word of mouth. A candle was brought, and held close to the paper while he read. The rain fell in torrents; it was difficult to keep the light from being extinguished. The captain rendered the capitulation, article by article, in mongrel English, while Washington and his officers stood listening, endeavoring to disentangle the meaning. One article stipulated that on surrendering the fort they should leave all their military stores, munitions, and artillery in possession of the French. This was objected to, and was readily modified.

The main articles, as Washington and his officers understood them, were, that they should be allowed to return to the settlements without molestation from French or Indians. That they should march out of the fort with the honors of war, drums beating and colors flying, and with all their effects and military stores excepting the artillery, which should be destroyed. That they should be allowed to deposit their effects in some secret place, and leave a guard to protect them until they could send horses to bring them away; their horses having been nearly all killed or lost during the action. That they should give their word of honor not to attempt any buildings or improvements on the lands of his most Christian Majesty for the space of a year. That the prisoners taken in the skirmish of Jumonville should be restored, and until their delivery Captain Van Braam and Captain Stobo should remain with the French as hostages.

The next morning, accordingly, Washington and his men marched out of their forlorn fortress with the honors of war, bearing with them their regimental colors, but leaving behind a large flag, too cumbrous to be transported. Scarcely had they begun their march, however, when, in defiance of the terms of capitulation, they were beset by a large body of Indians, allies of the French, who began plundering the baggage, and committing other irregularities. Seeing that the French did not, or could not, prevent them, and that all the baggage which could not be transported on the shoulders of his troops would fall into the hands of these savages,

Washington ordered it to be destroyed, as well as the artillery, gunpowder, and other military stores. All this detained him until ten o'clock, when he set out on his melancholy march, and continued on until three miles from Fort Necessity, where he encamped for the night.

In the following days' march the troops seemed jaded and disheartened; they were encumbered and delayed by the wounded; provisions were scanty, and they had seventy weary miles to accomplish before they could meet with supplies. Washington, however, encouraged them by his own steadfast and cheerful demeanor, and by sharing all their toils and privations; and at length conducted them in safety to Wills' Creek, where they found ample provisions in the military magazines. Leaving them here to recover their strength, he proceeded with Captain Mackay to Williamsburg, to make his military report to the governor.

A copy of the capitulation was subsequently laid before the Virginia House of Burgesses, with explanations. Notwithstanding the unfortunate result of the campaign, the conduct of Washington and his officers was properly appreciated, and they received a vote of thanks for their bravery, and gallant defence of their country. From the vote of thanks, two officers were excepted; Major Stobo, who was charged with cowardice, and Washington's unfortunate master of fence and blundering interpreter, Jacob Van Braam, who was accused of treachery, in purposely misinterpreting the articles of capitulation.

We will here anticipate dates to record the fortunes of the half-king after his withdrawal from the camp. He and several of his warriors, with their wives and children, retreated to Aughquick, in the back part of Pennsylvania, where George Croghan had an agency, and was allowed money from time to time for the maintenance of Indian allies. The half-king expressed himself perfectly disgusted with the white man's mode of warfare. The French, he said, were cowards; the English, fools. Washington was a good man, but wanted experience; he would not take advice of the Indians, and was always driving them to fight according to his own notions. For this reason he (the half-king) had carried off his wife and children to a place of safety. After a time the chieftain fell dangerously ill, and on his death, which took place shortly afterwards, there was great lamentation.

Early in August Washington rejoined his regiment, which had arrived at Alexandria by the way of Winchester. Letters from Governor Dinwiddie urged him to recruit it to the former number of three hundred men, and join Colonel Innes at Wills' Creek, where that officer was stationed with Mackay's independent company of South Carolinians, and two independent companies from New York; and had been employed in erecting a work to serve as a frontier post and rally point; which work received the name of Fort Cumberland, in honor of the Duke of Cumberland, captain-general of the British army.

In the meantime the French, elated by their recent triumph, and thinking no danger at hand, relaxed their vigilance at Fort Duquesne. Stobo, who was a kind of prisoner at large there, found means to send a letter secretly by an Indian, dated July 28, and directed to the commander of the English troops. It was accompanied by a plan of the fort. "There are two hundred men here," writes he, "and two hundred expected; the rest have gone off in detachments to the amount of one thousand, besides Indians. None lodge in the fort but Contrecoeur and the guard, consisting of forty men and five officers; the rest lodge in bark cabins around the fort. The Indians have access day and night, and come and go when they please. If one hundred trusty Shawnees, Mingoes, and Delawares were picked out, they might surprise the fort, lodging themselves under the palisades by day, and at night secure the guard with their tomahawks, shut the sally-gate, and the fort is ours."

The Indian messenger carried the letter to Aughquick and delivered it into the hands of George Croghan. The Indian chiefs who were with him insisted upon his opening it. He did so, but on finding the tenor of it, transmitted it to the governor of Pennsylvania. The secret information communicated by Stobo may have been the cause of a project suddenly conceived by Governor Dinwiddie, of a detachment which, by a forced march across the mountains, might descend upon the French and take Fort Duquesne at a single blow; or, failing that, might build a rival fort in its vicinity. He accordingly wrote to Washington to march forthwith for Wills' Creek, with such companies as were complete, leaving orders with the officers to follow as soon as they should have enlisted men sufficient to make up their companies.

The ignorance of Dinwiddie in military affairs and his want of forecast, led him perpetually into blunders. Washington saw the rashness of an attempt to dispossess the French with a force so inferior that it could be harassed and driven from place to place at their pleasure. Before the troops could be collected, and munitions of war provided, the season would be too far advanced. There would be no forage for the horses; the streams would be swollen and unfordable; the mountains rendered impassable by snow, and frost, and slippery roads.

Such are a few of the cogent reasons urged by Washington in a letter to his friend William Fairfax, then in the House of Burgesses, which no doubt was shown to Governor Dinwiddie, and probably had an effect in causing the rash project to be abandoned.

In the month of October the House of Burgesses made a grant of twenty thousand pounds for the public service; and ten thousand more were sent out from England, beside a supply of fire-arms. The governor now applied himself to military matters with renewed spirit; increased the actual force to ten companies; and as there had been difficulties among the different kinds of troops with regard to precedence, he reduced them all to independent companies; so that there would be no officer in a Virginia regiment above the rank of captain. This shrewd measure, upon which Dinwiddie secretly prided himself as calculated to put an end to the difficulties in question, immediately drove Washington out of the service; considering it derogatory to his character to accept a lower commission than that under which his conduct had gained him a vote of thanks from the Legislature.

Governor Sharpe, of Maryland, appointed by the king commander-in-chief of all the forces engaged against the French, sought to secure his valuable services, and authorized Colonel Fitzhugh, whom he had placed in temporary command of the army, to write to him to that effect. The reply of Washington (15th Nov.) is full of dignity and spirit, and shows how deeply he felt his military degradation. "You make mention," says he, "of my continuing in the service and retaining my colonel's commission. This idea has filled me with surprise; for if you think me capable of holding a commission that has neither rank nor emolument annexed to it, you must maintain a very contemptible opinion of my weakness, and believe me more empty than the commission itself. I herewith inclose Governor Sharpe's letter which I beg you will return to him with my acknowledgements for the favor he intended me."

Even had Washington hesitated to take this step, it would have been forced upon him by a further regulation of government, in the course of the ensuing winter, settling the rank of officers of his majesty's forces when joined or serving with the provincial forces in North America, "which directed that all such as were commissioned by the king, or by his general commander-in-chief in North America, should take rank of all officers commissioned by the governors of the respective provinces. And further, that the general and field officers of the provincial troops should have no rank when serving with the general and field officers commissioned by the crown; but that all captains and other inferior officers of the royal troops should take rank over provincial officers of the same grade, having older commissions." These regulations, originating in that supercilious assumption of superiority which sometimes overruns and degrades true British pride, would have been spurned by Washington, as insulting to the character and conduct of his high-minded brethren of the colonies. Another cause of vexation to Washington was the refusal of Governor Dinwiddie to give up the French prisoners, taken in the affair of De Jumonville, in fulfillment of the articles of capitulation. His plea was, that since the capitulation, the French had taken several British subjects, and sent them prisoners to Canada, he considered himself justifiable in detaining those Frenchmen which he had in his custody. Washington felt deeply mortified by this obtuseness of the governor on a point of military punctilio and honorable faith, but his remonstrances were unavailing. La Force not having acted in a military capacity, and having offended against the peace and security of the frontier, by his intrigues among the Indians, was kept in close durance.

The refusal of Governor Dinwiddie to fulfill the article of the capitulation respecting the prisoners, and the rigorous treatment of La Force, operated hardly upon the hostages, Stobo and Van Braam, who, in retaliation, were confined in prison in Quebec.

CHAPTER VII.
A CAMPAIGN UNDER GENERAL BRADDOCK.

Having resigned his commission, and disengaged himself from public affairs, Washington's first care was to visit his mother, inquire into the state of domestic concerns, and attend to the welfare of his brothers and sisters. In these matters he was ever his mother's adjunct and counsellor, discharging faithfully the duties of an eldest son, who should consider himself a second father to the family. He now took up his abode at Mount Vernon, and prepared to engage in those agricultural pursuits, for which, even in his youthful days, he had as keen a relish as for the profession of arms. Scarcely had he entered upon his rural occupations, however, when the service of his country once more called him to the field.

The disastrous affair at the Great Meadows, and the other acts of French hostility on the Ohio, had roused the attention of the British ministry, who now prepared for military operations in America; none of them professedly aggressive, but rather to resist and counteract aggressions. A plan of campaign was devised for 1755, having four objects: To eject the French from lands which they held unjustly, in the province of Nova Scotia; to dislodge them from a fortress which they had erected at Crown Point, on Lake Champlain, within what was claimed as British territory; to dispossess them of the fort which they had constructed at Niagara, between Lake Ontario and Lake Erie; to drive them from the frontiers of Pennsylvania and Virginia, and recover the valley of the Ohio. The Duke of Cumberland, captain-general of the British army, had the organization of this campaign; and through his patronage, Major-general Edward Braddock was intrusted with the execution of it, being appointed generalissimo of all the forces in the colonies.

Braddock was a veteran in service, and had been upwards of forty years in the guards, that school of exact discipline and technical punctilio. He was a brave and experienced officer; but his experience was that of routine, and rendered him pragmatical and obstinate, impatient of novel expedients, and his military precision, which would have been brilliant on parade, was a constant obstacle to alert action in the wilderness. He was to lead in person the grand enterprise of the campaign, that destined for the frontiers of Virginia and Pennsylvania; it was the enterprise in which Washington became enlisted, and, therefore, claims our especial attention.

Prior to the arrival of Braddock, came out from England Lieutenant-Colonel Sir John St. Clair, deputy quartermaster-general, eager to make himself acquainted with the field of operations. He made a tour of inspection, in company with Governor Sharpe, of Maryland, and appears to have been dismayed at sight of the impracticable wilderness, the region of Washington's campaign. From Fort Cumberland, he wrote in February to Governor Morris, of Pennsylvania, to have the road cut, or repaired, toward the head of the river Youghiogeny, and another opened from Philadelphia for the transportation of supplies. Unfortunately the governor of Pennsylvania had no money at his command, and was obliged, for expenses, to apply to his Assembly, "a set of men," writes he, "quite unacquainted with every kind of military service and exceedingly unwilling to part with money on any terms." However, by dint of exertions, he procured the appointment of commissioners to explore the country, and survey and lay out the roads required. At the head of the commission was George Croghan, the Indian trader, whose mission to the Twightwees we have already spoken of.

When Sir John St. Clair had finished his tour of inspection he descended Wills' Creek and the Potomac for two hundred miles in a canoe to Alexandria, and repaired to Virginia to meet General Braddock. The latter had landed on the 20th of February, at Hampton, in Virginia, and proceeded to Williamsburg to consult with Governor Dinwiddie. Shortly afterwards he was joined there by Commodore Keppel, whose squadron of two ships-of-war, and several transports, had anchored in the Chesapeake. On board of these ships were two prime regiments of about five hundred men each—one commanded by Sir Peter Halket, the other by Colonel Dunbar; together with a train of artillery, and the necessary munitions of war. The regiments were to be augmented to seven hundred men, each by men selected by Sir John St. Clair from Virginia companies recently raised. Alexandria was fixed upon as the place where the troops should disembark and encamp. The ships were accordingly ordered up to that place, and the levies directed to repair thither.

The plan of the campaign included the use of Indian allies. Governor Dinwiddie had already sent Christopher Gist to engage the Cherokees and Catawbas, the bravest of the Southern tribes, who he had no doubt would take up the hatchet for the English, peace being first concluded, through the mediation of his government, between them and the Six Nations; and he gave Braddock reason to expect at least four hundred Indians to join him at Fort Cumberland. General Braddock apprehended difficulty in procuring wagons and horses sufficient to attend him in his march. Sir John St. Clair, in the course of his tour of inspection, had met with two Dutch settlers, at the foot of the Blue Ridge, who engaged to furnish two hundred wagons and fifteen hundred carrying horses, to be at Fort Cumberland early in May. Governor Sharpe was to furnish above a hundred wagons for the transportation of stores, on the Maryland side of the Potomac. Keppel furnished four cannons from his ships, for the attack on Fort Duquesne, and thirty picked seamen to assist in dragging them over the mountains. They were to aid also in passing the troops and artillery on floats or in boats, across the rivers, and were under the command of a midshipman and lieutenant.

Trusting to these arrangements, Braddock proceeded to Alexandria. The troops had all been disembarked before his arrival, and the Virginia levies, selected by Sir John St. Clair to join the regiments of regulars, were arrived. There were beside two companies of hatchet men, or carpenters, six of rangers, and one troop of light horse. The levies, having been clothed, were ordered to march immediately for Winchester to be armed. The light horse were retained by the general as his escort and body guard.

The din and stir of warlike preparation disturbed the quiet of Mount Vernon. Washington looked down from his rural retreat upon the ships of war and transports as they passed up the Potomac, with the array of arms gleaming along their decks. The booming of cannon echoed among his groves. Alexandria was but a few miles distant. Occasionally he mounted his horse, and rode to that place; it was like a garrisoned town, teeming with troops, and resounding with the drum and fife. A brilliant campaign was about to open under the auspices of an experienced general, and with all the means and appurtenances of European warfare. How different from the starveling expeditions he had hitherto been doomed to conduct! What an opportunity to efface the memory of his recent disaster! All his thoughts of rural life were put to flight. The military part of his character was again in the ascendant; his great desire was to join the expedition as a volunteer. It was reported to General Braddock. The latter was apprised by Governor Dinwiddie, and others, of Washington's personal merits, his knowledge of the country, and his experience in frontier service. The consequence was a letter from Captain Robert Orme, one of Braddock's aides-de-camp, written by the general's order, inviting Washington to join his staff.

A volunteer situation on the staff of General Braddock offered no emolument nor command, and would be attended with considerable expense, still he did not hesitate a moment to accept the invitation. In the position offered to him, all the questions of military rank which had hitherto annoyed him would be obviated, and he could indulge his passion for arms without any sacrifice of dignity. His arrival at head-quarters was hailed by his young associates, Captains Orme and Morris, the general's aides-de-camp, who at once received him into frank companionship, and a cordial intimacy commenced between them that continued throughout the campaign. He experienced a courteous reception from the general, who expressed in flattering terms the impression he had received of his merits.

There were at that time four governors, beside Dinwiddie, assembled at Alexandria, at Braddock's request, to concert a plan of military operations—Governor Shirley, of Massachusetts; Lieutenant-Governor Delancey, of New York; Lieutenant-Governor Sharpe, of Maryland; Lieutenant-Governor Morris, of Pennsylvania. Washington was presented to them in a manner that showed how well his merits were already appreciated.

A grand council was held on the 14th of April, composed of General Braddock, Commodore Keppel, and the governors. In discussing the campaign, the governors were of opinion that New York should be made the centre of operations, as it afforded easy access by water to the heart of the French possessions in Canada. Braddock, however, did not feel at liberty to depart from his instructions, which specified the recent establishments of the French on the Ohio as the objects of his expedition.

Niagara and Crown Point were to be attacked about the same time with Fort Duquesne, the former by Governor Shirley, with his own and Sir William Pepperell's regiments, and some New York companies; the latter by Colonel William Johnson, sole manager and director of Indian affairs—a personage worthy of especial note. He was a native of Ireland, and had come out to this country in 1734 to manage the landed estates owned by his uncle, Commodore Sir Peter Warren, in the Mohawk country. By his agency and his dealings with the native tribes, he had acquired great wealth, and become a kind of potentate in the Indian country. His influence over the Six Nations was said to be unbounded.

The business of the Congress being finished, General Braddock would have set out for Fredericktown, in Maryland, but few wagons or teams had yet come to remove the artillery. Washington had looked with wonder and dismay at the huge paraphernalia of war and the world of superfluities to be transported across the mountains, recollecting the difficulties he had experienced in getting over them with his nine swivels and scanty supplies. "If our march is to be regulated by the slow movements of the train," said he, "it will be tedious, very tedious indeed."

In the meanwhile, Sir John St. Clair, who had returned to the frontier, was storming at the camp at Fort Cumberland. The road required of the Pennsylvania government had not been commenced. George Croghan and the other commissioners were but just arrived in camp. Sir John, according to Croghan, received them in a very disagreeable manner, would not look at their draughts, nor suffer any representations to be made to him in regard to the province, "but stormed like a lion rampant;" declaring that the want of the road and of the provisions promised by Pennsylvania had retarded the expedition and might cost them their lives from the fresh numbers of French that might be poured into the country, and that if the French defeated them, by the delays of Pennsylvania, he would, with his sword drawn, pass through the province and treat the inhabitants as a parcel of traitors to his master. The explosive wrath of Sir John, which was not to be appeased, shook the souls of the commissioners, and they wrote to Governor Morris, urging that people might be set at work upon the road. In reply, Mr. Richard Peters, Governor Morris's secretary, wrote in his name: "Get a number of hands immediately, and further the work by all possible methods."

A commission, of a different kind, was intrusted to George Croghan. Governor Morris, by letter, requested him to convene at Aughquick, in Pennsylvania, as many warriors as possible of the mixed tribes of the Ohio, distribute among them wampum belts sent for the purpose, and engage them to meet General Braddock when on the march and render him all the assistance in their power. In reply, Croghan engaged to enlist a strong body of Indians, being sure of the influence of Scarooyadi, successor to the half-king, and of his adjunct, White Thunder, keeper of the speech-belts. At the instance of Governor Morris, Croghan secured the services of another kind of force. This was a band of hunters, resolute men, well acquainted with the country and inured to hardships. They were under the command of Captain Jack, one of the most remarkable characters of Pennsylvania; a complete hero of the wilderness. He had been for many years a captive among the Indians; and, having learnt their ways, had formed this association for the protection of the settlements. The band had become famous for its exploits, and was a terror to the Indians.

General Braddock set out from Alexandria on the 20th of April. Washington remained behind a few days to arrange his affairs, and then rejoined him at Fredericktown, in Maryland, where, on the 10th of May, he was proclaimed one of the general's aides-de-camp. The troubles of Braddock had already commenced. The Virginian contractors failed to fulfil their engagements; of all the immense means of transportation so confidently promised, but fifteen wagons and a hundred draught-horses had arrived, and there was no prospect of more. There was equal disappointment in provisions, both as to quantity and quality, and he had to send round the country to buy cattle for the subsistence of the troops.

Fortunately, while the general was venting his spleen in anathemas against army contractors, Benjamin Franklin arrived at Fredericktown. That eminent man, then about forty-nine years of age, had been for many years member of the Pennsylvania Assembly, and was now postmaster-general for America. The Assembly understood that Braddock was incensed against them, supposing them adverse to the service of the war. They had procured Franklin to wait upon him, not as if sent by them, but as if he came in his capacity of postmaster-general, to arrange for the sure and speedy transmission of dispatches between the commander-in-chief and the governors of the provinces.

He was well received, and became a daily guest at the general's table. As the whole delay of the army was caused by the want of conveyances, Franklin observed one day to the general that it was a pity the troops had not been landed in Pennsylvania, where almost every farmer had his wagon. "Then, sir," replied Braddock, "you who are a man of interest there can probably procure them for me, and I beg you will." Franklin consented. An instrument in writing was drawn up, empowering him to contract for one hundred and fifty wagons, with four horses to each wagon, and fifteen hundred saddle or pack-horses for the service of his majesty's forces, to be at Wills' Creek on or before the 20th of May, and he promptly departed for Lancaster to execute the commission.

After his departure, Braddock, attended by his staff, and his guard of light horse, set off for Wills' Creek by the way of Winchester, the road along the north side of the Potomac not being yet made. "This gave him," writes Washington, "a good opportunity to see the absurdity of the route, and of damning it very heartily." Three of Washington's horses were knocked up before they reached Winchester, and he had to purchase others. The discomforts of the rough road were increased with the general, by his travelling with some degree of state in a chariot which he had purchased of Governor Sharpe. In this he arrived at Fort Cumberland, amid a thundering salute of seventeen guns. By this time the general discovered that he was not in a region fitted for such display, and his travelling chariot was abandoned.

By the 19th of May, the forces were assembled at Fort Cumberland. The two royal regiments, originally one thousand strong, now increased to fourteen hundred, by men chosen from the Maryland and Virginia levies; two provincial companies of carpenters, or pioneers, thirty men each, with subalterns and captains; a company of guides, composed of a captain, two aids, and ten men; the troop of Virginia light horse, commanded by Captain Stewart; the detachment of thirty sailors with their officers, and the remnants of two independent companies from New York, one of which was commanded by Captain Horatio Gates, of whom we shall have to speak much hereafter in course of this biography. Another person in camp, of subsequent notoriety, and who became a warm friend of Washington, was Dr. Hugh Mercer, a Scotchman, about thirty-three years of age. Another was Dr. James Craik, who had become strongly attached to Washington, being about the same age, and having been with him in the affair of the Great Meadows, serving as surgeon in the Virginia regiment, to which he still belonged.

Braddock's camp was a complete study for Washington during the halt at Fort Cumberland, where he had an opportunity of seeing military routine in its strictest forms. He had a specimen, too, of convivial life in the camp, which the general endeavored to maintain, even in the wilderness, keeping a hospitable table; for he is said to have been somewhat of a *bon vivant*.

There was great detention at the fort, caused by the want of forage and supplies, the road not having been finished from Philadelphia. Mr. Richard Peters, the secretary of Governor Morris, was in camp, to attend to the matter. He had to bear the brunt of Braddock's complaints. The general declared he would not stir from Wills' Creek until he had the governor's assurance that the road would be opened in time. Braddock was also completely chagrined and disappointed about the Indians. The Cherokees and Catawbas, whom Dinwiddie had given him reason to expect in such numbers, never arrived. George Croghan reached the camp with but about fifty warriors, whom he had brought from Aughquick. At the general's request he sent a messenger to invite the Delawares and Shawnees from the Ohio, who returned with two chiefs of the former tribe. Among the sachems thus assembled were some of Washington's former allies—Scarooyadi, alias Monacatoocha, successor to the half-king; White Thunder, the keeper of the speech-belts, and Silver-heels, so called, probably, from being swift of foot.

Notwithstanding his secret contempt for the Indians, Braddock, agreeably to his instructions, treated them with great ceremony. A grand council was held in his tent, where all his officers attended. The chiefs, and all the warriors, came painted and decorated for war. They were received with military honors, the guards resting on their fire-arms. The general made them a speech through his interpreter, expressing the grief of their father, the great king of England, at the death of the half-king, and made them presents to console them. They in return promised their aid as guides and scouts, and declared eternal enmity to the French, following the declaration with the war song, "making a terrible noise."

For a time all went well. The Indians had their separate camp, where they passed half the night singing, dancing and howling. The British were amused by their strange ceremonies, their savage antics, and savage decorations. The Indians, on the other hand, loitered by day about the English camp, fiercely painted and arrayed, gazing with silent admiration at the parade of the troops, their marchings and evolutions; and delighted with the horse-races, with which the young officers recreated themselves. Unluckily the warriors had brought their families with them to Wills' Creek, and the women were even fonder than the men of loitering about the British camp. The jealousy of the warriors was aroused. To prevent discord, the squaws were forbidden to come into the British camp. This did not prevent their being sought elsewhere. It was ultimately found necessary, for the sake of quiet, to send the women and children back to Aughquick. White Thunder, and several of the warriors, accompanied them for their protection. As to the three Delaware chiefs, they returned to the Ohio, promising the general they would collect their warriors together and meet him on his march. They never kept their word.

During the halt of the troops at Wills' Creek, Washington had been sent to Williamsburg to bring on four thousand pounds for the military chest. He returned after a fortnight's absence. He found the general out of all patience and temper at the delays and disappointments in regard to horses, wagons, and forage, making no allowances for the difficulties incident to a new country, and to the novel and great demands upon its scanty and scattered resources. He accused the army contractors of want of faith, honor and honesty; and in his moments of passion, which were many, extended the stigma to the whole country. This stung the patriotic sensibility of Washington, and overcame his usual self-command, and the proud and passionate commander was occasionally surprised by a well-merited rebuke from his aid-de-camp.

The same pertinacity was maintained with respect to the Indians. George Croghan informed Washington that the sachems considered themselves treated with slight, in never being consulted in war matters; that he himself had repeatedly offered the services of the warriors under his command as scouts and outguards, but his offers had been rejected. Washington ventured to interfere, and to urge their importance for such purposes, especially now when they were approaching the stronghold of the enemy. As usual, the general remained bigoted in his belief of the all-sufficiency of well-disciplined troops. Either from disgust thus caused, or from being actually dismissed, the warriors began to disappear from the camp. Before Braddock recommenced his march, none remained to accompany him but Scarooyadi, and eight of his warriors.

Seeing the general's impatience at the non-arrival of conveyances, Washington again represented to him the difficulties he would encounter in attempting to traverse the mountains with such a train of wheel-carriages, assuring him it would be the most arduous part of the campaign; and recommended, from his own experience, the substitution, as much as possible, of pack-horses. Braddock, however, had not been sufficiently harassed by frontier campaigning to depart from his European modes, or to be swayed in his military operations by so green a counsellor. At length the general was relieved from present perplexities by the arrival of the horses and wagons which Franklin had undertaken to procure.

CHAPTER VIII.

BRADDOCK'S ADVANCE.—HIS DEFEAT.

On the 10th of June, Braddock set off from Fort Cumberland with his aides-de-camp, and others of his staff, and his body guard of light horse. Sir Peter Halket, with his brigade, had marched three days previously; and a detachment of six hundred men, under the command of Colonel Chapman and the supervision of Sir John St. Clair, had been employed upwards of ten days in cutting down trees, removing rocks, and opening a road. The march over the mountains proved, as Washington had foretold, a "tremendous undertaking." It was with difficulty the heavily laden wagons could be dragged up the steep and rugged roads, newly made, or imperfectly repaired. Often they extended for three or four miles in a straggling and broken line, with the soldiers so dispersed, in guarding them, that an attack on any side would have thrown the whole in confusion.

By the time the advanced corps had struggled over two mountains, and through the intervening forest, and reached (16th June) the Little Meadows, where Sir John St. Clair had made a temporary camp, General Braddock had become aware of the difference between campaigning in a new country, or on the old well-beaten battle-grounds of Europe. He now, of his own accord, turned to Washington for advice. Thus unexpectedly called on, Washington gave his counsel with becoming modesty, but with his accustomed clearness. There was just now an opportunity to strike an effective blow at Fort Duquesne, but it might be lost by delay. The garrison, according to credible reports, was weak; large reinforcements and supplies, which were on their way, would be detained by the drought, which rendered the river by which they must come low and unnavigable. The blow must be struck before they could arrive. He advised the general, therefore, to divide his forces; leave one part to come on with the stores and baggage, and all the cumbrous appurtenances of an army, and to throw himself in the advance with the other part, composed of his choicest troops, lightened of every thing superfluous that might impede a rapid march.

His advice was adopted. Twelve hundred men, selected out of all the companies, and furnished with ten field-pieces, were to form the first division, their provisions, and necessaries, to be carried on pack-horses. The second division, with all the stores, munitions, and heavy baggage, was to be brought on by Colonel Dunbar. The least practicable part of the arrangement was with regard to the officers of the advance. Washington had urged a retrenchment of their baggage and camp equipage, that as many of their horses as possible might be used as pack-horses. Here was the difficulty. Brought up, many of them, in fashionable and luxurious life, or the loitering indulgence of country quarters, they were so encumbered with what they considered indispensable necessaries, that out of two hundred and twelve horses generally appropriated to their use, not more than a dozen could be spared by them for the public service.

During the halt at the Little Meadows, Captain Jack and his band of forest rangers, whom Croghan had engaged at Governor Morris's suggestion, made their appearance in the camp. The captain asked an interview with the general, by whom, it would seem, he was not expected. Braddock received him in his tent, in his usual stiff and stately manner. The "Black Rifle" spoke of himself and his followers as men inured to hardships, and accustomed to deal with Indians, who preferred stealth and stratagem to open warfare. He requested his company should be employed as a reconnoitring party, to beat up the Indians in their lurking-places and ambuscades. Braddock, who had a sovereign contempt for the chivalry of the woods, and despised their boasted strategy, replied to the hero of the Pennsylvania settlements in a manner to which he had not been accustomed. "There was time enough," he said, "for making arrangements; and he had experienced troops, on whom he could completely rely for all purposes." Captain Jack withdrew, indignant at so haughty a reception, and informed his leathern-clad followers of his rebuff. They forthwith shouldered their rifles and turned their backs upon the camp.

On the 19th of June, Braddock's first division set out, with less than thirty carriages, including those that transported ammunition for the artillery, all strongly horsed. The Indians marched with the advanced party. In the course of the day, Scarooyadi and his son being at a small distance from the line of march, was surrounded and taken by some French and Indians. His son escaped, and brought intelligence to his warriors; they hastened to rescue or revenge him, but found him tied to a tree. The French had been disposed to shoot him, but their savage allies declared they would abandon them should they do so; having some tie of friendship or kindred with the chieftain, who thus rejoined the troops unharmed.

For several days Washington had suffered from fever, accompanied by intense headache, and his illness increased in violence to such a degree that he was unable to ride, and had to be conveyed for a part of the time in a covered wagon. He was unable to bear the jolting of the wagon, but it needed an interposition of the kindly-intended authority of General Braddock to bring him to a halt at the great crossings of the Youghiogeny. There the general assigned him a guard, provided him with necessaries, and requested him to remain, under care of his physician, Dr. Craik, until the arrival of Colonel Dunbar's detachment, which was two days' march in the rear; giving him his word of honor that he should, at all events, be enabled to rejoin the main division before it reached the French fort.

[The march of the army, after leaving Washington, was excessively slow. In the course of the first day, (June 24th) they came to a deserted Indian camp, the trees about it being stripped and painted with threats and scurrilous taunts written in the French language, showing that white men were with the savages. On the next day, Indians were seen hovering in the woods. In crossing a mountain the carriages had to be lowered with the assistance of the sailors, by means of tackle. On the 26th there was a laborious march of but four miles. In the evening they came to a deserted camp, the fires of which were yet burning. The march continued to be toilful and difficult. On one day it did not exceed two miles, having to cut a passage over a mountain. On July 4th they encamped at Thicketty Run. The general now supposed himself to be within thirty miles of Fort Duquesne. Two Indians consented to reconnoitre it. They returned on the 6th, having been close to the fort. But few men were to be seen, and few tracks, if any. Gist, who had also reconnoitred the fort, returned and corroborated their story. He had, however, observed a smoke between the camp and the fort, made probably by some scouting party.]

On the same day, during the march, three or four men, loitering in the rear of the grenadiers, were killed and scalped. Several of the grenadiers set off to take revenge. They came upon a party of Indians, who held up boughs and grounded their arms—the concerted sign of amity. Not perceiving or understanding it, the grenadiers fired upon them and one fell. It proved to be the son of Scarooyadi. Aware too late of their error, the grenadiers brought the body to the camp. The conduct of Braddock was admirable on the occasion. He sent for the father and the other Indians, and condoled with them on the lamentable occurrence; making them the customary presents of expiation. But what was more to the point, he caused the youth to be buried with the honors of war; at his request the officers attended the funeral, and a volley was fired over the grave. These soldier-like tributes of respect to the deceased, and sympathy with the survivors, soothed the feelings and gratified the pride of the father, and attached him more firmly to the service.

We will return now to Washington in his sick encampment on the banks of the Youghiogeny, where he was left repining at the departure of the troops without him. He now considered himself sufficiently recovered to rejoin the troops, and his only anxiety was that he should not be able to do it in time for the great blow. He was rejoiced, therefore, on the 3d of July, by the arrival of an advanced party of one hundred men convoying provisions. Being still too weak to mount his horse, he set off with the escort in a covered wagon; and after a most fatiguing journey, over mountain and through forest, reached Braddock's camp on the 8th of July. It was on the east side of the Monongahela, about two miles from the river, and about fifteen miles from Fort Duquesne.

Washington was warmly received on his arrival, especially by his fellow aides-de-camp, Morris and Orme. He was just in time, for the attack upon Fort Duquesne was to be made on the following day. The neighboring country had been reconnoitred to determine upon a plan of attack. The fort stood on the same side of the Monongahela with the camp, but there was a narrow pass between them of about two miles, with the river on the left and a very high mountain on the right, and in its present state quite impassable for carriages. The route determined on was to cross the Monongahela by a ford immediately opposite to the camp; proceed along the west bank of the river, for about five miles, then recross by another ford to the eastern side, and push on to the fort. The river at these fords was shallow, and the banks were not steep.

According to the plan of arrangement, Lieutenant-Colonel Gage, with the advance, was to cross the river before daybreak, march to the second ford, and re-crossing there, take post to secure the passage of the main force. The advance was to be composed of two companies of grenadiers, one hundred and sixty infantry, the independent company of Captain Horatio Gates, and two six-pounders. Washington, who had already seen enough of regular troops to doubt their infallibility in wild bush-fighting, and who knew the dangerous nature of the ground they were to traverse, ventured to suggest that the Virginia rangers, being accustomed to the country and to Indian warfare, might be thrown in the advance. The proposition drew an angry reply from the general, indignant, very probably, that a young provincial officer should presume to school a veteran like himself.

Early next morning (July 9th), before daylight, Colonel Gage crossed with the advance. He was followed, at some distance, by Sir John St. Clair, with a working party of two hundred and fifty men, to make roads for the artillery and baggage. They had with them their wagons of tools, and two six-pounders. By sunrise, the main body turned out in full uniform. All looked as if arrayed for a fête, rather than a battle. As it was supposed the enemy would be on the watch for the crossing of the troops, it had been agreed that they should do it in the greatest order, with bayonets fixed, colors flying, and drums and fifes beating and playing. They accordingly made a gallant appearance as they forded the Monongahela and wound along its banks and through the open forests. About noon they reached the second ford. Gage, with the advance, was on the opposite side of the Monongahela, posted according to orders; but the river bank had not been sufficiently sloped. The artillery and baggage drew up along the beach and halted until one, when the second crossing took place. When all had passed, there was again a halt close by a small stream called Frazier's Run, until the general arranged the order of march.

First went the advance, under Gage, preceded by the engineers and guides, and six light horsemen. Then, Sir John St. Clair and the working party, with their wagons and the two six-pounders. On each side were thrown out four flanking parties. Then, at some distance, the general was to follow with the main body, the artillery and baggage preceded and flanked by light horse and squads of infantry; while the Virginian, and other provincial troops, were to form the rear guard.

The ground before them was level until about half a mile from the river, where a rising ground, covered with long grass, low bushes, and scattered trees, sloped gently up to a range of hills. The whole country, generally speaking, was a forest, with no clear opening but the road, which was about twelve feet wide, and flanked by two ravines, concealed by trees and thickets. Had Braddock been schooled in the warfare of the woods, he would have thrown out Indian scouts or Virginia rangers in the advance, and on the flanks, to beat up the woods and ravines; but he suffered his troops to march forward through the centre of the plain, with merely their usual guides and flanking parties.

It was now near two o'clock. The advanced party and the working party had crossed the plain and were ascending the rising ground. Braddock was about to follow with the main body and had given the word to march, when he heard an excessively quick and heavy firing in front. Washington, who was with the general, surmised that the evil he had apprehended had come to pass. For want of scouting parties ahead, the advance parties were suddenly and warmly attacked. Braddock ordered Lieutenant-Colonel Burton to hasten to their assistance with the vanguard of the main body, eight hundred strong. The residue, four hundred, were halted, and posted to protect the artillery and baggage. The firing continued, with fearful yelling. There was a terrible uproar. By the general's orders an aide-de-camp spurred forward to bring him an account of the nature of the attack. Without waiting for his return the general himself, finding the turmoil increase, moved forward, leaving Sir Peter Halket with the command of the baggage.

The van of the advance had indeed been taken by surprise. It was composed of two companies of carpenters or pioneers to cut the road, and two flank companies of grenadiers to protect them. Suddenly the engineer who preceded them to mark out the road gave the alarm, "French and Indians!" A body of them was approaching rapidly. There was sharp firing on both sides at first. Several of the enemy fell; among them their leader; but a murderous fire broke out from among trees and a ravine on the right, and the woods resounded with unearthly whoops and yellings. The Indian rifle was at work, levelled by unseen hands. Most of the grenadiers and many of the pioneers were shot down. The survivors were driven in on the advance.

Gage ordered his men to fix bayonets and form in order of battle. They did so in hurry and trepidation. He would have scaled a hill on the right, whence there was the severest firing. Not a platoon would quit the line of march. They were more dismayed by the yells than by the rifles of the unseen savages. The latter extended themselves along the hill and in the ravines; but their whereabouts was only known by their demoniac cries and the puffs of smoke from their rifles. The soldiers fired wherever they saw the smoke. The officers tried in vain to restrain them until they should see their foe. All orders were unheeded; in their fright they shot at random, killing some of their own flanking parties, and of the vanguard, as they came running in. The covert fire grew more intense. In a short time most of the officers and many of the men of the advance were killed or wounded. Colonel Gage himself received a wound. The advance fell back in dismay upon Sir John St. Clair's corps, which was equally dismayed. The cannon belonging to it were deserted.

Colonel Burton had come up with the reinforcement, and was forming his men to face the rising ground on the right, when both of the advanced detachments fell back upon him, and all now was confusion. By this time the general was upon the ground. He tried to rally the men. The colors were advanced in different places to separate the men of the two regiments. The general ordered the officers to form the men, tell them off into small divisions, and advance with them; but the soldiers could not be prevailed upon either by threats or entreaties. The Virginia troops, accustomed to the Indian mode of fighting, scattered themselves, and took post behind trees, whence they could pick off the lurking foe. In this way they, in some degree, protected the regulars. Washington advised General Braddock to adopt the same plan with the regulars; but he persisted in forming them into platoons; consequently they were cut down from behind logs and trees as fast as they could advance. Several attempted to take to the trees, without orders, but the general stormed at them, called them cowards, and even struck them with the flat of his sword. Several of the Virginians, who had taken post and were doing good service in this manner, were slain by the fire of the regulars, directed wherever a smoke appeared among the trees.

The officers behaved with consummate bravery; and Washington beheld with admiration those who, in camp or on the march, had appeared to him to have an almost effeminate regard for personal ease and convenience, now exposing themselves to imminent death, with a courage that kindled with the thickening horrors. In the vain hope of inspiriting the men to drive off the enemy from the flanks and regain the cannon, they would dash forward singly or in groups. They were invariably shot down; for the Indians aimed at every one who appeared to have command. Some were killed by random shot of their own men, who, crowded in masses, fired with affrighted rapidity, but without aim. Soldiers in the front ranks were killed by those in the rear. Between friend and foe, the slaughter of the officers was terrible.

Throughout this disastrous day, Washington distinguished himself by his courage and presence of mind. His brother aids, Orme and Morris, were wounded and disabled early in the action, and the whole duty of carrying the orders of the general devolved on him. His danger was imminent and incessant. He was in every part of the field, a conspicuous mark for the murderous rifle. Two horses were shot under him. Four bullets passed through his coat. His escape without a wound was almost miraculous. At one time he was sent to the main body to bring the artillery into action. All there was likewise in confusion; for the Indians had extended themselves along the ravine so as to flank the reserve and carry slaughter into the ranks. Sir Peter Halket had been shot down at the head of his regiment. The men who should have served the guns were paralyzed. Had they raked the ravines with grapeshot the day might have been saved. In his ardor, Washington sprang from his horse, wheeled and pointed a brass field-piece with his own hand, and directed an effective discharge into the woods; but neither his efforts nor example were of avail. The men could not be kept to the guns.

Braddock still remained in the centre of the field, in the desperate hope of retrieving the fortunes of the day. His secretary, Shirley, had fallen by his side. Five horses had been killed under him; still he kept his ground, vainly endeavoring to check the flight of his men, or at least to effect their retreat in good order. At length a bullet passed through his right arm, and lodged itself in his lungs. He fell from his horse, but was caught by Captain Stewart, of the Virginia guards, who, with the assistance of another American and a servant, placed him in a tumbril. It was with much difficulty they got him out of the field — in his despair he desired to be left there.

The rout now became complete. Baggage, stores, artillery, everything was abandoned. The wagoners took each a horse out of his team and fled. The officers were swept off with the men in this headlong flight. It was rendered more precipitate by the shouts and yells of the savages, numbers of whom rushed forth from their coverts and pursued the fugitives to the river side. Fortunately for the latter, the victors gave up the pursuit in their eagerness to collect the spoil. The shattered army continued its flight after it had crossed the Monongahela, a wretched wreck of the brilliant little force that had recently gleamed along its banks, confident of victory. Out of eighty-six officers, twenty-six had been killed, and thirty-six wounded. The number of rank and file killed and wounded was upwards of seven hundred.

About a hundred men were brought to a halt about a quarter of a mile from the ford of the river. Here was Braddock, with his wounded aides-de-camp and some of his officers. Braddock was still able to give orders, and had a faint hope of being able to keep possession of the ground until reinforced. Most of the men were stationed in a very advantageous spot about two hundred yards from the road; and Lieutenant-Colonel Burton posted out small parties and sentinels. Before an hour had elapsed most of the men had stolen off. Being thus deserted, Braddock and his officers continued their retreat; he would have mounted his horse but was unable, and had to be carried by soldiers. Orme and Morris were placed on litters borne by horses. They were subsequently joined by Colonel Gage with eighty men whom he had rallied.

Washington, in the meantime, notwithstanding his weak state, being found most efficient in frontier service, was sent to Colonel Dunbar's camp, forty miles distant, with orders for him to hurry forward provisions, hospital stores, and wagons for the wounded, under the escort of two grenadier companies. It was a hard and a melancholy ride throughout the night and the following day. The tidings of the defeat preceded him, borne by the wagoners who had mounted their horses, on Braddock's fall, and fled from the field of battle.

Washington arrived at the camp in the evening. The orders which he brought were executed during the night and he was in the saddle early in the morning accompanying the convoy of supplies. At Gist's plantation, about thirteen miles off, he met Gage and his scanty force escorting Braddock and his wounded officers. Captain Stewart, and a sad remnant of the Virginia light horse, still accompanied the general as his guard. The Captain had been unremitting in his attentions to him during the retreat. There was a halt of one day at Dunbar's camp for the repose and relief of the wounded. On the 13th they resumed their melancholy march, and that night reached the Great Meadows.

The proud spirit of Braddock was broken by his defeat. He remained silent the first evening after the battle, only ejaculating at night, "Who would have thought it!" He was equally silent the following day; yet hope still seemed to linger in his breast, from another ejaculation: "We shall better know how to deal with them another time!" He was grateful for the attentions paid to him by Captain Stewart and Washington, and more than once, it is said, expressed his admiration of the gallantry displayed by the Virginians in the action. He died on the night of the 13th, at the Great Meadows, the place of Washington's discomfiture in the previous year. His obsequies were performed before break of day. The chaplain having been wounded, Washington read the funeral service.

Reproach spared him not, even when in his grave. The failure of the expedition was attributed both in England and America to his obstinacy, his technical pedantry, and his military conceit. He had been continually warned to be on his guard against ambush and surprise, but without avail. Had he taken the advice urged on him by Washington and others, to employ scouting parties of Indians and rangers, he would never have been so signally surprised and defeated. Still his dauntless conduct on the field of battle shows him to have been a man of fearless spirit; and he was universally allowed to be an accomplished disciplinarian.

The obsequies of the unfortunate Braddock being finished, the escort continued its retreat with the sick and wounded. On the 17th, the sad cavalcade reached the fort, and were relieved from the incessant apprehension of pursuit. Here, too, flying reports had preceded them, brought by fugitives from the battle, who, with the disposition usual in such cases to exaggerate, had represented the whole army as massacred. Dunbar arrived shortly afterward with the remainder of the army.

The true reason why the enemy did not pursue the retreating army was not known until some time afterwards, and added to the disgrace of the defeat. They were not the main force of the French, but a mere detachment of 72 regulars, 146 Canadians, and 637 Indians—855 in all, led by Captain de Beaujeu. De Contrecoeur, the commander of Fort Duquesne, had received information, through his scouts, that the English, three thousand strong, were within six leagues of his fort. Despairing of making an effectual defence against such a superior force, he was balancing in his mind whether to abandon his fort without awaiting their arrival, or to capitulate on honorable terms. In this dilemma, Beaujeu prevailed on him to let him sally forth with a detachment to form an ambush and give check to the enemy. De Beaujeu was to have taken post at the river, and disputed the passage at the ford. For that purpose he was hurrying forward when discovered by the pioneers of Gage's advance party. He was a gallant officer, and fell at the beginning of the fight. The whole number of killed and wounded of French and Indians did not exceed seventy.

The affair of Braddock remains a memorable event in American history, and has been characterized as "the most extraordinary victory ever obtained, and the farthest flight ever made." It struck a fatal blow to the deference for British prowess, which once amounted almost to bigotry, throughout the provinces.

CHAPTER IX.

WASHINGTON IN COMMAND.—PANICS ON THE FRONTIER.

Washington arrived at Mount Vernon on the 26th of July, still in feeble condition from his long illness. His campaigning, thus far, had trenched upon his private fortune, and impaired one of the best of constitutions. His connection with the army ceased at the death of Braddock, but his military duties continued as adjutant-general of the northern division of the province, and he immediately issued orders for the county lieutenants to hold the militia in readiness for parade and exercise, foreseeing that, in the present defenceless state of the frontier, there would be need of their services.

Tidings of the rout and retreat of the army had circulated far and near, and spread consternation throughout the country. Immediate incursions both of French and Indians were apprehended; and volunteer companies began to form, for the purpose of marching across the mountains to the scene of danger.

On the 4th of August, Governor Dinwiddie convened the Assembly to devise measures for the public safety. The sense of danger had quickened the slow patriotism of the burgesses; they no longer held back supplies; forty thousand pounds were promptly voted, and orders issued for the raising of a regiment of one thousand men.

Washington's friends urged him to present himself at Williamsburg as a candidate for the command; they were confident of his success, notwithstanding that strong interest was making for the governor's favorite, Colonel Innes. With mingled modesty and pride, Washington declined to be a solicitor. The only terms, he said, on which he would accept a command were a certainty as to rank and emoluments, a right to appoint his field officers, and the supply of a sufficient military chest; but to solicit the command, and, at the same time, to make stipulations, would be a little incongruous, and carry with it the face of self-sufficiency.

While this was in agitation, he received letters from his mother, again imploring him not to risk himself in these frontier wars. His answer was characteristic: "Honored Madam—If it is in my power to avoid going to the Ohio again, I shall; but if the command is pressed upon me by the general voice of the country, and offered upon such terms as cannot be objected against, it would reflect dishonor on me to refuse it; and that, I am sure, must, and ought, to give you greater uneasiness than my going in an honorable command. Upon no other terms will I accept it."

On the very day that this letter was despatched (Aug. 14), he received intelligence of his appointment to the command on the terms specified in his letters to his friends. His commission nominated him commander-in-chief of all the forces raised, or to be raised in the colony. The Assembly also voted three hundred pounds to him, and proportionate sums to the other officers and to the privates of the Virginia companies, in consideration of their gallant conduct and their losses in the late battle. The officers next in command under him were Lieutenant-Colonel Adam Stephens and Major Andrew Lewis.

The appointment of Washington to his present station was the more gratifying and honorable from being a popular one, made in deference to public sentiment; to which Governor Dinwiddie was obliged to sacrifice his strong inclination in favor of Colonel Innes. It is thought that the governor never afterwards regarded Washington with a friendly eye. His conduct towards him subsequently was on various occasions cold and ungracious.

Having held a conference with Governor Dinwiddie at Williamsburg, and received his instructions, Washington repaired on the 14th of September to Winchester, where he fixed his head-quarters. It was a place as yet of trifling magnitude, but important from its position; being a central point where the main roads met, leading from north to south and east to west, and commanding the channels of traffic and communication between some of the most important colonies and a great extent of frontier.

Here he was brought into frequent and cordial communication with his old friend, Lord Fairfax. The stir of war had revived a spark of that military fire which animated the veteran nobleman in the days of his youth, when an officer in the cavalry regiment of the Blues. He was lord-lieutenant of the county. Greenway Court was his head-quarters. He had organized a troop of horse, which occasionally was exercised about the lawn of his domain, and he was now as prompt to mount his steed for a cavalry parade as he ever was for a fox-chase.

His services were soon put in requisition. Washington, having visited the frontier posts, established recruiting places and taken other measures of security, had set off for Williamsburg on military business, when an express arrived at Winchester from Colonel Stephens, who commanded at Fort Cumberland, giving the alarm that a body of Indians were ravaging the country, burning the houses and slaughtering the inhabitants. The express was instantly forwarded after Washington; in the meantime, Lord Fairfax sent out orders for the militia of Fairfax and Prince William counties to arm and hasten to the defence of Winchester, where all was confusion and affright. One fearful account followed another. The whole country beyond it was said to be at the mercy of the savages. They had blockaded the rangers in the little fortresses or outposts provided for the protection of neighborhoods. They were advancing upon Winchester with fire, tomahawk and scalping-knife. The country people were flocking into the town for safety—the townspeople were moving off to the settlements beyond the Blue Ridge. The beautiful valley of the Shenandoah was likely to become a scene of savage desolation.

In the height of the confusion, Washington rode into the town. He had been overtaken by Colonel Stephens' express. His presence inspired some degree of confidence, and he succeeded in stopping most of the fugitives.

Expresses were sent off to hurry up the militia ordered out by Lord Fairfax. Scouts were ordered out to discover the number of the foe, and convey assurances of succor to the rangers said to be blocked up in the fortresses, though Washington suspected the latter to be "more encompassed by fear than by the enemy." Smiths were set to work to furbish up and repair such firearms as were in the place, and wagons were sent off for musket balls, flints, and provisions. Instead, however, of animated co-operation, Washington was encountered by difficulties at every step. The wagons in question had to be impressed, and the wagoners compelled by force to assist. "No orders," writes he, "are obeyed, but such as a party of soldiers or my own drawn sword enforces. Without this, not a single horse, for the most earnest occasion, can be had."

In the meantime the panic and confusion increased. On Sunday an express hurried into town, breathless with haste and terror. The Indians, he said, were but twelve miles off; they had attacked the house of Isaac Julian; the inhabitants were flying for their lives. Washington immediately ordered the town guards to be strengthened; armed some recruits who had just arrived, and sent out two scouts to reconnoitre the enemy. It was a sleepless night in Winchester. Horror increased with the dawn; before the men could be paraded, a second express arrived, ten times more terrified than the former. The Indians were within four miles of the town, killing and destroying all before them. He had heard the constant firing of the savages and the shrieks of their victims.

The terror of Winchester now passed all bounds. Washington put himself at the head of about forty men, militia and recruits, and pushed for the scene of carnage. The result is almost too ludicrous for record. The whole cause of the alarm proved to be three drunken troopers, carousing, hallooing, and ever and anon firing off their pistols. Washington interrupted them in the midst of their revel and blasphemy and conducted them prisoners to town. The alarm thus originating had spread throughout the country. A captain, who arrived with recruits from Alexandria, reported that he had found the road across the Blue Ridge obstructed by crowds of people flying for their lives, whom he endeavored in vain to stop. They declared that Winchester was in flames!

At length the band of Indians, whose ravages had produced this consternation throughout the land, and whose numbers did not exceed one hundred and fifty, being satiated with carnage, conflagration and plunder, retreated, bearing off spoils and captives. Intelligent scouts sent out by Washington followed their traces, and brought back certain intelligence that they had recrossed the Alleghany Mountains and returned to their homes on the Ohio. This report allayed the public panic and restored temporary quiet to the harassed frontier. Most of the Indians engaged in these ravages were Delawares and Shawnees, who, since Braddock's defeat, had been gained over by the French. Scarooyadi, successor to the half-king, remained true to the English, and vindicated his people to the governor and council of Pennsylvania from the charge of having had any share in the late massacres.

[Washington now learned the fate of the other enterprises included in the plan of military operations. The defeat of Braddock paralyzed the expedition against Niagara. The troops assembled at Albany were struck with consternation, and deserted. By the end of August, Shirley was in force at Oswego. But storms, sickness, and other impediments caused the completion of the enterprise to be deferred until the following year.

Gen. Wm. Johnson, it will be recollected, had the command of the expedition against Crown Point, on Lake Champlain. A fort was erected at the carrying-place on the Hudson, between that river and Lake George, subsequently called Fort Edward. Part of the force were left to garrison it; the main body advanced to Lake George. Meanwhile there was great consternation in Canada. Three thousand troops, under Baron de Dieskaw, had arrived at Quebec. Yielding to public importunities, he advanced to Crown Point for its defence. His force was augmented by eight hundred Canadians and seven hundred Indians, the latter under command of the Chevalier St. Pierre.

In the meantime, Johnson remained encamped on the south end of Lake George. On September 7th, news was received that the French had been seen within four miles of the carrying-place. A detachment was sent to intercept them, which was attacked and driven back. A panic seized upon the camp as the French emerged from the forest in battle array, led by Dieskaw. But the Canadians and Indians held back. The camp recovered from its panic, artillery and musketry opened on the assailants, whose fire began to slacken. Johnson's men and the Indians leaped over the breastworks and a medley fight ensued, that ended in the slaughter, rout, or capture of the enemy. Dieskaw was mortally wounded; St. Pierre was slain in the attack on the detachment. The baron had intended the surprise of Fort Edward, but the Indians and Canadians refused to attack it, fearful of the cannon: he here changed his plan therefor, and attempted to surprise the camp. Johnson, having erected a stockaded fort, which received the name of William Henry, garrisoned it, and returned to Albany. In reward for his services he received five thousand pounds and a baronetcy.]

Mortifying experience had convinced Washington of the inefficiency of the militia laws, and he now set about effecting a reformation. Through his great and persevering efforts, an act was passed in the Virginia Legislature giving prompt operation to court-martial; punishing insubordination, mutiny and desertion with adequate severity; strengthening the authority of a commander, so as to enable him to enforce order and discipline among officers as well as privates; and to avail himself, in time of emergency and for the common safety, of the means and services of individuals. In disciplining his men, they were instructed not merely in ordinary and regular tactics, but in all the strategy of Indian warfare, and what is called "bush-fighting"—a knowledge indispensable in the wild wars of the wilderness. Stockaded forts, too, were constructed at various points, as places of refuge and defence, in exposed neighborhoods.

His exertions, however, were impeded by one of those questions of precedence which had so often annoyed him, arising from the difference between crown and provincial commissions. Maryland, having by a scanty appropriation raised a small militia force, stationed Captain Dagworthy, with a company of thirty men, at Fort Cumberland, which stood within the boundaries of that province. Dagworthy had served in Canada in the preceding war, and had received a king's commission. This he had since commuted for half-pay, and, of course, had virtually parted with its privileges. He was nothing more, therefore, than a Maryland provincial captain, at the head of thirty men. He now, however, assumed to act under his royal commission, and refused to obey the orders of any officer, however high his rank, who merely held his commission from a governor. Nay, when Governor, or rather Colonel Innes, who commanded at the fort, was called away to North Carolina by his private affairs, the captain took upon himself the command and insisted upon it as his right.

Parties instantly arose, and quarrels ensued among the inferior officers; grave questions were agitated between the Governors of Maryland and Virginia as to the fort itself; the former claiming it as within his province, the latter insisting that, as it had been built according to orders sent by the king, it was the king's fort, and could not be subject to the authority of Maryland.

Washington refrained from mingling in this dispute; but intimated that if the commander-in-chief of the forces of Virginia must yield precedence to a Maryland captain of thirty men, he should have to resign his commission, as he had been compelled to do before, by a question of military rank.

So difficult was it, however, to settle these disputes of precedence, especially where the claims of two governors came in collision, that it was determined to refer the matter to Major-general Shirley, who had succeeded Braddock in the general command of the colonies. For this purpose Washington was to go to Boston, obtain a decision from Shirley of the point in dispute, and a general regulation by which these difficulties could be prevented in future. It was thought, also, that in a conference with the commander-in-chief he might inform himself of the military measures in contemplation.

Accordingly, on the 4th of February (1756), leaving Colonel Adam Stephens in command of the troops, Washington set out on his mission, accompanied by his aide-de-camp, Captain George Mercer, of Virginia, and Captain Stewart, of the Virginia light horse. The party travelled in Virginia style, on horseback, attended by their black servants in livery. In this way they accomplished a journey of five hundred miles in the depth of winter; stopping for some days at Philadelphia and New York. Those cities were then comparatively small, and the arrival of a party of young Southern officers attracted attention. The late disastrous battle was still the theme of every tongue, and the honorable way in which these young officers had acquitted themselves in it made them objects of universal interest. Washington's fame, especially, had gone before him; having been spread by the officers who had served with him and by the public honors decreed him by the Virginia Legislature.

The mission to General Shirley was entirely successful as to the question of rank. A written order from the commander-in-chief determined that Dagworthy was entitled to the rank of a provincial captain only, and of course, must on all occasions give precedence to Colonel Washington as a provincial field officer. The latter was disappointed, however, in the hope of getting himself and his officers put upon the regular establishment, with commissions from the king, and had to remain subjected to mortifying questions of rank and etiquette when serving in company with regular troops.

From General Shirley he learnt that the main objects of the ensuing campaign would be the reduction of Fort Niagara, so as to cut off the communication between Canada and Louisiana, the capture of Ticonderoga and Crown Point, as a measure of safety for New York, the besieging of Fort Duquesne, and the menacing of Quebec by a body of troops which were to advance by the Kennebec River.

The official career of General Shirley was drawing to a close. He was recalled to England, and was to be superseded by General Abercrombie. The general command in America, however, was to be held by the Earl of Loudoun, who was invested with powers almost equal to those of a viceroy, being placed above all the colonial governors. Beside his general command he was to be governor of Virginia and colonel of a royal American regiment of four battalions, to be raised in the colonies, but furnished with officers who, like himself, had seen foreign service. The campaign would open on his arrival, which it was expected would be early in the spring; and brilliant results were anticipated.

Washington remained ten days in Boston, receiving the most hospitable attentions from the polite and intelligent society of the place, after which he returned to New York. Tradition gives very different motives from those of business for his sojourns in the latter city. He found there an early friend and school-mate, Beverly Robinson, son of John Robinson, speaker of the Virginia House of Burgesses. He was living happily and prosperously with a young and wealthy bride, having married one of the nieces and heiresses of Mr. Adolphus Philipse, a rich landholder. At the house of Mr. Beverly Robinson, Washington met Miss Mary Philipse, sister of Mrs. Robinson, a young lady whose personal attractions are said to have rivalled her reputed wealth. A life of constant activity and care, passed for the most part in the wilderness and on the frontier, far from female society, had left Washington little mood or leisure for the indulgence of the tender sentiment; but made him more sensible, in the present brief interval of gay and social life, to the attractions of an elegant woman, brought up in the polite circle of New York. That he was an open admirer of Miss Philipse is an historical fact; that he sought her hand, but was refused, is traditional. The most probable version of the story is, that he was called away by his public duties before he had made sufficient approaches in his siege of the lady's heart to warrant a summons to surrender. In the latter part of March we find him at Williamsburg attending the opening of the Legislature of Virginia, eager to promote measures for the protection of the frontier and the capture of Fort Duquesne—the leading object of his ambition. While thus engaged, he received a letter from a friend and confidant in New York, warning him to hasten back to that city before it was too late, as Captain Morris, who had been his fellow aide-de-camp under Braddock, was laying close siege to Miss Philipse. Sterner alarms, however, summoned him in another direction. Expresses from Winchester brought word that the French had made another sortie from Fort Duquesne, accompanied by a band of savages, and were spreading terror and desolation through the country. In this moment of exigency all softer claims were forgotten; Washington repaired in all haste to his post at Winchester, and Captain Morris was left to urge his suit unrivalled and carry off the prize.

Report had not exaggerated the troubles of the frontier. It was marauded by merciless bands of savages, led, in some instances, by Frenchmen. Travellers were murdered, farm houses burnt down, families butchered, and even stockaded forts, or houses of refuge, attacked in open day. The marauders had crossed the mountains and penetrated the valley of the Shenandoah. Washington, on his arrival at Winchester, found the inhabitants in great dismay. He resolved immediately to organize a force, composed partly of troops from Fort Cumberland, partly of militia from Winchester and its vicinity, to put himself at its head, and "scour the woods and suspected places in all the mountains and valleys of this part of the frontier, in quest of the Indians and their more cruel associates."

He accordingly despatched an express to Fort Cumberland with orders for a detachment from the garrison; "but how," said he, "are men to be raised at Winchester, since orders are no longer regarded in the county?" Lord Fairfax, and other militia officers with whom he consulted, advised that each captain should call a private muster of his men, and read before them an address, or "exhortation" as it was called, being an appeal to their patriotism and fears, and a summons to assemble on the 15th of April to enroll themselves for the projected mountain foray. This measure was adopted; the private musterings occurred; the exhortation was read; the time and place of assemblage appointed; but, when the day of enrollment arrived, not more than fifteen men appeared upon the ground. In the meantime the express returned with sad accounts from Fort Cumberland. No troops could be furnished from that quarter. The garrison was scarcely strong enough for self-defence, having sent out detachments in different directions.

Horrors accumulated at Winchester. Every hour brought its tale of terror, true or false, of houses burnt, families massacred, or beleaguered and famishing in stockaded forts. The danger approached. A scouting party had been attacked in the Warm Spring Mountain, about twenty miles distant, by a large body of French and Indians, mostly on horseback. The captain of the scouting party and several of his men had been slain, and the rest put to flight. An attack was apprehended, and the terrors of the people rose to agony. They now turned to Washington as their main hope. The women surrounded him, holding up their children and imploring him with tears and cries to save them from the savages. The youthful commander looked round on the suppliant crowd with a countenance beaming with pity and a heart wrung with anguish. A letter to Governor Dinwiddie drew from him an instant order for a militia force from the upper counties to his assistance; but the Virginia newspapers, in descanting on the frontier troubles, threw discredit on the army and its officers, and attached blame to its commander. Stung to the quick by this injustice, Washington publicly declared that nothing but the imminent danger of the times prevented him from instantly resigning a command from which he could never reap either honor or benefit. His sensitiveness called forth strong letters from his friends, assuring him of the high sense entertained at the seat of government, and elsewhere, of his merits and services.

In fact, the situation and services of the youthful commander, shut up in a frontier town, destitute of forces, surrounded by savage foes, gallantly, though despairingly, devoting himself to the safety of a suffering people, were properly understood throughout the country, and excited a glow of enthusiasm in his favor. The Legislature, too, began at length to act, but timidly and inefficiently. Its measure of relief was an additional appropriation of twenty thousand pounds, and an increase of the provincial force to fifteen hundred men. With this, it was proposed to erect and garrison a chain of frontier forts, extending through the ranges of the Alleghany Mountains, from the Potomac to the borders of North Carolina; a distance of between three and four hundred miles. This was one of the inconsiderate projects devised by Governor Dinwiddie.

Washington, in letters to the governor and to the speaker of the House of Burgesses, urged the impolicy of such a plan, with their actual force and means. The forts, he observed, ought to be within fifteen or eighteen miles of each other, that their spies might be able to keep watch over the intervening country, otherwise the Indians would pass between them unperceived, effect their ravages, and escape to the mountains, swamps and ravines before the troops from the forts could be assembled to pursue them. They ought each to be garrisoned with eighty or a hundred men, so as to afford detachments of sufficient strength, without leaving the garrison too weak. It was evident, therefore, observed he, that to garrison properly such a line of forts would require at least two thousand men. And even then, a line of such extent might be broken through at one end before the other end could yield assistance. His idea of a defensive plan was to build a strong fort at Winchester, the central point, where all the main roads met of a wide range of scattered settlements, where tidings could soonest be collected from every quarter, and whence reinforcements and supplies could most readily be forwarded. It was to be a grand deposit of military stores, a residence for commanding officers, a place of refuge for the women and children in time of alarm, when the men had suddenly to take the field; in a word, it was to be the citadel of the frontier. Beside this, he would have three or four large fortresses erected at convenient distances upon the frontiers, with powerful garrisons, so as to be able to throw out, in constant succession, strong scouting parties to range the country. Fort Cumberland he condemned as being out of the province and out of the track of Indian incursions.

His representations with respect to military laws and regulations were equally cogent. In the late act of the Assembly for raising a regiment it was provided that, in cases of emergency, if recruits should not offer in sufficient number, the militia might be drafted to supply the deficiencies, but only to serve until December, and not to be marched out of the province. In this case, said he, before they have entered upon service, or got the least smattering of duty, they will claim a discharge; if they are pursuing an enemy who has committed the most unheard-of cruelties, he has only to step across the Potomac and he is safe. Then as to the limits of service, they might just as easily have been enlisted for seventeen months as seven.

Then as to punishments: death, it was true, had been decreed for mutiny and desertion; but there was no punishment for cowardice; for holding correspondence with the enemy; for quitting, or sleeping on one's post; all capital offences, according to the military codes of Europe. Neither were there provisions for quartering or billeting soldiers, or impressing wagons and other conveyances, in times of exigency. To crown all, no court-martial could sit out of Virginia; a most embarrassing regulation, when troops were fifty or a hundred miles beyond the frontier. He earnestly suggested amendments on all these points, as well as with regard to the soldiers' pay; which was less than that of the regular troops, or the troops of most of the other provinces.

All these suggestions, showing at this youthful age that forethought and cir-cumspection which distinguished him throughout life, were repeatedly and el-oquently urged upon Governor Dinwiddie, with very little effect. The plan of a frontier line of twenty-three forts was persisted in. Fort Cumberland was pertina-ciously kept up at a great and useless expense of men and money, and the militia laws remained lax and inefficient. It was decreed, however, that the great central fort at Winchester, recommended by Washington, should be erected.

In the height of the alarm a company of one hundred gentlemen, mounted and equipped, volunteered their services to repair to the frontier. They were headed by Peyton Randolph. No doubt they would have conducted themselves gallantly had they been put to the test; but before they arrived near the scene of danger the alarm was over. About the beginning of May, scouts brought in word that the tracks of the marauding savages tended toward Fort Duquesne, as if on the return. In a little while it was ascertained that they had recrossed the Alleghany Mountain to the Ohio in such numbers as to leave a beaten track, equal to that made in the preceding year by the army of Braddock.

The repeated inroads of the savages called for an effectual and permanent check. The idea of being constantly subject to the irruptions of a deadly foe, that moved with stealth and mystery, and was only to be traced by its ravages and counted by its footprints, discouraged all settlement of the country. The beautiful valley of the Shenandoah was fast becoming a deserted and a silent place. Her peo-ple, for the most part, had fled to the older settlements south of the mountains, and the Blue Ridge was likely soon to become virtually the frontier line of the province.

CHAPTER X.
FRONTIER SERVICE.

Throughout the summer of 1756, Washington exerted himself diligently in carrying out measures determined upon for frontier security. The great fortress at Winchester was commenced, and the work urged forward as expeditiously as the delays and perplexities incident to a badly organized service would permit. It received the name of Fort Loudoun, in honor of the commander-in-chief, whose arrival in Virginia was hopefully anticipated.

As to the sites of the frontier posts, they were decided upon by Washington and his officers, after frequent and long consultations; parties were sent out to work on them, and men recruited and militia drafted to garrison them. Washington visited occasionally such as were in progress, and near at hand. In the autumn, he made a tour of inspection along the whole line, accompanied by his friend, Captain Hugh Mercer. This tour furnished repeated proofs of the inefficiency of the militia system. In one place he attempted to raise a force with which to scour a region infested by roving bands of savages. After waiting several days, but five men answered to his summons. In another place, where three companies had been ordered to the relief of a fort attacked by the Indians, all that could be mustered were a captain, a lieutenant, and seven or eight men. When the militia were drafted, and appeared under arms, the case was not much better. It was now late in the autumn: their term of service, by the act of the Legislature, expired in December, — half of the time, therefore, was lost in marching out and home. Their waste of provisions was enormous. To be put on allowance, like other soldiers, they considered an indignity. For want of proper military laws, they were obstinate, self-willed and perverse. The garrisons were weak for want of men, but more so from indolence and irregularity. Not one was in a posture of defence; few but might be surprised with the greatest ease. At one fort the Indians rushed from their lurking-place, pounced upon several children playing under the walls, and bore them off before they were discovered. Another fort was surprised, and many of the people massacred in the same manner.

What rendered this year's service peculiarly irksome and embarrassing to Washington, was the nature of his correspondence with Governor Dinwiddie. That gentleman, either from the natural hurry and confusion of his mind, or from a real disposition to perplex, was extremely ambiguous and unsatisfactory in most of his orders and replies. In nothing was this disposition to perplex more apparent than in the governor's replies respecting Fort Cumberland. Washington had repeatedly urged the abandonment of this fort as a place of frontier deposit, being within the bounds of another province and out of the track of Indian incursion; so that often the alarm would not reach there until after the mischief had been effected. He applied, at length, for particular and positive directions from the governor on this head. "The following," says he, "is an exact copy of his answer: 'Fort Cumberland is a *king's* fort, and built chiefly at the charge of the colony, therefore properly under our direction until a new governor is appointed.' Now, whether I am to understand this aye or no to the plain simple question asked, Is the fort to be continued or removed? I know not. But in all important matters I am directed in this ambiguous and uncertain way."

Governor Dinwiddie subsequently made himself explicit on this point. Taking offence at some of Washington's comments on the military affairs on the frontier, he made the stand of a self-willed and obstinate man, in the case of Fort Cumberland; and represented it in such a light to Lord Loudoun as to draw from his lordship an order that it should be kept up, and an implied censure of the conduct of Washington in slighting a post of such paramount importance. Thus powerfully supported, Dinwiddie went so far as to order that the garrisons should be withdrawn from the stockades and small frontier forts, and most of the troops from Winchester, to strengthen Fort Cumberland, which was now to become head-quarters. By these meddlesome moves all previous arrangements were reversed, everything was thrown into confusion, and enormous losses and expenses were incurred. Governor Dinwiddie had never recovered from the pique caused by the popular elevation of Washington to the command in preference to his favorite, Colonel Innes. His irritation was kept alive by a little Scottish faction, who were desirous of disgusting Washington with the service, so as to induce him to resign and make way for his rival. They might have carried their point during the panic at Winchester, had not his patriotism and his sympathy with the public distress been more powerful than his self-love. He determined, he said, to bear up under these embarrassments in the hope of better regulations when Lord Loudoun should arrive; to whom he looked for the future fate of Virginia.

[While these events were occurring on the Virginia frontier, military events went on tardily and heavily at the north. The campaign against Canada hung fire. The armament coming out for the purpose under Lord Loudoun was delayed. Gen. Abercrombie reached Albany June 25th, with two regiments. July 12th word was received that the forts Ontario and Oswego were menaced by the French. Relief was delayed until the arrival of Lord Loudoun, which took place on the 29th of July. After some delays Gen. Webb left Albany, August 12th, for the relief of Oswego. But while the British commanders had debated, Field-marshal the Marquis de Montcalm had acted.] He was a different kind of soldier from Abercrombie or Loudoun. A capacious mind and enterprising spirit animated a small, but active and untiring frame. Quick in thought, quick in speech, quicker still in action, he comprehended every thing at a glance, and moved from point to point of the province with a celerity and secrecy that completely baffled his slow and pondering antagonists. Crown Point and Ticonderoga were visited, and steps taken to strengthen their works; then, hastening to Montreal, he put himself at the head of a force of regulars, Canadians, and Indians; ascended the St. Lawrence to Lake Ontario;

blocked up the mouth of the Oswego by his vessels, landed his guns, and besieged the two forts; drove the garrison out of one into the other; killed the commander, Colonel Mercer, and compelled the garrisons to surrender prisoners of war. His blow achieved, Montcalm returned in triumph to Montreal.

The season was now too far advanced for Lord Loudoun to enter upon any great military enterprise; he postponed, therefore, the great northern campaign, so much talked of and debated, until the following year.

Circumstances had led Washington to think that Lord Loudoun "had received impressions to his prejudice by false representations of facts," and that a wrong idea prevailed at head-quarters respecting the state of military affairs in Virginia. He was anxious, therefore, for an opportunity of placing all these matters in a proper light; and, understanding that there was to be a meeting in Philadelphia in the month of March, between Lord Loudoun and the southern governors, to consult about measures of defence for their respective provinces, he wrote to Governor Dinwiddie for permission to attend it. "I cannot conceive," writes Dinwiddie in reply, "what service you can be of in going there, as the plan concerted will, in course, be communicated to you and the other officers. However, as you seem so earnest to go, I now give you leave."

This ungracious reply seemed to warrant the suspicions entertained by some of Washington's friends, that it was the busy pen of Governor Dinwiddie which had given the "false representation of facts" to Lord Loudoun. About a month, therefore, before the time of the meeting, Washington addressed a long letter to his lordship, explanatory of military affairs in the quarter where he had commanded. In this he set forth the various defects in the militia laws of Virginia; the errors in its system of defence, and the inevitable confusion which had thence resulted.

The manner in which Washington was received by Lord Loudoun on arriving in Philadelphia, showed him at once that his long, explanatory letter had produced the desired effect, and that his character and conduct were justly appreciated. During his sojourn in Philadelphia he was frequently consulted on points of frontier service, and his advice was generally adopted. On one point it failed. He advised that an attack should be made on Fort Duquesne, simultaneous with the attempts on Canada. At such time a great part of the garrison would be drawn away to aid in the defence of that province, and a blow might be struck more likely to insure the peace and safety of the southern frontier than all its forts and defences. Lord Loudoun, however, was not to be convinced, or at least persuaded. According to his plan, the middle and southern provinces were to maintain a merely defensive warfare.

Washington was also disappointed a second time in the hope of having his regiment placed on the same footing as the regular army and of obtaining a king's commission; the latter he was destined never to hold. His representations with respect to Fort Cumberland had the desired effect in counteracting the mischievous intermeddling of Dinwiddie. The Virginia troops and stores were ordered to be again removed to Fort Loudoun, at Winchester, which once more became head-quarters, while Fort Cumberland was left to be occupied by a Maryland garrison.

The great plan of operations at the north was again doomed to failure. The reduction of Crown Point, on Lake Champlain, which had long been meditated, was laid aside, and the capture of Louisburg substituted, as an acquisition of far greater importance. This was a place of great consequence, situated on the isle of Cape Breton, and strongly fortified. It commanded the fisheries of Newfoundland, overawed New England, and was a main bulwark to Acadia. [In July, Loudoun set sail for Halifax, with nearly six thousand men, to join with Admiral Holbourne, who had arrived at that port with eleven ships of the line, and transports having on board six thousand men. With this united force Lord Loudoun anticipated the certain capture of Louisburg. But the French were again too quick for him. Admiral de Bois de la Mothe had arrived at Louisburg with seventeen ships of the line and three frigates. The place was ascertained to be well fortified and garrisoned. Lord Loudoun, aware of the probability of defeat and the ruin it would bring upon British arms in America, wisely, though ingloriously, returned to New York.

Scarce had the tidings of his lordship's departure for Louisburg reached Canada, when Montcalm took the fort. Fort William Henry, on the southern shore of Lake George, was now his object. Colonel Munro, with five hundred men, formed the garrison. With eight thousand men Montcalm invested the fort, and after an obstinate resistance the brave Colonel Munro surrendered, but not until most of his cannon were burst and his ammunition expended. He obtained honorable terms. Montcalm demolished the fort, and returned to Canada.]

During these unfortunate operations to the north, Washington was stationed at Winchester, shorn of part of his force by a detachment to South Carolina, and left with seven hundred men to defend a frontier of more than three hundred and fifty miles in extent. The capture and demolition of Oswego by Montcalm had produced a disastrous effect. The whole country of the five nations was abandoned to the French. The frontiers of Pennsylvania, Maryland and Virginia were harassed by repeated inroads of French and Indians, and Washington had the mortification to see the noble valley of the Shenandoah almost deserted by its inhabitants and fast relapsing into a wilderness.

The year wore away on his part in the harassing service of defending a wide frontier with an insufficient and badly organized force, and the vexations he experienced were heightened by continual misunderstandings with Governor Dinwiddie, who was evidently actuated by the petty pique of a narrow and illiberal mind, impatient of contradiction, even when in error. He took advantage of his official station to vent his spleen and gratify his petulance in a variety of ways incompatible with the courtesy of a gentleman. It may excite a grave smile at the present day to find Washington charged by this very small-minded man with looseness in his way of writing to him: with remissness in his duty towards him; and even with impertinence in the able and eloquent representations which he felt compelled to make of disastrous mismanagement in military affairs.

The multiplied vexations which Washington experienced from this man had preyed upon his spirits, and contributed, with his incessant toils and anxieties, to undermine his health. For some time he struggled with repeated attacks of dysentery and fever, and continued in the exercise of his duties; but the increased violence of his malady, and the urgent advice of his friend, Dr. Craik, the army surgeon, induced him to relinquish his post towards the end of the year and retire to Mount Vernon. The administration of Dinwiddie, however, was now at an end. He set sail for England in January, 1758.

CHAPTER XI.

OPERATIONS AGAINST THE FRENCH.—WASHING-TON'S MARRIAGE.

For several months Washington was afflicted by returns of his malady, accompanied by symptoms indicative, as he thought, of a decline. A gradual improvement in his health and a change in his prospects encouraged him to continue in what really was his favorite career, and at the beginning of April he was again in command at Fort Loudoun. Mr. Francis Fauquier had been appointed successor to Dinwiddie, and, until he should arrive, Mr. John Blair, president of the council, had, from his office, charge of the government. In the latter Washington had a friend who appreciated his character and services, and was disposed to carry out his plans.

The general aspect of affairs, also, was more animating. Under the able and intrepid administration of William Pitt, who had control of the British cabinet, an effort was made to retrieve the disgraces of the late American campaign, and to carry on the war with greater vigor. The instructions for a common fund were discontinued; there was no more talk of taxation by Parliament. Lord Loudoun, from whom so much had been anticipated, had disappointed by his inactivity, and been relieved from a command in which he had attempted much and done so little.

On the return of his lordship to England, the general command in America devolved on Major-general Abercrombie, and the forces were divided into three detached bodies; one, under Major-general Amherst, was to operate in the north with the fleet under Boscawen, for the reduction of Louisburg and the island of Cape Breton; another, under Abercrombie himself, was to proceed against Ticonderoga and Crown Point on Lake Champlain; and the third, under Brigadier-general Forbes, who had the charge of the middle and southern colonies, was to undertake the reduction of Fort Duquesne. The colonial troops were to be supplied, like the regulars, with arms, ammunition, tents and provisions at the expense of the government, but clothed and paid by the colonies; for which the king would recommend to Parliament a proper compensation. The provincial officers appointed by the governors, and of no higher rank than colonel, were to be equal in command, when united in service with those who held direct from the king, according to the date of their commissions. By these wise provisions of Mr. Pitt a fertile cause of heartburnings and dissensions was removed.

It was with the greatest satisfaction Washington saw his favorite measure at last adopted, the reduction of Fort Duquesne; and he resolved to continue in the service until that object was accomplished. He had the satisfaction subsequently of enjoying the fullest confidence of General Forbes (who was to command the expedition), who knew too well the sound judgment and practical ability evinced by him in the unfortunate campaign of Braddock not to be desirous of availing himself of his counsels. Washington still was commander-in-chief of the Virginia troops, now augmented, by an act of the Assembly, to two regiments of one thousand men each; one led by himself, the other by Colonel Byrd; the whole destined to make a part of the army of General Forbes in the expedition against Fort Duquesne.

Before we proceed to narrate the expedition against Fort Duquesne, however, we will briefly notice the conduct of the two other expeditions, which formed important parts in the plan of military operations for the year. And first, of that against Louisburg and the Island of Cape Breton. [Major-general Amherst embarked in May with nearly twelve thousand men from Halifax in the fleet of Admiral Boscawen. With him went Brigadier-general Wolfe, who was destined to gain an almost romantic celebrity. On the 2d of June, the fleet arrived at the bay of Gabarus, seven miles from Louisburg. Boisterous weather prevented the landing until the 8th of June. Three divisions, under Brigadiers Wolfe, Whetmore and Laurens, attempted the landing west of the harbor at a place feebly secured. The boats forced their way through a high surf, and under a heavy fire from the batteries. Wolfe sprang into the water when the boats grounded, dashed through the surf with his men, stormed the enemy's breastworks and batteries, and drove them from the shore. By the side of Wolfe was an Irish youth, twenty-one years of age, whom, for his gallantry, Wolfe promoted to a lieutenancy. His name was Richard Montgomery. The other divisions effected a landing, and Louisburg was formally invested. The weather continued boisterous, and the siege advanced slowly. Chevalier Drucour, who commanded at Louisburg, made a brave defence. His ships were at last all either fired or captured, his cannon dismounted, and being threatened with a general assault he capitulated at the earnest entreaty of the inhabitants.

The second expedition was against the French forts on Lakes George and Champlain. Early in July, Abercrombie was on Lake George with seven thousand regulars and nine thousand provincials. Major Israel Putnam, who had served under Johnson, was present, and with a scouting party reconnoitred the neighborhood. Upon his return, Abercrombie proceeded against Ticonderoga. The force embarked on the 5th of July, in a vast flotilla of whaleboats, rafts, bateaux, etc. With Abercrombie went Lord Howe, a young nobleman who had greatly endeared himself to the army and the people. They landed at the entrance of the strait leading to Lake Champlain, formed into three columns and pushed forward. The van of the centre column under Lord Howe encountered a detachment of the foe; a severe conflict ensued; the enemy were routed, and Lord Howe was killed. With him expired the master-spirit of the enterprise. Abercrombie fell back to the landing-place; sent out detachments to secure a saw-mill, within two miles of the fort: this done he advanced with his whole force and took post at the mill. Montcalm was strongly posted behind deep intrenchments, with an abatis of felled trees in front of his lines. The strength of his position was underrated, and an assault was ordered, which was repulsed with dreadful havoc. After four hours of desperate and fruitless fighting, Abercrombie retreated to the landing-place, and, dismayed at the failure of the rash assault, which had been made against the advice of his most judicious officers, he embarked his troops and returned across the lake. While stationed here, planning fortifications, Colonel Bradstreet was permitted to undertake an expedition against Fort Frontenac, on the south side of Lake Ontario, which was entirely successful.]

Operations went on slowly in that part of the year's campaign in which Washington was immediately engaged—the expedition against Fort Duquesne. Brigadier-general Forbes, who was commander-in-chief, was detained at Philadelphia by those delays and cross-purposes incident to military affairs in a new country. Colonel Bouquet, who was to command the advanced division, took his station, with a corps of regulars, at Raystown, in the centre of Pennsylvania. There slowly assembled troops from various parts. Three thousand Pennsylvanians, twelve hundred and fifty South Carolinians, and a few hundred men from elsewhere.

Washington, in the meantime, gathered together his scattered regiment at Winchester, some from a distance of two hundred miles, and diligently disciplined his recruits. He had two Virginia regiments under him, amounting, when complete, to about nineteen hundred men. Seven hundred Indian warriors, also, came lagging into his camp, lured by the prospect of a successful campaign.

The force thus assembling was in want of arms, tents, field-equipage, and almost every requisite. Washington had made repeated representations, by letter, of the destitute state of the Virginia troops, but without avail; he was now ordered by Sir John St. Clair, the quartermaster-general of the forces under General Forbes, to repair to Williamsburg and lay the state of the case before the council. He set off promptly on horseback, attended by Bishop, the well-trained military servant who had served the late General Braddock. It proved an eventful journey, though not in a military point of view. In crossing a ferry of the Pamunkey, a branch of York River, he fell in company with a Mr. Chamberlayne, who lived in the neighborhood, and who, in the spirit of Virginian hospitality, claimed him as a guest. It was with difficulty Washington could be prevailed on to halt for dinner, so impatient was he to arrive at Williamsburg and accomplish his mission.

Among the guests at Mr. Chamberlayne's was a young and blooming widow, Mrs. Martha Custis, daughter of Mr. John Dandridge, both patrician names in the province. Her husband, John Parke Custis, had been dead about three years, leaving her with two young children, and a large fortune. She is represented as being rather below the middle size, but extremely well shaped, with an agreeable countenance, dark hazel eyes and hair, and those frank, engaging manners, so captivating in Southern women. Washington's heart appears to have been taken by surprise. The dinner, which in those days was an earlier meal than at present, seemed all too short. The afternoon passed away like a dream. Bishop was punctual to the orders he had received on halting; the horses pawed at the door; but for once Washington loitered in the path of duty. The horses were countermanded, and it was not until the next morning that he was again in the saddle, spurring for Williamsburg. Happily the White House, the residence of Mrs. Custis, was in New Kent County, at no great distance from that city, so that he had opportunities of visiting her in the intervals of business. His time for courtship, however, was brief. Military duties called him back almost immediately to Winchester; but he feared, should he leave the matter in suspense, some more enterprising rival might supplant him during his absence, as in the case of Miss Philipse, at New York. He improved, therefore, his brief opportunity to the utmost. In a word, before they separated, they had mutually plighted their faith, and the marriage was to take place as soon as the campaign against Fort Duquesne was at an end.

On arriving at Winchester, he found his troops restless and discontented from prolonged inaction; the inhabitants impatient of the burdens imposed on them, and of the disturbances of an idle camp; while the Indians, as he apprehended, had deserted outright. It was a great relief, therefore, when he received orders from the commander-in-chief to repair to Fort Cumberland. He arrived there on the 2d of July, and proceeded to open a road between that post and head-quarters at Raystown, thirty miles distant, where Colonel Bouquet was stationed. His troops were scantily supplied with regimental clothing. The weather was oppressively warm. He now conceived the idea of equipping them in the light Indian hunting garb, and even of adopting it himself. Two companies were accordingly equipped in this style, and sent under the command of Major Lewis to head-quarters. The experiment was successful.

The array was now annoyed by scouting parties of Indians hovering about the neighborhood. Expresses passing between the posts were fired upon; a wagoner was shot down. Washington sent out counter-parties of Cherokees. Colonel Bouquet required that each party should be accompanied by an officer and a number of white men. Washington complied with the order, though he considered them an encumbrance rather than an advantage. On the other hand, he earnestly discountenanced a proposition of Colonel Bouquet, to make an irruption into the enemy's country with a strong party of regulars. Such a detachment, he observed, could not be sent without a cumbersome train of supplies, which would discover it to the enemy, who must at that time be collecting his whole force at Fort Duquesne; the enterprise, therefore, would be likely to terminate in a miscarriage, if not in the destruction of the party. We shall see that his opinion was oracular.

As Washington intended to retire from military life at the close of this campaign, he had proposed himself to the electors of Frederick County as their representative in the House of Burgesses. The election was coming on at Winchester; his friends pressed him to attend it, and Colonel Bouquet gave him leave of absence; but he declined to absent himself from his post for the promotion of his political interests. There were three competitors in the field, yet so high was the public opinion of his merit, that, though Winchester had been his head-quarters for two or three years past, and he had occasionally enforced martial law with a rigorous hand, he was elected by a large majority.

On the 21st of July arrived tidings of the brilliant success of that part of the scheme of the year's campaign conducted by General Amherst and Admiral Boscawen. This intelligence increased Washington's impatience at the delays of the expedition with which he was connected. He wished to rival these successes by a brilliant blow in the south. Understanding that the commander-in-chief had some thoughts of throwing a body of light troops in the advance, he wrote to Colonel Bouquet, earnestly soliciting his influence to have himself and his Virginia regiment included in the detachment.

He soon learnt to his surprise that the road to which his men were accustomed, and which had been worked by Braddock's troops in his campaign, was not to be taken in the present expedition, but a new one opened through the heart of Pennsylvania, from Raystown to Fort Duquesne, on the track generally taken by the northern traders. He instantly commenced long and repeated remonstrances on the subject; but the officers of the regular service had received a fearful idea of Braddock's road from his own despatches, wherein he had described it as lying "across mountains and rocks of an excessive height, vastly steep, and divided by torrents and rivers," whereas the Pennsylvania traders, who were anxious for the opening of the new road through their province, described the country through which it would pass as less difficult; above all, it was a direct line, and fifty miles nearer. This route, therefore, to the great regret of Washington, was definitely adopted, and sixteen hundred men were immediately thrown in the advance from Raystown to work upon it.

The first of September found Washington still encamped at Fort Cumberland, his troops sickly and dispirited, and the brilliant expedition which he had anticipated, dwindling down into a tedious operation of road-making. At length, in the month of September, he received orders from General Forbes to join him with his troops at Raystown, where he had just arrived, having been detained by severe illness. He was received by the general with the highest marks of respect. On all occasions, both in private and at councils of war, that commander treated his opinions with the greatest deference. He, moreover, adopted a plan drawn out by Washington for the march of the army, and an order of battle which still exists, furnishing a proof of his skill in frontier warfare.

It was now the middle of September; yet the great body of men engaged in opening the new military road, after incredible toil, had not advanced above forty-five miles, to a place called Loyal Hannan, a little beyond Laurel Hill. Colonel Bouquet, who commanded the division of nearly two thousand men sent forward to open this road, had halted at Loyal Hannan to establish a military post and deposit. He was upwards of fifty miles from Fort Duquesne, and was tempted to adopt the measure, so strongly discountenanced by Washington, of sending a party on a foray into the enemy's country. He accordingly detached Major Grant with eight hundred picked men, some of them Highlanders, others in Indian garb, the part of Washington's Virginian regiment sent forward by him from Cumberland under command of Major Lewis. [The enterprise proved a disastrous one. Major Grant conducted it with foolhardy bravado; suffered himself to be led into an ambuscade; and a scene ensued similar to that at the defeat of Braddock. The whole detachment was put to rout with dreadful carnage. Captain Bullitt, with fifty Virginians, who were in charge of the baggage, formed a barricade with the wagons, rallied some of the fugitives, succeeded in checking the enemy for a time, and, collecting the wounded, effected a rapid retreat. Lewis, when surrounded by Indians, saved his life by surrendering to a French officer. Grant surrendered himself in like manner.]

Washington, who was at Raystown when the disastrous news arrived, was publicly complimented by General Forbes on the gallant conduct of his Virginian troops, and Bullitt's behavior was "a matter of great admiration." The latter was soon after rewarded with a major's commission. As a further mark of the high opinion now entertained of provincial troops for frontier service, Washington was given the command of a division, partly composed of his own men, to keep in the advance of the main body, clear the roads, throw out scouting parties, and repel Indian attacks.

It was the 5th of November before the whole army assembled at Loyal Hannan. Winter was now at hand, and upwards of fifty miles of wilderness were yet to be traversed, by a road not yet formed, before they could reach Fort Duquesne. Again, Washington's predictions seemed likely to be verified, and the expedition to be defeated by delay; for in a council of war it was determined to be impracticable to advance further with the army that season. Three prisoners, however, who were brought in gave such an account of the weak state of the garrison at Fort Duquesne, its want of provisions and the defection of the Indians, that it was determined to push forward. The march was accordingly resumed, but without tents or baggage, and with only a light train of artillery.

Washington still kept the advance. After leaving Loyal Hannan, the road presented traces of the late defeat of Grant; being strewed with human bones. At length the army arrived in sight of Fort Duquesne, advancing with great precaution, and expecting a vigorous defence; but that formidable fortress, the terror and scourge of the frontier and the object of such warlike enterprise, fell without a blow. The recent successes of the English forces in Canada, particularly the capture and destruction of Fort Frontenac, had left the garrison without hope of reinforcements and supplies. The whole force, at the time, did not exceed five hundred men, and the provisions were nearly exhausted. The commander, therefore, waited only until the English army was within one day's march, when he embarked his troops at night in bateaux, blew up his magazines, set fire to the fort, and retreated down the Ohio by the light of the flames. On the 25th of November, Washington, with the advanced guard, marched in, and planted the British flag on the yet smoking ruins.

The ruins of the fortress were now put in a defensible state, and garrisoned by two hundred men from Washington's regiment; the name was changed to that of Fort Pitt, in honor of the illustrious British minister; it has since been modified into Pittsburg, and designates one of the most busy and populous cities of the interior. The reduction of Fort Duquesne terminated, as Washington had foreseen, the troubles and dangers of the southern frontier. The French domination of the Ohio was at an end; the Indians, as usual, paid homage to the conquering power, and a treaty of peace was concluded with all the tribes between the Ohio and the lakes.

With this campaign ended, for the present, the military career of Washington.

His great object was attained, the restoration of quiet and security to his native province; and, having abandoned all hope of attaining rank in the regular army, and his health being much impaired, he gave up his commission at the close of the year, and retired from the service, followed by the applause of his fellow-soldiers and the gratitude and admiration of all his countrymen.

His marriage with Mrs. Custis took place shortly after his return. It was celebrated on the 6th of January, 1759, at the White House, the residence of the bride, in the good old hospitable style of Virginia, amid a joyous assemblage of relatives and friends.

CHAPTER XII.

CAMPAIGNS IN THE NORTH.—WASHINGTON AT MOUNT VERNON.

[Before following Washington into the retirement of domestic life, we think it proper to notice the events which closed the great struggle between England and France for empire in America. Abercrombie had been superseded in command by Major-general Amherst. According to the plan of operations for 1759, General Wolfe was to ascend the St. Lawrence in a fleet of ships of war with eight thousand men, and lay siege to Quebec. General Amherst, in the meantime, was to advance against Ticonderoga and Crown Point, reduce them, and push on to the St. Lawrence to co-operate with Wolfe. A third expedition, under Brigadier-general Prideaux, aided by Sir William Johnson, was to attack Fort Niagara. Having reduced this fort he was to proceed against Montreal.

The last mentioned expedition was the first executed. The fort was invested by General Prideaux, early in July. The garrison, six hundred strong, made a resolute defence. Prideaux was killed on the 20th of July while visiting his trenches, and General Gage was sent to succeed him in command. Meantime the siege was pressed with vigor by Sir William Johnson. Learning that twelve hundred regular troops were hastening to the rescue of the besieged, he despatched a force to intercept them. They met within distant view of the fort, and after a sharp conflict the French were routed and pursued through the woods. The garrison, having now no alternative, surrendered, the terms offered being honorable.

Meanwhile, General Amherst with twelve thousand men had descended Lake George. On the 23d they debarked, and proceeded toward Ticonderoga. Montcalm was absent for the protection of Quebec. The garrison did not exceed four hundred men. A defence against Amherst's overwhelming force would have been madness; and Bourlamarque, who was in command, consequently dismantled the fortifications, as he did likewise those of Crown Point, and retreated down the lake. Instead of following him up and hastening to co-operate with Wolfe, General Amherst proceeded to repair the forts, though neither was in present danger of being attacked. His delay enabled the enemy to rally their forces at Isle Aux Noix, and deprive Wolfe of the aid essential to the general success of the campaign.

Wolfe ascended the St. Lawrence in June. With him were Colonel Guy Carlton, and Lieutenant-Colonel William Howe, both destined to achieve celebrity in the annals of the American Revolution. The troops debarked on the Isle of Orleans, a little below Quebec. Quebec is built around the point of a rocky promontory, and flanked by precipices. The St. Lawrence sweeps by it on the right, and the St. Charles on the left. The place was not then, as now, rendered impregnable by fortifications. Montcalm commanded the post. His forces were drawn out along the northern shore below the city, from the St. Charles to the Falls of Montmorency, and their position was secured by intrenchments. Wolfe established batteries at the west point of the Isle of Orleans, and at Point Levi, on the south bank of the St. Lawrence, within cannon range of the city. From Point Levi the city was cannonaded; the lower town was reduced to rubbish, and many houses in the upper town were fired. Anxious for a decisive action, Wolfe, on the 9th of July crossed to the north bank of the St. Lawrence, and encamped below the Montmorency. He determined to attack Montcalm in his camp, however difficult to be approached, and however strongly posted. The plan of attack was complicated; orders were misunderstood; confusion ensued; and the attack proved a disastrous failure. News was now received of the capture of Fort Niagara, Ticonderoga, and Crown Point. Their successes fired the sensitive commander, and he declared he would never return without success. He made a reconnoitering expedition above Quebec. Rugged cliffs rose from the water's edge; above them was a plain called the Plains of Abraham, by which the upper town might be approached on its weakest side. It was determined to attempt reaching the Plains by scaling the cliffs at night. On the 13th of September, in flat-bottomed boats the troops passed the town undetected; landed in a cove called Cape Diamond; scrambled and struggled with difficulty up a cragged path; put to flight a sergeant's guard at the summit, and by break of day were in possession of the Plains.

Montcalm was thunderstruck when intelligence of the fact was brought to him. He hastened to the defence of the approaches to the city; a desperate battle ensued on the fated Plains. Wolfe, who was in front of the English line, was wounded in the wrist. A second ball struck him in the breast. He was borne to the rear. "It is all over with me," said he, and desired those about him to lay him down. Presently they cried, "They run! they run! see how they run!" "Who runs?" asked Wolfe eagerly, rousing from a lethargy into which he had fallen. "The enemy, sir: they give way everywhere." "Now, God be praised, I will die in peace," exclaimed the dying hero, and, turning upon his side, expired. The English had indeed obtained a complete victory; and among the enemy's losses was that of their gallant leader, Montcalm. The English, now in strong position on the Plains, hastened to fortify. Preparations were now made for the attack by both army and fleet on the upper and lower town, but the spirit of the garrison was broken, and they capitulated on the 17th of September.

Had Amherst followed up his successors, the year's campaign would have ended in the subjugation of Canada. His delay gave De Levi, the successor of Montcalm, time to rally and struggle for the salvation of the province. He laid siege to Quebec in the spring, and was on the eve of success, when the arrival of a British fleet reversed the scene. The besieging army retreated, and made a last stand at Montreal; but being invested with an overwhelming force, defence was hopeless. On the 8th of September, Montreal, and with it all Canada, surrendered, and the contest between France and England for dominion in America was ended.]

For three months after his marriage, Washington resided with his bride at the White House. During his sojourn there, he repaired to Williamsburg, to take his seat in the House of Burgesses. By a vote of the House it had been determined to greet his installation by a signal testimonial of respect. Accordingly, as soon as he took his seat, Mr. Robinson, the Speaker, in eloquent language, dictated by the warmth of private friendship, returned thanks, on behalf of the colony, for the distinguished military services he had rendered to his country. Washington rose to reply; blushed—stammered—trembled, and could not utter a word. "Sit down, Mr. Washington," said the Speaker, with a smile, "your modesty equals your valor, and that surpasses the power of any language I possess." Such was Washington's first launch into civil life, in which he was to be distinguished by the same judgment, devotion, courage, and magnanimity exhibited in his military career. He attended the House frequently during the remainder of the session, after which he conducted his bride to his favorite abode of Mount Vernon. "I am now, I believe," he writes, "fixed in this seat, with an agreeable partner for life, and I hope to find more happiness in retirement than I ever experienced in the wide and bustling world."

Mount Vernon was his harbor of repose, where he repeatedly furled his sail, and fancied himself anchored for life. No impulse of ambition tempted him thence; nothing but the call of his country and his devotion to the public good. The place was endeared to him by the remembrance of his brother Lawrence, and of the happy days he had passed here with that brother in the days of boyhood: but it was a delightful place in itself, and well calculated to inspire the rural feeling. The mansion was beautifully situated on a swelling height, crowned with wood, and commanding a magnificent view up and down the Potomac. The grounds immediately about it were laid out somewhat in the English taste. The estate was apportioned into separate farms, devoted to different kinds of culture, each having its allotted laborers. Much, however, was still covered with wild woods, seamed with deep dells and runs of water, and indented with inlets; haunts of deer, and lurking-places of foxes.

These were, as yet, the aristocratical days of Virginia. The estates were large, and continued in the same families by entails. Many of the wealthy planters were connected with old families in England. The young men, especially the elder sons, were often sent to finish their education there, and on their return brought out the tastes and habits of the mother country. The governors of Virginia were from the higher ranks of society, and maintained a corresponding state. A style of living prevailed that has long since faded away. The houses were spacious, commodious, liberal in all their appointments, and fitted to cope with the free-handed, open hearted hospitality of the owners. Nothing was more common than to see handsome services of plate, elegant equipages, and superb carriage-horses—all imported from England.

Washington, by his marriage, had added above one hundred thousand dollars to his already considerable fortune, and was enabled to live in ample and dignified style. His intimacy with the Fairfaxes, and his intercourse with British officers of rank, had perhaps had their influence on his mode of living. He had his chariot and four, with black postilions in livery, for the use of Mrs. Washington and her lady visitors. As for himself, he always appeared on horseback. His stable was well filled and admirably regulated. His stud was thoroughbred and in excellent order.

A large Virginia estate, in those days, was a little empire. The mansion-house was the seat of government, with its numerous dependencies, such as kitchens, smoke-house, workshops and stables. In this mansion the planter ruled supreme; his steward or overseer was his prime minister and executive officer; he had his legion of house negroes for domestic service, and his host of field negroes for the culture of tobacco, Indian corn, and other crops, and for other out-of-door labor. Their quarter formed a kind of hamlet apart, composed of various huts, with little gardens and poultry yards, all well stocked, and swarms of little negroes gambolling in the sunshine. Then there were large wooden edifices for curing tobacco, the staple and most profitable production, and mills for grinding wheat and Indian corn, of which large fields were cultivated for the supply of the family and the maintenance of the negroes.

Washington carried into his rural affairs the same method, activity and circumspection that had distinguished him in military life. He kept his own accounts, posted up his books and balanced them with mercantile exactness. The products of his estate became so noted for the faithfulness, as to quality and quantity, with which they were put up, that it is said any barrel of flour that bore the brand of George Washington, Mount Vernon, was exempted from the customary inspection in the West India ports.

He was an early riser, often before daybreak in the winter when the nights were long. He breakfasted at seven in summer, at eight in winter. Two small cups of tea and three or four cakes of Indian meal (called hoe cakes), formed his frugal repast. Immediately after breakfast he mounted his horse and visited those parts of the estate where any work was going on, seeing to every thing with his own eyes, and often aiding with his own hand. Dinner was served at two o'clock. He ate heartily, but was no epicure, nor critical about his food. His beverage was small beer or cider, and two glasses of old Madeira. He took tea, of which he was very fond, early in the evening, and retired for the night about nine o'clock.

Washington delighted in the chase. In the hunting season, when he rode out early in the morning to visit distant parts of the estate where work was going on, he often took some of the dogs with him for the chance of starting a fox, which he occasionally did, though he was not always successful in killing him. He was a bold rider and an admirable horseman, though he never claimed the merit of being an accomplished fox-hunter. In the height of the season, however, he would be out with the fox-hounds two or three times a week, accompanied by his guests at Mount Vernon and the gentlemen of the neighborhood, especially the Fairfaxes of Belvoir, of which estate his friend George William Fairfax was now the proprietor. On such occasions there would be a hunting dinner at one or other of those establishments, at which convivial repasts Washington is said to have enjoyed himself with unwonted hilarity.

MOUNT VERNON.
VOL. I

The waters of the Potomac also afforded occasional amusement in fishing and shooting. The fishing was sometimes on a grand scale, when the herrings came up the river in shoals, and the negroes of Mount Vernon were marshalled forth to draw the seine, which was generally done with great success. Canvas-back ducks abounded at the proper season, and the shooting of them was one of Washington's favorite recreations. The river border of his domain, however, was somewhat subject to invasion. An oysterman once anchored his craft at the landing-place, and disturbed the quiet of the neighborhood by the insolent and disorderly conduct of himself and crew. It took a campaign of three days to expel these invaders from the premises. A more summary course was pursued with another interloper. This was a vagabond who infested the creeks and inlets which bordered the estate, lurking in a canoe among the reeds and bushes, and making great havoc among the canvas-back ducks. He had been warned off repeatedly, but without effect. As Washington was one day riding about the estate he heard the report of a gun from the margin of the river. Spurring in that direction he dashed through the bushes and came upon the culprit just as he was pushing his canoe from shore. The latter raised his gun with a menacing look; but Washington rode into the stream, seized the painter of the canoe, drew it to shore, sprang from his horse, wrested the gun from the hands of the astonished delinquent, and inflicted on him a lesson in "Lynch law" that effectually cured him of all inclination to trespass again on these forbidden shores.

Occasionally he and Mrs. Washington would pay a visit to Annapolis, at that time the seat of government of Maryland, and partake of the gayeties which prevailed during the session of the legislature. Dinners and balls abounded, and there were occasional attempts at theatricals. The latter was an amusement for which Washington always had a relish, though he never had an opportunity of gratifying it effectually. Neither was he disinclined to mingle in the dance, and we remember to have heard venerable ladies, who had been belles in his day, pride themselves on having had him for a partner, though, they added, he was apt to be a ceremonious and grave one.

In this round of rural occupation, rural amusements and social intercourse, Washington passed several tranquil years, the halcyon season of his life. His marriage was unblessed with children; but those of Mrs. Washington experienced from him parental care and affection, and the formation of their minds and manners was one of the dearest objects of his attention. His domestic concerns and social enjoyments, however, were not permitted to interfere with his public duties. He was active by nature, and eminently a man of business by habit. As judge of the county court, and member of the House of Burgesses, he had numerous calls upon his time and thoughts, and was often drawn from home; for whatever trust he undertook, he was sure to fulfil with scrupulous exactness.

About this time we find him engaged, with other men of enterprise, in a project to drain the great Dismal Swamp, and render it capable of cultivation. This vast morass was about thirty miles long, and ten miles wide, and its interior but little known. With his usual zeal and hardihood he explored it on horseback and on foot. In many parts it was covered with dark and gloomy woods of cedar, cypress, and hemlock, or deciduous trees, the branches of which were hung with long, drooping moss. Other parts were almost inaccessible, from the density of brakes and thickets, entangled with vines, briers and creeping plants, and intersected by creeks and standing pools. In the centre of the morass he came to a great piece of water, six miles long, and three broad, called Drummond's Pond, but more poetically celebrated as the Lake of the Dismal Swamp. It was more elevated than any other part of the swamp, and capable of feeding canals, by which the whole might be traversed. Having made the circuit of it and noted all its characteristics, he encamped for the night upon the firm land which bordered it, and finished his explorations on the following day. In the ensuing session of the Virginia Legislature, the association in behalf of which he had acted was chartered under the name of the Dismal Swamp Company; and to his observations and forecast may be traced the subsequent improvement and prosperity of that once desolate region.

CHAPTER XIII.
COLONIAL DISCONTENTS.

Tidings of peace gladdened the colonies in the spring of 1763. The definite treaty between England and France had been signed at Fontainbleau. Now, it was trusted, there would be an end to these horrid ravages that had desolated the interior of the country. The month of May proved the fallacy of such hopes. In that month the famous insurrection of the Indian tribes broke out, which, from the name of the chief who was its prime mover and master-spirit, is commonly called Pontiac's war. The Delawares and Shawnees, and other of those emigrant tribes of the Ohio, among whom Washington had mingled, were foremost in this conspiracy. Some of the chiefs who had been his allies had now taken up the hatchet against the English. The plot was deep laid, and conducted with Indian craft and secrecy. At a concerted time an attack was made upon all the posts from Detroit to Fort Pitt (late Fort Duquesne). Several of the small stockaded forts, the places of refuge of woodland neighborhoods, were surprised and sacked with remorseless butchery. The frontiers of Pennsylvania, Maryland and Virginia were laid waste; and a considerable time elapsed before the frontier was restored to tolerable tranquility.

Fortunately, Washington's retirement from the army prevented his being entangled in this savage war, which raged throughout the regions he had repeatedly visited, or rather his active spirit had been diverted into a more peaceful channel, for he was at this time occupied in the enterprise just noticed, for draining the great Dismal Swamp.

Public events were now taking a tendency which, without any political aspirations or forethought of his own, was destined gradually to bear him away from his quiet home and individual pursuits, and launch him upon a grander and wider sphere of action than any in which he had hitherto been engaged.

Whatever might be the natural affection of the colonies for the mother country—and there are abundant evidences to prove that it was deep-rooted and strong—it had never been properly reciprocated. They yearned to be considered as children; they were treated by her as changelings. Her navigation laws had shut their ports against foreign vessels; obliged them to export their productions only to countries belonging to the British crown; to import European goods solely from England, and in English ships; and had subjected the trade between the colonies to duties. All manufactures, too, in the colonies that might interfere with those of the mother country had been either totally prohibited or subjected to intolerable restraints. The acts of Parliament imposing these prohibitions and restrictions had at various times produced sore discontent and opposition on the part of the colonies. There was nothing, however, to which the jealous sensibilities of the colonies were more alive than to any attempt of the mother country to draw a revenue from them by taxation. From the earliest period of their existence they had maintained the principle that they could only be taxed by a Legislature in which they were represented.

In 1760 there was an attempt in Boston to collect duties on foreign sugar and molasses imported into the colonies. Writs of assistance were applied for by the custom-house officers, authorizing them to break open ships, stores and private dwellings, in quest of articles that had paid no duty; and to call the assistance of others in the discharge of their odious task. The merchants opposed the execution of the writ on constitutional grounds. The question was argued in court, where James Otis spoke so eloquently in vindication of American rights that all his hearers went away ready to take arms against writs of assistance. Another ministerial measure was to instruct the provincial governors to commission judges. Not as theretofore "during good behavior," but "during the king's pleasure." New York was the first to resent this blow at the independence of the judiciary. The lawyers appealed to the public through the press against an act which subjected the halls of justice to the prerogative. Their appeals were felt beyond the bounds of the province, and awakened a general spirit of resistance.

Thus matters stood at the conclusion of the war. One of the first measures of ministers, on the return of peace, was to enjoin on all naval officers stationed on the coasts of the American colonies the performance, under oath, of the duties of custom-house officers, for the suppression of smuggling. This fell ruinously upon a clandestine trade which had long been connived at between the English and Spanish colonies, profitable to both, but especially to the former, and beneficial to the mother country, opening a market to her manufactures. As a measure of retaliation the colonists resolved not to purchase British fabrics, but to clothe themselves as much as possible in home manufactures. The demand for British goods in Boston alone was diminished upwards of £10,000 sterling in the course of a year.

In 1764 George Grenville, now at the head of government, ventured upon the policy from which Walpole [his predecessor] had wisely abstained. Early in March the eventful question was debated, "whether they had a right to tax America." It was decided in the affirmative. Next followed a resolution, declaring it proper to charge certain stamp duties in the colonies and plantations, but no immediate step was taken to carry it into effect. Mr. Grenville, however, gave notice to the American agents in London that he should introduce such a measure on the ensuing session of Parliament. In the meantime Parliament perpetuated certain duties on sugar and molasses—heretofore subjects of complaint and opposition—now reduced and modified so as to discourage smuggling, and thereby to render them more productive. Duties, also, were imposed on other articles of foreign produce or manufacture imported into the colonies. To reconcile the latter to these impositions, it was stated that the revenue thus raised was to be appropriated to their protection and security; in other words, to the support of a standing army, intended to be quartered upon them. We have here briefly stated but a part of what Burke terms an "infinite variety of paper chains," extending through no less than twenty-nine acts of Parliament, from 1660 to 1764, by which the colonies had been held in thraldom.

The New Englanders were the first to take the field against the project of taxation. They denounced it as a violation of their rights as freemen; of their chartered rights, by which they were to tax themselves for their support and defence; of their rights as British subjects, who ought not to be taxed but by themselves or their representatives. They sent petitions and remonstrances on the subject to the king, the lords and the commons, in which they were seconded by New York and Virginia. All was in vain. In March, 1765, the act was passed, according to which all instruments in writing were to be executed on stamped paper, to be purchased from the agents of the British government. What was more, all offences against the act could be tried in any royal, marine or admiralty court throughout the colonies, however distant from the place where the offence had been committed; thus interfering with that most inestimable right, a trial by jury.

It was an ominous sign that the first burst of opposition to this act should take place in Virginia. That colony had hitherto been slow to accord with the republican spirit of New England. Founded at an earlier period of the reign of James I., before kingly prerogative and ecclesiastical supremacy had been made matters of doubt and fierce dispute, it had grown up in loyal attachment to king, church, and constitution; was aristocratical in its tastes and habits, and had been remarked above all the other colonies for its sympathies with the mother country. Moreover, it had not so many pecuniary interests involved in these questions as had the people of New England, being an agricultural rather than a commercial province; but the Virginians are of a quick and generous spirit, readily aroused on all points of honorable pride, and they resented the stamp act as an outrage on their rights.

Washington occupied his seat in the House of Burgesses, when, on the 29th of May, the stamp act became a subject of discussion. Among the Burgesses sat Patrick Henry, a young lawyer who had recently distinguished himself by pleading against the exercise of the royal prerogative in church matters, and who was now for the first time a member of the House. Rising in his place, he introduced his celebrated resolutions, declaring that the General Assembly of Virginia had the exclusive right and power to lay taxes and impositions upon the inhabitants, and that whoever maintained the contrary should be deemed an enemy to the colony. The speaker, Mr. Robinson, objected to the resolutions, as inflammatory. Henry vindicated them, as justified by the nature of the case; went into an able and constitutional discussion of colonial rights, and an eloquent exposition of the manner in which they had been assailed.

The resolutions were modified, to accommodate them to the scruples of the speaker and some of the members, but their spirit was retained. The Lieutenant-governor (Fauquier), startled by this patriotic outbreak, dissolved the Assembly, and issued writs for a new election; but the clarion had sounded.

Washington returned to Mount Vernon full of anxious thoughts inspired by the political events of the day, and the legislative scene which he witnessed. His recent letters had spoken of the state of peaceful tranquillity in which he was living; those now written from his rural home show that he fully participated in the popular feeling, and that while he had a presentiment of an arduous struggle, his patriotic mind was revolving means of coping with it. In the meantime, from his quiet abode at Mount Vernon, he seemed to hear the patriotic voice of Patrick Henry, which had startled the House of Burgesses, echoing throughout the land, and rousing one legislative body after another to follow the example of that of Virginia. At the instigation of the General Court or Assembly of Massachusetts, a Congress was held in New York in October, composed of delegates from Massachusetts, Rhode Island, Connecticut, New York, New Jersey, Pennsylvania, Delaware, Maryland, and South Carolina. In this they denounced the acts of Parliament imposing taxes on them without their consent, and extending the jurisdiction of the courts of admiralty, as violations of their rights and liberties as natural born subjects of Great Britain, and prepared an address to the king, and a petition to both Houses of Parliament, praying for redress. Similar petitions were forwarded to England by the colonies not represented in the Congress.

The very preparations for enforcing the stamp act called forth popular tumults in various places. In Boston the stamp distributor was hanged in effigy; his windows were broken; a house intended for a stamp office was pulled down, and the effigy burnt in a bonfire made of the fragments. In Virginia, Mr. George Mercer had been appointed distributor of stamps, but on his arrival at Williamsburg publicly declined officiating. It was a fresh triumph to the popular cause. The bells were rung for joy; the town was illuminated, and Mercer was hailed with acclamations of the people. The 1st of November, the day when the act was to go into operation, was ushered in with portentous solemnities. There was great tolling of bells and burning of effigies in the New England colonies. At Boston the ships displayed their colors but half-mast high. Many shops were shut; funeral knells resounded from the steeples, and there was a grand auto-da-fe, in which the promoters of the act were paraded, and suffered martyrdom in effigy. At New York the printed act was carried about the streets on a pole, surmounted by a death's head, with a scroll bearing the inscription, "The folly of England and ruin of America."

These are specimens of the marks of popular reprobation with which the stamp act was universally nullified. No one would venture to carry it into execution. In fact no stamped paper was to be seen; all had been either destroyed or concealed. All transactions which required stamps to give them validity were suspended, or were executed by private compact. The courts of justice were closed, until at length some conducted their business without stamps. Union was becoming the watch-word. The merchants of New York, Philadelphia, Boston, and such other colonies as had ventured publicly to oppose the stamp act, agreed to import no more British manufactures after the 1st of January unless it should be repealed. So passed away the year 1765.

The dismissal of Mr. Grenville from the cabinet gave a temporary change to public affairs. The stamp act was repealed on the 18th of March, 1766, to the great joy of the sincere friends of both countries, still, there was a fatal clause in the repeal, which declared that the king, with the consent of Parliament, had power and authority to make laws and statutes of sufficient force and validity to "bind the colonies, and people of America, in all cases whatsoever." As the people of America were contending for principles, not mere pecuniary interests, this reserved power of the crown and Parliament left the dispute still open, and chilled the feeling of gratitude which the repeal might otherwise have inspired. Further aliment for public discontent was furnished by other acts of Parliament. One imposed duties on glass, pasteboard, white and red lead, painters' colors, and tea; the duties to be collected on the arrival of the articles in the colonies; another empowered naval officers to enforce the acts of trade and navigation. Another wounded to the quick the pride and sensibilities of New York. The mutiny act had recently been extended to America, with an additional clause, requiring the provincial Assemblies to provide the troops sent out with quarters, and to furnish them with fire, beds, candles, and other necessaries, at the expense of the colonies. The Governor and Assembly of New York refused to comply with this requisition as to stationary forces, insisting that it applied only to troops on a march. An act of Parliament now suspended the powers of the governor and Assembly until they should comply.

Boston continued to be the focus of what the ministerialists termed sedition. The General Court of Massachusetts, not content with petitioning the king for relief against the recent measures of Parliament, especially those imposing taxes as a means of revenue, drew up a circular, calling on the other colonial Legislatures to join with them in suitable efforts to obtain redress. In the ensuing session, Governor Sir Francis Bernard called upon them to rescind the resolution on which the circular was founded,—they refused to comply, and the General Court was consequently dissolved. The governors of other colonies required of their Legislatures an assurance that they would not reply to the Massachusetts circular—these Legislatures likewise refused compliance, and were dissolved. All this added to the growing excitement.

Nothing, however, produced a more powerful effect upon the public sensibilities throughout the country than certain military demonstrations at Boston. [In consequence of repeated collisions between the people of that place and the commissioners of customs, two regiments of troops were sent from Halifax to overawe the disaffected citizens. It was resolved in a town meeting that the king had no right to send troops thither without the consent of the Assembly. The selectmen accordingly refused to find quarters for the soldiers, and while some encamped on the common, others were quartered, to the great indignation of the public, in Faneuil Hall.]

Throughout these public agitations, Washington endeavored to preserve his equanimity. Still he was too true a patriot not to sympathize in the struggle for colonial rights which now agitated the whole country, and we find him gradually carried more and more into the current of political affairs. A letter written on the 5th of April, 1769, to his friend, George Mason, shows the important stand he was disposed to take. In the previous year the merchants and traders of Boston, Salem, Connecticut and New York, had agreed to suspend for a time the importation of all articles subject to taxation. Similar resolutions had recently been adopted by the merchants of Philadelphia. Washington's letter is emphatic in support of the measure. "At a time," writes he, "when our lordly masters in Great Britain will be satisfied with nothing less than the deprivation of American freedom, it seems highly necessary that something should be done to avert the stroke, and maintain the liberty which we have derived from our ancestors."

Mason, in his reply, concurred with him in opinion. "Our all is at stake," said he, "and the little conveniences and comforts of life, when set in competition with our liberty, ought to be rejected, not with reluctance but with pleasure." The result of the correspondence was the draft by the latter of a plan of association, the members of which were to pledge themselves not to import or use any articles of British merchandise or manufacture subject to duty. This paper Washington was to submit to the consideration of the House of Burgesses, at the approaching session in the month of May.

The Legislature of Virginia opened on this occasion with a brilliant pageant. While military force was arrayed to overawe the republican Puritans of the east, it was thought to dazzle the aristocratical descendants of the cavaliers by the reflex of regal splendor. Lord Botetourt, one of the king's lords of the bed-chamber, had recently come out as governor of the province. Junius described him as "a cringing, bowing, fawning, sword-bearing courtier." The words of political satirists, however, are always to be taken with great distrust. However his lordship may have bowed in presence of royalty, he elsewhere conducted himself with dignity, and won general favor by his endearing manners.

He had come out, however, with a wrong idea of the Americans. They had been represented to him as factious, immoral, and prone to sedition; but vain and luxurious, and easily captivated by parade and splendor. The latter foibles were aimed at in his appointment and fitting out. It was supposed that his titled rank would have its effect. Then to prepare him for occasions of ceremony, a coach of state was presented to him by the king. His opening of the session was in the style of the royal opening of Parliament. He proceeded in due parade from his dwelling to the capitol, in his state coach, drawn by six milk-white horses. Having delivered his speech according to royal form, he returned home with the same pomp and circumstance.

The time had gone by, however, for such display to have the anticipated effect. The Virginian legislators penetrated the intention of this pompous ceremonial, and regarded it with a depreciating smile. Sterner matters occupied their thoughts; they had come prepared to battle for their rights, and their proceedings soon showed Lord Botetourt how much he had mistaken them. Spirited resolutions were passed, denouncing the recent act of Parliament imposing taxes; the power to do which, on the inhabitants of this colony, "was legally and constitutionally vested in the House of Burgesses, with consent of the council and of the king, or of his governor, for the time being." Copies of these resolutions were ordered to be forwarded by the speaker to the Legislatures of the other colonies, with a request for their concurrence.

Other proceedings of the Burgesses showed their sympathy with their fellow-patriots of New England. A joint address of both Houses of Parliament had recently been made to the king, assuring him of their support in any further measures for the due execution of the laws in Massachusetts, and beseeching him that all persons charged with treason, or misprision of treason, committed within that colony since the 30th of December, 1767, might be sent to Great Britain for trial. As Massachusetts had no General Assembly at this time, having been dissolved by government, the Legislature of Virginia generously took up the cause. An address to the king was resolved on, stating, that all trials for treason, or misprision of treason, or for any crime whatever committed by any person residing in a colony, ought to be in and before his majesty's courts within said colony; and beseeching the king to avert from his royal subjects those dangers and miseries which would ensue from seizing and carrying beyond sea any person residing in America suspected of any crime whatever, thereby depriving them of the inestimable privilege of being tried by a jury from the vicinage, as well as the liberty of producing witnesses on such trial.

Lord Botetourt was astonished and dismayed when he heard of these high-toned proceedings. Repairing to the capitol on the following day at noon, he summoned the speaker and members to the council chamber, and addressed them in the following words: "Mr. Speaker, and gentlemen of the House of Burgesses, I have heard of your resolves, and augur ill of their effects. You have made it my duty to dissolve you, and you are dissolved accordingly."

The spirit conjured up by late decrees of Parliament was not so easily allayed. The Burgesses adjourned to a private house. Peyton Randolph, their late speaker, was elected moderator. Washington now brought forward a draft of the articles of association, concerted between him and George Mason. They formed the groundwork of an instrument signed by all present, pledging themselves neither to import, nor use any goods, merchandise, or manufactures taxed by Parliament to raise a revenue in America. This instrument was sent throughout the country for signature, and the scheme of non-importation, hitherto confined to a few northern colonies, was soon universally adopted.

The popular ferment in Virginia was gradually allayed by the amiable and conciliatory conduct of Lord Botetourt, His lordship soon became aware of the erroneous notions with which he had entered upon office. His semi-royal equipage and state were laid aside. He examined into public grievances; became a strenuous advocate for the repeal of taxes; and, authorized by his despatches from the ministry, assured the public that such repeal would speedily take place. His assurance was received with implicit faith, and for a while Virginia was quieted.

[In the month of May the General Court of Massachusetts, hitherto prorogued met according to charter. A committee immediately waited on the governor declaring that it was impossible to do business with dignity and freedom while the town was invested by sea and land, and a military guard was stationed at the state-house; and they requested the governor as his] majesty's representative, to have such forces removed out of the port and gates of the city during the session of the Assembly. The governor replied that he had no authority over either the ships or troops. The court persisted in refusing to transact business while so circumstanced, and the governor was obliged to transfer the session to Cambridge. There he addressed a message to that body in July, requiring funds for the payment of the troops, and quarters for their accommodation. The Assembly, after ample discussion of past grievances, resolved, that the establishment of a standing army in the colony in a time of peace was an invasion of natural rights; that a standing army was not known as a part of the British constitution, and that the sending an armed force to aid the civil authority was unprecedented, and highly dangerous to the people.

After waiting some days without receiving an answer to his message, the governor sent to know whether the Assembly would, or would not, make provision for the troops. In their reply, they followed the example of the Legislature of New York, by declining to furnish funds for the purposes specified, "being incompatible with their own honor and interest, and their duty to their constituents." They were in consequence again prorogued, to meet in Boston on the 10th of January.

So stood affairs in Massachusetts. In the meantime, the non-importation associations, being generally observed throughout the colonies, produced the effect on British commerce which Washington had anticipated, and Parliament was incessantly importuned by petitions from British merchants imploring its intervention to save them from ruin.

Early in 1770, an important change took place in the British cabinet. The Duke of Grafton suddenly resigned, and the reins of government passed into the hands of Lord North. He was a man of limited capacity, but a favorite of the king, and subservient to his narrow colonial policy. His administration, so eventful to America, commenced with an error. In the month of March an act was passed, revoking all the duties laid in 1767, *excepting that on tea*. This single tax was continued, as he observed, "to maintain the parliamentary right of taxation," — the very right which was the grand object of contest. Here was the stumbling-block at the threshold of Lord North's administration. In vain the members of the opposition urged that this single exception, while it would produce no revenue, would keep alive the whole cause of contention; that so long as a single external duty was enforced, the colonies would consider their rights invaded, and would remain unappeased. Lord North was not to be convinced. On the very day in which this ominous bill was passed in Parliament, a sinister occurrence took place in Boston. Some of the young men of the place insulted the military while under arms; the latter resented it; the young men, after a scuffle, were put to flight, and pursued. The alarm bells rang, a mob assembled; the custom-house was threatened; the troops, in protecting it, were assailed with clubs and stones, and obliged to use their fire-arms before the tumult could be quelled. Four of the populace were killed, and several wounded. The troops were now removed from the town, which remained in the highest state of exasperation; and this untoward occurrence received the opprobrious and somewhat extravagant name of "the Boston massacre."

In Virginia the public discontents, which had been allayed by the conciliatory conduct of Lord Botetourt, and by his assurances, made on the strength of letters received from the ministry, that the grievances complained of would be speedily redressed, now broke out with more violence than ever. The Virginians spurned the mock-remedy which left the real cause of complaint untouched. His lordship also felt deeply wounded by the disingenuousness of ministers which had led him into such a predicament, and wrote home demanding his discharge. Before it arrived, an attack of bilious fever, acting upon a delicate and sensitive frame, enfeebled by anxiety and chagrin, laid him in his grave. He left behind him a name endeared to the Virginians by his amiable manners, his liberal patronage of the arts, and, above all, by his zealous intercession for their rights.

CHAPTER XIV.
EXPEDITION TO THE OHIO.—TEA TAX.

In the midst of these popular turmoils, Washington was induced, by public as well as private considerations, to make another expedition to the Ohio. He was one of the Virginia Board of Commissioners, appointed at the close of the late war to settle the military accounts of the colony. Among the claims which came before the board were those of the officers and soldiers who had engaged to serve until peace, under the proclamation of Governor Dinwiddie, holding forth a bounty of two hundred thousand acres of land, to be apportioned among them according to rank. Those claims were yet unsatisfied. Washington became the champion of those claims, and an opportunity now presented itself for their liquidation. The Six Nations, by a treaty in 1768, had ceded to the British crown, in consideration of a sum of money, all the lands possessed by them south of the Ohio. Land offices would soon be opened for the sale of them. Washington determined at once to visit the lands thus ceded; affix his mark on such tracts as he should select, and apply for a grant from government in behalf of the "soldiers' claim."

Washington had for a companion in this expedition his friend and neighbor, Dr. Craik. They set out on the 5th of October with three negro attendants, two belonging to Washington, and one to the doctor. The whole party was mounted, and there was a led horse for the baggage. After twelve days' travelling they arrived at Fort Pitt (late Fort Duquesne). It was garrisoned by two companies of royal Irish, commanded by a Captain Edmonson. A hamlet of about twenty log-houses, inhabited by Indian traders, had sprung up within three hundred yards of the fort, and was called "the town." It was the embryo city of Pittsburg, now so populous. At one of the houses, a tolerable frontier inn, they took up their quarters; but during their brief sojourn they were entertained with great hospitality at the fort. Here at dinner Washington met his old acquaintance, George Croghan, who had figured in so many capacities and experienced so many vicissitudes on the frontier. He was now Colonel Croghan, deputy-agent to Sir William Johnson.

On the day following the repast at the fort, Washington visited Croghan at his abode on the Alleghany River, where he found several of the chiefs of the Six Nations assembled. One of them, the White Mingo by name, made him a speech, accompanied, as usual, by a belt of wampum.

At Pittsburg the travellers left their horses, and embarked in a large canoe, to make a voyage down the Ohio as far as the Great Kanawha. Colonel Croghan engaged two Indians for their service, and an interpreter named John Nicholson.

The colonel and some of the officers of the garrison accompanied them as far as Logstown, the scene of Washington's early diplomacy, and his first interview with the half-king. Here they breakfasted together; after which they separated, the colonel and his companions cheering the voyagers from the shore, as the canoe was borne off by the current of the beautiful Ohio.

Washington's propensities as a sportsman had here full play. Deer were continually to be seen coming down to the water's edge to drink, or browsing along the shore; there were innumerable flocks of wild turkeys, and streaming flights of ducks and geese; so that as the voyagers floated along, they were enabled to load their canoe with game. At night they encamped on the river bank, lit their fire and made a sumptuous hunter's repast. About seventy-five miles below Pittsburg the voyagers landed at a Mingo town, which they found in a stir of warlike preparation — sixty of the warriors being about to set off on a foray into the Cherokee country against the Catawbas.

On the 24th, about three o'clock in the afternoon, they arrived at Captema Creek, and two days more of voyaging brought them to an Indian hunting camp, near the mouth of the Muskingum. Here it was necessary to land and make a ceremonious visit, for the chief of the hunting party was Kiashuta, a Seneca sachem, the head of the river tribes. He was noted to have been among the first to raise the hatchet in Pontiac's conspiracy, and almost equally vindictive with that potent warrior. As Washington approached the chieftain, he recognized him for one of the Indians who had accompanied him on his mission to the French in 1753. Kiashuta retained a perfect recollection of the youthful ambassador, though seventeen years had matured him into thoughtful manhood. With hunter's hospitality he gave him a quarter of a fine buffalo just slain, but insisted that they should encamp together for the night.

At the mouth of the Great Kanawha the voyagers encamped for a day or two to examine the lands in the neighborhood, and Washington set up his mark upon such as he intended to claim on behalf of the soldiers' grant. Here Washington was visited by an old sachem, who approached him with great reverence, at the head of several of his tribe, and addressed him through Nicholson, the interpreter. He had heard, he said, of his being in that part of the country, and had come from a great distance to see him. On further discourse, the sachem made known that he was one of the warriors in the service of the French, who lay in ambush on the banks of the Monongahela and wrought such havoc in Braddock's army. He declared that he and his young men had singled out Washington, as he made himself conspicuous riding about the field of battle with the general's orders, and had fired at him repeatedly, but without success; whence they had concluded that he was under the protection of the Great Spirit, had a charmed life, and could not be slain in battle. At the Great Kanawha Washington's expedition down the Ohio terminated; having visited all the points he wished to examine. His return to Fort Pitt, and thence homeward, affords no incident worthy of note.

The discontents of Virginia, which had been partially soothed by the amiable administration of Lord Botetourt, were irritated anew under his successor, the Earl of Dunmore. This nobleman had for a short time held the government of New

York. When appointed to that of Virginia, he lingered for several months at his former post. In the meantime he sent his military secretary, Captain Foy, to attend to the despatch of business until his arrival; awarding to him a salary and fees to be paid by the colony. The pride of the Virginians was piqued at his lingering at New York, as if he preferred its gayety and luxury to the comparative quiet and simplicity of Williamsburg. The first measure of the Assembly, at its opening, was to demand by what right he had awarded a salary and fees to his secretary without consulting it; and to question whether it was authorized by the crown. His lordship had the good policy to rescind the unauthorized act, and in so doing mitigated the ire of the Assembly: but he lost no time in proroguing a body which, from various symptoms, appeared to be too independent, and disposed to be untractable.

He continued to prorogue it from time to time, seeking in the interim to conciliate the Virginians, and soothe their irritated pride. At length, after repeated prorogations he was compelled by circumstances to convene it on the 1st of March, 1773. Washington was prompt in his attendance on the occasion, and foremost among the patriotic members who eagerly availed themselves of this long wished for opportunity to legislate upon the general affairs of the colonies. One of their most important measures was the appointment of a committee of eleven persons, "whose business it should be to obtain the most clear and authentic intelligence of all such acts and resolutions of the British Parliament, or proceedings of administration, as may relate to or affect the British colonies, and to maintain with their sister colonies a correspondence and communication." The plan thus proposed by their "noble, patriotic sister colony of Virginia" was promptly adopted by the people of Massachusetts, and soon met with general concurrence. These corresponding committees, in effect, became the executive power of the patriot party, producing the happiest concert of design and action throughout the colonies.

Notwithstanding the decided part taken by Washington in the popular movement, very friendly relations existed between him and Lord Dunmore. The latter appreciated his character, and sought to avail himself of his experience in the affairs of the province. It was even concerted that Washington should accompany his lordship on an extensive tour, which the latter intended to make in the course of the summer along the western frontier. A melancholy circumstance occurred to defeat this arrangement.

We have spoken of Washington's paternal conduct towards the two children of Mrs. Washington. The daughter, Miss Custis had long been an object of extreme solicitude. She was of a fragile constitution, and for some time past had been in very declining health. Early in the present summer, symptoms indicated a rapid change for the worse. Washington was absent from home at the time. On his return to Mount Vernon he found her in the last stage of consumption. Though not a man given to bursts of sensibility, he is said on the present occasion to have evinced the deepest affliction; kneeling by her bedside, and pouring out earnest prayers for her recovery. She expired on the 19th of June, in the seventeenth year of her age. This, of course put an end to Washington's intention of accompanying Lord Dunmore to the frontier: he remained at home to console Mrs. Washington in her affliction—furnishing his lordship, however, with travelling hints and directions, and recommending proper guides.

The general covenant throughout the colonies against the use of taxed tea had operated disastrously against the interests of the East India Company, and produced an immense accumulation of the proscribed article in their warehouses. To remedy this Lord North brought in a bill (1773), by which the company were allowed to export their teas from England to any part whatever, without paying export duty. This, by enabling them to offer their teas at a low price in the colonies would, he supposed, tempt the Americans to purchase large quantities, thus relieving the company, and at the same time benefiting the revenue by the impost duty. Confiding in the wisdom of this policy, the company disgorged their warehouses, freighted several ships with tea, and sent them to various parts of the colonies. This brought matters to a crisis. One sentiment, one determination, pervaded the whole continent. Taxation was to receive its definitive blow. Whoever submitted to it was an enemy to his country. From New York and Philadelphia the ships were sent back, unladen, to London. In Charleston the tea was unloaded, and stored away in cellars and other places, where it perished. At Boston the action was still more decisive. The ships anchored in the harbor. Some small parcels of tea were brought on shore, but the sale of them was prohibited.

To settle the matter completely, and prove that on a point of principle they were not to be trifled with, a number of inhabitants, disguised as Indians, boarded the ships in the night (18th December), broke open all the chests of tea, and emptied the contents into the sea. The general opposition of the colonies to the principle of taxation had given great annoyance to government, but this individual act concentrated all its wrath upon Boston. A bill was forthwith passed in Parliament (commonly called the Boston port bill), by which all lading and unlading of goods, wares, and merchandise, were to cease in that town and harbor on and after the 4th of June, and the officers of the customs to be transferred to Salem.

Another law, passed soon after, altered the charter of the province, decreeing that all counsellors, judges, and magistrates, should be appointed by the crown, and hold office during the royal pleasure. This was followed by a third, intended for the suppression of riots; and providing that any person indicted for murder, or other capital offence, committed in aiding the magistracy, might be sent by the governor to some other colony, or to Great Britain, for trial.

Such was the bolt of Parliamentary wrath fulminated against the devoted town of Boston. Before it fell there was a session in May of the Virginia House of Burgesses. The social position of Lord Dunmore had been strengthened in the province by the arrival of his lady, and a numerous family of sons and daughters. The House of Burgesses was opened in form, and one of its first measures was an address of congratulation to the governor on the arrival of his lady. It was followed up by an agreement among the members to give her ladyship a splendid ball, on the 27th of the month.

All things were going on smoothly and smilingly, when a letter, received through the corresponding committee, brought intelligence of the vindictive measure of Parliament, by which the port of Boston was to be closed on the approaching 1st of June. The letter was read in the House of Burgesses, and produced a general burst of indignation. All other business was thrown aside, and this became the sole subject of discussion. A protest against this and other recent acts of Parliament was entered upon the journal of the House, and a resolution was adopted, on the 24th of May, setting apart the 1st of June as a day of fasting, prayer, and humiliation. On the following morning the Burgesses were summoned to attend Lord Dunmore in the council chamber, where he made them the following laconic speech: "Mr. Speaker, and Gentlemen of the House of Burgesses: I have in my hand a paper, published by order of your House, conceived in such terms as reflect highly upon his majesty, and the Parliament of Great Britain, which makes it necessary for me to dissolve you, and you are dissolved accordingly."

As on a former occasion, the Assembly, though dissolved was not dispersed. The members adjourned to the long room of the old Raleigh tavern, and passed resolutions denouncing the Boston port bill as a most dangerous attempt to destroy the constitutional liberty and rights of all North America; recommending their countrymen to desist from the use, not merely of tea, but of all kinds of East Indian commodities; pronouncing an attack on one of the colonies, to enforce arbitrary taxes, an attack on all; and ordering the committee of correspondence to communicate with the other corresponding committees on the expediency of appointing deputies from the several colonies of British America to meet annually in GENERAL CONGRESS, at such place as might be deemed expedient, to deliberate on such measures as the united interests of the colonies might require.

This was the first recommendation of a General Congress by any public assembly, though it had been previously proposed in town meetings at New York and Boston. A resolution to the same effect was passed in the Assembly of Massachusetts before it was aware of the proceedings of the Virginia Legislature. The measure recommended met with prompt and general concurrence throughout the colonies, and the fifth day of September next ensuing was fixed upon for the meeting of the first Congress, which was to be held at Philadelphia.

On the 29th, letters arrived from Boston giving the proceedings of a town meeting, recommending that a general league should be formed throughout the colonies suspending all trade with Great Britain. But twenty-five members of the late House of Burgesses, including Washington, were at that time remaining in Williamsburg. They held a meeting on the following day, at which Peyton Randolph presided as moderator. After some discussion it was determined to issue a printed circular, bearing their signatures, and calling a meeting of all the members of the late House of Burgesses, on the 1st of August, to take into consideration this measure of a general league. The circular recommended them, also, to collect, in the meantime, the sense of their respective counties.

In the meantime the Boston port bill had been carried into effect. On the 1st of June the harbor of Boston was closed at noon, and all business ceased. The two other parliamentary acts altering the charter of Massachusetts were to be enforced. No public meetings, excepting the annual town meetings in March and May, were to be held without permission of the governor.

General Thomas Gage had recently been appointed to the military command of Massachusetts, and the carrying out of these offensive acts. As lieutenant-colonel, he had led the advance guard on the field of Braddock's defeat. Fortune had since gone well with him. Rising in the service, he had been governor of Montreal, and had succeeded Amherst in the command of the British forces on this continent. He was linked to the country also by domestic ties, having married into one of the most respectable families of New Jersey. In the various situations in which he had hitherto been placed he had won esteem, and rendered himself popular. But with all his experience in America he had formed a most erroneous opinion of the character of the people. "The Americans," said he to the king, "will be lions only as long as the English are lambs;" and he engaged, with five regiments, to keep Boston quiet!

The manner in which his attempts to enforce the recent acts of Parliament were resented, showed how egregiously he was in error. At the suggestion of the Assembly, a paper was circulated through the province by the committee of correspondence, entitled "a solemn league and covenant," the subscribers to which bound themselves to break off all intercourse with Great Britain from the 1st of August, until the colony should be restored to the enjoyment of its chartered rights; and to renounce all dealings with those who should refuse to enter into this compact.

The very title of league and covenant had an ominous sound, and startled General Gage. He issued a proclamation, denouncing it as illegal and traitorous. Furthermore, he encamped a force of infantry and artillery on Boston Common, as if prepared to enact the lion. An alarm spread through the adjacent country. "Boston is to be blockaded! Boston is to be reduced to obedience by force or famine!" The spirit of the yeomanry was aroused. They sent in word to the inhabitants promising to come to their aid if necessary; and urging them to stand fast to the faith.

CHAPTER XV.
THE FIRST GENERAL CONGRESS.

Shortly after Washington's return to Mount Vernon, in the latter part of June, he presided as moderator at a meeting of the inhabitants of Fairfax County, wherein, after the recent acts of Parliament had been discussed, a committee was appointed, with himself as chairman, to draw up resolutions expressive of the sentiments of the present meeting, and to report the same at a general meeting of the county, to be held in the court-house on the 18th of July.

The committee met according to appointment, with Washington as chairman. The resolutions framed at the meeting insisted, as usual, on the right of self-government, and the principle that taxation and representation were in their nature inseparable: that the various acts of Parliament for raising revenue, taking away trials by jury, ordering that persons might be tried in a different country from that in which the cause of accusation originated, closing the port of Boston, abrogating the charter of Massachusetts Bay, etc., etc., were all part of a premeditated design and system to introduce arbitrary government into the colonies; that the sudden and repeated dissolutions of Assemblies whenever they presumed to examine the illegality of ministerial mandates, or deliberated on the violated rights of their constituents, were part of the same system, and calculated and intended to drive the people of the colonies to a state of desperation, and to dissolve the compact by which their ancestors bound themselves and their posterity to remain dependent on the British crown. The resolutions, furthermore, recommended the most perfect union and co-operation among the colonies; solemn covenants with respect to non-importation and non-intercourse, and a renunciation of all dealings with any colony, town, or province that should refuse to agree to the plan adopted by the General Congress. They also recommended a dutiful petition and remonstrance from the Congress to the king, asserting their constitutional rights and privileges; lamenting the necessity of entering into measures that might be displeasing; declaring their attachment to his person, family, and government, and their desire to continue in dependence upon Great Britain; beseeching him not to reduce his faithful subjects of America to desperation, and to reflect that *from our sovereign there can be but one appeal.*

The resolutions reported by the committee were adopted, and Washington was chosen a delegate to represent the county at the General Convention of the province, to be held at Williamsburg on the 1st of August. [On the date appointed the convention assembled.] Washington appeared on behalf of Fairfax County, and presented the resolutions, already cited, as the sense of his constituents. He is said, by one who was present, to have spoken in support of them in a strain of uncommon eloquence. The Convention was six days in session. Resolutions, in the same spirit with those passed in Fairfax County, were adopted, and Peyton Randolph, Richard Henry Lee, George Washington, Patrick Henry, Richard Bland, Benjamin Harrison, and Edmund Pendleton, were appointed delegates, to represent the people of Virginia in the General Congress.

General Gage from the time of taking command at Boston, had been perplexed how to manage its inhabitants. Had they been hot-headed, impulsive, and prone to paroxysm, his task would have been comparatively easy; but it was the cool, shrewd common sense, by which all their movements were regulated, that confounded him. There was no uproar, no riots; everything was awfully systematic and according to rule. Town meetings were held, in which public rights and public measures were eloquently discussed by John Adams, Josiah Quincy, and other eminent men. Over these meetings Samuel Adams presided as moderator; a man clear in judgment, calm in conduct, inflexible in resolution, deeply grounded in civil and political history, and infallible on all points of constitutional law.

Gage was at a loss how to act. It would not do to disperse these assemblages by force of arms; for the people who composed them mingled the soldier with the polemic; and like their prototypes, the covenanters of yore, if prone to argue, were as ready to fight. So the meetings continued to be held pertinaciously. Faneuil Hall was at times unable to hold them, and they swarmed from that revolutionary hive into old South Church. The liberty tree became a rallying place for any popular movement, and a flag hoisted on it was saluted by all processions as the emblem of the popular cause.

When the time approached for the meeting of the General Congress at Philadelphia, Washington was joined at Mount Vernon by Patrick Henry and Edmund Pendleton, and they performed the journey together on horseback. It was a noble companionship. Henry was then in the youthful vigor and elasticity of his bounding genius, ardent, acute, fanciful, eloquent; Pendleton, schooled in public life, a veteran in council, with native force of intellect, and habits of deep reflection; Washington, in the meridian of his days, mature in wisdom, comprehensive in mind, sagacious in foresight. Such were the apostles of liberty, repairing on their august pilgrimage to Philadelphia from all parts of the land, to lay the foundations of a mighty empire.

Congress assembled on Monday, the 5th of September, in a large room in Carpenter's Hall. There were fifty-one delegates, representing all the colonies excepting Georgia. The meeting has been described as "awfully solemn." The most eminent men of the various colonies were now for the first time brought together; they were known to each other by fame, but were, personally, strangers. The object which had called them together was of incalculable magnitude. The liberties of no less than three millions of people, with that of all their posterity, were staked on the wisdom and energy of their councils.

There being an inequality in the number of delegates from the different colonies, a question arose as to the mode of voting; whether by colonies, by the poll, or by interests. After some debate, it was determined that each colony should have but one vote, whatever might be the number of its delegates. The deliberations of the House were to be with closed doors, and nothing but the resolves promulgated, unless by order of the majority. To give proper dignity and solemnity to the proceedings, it was moved on the following day that each morning the session should be opened by prayer. In the course of the day, a rumor reached Philadelphia that Boston had been cannonaded by the British. It produced a strong sensation; and when Congress met on the following morning (7th), the effect was visible in every countenance. The delegates from the east were greeted with a warmer grasp of the hand by their associates from the south. [The rumor proved to be erroneous.]

Owing to closed doors, and the want of reporters, no record exists of the discussions and speeches made in the first Congress. The first public measure was a resolution declaratory of their feelings with regard to the recent acts of Parliament, violating the rights of the people of Massachusetts, and of their determination to combine in resisting any force that might attempt to carry those acts into execution.

A committee of two from each province reported a series of resolutions, which were adopted and promulgated by Congress, as a "declaration of colonial rights." In this were enumerated their natural rights to the enjoyment of life, liberty, and property; and their rights as British subjects. Among the latter was participation in legislative councils. This they could not exercise through representatives in Parliament; they claimed, therefore, the power of legislating in their provincial assemblies; consenting, however, to such acts of Parliament as might be essential to the regulation of trade; but excluding all taxation, internal or external, for raising revenue in America. The common law of England was claimed as a birthright, including the right of trial by a jury of the vicinage; of holding public meetings to consider grievances; and of petitioning the king. The benefits of all such statutes as existed at the time of the colonization were likewise claimed; together with the immunities and privileges granted by royal charters, or secured by provincial laws. The maintenance of a standing army in any colony in time of peace, without the consent of its legislature, was pronounced contrary to law. The exercise of the legislative power in the colonies by a council appointed during pleasure by the crown, was declared to be unconstitutional, and destructive to the freedom of American legislation. Then followed a specification of the acts of Parliament, passed during the reign of George III., infringing and violating these rights. These were—the sugar act; the stamp act; the two acts for quartering troops; the tea act; the act suspending the New York legislature; the two acts for the trial in Great Britain of offences committed in America; the Boston port bill; the act for regulating the government of Massachusetts, and the Quebec act.

"To these grievous acts and measures," it was added, "Americans cannot submit; but in hopes their fellow subjects in Great Britain will, on a revision of them, restore us to that state in which both countries found happiness and prosperity, we have for the present, only resolved to pursue the following peaceable measures: 1st. To enter into a non-importation, non-consumption, and non-exportation agreement, or association. 2d. To prepare an address to the people of Great

Britain, and a memorial to the inhabitants of British America. 3d. To prepare a loyal address to his majesty." The above-mentioned association was accordingly formed, and committees were to be appointed in every county, city and town to maintain it vigilantly and strictly.

Masterly state papers were issued by Congress in conformity to the resolutions: viz, a petition to the king, drafted by Mr. Dickinson, of Philadelphia; an address to the people of Canada by the same hand, inviting them to join the league of the colonies; another to the people of Great Britain, drafted by John Jay, of New York; and a memorial to the inhabitants of the British colonies by Richard Henry Lee, of Virginia.

The Congress remained in session fifty-one days. Every subject, according to Adams, was discussed "with a moderation, an acuteness, and a minuteness equal to that of Queen Elizabeth's privy council." The papers issued by it have deservedly been pronounced masterpieces of practical talent and political wisdom. From the secrecy that enveloped its discussions, we are ignorant of the part taken by Washington in the debates; the similarity of the resolutions, however, in spirit and substance to those of the Fairfax County meeting, in which he presided, and the coincidence of the measures adopted with those therein recommended, show that he had a powerful agency in the whole proceedings of this eventful assembly. Patrick Henry, being asked, on his return home, whom he considered the greatest man in Congress, replied: "If you speak of eloquence, Mr. Rutledge, of South Carolina, is by far the greatest orator; but if you speak of solid information and sound judgment, Colonel Washington is unquestionably the greatest man on that floor."

On the breaking up of Congress, Washington hastened back to Mount Vernon, where his presence was more than usually important to the happiness of Mrs. Washington, from the loneliness caused by the recent death of her daughter and the absence of her son. The cheerfulness of the neighborhood had been diminished of late by the departure of George William Fairfax for England, to take possession of estates which had devolved to him in that kingdom. His estate of Belvoir, so closely allied with that of Mount Vernon by family ties and reciprocal hospitality, was left in charge of a steward, or overseer. Through some accident the house took fire, and was burnt to the ground. It was never rebuilt. The course of political events which swept Washington from his quiet home into the current of public and military life, prevented William Fairfax, who was a royalist, though a liberal one, from returning to his once happy abode, and the hospitable intercommunion of Mount Vernon and Belvoir was at an end for ever.

CHAPTER XVI.

MILITARY MEASURES.—AFFAIRS AT LEXINGTON.

The rumor, at the opening of Congress, of the cannonading of Boston had been caused by measures of Governor Gage. The public mind in Boston and its vicinity had been rendered excessively jealous and sensitive by the landing and encamping of artillery upon the Common and Welsh Fusiliers on Fort Hill, and by the planting of four large field-pieces on Boston Neck, the only entrance to the town by land. The country people were arming and disciplining themselves in every direction, and collecting and depositing arms and ammunition in places where they would be at hand in case of emergency. Gage, on the other hand, issued orders that the munitions of war in all the public magazines should be brought to Boston. One of these magazines was the arsenal in the north-west part of Charlestown, between Medford and Cambridge. Two companies of the king's troops passed silently in boats up Mystic River in the night; took possession of a large quantity of gunpowder deposited there, and conveyed it to Castle Williams. Intelligence of this sacking of the arsenal flew with lightning speed through the neighborhood. In the morning several thousands of patriots were assembled at Cambridge, weapon in hand, and were with difficulty prevented from marching upon Boston to compel a restitution of the powder. In the confusion and agitation, a rumor stole out into the country that Boston was to be attacked; followed by another that the ships were cannonading the town, and the soldiers shooting down the inhabitants. The whole country was forthwith in arms. Numerous bodies of the Connecticut people had made some marches before the report was contradicted.

Gage, on the 1st of September, before this popular agitation, had issued writs for an election of an assembly to meet at Salem in October; seeing, however, the irritated state of the public mind, he now countermanded the same by proclamation. The people, disregarding the countermand, carried the election, and ninety of the new members thus elected met at the appointed time. They waited a whole day for the governor to attend, administer the oaths, and open the session; but as he did not make his appearance, they voted themselves a provincial Congress, and chose for president of it John Hancock,—a man of great wealth, popular, and somewhat showy talents, and ardent patriotism; and eminent from his social position. This self-constituted body adjourned to Concord, about twenty miles from Boston; quietly assumed supreme authority, and issued a remonstrance to the governor, virtually calling him to account for his military operations in fortifying Boston Neck, and collecting warlike stores about him, thereby alarming the fears of the whole province and menacing the lives and property of the Bostonians.

General Gage, overlooking the irregularity of its organization, entered into explanations with the Assembly, but failed to give satisfaction. As winter approached, he found his situation more and more critical. Boston was the only place in Massachusetts that now contained British forces, and it had become the refuge of all the *"tories"* of the province; that is to say, of all those devoted to the British government. There was animosity between them and the principal inhabitants, among whom revolutionary principles prevailed. The town itself, almost insulated by nature, and surrounded by a hostile country, was like a place besieged.

The provincial Congress conducted its affairs with the order and system so formidable to General Gage. Having adopted a plan for organizing the militia, it had nominated general officers, two of whom, Artemas Ward and Seth Pomeroy, had accepted. The executive powers were vested in a committee of safety. This was to determine when the services of the militia were necessary; was to call them forth,—to nominate their officers to the Congress,—to commission them, and direct the operations of the army. Another committee was appointed to furnish supplies to the forces when called out; hence, named the Committee of Supplies. Under such auspices, the militia went on arming and disciplining itself in every direction.

Arrangements had been made for keeping up an active correspondence between different parts of the country, and spreading an alarm in case of any threatening danger. Under the direction of the committees just mentioned, large quantities of military stores had been collected and deposited at Concord and Worcester.

This semi-belligerent state of affairs in Massachusetts produced a general restlessness throughout the land. The weak-hearted apprehended coming troubles; the resolute prepared to brave them. Military measures, hitherto confined to New England, extended to the middle and southern provinces, and the roll of the drum resounded through the villages. Virginia was among the first to buckle on its armor. It had long been a custom among its inhabitants to form themselves into independent companies, equipped at their own expense, having their own peculiar uniform, and electing their own officers, though holding themselves subject to militia law. They had hitherto been self-disciplined; but now they continually resorted to Washington for instruction and advice; considering him the highest authority on military affairs. He was frequently called from home, therefore, in the course of the winter and spring, to different parts of the country to review independent companies; all of which were anxious to put themselves under his command as field-officer.

Mount Vernon, therefore, again assumed a military tone as in former days, when he took his first lessons there in the art of war. Two occasional and important guests in this momentous crisis, were General Charles Lee,[1] and Major Horatio

---

[1] General Charles Lee was an Englishman by birth, and a highly cultivated production of European warfare. He was born in 1731, and may almost be said to have been cradled in the army, for he received a commission by the time he was eleven years of age. He served in the French war of America; in 1762 obtained a colonel's commission, and went with Burgoyne to Portugal. Having a caustic pen he undertook to write on colonial questions, and thereby lost the favor of the ministry. He then went to Poland; won the favor of

Gates.[2] To Washington the visits of these gentlemen were extremely welcome at this juncture, from their military knowledge and experience, especially as much of it had been acquired in America, in the same kind of warfare, if not the very same campaigns in which he himself had mingled. Both were interested in the popular cause. Lee was full of plans for the organization and disciplining of the militia, and occasionally accompanied Washington in his attendance on provincial reviews. He was subsequently very efficient at Annapolis in promoting and superintending the organization of the Maryland militia.

In the month of March the second Virginia convention was held at Richmond. Washington attended as delegate from Fairfax County. In this assembly, Patrick Henry, with his usual ardor and eloquence, advocated measures for embodying, arming and disciplining a militia force, and providing for the defence of the colony. Washington joined him in the conviction, and was one of a committee that reported a plan for carrying those measures into effect. He was not an impulsive man to raise the battle cry, but the executive man to marshal the troops into the field and carry on the war.

While the spirit of revolt was daily gaining strength and determination in America, a strange infatuation reigned in the British councils. While the wisdom and eloquence of Chatham were exerted in vain in behalf of American rights, an empty braggadocio, elevated to a seat in Parliament, was able to captivate the attention of the members and influence their votes by gross misrepresentations of the Americans and their cause. This was no other than Colonel Grant, the same shallow soldier who had been guilty of a foolhardy bravado before the walls of Fort Duquesne, which brought slaughter and defeat upon his troops. We are told that he entertained Parliament, especially the ministerial side of the House, with ludicrous stories of the cowardice of Americans. This taunting and braggart speech was made in the face of the conciliatory bill of the venerable Chatham, devised with a view to redress the wrongs of America. The councils of the arrogant and scornful prevailed; and instead of the proposed bill, further measures of a stringent nature were adopted, coercive of some of the middle and southern colonies, but ruinous to the trade and fisheries of New England.

At length the bolt, so long suspended, fell! The troops at Boston had been augmented to about four thousand men. Goaded on by the instigations of the tories, and alarmed by the energetic measures of the whigs, General Gage now

---

King Stanislaus; in 1769 obtained the rank of major-general in the Polish army, and served in a campaign against the Turks. Leaving the Polish army he led a restless life about Europe, and in 1773, coming to America, openly espoused the colonial cause. He was a man of eccentric habits, caustic humor, extensive military experience, and was considered a prodigious acquisition to the patriot cause.

[2] Major Horatio Gates was an Englishman by birth. When twenty he served as a volunteer under Cornwallis, governor of Halifax; next as captain under Braddock; accompanied General Monckton as aide-de-camp to the West Indies, gained credit at the capture of Martinico, and was promoted to the rank of major. His promotion did not equal his expectations, and went to England, and failing to attain his desires, came to Virginia in 1772, and purchased an estate in Berkeley County, where he settled. He was now forty-six years of age.

resolved to deal the latter a crippling blow. This was to surprise and destroy their magazine of military stores at Concord, about twenty miles from Boston. It was to be effected on the night of the 18th of April by a force detached for the purpose. Preparations were made with great secrecy. Boats for the transportation of troops were launched, and moored under the sterns of the men-of-war. Grenadiers and light infantry were relieved from duty and held in readiness. On the 18th, officers were stationed on the roads leading from Boston to prevent any intelligence of the expedition getting into the country. At night orders were issued by General Gage that no person should leave the town. About ten o'clock from eight to nine hundred men, grenadiers, light infantry and marines, commanded by Lieutenant-colonel Smith, embarked in the boats at the foot of Boston Common and crossed to Lechmere Point, in Cambridge, whence they were to march silently and without beat of drum to the place of destination.

The measures of General Gage had not been shrouded in all the secrecy he imagined. Dr. Joseph Warren, one of the committee of safety, had observed the preparatory disposition of the boats and troops, and surmised some sinister intention. He sent notice of these movements to John Hancock and Samuel Adams, both members of the provincial Congress, but at that time privately sojourning with a friend at Lexington. A design on the magazine at Concord was suspected, and the committee of safety ordered that the cannon collected there should be secreted and part of the stores removed. On the night of the 18th, Dr. Warren sent off two messengers by different routes to give the alarm that the king's troops were actually sallying forth. The messengers got out of Boston just before the order of General Gage went into effect, to prevent any one from leaving the town. About the same time a lantern was hung out of an upper window of the north church, in the direction of Charlestown. This was a preconcerted signal to the patriots of that place who instantly despatched swift messengers to rouse the country.

In the meantime, Colonel Smith set out on his nocturnal march from Lechmere Point by an unfrequented path across marshes, where at times the troops had to wade through water. He had proceeded but a few miles when alarm guns, booming through the night air, and the clang of village bells, showed that the news of his approach was travelling before him, and the people were rising. He now sent back to General Gage for a reinforcement, while Major Pitcairn was detached with six companies to press forward and secure the bridges at Concord.

Pitcairn advanced rapidly, capturing every one that he met or overtook. Within a mile and a half of Lexington, however, a horseman was too quick on the spur for him, and galloping to the village, gave the alarm that the redcoats were coming. Drums were beaten; guns fired. By the time that Pitcairn entered the village about seventy or eighty of the yeomanry, in military array, were mustered on the green near the church. The sound of drum, and the array of men in arms, indicated a hostile determination. Pitcairn halted his men within a short distance of the church, and ordered them to prime and load. They then advanced at double quick time. The major, riding forward ordered the rebels, as he termed them, to disperse. The order was disregarded. A scene of confusion ensued, with firing on both sides; which party commenced it has been a matter of dispute. The firing of the Americans was irregular and without much effect; that of the British was more fatal. Eight of the patriots were killed and ten wounded, and the whole put to flight. Colonel Smith soon arrived with the residue of the detachment, and they all marched on towards Concord, about six miles distant.

The alarm had reached that place in the dead hour of the preceding night. The church bell roused the inhabitants. They gathered together in anxious consultation. The militia and minute men seized their arms and repaired to the parade ground near the church. Exertions were now made to remove and conceal the military stores. A scout, who had been sent out for intelligence, brought word that the British had fired upon the people at Lexington and were advancing upon Concord. There was great excitement and indignation. Part of the militia marched down the Lexington road to meet them, but returned, reporting their force to be three times that of the Americans. The whole of the militia now retired to an eminence about a mile from the centre of the town, and formed themselves into two battalions.

About seven o'clock the British came in sight. They entered in two divisions by different roads. Concord is traversed by a river of the same name, having two bridges, the north and the south. The grenadiers and light infantry took post in the centre of the town, while strong parties of light troops were detached to secure the bridges, and destroy the military stores. Two hours were expended in the work of destruction without much success, so much of the stores having been removed, or concealed. During all this time the yeomanry from the neighboring towns were hurrying in with such weapons as were at hand, and joining the militia on the height, until the little cloud of war gathering there numbered about four hundred and fifty. About ten o'clock, a body of three hundred undertook to dislodge the British from the north bridge. As they approached, the latter fired upon them, killing two, and wounding a third. The patriots returned the fire with spirit and effect. The British retreated to the main body, the Americans pursuing them across the bridge.

By this time all the military stores which could be found had been destroyed; Colonel Smith, therefore, made preparations for a retreat. About noon he commenced his retrograde march for Boston. It was high time. His troops were jaded by the night march and the morning's toils and skirmishings.

The country was thoroughly alarmed. The yeomanry were hurrying from every quarter to the scene of action. As the British began their retreat, the Americans began the work of sore and galling retaliation. Along the open road the former were harassed incessantly by rustic marksmen, who took deliberate aim from behind trees or over stone fences. It was in vain they threw out flankers and endeavored to dislodge their assailants; each pause gave time for other pursuers to come within reach and open attacks from different quarters. For several miles they urged their way along woody defiles, or roads skirted with fences and stone walls, the retreat growing more and more disastrous. Before reaching Lexington, Colonel Smith received a severe wound in the leg, and the situation of the retreating troops was becoming extremely critical, when, about two o'clock, they were met by Lord Percy, with a brigade of one thousand men and two field-pieces. Opening his brigade to the right and left, he received the retreating troops into a hollow square; where, fainting and exhausted, they threw themselves on the ground to rest. His lordship showed no disposition to advance upon their assailants, but contented himself with keeping them at bay with his field-pieces, which opened a vigorous fire from an eminence.

Hitherto the Provincials, being hasty levies, without a leader, had acted from individual impulse, without much concert; but now General Heath was upon the ground. He was one of those authorized to take command when the minute men should be called out. Dr. Warren also arrived on horseback, having spurred from Boston on receiving news of the skirmishing. In the subsequent part of the day he was one of the most active and efficient men in the field. His presence, like that of General Heath, regulated the infuriated ardor of the militia and brought it into system.

Lord Percy, having allowed the troops a short interval for repose and refreshment, continued the retreat toward Boston. As soon as he got under march, the galling assault by the pursuing yeomanry was recommenced in flank and rear. The British soldiery, irritated in turn, acted as if in an enemy's country. Houses and shops were burnt down in Lexington; private dwellings along the road were plundered, and their inhabitants maltreated. Their march became more and more impeded by the number of their wounded. Lord Percy narrowly escaped death from a musket-ball, which struck off a button of his waistcoat. The provincials pressed upon him in rear, others were advancing from Roxbury, Dorchester, and Milton; Colonel Pickering, with the Essex militia, seven hundred strong, was at hand; there was danger of being intercepted in the retreat to Charlestown. The field-pieces were again brought into play to check the ardor of the pursuit; but they were no longer objects of terror. The pursuit terminated a little after sunset at Charlestown Common, where General Heath brought the minute men to a halt.

In this memorable affair the British loss was seventy-three killed, one hundred and seventy-four wounded and twenty-six missing. Among the slain were eighteen officers. The loss of the Americans was forty-nine killed, thirty-nine wounded, and five missing. This was the first blood shed in the revolutionary struggle. The cry went through the land. None felt the appeal more than the old soldiers of the French war. It roused John Stark, of New Hampshire—a trapper and hunter in his youth, a veteran in Indian warfare, a campaigner under Abercrombie and Amherst. Within ten minutes after receiving the alarm, he was spurring towards the sea-coast. Equally alert was his old comrade in frontier exploits, Colonel Israel Putnam.[3] A man on horseback, with a drum, passed through his neighborhood in Connecticut, proclaiming British violence at Lexington. Putnam was in the field ploughing, assisted by his son. In an instant the team was unyoked; the plough left in the furrow; the lad sent home to give word of his father's departure; and Putnam, on horseback in his working garb, urging with all speed to the camp.

---

[3] Israel Putnam was a soldier of native growth. He had served at Louisburg, Fort Duquesne, and Crown Point; had signalized himself in Indian warfare: been captured by the savages, tortured, and rescued from the stake at the eleventh hour. Since the peace he had resided on his farm at Pomfret, in Connecticut.

The news reached Virginia at a critical moment. Lord Dunmore, obeying a general order issued by the ministry to all the provincial governors, had seized upon the military munitions of the province. Here was a similar measure to that of Gage. The cry went forth that the subjugation of the colonies was to be attempted. All Virginia was in combustion. The standard of liberty was reared in every county; there was a general cry to arms. Washington was looked to from various quarters to take command. His old comrade in arms, Hugh Mercer, was about marching down to Williamsburg at the head of a body of resolute men, seven hundred strong, entitled "The friends of constitutional liberty and America," whom he had organized and drilled in Fredericksburg, and nothing but a timely concession of Lord Dunmore, with respect to some powder which he had seized, prevented his being beset in his palace.

CHAPTER XVII.

CAPTURE OF TICONDEROGA AND CROWN POINT.—WASHINGTON APPOINTED COMMANDER-IN-CHIEF.

At the eastward, the march of the Revolution went on with accelerated speed. Thirty thousand men had been deemed necessary for the defence of the country. The provincial Congress of Massachusetts resolved to raise thirteen thousand six hundred, as its quota. Circular letters also were issued by the committee of safety, urging the towns to enlist troops with all speed, and calling for military aid from the other New England provinces.

Their appeals were promptly answered. Bodies of militia and parties of volunteers from New Hampshire, Rhode Island and Connecticut hastened to join the minute men of Massachusetts in forming a camp in the neighborhood of Boston. The command of the camp was given to General Artemas Ward, already mentioned. He was a native of Shrewsbury, in Massachusetts, and a veteran of the seven years' war—having served as lieutenant-colonel under Abercrombie.

As affairs were now drawing to a crisis and war was considered inevitable, some bold spirits in Connecticut conceived a project for the outset. This was the surprisal of the old forts of Ticonderoga and Crown Point, already famous in the French war. Their situation on Lake Champlain gave them the command of the main route to Canada; so that the possession of them would be all-important in case of hostilities. They were feebly garrisoned and negligently guarded, and abundantly furnished with artillery and military stores, so much needed by the patriot army. This scheme was set on foot in the purlieus, as it were, of the provincial Legislature of Connecticut, then in session. It was not openly sanctioned by that body, but secretly favored, and money lent from the treasury to those engaged in it. Sixteen men were thus enlisted in Connecticut, a greater number in Massachusetts, but the greatest accession of force was from what was called the "New Hampshire Grants." This was a region forming the present State of Vermont. It had long been a disputed territory, claimed by New York and New Hampshire. The settlers had resisted the attempts of New York to eject them, and formed themselves into an association called "The Green Mountain Boys," with Ethan Allen at their head. He and his lieutenants, Seth Warner and Remember Baker, were outlawed by the Legislature of New York, and Allen was becoming a kind of Robin Hood among the mountains when the present crisis changed the relative position of things as if by magic. Boundary feuds were forgotten amid the great questions of colonial rights. Ethan Allen at once stepped forward, a patriot, and volunteered with his Green Mountain Boys to serve in the popular cause. Thus reinforced, the party, now two hundred and seventy strong, pushed forward to Castleton, a place within a few miles of the head of Lake Champlain. Here a council of war was held on the 2d of May. Ethan Allen was placed at the head of the expedition. [At this juncture Benedict Arnold, afterwards so sadly renowned, arrived at Castleton. He too had conceived the project of surprising Ticonderoga and Crown Point; his plan had been approved by the Massachusetts committee of safety, and he had received a colonel's commission. He claimed the right to command the expedition, but the Green Mountain Boys would follow no leader but Allen. Arnold was fain to acquiesce. The party arrived at Shoreham, opposite Ticonderoga, on the night of the 9th of May. The boats were few, and by day-break a part of the force only had crossed. Allen announced his intention to make a dash at the fort at once, before the garrison should wake.]

They mounted the hill briskly but in silence, guided by a boy from the neighborhood. The day dawned as Allen arrived at a sally port. A sentry pulled trigger on him, but his piece missed fire. He retreated through a covered way. Allen and his men followed. Another sentry was struck down by Allen, and begged for quarter. It was granted on condition of his leading the way instantly to the quarters of the commandant, Captain Delaplace, who was yet in bed. Being arrived there, Allen thundered at the door, and demanded a surrender of the fort. By this time his followers had formed into two lines on the parade-ground, and given three hearty cheers. The commandant appeared at his door half-dressed. He gazed at Allen in bewildered astonishment. "By whose authority do you act?" exclaimed he. "In the name of the great Jehovah, and the Continental Congress!" replied Allen with a flourish of his sword and an oath which we do not care to subjoin. There was no disputing the point. The garrison, like the commander, had been startled from sleep, and made prisoners as they rushed forth in their confusion. A surrender accordingly took place. A great supply of military and naval stores, so important in the present crisis, was found in the fortress.

Colonel Seth Warner was now sent with a detachment against Crown Point, which surrendered on the 12th of May without firing a gun; the whole garrison being a sergeant and twelve men. Here were taken upward of a hundred cannon. [A plan was also concerted to surprise St. John's on the Sorel River, the frontier post of Canada. It was led by Arnold and was eminently successful; a king's sloop of seventy tons, with two brass six-pounders, four bateaux, and many valuable stores were captured. The approach of troops from Montreal rendered it necessary to abandon the post.]

Thus a partisan band, unpractised in the art of war, had, by a series of daring exploits and almost without the loss of a man, won for the patriots the command of Lakes George and Champlain, and thrown open the great highway to Canada.

The second General Congress assembled at Philadelphia on the 10th of May. Peyton Randolph was again elected as president; but being obliged to return and occupy his place as speaker of the Virginia Assembly, John Hancock, of Massachusetts, was elevated to the chair.

A lingering feeling of attachment to the mother country, struggling with the growing spirit of self-government, was manifested in the proceedings of this remarkable body. Many of those most active in vindicating colonial rights, and Washington among the number, still indulged the hope of an eventual reconciliation, while few entertained, or at least avowed the idea of complete independence. A second "humble and dutiful" petition to the king was moved, but met with strong opposition. John Adams condemned it as an imbecile measure, calculated to embarrass the proceedings of Congress. He was for prompt and vigorous action. Other members concurred with him.

A federal union was formed, leaving to each colony the right of regulating its internal affairs according to its own individual constitution, but vesting in Congress the power of making peace or war; of entering into treaties and alliances; of regulating general commerce; in a word, of legislating on all such matters as regarded the security and welfare of the whole community. The executive power was to be vested in a council of twelve, chosen by Congress from among its own members, and to hold office for a limited time. Such colonies as had not sent delegates to Congress might yet become members of the confederacy by agreeing to its conditions. Georgia, which had hitherto hesitated, soon joined the league, which thus extended from Nova Scotia to Florida.

Congress lost no time in exercising their federated powers. In virtue of them, they ordered the enlistment of troops, the construction of forts in various parts of the colonies, the provision of arms, ammunition, and military stores; while to defray the expense of these, and other measures, avowedly of self-defence, they authorized the emission of notes to the amount of three millions of dollars, bearing the inscription of "The United Colonies;" the faith of the confederacy being pledged for their redemption.

The public sense of Washington's military talents and experience, was evinced in his being chairman of all the committees appointed for military affairs. Most of the rules and regulations for the army, and the measures for defence, were devised by him.

The situation of the New England army, actually besieging Boston, became an early and absorbing consideration. It was without munitions of war, without arms, clothing, or pay; in fact, without legislative countenance or encouragement. Unless sanctioned and assisted by Congress, there was danger of its dissolution. All this was the subject of much discussion out of doors. The disposition to uphold the army was general; but the difficult question was, who should be commander-in-chief? [There was a southern party in Congress who were urgent for the appointment of a southern general to command, and "so many of our stanchest men," says Adams, "were in the plan, that we could carry nothing without it." On the other hand Hancock himself had an ambition to be appointed to the command. The opinion, however, evidently inclined in favor of Washington. Adams, rising in his place one day, urged upon Congress that they should adopt the army at Cambridge, and appoint a general. He then proceeded to advance the name of Washington. The subject was postponed to a future day. On the 15th of June, the army was regularly adopted by Congress, and the pay of the commander-in-chief fixed at five hundred dollars a month.]

In this stage of the business Mr. Johnson, of Maryland, rose and nominated Washington for the station of commander-in-chief. The election was by ballot, and was unanimous. It was formally announced to him by the president on the following day, when he had taken his seat in Congress. Rising in his place, he briefly expressed his high and grateful sense of the honor conferred on him and his sincere devotion to the cause. "But," added he, "lest some unlucky event should happen unfavorable to my reputation, I beg it may be remembered by every gentleman in the room, that I this day declare with the utmost sincerity I do not think myself equal the command I am honored with. As to pay, I beg leave to assure the Congress that, as no pecuniary consideration could have tempted me to accept this arduous employment, at the expense of my domestic ease and happiness, I do not wish to make any profit of it. I will keep an exact account of my expenses. Those, I doubt not, they will discharge, and that is all I desire."

Four major-generals were to be appointed. General Ward was elected the second in command, and Lee the third. The other two major-generals were Philip Schuyler, of New York, and Israel Putnam, of Connecticut. Eight brigadier-generals were likewise appointed; Seth Pomeroy, Richard Montgomery, David Wooster, William Heath, Joseph Spencer, John Thomas, John Sullivan, and Nathaniel Greene.

At Washington's express request, his old friend, Major Horatio Gates, then absent at his estate in Virginia, was appointed adjutant-general, with the rank of brigadier.

In this momentous change in his condition, which suddenly altered all his course of life, and called him immediately to the camp, Washington's thoughts recurred to Mount Vernon and its rural delights, so dear to his heart, whence he was to be again exiled. His chief concern, however, was on account of the distress it might cause to his wife. His letter to her on the subject is written in a tone of manly tenderness. "You may believe me," writes he, "when I assure you, in the most solemn manner, that, so far from seeking this appointment, I have used every endeavor in my power to avoid it, not only from my unwillingness to part with you and the family, but from a consciousness of its being a trust too great for my capacity; and I should enjoy more real happiness in one month with you at home than I have the most distant prospect of finding abroad if my stay were to be seven times seven years. But as it has been a kind of destiny that has thrown me upon this service, I shall hope that my undertaking it is designed to answer some good purpose...."

On the 20th of June he received his commission from the president of Congress. The following day was fixed upon for his departure for the army. He reviewed previously, at the request of their officers, several militia companies of horse and foot. Every one was anxious to see the new commander, and rarely has the public *beau ideal* of a commander been so fully answered. He was now in the vigor of his days, forty-three years of age, stately in person, noble in his demeanor, calm and dignified in his deportment; as he sat his horse, with manly grace, his

whom had seized their rifles and fowling-pieces and turned out in their working clothes and homespun country garbs. Such was the army spread over an extent of ten or twelve miles, and keeping watch upon the town of Boston, containing at that time a population of seventeen thousand souls, and garrisoned with more than ten thousand British troops, disciplined and experienced in the wars of Europe.

In the disposition of these forces, General Ward had stationed himself at Cambridge, with the main body of about nine thousand men and four companies of artillery. Lieutenant-general Thomas, second in command, was posted, with five thousand Massachusetts, Connecticut and Rhode Island troops, and three or four companies of artillery, at Roxbury and Dorchester, forming the right wing of the army; while the left, composed in a great measure of New Hampshire troops, stretched through Medford to the hills of Chelsea.

We have already mentioned the peninsula of Charlestown (called from a village of the same name), which lies opposite to the north side of Boston. The heights which swell up in rear of the village overlook the town and shipping. The project was conceived in the besieging camp to seize and occupy those heights. A council of war was held upon the subject. General Putnam was one of the most strenuous in favor of the measure. Some of the more wary and judicious, among whom were General Ward and Dr. Warren, doubted the expediency of intrenching themselves on those heights and the possibility of maintaining so exposed a post. Putnam made light of the danger. He was seconded by General Pomeroy, a leader of like stamp, and another veteran of the French war. The daring councils of such men are always captivating to the inexperienced; but in the present instance they were sanctioned by one whose opinion in such matters, and in this vicinity, possessed peculiar weight. This was Colonel William Prescott, of Pepperell, who commanded a regiment of minute men. He, too, had seen service in the French war, and acquired reputation as a lieutenant of infantry at the capture of Cape Breton. This was sufficient to constitute him an oracle in the present instance. He was now about fifty years of age, tall and commanding in his appearance, and retaining the port of a soldier. His opinion, probably, settled the question; and it was determined to seize on and fortify Bunker's Hill and Dorchester Heights.

Secret intelligence hurried forward the project. General Gage, it was said, intended to take possession of Dorchester Heights on the night of the 18th of June. These heights lay on the opposite side of Boston, and the committee were ignorant of their localities. Those on Charlestown Neck, being near at hand, had some time before been reconnoitered by Colonel Richard Gridley, and other of the engineers. It was determined to seize and fortify these heights on the night of Friday, the 16th of June, in anticipation of the movement of General Gage. Troops were drafted for the purpose, and Colonel Prescott, from his experience in military matters was chosen by General Ward to conduct the enterprise. His written orders were to fortify Bunker's Hill, and defend the works until he should be relieved. Colonel Richard Gridley, the chief engineer, was to accompany him and plan the fortifications. The detachment left Cambridge about nine o'clock, Colonel Prescott taking the lead. At Charlestown Neck they were joined by Major Brooks, of Bridges' regiment, and General Putnam; and here were the wagons laden with intrenching tools, which first gave the men an indication of the nature of the enterprise.

Charlestown Neck is a narrow isthmus, connecting the peninsula with the main land; having the Mystic River, about half a mile wide, on the north, and a large embayment of Charles River on the south or right side. It was now necessary to proceed with the utmost caution, for they were coming on ground over which the British kept jealous watch. They had erected a battery at Boston on Copp's Hill, immediately opposite to Charlestown. Five of their vessels of war were stationed so as to bear upon the peninsula from different directions, and the guns of one of them swept the isthmus or narrow neck just mentioned.

Across this isthmus, Colonel Prescott conducted the detachment undiscovered, and up the ascent of Bunker's Hill. This commences at the Neck, and slopes up for about three hundred yards to its summit, which is about one hundred and twelve feet high. It then declines toward the south, and is connected by a ridge with Breed's Hill, about sixty or seventy feet high. The crests of the two hills are about seven hundred yards apart. On attaining the heights, a question rose which of the two they should proceed to fortify. Bunker's Hill was specified in the written orders given to Colonel Prescott by General Ward, but Breed's Hill was much nearer to Boston, and had a better command of the town and shipping. Bunker's Hill, also, being on the upper and narrower part of the peninsula, was itself commanded by the same ship which raked the Neck. Putnam was clear for commencing at Breed's Hill, and making the principal work there, while a minor work might be thrown up at Bunker's Hill, as a protection in the rear, and a rallying point, in case of being driven out of the main work. Others concurred with this opinion. Gridley marked out the lines for the fortifications; the men stacked their guns; threw off their packs; seized their trenching tools, and set to work with great spirit. So spiritedly, though silently, was the labor carried on, that by morning a strong redoubt was thrown up as a main work, flanked on the left by a breastwork, partly cannon-proof, extending down the crest of Breed's Hill to a piece of marshy ground called the Slough. To support the right of the redoubt, some troops were thrown into the village of Charlestown, at the southern foot of the hill.

At dawn of day, the Americans at work were espied by the sailors on board of the ships of war, and the alarm was given. The captain of the Lively, the nearest ship, without waiting for orders, put a spring upon her cable, and bringing her guns to bear, opened a fire upon the hill. The other ships and a floating battery followed his example. Their shot did no mischief to the works. The cannonading roused the town of Boston. General Gage could scarcely believe his eyes when he beheld on the opposite hill a fortification full of men, which had sprung up in the course of the night. He called a council of war. The Americans might intend to cannonade Boston from this new fortification; it was unanimously resolved to dislodge them. How was this to be done? A majority of the council, including Clinton and Grant, advised that a force should be landed on Charlestown Neck, under the protection of their batteries, so as to attack the Americans in rear and cut off their retreat. General Gage objected that it would place his troops between two armies; one at Cambridge, superior in numbers, the other on the heights, strongly fortified. He was for landing in front of the works, and pushing directly up the hill; a plan adopted through a confidence that raw militia would never stand their ground against the assault of veteran troops.

The sound of drum and trumpet, the clatter of hoofs, the rattling of gun-carriages, and all the other military din and bustle in the streets of Boston, soon apprised the Americans on their rudely fortified height of an impending attack. They were ill-fitted to withstand it, being jaded by the night's labor, and want of sleep; hungry and thirsty, having brought but scanty supplies, and oppressed by the heat of the weather. Prescott sent repeated messages to General Ward, asking reinforcements and provisions. Ward issued orders for Colonels Stark and Read, then at Medford, to march to the relief of Prescott with their New Hampshire regiments.

In the meantime, the Americans on Breed's Hill were sustaining the fire from the ships, and from the battery on Copp's Hill, which opened upon them about ten o'clock. They returned an occasional shot from one corner of the redoubt, without much harm to the enemy, and continued strengthening their position until about eleven o'clock, when they ceased to work, piled their intrenching tools in the rear, and looked out anxiously and impatiently for the anticipated reinforcements and supplies. The tools were ultimately carried to Bunker's Hill, and a breastwork commenced by order of General Putnam. The importance of such a work was afterwards made apparent.

About noon the Americans descried twenty-eight barges crossing from Boston in parallel lines. They contained a large detachment of grenadiers, rangers, and light infantry, admirably equipped, and commanded by Major-general Howe. A heavy fire from the ships and batteries covered their advance, but no attempt was made to oppose them, and they landed about one o'clock at Moulton's Point, a little to the north of Breed's Hill. Here General Howe made a pause. On reconnoitering the works from this point, the Americans appeared to be much more strongly posted than he had imagined, and he immediately sent over to General Gage for more forces. While awaiting their arrival, refreshments were served out to the troops. The Americans meanwhile took advantage of the delay to strengthen their position. The breastwork on the left of the redoubt extended to what was called the Slough, but beyond this, the ridge of the hill, and the slope toward Mystic River, were undefended, leaving a pass by which the enemy might turn the left flank of the position, and seize upon Bunker's Hill. Putnam ordered his chosen officer, Captain Knowlton, to cover this pass with the Connecticut troops under his command. A novel kind of rampart, savoring of rural device was suggested by the rustic general. About six hundred feet in the rear of the redoubt, and about one hundred feet to the left of the breastwork, was a post and rail-fence, set in a low foot-wall of stone, and extending down to Mystic River. The posts and rails of another fence were hastily pulled up, and set a few feet in behind this, and the intermediate space was filled up with new mown hay from the adjacent meadows. This double fence, it will be found, proved an important protection to the redoubt, although there still remained an unprotected interval of about seven hundred feet.

While Knowlton and his men were putting up this fence, Putnam proceeded with other of his troops to throw up the work on Bunker's Hill, despatching his son, Captain Putnam, on horseback, to hurry up the remainder of his men from

Cambridge. By this time Stark made his appearance with the New Hampshire troops, five hundred strong. Putnam detained some of Stark's men to aid in throwing up the works on Bunker's Hill, and directed him to reinforce Knowlton with the rest. About two o'clock, Warren arrived on the heights, ready to engage in their perilous defence, although he had opposed the scheme of their occupation. He had recently been elected a major-general, but had not received his commission. Putnam offered him the command at the fence; he declined it, and merely asked where he could be of most service as a volunteer.

The British now prepared for a general assault. An easy victory was anticipated; the main thought was, how to make it most effectual. The left wing, commanded by General Pigot, was to mount the hill and force the redoubt, while General Howe, with the right wing, was to push on between the fort and Mystic River, turn the left flank of the Americans, and cut off their retreat. General Pigot, accordingly advanced up the hill under cover of a fire from field-pieces and howitzers planted on a small height near the landing-place on Moulton's Point. His troops commenced a discharge of musketry while yet at a long distance from the redoubts. The Americans within the works, obedient to strict command, retained their fire until the enemy were within thirty or forty paces, when they opened upon them with a tremendous volley. Being all marksmen, accustomed to take deliberate aim, the slaughter was immense, and especially fatal to officers. The assailants fell back in some confusion; but, rallied on by their officers, advanced within pistol shot. Another volley, more effective than the first, made them again recoil. To add to their confusion, they were galled by a flanking fire from the handful of Provincials posted in Charlestown. Shocked at the carnage and seeing the confusion of his troops, General Pigot was urged to give the word for a retreat.

In the meantime, General Howe, with the right wing, advanced along Mystic River toward the fence where Stark, Read, and Knowlton were stationed, thinking to carry this slight breastwork with ease, and so get in the rear of the fortress. His artillery proved of little avail, being stopped by a swampy piece of ground, while his columns suffered from two or three field-pieces with which Putnam had fortified the fence. Howe's men kept up a fire of musketry as they advanced; but not taking aim, their shot passed over the heads of the Americans. The latter had received the same orders with those in the redoubt, not to fire until the enemy should be within thirty paces. When the British arrived within the stated distance a sheeted fire opened upon them from rifles, muskets, and fowling-pieces, all levelled with deadly aim. The carnage, as in the other instance, was horrible. The British were thrown into confusion and fell back; some even retreated to the boats.

There was a general pause on the part of the British. The American officers availed themselves of it to prepare for another attack, which must soon be made. Prescott mingled among his men in the redoubt, who were all in high spirits at the severe check they had given "the regulars." He praised them for their steadfastness in maintaining their post, and their good conduct in reserving their fire until the word of command, and exhorted them to do the same in the next attack. Putnam rode about Bunker's Hill and its skirts, to rally and bring on reinforcements which had been checked or scattered in crossing Charlestown Neck by the raking fire from the ships and batteries. Before many could be brought to the scene of action the British had commenced their second attack. They again ascended the hill to storm the redoubt; their advance was covered as before by discharges of artillery. Charlestown, which had annoyed them on their first attack by a flanking fire, was in flames, by shells thrown from Copp's Hill, and by marines from the ships. The thunder of artillery from batteries and ships, the bursting of bomb-shells; the sharp discharges of musketry; the shouts and yells of the combatants; the crash of burning buildings, arid the dense volumes of smoke, which obscured the summer sun, all formed a tremendous spectacle.

The American troops, although unused to war, stood undismayed amidst a scene where it was bursting upon them with all its horrors. Reserving their fire, as before, until the enemy was close at hand, they again poured forth repeated volleys with the fatal aim of sharpshooters. The British stood the first shock, and continued to advance; but the incessant stream of fire staggered them. Their officers remonstrated, threatened, and even attempted to goad them on with their swords, but the havoc was too deadly; whole ranks were mowed down; many of the officers were either slain or wounded, and among them several of the staff of General Howe. The troops again gave way and retreated down the hill.

A third attack was now determined on, though some of Howe's officers remonstrated, declaring it would be downright butchery. A different plan was adopted. Instead of advancing in front of the redoubt, it was to be taken in flank on the left, where the open space between the breastwork and the fortified fence presented a weak point. It having been accidentally discovered that the ammunition of the Americans was nearly expended, preparations were made to carry the works at the point of the bayonet. General Howe, with the main body, now made a feint of attacking the fortified fence; but, while a part of his force was thus engaged, the rest brought some of the field-pieces to enfilade the breastwork on the left of the redoubt. A raking fire soon drove the Americans out of this exposed place into the enclosure. The troops were now led on to assail the works. The Americans again reserved their fire until their assailants were close at hand, and then made a murderous volley, by which several officers were laid low, and General Howe himself was wounded in the foot. The British soldiery this time likewise reserved their fire and rushed on with fixed bayonet. Clinton and Pigot had reached the southern and eastern sides of the redoubt, and it was now assailed on three sides at once. Prescott ordered those who had no bayonets to retire to the back part of the redoubt and fire on the enemy as they showed themselves on the parapet. The Americans, however, had fired their last round, their ammunition was exhausted; and now succeeded a desperate and deadly struggle, hand to hand, with bayonets, stones, and the stocks of their muskets. At length, as the British continued to pour in, Prescott gave the order to retreat. His men had to cut their way through two divisions of the enemy who were getting in rear of the redoubt, and they received a destructive volley from those who had formed on the captured works. By that volley fell the patriot Warren, who had distinguished himself throughout the action.

While the Americans were thus slowly dislodged from the redoubt, Stark, Read and Knowlton maintained their ground at the fortified fence; which, indeed, had been nobly defended throughout the action. The resistance at this hastily constructed work was kept up after the troops in the redoubt had given way, and until Colonel Prescott had left the hill; thus defeating General Howe's design of cutting off the retreat of the main body; which would have produced a scene of direful confusion and slaughter. Having effected their purpose, the brave associates at the fence abandoned their weak outpost, retiring slowly, and disputing the ground inch by inch, with a regularity remarkable in troops many of whom had never before been in action.

The main retreat was across Bunker's Hill, where Putnam had endeavored to throw up a breastwork. The veteran, sword in hand, rode to the rear of the retreating troops, regardless of the balls whistling about him. His only thought was to rally them at the unfinished works. It was impossible, however, to bring the troops to a stand. They continued on down the hill to the Neck and across it to Cambridge, exposed to a raking fire from the ships and batteries, and only protected by a single piece of ordnance. The British were too exhausted to pursue them; they contented themselves with taking possession of Bunker's Hill, were reinforced from Boston, and threw up additional works during the night.

Thus ended the first regular battle between the British and the Americans, and most eventful in its consequences. The former had gained the ground for which they contended; but, if a victory, it was more disastrous and humiliating to them than an ordinary defeat. According to their own returns, their killed and wounded, out of a detachment of two thousand men, amounted to one thousand and fifty-four, and a large proportion of them officers. The loss of the Americans did not exceed four hundred and fifty.

To the latter this defeat, if defeat it might be called, had the effect of a triumph. It gave them confidence in themselves and consequence in the eyes of their enemies. They had proved to themselves and to others that they could measure weapons with the disciplined soldiers of Europe, and inflict the most harm in the conflict.

Among the British officers slain was Major Pitcairn, who, at Lexington, had shed the first blood in the Revolutionary war. In the death of Warren the Americans had to lament the loss of a distinguished patriot and a most estimable man. It was deplored as a public calamity. He was one of the first who fell in the glorious cause of his country, and his name has become consecrated in its history.

CHAPTER XIX.

WASHINGTON ON HIS WAY TO THE CAMP.

In a preceding chapter we left Washington preparing to depart from Philadelphia for the army before Boston. He set out on horseback on the 21st of June, having for military companions of his journey Major-generals Lee and Schuyler, and being accompanied for a distance by several private friends. As an escort he had a "gentleman troop" of Philadelphia, commanded by Captain Markoe; the whole formed a brilliant cavalcade.

General Schuyler was a man eminently calculated to sympathize with Washington in all his patriotic views and feelings, and became one of his most faithful coadjutors. Sprung from one of the earliest and most respectable Dutch families which colonized New York, all his interests and affections were identified with the country. He had received a good education; applied himself at an early age to the exact sciences, and became versed in finance, military engineering, and political economy. He was one of those native born soldiers who had acquired experience in that American school of arms, the old French war. Since the close of the French war he had served his country in various civil stations, and been one of the most zealous and eloquent vindicators of colonial rights.

They had scarcely proceeded twenty miles from Philadelphia when they were met by a courier, spurring with all speed, bearing despatches from the army to Congress, communicating tidings of the battle of Bunker's Hill. Washington eagerly inquired particulars; above all, how acted the militia? When told that they stood their ground bravely, sustained the enemy's fire—reserved their own until at close quarters, and then delivered it with deadly effect, it seemed as if a weight of doubt and solicitude were lifted from his heart. "The liberties of the country are safe!" exclaimed he.

The news of the battle of Bunker's Hill had startled the whole country; and this clattering cavalcade, escorting the commander-in-chief to the army, was the gaze and wonder of every town and village.

The journey may be said to have been a continual council of war between Washington and the two generals. One of the most frequent subjects of conversation was the province of New York. Its power and position rendered it the great link of the confederacy; what measures were necessary for its defence, and most calculated to secure its adherence to the cause? The population of New York was more varied in its elements than that of almost any other of the provinces, and had to be cautiously studied. The New Yorkers were of a mixed origin, and stamped with the peculiarities of their respective ancestors. The descendants of the old Dutch and Huguenot families, the earliest settlers, were still among the soundest and best of the population. They inherited the love of liberty, civil and religious, of their forefathers, and were those who stood foremost in the present struggle for popular rights. A great proportion of the more modern families, dating from the downfall of the Dutch government in 1664, were English and Scotch, and among these were many loyal adherents to the crown.

There was a power, too, of a formidable kind within the interior of the province, which was an object of much solicitude. This was the "Johnson Family." We have repeatedly had occasion to speak of Sir William Johnson, his majesty's general agent for Indian affairs, of his great wealth, and his almost sovereign sway over the Six Nations. In the recent difficulties between the crown and colonies, Sir William had naturally been in favor of the government which had enriched and honored him, but he had viewed with deep concern the acts of Parliament which were goading the colonists to armed resistance. In the height of his solicitude, he received despatches ordering him, in case of hostilities, to enlist the Indians in the cause of government. To the agitation of feelings produced by these orders many have attributed a stroke of apoplexy, of which he died, on the 11th of July, 1774, about a year before the time of which we are treating. His son and heir, Sir John Johnson, and his sons-in-law, Colonel Guy Johnson and Colonel Claus felt none of the reluctance of Sir William to use harsh measures in support of royalty. They lived in a degree of rude feudal style in stone mansions capable of defence, situated on the Mohawk River and in its vicinity; they had many Scottish Highlanders for tenants; and among their adherents were violent men, such as the Butlers of Tryon County, and Brant, the Mohawk sachem, since famous in Indian warfare. They had recently gone about with armed retainers, overawing and breaking up patriotic assemblages, and it was known they could at any time bring a force of warriors in the field.

Tryon, the governor of New York, was at present absent in England, having been called home by the ministry to give an account of the affairs of the province, and to receive instructions for its management. He was a tory in heart, and had been a zealous opponent of all colonial movements, and his talents and address gave him great influence over an important part of the community. Should he return with hostile instructions, and should he and the Johnsons co-operate, the one controlling the bay and harbor of New York and the waters of the Hudson by means of ships and land forces; the others overrunning the valley of the Mohawk and the regions beyond Albany with savage hordes, this great central province might be wrested from the confederacy, and all intercourse broken off between the eastern and southern colonies. All these circumstances and considerations, many of which came under discussion in the course of this military journey, rendered the command of New York a post of especial trust and importance, and determined Washington to confide it to General Schuyler. He was peculiarly fitted for it by his military talents, his intimate knowledge of the province and its concerns, especially what related to the upper parts of it, and his experience in Indian affairs.

At Newark, in the Jerseys, Washington was met on the 25th by a committee of the provincial Congress, sent to conduct him to the city. The Congress was in a perplexity. It had in a manner usurped and exercised the powers of Governor Tryon during his absence, while at the same time it professed allegiance to the crown which had appointed him. He was now in the harbor, just arrived from England, and hourly expected to land. Washington, too, was approaching. How were these double claims to ceremonious respect happening at the same time to be managed?

In this dilemma a regiment of militia was turned out, and the colonel instructed to pay military honors to whichever of the distinguished functionaries should first arrive. Washington was earlier than the governor by several hours, and received those honors. The landing of Governor Tryon took place about eight o'clock in the evening. The military honors were repeated; he was received with great respect by the mayor and common council, and transports of loyalty by those devoted to the crown. It was unknown what instructions he had received from the ministry, but it was rumored that a large force would soon arrive from England, subject to his directions. At this very moment a ship of war, the Asia, lay anchored opposite the city; its grim batteries bearing upon it, greatly to the disquiet of the faint-hearted among its inhabitants. In this situation of affairs Washington was happy to leave such an efficient person as General Schuyler in command of the place.

In the meantime the provincial Congress of Massachusetts, then in session at Watertown, had made arrangements for the expected arrival of Washington. It sent on a deputation which met Washington at Springfield, on the frontiers of the province, and provided escorts and accommodations for him along the road. Thus honorably attended from town to town, and escorted by volunteer companies and cavalcades of gentlemen, he arrived at Watertown on the 2d of July, where he was greeted by Congress with a congratulatory address, in which, however, was frankly stated the undisciplined state of the army he was summoned to command. An address of cordial welcome was likewise made to General Lee.

The ceremony over, Washington was again in the saddle, and escorted by a troop of light horse and a cavalcade of citizens, proceeded to the head-quarters provided for him at Cambridge, three miles distant. As he entered the confines of the camp, the shouts of the multitude and the thundering of artillery gave note to the enemy beleaguered in Boston of his arrival.

His military reputation had preceded him and excited great expectations. They were not disappointed. His personal appearance, notwithstanding the dust of travel, was calculated to captivate the public eye. As he rode through the camp, amidst a throng of officers, he was the admiration of the soldiery and of a curious throng collected from the surrounding country. Happy was the countryman who could get a full view of him to carry home an account of it to his neighbors.

With Washington, modest at all times, there was no false excitement on the present occasion; nothing to call forth emotions of self-glorification. The honors and congratulations with which he was received, the acclamations of the public, the cheerings of the army, only told him how much was expected from him; and when he looked round upon the raw and rustic levies he was to command, "a mixed multitude of people, under very little discipline, order, or government," scattered in rough encampments about hill and dale, beleaguering a city garrisoned by veteran troops, with ships of war anchored about its harbor, and strong outposts guarding it, he felt the awful responsibility of his situation, and the complicated and stupendous task before him. He spoke of it, however, not despondingly nor boastfully and with defiance; but with that solemn and sedate resolution, and that hopeful reliance on Supreme Goodness, which belonged to his magnanimous nature.

CHAPTER XX.
SIEGE OF BOSTON.

On the 3d of July, the morning after his arrival at Cambridge, Washington took formal command of the army. Accompanied by General Lee, on whose military judgment he had great reliance, he visited the different American posts, and rode to the heights commanding views over Boston and its environs, being anxious to make himself acquainted with the strength and relative position of both armies.

In visiting the different posts, Washington halted for a time at Prospect Hill, which, as its name denotes, commanded a wide view over Boston and the surrounding country. Here Putnam had taken his position after the battle of Bunker's Hill, fortifying himself with works which he deemed impregnable; and here the veteran was enabled to point out to the commander-in-chief, and to Lee, the main features of the belligerent region, which lay spread out like a map before them. Bunker's Hill was but a mile distant to the west; the British standard floating as if in triumph on its summit. The main force under General Howe was intrenching itself strongly about half a mile beyond the place of the recent battle. Howe's sentries extended a hundred and fifty yards beyond the neck or isthmus, over which the Americans retreated after the battle. A large force was intrenched south of the town on the neck leading to Roxbury—the only entrance to Boston by land. The troops were irregularly distributed in a kind of semicircle, eight or nine miles in extent; the left resting on Winter Hill, the most northern post, the right extending on the south to Roxbury and Dorchester Neck.

Washington reconnoitred the British posts from various points of view. Everything about them was in admirable order. The works appeared to be constructed with military science, the troops to be in a high state of discipline. The American camp, on the contrary, disappointed him. He had expected to find eighteen or twenty thousand men under arms; there were not much more than fourteen thousand. He had expected to find some degree of system and discipline; whereas all were raw militia. He had expected to find works scientifically constructed, and proofs of knowledge and skill in engineering; whereas, what he saw of the latter was very imperfect, and confined to the mere manual exercise of cannon.

In riding throughout the camp, Washington observed that nine thousand of the troops belonged to Massachusetts; the rest were from other provinces. They were encamped in separate bodies, each with its own regulations, and officers of its own appointment. Some had tents, others were in barracks, and others sheltered themselves as best they might. Many were sadly in want of clothing, and all, said Washington, were strongly imbued with the spirit of insubordination, which they mistook for independence.

One of the encampments, however, was in striking contrast with the rest, and might vie with those of the British for order and exactness. Here were tents and marquees pitched in the English style; soldiers well drilled and well equipped; everything had an air of discipline and subordination. It was a body of Rhode Island troops, which had been raised, drilled, and brought to the camp by Brigadier-general Greene,[4] of that province.

Having taken his survey of the army, Washington wrote to the President of Congress, representing its various deficiencies, and, among other things, urging the appointment of a commissary-general, a quartermaster-general, a commissary of musters, and a commissary of artillery. Above all things, he requested a supply of money as soon as possible. "I find myself already much embarrassed for want of a military chest." In one of his recommendations we have an instance of frontier expediency, learnt in his early campaigns. Speaking of the ragged condition of the army, and the difficulty of procuring the requisite kind of clothing, he advises that a number of hunting-shirts, not less than ten thousand, should be provided; as being the cheapest and quickest mode of supplying this necessity.

The justice and impartiality of Washington were called into exercise as soon as he entered upon his command in allaying discontents among his general officers, caused by the recent appointments and promotions made by the Continental Congress. General Spencer was so offended that Putnam should be promoted over his head that he left the army without visiting the commander-in-chief; but was subsequently induced to return. General Thomas felt aggrieved by being outranked by the veteran Pomeroy; the latter however declining to serve, he found himself senior brigadier, and was appeased.

The Congress of Massachusetts manifested considerate liberality with respect to head-quarters. According to their minutes, a committee was charged to procure a steward, a housekeeper, and two or three women cooks. The wishes of Washington were to be consulted in regard to the supply of his table. This his station, as commander-in-chief, required should be kept up in ample and hospitable style. Every day a number of his officers dined with him. As he was in the neighborhood of the seat of the Provincial Government, he would occasionally have members of Congress and other functionaries at his board. Though social, however, he was not convivial in his habits. He received his guests with courtesy; but his mind and time were too much occupied by grave and anxious concerns to permit him the genial indulgence of the table. He would retire early from the board, leaving an aide-de-camp or one of his officers to take his place. Colonel Mifflin was the first person who officiated as aide-de-camp. He was a Philadelphia gentleman of high respectability, who had accompanied him from that city, and received his appoint-

---

[4] Nathaniel Greene was born in Rhode Island in May, 1742; was the son of Quaker parents; in his boyhood aided his father on a farm and in a mill, but having a thirst for knowledge applied himself sedulously to various studies. Public affairs had aroused his martial spirit and he had applied himself to military studies. In the month of May he had been elected commander of the Rhode Island contingent.

ment shortly after their arrival at Cambridge. The second aide-de-camp was John Trumbull,[5] son of the governor of Connecticut. Trumbull was young, and unaccustomed to society, and soon found himself, he says, unequal to the elegant duties of his situation; he gladly exchanged it, therefore, for that of major of brigade.

The member of Washington's family most deserving of mention at present, was his secretary, Mr. Joseph Reed. With this gentleman he had formed an intimacy in the course of his visits to Philadelphia, to attend the sessions of the Continental Congress. Mr. Reed was an accomplished man, had studied law in America, and at the Temple in London, and had gained a high reputation at the Philadelphia bar. He had since been highly instrumental in rousing the Philadelphians to co-operate with the patriots of Boston. A sympathy of views and feelings had attached him to Washington, and induced him to accompany him to the camp.

The arrival of Gates in camp was heartily welcomed by the commander-in-chief, who had received a letter from that officer, gratefully acknowledging his friendly influence in procuring him the appointment of adjutant-general. Washington may have promised himself much cordial co-operation from him, recollecting the warm friendship professed by him when he visited at Mount Vernon, and they talked together over their early companionship in arms; but of that kind of friendship there was no further manifestation. Gates was certainly of great service, from his practical knowledge and military experience at this juncture, when the whole army had in a manner to be organized; but from the familiar intimacy of Washington he gradually estranged himself. A contemporary has accounted for this by alleging that he was secretly chagrined at not having received the appointment of major-general, to which he considered himself well fitted by his military knowledge and experience and which he thought Washington might have obtained for him had he used his influence with Congress.

The hazardous position of the army from the great extent and weakness of its lines, was what most pressed on the immediate attention of Washington; and he summoned a council of war, to take the matter into consideration. In this it was urged that, to abandon the line of works, after the great labor and expense of their construction, would be dispiriting to the troops and encouraging to the enemy, while it would expose a wide extent of the surrounding country to maraud and ravage. Beside, no safer position presented itself, on which to fall back. This being generally admitted, it was determined to hold on to the works, and defend them as long as possible; and, in the meantime, to augment the army to at least twenty thousand men.

Washington now hastened to improve the defences of the camp, strengthen the weak parts of the line, and throw up additional works around the main forts. The army was distributed into three grand divisions. One, forming the right wing, was stationed on the heights of Roxbury. It was commanded by Major-general Ward, who had under him Brigadier-generals Spencer and Thomas. Another, forming the left wing, under Major-general Lee, having with him Brigadier-generals Sullivan and Greene, was stationed on Winter and Prospect Hills; while the centre, under Major-general Putnam and Brigadier-general Heath, was stationed

[5] In after years distinguished as a historical painter.

at Cambridge. At Washington's recommendation, Joseph Trumbull, the eldest son of the governor, received on the 24th of July the appointment of commissary-general of the continental army. He had already officiated with talent in that capacity in the Connecticut militia.

Nothing excited more gaze and wonder among the rustic visitors to the camp than the arrival of several rifle companies, fourteen hundred men in all, from Pennsylvania, Maryland, and Virginia; such stalwart fellows as Washington had known in his early campaigns. Stark hunters and bush fighters; many of them upwards of six feet high, and of vigorous frame; dressed in fringed frocks, or rifle shirts, and round hats. Their displays of sharp shooting were soon among the marvels of the camp. One of these companies was commanded by Captain Daniel Morgan, a native of New Jersey, whose first experience in war had been to accompany Braddock's army as a wagoner. He had since carried arms on the frontier and obtained a command. He and his riflemen in coming to the camp had marched six hundred miles in three weeks.

While all his forces were required for the investment of Boston, Washington was importuned by the Legislature of Massachusetts and the Governor of Connecticut, to detach troops for the protection of different points of the sea-coast, where depredations by armed vessels were apprehended. The case of New London was specified by Governor Trumbull, where Captain Wallace of the Rose frigate, with two other ships of war, had entered the harbor, landed men, spiked the cannon, and gone off threatening future visits.

Washington referred to his instructions, and consulted with his general officers and such members of the Continental Congress as happened to be in camp, before he replied to these requests; he then respectfully declined compliance. In his reply he stated frankly and explicitly the policy and system on which the war was to be conducted. "It has been debated in Congress and settled," writes he, "that the militia, or other internal strength of each province, is to be applied for defence against those small and particular depredations, which were to be expected, and to which they were supposed to be competent. This will appear the more proper, when it is considered that every town, and indeed every part of our sea-coast, which is exposed to these depredations, would have an equal claim upon this army. The great advantage the enemy have of transporting troops, by being masters of the sea, will enable them to harass us by diversions of this kind; and should we be tempted to pursue them, upon every alarm, the army must either be so weakened as to expose it to destruction, or a great part of the coast be still left unprotected.... I wish I could extend protection to all, but the numerous detachments necessary to remedy the evil would amount to a dissolution of the army, or make the most important operations of the campaign depend upon the piratical expeditions of two or three men-of-war and transports."

His refusal to grant the required detachments gave much dissatisfaction in some quarters, until sanctioned and enforced by the Continental Congress. All at length saw and acquiesced in the justice and wisdom of his decision. It was in fact a vital question, involving the whole character and fortune of the war; and it was acknowledged that he met it with a forecast and determination befitting a commander-in-chief.

The great object of Washington at present was to force the enemy to come out of Boston and try a decisive action. His lines had for some time cut off all communication of the town with the country, and he had caused the live stock within a considerable distance of the place to be driven back from the coast, out of reach of the men-of-war's boats. At this critical juncture, when endeavoring to provoke a general action, a startling fact came to light; the whole amount of powder in the camp would not furnish more than nine cartridges to a man!

A gross error had been made by the committee of supplies when Washington, on taking command, had required a return of the ammunition. They had returned the whole amount of powder collected by the province, upwards of three hundred barrels; without stating what had been expended. The blunder was detected on an order being issued for a new supply of cartridges. It was found that there were but thirty-two barrels of powder in store. This was an astounding discovery. Washington instantly despatched letters and expresses to Rhode Island, the Jerseys, Ticonderoga and elsewhere, urging immediate supplies of powder and lead; no quantity, however small, to be considered beneath notice.

A correspondence of an important character now took place between Washington and General Gage. It was one intended to put the hostile services on a proper footing. A strong disposition had been manifested among the British officers to regard those engaged in the patriot cause as malefactors, outlawed from the courtesies of chivalric warfare. Washington was determined to have a full understanding on this point. He was peculiarly sensitive with regard to Gage. They had been companions in arms in their early days; but Gage might now affect to look down upon him as the chief of a rebel army. Washington took an early opportunity to let him know that he claimed to be the commander of a legitimate force, engaged in a legitimate cause, and that both himself and his army were to be treated on a footing of perfect equality.

CHAPTER XXI.
PROJECTS FOR THE INVASION OF CANADA.

We must interrupt our narrative of the siege of Boston to give an account of events in other quarters, requiring the superintending care of Washington as commander-in-chief. Letters from General Schuyler, received in the course of July, had awakened apprehensions of danger from the interior. The Johnsons were said to be stirring up the Indians in the western parts of New York to hostility, and preparing to join the British forces in Canada.

Great rivalry, since the exploits of Ethan Allen and Benedict Arnold, at Ticonderoga and on Lake Champlain, had arisen between these doughty leaders. Allen claimed command at Ticonderoga, on the authority of the committee from the Connecticut Assembly, which had originated the enterprise. Arnold claimed it on the strength of his instructions from the Massachusetts committee of safety. The public bodies themselves seemed perplexed what to do with the prize, so bravely seized upon by these bold men. The Continental Congress at length legitimated the exploit, and as it were accepted the captured fortress. [The custody of it was committed to New York, with the power to call on the New England colonies for aid. The call was made, and one thousand troops under Colonel Hinman were sent forward by the governor of Connecticut.]

It had been the idea of the Continental Congress to have those posts dismantled, and the cannon and stores removed to the south end of Lake George, where a strong post was to be established. But both Allen and Arnold exclaimed against such a measure; vaunting, and with reason, the importance of those forts. Both were ambitious of further laurels. Both were anxious to lead an expedition into Canada; and Ticonderoga and Crown Point would open the way to it. "The Key is ours," writes Allen to the New York Congress. "If the colonies would suddenly push an army of two or three thousand men into Canada, they might make an easy conquest of all that would oppose them in the extensive province of Quebec, except a reinforcement from England should prevent it. Such a diversion would weaken Gage and insure us Canada."

A letter to the same purport was written by Allen to Trumbull, the governor of Connecticut. Arnold urged the same project upon the attention of the Continental Congress. His letter was dated from Crown Point, where he had a little squadron, composed of the sloop captured at St. Johns, a schooner, and a flotilla of bateaux. All these he had equipped, armed, maimed, and officered; and his crews were devoted to him.

Within a few days after the date of this letter, Colonel Hinman with the Connecticut troops arrived. The greater part of the Green Mountain Boys now returned home, their term of enlistment having expired. Ethan Allen and his brother in arms, Seth Warner, repaired to Congress to get pay for their men, and authority to raise a new regiment. They were received with distinguished honor by that body. As to Arnold, difficulties instantly took place between him and Colonel Hinman. Arnold refused to give up to him the command of either post, claiming on the strength of his instructions from the committee of safety of Massachusetts, a right to the command of all the posts and fortresses at the south end of Lake Champlain and Lake George. At this juncture arrived a committee of three members of the Congress of Massachusetts, sent by that body to inquire into the manner in which he had executed his instructions; complaints having been made of his arrogant and undue assumption of command. Arnold, thunderstruck at being subjected to inquiry, when he had expected an ovation, disbanded his men and threw up his commission. Quite a scene ensued. His men became turbulent; some refused to serve under any other leader; others clamored for their pay, which was in arrears. The storm was allayed by the interference of several of the officers, and the assurances of the committee that every man should be paid.

The project of an invasion of Canada had at first met with no favor with the Continental Congress. Intelligence subsequently received induced it to change its plans. Sir Guy Carleton was said to be strengthening the fortifications and garrison at St. Johns, and preparing to launch vessels on the lake wherewith to regain command of it, and retake the captured posts. Powerful reinforcements were coming from England and elsewhere. Guy Johnson was holding councils with the fierce Cayugas and Senecas, and stirring up the Six Nations to hostility. On the other hand, Canada was full of religious and political dissensions. The late exploits of the Americans on Lake Champlain, had produced a favorable effect on the Canadians, who would flock to the patriot standard if unfurled among them by an imposing force. Now was the time to strike a blow to paralyze all hostility from this quarter; now, while Carleton's regular force was weak, and before the arrival of additional troops. Influenced by these considerations, Congress now determined to extend the revolution into Canada, but it was an enterprise too important to be entrusted to any but discreet hands. General Schuyler, then in New York, was accordingly ordered, on the 27th of June, to proceed to Ticonderoga, and "should he find it practicable, and not disagreeable to the Canadians, immediately to take possession of St. Johns and Montreal, and pursue such other measures in Canada as might have a tendency to promote the peace and security of these provinces."

Schuyler arrived at Ticonderoga on the 18th of July. Colonel Hinman, it will be recollected, was in temporary command at Ticonderoga. The garrison was about twelve hundred strong; the greater part Connecticut men, brought by himself; some were New York troops, and some few Green Mountain Boys. Schuyler, on taking command, despatched a confidential agent into Canada, Major John Brown, an American, who resided on the Sorel River, and was popular among the Canadians. He was to collect information as to the British forces and fortifications, and to ascertain how an invasion and an attack on St. Johns would be considered by the people of the province; in the meantime, Schuyler set diligently to work to build boats and prepare for the enterprise, should it ultimately be ordered by Congress.

Schuyler was excessively annoyed by the confusion and negligence prevalent around him, and the difficulties and delays thereby occasioned. He chafed in spirit at the disregard of discipline among his yeoman soldiery, and their opposition to all system and regularity. This was especially the case with the troops from Connecticut, officered generally by their own neighbors and familiar companions, and unwilling to acknowledge the authority of a commander from a different province.

He had calculated on being joined by this time by the regiment of Green Mountain Boys which Ethan Allen and Seth Warner had undertaken to raise in the New Hampshire Grants. Unfortunately a quarrel had arisen between those brothers in arms, which filled the Green Mountains with discord and party feuds. The election of officers took place on the 27th of July. It was made by committees from the different townships. Ethan Allen was entirely passed by, and Seth Warner nominated as Lieutenant-colonel of the regiment. Allen was thunderstruck at finding himself thus suddenly dismounted. His patriotism and love of adventure, however, were not quelled: and he forthwith repaired to the army at Ticonderoga to offer himself as a volunteer.

Schuyler was on the alert with respect to the expedition against Canada. From his agent, Major Brown, and from other sources, he had learnt that there were about seven hundred king's troops in that province; three hundred of them at St. Johns, about fifty at Quebec, the remainder at Montreal, Chamblee, and the upper posts. Colonel Guy Johnson was at Montreal with three hundred men, mostly his tenants, and with a number of Indians. Two batteries had been finished at St. Johns, mounting nine guns each: other works were intrenched and picketed. Two large row galleys were on the stocks, and would soon be finished. Now was the time, according to his informants, to carry Canada. It might be done with great ease and little cost. The Canadians were disaffected to British rule, and would join the Americans, and so would many of the Indians. "I am prepared," writes he to Washington, "to move against the enemy, unless your Excellency and Congress should direct otherwise."

While awaiting orders on this head, he repaired to Albany, to hold a conference and negotiate a treaty with the Caughnawagas, and the warriors of the Six Nations, whom, as one of the commissioners of Indian affairs, he had invited to meet him at that place. General Richard Montgomery was to remain in command at Ticonderoga, during his absence, and to urge forward the military preparations. The subsequent fortunes of this gallant officer are inseparably connected with the Canadian campaign, and have endeared his name to Americans.[6]

While these things were occurring at Ticonderoga, several Indian chiefs made their appearance in the camp at Cambridge. They came in savage state and costume, as ambassadors from their respective tribes, to have a talk about the im-

[6] Richard Montgomery was born in the north of Ireland in 1736. He entered the army at eighteen years of age; served in the French war with gallantry; afterward returned to England. About three years before the Revolution he sold his commission and emigrated to New York, where he married a daughter of Judge Robert R. Livingston.

pending invasion of Canada. One was chief of the Caughnawaga tribe, whose residence was on the banks of the St. Lawrence, six miles above Montreal. Others were from St. Francis, about forty-five leagues above Quebec, and were of a warlike tribe, from which hostilities had been especially apprehended. Washington, accustomed to deal with the red warriors of the wilderness, received them with great ceremonial. They dined at head-quarters among his officers, and it is observed that to some of the latter they might have served as models; such was their grave dignity and decorum.

A council fire was held. The sachems all offered, on behalf of their tribes, to take up the hatchet for the Americans, should the latter invade Canada. The offer was embarrassing. Congress had publicly resolved to seek nothing but neutrality from the Indian nations, unless the ministerial agents should make an offensive alliance with them. The chief of the St. Francis tribe declared that Governor Carleton had endeavored to persuade him to take up the hatchet against the Americans, but in vain.

Washington wished to be certain of the conduct of the enemy, before he gave a reply to these Indian overtures. He wrote by express, therefore, to General Schuyler, requesting him to ascertain the intentions of the British governor with respect to the native tribes. By the same express, he communicated a plan which had occupied his thoughts for several days. As the contemplated movement of Schuyler would probably cause all the British force in Canada to be concentrated in the neighborhood of Montreal and St. Johns, he proposed to send off an expedition of ten or twelve hundred men, to penetrate to Quebec by the way of the Kennebec River.

The express found Schuyler in Albany, where he had been attending the conference with the Six Nations. He had just received intelligence which convinced him of the propriety of an expedition into Canada; had sent word to General Montgomery to get everything ready for it, and was on the point of departing for Ticonderoga to carry it into effect. In reply to Washington, he declared his conviction, from various accounts which he had received, that Carleton and his agents were exciting the Indian tribes to hostility. "I should, therefore, not hesitate one moment," adds he, "to employ any savages that might be willing to join us." He expressed himself delighted with Washington's project of sending off an expedition to Quebec, regretting only that it had not been thought of earlier.

Having sent off these despatches, Schuyler hastened back to Ticonderoga. Before he reached there, Montgomery had received intelligence that Carleton had completed his armed vessels at St. Johns, and was about to send them into Lake Champlain by the Sorel River. No time, therefore, was to be lost in getting possession of the Isle aux Noix, which commanded the entrance to that river. Montgomery hastened, therefore, to embark with about a thousand men, which were as many as the boats now ready could hold, taking with him two pieces of artillery; with this force he set off down the lake. A letter to General Schuyler explained the cause of his sudden departure, and entreated him to follow on in a whale-boat, leaving the residue of the artillery to come on as soon as conveyances could be procured.

Schuyler arrived at Ticonderoga on the night of the 30th of August, but too ill of a bilious fever to push on in a whale-boat. He caused, however, a bed to be prepared for him in a covered bateau, and, ill as he was, continued forward on the following day. On the 4th of September he overtook Montgomery at the Isle la Motte, where he had been detained by contrary weather, and assuming command of the little army, kept on the same day to the Isle aux Noix, about twelve miles south of St. Johns.

The siege of Boston had been kept up for several weeks without any remarkable occurrence. The British remained within their lines, diligently strengthening them; the besiegers having received further supplies of ammunition, were growing impatient of a state of inactivity. Towards the latter part of August there were rumors from Boston that the enemy were preparing for a sortie. Washington was resolved to provoke it by a kind of challenge. He accordingly detached fourteen hundred men to seize at night upon a height within musket shot of the enemy's line on Charlestown Neck, presuming that the latter would sally forth on the following day to dispute possession of it, and thus be drawn into a general battle. The task was executed with silence and celerity, and by daybreak the hill presented to the astonished foe the aspect of a fortified post.

The challenge was not accepted. The British opened a heavy cannonade from Bunker's Hill, but kept within their works. The Americans, scant of ammunition, could only reply with a single nine-pounder; this however sank one of the floating batteries which guarded the neck. The evident unwillingness of the British to come forth was perplexing. Perhaps they persuaded themselves that the American army, composed of crude, half-disciplined levies from different and distant quarters, would gradually fall asunder and disperse, or that its means of subsistence would be exhausted.

In the meantime as it was evident the enemy did not intend to come out, but were only strengthening their defences and preparing for winter, Washington was enabled to turn his attention to the expedition to be sent into Canada by the way of the Kennebec River. A detachment of about eleven hundred men, chosen for the purpose, was soon encamped on Cambridge Common. The proposed expedition was wild and perilous, and required a hardy, skilful and intrepid leader. Such a one was at hand. Benedict Arnold was at Cambridge, occupied in settling his accounts with the Massachusetts committee of safety. Whatever faults may have been found with his conduct in some particulars, his exploits on Lake Champlain had atoned for them, for valor in time of war covers a multitude of sins.

Washington had given him an honorable reception at head-quarters, and now considered him the very man for the present enterprise. As he would be intrusted with dangerous powers, Washington, beside a general letter of instructions, addressed a special one to him individually, full of cautious and considerate advice. He was furnished with handbills for distribution in Canada, setting forth the friendly objects of the present expedition, as well as of that under General Schuyler; and calling on the Canadians to furnish necessaries and accommodations of every kind; for which they were assured ample compensation.

On the 13th of September, Arnold struck his tents and set out in high spirits. Washington enjoined upon him to push forward, as rapidly as possible, success depending upon celerity; and counted the days as they elapsed after his departure, impatient to receive tidings of his progress up the Kennebec, and expecting that the expedition would reach Quebec about the middle of October. In the interim came letters from General Schuyler, giving particulars of the main expedition.

In a preceding chapter we left the general and his little army at the Isle aux Noix, near the Sorel River, the outlet of the lake. Thence, on the 5th of September, he sent Colonel Ethan Allen and Major Brown to reconnoitre the country between that river and the St. Lawrence, to distribute friendly addresses among the people and ascertain their feelings. This done, and having landed his baggage and provisions, the general proceeded along the Sorel River the next day with his boats, until within two miles of St. Johns, when a cannonade was opened from the fort.

In the night the camp was visited secretly by a person who informed General Schuyler of the state of the fort. The works were completed, and furnished with cannon. A vessel pierced for sixteen guns was launched, and would be ready to sail in three or four days. It was not probable that any Canadians would join the army, being disposed to remain neutral. This intelligence being discussed in a council of war in the morning, it was determined that they had neither men nor artillery sufficient to undertake a siege. They returned, therefore, to the Isle aux Noix, cast up fortifications, and threw a boom across the channel of the river to prevent the passage of the enemy's vessels into the lake, and awaited the arrival of artillery and reinforcements from Ticonderoga. In the course of a few days the expected reinforcements arrived, and with them a small train of artillery. Ethan Allen also returned from his reconnoitring expedition, of which he made a most encouraging report.

Preparations were now made for the investment of St. Johns, by land and water. Major Brown, who had already acted as a scout, was sent with one hundred Americans and about thirty Canadians towards Chamblee, to make friends in that quarter, and to join the army as soon as it should arrive at St. Johns. To quiet the restless activity of Ethan Allen, who had no command in the army, he was sent with an escort of thirty men to retrace his steps, penetrate to La Prairie, and beat up for recruits among the people whom he had recently visited.

For some time past, General Schuyler had been struggling with a complication of maladies, but exerting himself to the utmost in the harassing business of the camp. When everything was nearly ready, he was attacked in the night by a severe access of his disorder, which confined him to his bed, and compelled him to surrender the conduct of the expedition to General Montgomery. Since he could be of no further use, therefore, in this quarter, he caused his bed, as before, to be placed on board a covered bateau, and set off for Ticonderoga, to hasten forward reinforcements and supplies.

On the 16th of September, the day after Schuyler's departure, Montgomery proceeded to carry out the plans which had been concerted between them. Landing on the 17th at the place where they had formerly encamped, within a mile and a half of the fort, he detached a force of five hundred men to take a position at the junction of two roads leading to Montreal and Chamblee, so as to intercept relief from those points. He now proceeded to invest St. Johns, which had a garrison of five or six hundred regulars and two hundred Canadian militia. Its commander, Major Preston, made a brave resistance. Montgomery had not proper battering cannon; his mortars were defective; his artillerists unpractised, and the engineer ignorant. The siege went on slowly, until the arrival of an artillery company under Captain Lamb. Lamb, who was an able officer, immediately bedded a thirteen-inch mortar, and commenced a fire of shot and shells upon the fort. The distance, however, was too great, and the positions of the batteries were ill chosen.

A flourishing letter was received by the general from Colonel Ethan Allen, giving hope of further reinforcement. "I am now," writes he, "at the Parish of St. Ours, four leagues from Sorel to the south. I have two hundred and fifty Canadians under arms. As I march, they gather fast. You may rely on it that I shall join you in about three days, with five hundred or more Canadian volunteers."

But when on his way towards St. Johns, when between Longueil and La Prairie, Allen met Colonel Brown with his party of Americans and Canadians. A conversation took place between them. Brown assured him that the garrison at Montreal did not exceed thirty men, and might easily be surprised. Allen's partisan spirit was instantly excited. Here was a chance for another bold stroke equal to that at Ticonderoga. A plan was forthwith agreed upon. Allen was to return to Longueil, which is nearly opposite Montreal, and cross the St. Lawrence in canoes in the night, so as to land a little below the town. Brown, with two hundred men, was to cross above, and Montreal was to be attacked simultaneously at opposite points.

All this was arranged and put in action without the consent or knowledge of General Montgomery. Allen was again the partisan leader, acting from individual impulse. The whole force with which he undertook his part of this inconsiderate enterprise was thirty Americans and eighty Canadians. With these he crossed the river on the night of the 24th of September. Guards were stationed on the roads to prevent any one passing and giving the alarm in Montreal. Day dawned, but there was no signal of Major Brown having performed his part of the scheme. The day advanced, but still no signal; it was evident Major Brown had not crossed. Allen would gladly have recrossed the river, but it was too late. An alarm had been given to the town, and he soon found himself encountered by about forty regular soldiers and a hasty levy of Canadians and Indians. A smart action ensued; most of Allen's Canadian recruits gave way and fled, a number of Americans were slain, and he at length surrendered. This reckless dash at Montreal was viewed with concern by the American commander. "I am apprehensive of disagreeable consequences arising from Mr. Allen's imprudence," writes General Schuyler. The conduct of Allen was also severely censured by Washington. "His misfortune," said he, "will, I hope, teach a lesson of prudence and subordination to others."

Washington, who was full of solicitude about the fate of Arnold, received a despatch from him, dated October 13th, from the great portage or carrying-place between the Kennebec and Dead Rivers. The toils of the expedition up the Kennebec River had been excessive. Part of the men of each division managed the boats—

part marched along the banks. Those on board had to labor against swift currents; to unload at rapids; transport the cargoes, and sometimes the boats themselves, for some distance on their shoulders, and then to reload. Those on land had to scramble over rocks and precipices, to struggle through swamps and fenny streams; or cut their way through tangled thickets, which reduced their clothes to rags. With all their efforts, their progress was but from four to ten miles a day.

By the time they arrived at the place whence the letter was written, fatigue, swamp fevers and desertion had reduced their numbers to about nine hundred and fifty effective men. Arnold, however, wrote in good heart. "The last division," said he, "is just arrived; three divisions are over the first carrying-place, and as the men are in high spirits, I make no doubt of reaching the river Chaudiere in eight or ten days, the greatest difficulty being, I hope, already past."

CHAPTER XXII.

WAR ALONG THE COAST.—PROGRESS OF THE SIEGE.

While the two expeditions were threatening Canada from different quarters, the war was going on along the seaboard. The British in Boston, cut off from supplies by land, fitted out small armed vessels to seek them along the coast of New England. The inhabitants drove their cattle into the interior, or boldly resisted the aggressors. Parties landing to forage were often repulsed by hasty levies of the yeomanry. Scenes of ravage and violence occurred. Stonington was cannonaded, and further measures of vengeance were threatened by Captain Wallace of the Rose man-of-war, a naval officer, who had acquired an almost piratical reputation along the coast, and had his rendezvous in the harbor of Newport: domineering over the waters of Rhode Island.

To check these maraudings, and to capture the enemy's transports laden with supplies, the provinces of Massachusetts, Rhode Island and Connecticut fitted out two armed vessels each, at their own expense, without seeking the sanction or aid of Congress. Washington, also, on his own responsibility ordered several to be equipped for like purpose.

Among the sturdy little New England seaports, which had become obnoxious to punishment by resistance to nautical exactions, was Falmouth (now Portland), in Maine. On the evening of the 11th of October, Lieutenant Mowat, of the royal navy, appeared before it with several armed vessels, and sent a letter on shore, apprising the inhabitants that he was come to execute a just punishment on them for their "premeditated attacks on the legal prerogatives of the best of sovereigns." Two hours were given them, "to remove the human species out of the town." With much difficulty, and on the surrendering of some arms, a respite was obtained until nine o'clock the next morning, and the inhabitants employed the interval in removing their families and effects. About half-past nine o'clock the signal gun was fired, and within five minutes several houses were in flames. The inhabitants, standing on the heights, were spectators of the conflagration. All the vessels in the harbor were destroyed or carried away as prizes, and the town left a smoking ruin.

The conflagration of Falmouth was as a bale of fire throughout the country. [Lieutenant Mowat had declared to the people of Falmouth that he had orders from Admiral Graves to set fire to all the seaport towns between Boston and Halifax. Washington supposed such to be the case.] General Sullivan was sent to Portsmouth, where there was a fortification of some strength, to give the inhabitants his advice and assistance in warding off the menaced blow. Newport, also, was put on the alert, and recommended to fortify itself. Under the feeling roused by these reports, the General Court of Massachusetts, exercising a sovereign power, passed an act for encouraging the fitting out of armed vessels to defend the sea-coast of America, and for erecting a court to try and condemn all vessels that should be found infesting the same. This act, granting letters of marque and reprisal, anticipated any measure of the kind on the part of the General Government.

The British ministry have, in later days, been exculpated from the charge of issuing such a desolating order as that said to have been reported by Lieutenant Mowat. The orders under which that officer acted, we are told, emanated from General Gage and Admiral Graves. Whatever part General Gage may have had in this most ill-advised and discreditable measure, it was the last of his military government, and he did not remain long enough in the country to see it carried into effect. He sailed for England on the 10th of October, not absolutely superseded, but called home, "in order," as it was considerately said, "to give his majesty exact information of everything, and suggest such matters as his knowledge and experience of the service might enable him to furnish." During his absence, Major-general Howe would act as commander-in-chief. He never returned to America.

On the 15th of October a committee from Congress arrived in camp, sent to hold a conference with Washington, and with delegates from the governments of Connecticut, Rhode Island, Massachusetts and New Hampshire, on the subject of a new organization of the army. The committee consisted of Benjamin Franklin, Thomas Lynch of Carolina, and Colonel Harrison of Virginia. Washington was president of the board of conference, and Mr. Joseph Reed secretary. The committee brought an intimation from Congress that an attack upon Boston was much desired, if practicable. Washington called a council of war of his generals on the subject; they were unanimously of the opinion that an attack would not be prudent at present.

The board of conference was repeatedly in session for three or four days. The report of its deliberations rendered by the committee, produced a resolution of Congress that a new army of twenty-two thousand two hundred and seventy-two men and officers should be formed, to be recruited as much as possible from the troops actually in service. Unfortunately the term for which they were to be enlisted was to be *but for one year*. It formed a precedent which became a recurring cause of embarrassment throughout the war.

Washington's secretary, Mr. Reed, had, after the close of the conference, signified to him his intention to return to Philadelphia, where his private concerns required his presence. His departure was deeply regretted. On the departure of Mr. Reed, his place as secretary was temporarily supplied by Mr. Robert Harrison of Maryland, and subsequently by Colonel Mifflin; neither, however, attained to the affectionate confidence reposed in their predecessor.

The measures which General Howe had adopted after taking command in Boston, rejoiced the royalists, seeming to justify their anticipations. He proceeded to strengthen the works on Bunker's Hill and Boston Neck, and to clear away houses and throw up redoubts on eminences within the town. The patriot inhabitants were shocked by the desecration of the Old South Church, which was converted into a riding-school. The North Church was entirely demolished and used for fuel.

About the last of October, Howe issued three proclamations. The first forbade all persons to leave Boston without his permission under pain of military execution; the second forbade any one, so permitted, to take with him more than five pounds sterling, under pain of forfeiting all the money found upon his person and being subject to fine and imprisonment; the third called upon the inhabitants to arm themselves for the preservation of order within the town; they to be commanded by officers of his appointment.

Washington had recently been incensed by the conflagration of Falmouth; the conduct of Governor Dunmore who had proclaimed martial law in Virginia and threatened ruin to the patriots, had added to his provocation; the measures of General Howe seemed of the same harsh character, and he determined to retaliate. "Would it not be prudent," writes he to Governor Trumbull of Connecticut, "to seize those tories who have been, are, and we know will be active against us? Why should persons who are preying upon the vitals of their country, be suffered to stalk at large, whilst we know they will do us every mischief in their power?"

In this spirit he ordered General Sullivan, who was fortifying Portsmouth, "to seize upon such persons as held commissions under the crown, and were acting as open and avowed enemies to their country, and hold them as hostages for the security of the town." Still he was moderate in his retaliation, and stopped short of private individuals.

The season was fast approaching when the bay between the camp and Boston would be frozen over, and military operations might be conducted upon the ice. General Howe, if reinforced, would then very probably "endeavor to relieve himself from the disgraceful confinement in which the ministerial troops had been all summer." Washington felt the necessity, therefore, of guarding the camps wherever they were most assailable: and of throwing up batteries for the purpose. He had been embarrassed throughout the siege by the want of artillery and ordnance stores; but never more so than at the present moment. In this juncture, Mr. Henry Knox stepped forward, and offered to proceed to the frontier forts on Champlain in quest of a supply. Knox was one of the patriots who had fought on Bunker's Hill, since when he had aided in planning the defences of the camp before Boston. The aptness and talent here displayed by him as an artillerist, had recently induced Washington to recommend him to Congress for the command of a regiment of artillery. Congress had not yet acted on that recommendation; in the meantime Washington availed himself of the offered services of Knox in the present instance. He was instructed to take an account of the cannon, mortars, shells, lead and ammunition that were wanting. He was to hasten to New York, procure and forward all that could be had there; and thence proceed to the head-quarters of General Schuyler, who was requested by letter to aid him in obtaining what further supplies of the kind were wanting from the forts at Ticonderoga, Crown Point, St. Johns, and even Quebec, should it be in the hands of the Americans. Knox set off on his errand with promptness and alacrity.

The re-enlistment of troops actually in service was now attempted, and proved a fruitful source of perplexity. In a letter to the President of Congress, Washington observes that half of the officers of the rank of captain were inclined to retire; and it was probable their example would influence their men. Of those who were disposed to remain, the officers of one colony were unwilling to mix in the same regiment with those of another. Many sent in their names, to serve in expectation of promotion; others stood aloof, to see what advantages they could make for themselves; while those who had declined sent in their names again to serve. The difficulties were greater, if possible, with the soldiers than with the officers. They would not enlist unless they knew their colonel, lieutenant-colonel and captain; Connecticut men being unwilling to serve under officers from Massachusetts, and Massachusetts men under officers from Rhode Island: so that it was necessary to appoint the officers first.

Twenty days later he again writes to the President of Congress: "I am sorry to be necessitated to mention to you the egregious want of public spirit which prevails here. Instead of pressing to be engaged in the cause of their country, which I vainly flattered myself would be the case, I find we are likely to be deserted in a most critical time.... Our situation is truly alarming, and of this General Howe is well apprised. No doubt when he is reinforced he will avail himself of the information." In a letter to Reed he disburdened his heart more completely. "Such dearth of public spirit, and such want of virtue; such stock-jobbing, and fertility in all the low arts to obtain advantage of one kind or another in this great change of military arrangement, I never saw before, and I pray God's mercy that I may never be witness to again."

CHAPTER XXIII.

AFFAIRS IN CANADA.

[Despatches from Schuyler, dated October 26th, gave Washington another chapter of the Canada expedition. Chamblee, an inferior fort within five miles of St. Johns, had been captured. Montgomery now pressed the siege of St. Johns with vigor. Major Preston, although suffering for want of provisions, still held out manfully, hoping for relief from General Carleton. Colonel Maclean, a brave and veteran Scot, had enlisted three hundred of his countrymen at Quebec, and was to land at the mouth of the Sorel, where it empties into the St. Lawrence, and proceeding along the latter river join Carleton at St. Johns, who would repair thither by the way of Longueil.

On September 31st, Carleton embarked his force at Montreal in thirty-four boats, to cross the St. Lawrence, and land at Longueil. As the boats approached the shore, a terrible fire of artillery and musketry opened upon them from a detachment of Green Mountain Boys and New York troops stationed there under the command of Colonel Seth Warner. The boats were thrown into confusion; some were disabled, others were driven on shore on an island, and Carleton retreated with the rest to Montreal. This disorder led to the surrender of St. Johns, the garrison of which consisted of five hundred regulars and one hundred Canadians. Colonel Maclean, who was to have co-operated with Carleton, met with no better fortune than that commander.] While in full march for St. Johns he encountered Majors Brown and Livingston, who pressed him back to the mouth of the Sorel, where, hearing of the repulse of Carleton, and being deserted by his Canadian recruits, he embarked the residue of his troops, and set off down the St. Lawrence to Quebec. The Americans now took post at the mouth of the Sorel, where they erected batteries so as to command the St. Lawrence, and prevent the descent of any armed vessels from Montreal.

[Arnold, meanwhile, was advancing with severe toil and difficulty. His troops and effects were transported across the carrying-point between the Kennebec and Dead Rivers. On the latter river they landed their boats, and navigated its sluggish waters to the foot of snow crowned mountains. Here they experienced heavy rains; some of their boats were overturned by torrents from the mountains, and many of their provisions lost. The sick list increased, and the spirits of the army gave way. But the energy of Arnold was unabated. He pushed on, and at Lake Megantic, the source of the Chaudiere, he met an emissary whom he had sent forward to sound the feelings of the French yeomanry. His report being favorable, Arnold divided his provisions among his troops, and with a light foraging party pushed rapidly ahead to procure and send back supplies. Chaudiere is little better than a mountain torrent, full of rocks and rapids. Arnold embarked upon it with his little party in five bateaux and a birch canoe. Three of the boats were dashed to pieces, the cargoes lost, and the crews saved with difficulty.] At length they reached Sertigan, the first French settlement, where they were cordially received. Here Arnold bought provisions, which he sent back by the Canadians and Indians to his troops. The latter were in a state of starvation.

Arnold halted for a short time in the hospitable valley of Chaudiere to give his troops repose, and distributed among the inhabitants the printed manifesto with which he had been furnished by Washington. Here he was joined by about forty Norridgewock Indians. On the 9th of November, the little army emerged from the woods at Point Levi, on the St. Lawrence, opposite to Quebec.

Leaving Arnold in full sight of Quebec, we turn to narrate the events of the upper expedition into Canada. Montgomery appeared before Montreal on the 12th of November. General Carleton had embarked with his little garrison and several of the civil officers of the place, on board of a flotilla of ten or eleven small vessels, and made sail in the night. The town capitulated, of course; and Montgomery took quiet possession. His urbanity and kindness soon won the good will of the inhabitants, both English and French, and made the Canadians sensible that he really came to secure their rights, not to molest them. Intercepted letters acquainted him with Arnold's arrival in the neighborhood of Quebec.

His great immediate object was the capture of Carleton; which would form a triumphal close to the enterprise, and might decide the fate of Canada. The flotilla in which the general was embarked had made repeated attempts to escape down the St. Lawrence; but had as often been driven back by the batteries thrown up by the Americans at the mouth of the Sorel. It now lay anchored about fifteen miles above the river; and Montgomery prepared to attack it with bateaux and light artillery, so as to force it down upon the batteries. Carleton saw his imminent peril. Disguising himself as a Canadian voyager, he set off on a dark night accompanied by six peasants, in a boat with muffled oars, which he assisted to pull; slipped quietly and silently past all the batteries and guard-boats, and effected his escape to Three Rivers, where he embarked in a vessel for Quebec. After his departure the flotilla surrendered.

Montgomery now placed garrisons in Montreal, St. Johns and Chamblee, and made final preparations for descending the St. Lawrence, and co-operating with Arnold against Quebec. To his disappointment and deep chagrin, he found but a handful of his troops disposed to accompany him. Some pleaded ill health; the term of enlistment of many had expired, and they were bent on returning home; and others, who had no such excuses to make became exceedingly turbulent, and mutinous. Nothing but a sense of public duty and gratitude to Congress for an unsought commission, had induced Montgomery to engage in the service; wearied by the continual vexations which beset it, he avowed, in a letter to Schuyler, his determination to retire as soon as the intended expedition against Quebec was finished.

[General Montgomery had been thwarted continually in his efforts by the want of subordination and discipline among his troops, "who," said he, "carry the spirit of freedom into the camp and think for themselves." Accustomed as he had been, in his former military experience, to the implicit obedience of European troops, the insubordination of these yeoman soldiery was intolerable to him.]

The tidings of the capture of Montreal gave Washington the liveliest satisfaction. He now looked forward to equal success in the expedition against Quebec. Certain passages of Schuyler's letters, however, gave him deep concern, wherein that general complained of the embarrassments and annoyances he had experienced from the insubordination of the army. "Habituated to order," said he, "I cannot without pain see that disregard of discipline, confusion and inattention which reign so generally in this quarter, and I am determined to retire. Of this resolution I have advised Congress."

He had indeed done so. In communicating to the President of Congress the complaints of General Montgomery, and his intention to retire, "my sentiments," said he, "exactly coincide with his. I shall, with him, do everything in my power to put a finishing stroke to the campaign, and make the best arrangement in my power, in order to insure success to the next. This done, I must beg leave to retire." Congress, however, was too well aware of his value, readily to dispense with his services. His letter produced a prompt resolution expressive of their high sense of his attention and perseverance, "which merited the thanks of the United Colonies."

What, however, produced a greater effect upon Schuyler than any encomium or entreaty on the part of Congress, were the expostulations of Washington, inspired by strong friendship and kindred sympathies. "I am exceedingly sorry," writes the latter, "that you and General Montgomery incline to quit the service. Let me ask you, sir, when is the time for brave men to exert themselves in the cause of liberty and their country, if this is not? Should any difficulties that they may have to encounter at this important crisis deter them? God knows there is not a difficulty that you both very justly complain of, that I have not in an eminent degree experienced, that I am not every day experiencing; but we must bear up against them, and make the best of mankind, as they are, since we cannot have them as we wish. Let me therefore conjure you, and Mr. Montgomery, to lay aside such thoughts—as thoughts injurious to yourselves and extremely so to your country, which calls aloud for gentlemen of your ability."

This noble appeal went straight to the heart of Schuyler, and brought out a magnanimous reply. "I do not hesitate," writes he, "to answer my dear general's question in the affirmative, by declaring that now or never is the time for every virtuous American to exert himself in the cause of liberty and his country; and that it is become a duty cheerfully to sacrifice the sweets of domestic felicity to attain the honest and glorious end America has in view."

[The true cause of Schuyler's wish to retire from official station was the annoyance he had suffered through the campaign from sectional prejudices. The eastern troops persistently declared that the general commanding in that quarter ought to be of the colony whence the majority of the troops came. His liberal treatment of British and Canadian prisoners was also a cause of offence, and rendered him unpopular.]

CHAPTER XXIV.
INCIDENTS OF THE CAMP.—ARNOLD BEFORE QUEBEC.

The forming even of the skeleton of an army under the new regulations, had been a work of infinite difficulty; to fill it up was still more difficult. The first burst of revolutionary zeal had passed away; enthusiasm had been chilled by the inaction and monotony of a long encampment; an encampment, moreover, destitute of those comforts which, in experienced warfare, are provided by a well-regulated commissariat. The troops had suffered privations of every kind, want of fuel, clothing, provisions. They looked forward with dismay to the rigors of winter, and longed for their rustic homes and their family firesides.

[The Connecticut troops, whose time was expiring, were urged to remain until December 10th, when their place would be supplied by new levies. They refused, and withdrew on the 1st, thereby greatly weakening the lines. This conduct excited great indignation, and the homeward-bound warriors met with a reception on their arrival at home which prompted many to return again to camp.]

On the very day after the departure homeward of these troops, and while it was feared their example would be contagious, a long, lumbering train of wagons, laden with ordnance and military stores, and decorated with flags, came wheeling into the camp escorted by continental troops and country militia. They were part of the cargo of a large brigantine laden with munitions of war, captured and sent in to Cape Ann by the schooner Lee, Captain Manly, one of the cruisers sent out by Washington. Beside the ordnance captured, there were two thousand stand of arms, one hundred thousand flints, thirty thousand round shot, and thirty-two tons of musket balls.

It was a cheering incident, and was eagerly turned to account. Among the ordnance was a huge brass mortar of a new construction, weighing near three thousand pounds. It was considered a glorious trophy, and there was a resolve to christen it. Mifflin, Washington's secretary, suggested the name. The mortar was fixed in a bed; old Putnam mounted it, dashed on it a bottle of rum, and gave it the name of "Congress."

With Washington, this transient gleam of nautical success was soon overshadowed by the conduct of the cruisers he had sent to the St. Lawrence. Failing to intercept the brigantines, the objects of their cruise, they landed on the Island of St. Johns, plundered the house of the governor and several private dwellings, and brought off three of the principal inhabitants prisoners; one of whom, Mr. Callbeck, was president of the council, and acted as governor. These gentlemen made a memorial to Washington of this scandalous maraud. He instantly ordered the restoration of the effects which had been pillaged.

Shortly after the foregoing occurrence, information was received of the indignities which had been heaped upon Colonel Ethan Allen, [who was loaded with chains and thrown into prison,] when captured at Montreal by General Prescott, who himself was now a prisoner in the hands of the Americans. It touched Washington on a point on which he was most sensitive and tenacious, the treatment of American officers when captured.

[A correspondence ensued between Washington and General Howe, in which the former threatened as retaliation to inflict upon General Prescott the same treatment and fate which Colonel Allen should experience. In reply, Howe asserted that his command did not extend to Canada and that he had no knowledge of Allen or his fate. General Carleton, he assumed, would not in this case forfeit his past pretensions to decency and humanity. The measure of retaliation threatened by Washington was actually meted out by Congress on the arrival of General Prescott in Philadelphia. He was ordered into close confinement in jail, though not put in irons; but subsequently, on account of his health, he was released.]

At the time of this correspondence with Howe, Washington was earnestly occupied preparing works for the bombardment of Boston, should that measure be resolved upon by Congress. General Putnam, in the preceding month, had taken possession in the night of Cobble Hill without molestation from the enemy, though a commanding eminence; and in two days had constructed a work, which, from its strength, was named Putnam's impregnable fortress. He was now engaged on another work on Lechmere Point, to be connected with the works at Cobble Hill by a bridge thrown across Willis's Creek, and a covered way. Lechmere Point is immediately opposite the north part of Boston; and the Scarborough ship-of-war was anchored near it. Putnam availed himself of a dark and foggy day (Dec. 17), to commence operations, and broke ground with four hundred men, at ten o'clock in the morning, on a hill at the Point. "The mist," says a contemporary account, "was so great as to prevent the enemy from discovering what he was about until near twelve o'clock, when it cleared up, and opened to their view our whole party at the Point, and another at the causeway throwing a bridge over the creek. The Scarborough, anchored off the Point, poured in a broadside. The enemy from Boston threw shells. The garrison at Cobble Hill returned fire. Our men were obliged to decamp from the Point, but the work was resumed by the brave old general at night."

On the next morning, General Heath was detached with a party of men to carry on the work which Putnam had commenced. It was to consist of two redoubts, on one of which was to be a mortar battery. There was, as yet, a deficiency of ordnance; but the prize mortar was to be mounted which Putnam had recently christened, "The Congress." For several days the labor at the works was continued; the redoubts were thrown up, and a covered way was constructed leading down to the bridge. All this was done notwithstanding the continual fire of the enemy. Putnam anticipated great effects from this work, and especially from his grand mortar. Shells there were in abundance for a bombardment; the only thing wanting was a supply of powder.

Amid the various concerns of the war, and the multiplied perplexities of the camp, the thoughts of Washington continually reverted to his home on the banks of the Potomac. A constant correspondence was kept up between him and his agent, Mr. Lund Washington, who had charge of his various estates. The general gave clear and minute directions as to their management, and the agent rendered as clear and minute returns of everything that had been done in consequence. According to recent accounts, Mount Vernon had been considered in danger. Lord Dunmore was exercising martial law in the Ancient Dominion, and it was feared that the favorite abode of the "rebel commander-in-chief" would be marked out for hostility, and that the enemy might land from their ships in the Potomac and lay it waste. Washington's brother, John Augustine, had entreated Mrs. Washington to leave it. The people of Loudoun had advised her to seek refuge beyond the Blue Ridge, and had offered to send a guard to escort her. She had declined the offer, not considering herself in danger. Lund Washington was equally free from apprehensions on the subject. Though alive to everything concerning Mount Vernon, Washington agreed with them in deeming it in no present danger of molestation by the enemy. Still he felt for the loneliness of Mrs. Washington's situation, heightened as it must be by anxiety on his own account. He wrote to her, therefore, by express, in November, inviting her to join him at the camp. He at the same time wrote to Lund Washington, engaging his continued services as an agent. This person, though bearing the same name, and probably of the same stock, does not appear to have been in any near degree of relationship.

Mrs. Washington came on with her own carriage and horses, accompanied by her son, Mr. Custis, and his wife. Escorts and guards of honor attended her from place to place, and she was detained some time at Philadelphia by the devoted attention of the inhabitants. Her arrival at Cambridge was a glad event in the army.

[Mrs. Washington presided at head-quarters with dignity and affability. Some questions of ceremony had arisen, and jealousies had been excited in reference to invitations to head-quarters. The presence of Mrs. Washington relieved the general from numerous perplexities of this character. After her arrival the camp assumed a more convivial tone than before, and parties became common.]

While giving these familiar scenes and occurrences we are tempted to subjoin one furnished from the manuscript memoir of an eye witness. A large party of Virginia riflemen, who had recently arrived in camp, were strolling about Cambridge, and viewing the collegiate buildings, now turned into barracks. Their half-Indian equipments, and fringed and ruffled hunting garbs, provoked the merriment of some troops from Marblehead, chiefly fishermen and sailors, who thought nothing equal to the round jacket and trowsers. A bantering ensued between them. There was snow upon the ground, and snowballs began to fly when jokes were wanting. The parties waxed warm with the contest. They closed, and came to blows; both sides were reinforced, and in a little while at least a thousand were at fisticuffs, and there was a tumult in the camp worthy of the days of Homer. "At this juncture," writes our informant, "Washington made his appearance, whether by accident or design, I never knew. I saw none of his aides with him; his black servant was just behind him mounted. He threw the bridle of his own horse into his servant's hands, sprang from his seat, rushed into the thickest of the melée, seized two tall brawny riflemen by the throat, keeping them at arm's-length, talking to and shaking them."

As they were from his own province, he may have felt peculiarly responsible for their good conduct; they were engaged, too, in one of those sectional brawls which were his especial abhorrence; his reprimand must, therefore, have been a vehement one. He was commanding in his serenest moments, but irresistible in his bursts of indignation. On the present occasion, we are told, his appearance and strong-handed rebuke put an instant end to the tumult. The combatants dispersed in all directions, and in less than three minutes none remained on the ground but the two he had collared.

The invasion of Canada still shared the anxious thoughts of Washington. His last accounts of the movements of Arnold, left him at Point Levi, opposite to Quebec. It was his intention to cross the river immediately. At Point Levi, however, he was brought to a stand; not a boat was to be found there. Letters to Generals Schuyler and Montgomery had been carried by his faithless messengers, to Caramhé, the lieutenant-governor, who, had caused all the boats of Point Levi to be either removed or destroyed.

Arnold was not a man to be disheartened by difficulties. With great exertions he procured about forty birch canoes, but stormy winds arose, and for some days the river was too boisterous for such frail craft. In the meantime the garrison at Quebec was gaining strength. The veteran Maclean arrived down the river with his corps of Royal Highland Emigrants, and threw himself into the place. The Lizard frigate, the Hornet sloop-of-war, and two armed schooners were stationed in the river, and guard-boats patrolled at night.

On the 13th of November, Arnold received intelligence that Montgomery had captured St. Johns. He was instantly roused to emulation. His men, too, were inspirited by the news. The wind had abated: he determined to cross the river that very night. At a late hour in the evening he embarked with the first division. By four o'clock in the morning a large part of his force had crossed without being perceived, and landed about a mile and a half above Cape Diamond, at Wolfe's Cove, so called from being the landing-place of that gallant commander. Just then a guard-boat, belonging to the Lizard, came slowly along shore and discovered them. They hailed it, and ordered it to land. Not complying, it was fired into and three men were killed. The boat instantly pulled for the frigate, giving vociferous alarm.

Without waiting the arrival of the residue of his men, for whom the canoes had been despatched, Arnold led those who had landed to the foot of the cragged defile, once scaled by the intrepid Wolfe, and scrambled up it in all haste. By daylight he had planted his daring flag on the far-famed Heights of Abraham. Here the main difficulty stared him in the face. A strong line of walls and bastions traversed the promontory from one of its precipitous sides to the other; enclosing the upper and lower towns. On the right, the great bastion of Cape Diamond crowned the rocky height of that name. On the left was the bastion of La Potasse, close by the gate of St. Johns, opening upon the barracks.

A council of war was now held. Arnold, who had some knowledge of the place, was for dashing forward at once and storming the gate of St. Johns. Had they done so, they might have been successful. The gate was open and unguarded. Through some blunder and delay, a message from the commander of the Lizard to the lieutenant-governor had not yet been delivered, and no alarm had reached the fortress. The formidable aspect of the place, however, awed Arnold's associates. Cautious counsel is often fatal to a daring enterprise. While the counsel of war deliberated, the favorable moment passed away. The lieutenant-governor received the tardy message. He hastily assembled the merchants, officers of militia, and captains of merchant vessels. All promised to stand by him, and the walls looking upon the heights were soon manned by the military. Arnold paraded his men within a hundred yards of the walls, and caused them to give three hearty cheers; hoping to excite a revolt in the place, or to provoke the scanty garrison to a sally. There was some firing on the part of the Americans, but merely as an additional taunt; they were too far off for their musketry to have effect. A large cannon on the ramparts was brought to bear on them, and a few shots obliged the Americans to retire and encamp.

In the evening Arnold sent a flag, demanding in the name of the United Colonies the surrender of the place. Some of the disaffected and the faint-hearted were inclined to open the gates, but were held in check by the mastiff loyalty of Maclean. The inhabitants gradually recovered from their alarm, and armed themselves to defend their property. The sailors and marines proved a valuable addition to the garrison, which now really meditated a sortie. Arnold received information of all this from friends within the walls; he heard about the same time of the capture of Montreal, and that General Carleton, having escaped from that place, was on his way down to Quebec. He thought at present, therefore, to draw off on the 19th to *Point aux Trembles* (Aspen-tree Point), twenty miles above Quebec, there to await the arrival of General Montgomery with troops and artillery. As his little army wended its way along the high bank of the river towards its destined encampment, a vessel passed below, which had just touched at Point aux Trembles. On board of it was General Carleton, hurrying on to Quebec.

CHAPTER XXV.

WASHINGTON'S PERPLEXITIES.—NEW YORK IN DANGER.

In the month of December a vessel had been captured, bearing supplies from Lord Dunmore to the army at Boston. A letter on board, from his lordship to General Howe, invited him to transfer the war to the southern colonies; or, at all events, to send reinforcements thither; intimating at the same time his plan of proclaiming liberty to indentured servants, negroes, and others appertaining to rebels, and inviting them to join his majesty's troops. In a word, to inflict upon Virginia the horrors of a servile war. "If this man is not crushed before spring," writes Washington, "he will become the most formidable enemy America has. His strength will increase as a snowball."

General Lee took the occasion to set forth his own system of policy. "Had my opinion been thought worthy of attention," would he say, "Lord Dunmore would have been disarmed of his teeth and claws." He would seize Tryon too, "and every governor, government man, placeman, tory and enemy to liberty on the continent, and confiscate their estates, or at least lay them under heavy contributions for the public. Their persons should be secured, in some of the interior towns, as hostages for the treatment of those of our party whom the fortune of war shall throw into their hands; they should be allowed a reasonable pension out of their fortunes for their maintenance."

Such was the policy advocated by Lee in his letters and conversation, and he soon had an opportunity of carrying it partly into operation. [Newport being threatened by a naval armament from Boston, General Lee was despatched, at the request of the governor, to put the island in a state of defence. Lee set out with alacrity. Having laid out works, and given directions for fortifications, he summoned before him a number of persons who had been in the habit of supplying the enemy, and compelled them all to take an oath of fidelity to the continental claim. Those who refused were put under guard and sent to Providence. Congress was disposed to consider these measures too highhanded, but Washington approved of them.]

December had been throughout a month of severe trial to Washington; during which he saw his army dropping away piece-meal before his eyes. Homeward every face was turned as soon as the term of enlistment was at an end. Scarce could the disbanding troops be kept a few days in camp until militia could be procured to supply their place. Washington made repeated and animated appeals to their patriotism; they were almost unheeded. He caused popular and patriotic songs to be sung about the camp. They passed by like the idle wind. Home! home! home! throbbed in every heart. "The desire of retiring into a chimney-corner," says Washington reproachfully, "seized the troops as soon as their terms expired."

Greene, throughout this trying month, was continually by Washington's side. His letters expressing the same cares and apprehensions, and occasionally in the same language with those of the commander-in-chief, show how completely he was in his councils. The 31st of December arrived, the crisis of the army; for with that month expired the last of the old terms of enlistment. "We never have been so weak," writes Greene, "as we shall be to-morrow, when we dismiss the old troops." On this day Washington received cheering intelligence from Canada. A junction had taken place, a month previously, between Arnold and Montgomery at Point aux Trembles. They were about two thousand strong, and were making every preparation for attacking Quebec.

On the following morning (January 1st, 1776,) his army did not amount to ten thousand men, and was composed of but half-filled regiments. Even in raising this inadequate force, it had been necessary to indulge many of the men with furloughs, that they might visit their families and friends. The detachments of militia from the neighboring provinces which replaced the disbanding troops, remained but for brief periods; so that, in despite of every effort, the lines were often but feebly manned, and might easily have been forced.

The anxiety of Washington in this critical state of the army, may be judged from his correspondence with Reed. "It is easier to conceive than to describe the situation of my mind for some time past, and my feelings under our present circumstances," writes he, on the 4th of January. "Search the volumes of history through, and I much question whether a case similar to ours is to be found; namely, to maintain a post against the power of the British troops for six months together, without powder, and then to have one army disbanded and another raised within the same distance (musket shot) of a reinforced enemy. What may be the issue of the last manoeuvre, time only can unfold. I wish this month were well over our head."

In the midst of his discouragements, Washington received letters from Knox, showing the spirit and energy with which he was executing his mission, in quest of cannon and ordnance stores. He had struggled manfully and successfully with all kinds of difficulties from the advanced season, and head winds, in getting them from Ticonderoga to the head of Lake George. "Three days ago," writes he, on the 17th of December, "it was very uncertain whether we could get them over until next spring; but now, please God, they shall go. I have made forty-two exceedingly strong sleds, and have provided eighty yoke of oxen to drag them as far as Springfield, where I shall get fresh cattle to take them to camp."

Early in the month of January, there was a great stir of preparation in Boston harbor. A fleet of transports were taking in supplies, and making arrangements for the embarkation of troops. Bomb-ketches and flat-bottomed boats were getting ready for sea, as were two sloops-of-war, which were to convey the armament. Its destination was kept secret; but was confidently surmised by Washington.

In the preceding month of October, a letter had been laid before Congress, written by some person in London of high credibility, and revealing a secret plan of operations said to have been sent out by ministers to the commanders in Boston. The following is the purport: Possession was to be gained of New York and Albany, through the assistance of Governor Tryon, on whose influence with the tory part of the population, much reliance was placed. These cities were to be very strongly garrisoned. All who did not join the king's forces were to be declared rebels. The Hudson River, and the East River or Sound, were to be commanded by a number of small men-of-war and cutters, stationed in different parts, so as wholly to cut off all communication by water between New York and the provinces to the northward of it; and between New York and Albany, except for the king's service; and to prevent, also, all communication between the city of New York and the provinces of New Jersey, Pennsylvania, and those to the southward of them. "By these means," said the letter, "the administration and their friends fancy they shall soon either starve out or retake the garrisons of Crown Point and Ticonderoga, and open and maintain a safe intercourse and correspondence between Quebec, Albany, and New York; and thereby offer the fairest opportunity to their soldiery and the Canadians, in conjunction with the Indians to be procured by Guy Johnson, to make continual irruptions into New Hampshire, Massachusetts and Connecticut, and so distract and divide the Provincial forces, as to render it easy for the British army at Boston to defeat them, break the spirits of the Massachusetts people, depopulate their country, and compel an absolute subjection to Great Britain."

This information had already excited solicitude respecting the Hudson, and led to measures for its protection. It was now surmised that the expedition preparing to sail from Boston, and which was to be conducted by Sir Henry Clinton, might be destined to seize upon New York. How was the apprehended blow to be parried? General Lee, who was just returned from his energetic visit to Rhode Island, offered his advice and services in the matter. In a letter to Washington, he urged him to act at once, and on his own responsibility, without awaiting the tardy and doubtful sanction of Congress, for which, in military matters, Lee had but small regard.

"New York must be secured," writes he, "but it will never, I am afraid, be secured by due order of the Congress, for obvious reasons. They find themselves awkwardly situated on this head. You must step in to their relief. I am sensible no man can be spared from the lines under present circumstances; but I would propose that you should detach me into Connecticut, and lend your name for collecting a body of volunteers. I am assured that I shall find no difficulty in assembling a sufficient number for the purposes wanted. This body in conjunction (if there should appear occasion to summon them) with the Jersey regiment under the command of Lord Stirling, now at Elizabethtown, will effect the security of New York, and the expulsion or suppression of that dangerous banditti of tories who have appeared on Long Island with the professed intention of acting against the authority of Congress."

Washington, while he approved of Lee's military suggestions, was cautious in exercising the powers vested in him, and fearful of transcending them. John Adams was at that time in the vicinity of the camp, and he asked his opinion as to the practicability and expediency of the plan, and whether it "might not be regarded as beyond his line." Adams, resolute of spirit, thought the enterprise might easily be accomplished by the friends of liberty in New York, in connection with the Connecticut people, "who are very ready," said he, "upon such occasions."

Thus fortified, as it were, by congressional sanction, through one of its most important members, who pronounced New York as much within his command as Massachusetts; he gave Lee authority to carry out his plans. He was to raise volunteers in Connecticut; march at their head to New York; call in military aid from New Jersey; put the city and the post on the Hudson in a posture of security against surprise; disarm all persons on Long Island and elsewhere, inimical to the views of Congress, or secure them in some other manner if necessary; and seize upon all medicines, shirts and blankets, and send them on for the use of the American army.

Lee departed on his mission on the 8th of January. The people of New York were thrown into a panic on hearing that Lee was in Connecticut, on his way to take military possession of the city. They apprehended his appearance there would provoke an attack from the ships in the harbor. Some, who thought the war about to be brought to their own doors, packed up their effects, and made off into the country with their wives and children. Others beleaguered the committee of safety with entreaties against the deprecated protection of General Lee. The committee, through Pierre Van Cortlandt, their chairman, addressed a letter to Lee, inquiring into the motives of his coming with an army to New York, and stating the incapacity of the city to act hostilely against the ships of war in port, from deficiency of powder, and a want of military works.

Lee, in reply, dated Stamford, January 23d, disclaimed all intention of commencing actual hostilities against the men-of-war in the harbor; his instructions from the commander-in-chief being solely to prevent the enemy from taking post in the city, or lodging themselves on Long Island. Some subordinate purposes were likewise to be executed, which were much more proper to be communicated by word of mouth than by writing. In compliance with the wishes of the committee, he promised to carry with him into the town just troops enough to secure it against any present designs of the enemy, leaving his main force on the western border of Connecticut. How he conducted himself on his arrival in the city, we shall relate in a future chapter.

CHAPTER XXVI.

ATTACK ON QUEBEC.—AFFAIRS IN NEW YORK.

From amid surrounding perplexities, Washington still turned a hopeful eye to Canada. He expected daily to receive tidings that Montgomery and Arnold were within the walls of Quebec. On the 18th of January came dispatches to him from General Schuyler, containing withering tidings. The following is the purport. Montgomery, on the 2d of December, the day after his arrival at Point aux Trembles, set off in face of a driving snow-storm for Quebec, and arrived before it on the 5th. The works, from their great extent, appeared to him incapable of being defended by the actual garrison; made up, as he said, of "Maclean's banditti," the sailors from the frigates and other vessels, together with the citizens obliged to take up arms.

On the day of his arrival, he sent a flag with a summons to surrender. It was fired upon, and obliged to retire. Exasperated at this outrage, Montgomery wrote an indignant letter to Carleton, reiterating the demand, magnifying the number of his troops, and warning him against the consequences of an assault. Finding it was rejected from the walls, he prepared for an attack. The ground was frozen to a great depth, and covered with snow. By dint of excessive labor a breastwork was thrown up, four hundred yards distant from the walls and opposite to the gate of St. Louis, which is nearly in the centre. It was formed of gabions, ranged side by side, and filled with snow, over which water was thrown until thoroughly frozen. Here Captain Lamb mounted five light pieces and a howitzer. Several mortars were placed in the suburbs of St. Roque, which extends on the left of the promontory, below the heights, and nearly on a level with the river.

From the "Ice Battery" Captain Lamb opened a well-sustained and well-directed fire upon the walls, but his field-pieces were too light to be effective. With his howitzer he threw shells into the town and set it on fire in several places.

On the evening of the fifth day, Montgomery paid a visit to the ice battery. The heavy artillery from the wall had repaid its ineffectual fire with ample usury. The brittle ramparts had been shivered like glass; several of the guns had been rendered useless. The general saw the insufficiency of the battery, and, on retiring, gave Captain Lamb permission to leave it whenever he thought proper. The veteran waited until after dark, when, securing all the guns, he abandoned the ruined redoubt.

Nearly three weeks had been consumed in these futile operations. The army, ill-clothed, and ill-provided, was becoming impatient of the rigors of a Canadian winter; the term for which part of the troops had enlisted would expire with the year, and they already talked of returning home. Montgomery was sadly conscious of the insufficiency of his means; still he could not endure the thoughts of retiring from before the place without striking a blow. He determined, therefore, to attempt to carry the place by *escalade*. Colonel Livingston was to make a false attack on the gate of St. Johns and set fire to it; Major Brown, with another detachment, was to menace the bastion of Cape Diamond. Arnold with three hundred and fifty of the hardy fellows who had followed him through the wilderness, strengthened by Captain Lamb and forty of his company, was to assault the suburbs and batteries of St. Roque; while Montgomery, with the residue of his forces, was to pass below the bastion at Cape Diamond, defile along the river, carry the defences at Drummond's Wharf, and thus enter the lower town on one side, while Arnold forced his way into it on the other. These movements were all to be made at the same time, on the discharge of signal rockets, thus distracting the enemy, and calling their attention to four several points.

On the 31st of December, at two o'clock in the morning, the troops repaired to their several destinations, under cover of a violent snow-storm. By some mistake the signal rockets were let off before the lower divisions had time to get to their fighting ground. They were descried by one of Maclean's Highland officers, who gave the alarm. Livingston also failed to make the false attack on the gate of St. Johns, which was to have caused a diversion favorable to Arnold's attack on the suburb below.

The feint by Major Brown, on the bastion of Cape Diamond, was successful, and concealed the march of General Montgomery. That gallant commander descended from the heights to Wolfe's Cove, and led his division along the shore of the St. Lawrence, round the beetling promontory of Cape Diamond. The narrow approach to the lower town in that direction was traversed by a picket or stockade, defended by Canadian militia; beyond which was a second defence, a kind of block-house. The aim of Montgomery was to come upon these barriers by surprise. The pass which they defended is formidable at all times, having a swift river on one side, and overhanging precipices on the other; but at this time was rendered peculiarly difficult by drifting snow, and by great masses of ice piled on each other at the foot of the cliffs.

The troops made their way painfully, in extended and straggling files, along the narrow footway, and over the slippery piles of ice. Among the foremost, were some of the first New York regiment, led on by Captain Cheeseman. Montgomery, in his eagerness, threw himself far in the advance with his pioneers and a few officers, and made a dash at the first barrier. The Canadians stationed there, taken by surprise, made a few random shots, then threw down their muskets and fled. Montgomery sprang forward, aided with his own hand to pluck down the pickets, which the pioneers were sawing, and having made a breach sufficiently wide to admit three or four men abreast, entered sword in hand. The Canadians had fled from the picket to the battery or block-house. Montgomery again dashed forward, but when within forty paces of the battery, a discharge of grape-shot from a single cannon made deadly havoc. Montgomery, and McPherson, one of his aides, were killed on the spot. Captain Cheeseman received a canister shot through the body; with him fell his orderly sergeant and several of his men. This fearful slaughter, and the death of their general, threw everything in confusion. Colonel Campbell, quarter-master general, took the command and ordered a retreat.

While all this was occurring on the side of Cape Diamond, Arnold led his division against the opposite side of the lower town along the suburb and street of St. Roque. Like Montgomery, he took the advance at the head of a forlorn hope of twenty-five men. Captain Lamb and his artillery company came next, with a field-piece mounted on a sledge. Then came a company with ladders and scaling implements, followed by Morgan and his riflemen. In the rear of all these came the main body. A battery on a wharf commanded the narrow pass by which they had to advance. This was to be attacked with the field-piece, and then scaled with ladders by the forlorn hope; while Captain Morgan, with his riflemen, was to pass round the wharf on the ice.

The false attack which was to have been made by Livingston on the gate of St. Johns, by way of diversion, had not taken place; there was nothing, therefore, to call off the attention of the enemy in this quarter from the detachment. The troops, as they straggled along in lengthened file through the drifting snow were sadly galled by a flanking fire on the right, from walls and pickets. The field-piece at length became so deeply embedded in a snow-drift that it could not be moved. Lamb sent word to Arnold of the impediment; in the meantime, he and his artillery company were brought to a halt. The company with the scaling ladders would have halted also, having been told to keep in the rear of the artillery; but they were urged on by Morgan with a thundering oath, who pushed on after them with his riflemen, the artillery company opening to the right and left to let them pass.

They arrived in the advance, just as Arnold was leading on his forlorn hope to attack the barrier. Before he reached it a severe wound in the right leg with a musket ball completely disabled him, and he had to be borne from the field. Morgan instantly took the command. Just then Lamb came up with his company, armed with muskets and bayonets, having received orders to abandon the field-piece, and support the advance. Oswald joined him with the forlorn hope. The battery which commanded the defile mounted two pieces of cannon. There was a discharge of grape-shot when the assailants were close under the muzzles of the guns, yet but one man was killed. Before there could be a second discharge, the battery was carried by assault, some firing in to the embrasures; others scaling the walls. The captain and thirty of his men were taken prisoners.

The day was just dawning as Morgan led on to attack the second barrier, and his men had to advance under a fire from the town walls on their right, which incessantly thinned their ranks. The second barrier was reached; they applied their scaling ladders to storm it. The defence was brave and obstinate, but the defenders were at length driven from their guns, and the battery was gained. At the last moment one of the gunners ran back, linstock in hand, to give one more shot. Captain Lamb snapped a fusee at him. It missed fire. The cannon was discharged, and a grape-shot wounded Lamb in the head, carrying away part of the cheek-bone. He was borne off senseless to a neighboring shed.

The two barriers being now taken, the way on this side into the lower town seemed open. Morgan prepared to enter it with the victorious vanguard; first stationing Captain Dearborn and some provincials at Palace Gate, which opened down into the defile from the upper town. By this time, however, the death of Montgomery and retreat of Campbell had enabled the enemy to turn all their attention in this direction. A large detachment sent by General Carleton, sallied out of Palace Gate after Morgan had passed it, surprised and captured Dearborn and the guard, and completely cut off the advanced party. The main body, informed of the death of Montgomery, and giving up the game as lost, retreated to the camp, leaving behind the field-piece which Lamb's company had abandoned, and the mortars in the battery of St. Roque. Morgan and his men were now hemmed in on all sides, and obliged to take refuge in a stone house from the inveterate fire which assailed them. From the windows of this house they kept up a desperate defence, until cannon were brought to bear upon it. Then, hearing of the death of Montgomery, and seeing that there was no prospect of relief, Morgan and his gallant handful of followers were compelled to surrender themselves prisoners of war.

Thus foiled at every point, the wrecks of the little army abandoned their camp, and retreated about three miles from the town; where they hastily fortified themselves, apprehending a pursuit by the garrison. General Carleton, however, contented himself with having secured the safety of the place, and remained cautiously passive until he should be properly reinforced.

The remains of the gallant Montgomery received a soldier's grave within the fortifications of Quebec, by the care of Cramahé, the lieutenant-governor, who had formerly known him.

Arnold took temporary command of the shattered army, until General Wooster should arrive from Montreal, to whom he sent an express, urging him to bring on succor. "On this occasion," says a contemporary writer, "he discovered the utmost vigor of a determined mind, and a genius full of resources. Defeated and wounded as he was, he put his troops into such a situation as to keep them still formidable." With a mere handful of men, at one time not exceeding five hundred, he maintained a blockade of the strong fortress from which he had just been repulsed.

General Schuyler, who was now in Albany, urged the necessity of an immediate reinforcement of three thousand men for the army in Canada. Washington had not a man to spare from the army before Boston. He applied, therefore, on his own responsibility, to Massachusetts, New Hampshire and Connecticut, for three regiments which were granted. His prompt measure received the approbation of Congress, and further reinforcements were ordered from the same quarters.

Solicitude was awakened about the interior of the province of New York. Arms and ammunition were said to be concealed in Tryon County, and numbers of the tories in that neighborhood preparing for hostilities. Sir John Johnson had fortified Johnson Hall, gathered about him his Scotch Highland tenants and Indian allies, and it was rumored he intended to carry fire and sword along the valley of the Mohawk.

Schuyler, in consequence, received orders from Congress to take measures for securing the military stores, disarming the disaffected, and apprehending their chiefs. He forthwith hastened from Albany, at the head of a body of soldiers; was joined by Colonel Herkimer, with the militia of Tryon County marshalled forth on the frozen bosom of the Mohawk River, and appeared before Sir John's stronghold, near Johnstown, on the 19th of January. Thus beleaguered, Sir John, after much negotiation, capitulated. He was to surrender all weapons of war and military stores in his possession, and to give his parole not to take arms against America.

The recent reverses in Canada had heightened the solicitude of Washington about the province of New York. That province was the central and all-important link in the confederacy; but he feared it might prove a brittle one. We have already mentioned the adverse influences in operation there. A large number of friends to the crown, among the official and commercial classes; rank tories, (as they were called,) in the city and about the neighboring country; particularly on Long and Staten Islands; king's ships at anchor in the bay and harbor, keeping up a suspicious intercourse with the citizens; while Governor Tryon, castled, as it were, on board one of these ships, carried on intrigues with those disaffected to the popular cause, in all parts of the neighborhood.

Lee arrived at New York on the 4th of February, his caustic humors sharpened by a severe attack of the gout, which had rendered it necessary, while on the march, to carry him for a considerable part of the way in a litter. By a singular coincidence, on the very day of his arrival, Sir Henry Clinton, with the squadron which had sailed so mysteriously from Boston, looked into the harbor. "Though it was Sabbath," says a letter-writer of the day, "it threw the whole city into such a convulsion as it never knew before. Many of the inhabitants hastened to move their effects into the country, expecting an immediate conflict."

Clinton sent for the mayor, and expressed much surprise and concern at the distress caused by his arrival; which was merely, he said, on a short visit to his friend Tryon, and to see how matters stood. He professed a juvenile love for the place, and desired that the inhabitants might be informed of the purport of his visit, and that he would go away as soon as possible. For this time, the inhabitants of New York were let off for their fears. Clinton, after a brief visit, continued his mysterious cruise, openly avowing his destination to be North Carolina—which nobody believed, simply because he avowed it.

The necessity of conferring with committees at every step was a hard restraint upon a man of Lee's ardent and impatient temper, who had a soldierlike contempt for the men of peace around him; yet at the outset he bore it better than might have been expected. "The Congress committees, a certain number of the committees of safety, and your humble servant," writes he to Washington, "have had two conferences. The result is such as will agreeably surprise you. It is in the first place agreed, and justly, that to fortify the town against shipping is impracticable; but we are to fortify lodgements on some commanding part of the city for two thousand men. We are to erect enclosed batteries on both sides of the water, near Hell Gate, which will answer the double purpose of securing the town against piracies through the Sound, and secure our communication with Long Island, now become a more important point than ever; as it is determined to form a strong fortified camp of three thousand men, on the Island, immediately opposite to New York. The pass in the Highlands is to be made as respectable as possible, and guarded by a battalion. In short, I think the plan judicious and complete."

The pass in the Highlands above alluded to, is that grand defile of the Hudson where, for upwards of fifteen miles, it wends its deep channel between stern, forest-clad mountains and rocky promontories. Two forts, about six miles distant from each other, and commanding narrow parts of the river at its bends through these Highlands, had been commenced in the preceding autumn, by order of the Continental Congress; but they were said to be insufficient for the security of that important pass, and were to be extended and strengthened.

Washington had charged Lee, in his instructions, to keep a stern eye upon the tories, who were active in New York. "You can seize upon the persons of the principals," said he; "they must be so notoriously known, that there will be little danger of committing mistakes." Lee acted up to the letter of these instructions, and weeded out with a vigorous hand some of the rankest of the growth.

In the exercise of his military functions, Lee set Governor Tryon and the captain of the Asia at defiance. "They had threatened perdition to the town," writes he to Washington, "if the cannon were removed from the batteries and wharves, but I ever considered their threats as a *brutum fulmen,* and even persuaded the town to be of the same way of thinking. We accordingly conveyed them to a place of safety in the middle of the day, and no cannonade ensued."

Lee now proceeded with his plan of defences. A strong redoubt, capable of holding three hundred men, was commenced at Horen's Hook, commanding the pass at Hell Gate, so as to block up from the enemy's ships the passage between the mainland and Long Island. A regiment was stationed on the island, making fascines, and preparing other materials for constructing the works for an intrenched camp, which Lee hoped would render it impossible for the enemy to get a footing there. "What to do with this city," writes he, "I own, puzzles me. It is so encircled with deep navigable water, that whoever commands the sea must command the town. To-morrow I shall begin to dismantle that part of the fort next to the town, to prevent its being converted into a citadel. I shall barrier the principal streets, and, at least, if I cannot make it a continental garrison, it shall be a disputable field of battle." Batteries were to be erected on an eminence behind Trinity Church, to keep the enemy's ships at so great a distance as not to injure the town.

King's Bridge, at the upper end of Manhattan or New York Island, linking it with the mainland, was pronounced by Lee "a most important pass, without which the city could have no communication with Connecticut." It was, therefore, to be made as strong as possible. Heavy cannon were to be sent up to the forts in the Highlands; which were to be enlarged and strengthened.

In the midst of his schemes, Lee received orders from Congress to the command in Canada, vacant by the death of Montgomery. He bewailed the defenceless condition of the city; the Continental Congress, as he said, not having, as yet, taken the least step for its security. "The instant I leave it," said he, "I conclude the Provincial Congress, and inhabitants in general, will relapse into their former hysterics. The men-of-war and Mr. Tryon will return to their old station at the wharves, and the first regiments who arrive from England will take quiet possession of the town and Long Island."

CHAPTER XXVII.

MOVEMENTS BEFORE BOSTON.—ITS EVACUA-TION.

The siege of Boston continued through the winter without any striking incident to enliven its monotony. The British remained within their works, leaving the beleaguering army slowly to augment its forces. The country was dissatisfied with the inaction of the latter. Even Congress was anxious for some successful blow that might revive popular enthusiasm. Washington shared this anxiety, and had repeatedly, in councils of war, suggested an attack upon the town, but had found a majority of his general officers opposed to it. He had hoped some favorable opportunity would present itself, when, the harbor being frozen, the troops might approach the town upon the ice. The winter, however, though severe at first, proved a mild one, and the bay continued open. General Putnam, in the meantime, having completed the new works at Lechmere Point, and being desirous of keeping up the spirit of his men, resolved to treat them to an exploit. Accordingly, from his "impregnable fortress" of Cobble Hill, he detached a party of about two hundred, under his favorite officer, Major Knowlton, to surprise and capture a British guard stationed at Charlestown. It was a daring enterprise, and executed with spirit. As Charlestown Neck was completely protected, Knowlton led his men across the mill-dam, round the base of the hill, and immediately below the fort; set fire to the guard-house and some buildings in its vicinity; made several prisoners, and retired without loss; although thundered upon by the cannon of the fort.

Meanwhile, Washington was incessantly goaded by the impatient murmurs of the public, as we may judge by his letters to Mr. Reed. "I know the integrity of my own heart," writes he, on the 10th of February, "but to declare it, unless to a friend, may be an argument of vanity. I know the unhappy predicament I stand in; I know that much is expected of me; I know that, without men, without arms, without ammunition, without anything fit for the accommodation of a soldier, little is to be done; and, what is mortifying, I know that I cannot stand justified to the world without exposing my own weakness, and injuring the cause, by declaring my wants; which I am determined not to do, further than unavoidable necessity brings every man acquainted with them."

He still adhered to his opinion in favor of an attempt upon the town. He was aware that it would be attended with considerable loss, but believed it would be successful if the men should behave well. Within a few days after the date of this letter, the bay became sufficiently frozen for the transportation of troops. "This," writes he to Reed, "I thought, knowing the ice would not last, a favorable opportunity to make an assault upon the troops in town. I proposed it in council; but behold, though we had been waiting all the year for this favorable event, the enterprise was thought too dangerous."

At length the camp was rejoiced by the arrival of Colonel Knox, with his long train of sledges drawn by oxen, bringing more than fifty cannon, mortars, howitzers, beside supplies of lead and flints. The zeal and perseverance which he had displayed in his wintry expedition across frozen lakes and snowy wastes, and the intelligence with which he had fulfilled his instructions, won him the entire confidence of Washington. His conduct in this enterprise was but an earnest of that energy and ability which he displayed throughout the war.

Further ammunition being received from the royal arsenal at New York, and other quarters, and a reinforcement of ten regiments of militia, Washington no longer met with opposition to his warlike measures. Lechmere Point, which Putnam had fortified, was immediately to be supplied with mortars and heavy cannon, so as to command Boston on the north; and Dorchester Heights, on the south of the town, were forthwith to be taken possession of. Their possession would enable him to push his works to Nook's Hill, and other points opposite Boston, whence a cannonade and bombardment must drive the enemy from the city.

The council of Massachusetts, at his request, ordered the militia of the towns contiguous to Dorchester and Roxbury to hold themselves in readiness to repair to the lines at those places with arms, ammunition and accoutrements, on receiving a preconcerted signal.

Washington felt painfully aware how much depended upon the success of this attempt. There was a cloud of gloom and distrust lowering upon the public mind. Danger threatened on the north and on the south. Montgomery had fallen before the walls of Quebec. The army in Canada was shattered. Tryon and the tories were plotting mischief in New York. Dunmore was harassing the lower part of Virginia, and Clinton and his fleet were prowling along the coast on a secret errand of mischief.

In the general plan it was concerted that, should the enemy detach a large force to dislodge our men from Dorchester Heights, as had been done in the affair of Bunker's Hill, an attack upon the opposite side of the town should forthwith be made by General Putnam. For this purpose he was to have four thousand picked men in readiness, in two divisions, under Generals Sullivan and Greene. At a concerted signal from Roxbury, they were to embark in boats near the mouth of Charles River, cross under cover of the fire of three floating batteries, land in two places in Boston, secure its strong posts, force the gates and works at the Neck, and let in the Roxbury troops.

The evening of Monday, the 4th of March, was fixed upon for the occupation of Dorchester Heights. The ground was frozen too hard to be easily intrenched; fascines, therefore, and gabions, and bundles of screwed hay, were collected during the two preceding nights, with which to form breastworks and redoubts. During these two busy nights the enemy's batteries were cannonaded and bombarded from opposite points, to occupy their attention, and prevent their noticing these preparations. They replied with spirit, and the incessant roar of artillery thus kept up, covered completely the rumbling of wagons and ordnance.

As soon as the firing commenced, the detachment under General Thomas set out on its cautious and secret march from the lines of Roxbury and Dorchester. Everything was conducted as regularly and quietly as possible. A covering party of eight hundred men preceded the carts with the intrenching tools; then came General Thomas with the working party, twelve hundred strong, followed by a train of three hundred wagons, laden with fascines, gabions, and hay screwed into bundles of seven or eight hundred weight. A great number of such bundles were ranged in a line along Dorchester Neck on the side next the enemy, to protect the troops, while passing, from being raked by the fire of the enemy. Fortunately, although the moon, as Washington writes, was shining in its full lustre, the flash and roar of cannonry from opposite points, and the bursting of bombshells high in the air, so engaged and diverted the attention of the enemy, that the detachment reached the heights about eight o'clock without being heard or perceived. The covering party then divided; one half proceeded to the point nearest Boston, the other to the one nearest to Castle Williams. The working party commenced to fortify, under the directions of Gridley, the veteran engineer, who had planned the works on Bunker's Hill. It was severe labor, for the earth was frozen eighteen inches deep; but the men worked with more than their usual spirit; for the eye of the commander-in-chief was upon them. Though not called there by his duties, Washington could not be absent from this eventful operation.

The labors of the night were carried on with activity and address. When a relief party arrived at four o'clock in the morning, two forts were in sufficient forwardness to furnish protection against small-arms and grape-shot; and such use was made of the fascines and bundles of screwed hay, that, at dawn, a formidable-looking fortress frowned along the height. Howe gazed at the mushroom fortress with astonishment, as it loomed indistinctly, but grandly, through a morning fog. "The rebels," exclaimed he, "have done more work in one night than my whole army would have done in one month."

Washington had watched with intense anxiety the effect of the revelation at daybreak. An American, who was on Dorchester Heights, gives a picture of the scene. A tremendous cannonade was commenced from the forts in Boston and the shipping in the harbor. "Cannon shot," writes he, "are continually rolling and rebounding over the hill, and it is astonishing to observe how little our soldiers are terrified by them. The royal troops are perceived to be in motion, as if embarking to pass the harbor and land on Dorchester shore, to attack our works. The hills and elevations in this vicinity are covered with spectators, to witness deeds of horror in the expected conflict."

General Thomas was reinforced with two thousand men. Old Putnam stood ready to make a descent upon the north side of the town, with his four thousand picked men, as soon as the heights on the south should be assailed. As Washington rode about the heights, he reminded the troops that it was the 5th of March, the anniversary of the Boston massacre, and called on them to revenge the slaughter of their brethren. They answered him with shouts.

Howe, in the meantime, was perplexed between his pride and the hazards of his position. In his letters to the ministry, he had scouted the idea of "being in danger from the rebels." He had "hoped they would attack him." Apparently, they were about to fulfil his hopes, and with formidable advantages of position. He must dislodge them from Dorchester Heights, or evacuate Boston. The latter was an alternative too mortifying to be readily adopted. He resolved on an attack, but it was to be a night one.

In the evening the British began to move. Lord Percy was to lead the attack. Twenty-five hundred men were embarked in transports, which were to convey them to the rendezvous at Castle William. A violent storm set in from the east. The transports could not reach their place of destination. The men-of-war could not cover and support them. A furious surf beat on the shore where the boats would have to land. The attack was consequently postponed until the following day. That day was equally unpropitious. The storm continued, with torrents of rain. The attack was again postponed. In the meantime, the Americans went on strengthening their works; by the time the storm subsided, General Howe deemed them too strong to be easily carried; the attempt, therefore, was relinquished altogether.

What was to be done? The shells thrown from the heights into the town proved that it was no longer tenable. The fleet was equally exposed. Admiral Shuldham, the successor to Graves, assured Howe that if the Americans maintained possession of the heights, his ships could not remain in the harbor. It was determined, therefore, in a council of war, to evacuate the place as soon as possible. But now came on a humiliating perplexity. The troops, in embarking, would be exposed to a destructive fire. How was this to be prevented? General Howe's pride would not suffer him to make capitulations; he endeavored to work on the fears of the Bostonians, by hinting that if his troops were molested while embarking, he might be obliged to cover their retreat by setting fire to the town.

The hint had its effect. Several of the principal inhabitants communicated with him through the medium of General Robertson. The result of the negotiation was that a paper was concocted and signed by several of the "select men" of Boston, stating the fears they had entertained of the destruction of the place, but that those fears had been quieted by General Howe's declaration that it should remain uninjured, provided his troops were unmolested while embarking; the select men, therefore, begged "some assurance that so dreadful a calamity might not be brought on, by any measures from without."

This paper was sent out from Boston, on the evening of the 8th, with a flag of truce, which bore it to the American lines at Roxbury. There it was received by Colonel Learned, and carried by him to head-quarters. Washington consulted with such of the general officers as he could immediately assemble. The paper was not addressed to him, nor to any one else. It was not authenticated by the signature of General Howe; nor was there any other act obliging that commander to fulfil the promise asserted to have been made by him. It was deemed proper, therefore, that Washington should give no answer to the paper; but that Colonel Learned should signify in a letter his having laid it before the commander-in-chief, and the reasons assigned for not answering it. With this uncompromising letter, the flag returned to Boston. The Americans suspended their fire, but continued to fortify their positions.

Daily preparations were now made by the enemy for departure. By proclamation, the inhabitants were ordered to deliver up all linen and woollen goods, and all other goods that, in possession of the rebels, would aid them in carrying on the war. For some days the embarkation of the troops was delayed by adverse winds. Washington, who was imperfectly informed of affairs in Boston, feared that the movements there might be a feint. Determined to bring things to a crisis, he detached a force to Nook's Hill on Saturday, the 16th, which threw up a breastwork in the night regardless of the cannonading of the enemy. This commanded Boston Neck, and the south part of the town, and a deserter brought a false report to the British that a general assault was intended. The embarkation, so long delayed, began with hurry and confusion at four o'clock in the morning. The harbor of Boston soon presented a striking and tumultuous scene. There were seventy-eight ships and transports casting loose for sea, and eleven or twelve thousand men, soldiers, sailors, and refugees, hurrying to embark; many, especially of the latter, with their families and personal effects. The refugees, in fact, labored under greater disadvantages than the king's troops, being obliged to man their own vessels, as sufficient seamen could not be spared from the king's transports.

While this tumultuous embarkation was going on, the Americans looked on in silence from their batteries on Dorchester Heights, without firing a shot. At an early hour of the morning, the troops stationed at Cambridge and Roxbury had paraded, and several regiments under Putnam had embarked in boats, and dropped down Charles River, to Sewall's Point, to watch the movements of the enemy by land and water. About nine o'clock a large body of troops was seen marching down Bunker's Hill, while boats full of soldiers were putting off for the shipping. Two scouts were sent from the camp to reconnoitre. The works appeared still to be occupied, for sentries were posted about them with shouldered muskets. Observing them to be motionless, the scouts made nearer scrutiny, and discovered them to be mere effigies, set up to delay the advance of the Americans. Pushing on, they found the works deserted, and gave signal of the fact; whereupon, a detachment was sent from the camp to take possession.

Part of Putnam's troops were now sent back to Cambridge; a part were ordered forward to occupy Boston. General Ward, too, with five hundred men, made his way from Roxbury, across the neck, about which the enemy had scattered caltrops or crows' feet,[7] to impede invasion. The gates were unbarred and thrown open, and the Americans entered in triumph, with drums beating and colors flying.

By ten o'clock the enemy were all embarked and under way: Putnam had taken command of the city, and occupied the important points, and the flag of thirteen stripes, the standard of the Union, floated above all the forts. On the following day, Washington himself entered the town where he was joyfully welcomed.

---

[7] Iron balls, with four sharp points, to wound the feet of men or horses.

The eminent services of Washington throughout this arduous siege, his admirable management, by which, "in the course of a few months, *an undisciplined band of husbandmen* became soldiers, and were enabled to invest, for nearly a year, and finally to expel a brave army of veterans, commanded by the most experienced generals," drew forth the enthusiastic applause of the nation. On motion of John Adams, who had first moved his nomination as commander-in-chief, a unanimous vote of thanks to him was passed in Congress; and it was ordered that a gold medal be struck, commemorating the evacuation of Boston, bearing the effigy of Washington as its deliverer.

The British fleet bearing the army from Boston, had disappeared from the coast. "Whither they are bound, and where they next will pitch their tents," writes Washington, "I know not." He conjectured their destination to be New York, and made his arrangements accordingly; but he was mistaken. General Howe had steered for Halifax, there to await the arrival of strong reinforcements from England, and the fleet of his brother, Admiral Lord Howe; who was to be commander-in-chief of the naval forces on the North American station.

It was presumed the enemy, in the ensuing campaign, would direct their operations against the Middle and Southern colonies. Congress divided the colonies into two departments; one, comprehending New York, New Jersey, Pennsylvania, Delaware and Maryland, was to be under the command of a major-general, and two brigadier-generals; the other, comprising Virginia, the Carolinas and Georgia, to be under the command of a major-general and four brigadiers. In this new arrangement, the orders destining General Lee to Canada were superseded, and he was appointed to the command of the Southern department, where he was to keep watch upon the movements of Sir Henry Clinton. The command in Canada was given to General Thomas, who had distinguished himself at Roxbury and was promoted to the rank of major-general. It would have been given to Schuyler, but for the infirm state of his health; still Congress expressed a reliance on his efforts to complete the work "so conspicuously begun and well conducted" under his orders, in the last campaign; and, as not merely the success but the very existence of the army in Canada would depend on supplies sent from these colonies across the lakes, he was required, until further orders, to fix his head-quarters at Albany, where, without being exposed to the fatigue of the camp until his health was perfectly restored, he would be in a situation to forward supplies; to superintend the operations necessary for the defence of New York and the Hudson River, and the affairs of the whole middle department.

Lee set out for the South on the 7th of March, carrying with him his bold spirit, his shrewd sagacity, and his whimsical and splenetic humors. Brigadier-general Lord Stirling remained in temporary command at New York. Washington, presuming that the British fleet had steered for that port with the force which had evacuated Boston, hastened detachments thither under Generals Heath and Sullivan, and wrote for three thousand additional men to be furnished by Connecticut. The command of the whole he gave to General Putnam, who was ordered to fortify the city and the passes of the Hudson according to the plans of General Lee. In the meantime, Washington delayed to come on himself, until he should have pushed forward the main body of his army by divisions.

Lee's anticipations that laxity and confusion would prevail after his departure, were not realized. The veteran Putnam, on taking command, put the city under rigorous military rule. All communication between the "ministerial fleet" and shore was stopped; the ships were no longer to be furnished with provisions. Any person taken in the act of holding communication with them would be considered an enemy, and treated accordingly.

Washington came on by the way of Providence, Norwich and New London, expediting the embarkation of troops from these posts, and arrived at New York on the 13th of April. Many of the works which Lee had commenced were by this time finished; others were in progress. It was apprehended the principal operations of the enemy would be on Long Island, the high grounds of which, in the neighborhood of Brooklyn, commanded the city. Washington saw that an able and efficient officer was needed at that place. Greene was accordingly stationed there, with a division of the army. He immediately proceeded to complete the fortifications of that important post, and to make himself acquainted with the topography and the defensive points of the surrounding country.

The aggregate force distributed at several extensive posts in New York and its environs, and on Long Island, Staten Island and elsewhere, amounted to little more than ten thousand men; some of those were on the sick list, others absent on command, or on furlough; there were but about eight thousand available and fit for duty. These, too, were without pay; those recently enlisted without arms, and no one could say where arms were to be procured. Washington saw the inadequacy of the force to the purposes required and was full of solicitude about the security of a place, the central point of the Confederacy, and the grand deposit of ordnance and military stores. The process of fortifying the place had induced the ships of war to fall down into the outer bay, within the Hook, upwards of twenty miles from the city; but Governor Tryon was still on board of one of them, keeping up an active correspondence with the tories on Staten and Long Islands, and in other parts of the neighborhood.

In addition to his cares about the security of New York, Washington had to provide for the perilous exigencies of the army in Canada. Since his arrival in the city, four regiments of troops, a company of riflemen and another of artificers had been detached under the command of Brigadier-general Thompson, and a further corps of six regiments under Brigadier-general Sullivan, with orders to join General Thomas as soon as possible.

Still Congress inquired of him whether further reinforcements to the army in Canada would not be necessary, and whether they could be spared from the army in New York. His reply shows the peculiar perplexities of his situation and the tormenting uncertainty in which he was kept, as to where the next storm of war would break. "With respect to sending more troops to that country, I am really at a loss what to advise, as it is impossible, at present, to know the designs of the enemy. Should they send the whole force under General Howe up the river St. Lawrence, to relieve Quebec and recover Canada, the troops gone and now going will be insufficient to stop their progress; and, should they think proper to send that, or an equal force, this way from Great Britain, for the purpose of possessing this city and securing the navigation of Hudson's River, the troops left here will not be sufficient to oppose them; and yet, for anything we know, I think it not improbable they may attempt both; both being of the greatest importance to them, if they have men. I could wish, indeed, that the army in Canada should be more powerfully reinforced; at the same time, I am conscious that the trusting of this important post, which is now become the grand magazine of America, to the handful of men remaining here, is running too great a risk."

Washington at that time was not aware of the extraordinary expedients England had recently resorted to against the next campaign. The Duke of Brunswick, the Landgrave of Hesse Cassel, and the Hereditary Prince of Cassel, Count of Hanau, had been subsidized to furnish troops to assist in the subjugation of her colonies. Four thousand three hundred Brunswick troops, and nearly thirteen thousand Hessians, had entered the British service. Beside the subsidy exacted by the German princes, they were to be paid seven pounds four shillings and four pence sterling for every soldier furnished by them, and as much more for every one slain.

CHAPTER XXVIII.

REVERSES IN CANADA.—THE HIGHLANDS.— CLOSE OF THE INVASION OF CANADA.

We left Arnold before the walls of Quebec, wounded, crippled, almost disabled, yet not disheartened, blockading that "proud town" with a force inferior, by half, in number to that of the garrison. For his gallant services, Congress promoted him in January to the rank of brigadier-general. Throughout the winter he kept up the blockade with his shattered army; though had Carleton ventured upon a sortie, he might have been forced to decamp.

Arnold had difficulties of all kinds to contend with. His military chest was exhausted; his troops were in want of necessaries; sickness thinned his ranks. At one time, his force was reduced to five hundred men, and for two months, with all his recruitments of raw militia, did not exceed seven hundred. The failure of the attack on Quebec had weakened the cause among the Canadians; the peasantry had been displeased by the conduct of the American troops; they had once welcomed them as deliverers; they now began to regard them as intruders.

Notwithstanding all these discouragements, Arnold still kept up a bold face: cut off supplies occasionally, and harassed the place with alarms. Having repaired his batteries, he opened a fire upon the town, but with little effect; the best part of the artillerists, with Lamb, their capable commander, were prisoners within the walls. On the 1st day of April, General Wooster arrived from Montreal, with reinforcements, and took the command. The day after his arrival, Arnold, by the falling of his horse, again received an injury on the leg recently wounded, and was disabled for upwards of a week. Considering himself slighted by General Wooster, who did not consult him in military affairs, he obtained leave of absence until he should be recovered from his lameness, and repaired to Montreal, where he took command.

General Thomas arrived at the camp in the course of April, and found the army in a forlorn condition, scattered at different posts, and on the island of Orleans. It was numerically increased to upwards of two thousand men, but several hundred were unfit for service. The small-pox had made great ravages. They had inoculated each other. In their sick and debilitated state they were without barracks, and almost without medicine. A portion, whose term of enlistment had expired, refused to do duty, and clamored for their discharge. The winter was over, the river was breaking up, reinforcements to the garrison might immediately be expected, and then the case would be desperate. Observing that the river about Quebec was clear of ice, General Thomas determined on a bold effort. It was to send up a fire-ship with the flood, and, while the ships in the harbor were in flames, and the town in confusion, to scale the walls.

Accordingly, on the 3d of May the troops turned out with scaling ladders; the fire-ship came up the river under easy sail, and arrived near the shipping before it was discovered. It was fired into. The crew applied a slow match to the train and pulled off. The ship was soon in a blaze, but the flames caught and consumed the sails; her way was checked, and she drifted off harmlessly with the ebbing tide. The rest of the plan was, of course, abandoned.

Nothing now remained but to retreat before the enemy should be reinforced. Preparations were made in all haste to embark the sick and the military stores. While this was taking place, five ships made their way into the harbor, on the 6th of May, and began to land troops. Thus reinforced, General Carleton sallied forth with eight hundred or a thousand men. The Americans were in no condition to withstand the attack. They had no intrenchments, and could not muster three hundred men at any point. A precipitate retreat was the consequence, in which baggage, artillery, everything was abandoned. Even the sick were left behind; many of whom crawled away from the camp hospitals, and took refuge in the woods, or among the Canadian peasantry.

General Thomas came to a halt at point Deschambault, about sixty miles above Quebec, and called a council of war to consider what was to be done. The enemy's ships were hastening up the St. Lawrence; some were already but two or three leagues distant. The camp was without cannon; powder, forwarded by General Schuyler, had fallen into the enemy's hands; there were not provisions enough to subsist the army for more than two or three days; the men-of-war, too, might run up the river, intercept all their resources, and reduce them to the same extremity they had experienced before Quebec. It was resolved, therefore, to ascend the river still further. General Thomas, however, determined to send forward the invalids, but to remain at Point Deschambault, with about five hundred men, until he should receive orders from Montreal and learn whether such supplies could be forwarded immediately as would enable him to defend his position.

The despatches of General Thomas, setting forth the disastrous state of affairs, had a disheartening effect on Schuyler, who feared the army would be obliged to abandon Canada. Washington, on the contrary, spoke cheeringly on the subject. He regretted that the troops had not been able to make a stand at Point Deschambault, but hoped they would maintain a post as far down the river as possible.

[The reverses in Canada, which spread consternation through the New England frontier, now laid open to invasion, strengthened the ill-will and prejudice that prevailed in the Eastern States against General Schuyler. He was stigmatized as the cause of the late reverses, and was even accused of being untrue to his country. Committees, which the alarming state of affairs had caused to be organized in various counties, addressed Washington on the subject, which, reviling Schuyler, he at once demanded a court of inquiry. It is proper to add that the committees in question, after investigating the evidence, acknowledged to Washington that their suspicions had been wholly groundless.]

As the reverses in Canada would affect the fortunes of the Revolution elsewhere, Washington sent General Gates to lay the despatches concerning them before Congress. Scarce had Gates departed on his mission (May 19th), when Washington himself received a summons to Philadelphia, to advise with Congress concerning the opening campaign. He was informed also that Gates, on the 16th of May, had been promoted to the rank of major-general, and Mifflen to that of brigadier-general, and a wish was intimated that they might take the command of Boston.

Washington prepared to proceed to Philadelphia. In his parting instructions to Putnam, who, as the oldest major-general in the city, would have the command during his absence, Washington informed him of the intention of the Provincial Congress of New York to seize the principal tories and disaffected persons in the city and the surrounding country, especially on Long Island, and authorized him to afford military aid, if required, to carry the same into execution. He was also to send Lord Stirling, Colonel Putnam the engineer, and Colonel Knox, if he could be spared, up to the Highlands, to examine the state of the forts and garrisons, and report what was necessary to put them in a posture of defence.

The general, accompanied by Mrs. Washington, departed from New York on the 21st of May, and they were invited by Mr. Hancock, the President of Congress, to be his guests during their sojourn at Philadelphia.

Washington, in his conferences with Congress, roundly expressed his conviction that no accommodation could be effected with Great Britain on acceptable terms. Ministerialists had declared in Parliament that, the sword being drawn, the most coercive measures would be persevered in until there was complete submission. The recent subsidizing of foreign troops was a part of this policy, and indicated unsparing hostility. A protracted war, therefore, was inevitable; but it would be impossible to carry it on successfully with the scanty force actually embodied, and with transient enlistments of militia.

In consequence of his representations, resolutions were passed in Congress that soldiers should be enlisted for three years, with a bounty of ten dollars for each recruit; that the army at New York should be reinforced until the 1st of December with thirteen thousand eight hundred militia; that gondolas and fire-rafts should be built to prevent the men-of-war and enemy's ships from coming into New York Bay, or the Narrows; and that a flying camp of ten thousand militia, furnished by Pennsylvania, Delaware and Maryland, and likewise engaged until the 1st of December, should be stationed in the Jerseys for the defence of the Middle colonies. Washington was, moreover, empowered, in case of emergency, to call on the neighboring colonies for temporary aid with their militia.

Another important result of his conferences with Congress was the establishment of a war office. Military affairs had hitherto been referred in Congress to committees casually appointed, and had consequently been subject to great irregularity and neglect. Henceforth a permanent committee, entitled the Board of War and Ordnance, was to take cognizance of them. The first board was composed of five members—John Adams, Colonel Benjamin Harrison, Roger Sherman, James Wilson, and Edward Rutledge; with Richard Peters as secretary. It went into operation on the 12th of June.

While at Philadelphia, Washington had frequent consultations with George Clinton, one of the delegates from New York, concerning the interior defences of that province, especially those connected with the security of the Highlands of the Hudson, where part of the regiment of Colonel James Clinton, the brother of the delegate, was stationed. He was gratified, also, by procuring the appointment of his late secretary, Joseph Reed, to the post of adjutant-general, vacated by the promotion of General Gates, thus placing him once more by his side.

[Despatches from Canada continued to be disastrous. A post stationed at the Cedars, forty miles above Montreal consisting of about four hundred men, had been intimidated into a surrender by a body of Canadians and Indians. A force of one hundred men, sent to the relief of the post, was also captured. The enemy was pursued by Arnold, and overtaken near St. Anns, above the rapids of the St. Lawrence. The prisoners captured at the Cedars were threatened with massacre if Arnold should attack; and this led to negotiations which resulted in their exchange. While these events were occurring mischief was brewing in another quarter.

Colonel Guy Johnson, with Brant and the Butlers, had been holding councils with the Indians, and were threatening a maraud on the Mohawk country. A correspondence was carried on between Guy Johnson and his cousin, Sir John Johnson, who was said to be preparing to co-operate with his Scotch dependents. Schuyler considered this a breach of Sir John's parole, and sent Colonel Dayton to apprehend him. Sir John, with a number of his tenants, retreated for refuge among the Indians. Shortly after this came intelligence that Sir John, with his Scotch warriors and Indian allies, was actually coming down the valley of the Mohawk, bent on revenge, and prepared to lay everything to waste. Schuyler immediately collected a force at Albany to oppose him; letters from Washington directed Schuyler to detach Colonel Dayton with his regiment on that service, with instructions for him to secure a post upon the old site of Fort Stanwix. Washington also authorized Schuyler to hold a conference with the Six Nations, and secure their active services, without waiting further directions from Congress—that body having recently resolved to employ Indian allies.]

Lord Stirling, who, by Washington's orders, had visited and inspected the defences in the Highlands, rendered a report of their condition, of which we give the purport. Fort Montgomery, at the lower part of the Highlands, was on the west bank of the river, north of Dunderberg (or Thunder Hill). It was situated on a bank one hundred feet high. The river at that place was about half a mile wide. Opposite the fort was the promontory of Anthony's Nose, many hundred feet high, accessible only to goats, or men expert in climbing. A body of riflemen stationed here might command the decks of vessels. Fort Montgomery appeared to Lord Stirling the proper place for a guard post. Fort Constitution was about six miles higher up the river, on a rocky island of the same name, at a narrow strait where the Hudson, shouldered by precipices, makes a sudden bend round West Point. A redoubt, in the opinion of Lord Stirling, would be needed on the point, not only for the preservation of Fort Constitution, but for its own importance.

The garrison of that fort consisted of two companies of Colonel James Clinton's regiment, and Captain Wisner's company of minute men, in all one hundred and sixty rank and file. Fort Montgomery was garrisoned by three companies of the same regiment, about two hundred rank and file. Both garrisons were miserably armed. The direction of the works of both forts was in the hands of commissioners appointed by the Provincial Congress of New York. The general command of the posts required to be adjusted.

In view of all these circumstances, Washington, on the 14th of June, ordered Colonel James Clinton to take command of both posts, and of all the troops stationed at them. He seemed a fit custodian for them, having been a soldier from his youth; brought up on a frontier subject to Indian alarms and incursions, and acquainted with the strong points and fastnesses of the Highlands.

King's Bridge, and the heights adjacent, considered by General Lee of the utmost importance to the communication between New York and the mainland, and to the security of the Hudson, were reconnoitred by Washington on horseback, about the middle of the month; ordering where works should be laid out. Breastworks were to be thrown up for the defence of the bridge, and an advanced work (subsequently called Fort Independence) was to be built beyond it, on a hill commanding Spyt den Duivel Creek, as that inlet of the Hudson is called, which links it with the Harlem River. A strong work, intended as a kind of citadel, was to crown a rocky height between two and three miles south of the bridge, commanding the channel of the Hudson, and below it were to be redoubts on the banks of the river at Jeffrey's Point. In honor of the general, the citadel received the name of Fort Washington. While these preparations were made for the protection of the Hudson, the works about Brooklyn on Long Island were carried on with great activity, under the superintendence of General Greene. In a word, the utmost exertions were made at every point, to put the city, its environs, and the Hudson River, in a state of defence, before the arrival of another hostile armament.

Operations in Canada were now drawing to a disastrous close. General Thomas, finding it impossible to make a stand at Point Deschambault, had continued his retreat to the mouth of the Sorel, where he found General Thompson with part of the troops detached by Washington, from New York, who were making some preparations for defence. Shortly after his arrival, he was taken ill with the smallpox, and removed to Chamblee. He had prohibited inoculation among his troops, because it put too many of their scanty number on the sick list; he probably fell a victim to his own prohibition, as he died of that malady on the 2d of June.

On his death, General Sullivan, who had recently arrived with the main detachment of troops from New York, succeeded to the command; General Wooster having been recalled. He advanced immediately with his brigade to the mouth of the Sorel, where he found General Thompson with but very few troops to defend that post, having detached Colonel St. Clair, with six or seven hundred men, to Three Rivers, about fifty miles down the St. Lawrence, to give check to an advanced corps of the enemy of about eight hundred regulars and Canadians, under the veteran Scot, Colonel Maclean. Sullivan proceeded forthwith to complete the works on the Sorel; in the meantime he detached General Thompson with additional troops to overtake St. Clair and assume command of the whole party, which would then amount to two thousand men. He was by no means to attack the encampment at Three Rivers, unless there was great prospect of success, as his defeat might prove the total loss of Canada.

Sullivan was aiming at the command in Canada; and Washington soberly weighed his merits for the appointment, in a letter to the President of Congress. "He is active, spirited, and zealously attached to the cause. He has his wants and he has his foibles…. He wants experience to move upon a grand scale; for the limited and contracted knowledge, which any of us have in military matters, stands in very little stead." Scarce had Washington despatched this letter, when he received one from the President of Congress, dated the 18th of June, informing him that Major-general Gates had been appointed to command the forces in Canada, and requesting him to expedite his departure as soon as possible. The appointment of Gates has been attributed to the influence of the Eastern delegates, with whom he was a favorite; indeed, during his station at Boston, he had been highly successful in cultivating the good graces of the New England people. He departed for his command on the 26th of June, vested with extraordinary powers for the regulation of affairs in that "distant, dangerous, and shifting scene."

The actual force of the enemy in Canada had recently been augmented to about 13,000 men; several regiments having arrived from Ireland, one from England, another from General Howe, and a body of Brunswick troops under the Baron Reidesel. Of these, the greater part were on the way up from Quebec in divisions, by land and water, with Generals Carleton, Burgoyne, Philips and Reidesel; while a considerable number under General Frazer had arrived at Three Rivers, and others, under General Nesbit, lay near them on board of transports.

General Thompson coasted in bateaux along the right bank of the river at that expanse called Lake St. Pierre, and arrived at Nicolete, where he found St. Clair and his detachment. He crossed the river in the night, and landed a few miles above Three Rivers, intending to surprise the enemy before daylight; he was not aware at the time that additional troops had arrived under General Burgoyne. After landing, he marched with rapidity toward Three Rivers, but was led by treacherous guides into a morass, and obliged to return back nearly two miles. Day broke, and he was discovered from the ships. A cannonade was opened upon his men as they made their way slowly for an hour and a half through a swamp. At length they arrived in sight of Three Rivers, but it was to find a large force drawn up in battle array, under General Frazer, by whom they were warmly attacked, and after a brief stand thrown in confusion. Thompson attempted to rally his troops, and partly succeeded, until a fire was opened upon them in rear by Nesbit, who had landed from his ships. Their rout now was complete. General Thompson, Colonel Irvine, and about two hundred men were captured, twenty-five were slain, and the rest pursued for several miles through a deep swamp. After great fatigues and sufferings, they were able to get on board of their boats, which had been kept from falling into the hands of the enemy. In these they made their way back to the Sorel, bringing General Sullivan the alarming intelligence of the overpowering force that was coming up the river.

Sullivan made the desperate resolve to defend the mouth of the Sorel, but was induced to abandon it by the unanimous opinion of his officers, and the evident unwillingness of his troops. Dismantling his batteries, therefore, he retreated with his artillery and stores just before the arrival of the enemy, and was followed, step by step along the Sorel, by a strong column under General Burgoyne. On the 18th of June he was joined by General Arnold with three hundred men, the garrison of Montreal, who had crossed at Longueil just in time to escape a large detachment of the enemy. Thus reinforced, and the evacuation of Canada being determined on in a council of war, Sullivan succeeded in destroying everything at Chamblee and St. Johns that he could not carry away, breaking down bridges, and leaving forts and vessels in flames, and continued his retreat to the Isle aux Noix, where he made a halt for some days, until he should receive positive orders from Washington or General Schuyler. The low, unhealthy situation of the Isle aux Noix obliged him soon to remove his camp to the Isle la Motte, whence, on receiving orders to that effect from General Schuyler, he ultimately embarked with his forces, sick and well, for Crown Point.

Thus ended this famous invasion; an enterprise bold in its conceptions, daring and hardy in its execution; full of ingenious expedients, and hazardous exploits; and which, had not unforeseen circumstances counteracted its well-devised plans, might have added all Canada to the American confederacy.

CHAPTER XXIX.

THE ARMY IN NEW YORK.

The great aim of the British, at present, was to get possession of New York and the Hudson, and make them the basis of military operations. This they hoped to effect on the arrival of a powerful armament, hourly expected, and designed for operations on the seaboard.

At this critical juncture there was an alarm of a conspiracy among the tories in the city and on Long Island, suddenly to take up arms and co-operate with the British troops on their arrival. The wildest reports were in circulation concerning it. Some of the tories were to break down King's Bridge, others were to blow up the magazines, spike the guns, and massacre all the field-officers. Washington was to be killed or delivered up to the enemy. Some of his own body-guard were said to be in the plot. Several publicans of the city were pointed out as having aided or abetted it.

One of the most noted was Corbie, whose tavern was said to be "to the southeast of General Washington's house, to the westward of Bayard's Woods, and north of Lispenard's Meadows," from which it would appear that, at that time, the general was quartered at what was formerly called Richmond Hill; a mansion surrounded by trees, at a short distance from the city, in rather an isolated situation.

A committee of the New York Congress traced the plot up to Governor Tryon, who, from his safe retreat on shipboard, acted through agents on shore. The most important of these was David Matthews, the tory mayor of the city. He was accused of disbursing money to enlist men, purchase arms, and corrupt the soldiery. Washington was authorized and requested by the committee to cause the mayor to be apprehended, and all his papers secured. Matthews was at that time residing at Flatbush on Long Island, at no great distance from General Greene's encampment. Washington transmitted the warrant of the committee to the general on the 21st, with directions that it should "be executed with precision, and exactly by one o'clock of the ensuing morning, by a careful officer." Precisely at the hour of one, a detachment from Greene's brigade surrounded the house of the mayor, and secured his person; but no papers were found, though diligent search was made.

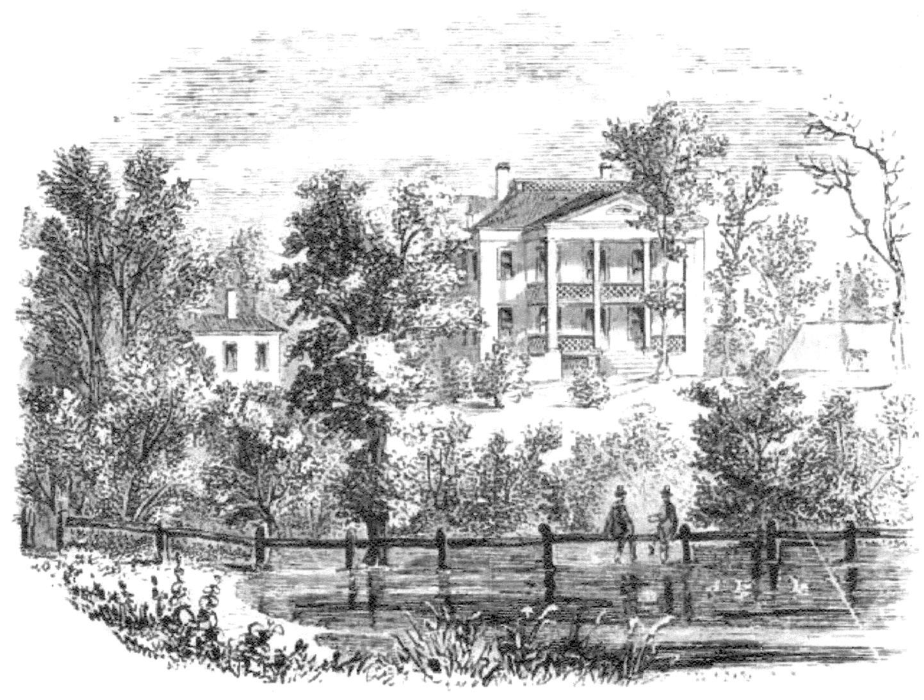

WASHINGTON'S HEAD-QUARTERS. RICHMOND HILL HOUSE, 1776.
VOL. II.

Numerous other arrests took place, and among the number, some of Washington's body-guard. A great dismay fell upon the tories. Some of those on Long Island who had proceeded to arm themselves, finding the plot discovered, sought refuge in woods and morasses. Washington directed that those arrested, who belonged to the army, should be tried by a court-martial, and the rest handed over to the secular power.

According to statements made before the committee, five guineas bounty was offered by Governor Tryon to each man who should enter the king's service; with a promise of two hundred acres of land for himself, one hundred for his wife, and fifty for each child. The men thus recruited were to act on shore, in co-operation with the king's troops when they came. Corbie's tavern, near Washington's quarters, was a kind of rendezvous of the conspirators. From this house a correspondence was kept up with Governor Tryon on shipboard, through a mulatto. At this tavern it was supposed Washington's body-guards were tampered with. Thomas Hickey, one of the guards, was said not only to be enlisted, but to have aided in corrupting his comrades.

Much of the evidence given was of a dubious kind. It was certain that persons had secretly been enlisted and sworn to hostile operations, but Washington did not think that any regular plan had been digested by the conspirators. According to the mayor's admission before the committee, he had been cognizant of attempts to enlist tories and corrupt Washington's guards, though he declared that he had discountenanced them. He, with a number of others, were detained in prison to await a trial. Thomas Hickey, the individual of Washington's guard, was tried before a court-martial. He was an Irishman, and had been a deserter from the British army. The court-martial found him guilty of mutiny and sedition, and treacherous correspondence with the enemy, and sentenced him to be hanged. The sentence was approved by Washington, and was carried promptly into effect June 28th.

While the city was still brooding over this event, four ships-of-war, portentous visitants, appeared off the Hook, stood quietly in at the Narrows, and dropped anchor in the bay. On the 29th of June an express from the look-out on Staten Island, announced that forty sail were in sight. They were, in fact, ships from Halifax, bringing between nine and ten thousand of the troops recently expelled from Boston; together with six transports filled with Highland troops, which had joined the fleet at sea. At sight of this formidable armament standing into the harbor, Washington instantly sent notice of its arrival to Colonel James Clinton, who had command of the posts in the Highlands, and urged all possible preparations to give the enemy a warm reception should they push their frigates up the river. Other arrivals swelled the number of ships in the bay of New York to one hundred and thirty men-of-war and transports. They made no movement to ascend the Hudson, but anchored off Staten Island, where they landed their troops, and the hill sides were soon whitened with their tents.

Washington beheld the gathering storm with an anxious eye, aware that General Howe only awaited the arrival of his brother, the admiral, to commence hostile operations. He wrote to the President of Congress, urging a call on the Massachusetts government for its quota of continental troops; and the formation of a flying camp of ten thousand men, to be stationed in the Jerseys as a central force, ready to act in any direction as circumstances might require. On the 2d of July he issued a general order, calling upon the troops to prepare for a momentous conflict which was to decide their liberties and fortunes. Those who should signalize themselves by acts of bravery would be noticed and rewarded; those who proved craven would be exposed and punished.

About this time, we have the first appearance in the military ranks of the Revolution of one destined to take an active and distinguished part in public affairs; and to leave the impress of his genius on the institutions of the country. As General Greene one day, on his way to Washington's head-quarters, was passing through a field—then on the outskirts of the city, now in the heart of its busiest quarter, and known as "the Park,"—he paused to notice a provincial company of artillery, and was struck with its able performances, and with the tact and talent of its commander. He was a mere youth, apparently about twenty years of age; small in person and stature, but remarkable for his alert and manly bearing. It was Alexander Hamilton.[8]

Greene was an able tactician, and quick to appreciate any display of military

[8] Hamilton was a native of the island of Nevis, in the West Indies. At an early age he was put in a counting house, but his nature was aspiring, and he devoted his leisure hours

science; a little conversation sufficed to convince him that the youth before him had a mind of no ordinary grasp and quickness. He invited him to his quarters, and from that time cultivated his friendship. Further acquaintance heightened the general's opinion of his extraordinary merits, and he took an early occasion to introduce him to the commander-in-chief, by whom we shall soon find him properly appreciated.

A valuable accession to the army, at this anxious time, was Washington's neighbor, and former companion in arms, Hugh Mercer. His military spirit was alert as ever; the talent he had shown in organizing the Virginia militia, and his zeal and efficiency as a member of the committee of safety, had been properly appreciated by Congress, and on the 5th of June he had received the commission of brigadier-general. He was greeted by Washington with the right hand of fellowship. The flying camp was about forming. Washington had the nomination of some continental officer to the command. He gave it to Mercer, and sent him over to Paulus Hook, in the Jerseys, to make arrangements for the militia as they should come in; recommending him to Brigadier-general William Livingston, as an officer on whose experience and judgment great confidence might be reposed. Livingston was a man inexperienced in arms, but of education, talent, sagacity and ready wit. Mercer and he were to consult together, and concert plans to repel invasions; the New Jersey militia, however, were distinct from the flying camp, and only called out for local defence.

While danger was gathering round New York, the General Congress at Philadelphia was discussing, with closed doors, what John Adams pronounced—"The greatest question ever debated in America, and as great as ever was or will be debated among men." The result was, a resolution passed unanimously, on the 2d of July, "that these United Colonies are, and of right ought to be, free and independent States." "The 2d of July," adds the same patriotic statesman, "will be the most memorable epoch in the history of America. I am apt to believe that it will be celebrated by succeeding generations as the great anniversary festival. It ought to be commemorated as the day of deliverance, by solemn acts of devotion to Almighty God. It ought to be solemnized with pomp and parade, with shows, games, sports, guns, bells, bonfires and illuminations, from one end of this continent to the other, from this time forth for evermore."

The glorious event has, indeed, given rise to an annual jubilee, but not on the day designated by Adams. The 4th of July is the day of national rejoicing, for on that day the "Declaration of Independence," that solemn and sublime document, was adopted. Washington hailed the declaration with joy. It is true, it was but a formal recognition of a state of things which had long existed, but it put an end to all those temporizing hopes of reconciliation which had clogged the military action of the country.

On the 9th of July he caused it to be read at six o'clock in the evening, at the head of each brigade of the army. "The general hopes," said he in his orders, "that

---

to study. Some early achievements of his pen gave such proof of talent that it was determined to give him the advantage of a regular education, and he was sent to King's (now Columbia) College at New York.

this important event will serve as a fresh incentive to every officer and soldier to act with fidelity and courage, as knowing that now the peace and safety of his country depend, under God, solely on the success of our arms; and that he is now in the service of a state, possessed of sufficient power to reward his merit and advance him to the highest honors of a free country."

The excitable populace of New York were not content with the ringing of bells to proclaim their joy. There was a leaden statue of George III. in the Bowling Green, in front of the fort. Since kingly rule is at an end, why retain its effigy? On the same evening, therefore, the statue was pulled down amid the shouts of the multitude, and broken up to be run into bullets "to be used in the cause of independence."

The exultation of the patriots of New York, caused by the Declaration of Independence, was soon overclouded. On the 12th of July several ships stood in from sea, and joined the naval force below. Every nautical movement was now a matter of speculation and alarm. Two ships-of-war were observed getting under way, and standing toward the city. One was the Phoenix, of forty guns; the other the Rose, of twenty guns, commanded by Captain Wallace. The troops were immediately at their alarm posts. It was about half-past three o'clock in the afternoon as the ships and three tenders came sweeping up the bay with the advantage of wind and tide, and shaped their course up the Hudson. The batteries of the city and of Paulus Hook, on the opposite Jersey shore, opened a fire upon them. They answered it with broadsides, but continued their course up the Hudson. They had merely fired upon the batteries as they passed; and on their own part had sustained but little damage, their decks having ramparts of sand-bags. The ships below remained in sullen quiet at their anchors, and showed no intention of following them. The firing ceased. The fear of a general attack upon the city died away, and the agitated citizens breathed more freely.

Washington, however, apprehended this movement of the ships might be with a different object. They might be sent to land troops and seize upon the passes of the Highlands. Forts Montgomery and Constitution were far from complete, and were scantily manned. A small force might be sufficient to surprise them. Thus thinking, he sent off an express to put General Mifflin on the alert, who was stationed with his Philadelphia troops at Fort Washington and King's Bridge. The same express carried a letter from him to the New York Convention, at that time holding its sessions at White Plains in Westchester County, apprising it of the impending danger.

Fortunately George Clinton, the patriotic legislator, had recently been appointed brigadier-general of the militia of Ulster and Orange counties. Called to his native State by his military duties in this time of danger, he had only remained in Congress to vote for the declaration of independence, and then hastened home. He was now at New Windsor, in Ulster County, just above the Highlands. Washington wrote to him on the afternoon of the 12th, urging him to collect as great a force as possible of the New York militia, for the protection of the Highlands against this hostile irruption. Long before the receipt of Washington's letter, Clinton had been put on the alert. About nine o'clock in the morning of the 13th, two river sloops came to anchor above the Highlands, before the general's residence.

Their captains informed him that New York had been attacked on the preceding afternoon. They had seen the cannonade from a distance, and judged from the subsequent firing, that the enemy's ships were up the river as far as King's Bridge. Clinton was as prompt a soldier as he had been an intrepid legislator. The neighboring militia were forthwith put in motion. Three regiments were ordered out; one was to repair to Fort Montgomery; another to Fort Constitution; the third to rendezvous at Newburgh, just above the Highlands, ready to hasten to the assistance of Fort Constitution, should another signal be given.

Another of his sagacious measures was to send expresses to all the owners of sloops and boats twenty miles up the west side of the river, to haul them off so as to prevent their grounding. Part of them were to be ready to carry over the militia to the forts; the rest were ordered down to Fort Constitution, where a chain of them might be drawn across the narrowest part of the river, to be set on fire, should the enemy's ships attempt to pass. Having made these prompt arrangements, he proceeded to Fort Montgomery, where he fixed his head-quarters. Here, on the following day (July 14th,) he received Washington's letter, written two days previously; but by this time he had anticipated its orders, and stirred up the whole country.

While the vigilant Clinton was preparing to defend the passes of the Highlands, danger was growing more imminent at the mouth of the Hudson. The agitation into which New York was thrown on the afternoon of the 12th of July, by the broadsides of the Phoenix and the Rose, was almost immediately followed by another. On the same evening there was a great booming of cannon, with clouds of smoke, from the shipping at anchor at Staten Island. Every spy-glass was again in requisition. The British fleet were saluting a ship of the line, just arrived from sea. She advanced grandly, every man-of-war thundering a salute as she passed. At her foretop masthead she bore St. George's flag. "It is the admiral's ship!" cried the nautical men on the look-out at the Battery. "It is the admiral's ship!" was echoed from mouth to mouth, and the word soon flew throughout the city, "Lord Howe is come!"

CHAPTER XXX.

PROCEEDINGS OF LORD HOWE.—GATES AND SCHUYLER.

Lord Howe was indeed come, and affairs now appeared to be approaching a crisis. In consequence of the recent conspiracy, the Convention of New York, seated at White Plains in Westchester County, had a secret committee stationed in New York for the purpose of taking cognizance of traitorous machinations. To this committee Washington addressed a letter the day after his lordship's arrival, suggesting the policy of removing from the city and its environs, "all persons of known disaffection and enmity to the cause of America;" especially those confined in jail for treasonable offences; who might become extremely dangerous in case of an attack and alarm. He took this step with great reluctance; but felt compelled to it by circumstances. In consequence of his suggestion, thirteen persons in confinement for traitorous offences, were removed to the jail of Litchfield in Connecticut. Among the number was the late mayor; but as his offence was not of so deep a dye as those whereof the rest stood charged, it was recommended by the president of the Convention that he should be treated with indulgence.

The proceedings of Lord Howe soon showed the policy of these precautions. His lordship had prepared a declaration, addressed to the people at large, informing them of the powers vested in his brother and himself as commissioners for restoring peace. He sent a flag on shore, bearing a circular letter, written in his civil and military capacity, to the colonial governor, requesting him to publish his address to the people as widely as possible.

The British officers, considering the Americans in arms rebels without valid commissions, were in the habit of denying them all military title. Washington's general officers had urged him not to submit to this tacit indignity, but to reject all letters directed to him without a specification of his official rank. An occasion now presented itself for the adjustment of this matter. Within a day or two an officer of the British navy, Lieutenant Brown, came with a flag from Lord Howe, seeking a conference with Washington. Colonel Reed, the adjutant-general, embarked in a barge, and met him half way between Governor's and Staten Islands. The lieutenant informed him that he was the bearer of a letter from Lord Howe to *Mr.* Washington. Colonel Reed replied that he knew no such person in the American army. The lieutenant produced and offered the letter. It was addressed to George Washington, Esquire. He was informed that it could not be received with such a direction. The lieutenant expressed much concern, while Reed maintained his coolness, politely declining to receive the letter, as inconsistent with his duty.

On the 19th an aide-de-camp of General Howe came with a flag, and requested to know, as there appeared to be an obstacle to a correspondence between the two generals, whether Colonel Patterson, the British adjutant-general, could be admitted to an interview with General Washington. Colonel Reed, who met the flag, consented in the name of the general, and pledged his honor for the safety of the adjutant-general during the interview, which was fixed for the following morning.

At the appointed time, Colonel Reed and Colonel Webb, one of Washington's aides, met the flag in the harbor, took Colonel Patterson into their barge and escorted him to town, passing in front of the grand battery. Washington received the adjutant-general at head-quarters with much form and ceremony, in full military array, with his officers and guards about him. Colonel Patterson, addressing him by the title of *your excellency*, produced, but did not offer, a letter addressed to George Washington, Esquire, etc., etc., hoping that the et ceteras, which implied everything, would remove all impediments. Washington replied that it was true the et ceteras implied everything, but they also implied anything. A letter, he added, addressed to a person acting in a public character should have some inscriptions to designate it from a mere private letter; and he should absolutely decline any letter addressed to himself as a private person, when it related to his public station.

Colonel Patterson, finding the letter would not be received, endeavored, as far as he could recollect, to communicate the scope of it in the course of a somewhat desultory conversation. What he chiefly dwelt upon was that Lord Howe and his brother had been specially nominated commissioners for the promotion of peace, which was esteemed a mark of favor and regard to America; that they had great powers, and would derive the highest pleasure from effecting an accommodation; and he concluded by adding, that he wished his visit to be considered as making the first advance toward that desirable object. Washington replied that, by what had appeared (alluding, no doubt, to Lord Howe's circular), their powers, it would seem, were only to grant pardons. Now those who had committed no fault needed no pardon; and such was the case with the Americans, who were only defending what they considered their indisputable rights.

Colonel Patterson avoided a discussion of this matter, which, he observed, would open a very wide field; so here the conference, which had been conducted on both sides with great courtesy, terminated. Washington received the applause of Congress and of the public for sustaining the dignity of his station. His conduct in this particular was recommended as a model to all American officers in corresponding with the enemy.

In the meantime, the irruption of the Phoenix and the Rose into the waters of the Hudson had roused a belligerent spirit along its borders. The lower part of that noble river is commanded on the eastern side by the bold woody heights of Manhattan Island and Westchester County, and on the western side by the rocky cliffs of the Palisades. Beyond those cliffs, the river expands into a succession of what may almost be termed lakes; first the Tappan Sea, then Haverstraw Bay, then the Bay of Peekskill; separated from each other by long stretching points, or high beetling promontories, but affording ample sea room and safe anchorage. Then come the redoubtable Highlands, that strait, fifteen miles in length, where the river bends its course, narrow and deep, between rocky, forest-clad mountains.

The New York Convention, aware of the impending danger, despatched military envoys to stir up the yeomanry along the river, and order out militia. Powder and ball were sent to Tarrytown, before which the hostile ships were anchored, and yeoman troops were stationed there and along the neighboring shores of the Tappan Sea. In a little while the militia of Dutchess County and Cortlandt's Manor were hastening, rudely armed, to protect the public stores at Peekskill, and mount guard at the entrance of the Highlands.

The ships-of-war which caused this alarm and turmoil, lay quietly anchored in the broad expanses of the Tappan Sea and Haverstraw Bay; shifting their ground occasionally, while their boats were out taking soundings quite up to the Highlands, evidently preparing for further operations. At night, too, their barges were heard rowing up and down the river on mysterious errands.

The ships, now acquainted with the channel, moved up within six miles of Fort Montgomery. General Clinton apprehended they might mean to take advantage of a dark night, and slip by him in the deep shadows of the mountains. To prevent this, he stationed a guard at night on the furthest point in view, about two miles and a half below the fort, prepared to kindle a blazing fire should the ships appear in sight. Large piles of dry brushwood mixed with combustibles were prepared at various places up and down the shore opposite to the fort, and men stationed to set fire to them as soon as a signal should be given from the lower point. The fort, therefore, while it remained in darkness, would have a fair chance with its batteries as the ships passed between it and these conflagrations.

A private committee sent up by the New York Convention, had a conference with the general, to devise further means of obstructing the passage of ships up the river. Fire rafts were to be brought from Poughkeepsie and kept at hand ready for action. These were to be lashed two together, with chains, between old sloops filled with combustibles, and sent down with a strong wind and tide, to drive upon the ships. An iron chain, also, was to be stretched obliquely across the river from Fort Montgomery to the foot of Anthony's Nose, thus, as it were, chaining up the gate of the Highlands. For a protection below the Highlands, it was proposed to station whale-boats about the coves and promontories of Tappan Sea and Haverstraw Bay; to reconnoitre the enemy, cruise about at night, carry intelligence from post to post, seize any river craft that might bring the ships supplies, and cut off their boats when attempting to land. Galleys, also, were prepared, with nine-pounders mounted at the bows.

While the security of the Hudson from invading ships was claiming the attention of Washington, he was equally anxious to prevent an irruption of the enemy from Canada. He was grieved, therefore, to find there was a clashing of authorities between the generals who had charge of the Northern frontier. Gates, on his way to take command of the army in Canada, had heard with surprise in Albany of its retreat across the New York frontier. He still considered it under his orders, and was proceeding to act accordingly, when General Schuyler observed that the resolution of Congress, and the instructions of Washington, applied to the army only while in Canada; the moment it retreated within the limits of New York, it came within his (Schuyler's) command.

That there might be no delay in the service at this critical juncture the two generals agreed to refer the question of command to Congress, and in the meantime to act in concert. They accordingly departed together for Lake Champlain, to prepare against an anticipated invasion by Sir Guy Carleton. They arrived at Crown Point on the 6th of July, and found there the wrecks of the army recently driven out of Canada. They had been harassed in their retreat by land; their transportation on the lake had been in leaky boats, without awnings, where the sick, suffering from small-pox, lay on straw, exposed to a burning July sun; no food but salt pork, often rancid, hard biscuit or unbaked flour, and scarcely any medicine. Not more than six thousand men had reached Crown Point, and half of those were on the sick list; the shattered remains of twelve or fifteen very fine battalions. In a council of war it was determined that, under present circumstances, the post of Crown Point was not tenable; and that, therefore, it was expedient to fall back, and take a strong position at Ticonderoga.

General Sullivan had been deeply hurt that Gates, his former inferior in rank, should have been appointed over him to the command of the army in Canada; considering it a tacit intimation that Congress did not esteem him competent to the trust which had devolved upon him. He now, therefore, requested leave of absence, in order to wait on the commander-in-chief. It was granted with reluctance.

On the 9th of July, Schuyler and Gates returned to Ticonderoga, accompanied by Arnold. Instant arrangements were made to encamp the troops, and land the artillery and stores as fast as they should arrive. Great exertions, also, were made to strengthen the defences of the place. Colonel John Trumbull, who was to have accompanied Gates to Canada, as adjutant-general, had been reconnoitring the neighborhood of Ticonderoga, and had pitched upon a place for a fortification on the eastern side of the lake, directly opposite the east point of Ticonderoga, where Fort Independence was subsequently built. He also advised the erection of a work on a lofty eminence, the termination of a mountain ridge, which separates Lake George from Lake Champlain. His advice was unfortunately disregarded. Preparations were made, also, to augment the naval force on the lakes. Ship carpenters from the Eastern States were employed at Skenesborough to build the hulls of galleys and boats, which, when launched, were to be sent down to Ticonderoga for equipment and armament, under the superintendence of General Arnold.

Schuyler soon returned to Albany, to superintend the general concerns of the Northern department. He was indefatigable in procuring and forwarding the necessary materials and artillery for the fortification of Ticonderoga. The question of command between him and Gates was apparently at rest. A letter from the President of Congress, dated July 8th, informed General Gates that, according to the resolution of that body under which he had been appointed, his command was totally independent of General Schuyler, *while the army was in Canada,* but no longer.

Gates professed himself entirely satisfied with the explanation he had received, and perfectly disposed to obey the commands of Schuyler.

As to General Sullivan, who repaired to Philadelphia and tendered his resignation, the question of rank which had aggrieved him was explained in a manner that induced him to continue in service. It was universally allowed that his retreat had been ably conducted through all kinds of difficulties and disasters.

A greater source of solicitude to Washington than this jealousy between commanders, was the sectional jealousy springing up among the troops. In a letter to Schuyler (July 17th), he says, "I must entreat your attention to do away the unhappy and pernicious distinctions and jealousies between the troops of different governments. Enjoin this upon the officers, and let them inculcate and press home to the soldiery, the necessity of order and harmony among those who are embarked in one common cause, and mutually contending for all that freemen hold dear." Nowhere were these sectional jealousies more prevalent than in the motley army assembled from distant quarters under Washington's own command. Reed, the adjutant-general, speaking on this subject, observes: "The Southern troops, comprising the regiments south of the Delaware, looked with very unkind feelings on those of New England; especially those from Connecticut, whose peculiarities of deportment made them the objects of ill-disguised derision among their fellow soldiers."

Among the troops thus designated as Southern, were some from Virginia under a Major Leitch; others from Maryland, under Colonel Smallwood; others from Delaware, led by Colonel Haslet. There were four Continental battalions from Pennsylvania commanded by Colonels Shee, St. Clair, Wayne, and Magaw; and provincial battalions, two of which were severally commanded by Colonels Miles and Atlee. The Continental battalion under Colonel Shee was chiefly from the city of Philadelphia, especially the officers; among whom were Lambert Cadwalader and William Allen, members of two of the principal and most aristocratic families, and Alexander Graydon, to whose memoirs we are indebted for some graphic pictures of the times. These Pennsylvania troops were under the command of Brigadier-general Mifflin, who, in the preceding year, had acted as Washington's aide-de-camp, and afterwards as quartermaster-general.

Smallwood's Maryland battalion was one of the brightest in point of equipment. The scarlet and buff uniforms of those Southerners contrasted vividly with the rustic attire of the yeoman battalions from the East. Their officers, too, looked down upon their Connecticut compeers, who could only be distinguished from their men by wearing a cockade. "There were none," says Graydon, "by whom an unofficer-like appearance and deportment could be tolerated less than by a city-bred Marylander; who, at this time, was distinguished by the most fashionable cut coat, the most *macaroni* cocked-hat, and hottest blood in the Union." In the same sectional spirit, he speaks of the Connecticut light-horse: "Old-fashioned men, truly irregulars; whether their clothing, equipments, or caparisons were regarded, it would have been difficult to have discovered any circumstance of uniformity. Instead of carbines and sabres, they generally carried fowling-pieces, some of them very long, such as in Pennsylvania are used for shooting ducks. Here and there one appeared in a dingy regimental of scarlet, with a triangular, tarnished, laced hat. These singular dragoons were volunteers, who came to make a tender of their services to the commander-in-chief."

The troops thus satirized were a body of between four and five hundred Connecticut light-horse, under Colonel Thomas Seymour. On an appeal for aid to the governor of their State, they had voluntarily hastened on in advance of the militia, to render the most speedy succor. Washington speaks of them as being for the most part, if not all, men of reputation and property. They were, in fact, mostly farmers. The Connecticut infantry which had been furnished by Governor Trumbull in the present emergency, likewise were substantial farmers, whose business would require their return, when the necessity of their further stay in the army should be over. They were all men of simple rural manners, from an agricultural State, where great equality of condition prevailed; the officers were elected by the men out of their own ranks, they were their own neighbors, and every way their equals. All this, as yet, was but little understood or appreciated by the troops from the South, among whom military rank was more defined and tenaciously observed, and where the officers were men of the cities, and of more aristocratic habits.

CHAPTER XXXI.

THE WAR IN THE SOUTH.—AFFAIRS IN THE HIGHLANDS.

Letters from General Lee gave Washington intelligence of the fate of Sir Henry Clinton's expedition to the South; that expedition which had been the subject of so much surmise and perplexity.

Within a year past, Charleston had been fortified at various points. Fort Johnson, on James Island, three miles from the city, and commanding the breadth of the channel, was garrisoned by a regiment of South Carolina regulars under Colonel Gadsden. A strong fort had recently been constructed nearly opposite, on the south-west point of Sullivan's Island, about six miles below the city. It was mounted with twenty-six guns, and garrisoned by three hundred and seventy-five regulars and a few militia, and commanded by Colonel William Moultrie, of South Carolina, who had constructed it. This fort, in connection with that on James Island, was considered the key of the harbor. Cannon had also been mounted on Haddrell's Point on the mainland, to the north-west of Sullivan's Island, and along the bay in front of the town.

The arrival of General Lee gave great joy to the people of Charleston, from his high reputation for military skill and experience. According to his own account in a letter to Washington, the town on his arrival was "utterly defenceless." He was rejoiced, therefore, when the enemy, instead of immediately attacking it, directed his whole force against the fort on Sullivan's Island.

The British ships, in fact, having passed the bar with some difficulty, landed their troops on Long Island, situated to the east of Sullivan's Island, and separated from it by a small creek called the Breach. Sir Henry Clinton meditated a combined attack with his land and naval forces on the fort commanded by Moultrie; the capture of which, he thought, would insure the reduction of Charleston. The Americans immediately threw up works on the north-eastern extremity of Sullivan's Island, to prevent the passage of the enemy over the Breach, stationing a force of regulars and militia there, under Colonel Thompson. General Lee encamped on Haddrell's Point, on the mainland, to the north of the island, whence he intended to keep up a communication by a bridge of boats, so as to be ready at any moment to aid either Moultrie or Thompson.

Sir Henry Clinton, on the other hand, had to construct batteries on Long Island, to oppose those of Thompson, and cover the passage of his troops by boats or by the ford. Thus time was consumed, and the enemy were, from the 1st to the

28th of June, preparing for the attack.

At length on the 28th of June, the Thunder Bomb commenced the attack, throwing shells at the fort as the fleet, under Sir Peter Parker, advanced. About eleven o'clock the ships dropped their anchors directly before the front battery. ["They commenced," says Lee, "the most furious fire I ever saw." The garrison, however, according to British authority, stuck with the greatest constancy and firmness to their guns; fired deliberately and slow, and took a cool, effective aim. The ships suffered accordingly, they were torn almost to pieces, and the slaughter was dreadful. The fire from the ships did not produce the expected effect.] The fortifications were low, composed of earth and palmetto wood, which is soft, and makes no splinters, and the merlons were extremely thick. At one time there was a considerable pause in the American fire, and the enemy thought the fort was abandoned. It was only because the powder was exhausted. As soon as a supply could be forwarded from the mainland by General Lee, the fort resumed its fire with still more deadly effect. Through unskilful pilotage, several of the ships ran aground, where one, the frigate Actæon, remained; the rest were extricated with difficulty. Those which bore the brunt of the action were much cut up. One hundred and seventy-five men were killed, and nearly as many wounded. Sir Henry Clinton, with two thousand troops and five or six hundred seamen, attempted repeatedly to cross from Long Island, and co-operate in the attack upon the fort, but was as often foiled by Colonel Thompson, with his battery of two cannons, and a body of South Carolina rangers and North Carolina regulars.

The combat slackened before sunset, and ceased before ten o'clock. Sir Peter Parker, who had received a severe contusion in the engagement, then slipped his cables, and drew off his shattered ships to Five Fathom Hole. The Actæon remained aground. On the following morning Sir Henry Clinton made another attempt to cross from Long Island to Sullivan's Island; but was again repulsed, and obliged to take shelter behind his breastworks. Sir Peter Parker, too, giving up all hope of reducing the fort in the shattered condition of his ships, ordered that the Actæon should be set on fire and abandoned. Within a few days the troops were re-embarked from Long Island: the attempt upon Charleston was for the present abandoned, and the fleet once more put to sea.

In this action, one of the severest in the whole course of the war, the loss of the Americans in killed and wounded was but thirty-five men. Colonel Moultrie derived the greatest glory from the defence of Sullivan's Island; though the thanks of Congress were voted as well to General Lee, Colonel Thompson and those under their command.

The tidings of this signal repulse of the enemy came most opportunely to Washington, when he was apprehending an attack upon New York.

General Putnam, beside his bravery in the field, was somewhat of a mechanical projector. The batteries at Fort Washington had proved ineffectual in opposing the passage of hostile ships up the Hudson. He was now engaged on a plan for obstructing the channel opposite the fort, so as to prevent the passing of any more ships. A letter from him to General Gales (July 26th) explains his project. "We are preparing chevaux-de-frise, at which we make great despatch by the help of ships, which are to be sunk. The two ships' sterns lie towards each other, about seventy feet apart. Three large logs, which reach from ship to ship, are fastened to them. The two ships and logs stop the river two hundred and eighty feet. The ships are to be sunk, and when hauled down on one side, the pricks will be raised to a proper height, and they must inevitably stop the river, if the enemy will let us sink them."

It so happened that one Ephraim Anderson, adjutant to the second Jersey battalion, had recently submitted a project to Congress for destroying the enemy's fleet in the harbor of New York. He had attempted an enterprise of the kind against the British ships in the harbor of Quebec during the siege, and, according to his own account, would have succeeded, had not the enemy discovered his intentions, and stretched a cable across the mouth of the harbor, and had he not accidentally been much burnt. His scheme was favorably entertained by Congress, and Washington, by a letter dated July 10th, was instructed to aid him in carrying it into effect. Anderson, accordingly, was soon at work at New York constructing fire-ships, with which the fleet was to be attacked. Simultaneous with the attack, a descent was to be made on the British camp on Staten Island, from the nearest point of the Jersey shore, by troops from Mercer's flying camp, and by others stationed at Bergen under Major Knowlton, Putnam's favorite officer for daring enterprises. Projectors are subject to disappointments. It was impossible to construct a sufficient number of fire-ships and galleys in time. The flying camp, too, recruited but slowly, and scarcely exceeded three thousand men; the combined attack by fire and sword had therefore to be given up.

In the course of a few days arrived a hundred sail, with large reinforcements, among which were one thousand Hessians, and as many more were reported to be on the way. The troops were disembarked on Staten Island, and fortifications thrown up on some of the most commanding hills. All projects of attack upon the enemy were now out of the question. Indeed, some of Washington's ablest advisers questioned the policy of remaining in New York, where they might be entrapped as the British had been in Boston.

During the latter part of July, and the early part of August, ships of war with their tenders continued to arrive, and Scotch Highlanders, Hessians, and other troops to be landed on Staten Island. At the beginning of August, the squadron with Sir Henry Clinton, recently repulsed at Charleston, anchored in the bay.

In the meantime, Putnam's contrivances for obstructing the channel had reached their destined place. A letter, dated Fort Washington, August 3d, says: "Four ships, chained and boomed, with a number of amazing large chevaux-de-frise, were sunk close by the fort under command of General Mifflin, which fort mounts thirty-two pieces of heavy cannon. We are thoroughly sanguine that they (the ships up the river) never will be able to join the British fleet, nor assistance from the fleet be afforded to them." Another letter, written at the same date from Tarrytown, on the borders of the Tappan Sea, gives an account of an attack made by six row galleys upon the Phoenix and the Rose. They fought bravely for two hours, hulling the ships repeatedly, but sustaining great damage in return; until their commodore, Colonel Tupper, gave the signal to draw off.

The force of the enemy collected in the neighborhood of New York was about thirty thousand men; that of the Americans a little more than seventeen thousand, but was subsequently increased to twenty thousand, for the most part, raw and undisciplined. One-fourth were on the sick list with bilious and putrid fevers and dysentery; others were absent on furlough or command; the rest had to be distributed over posts and stations fifteen miles apart.

Washington kept the most watchful eye upon the movements of the enemy. Beside their great superiority in point of numbers as well as discipline, to his own crude and scanty legions, they possessed a vast advantage in their fleet. "They would not be half the enemy they are," observed Colonel Reed, "if they were once separated from their ships." Every arrival and departure of these, therefore, was a subject of speculation and conjecture. Aaron Burr, at that time in New York, aide-de-camp to General Putnam, speaks in a letter to an uncle, of thirty transports, which, under convoy of three frigates, had put to sea on the 7th of August, with the intention of sailing round Long Island and coming through the Sound, and thus investing the city by the North and East Rivers. "They are then to land on both sides of the island," writes he, "join their forces, and draw a line across, which will hem us in, and totally cut off all communication; after which, they will have their own fun."

In this emergency, Washington wrote to General Mercer for 2,000 men from the flying camp. Colonel Smallwood's battalion was immediately furnished, as a part of them. The Convention of the State ordered out hasty levies of country militia, to form temporary camps on the shore of the Sound, and on that of the Hudson above King's Bridge, to annoy the enemy, should they attempt to land from their ships on either of these waters. Others were sent to reinforce the posts on Long Island. Many of the yeomen of the country, thus hastily summoned from the plough, were destitute of arms, in lieu of which they were ordered to bring with them a shovel, spade, or pickaxe, or a scythe straightened and fastened to a pole. This rustic array may have provoked the thoughtless sneers of city scoffers, such as those cited by Graydon; but it was in truth one of the glorious features of the Revolution, to be thus aided in its emergencies by "hasty levies of husbandmen."

By the authority of the New York Convention, Washington had appointed General George Clinton to the command of the levies on both sides of the Hudson. He now ordered him to hasten down with them to the fort just erected on the north side of King's Bridge; leaving two hundred men under the command of a brave and alert officer to throw up works at the pass of Anthony's Nose, where the main road to Albany crosses that mountain. Troops of horse also were to be posted by him along the river to watch the motions of the enemy.

Accounts of deserters, and other intelligence, informed Washington, on the 17th, that a great many of the enemy's troops had gone on board of the transports; that three days' provisions had been cooked, and other steps taken indicating an intention of leaving Staten Island. Putnam, also, came up from below with word that at least one-fourth of the fleet had sailed. There were many conjectures at head-quarters as to whither they were bound, or whether they had not merely shifted their station. Everything indicated, however, that affairs were tending to a crisis.

A gallant little exploit at this juncture, gave a fillip to the spirits of the community. Two of the fire-ships recently constructed, went up the Hudson to attempt the destruction of the ships which had so long been domineering over its waters. One succeeded in grappling the Phoenix, and would soon have set her in flames, but in the darkness got to leeward, and was cast loose without effecting any damage. The other, in making for the Rose, fell foul of one of the tenders, grappled and burnt her. The enterprise was conducted with spirit, and though it failed of its main object, had an important effect. The commanders of the ships determined to abandon those waters, where their boats were fired upon by the very yeomanry whenever they attempted to land; and where their ships were in danger from midnight incendiaries, while riding at anchor. Taking advantage of a brisk wind and favoring tide, they made all sail early on the morning of the 18th of August, and stood down the river, keeping close under the eastern shore, where they supposed the guns from Mount Washington could not be brought to bear upon them. Notwithstanding this precaution, the Phoenix was thrice hulled by shots from the fort, and one of the tenders once. The Rose, also, was hulled once by a shot from Burdett's Ferry. The men on board were kept close, to avoid being picked off by a party of riflemen posted on the river bank. The ships fired grape-shot as they passed, but without effecting any injury. Unfortunately, a passage had been left open in the obstructions on which General Putnam had calculated so sanguinely; it was to have been closed in the course of a day or two. Through this they made their way, guided by a deserter.

CHAPTER XXXII.
BATTLE OF LONG ISLAND.—RETREAT.

The movements of the British fleet, and of the camp on Staten Island, gave signs of a meditated attack; but as the nature of that attack was uncertain, Washington was obliged to retain the greater part of his troops in the city for its defence, holding them ready, however, to be transferred to any point in the vicinity. General Mifflin, with about five hundred of the Pennsylvania troops, of Colonels Shee and Magaw's regiments, were at King's Bridge, ready to aid at a moment's notice. General George Clinton was at that post, with about fourteen hundred of his yeomanry of the Hudson.

Reports from different quarters gave Washington reason to apprehend that the design of the enemy might be to land part of their force on Long Island, and endeavor to get possession of the heights of Brooklyn, which overlooked New York; while another part should land above the city. Thus, various disconnected points, distant from each other, and a great extent of intervening country, had to be defended by raw troops, against a superior force well disciplined, and possessed of every facility for operating by land and water.

General Greene, with a considerable force, was stationed at Brooklyn. He had acquainted himself with all the localities of the island, from Hell Gate to the Narrows, and made his plan of defence accordingly. His troops were diligently occupied in works which he laid out, about a mile beyond the village of Brooklyn, and facing the interior of the island, whence a land attack might be attempted. Brooklyn was immediately opposite to New York. The Sound, commonly called the East River, in that place about three quarters of a mile in width, swept its rapid tides between them. The village stood on a kind of peninsula, formed by the deep inlets of Wallabout Bay on the north, and Gowanus Cove on the south. A line of intrenchments and strong redoubts extended across the neck of the peninsula, from the bay to a swamp and creek emptying into the cove. To protect the rear of the works from the enemy's ships, a battery was erected at Red Hook, the south-west corner of the peninsula, and a fort on Governor's Island, nearly opposite.

About two miles and a half in front of the line of intrenchments and redoubts, a range of hills, densely wooded, extended from south-west to north-east, forming a natural barrier across the island. It was traversed by three roads. One, on the left of the works, stretched eastwardly to Bedford, and then by a pass through the Bedford Hills to the village of Jamaica; another, central and direct, led through the woody heights to Flatbush; a third, on the right of the lines, passed by Gowanus

Cove to the Narrows and Gravesend Bay. The occupation of this range of hills, and the protection of its passes, had been designed by General Greene; but unfortunately, in the midst of his arduous toils, he was taken down by a raging fever, which confined him to his bed; and General Sullivan, just returned from Lake Champlain, had the temporary command.

On the 21st came a letter, written in all haste by Brigadier-general William Livingston, of New Jersey. Movements of the enemy on Staten Island had been seen from his camp. He had sent over a spy at midnight, who brought back the following intelligence. Twenty thousand men had embarked to make an attack on Long Island, and up the Hudson. Fifteen thousand remained on Staten Island, to attack Bergen Point, Elizabethtown Point, and Amboy.

Washington sent a copy of the letter to the New York Convention. On the following morning (August 22d) the enemy appeared to be carrying their plans into execution. The reports of cannon and musketry were heard from Long Island, and columns of smoke were descried rising above the groves and orchards at a distance. The city, as usual, was alarmed, and had reason to be so; for word soon came that several thousand men, with artillery and light-horse, were landed at Gravesend; and that Colonel Hand, stationed there with the Pennsylvania rifle regiment, had retreated to the lines, setting fire to stacks of wheat, and other articles, to keep them from falling into the enemy's hands. Washington apprehended an attempt of the foe by a forced march, to surprise the lines at Brooklyn. He immediately sent over a reinforcement of six battalions. It was all that he could spare, as with the next tide the ships might bring up the residue of the army, and attack the city. Five battalions more, however, were ordered to be ready as a reinforcement, if required.

Nine thousand of the enemy had landed, with forty pieces of cannon. Sir Henry Clinton had the chief command, and led the first division. His associate officers were the Earls of Cornwallis and Percy, General Grant, and General Sir William Erskine. As their boats approached the shore, Colonel Hand, stationed, as has been said, in the neighborhood with his rifle regiment, retreated to the chain of wooded hills, and took post on a height commanding the central road leading from Flatbush. The enemy having landed without opposition, Lord Cornwallis was detached with the reserve to Flatbush, while the rest of the army extended itself from the ferry at the Narrows through Utrecht and Gravesend, to the village of Flatland. Cornwallis, with two battalions of light-infantry, Colonel Donop's corps of Hessians, and six field-pieces, advanced rapidly to seize upon the central pass through the hills. He found Hand and his riflemen ready to make a vigorous defence. This brought him to a halt, having been ordered not to risk an attack should the pass be occupied. He took post for the night, therefore, in the village of Flatbush.

On the 24th Washington crossed over to Brooklyn, to inspect the lines and reconnoitre the neighborhood. In this visit he felt sensibly the want of General Greene's presence, to explain his plans and point out the localities. The American advanced posts were in the wooded hills. Colonel Hand, with his riflemen, kept watch over the central road, and a strong redoubt had been thrown up in front of the pass, to check any advance of the enemy from Flatbush. Another road leading from Flatbush to Bedford, by which the enemy might get round to the left of the works at Brooklyn, was guarded by two regiments, one under Colonel Williams, posted on the north side of the ridge, the other by a Pennsylvanian rifle regiment, under Colonel Miles, posted on the south side. The enemy were stretched along the country beyond the chain of hills.

As yet nothing had taken place but skirmishing and irregular firing between the outposts. It was with deep concern Washington noticed a prevalent disorder and confusion in the camp. There was a want of system among the officers and co-operation among the troops, each corps seeming to act independently of the rest. Few of the men had any military experience, except, perchance, in bush-fighting with the Indians. Unaccustomed to discipline and the restraint of camps, they sallied forth whenever they pleased, singly or in squads, prowling about and firing upon the enemy, like hunters after game. Much of this was no doubt owing to the protracted illness of General Greene. On returning to the city, therefore, Washington gave the command on Long Island to General Putnam, warning him, however, in his letter of instructions, to summon the officers together, and enjoin them to put a stop to the irregularities which he had observed among the troops. In the meantime, the enemy were augmenting their forces on the island. Two brigades of Hessians, under Lieutenant-general De Heister, were transferred from the camp on Staten Island on the 25th. This movement did not escape the vigilant eye of Washington. He now concluded that the enemy were about to make a push with their main force for the possession of Brooklyn Heights. He accordingly sent over additional reinforcements, and among them Colonel John Haslet's well equipped and well disciplined Delaware regiment; which was joined to Lord Stirling's brigade, chiefly composed of Southern troops, and stationed outside of the lines.

On the 26th he crossed over to Brooklyn, accompanied by Reed, the adjutant-general. There was much movement among the enemy's troops, and their number was evidently augmented. In fact, General De Heister had reached Flatbush with his Hessians, and taken command of the centre; whereupon Sir Henry Clinton, with the right wing, drew off to Flatlands, in a diagonal line to the right of De Heister, while the left wing, commanded by General Grant, extended to the place of landing on Gravesend Bay.

Washington remained all day, aiding General Putnam with his counsels, who, new to the command, had not been able to make himself well acquainted with the fortified posts beyond the lines. In the evening, Washington returned to the city, full of anxious thought. A general attack was evidently at hand. Where would it be made? How would his inexperienced troops stand the encounter? What would be the defence of the city if assailed by the ships? It was a night of intense solicitude, and well might it be; for during that night a plan was carried into effect, fraught with disaster to the Americans.

The plan to which we allude was concerted by General Howe, the commander-in-chief. Sir Henry Clinton with the vanguard, composed of the choicest troops, was, by a circuitous march in the night to throw himself into the road leading from Jamaica to Bedford, seize upon a pass through the Bedford Hills, within three miles of that village, and thus turn the left of the American advanced posts. To divert the attention of the Americans from this stealthy march on their left, General Grant was to menace their right flank toward Gravesend before daybreak, and General De Heister to cannonade their centre, where Colonel Hand was stationed. Neither, however, was to press an attack until the guns of Sir Henry Clinton should give notice that he had effected his purpose, and turned the left flank of the Americans; then the latter were to be assailed at all points with the utmost vigor.

About nine o'clock in the evening of the 26th, Sir Henry Clinton began his march from Flatlands with the vanguard, composed of light infantry. Lord Percy followed with the grenadiers, artillery, and light dragoons, forming the centre. Lord Cornwallis brought up the rear-guard with the heavy ordnance. General Howe accompanied this division. It was a silent march, without beat of drum or sound of trumpet, under guidance of a Long Island tory, along by-roads traversing a swamp by a narrow causeway, and so across the country to the Jamaica road. About two hours before daybreak, they arrived within half a mile of the pass through the Bedford Hills, and halted to prepare for an attack. At this juncture they captured an American patrol, and learnt, to their surprise, that the Bedford pass was unoccupied. In fact, the whole road beyond Bedford, leading to Jamaica, had been left unguarded, excepting by some light volunteer troops. Colonels Williams and Miles, who were stationed to the left of Colonel Hand, among the wooded hills, had been instructed to send out parties occasionally to patrol the road, but no troops had been stationed at the Bedford pass. The road and pass may not have been included in General Greene's plan of defence, or may have been thought too far out of the way to need special precaution. The neglect of them, however, proved fatal.

Sir Henry Clinton immediately detached a battalion of light infantry to secure the pass; and, advancing with his corps at the first break of day, possessed himself of the heights. He was now within three miles of Bedford, and his march had been undiscovered. Having passed the heights, therefore, he halted his division for the soldiers to take some refreshment, preparatory to the morning's hostilities. There we will leave them, while we note how the other divisions performed their part of the plan.

About midnight General Grant moved from Gravesend Bay, with the left wing, composed of two brigades and a regiment of regulars, a battalion of New York loyalists, and ten field-pieces. He proceeded along the road leading past the Narrows and Gowanus Cove, toward the right of the American works. A picket guard of Pennsylvanian and New York militia, under Colonel Atlee, retired before him fighting to a position on the skirts of the wooded hills. In the meantime, scouts had brought in word to the American lines that the enemy were approaching in force upon the right. General Putnam instantly ordered Lord Stirling to hasten with the two regiments nearest at hand, and hold them in check. These were Haslet's Delaware, and Smallwood's Maryland regiments; the latter the *macaronis*, in scarlet and buff, who had outshone, in camp, their yeoman fellow-soldiers in home-spun. They turned out with great alacrity, and Stirling pushed forward with them on the road to the Narrows. By the time he had passed Gowanus Cove, daylight began to appear. Here, on a rising ground he met Colonel Atlee with his Pennsylvania

Provincials, and learned that the enemy were near. Indeed their front began to appear in the uncertain twilight. Stirling ordered Atlee to place himself in ambush in an orchard on the left of the road, and await their coming up, while he formed the Delaware and Maryland regiments along a ridge from the road, up to a piece of woods on the top of the hill.

Atlee gave the enemy two or three volleys as they approached, and then re-treated and formed in the wood on Lord Stirling's left. By this time his lordship was reinforced by Kichline's riflemen, part of whom he placed along a hedge at the foot of the hill, and part in front of the wood. General Grant threw his light troops in the advance, and posted them in an orchard and behind hedges, extending in front of the Americans, and about one hundred and fifty yards distant.

It was now broad daylight. A rattling fire commenced between the British light troops and the American riflemen, which continued for about two hours, when the former retired to their main body. In the meantime, Stirling's position had been strengthened by the arrival of Captain Carpenter with two field-pieces. These were placed on the side of the hill, so as to command the road and the approach for some hundred yards. General Grant, likewise, brought up his artillery within three hundred yards, and formed his brigades on opposite hills, about six hundred yards distant. There was occasional cannonading on both sides, but neither party sought a general action. Lord Stirling's object was merely to hold the enemy in check; and the instructions of General Grant, as we have shown, were not to press an attack until aware that Sir Henry Clinton was on the left flank of the Americans.

During this time, De Heister had commenced his part of the plan by opening a cannonade from his camp at Flatbush upon the redoubt, at the pass of the wooded hills, where Hand and his riflemen were stationed. On hearing this, General Sullivan, who was within the lines, rode forth to Colonel Hand's post to reconnoitre. De Heister, however, according to the plan of operations, did not advance from Flatbush, but kept up a brisk fire from his artillery on the redoubt in front of the pass, which replied as briskly. At the same time, a cannonade from a British ship upon the battery at Red Hook, contributed to distract the attention of the Americans.

In the meantime terror reigned in New York. The volleying of musketry and the booming of cannon at early dawn, had told of the fighting that had commenced. As the morning advanced, and platoon firing and the occasional discharge of a field-piece were heard in different directions, the terror increased. Washington was still in doubt whether this was but a part of a general attack, in which the city was to be included. Five ships of the line were endeavoring to beat up the bay. Were they to cannonade the city, or to land troops above it? Fortunately, a strong head-wind baffled their efforts; but one vessel of inferior force got up far enough to open the fire already mentioned upon the fort at Red Hook. Seeing no likeli-hood of an immediate attack upon the city, Washington hastened over to Brooklyn in his barge, and galloped up to the works. He arrived there in time to witness the catastrophe for which all the movements of the enemy had been concerted.

The thundering of artillery in the direction of Bedford, had given notice that

Sir Henry had turned the left of the Americans. De Heister immediately ordered Colonel Count Donop to advance with his Hessian regiment, and storm the redoubt, while he followed with his whole division. Sullivan did not remain to defend the redoubt. Sir Henry's cannon had apprised him of the fatal truth, that his flank was turned, and he in danger of being surrounded. He ordered a retreat to the lines, but it was already too late. Scarce had he descended from the height, and emerged into the plain, when he was met by the British light infantry, and dragoons, and driven back into the woods. By this time De Heister and his Hessians had come up, and now commenced a scene of confusion, consternation, and slaughter, in which the troops under Williams and Miles were involved. Hemmed in and entrapped between the British and Hessians, and driven from one to the other, the Americans fought for a time bravely, or rather desperately. Some were cut down and trampled by the cavalry, others bayoneted without mercy by the Hessians. Some rallied in groups, and made a brief stand with their rifles from rocks or behind trees. The whole pass was a scene of carnage, resounding with the clash of arms, the tramp of horses, the volleying of fire-arms and the cries of the combatants, with now and then the dreary braying of the trumpet. At length some of the Americans, by a desperate effort, cut their way through the host of foes, and effected a retreat to the lines, fighting as they went. Others took refuge among the woods and fastnesses of the hills, but a great part were either killed or taken prisoners. Among the latter was General Sullivan.

Washington, as we have observed, arrived in time to witness this catastrophe, but was unable to prevent it. He had heard the din of the battle in the woods, and seen the smoke rising from among the trees; but a deep column of the enemy was descending from the hills on the left; his choicest troops were all in action, and he had none but militia to man the works. His solicitude was now awakened for the safety of Lord Stirling and his corps, who had been all the morning exchanging cannonades with General Grant. He saw the danger to which these brave fellows were exposed, though they could not. Stationed on a hill within the lines, he commanded, with his telescope, a view of the whole field, and saw the enemy's reserve, under Cornwallis, marching down by a cross-road to get in their rear, and thus place them between two fires. With breathless anxiety he watched the result.

The sound of Sir Henry Clinton's cannon apprised Stirling that the enemy was between him and the lines. General Grant, too, aware that the time had come for earnest action, was closing up, and had already taken Colonel Atlee prisoner. His lordship now thought to effect a circuitous retreat to the lines, by crossing the creek which empties into Gowanus Cove, near what was called the Yellow Mills. There was a bridge and mill-dam, and the creek might be forded at low water, but no time was to be lost, for the tide was rising. Leaving part of his men to keep face toward General Grant, he advanced with the rest to pass the creek, but was suddenly checked by the appearance of Cornwallis and his grenadiers.

Washington, and some of his officers on the hill, who watched every movement, had supposed that Stirling and his troops, finding the case desperate, would surrender in a body without firing. On the contrary, his lordship boldly attacked Cornwallis with half of Smallwood's battalion, while the rest of his troops retreated across the creek. Washington wrung his hands in agony at the sight. "Good God!" cried he, "what brave fellows I must this day lose!"

It was, indeed, a desperate fight; and now Smallwood's *macaronis* showed their game spirit. They were repeatedly broken, but as often rallied and renewed the fight. "We were on the point of driving Lord Cornwallis from his station," writes Lord Stirling, "but large reinforcements arriving, rendered it impossible to do more than provide for safety." "Being thus surrounded, and no probability of a reinforcement," writes a Maryland officer, "his lordship ordered me to retreat with the remaining part of our men, and force our way to our camp."

Only five companies of Smallwood's battalion were now in action. There was a warm and close engagement for nearly ten minutes. The struggle became desperate on the part of the Americans. Broken and disordered, they rallied in a piece of woods, and made a second attack. They were again overpowered with numbers. Some were surrounded and bayoneted in a field of Indian corn; others joined their comrades who were retreating across the marsh. Lord Stirling had encouraged and animated his young soldiers by his voice and example, but when all was lost he sought out General De Heister, and surrendered himself as his prisoner. More than two hundred and fifty brave fellows perished in this deadly struggle, within sight of the lines of Brooklyn. That part of the Delaware troops who had first crossed the creek and swamp, made good their retreat to the lines with a trifling loss.

The enemy now concentrated their forces within a few hundred yards of the redoubts. The grenadiers were within musket shot. Washington expected they would storm the works, and prepared for a desperate defence. The discharge of a cannon and volleys of musketry from the part of the lines nearest to them, seemed to bring them to a pause. It was, in truth, the forbearance of the British commander that prevented a bloody conflict. His troops, heated with action and flushed with success, were eager to storm the works; but he was unwilling to risk the loss of life that must attend an assault, when the object might be attained at a cheaper rate, by regular approaches. Checking the ardor of his men, therefore, though with some difficulty, he drew them off to a hollow way in front of the lines, but out of reach of the musketry, and encamped there for the night.

The loss of the Americans in this disastrous battle has been variously stated, but is thought in killed, wounded and prisoners, to have been nearly two thousand; a large number, considering that not above five thousand were engaged. The enemy acknowledged a loss of 380 killed and wounded. The success of the enemy was attributed, in some measure, to the doubt in which Washington was kept as to the nature of the intended attack, and at what point it would chiefly be made. This obliged him to keep a great part of his forces in New York, and to distribute those at Brooklyn over a wide extent of country, and at widely distant places. Much of the day's disaster has been attributed, also, to a confusion in the command, caused by the illness of General Greene. Putnam, who had supplied his place in the emergency after the enemy had landed, had not time to make himself acquainted with the post and the surrounding country. The fatal error, however, and one probably arising from all these causes, consisted in leaving the passes through the wooded hills too weakly fortified and guarded; and especially in neglecting the eastern road, by which Sir Henry Clinton got in the rear of the advanced troops, cut them off from the lines, and subjected them to a cross fire of his own men and De Heister's Hessians.

The night after the battle was a weary, yet almost sleepless one to the Americans. Fatigued, dispirited, many of them sick and wounded, yet they were for the most part without tent or other shelter. To Washington it was a night of anxious vigil. Everything boded a close and deadly conflict. The enemy had pitched a number of tents about a mile distant. Their sentries were but a quarter of a mile off, and close to the American sentries. The morning broke lowering and dreary. Large encampments were gradually descried; to appearance, the enemy were twenty thousand strong. As the day advanced, their ordnance began to play upon the works. They were proceeding to intrench themselves, but were driven into their tents by a drenching rain.

Early in the morning General Mifflin arrived in camp with part of the troops which had been stationed at Fort Washington and King's Bridge. He brought with him Shee's prime Philadelphia regiment, and Magaw's Pennsylvania regiment, both well disciplined and officered, and accustomed to act together. They were so much reduced in number, however, by sickness, that they did not amount in the whole to more than eight hundred men. With Mifflin came also Colonel Glover's Massachusetts regiment, composed chiefly of Marblehead fishermen and sailors, hardy, adroit, and weather-proof; trimly clad in blue jackets and trousers. The detachment numbered, in the whole, about thirteen hundred men, all fresh and full of spirits. They were posted at the left extremity of the intrenchments towards the Wallabout.

There were skirmishes throughout the day between the riflemen on the advanced posts and the British "irregulars," which at times were quite severe; but no decided attack was attempted. The main body of the enemy kept within their tents until the latter part of the day; when they began to break ground at about five hundred yards distance from the works, as if preparing to carry them by regular approaches.

On the 29th there was a dense fog over the island, that wrapped everything in mystery. In the course of the morning, General Mifflin, with Adjutant-general Reed, and Colonel Grayson of Virginia, one of Washington's aides-de-camp, rode to the western outposts, in the neighborhood of Red Hook. While they were there, a light breeze lifted the fog from a part of the New York Bay, and revealed the British ships at their anchorage opposite Staten Island. There appeared to be an unusual bustle among them. Boats were passing to and from the admiral's ship, as if seeking or carrying orders. Some movement was apparently in agitation. The idea occurred to the reconnoitring party that the fleet was preparing, should the wind hold and the fog clear away, to come up the bay at the turn of the tide, silence the feeble batteries at Red Hook and the city, and anchor in the East River. In that case the army on Long Island would be completely surrounded and entrapped.

Alarmed at this perilous probability, they spurred back to head-quarters, to urge the immediate withdrawal of the army. As this might not be acceptable advice, Reed, emboldened by his intimacy with the commander-in-chief, undertook to give it. Washington instantly summoned a council of war. The difficulty was already apparent of guarding such extensive works with troops fatigued and dispirited, and exposed to the inclemencies of the weather. Other dangers now presented themselves. Their communication with New York might be cut off by the fleet from below. Other ships had passed round Long Island, and were at Flushing Bay on the Sound. These might land troops on the east side of Harlem River, and make themselves masters of King's Bridge; that key of Manhattan Island. Taking all these things into consideration, it was resolved to cross with the troops to the city that very night.

Never did retreat require greater secrecy and circumspection. Nine thousand men, with all the munitions of war, were to be withdrawn from before a victorious army, encamped so near that every stroke of spade and pickaxe from their trenches could be heard. The retreating troops, moreover, were to be embarked and conveyed across a strait three-quarters of a mile wide, swept by rapid tides. The least alarm of their movement would bring the enemy upon them, and produce a terrible scene of confusion and carnage at the place of embarkation. Washington made the preparatory arrangements with great alertness, yet profound secrecy. Verbal orders were sent to Colonel Hughes, who acted as quartermaster-general, to impress all water craft, largo and small, from Spyt den Duivel on the Hudson round to Hell Gate on the Sound, and have them on the east side of the city by evening. The order was issued at noon, and so promptly executed that, although some of the vessels had to be brought a distance of fifteen miles, they were all at Brooklyn at eight o'clock in the evening, and put under the management of Colonel Glover's amphibious Marblehead regiment.

To prepare the army for a general movement without betraying the object, orders were issued for the troops to hold themselves in readiness for a night attack upon the enemy. To keep the enemy from discovering the withdrawal of the Americans until their main body should have embarked in the boats and pushed off from the shore, General Mifflin was to remain at the lines with his Pennsylvania troops, and the gallant remains of Haslet, Smallwood and Hand's regiments, with guards posted and sentinels alert, as if nothing extraordinary was taking place; when the main embarkation was effected, they were themselves to move off quietly, march briskly to the ferry, and embark.

It was late in the evening when the troops began to retire from the breastworks. As one regiment quietly withdrew from their station on guard, the troops on the right and left moved up and filled the vacancy. There was a stifled murmur in the camp, unavoidable in a movement of the kind; but it gradually died away in the direction of the river, as the main body moved on in silence and order. The youthful Hamilton, whose military merits had won the favor of General Greene, and who had lost his baggage and a field-piece in the battle, brought up the rear of the retreating party.

The embarkation went on with all possible despatch, under the vigilant eye of Washington, who stationed himself at the ferry, superintending every movement.

In his anxiety for despatch, he sent back Colonel Scammel, one of his aides-de-camp, to hasten forward all the troops that were on the march. Scammel blundered in executing his errand, and gave the order to Mifflin likewise. The general instantly called in his pickets and sentinels, and set off for the ferry.

By this time the tide had turned; there was a strong wind from the north-east; the boats with oars were insufficient to convey the troops; those with sails could not make headway against wind and tide. There was some confusion at the ferry, and in the midst of it, General Mifflin came down with the whole covering party; adding to the embarrassment and uproar. "Good God! General Mifflin!" cried Washington, "I am afraid you have ruined us by so unseasonably withdrawing the troops from the lines." "I did so by your order," replied Mifflin with some warmth. "It cannot be!" exclaimed Washington. "By G—, I did!" was the blunt rejoinder. "Did Scammel act as aide-de-camp for the day, or did he not?" "He did." "Then," said Mifflin, "I had orders through him." "It is a dreadful mistake," rejoined Washington, "and unless the troops can regain the lines before their absence is discovered by the enemy, the most disastrous consequences are to be apprehended." Mifflin led back his men to the lines, which had been completely deserted for three-quarters of an hour. Fortunately, the dense fog had prevented the enemy from discovering that they were unoccupied. The men resumed their former posts, and remained at them until called off to cross the ferry.

The fog which prevailed all this time, seemed almost providential. While it hung over Long Island, and concealed the movements of the Americans, the atmosphere was clear on the New York side of the river. The adverse wind, too, died away, the river became so smooth that the row-boats could be laden almost to the gunwale; and a favoring breeze sprang up for the sail-boats. The whole embarkation of troops, artillery, ammunition, provisions, cattle, horses and carts, was happily effected, and by daybreak the greater part had safely reached the city, thanks to the aid of Glover's Marblehead men. Scarce anything was abandoned to the enemy, excepting a few heavy pieces of artillery. At a proper time, Mifflin with his covering party left the lines, and effected a silent retreat to the ferry. Washington, though repeatedly entreated, refused to enter a boat until all the troops were embarked; and crossed the river with the last.

This extraordinary retreat, which, in its silence and celerity, equalled the midnight fortifying of Bunker's Hill, was one of the most signal achievements of the war, and redounded greatly to the reputation of Washington, who, we are told, for forty-eight hours preceding the safe extricating of his army from their perilous situation, scarce closed his eyes, and was the greater part of the time on horseback.

CHAPTER XXXIII.

RETREAT FROM NEW YORK ISLAND.

The enemy had now possession of Long Island. British and Hessian troops garrisoned the works at Brooklyn, or were distributed at Bushwick, Newtown, Hell Gate and Flushing. Admiral Howe came up with the main body of the fleet, and anchored close to Governor's Island, within cannon shot of the city.

"Our situation is truly distressing," writes Washington to the President of Congress, on the 2d of September. "The check our detachment sustained on the 27th ultimo, has dispirited too great a proportion of our troops, and filled their minds with apprehension and despair. The militia, instead of calling forth their utmost efforts to a brave and manly opposition in order to repair our losses, are dismayed, intractable, and impatient to return. Great numbers of them have gone off; in some instances, almost by whole regiments, by half ones, and by companies, at a time.... With the deepest concern, I am obliged to confess my want of confidence in the generality of the troops.... Our number of men at present fit for duty is under twenty thousand. I have ordered General Mercer to send the men intended for the flying camp to this place, about a thousand in number, and to try with the militia, if practicable, to make a diversion upon Staten Island. Till of late, I had no doubt in my own mind of defending this place; nor should I have yet, if the men would do their duty, but this I despair of. If we should be obliged to abandon the town, ought it to stand as winter quarters for the enemy? They would derive great conveniences from it, on the one hand, and much property would be destroyed on the other. It is an important question, but will admit of but little time for deliberation. At present I daresay the enemy mean to preserve it if they can. If Congress, therefore, should resolve upon the destruction of it, the resolution should be a profound secret, as the knowledge will make a capital change in their plans."

On the night of Monday (Sept. 2d) a forty gun ship, taking advantage of a favorable wind and tide, passed between Governor's Island and Long Island, swept unharmed by the batteries which opened upon her, and anchored in Turtle Bay, above the city. In the morning, Washington despatched Major Crane of the artillery, with two twelve pounders and a howitzer to annoy her from the New York shore. They hulled her several times, and obliged her to take shelter behind Blackwell's Island. Several other ships-of-war, with transports and store-ships had made their appearance in the upper part of the Sound, having gone round Long Island.

As the city might speedily be attacked, Washington caused all the sick and wounded to be conveyed to Orangetown, in the Jerseys, and such military stores and baggage as were not immediately needed, to be removed, as fast as conveyances could be procured, to a post partially fortified at Dobbs' Ferry, on the eastern bank of the Hudson, about twenty-two miles above the city.

The thousand men ordered from the flying camp were furnished by General Mercer. They were Maryland troops under Colonels Griffith and Richardson, and were a seasonable addition to the effective forces; but the ammunition carried off by the disbanding militia was a serious loss at this critical juncture.

A work had been commenced on the Jersey shore, opposite Fort Washington, to aid in protecting Putnam's chevaux-de-frise which had sunk between them. This work had received the name of Fort Constitution (a name already borne by one of the forts in the Highlands). Troops were drawn from the flying camp to make a strong encampment in the vicinity of the fort, with an able officer to command it and a skilful engineer to strengthen the works. It was hoped, by the co-operation of these opposite forts and the chevaux-de-frise, to command the Hudson, and prevent the passing and repassing of hostile ships.

The British, in the meantime, forbore to press further hostilities. Lord Howe was really desirous of a peaceful adjustment of the strife between the colonies and the mother country, and supposed this a propitious moment for a new attempt at pacification. He accordingly sent off General Sullivan on parole, charged with an overture to Congress. In this he declared himself empowered and disposed to compromise the dispute between Great Britain and America, on the most favorable terms, and though he could not treat with Congress as a legally organized body, he was desirous of a conference with some of its members. These, for the time, he should consider only as private gentlemen, but if in the conference any probable scheme of accommodation should be agreed upon, the authority of Congress would afterwards be acknowledged to render the compact complete.

The message caused some embarrassment in Congress. To accede to the interview might seem to waive the question of independence; to decline it was to shut the door on all hope of conciliation, and might alienate the co-operation of some worthy whigs who still clung to that hope. After much debate, Congress, on the 5th September, replied that, being the representatives of the free and independent States of America, they could not send any members to confer with his lordship in their private characters, but that, ever desirous of establishing peace on reasonable terms, they would send a committee of their body to ascertain what authority he had to treat with persons authorized by Congress, and what propositions he had to offer. A committee was chosen on the 6th of September, composed of John Adams, Edward Rutledge, and Doctor Franklin.

The proposed conference was to take place on the 11th, at a house on Staten Island, opposite to Amboy; at which latter place the veteran Mercer was stationed with his flying camp. At Amboy, the committee found Lord Howe's barge waiting to receive them. The admiral met them on their landing, and conducted them through his guards to his house.

On opening the conference, his lordship again intimated that he could not treat with them as a committee of Congress, but only confer with them as private gentlemen of influence in the colonies, on the means of restoring peace between the two countries. The commissioners replied that as their business was to hear, he might consider them in what light he pleased; but that they should consider themselves in no other character than that in which they were placed by order of Congress. Lord Howe then entered into a discourse of considerable length, but made no explicit proposition of peace, nor promise of redress of grievances, excepting on condition that the colonies should return to their allegiance. This, the commissioners replied, was not now to be expected. Their repeated humble petitions to the king and parliament having been treated with contempt, and answered by additional injuries, and war having been declared against them, the colonies had declared their independence, and it was not in the power of Congress to agree for them that they should return to their former dependent state. His lordship expressed his sorrow that no accommodation was likely to take place; and the conference broke up.

The result of this conference had a beneficial effect. It showed that his lordship had no power but what was given by the act of Parliament; and put an end to the popular notion that he was vested with secret powers to negotiate an adjustment of grievances.

Since the retreat from Brooklyn, Washington had narrowly watched the movements of the enemy to discover their further plans. Their whole force, excepting about four thousand men, had been transferred from Staten to Long Island. A great part was encamped on the peninsula between Newtown Inlet and Flushing Bay. A battery had been thrown up near the extremity of the peninsula, to check an American battery at Horen's Hook opposite, and to command the mouth of Harlem River. Troops were subsequently stationed on the islands about Hell Gate. "It is evident," writes Washington, "the enemy mean to enclose us on the island of New York, by taking post in our rear, while the shipping secures the front, and thus, by cutting off our communication with the country, oblige us to fight them on their own terms, or surrender at discretion."

The question was, how could their plans be most successfully opposed? On every side, he saw a choice of difficulties; every measure was to be formed with some apprehension that all the troops would not do their duty. In a council of war, held on the 7th of September, the question was discussed, whether the city should be defended or evacuated. All admitted that it would not be tenable, should it be cannonaded and bombarded. Several of the council, among whom was General Putnam, were for a total and immediate removal from the city; urging that one part of the army might be cut off before the other could support it; the extremities being at least sixteen miles apart, and the whole, when collected, being inferior to the enemy. By removing, they would deprive the enemy of the advantage of their ships; they would keep them at bay; put nothing at hazard; keep the army together to be recruited another year, and preserve the unspent stores and the heavy artillery. Washington himself inclined to this opinion. Others, however, were unwilling to abandon a place which had been fortified with great cost and labor, and seemed defensible, and which, by some, had been considered the key to the northern country.

After much discussion a middle course was adopted. Putnam, with five thousand men, was to be stationed in the city. Heath, with nine thousand, was to keep guard on the upper part of the Island, and oppose any attempt of the enemy to land. His troops, among whom were Magaw's, Shee's, Hand's, and Miles's Pennsylvanian battalions, and Haslet's Delaware regiment, were posted about King's Bridge and its vicinity.

The third division, composed principally of militia, was under the command of Generals Greene and Spencer, the former of whom, however, was still unwell. It was stationed about the centre of the island, chiefly along Turtle Bay and Kip's Bay, where strong works had been thrown up, to guard against any landing of troops from the ships or from the encampments on Long Island. It was also to hold itself ready to support either of the other divisions. Washington himself had his head-quarters at a short distance from the city. A resolution of Congress, passed the 10th of September, left the occupation or abandonment of the city entirely at Washington's discretion.

Convinced of the propriety of evacuation, Washington prepared for it by ordering the removal of all stores, excepting such as were indispensable for the subsistence of the troops while they remained. A letter from a Rhode Island officer, on a visit to New York, gives an idea of its agitations. "On the 13th of September, just after dinner, three frigates and a forty-gun ship sailed up the East River with a gentle breeze, toward Hell Gate, and kept up an incessant fire, assisted by the cannon at Governor's Island."

On the 14th, Washington's baggage was removed to King's Bridge, whither head-quarters were to be transferred the same evening; it being clear that the enemy were preparing to encompass him on the island. About sunset of the same day, six more ships, two of them men-of-war, passed up the Sound and joined those above. Within half an hour came expresses spurring to head-quarters, one from Mifflin at King's Bridge, the other from Colonel Sargent at Horen's Hook. Three or four thousand of the enemy were crossing at Hell Gate to the islands at the mouth of Harlem River, where numbers were already encamped. An immediate landing at Harlem, or Morrisania, was apprehended. Washington was instantly in the saddle, spurring to Harlem Heights. The night, however, passed away quietly. In the morning the enemy commenced operations. Three ships of war stood up the Hudson, and anchored opposite Bloomingdale, a few miles above the city, and put a stop to the removal by water of stores and provisions to Dobbs' Ferry. About eleven o'clock, the ships in the East River commenced a heavy cannonade upon the breastworks between Turtle Bay and the city. At the same time two divisions of the troops encamped on Long Island, one British, under Sir Henry Clinton, the other Hessian, under Colonel Donop, emerged in boats from the deep, woody recesses of Newtown Inlet, and under cover of the fire from the ships, began to land at two points between Turtle and Kip's Bays. The breastworks were manned by militia who had recently served at Brooklyn. Disheartened by their late defeat, they fled at the first advance of the enemy. Two brigades of Putnam's Connecticut troops, which had been sent that morning to support them, caught the panic, and regardless of the commands and entreaties of their officers, joined in the general scamper.

At this moment Washington, who had mounted his horse at the first sound of the cannonade, came galloping to the scene of confusion; riding in among the fugitives, he endeavored to rally and restore them to order. All in vain. At the first appearance of sixty or seventy redcoats, they broke again without firing a shot, and fled in headlong terror. Losing all self-command at the sight of such dastardly conduct, he dashed his hat upon the ground in a transport of rage. "Are these the men," exclaimed he, "with whom I am to defend America!" In a paroxysm of passion and despair he snapped his pistols at some of them, threatened others with his sword, and was so heedless of his own danger that he might have fallen into the hands of the enemy, who were not eighty yards distant, had not an aide-de-camp seized the bridle of his horse, and absolutely hurried him away.

It was one of the rare moments of his life, when the vehement element of his nature was stirred up from its deep recesses. He soon recovered his self-possession, and took measures against the general peril. The enemy might land another force about Hell Gate, seize upon Harlem Heights, the strong central portion of the island, cut off all retreat of the lower divisions, and effectually sever his army. In all haste, therefore, he sent off an express to the forces encamped above, directing them to secure that position immediately; while another express to Putnam, ordered an immediate retreat from the city to those heights.

It was indeed a perilous moment. Had the enemy followed up their advantage, and seized upon the heights, before thus occupied, or had they extended themselves across the island, from the place where they had effected a landing, the result might have been most disastrous to the Americans. Fortunately, they contented themselves for the present with sending a strong detachment down the road along the East River, leading to the city, while the main body, British and Hessians, rested on their arms.

In the meantime, Putnam, on receiving Washington's express, called in his pickets and guards, and abandoned the city in all haste, leaving behind him a large quantity of provisions and military stores, and most of the heavy cannon. To avoid the enemy he took the Bloomingdale road, though this exposed him to be raked by the enemy's ships anchored in the Hudson. It was a forced march, on a sultry day, under a burning sun and amid clouds of dust. His army was encumbered with women and children, and all kinds of baggage. Many were overcome by fatigue and thirst, some perished by hastily drinking cold water; but Putnam rode backward and forward, hurrying every one on. All the loss sustained by him in his perilous retreat, was fifteen killed, and about three hundred taken prisoners.

The fortified camp, where the main body of the army was now assembled, was upon that neck of land several miles long, and for the most part not above a mile wide, which forms the upper part of Manhattan or New York Island. It forms a chain of rocky heights, and is separated from the mainland by Harlem River, a narrow strait, extending from Hell Gate on the Sound, to Spyt den Duivel, a creek or inlet of the Hudson. Fort Washington occupied the crest of one of the rocky heights above mentioned, overlooking the Hudson, and about two miles north of it was King's Bridge, crossing Spyt den Duivel Creek, and forming at that time the only pass from Manhattan Island to the mainland. About a mile and a half south of the fort, a double row of lines extended across the neck from Harlem River to the Hudson. They faced south towards New York, were about a quarter of a mile apart, and were defended by batteries.

There were strong advanced posts about two miles south of the outer line; one on the left of Harlem, commanded by General Spencer, the other on the right, at what was called McGowan's Pass, commanded by General Putnam. About a mile and a half beyond these posts the British lines extended across the island from Horen's Hook to the Hudson, being a continuous encampment, two miles in length, with both flanks covered by shipping. An open plain intervened between the hostile camps.

While thus posted, Washington was incessantly occupied in fortifying the approaches to his camp by redoubts, *abatis*, and deep intrenchments. In the course of his rounds of inspection, he was struck with the skill and science displayed in the construction of some of the works, which were thrown up under the direction of a youthful captain of artillery. It proved to be the same young officer, Alexander Hamilton, whom Greene had recommended to his notice. After some conversation with him, Washington invited him to his marquee, and thus commenced that intercourse which has indissolubly linked their memories together.

On the morning of the 16th, word was brought to head-quarters that the enemy were advancing in three large columns. There had been so many false reports, that Reed, the adjutant-general, obtained leave to sally out and ascertain the truth. Washington himself soon mounted his horse and rode towards the advanced posts. On arriving there he heard a brisk firing. It was kept up for a time with great spirit. There was evidently a sharp conflict. At length Reed came galloping back with information. A strong detachment of the enemy had attacked the most advanced post, which was situated on a hill skirted by a wood. It had been bravely defended by Lieutenant-colonel Knowlton. After skirmishing for a time, the party had been overpowered by numbers and driven in, and the outpost was taken possession of by the enemy.

Reed urged that troops should be sent to support the brave fellows who had behaved so well. While he was talking with Washington, "the enemy," he says, "appeared in open view, and sounded their bugles in the most insulting manner, as usual after a fox-chase. I never," adds he, "felt such a sensation before; it seemed to crown our disgrace."

Washington, too, was stung by the taunting note of derision; it recalled the easy triumph of the enemy at Kip's Bay. Resolved that something should be done to wipe out that disgrace, and rouse the spirits of the army, he ordered out three companies from Colonel Weedon's regiment just arrived from Virginia, and sent them under Major Leitch, to join Knowlton's rangers. The troops thus united were to get in the rear of the enemy, while a feigned attack was made upon them in front.

The plan was partially successful. As the force advanced to make the false attack, the enemy ran down the hill, and took what they considered an advantageous position behind some fences and bushes which skirted it. A firing commenced between them and the advancing party, but at too great distance to do much harm on either side. In the meantime, Knowlton and Leitch, ignorant of this change in the enemy's position, having made a circuit, came upon them in flank instead of in rear. They were sharply received. A vivid contest took place, in which Connecticut vied with Virginia in bravery. In a little while Major Leitch received three bullets in his side, and was borne off the field. Shortly afterward, a wound in the head from a musket ball, brought Knowlton to the ground. Colonel Reed placed him on his horse, and conveyed him to a distant redoubt. The men, undismayed by the fall of their leaders, fought with unflinching resolution under the command of their captains. The enemy were reinforced by a battalion of Hessians and a company of chasseurs. Washington likewise sent reinforcements of New England and Maryland troops. The action waxed hotter and hotter; the enemy were driven from the wood into the plain, and pushed for some distance; the Americans were pursuing them with ardor, when Washington, having effected the object of this casual encounter, and being unwilling to risk a general action, ordered a retreat to be sounded.

Colonel Knowlton did not long survive the action. "When gasping in the agonies of death," says Colonel Reed, "all his inquiry was whether he had driven in the enemy." The brave Leitch died of his wounds on the 1st of October.

In the dead of the night, on the 20th September, a great light was beheld by the picket guards, looming up from behind the hills in the direction of the city. It continued throughout the night, and was at times so strong that the heavens in that direction appeared to them, they said, as if in flames. At daybreak huge columns of smoke were still rising. It was evident there had been a great conflagration in New York. In the course of the morning Captain Montresor, aide-de-camp to General Howe, came out with a flag, bearing a letter to Washington on the subject of an exchange of prisoners. According to Montresor's account a great part of the city had been burnt down, and as the night was extremely windy, the whole might have been so, but for the exertions of the officers and men of the British army. The enemy were now bringing up their heavy cannon, preparatory to an attack upon the American camp by the troops and by the ships. What was the state of Washington's army? The terms of engagement of many of his men would soon be at an end, most of them would terminate with the year, nor did Congress hold out offers to encourage re-enlistments. "We are now, as it were, upon the eve of another dissolution of the army," writes he, "and unless some speedy and effectual measures are adopted by Congress, our cause will be lost." Under these gloomy apprehensions, he borrowed, as he said, "a few moments from the hours allotted to sleep," and on the night of the 24th of September, penned an admirable letter to the President of Congress, setting forth the total inefficiency of the existing military system, the total insubordination, waste, confusion, and discontent produced by it among the men, and the harassing cares and vexations to which it subjected the commanders. Nor did he content himself with complaining, but, in his full, clear, and sagacious manner, pointed out the remedies. To the achievements of his indefatigable pen, we may trace the most fortunate turns in the current of our revolutionary affairs. In the present instance his representations, illustrated by sad experience, produced at length a reorganization of the army, and the establishment of it on a permanent footing. It was decreed that eighty-eight battalions should be furnished in quotas, by the different States, according to their abilities. The pay of the officers was raised. The troops which engaged to serve throughout the war were to receive a bounty of twenty dollars and one hundred acres of land, besides a yearly suit of clothes while in service. Those who enlisted but for three years received no bounty in land. The bounty to officers was on a higher ratio. The States were to send commissioners to the army, to arrange with the commander-in-chief as to the appointment of officers in their quotas; but, as they might occasionally be slow in complying with this regulation, Washington was empowered to fill up all vacancies.

All this was a great relief to his mind. He was gratified, also, by effecting, after a long correspondence with the British commander, an exchange of prisoners, in which those captured in Canada were included. Among those restored to the service were Lord Stirling and Captain Daniel Morgan. The latter, in reward of his good conduct in the expedition with Arnold, and of "his intrepid behavior in the assault upon Quebec where the brave Montgomery fell," was recommended to Congress by Washington for the command of a rifle regiment about to be raised. We shall see how eminently he proved himself worthy of this recommendation.

Nothing perplexed Washington at this juncture more than the conduct of the enemy. He beheld before him a hostile army, armed and equipped at all points, superior in numbers, thoroughly disciplined, flushed with success, and abounding in the means of pushing a vigorous campaign, yet suffering day after day to elapse unimproved. What could be the reason of this supineness on the part of Sir William Howe? He must know the depressed and disorganized state of the American camp; the absolute chaos that reigned there. Did he meditate an irruption into the Jerseys? A movement towards Philadelphia? Did he intend to detach a part of his forces for a winter's campaign against the South?

In this uncertainty, Washington wrote to General Mercer, of the flying camp, to keep a vigilant watch from the Jersey shore on the movements of the enemy, by sea and land, and to station videttes on the Neversink Heights, to give immediate intelligence should any of the British fleet put to sea. At the same time he himself practised unceasing vigilance, visiting the different parts of his camp on horseback. Occasionally he crossed over to Fort Constitution, on the Jersey shore, of which General Greene had charge, and, accompanied by him, extended his reconnoitrings down to Paulus Hook, to observe what was going on in the city and among the enemy's ships. Greene had recently been promoted to the rank of major-general, and now had command of all the troops in the Jerseys. He had liberty to shift his quarters to Baskingridge or Bergen, as circumstances might require; but was enjoined to keep up a communication with the main army, east of the Hudson, so as to secure a retreat in case of necessity.

The security of the Hudson was at this time an object of great solicitude with

Congress, and much reliance was placed on Putnam's obstructions at Fort Washington. Four galleys, mounted with heavy guns and swivels, were stationed at the chevaux-de-frise, and two new ships were at hand, which, filled with stones, were to be sunk where they would block up the channel. A sloop was also at anchor, having on board a machine, invented by a Mr. Bushnell, for submarine explosion, with which to blow up the men-of-war; a favorite scheme with General Putnam. The obstructions were so commanded by batteries on each shore, that it was thought no hostile ship would be able to pass. On the 9th of October, however, the Roebuck and Phoenix, each of forty-four guns, and the Tartar of twenty guns, which had been lying for some time opposite Bloomingdale, got under way with their three tenders, at eight o'clock in the morning, and came standing up the river with an easy southern breeze. At their approach, the galleys and the two ships intended to be sunk, got under way with all haste, as did a schooner laden with rum, sugar and other supplies for the American army, and the sloop with Bushnell's submarine machine.

The Roebuck, Phoenix and Tartar broke through the vaunted barriers as through a cobweb. Seven batteries kept up a constant fire upon them, yet a gentleman was observed walking the deck of the second ship as coolly as if nothing were the matter. The hostile ships kept on their course, the American vessels scudding before them. The schooner was overhauled and captured; a well-aimed shot sent the sloop and Bushnell's submarine engine to the bottom of the river. The two new ships would have taken refuge in Spyt den Duivel Creek, but fearing there might not be water enough, they kept on and drove ashore at Philips' Mills at Yonkers. Two of the galleys got into a place of safety, where they were protected from the shore; the other two trusted to outsail their pursuers. The breeze freshened, and the frigates gained on them fast; at eleven o'clock began to fire on them with their bow-chasers, and at twelve o'clock overreached them, which caused them to bear in shore; at half-past one the galleys ran aground just above Dobbs' Ferry, and lay exposed to a shower of grape-shot. The crews, without stopping to burn or bilge them, swam on shore, and the enemy took possession of the two galleys.

One express after another brought Washington word of these occurrences. First, he sent off a party of rifle and artillery men, with two twelve-pounders, to secure the new ships which had run aground at Yonkers. Next, he ordered Colonel Sargent to march up along the eastern shore with five hundred infantry, a troop of light-horse, and a detachment of artillery, to prevent the landing of the enemy. Before the troops arrived at Dobbs' Ferry, the ships' boats had plundered a store there and set it on fire.

To prevent, if possible, the men-of-war already up the river from coming down, or others from below joining them, Washington gave orders to complete the obstructions. Two hulks which lay in Spyt den Duivel Creek, were hastily ballasted by men from General Heath's division, and men were sent up to get off the ships which had run aground at Philips' Mills, that they might be brought down and sunk immediately.

[This new irruption of hostile ships caused great excitement and alarm. It was rumored that bodies of disaffected citizens were organizing in order to assist the enemy, and it was feared that these ships were carrying arms and ammunition for these bodies of men, and also concealed troops to co-operate with them in over-powering the well-affected, and in seizing upon such passes as would cut off the communication between the army and the upper counties.]

Fugitive river crafts carried the news up to the Highlands that the frigates were already before Tarrytown in the Tappan Sea. Word was instantly despatched to Peter R. Livingston, president of the Provincial Congress, and startled that de-liberative body, which was then seated at Fishkill, just above the Highlands. Washington ordered up part of the militia from Massachusetts, under General Lincoln. As a further precaution, an express was sent off to Colonel Tash, who, with a regiment of New Hampshire militia, was on his way from Hartford to the camp, ordering him to repair with all possible dispatch to Fishkill, and there hold himself at the disposition of the committee of safety.

James Clinton, also, who had charge of the posts in the Highlands, was put on the alert. That trusty officer was now a brigadier-general, having been promoted by Congress, on the 8th of August. He was charged to have all boats passing up and down the river rigidly searched, and the passengers examined. Beside the usual sentries, a barge, well manned, was to patrol the river opposite to each fort every night; all barges, row-boats, and other small craft, between the forts in the Highlands and the army, were to be secured in a place of safety, to prevent their falling into the enemy's hands and giving intelligence. Moreover, a French engineer was sent up to aid in strengthening and securing the passes.

CHAPTER XXXIV.

RETREAT THROUGH WESTCHESTER COUNTY.— BATTLE OF WHITE PLAINS.

On the morning of the 12th of October, Washington received intelligence by express from General Heath, stationed above King's Bridge, that the enemy were landing with artillery on Throg's Neck in the Sound, about nine miles from the camp. Washington surmised that Howe was pursuing his original plan of getting into the rear of the American army, cutting off its supplies, which were chiefly derived from the East, and interrupting its communication with the main country. Officers were ordered to their alarm posts, and the troops to be ready, under arms, to act as occasion might require. Word, at the same time, was sent to General Heath to dispose of the troops on his side of King's Bridge, and of two militia regiments posted on the banks of Harlem River opposite the camp, in such manner as he should think necessary. Having made all his arrangements as promptly as possible, Washington mounted his horse, and rode over towards Throg's Neck to reconnoitre.

Throg's Neck is a peninsula in Westchester County, stretching upwards of two miles into the Sound. It was separated from the mainland by a narrow creek and a marsh, and was surrounded by water every high tide. A bridge across a creek connecting with a ruined causeway across the marsh, led to the mainland, and the upper end of the creek was fordable at low water. Early in the morning, eighty or ninety boats full of men had stood up the Sound from Montresor's Island, and Long Island, and had landed troops to the number of four thousand on Throg's Point, the extremity of the neck. Thence their advance pushed forward toward the causeway and bridge, to secure that pass to the mainland. General Heath had been too rapid for them. Colonel Hand and his Philadelphia riflemen had taken up the planks of the bridge, and posted themselves opposite the end of the causeway, whence they commenced firing with their rifles. They were soon reinforced by Colonel Prescott, of Bunker's Hill renown, with his regiment, and Lieutenant Bryant of the artillery, with a three-pounder. Checked at this pass, the British moved toward the head of the creek; here they found the Americans in possession of the ford, where they were reinforced by Colonel Graham of the New York line, with his regiment, and Lieutenant Jackson of the artillery, with a six-pounder. These skilful dispositions of his troops by General Heath had brought the enemy to a stand.

Having surveyed the ground, Washington ordered works to be thrown up at the passes from the neck to the mainland. The British also threw up a work at the end of the causeway. In the afternoon nine ships, with a great number of schooners, sloops, and flat-bottomed boats full of men, passed through Hell Gate, towards Throg's Point; and information received from two deserters, gave Washington reason to believe that the greater part of the enemy's forces were gathering in that quarter. General McDougall's brigade, in which were Colonel Smallwood and the independent companies, was sent in the evening to strengthen Heath's division at King's Bridge, and to throw up works opposite the ford of Harlem River. Greene, who had heard of the landing of the enemy at Throg's Neck, wrote over to Washington, from Fort Constitution, informing him that he had three brigades ready to join him if required.

[On the 14th, General Lee, whose return from the south had been anxiously expected, arrived in camp. The success of Lee at the south was contrasted by many with the defeat on Long Island and evacuation of New York, and they began to consider him the main hope of the army. His appearance was welcomed as the harbinger of good luck.] No one gave him a sincerer greeting than the commander-in-chief; who, diffident of his own military knowledge, had a high opinion of that of Lee. He immediately gave him command of the troops above King's Bridge, now the greatest part of the army, but desired that he would not exercise it for a day or two, until he had time to acquaint himself with the localities and arrangements of the post. Heath, in the interim, held the command.

In the meantime, Congress, on the 11th of October, having heard of the ingress of the Phoenix, Roebuck and Tartar, passed a resolution that General Washington be desired, if it be practicable, by every art, and at whatever expensive, to obstruct effectually the navigation of the North River between Fort Washington and Mount Constitution, as well to prevent the regress of the enemy's vessels lately gone up as to hinder them from receiving succors.

Washington held a council of war on the 16th, at Lee's head-quarters, at which all the major-generals were present excepting Greene, and all the brigadiers, as well as Colonel Knox, who commanded the artillery. Letters from the Convention and from individual members of it were read, concerning the turbulence of the disaffected in the upper parts of the State; intelligence gained from deserters was likewise stated, showing the intention of the enemy to surround the camp. The policy was then discussed of remaining in their present position on Manhattan Island, and awaiting there the menaced attack.

"After much consideration and debate," says the record of the council, "the following question was stated: Whether (it having appeared that the obstructions in the North River have proved insufficient, and that the enemy's whole force is now in our rear on Frog Point) it is now deemed possible, in our situation, to prevent the enemy from cutting off the communication with the country, and compelling us to fight them at all disadvantages or surrender prisoners at discretion?"

All agreed, with but one dissenting voice,[9] that it was not possible to prevent the communication from being cut off, and that one of the consequences mentioned in the question must follow.

[9] That of General George Clinton.

As the resolve of Congress seemed imperative with regard to Fort Washington, that post, it was agreed, should be "retained as long as possible." A strong garrison was accordingly placed in it, composed chiefly of troops from Magaw's and Shee's Pennsylvania regiments, the latter under Lieutenant-colonel Lambert Cadwalader, of Philadelphia. Shee having obtained leave of absence, Colonel Magaw was put in command of the post, and solemnly charged by Washington to defend it to the last extremity. The name of the opposite post on the Jersey shore, where Greene was stationed, was changed from Fort Constitution to Fort Lee, in honor of the general. Lee, in fact, was the military idol of the day.

Previous to decamping from Manhattan Island, Washington formed four divisions of the army, which were respectively assigned to Generals Lee, Heath, Sullivan (recently obtained in exchange for General Prescott), and Lincoln. Lee was stationed on Valentine's Hill, on the mainland immediately opposite King's Bridge, to cover the transportation across it of the military stores and heavy baggage. The other divisions were to form a chain of fortified posts, extending about thirteen miles along a ridge of hills on the west side of the Bronx, from Lee's camp up to the village of White Plains.

Washington's head-quarters continued to be on Harlem Heights for several days. By his skilful disposition of the army it was protected in its whole length by the Bronx, a narrow but deep stream, fringed with trees, which ran along the foot of the ridge; at the same time his troops faced and outflanked the enemy, and covered the roads along which the stores and baggage had to be transported. On the 21st, he shifted his head-quarters to Valentine's Hill, and on the 23d to White Plains, where he stationed himself in a fortified camp.

While he was thus incessantly in action, General, now Sir William Howe, remained for six days passive in his camp on Throg's Point, awaiting the arrival of supplies and reinforcements, instead of pushing across to the Hudson, and throwing himself between Washington's army and the upper country. His inaction lost him a golden opportunity. By the time his supplies arrived, the Americans had broken up the causeway leading to the mainland, and taken positions too strong to be easily forced. Finding himself headed in this direction, Sir William re-embarked part of his troops in flat boats on the 18th, crossed Eastchester Bay, and landed on Pell's Point, at the mouth of Hutchinson's River. Here he was joined in a few hours by the main body, with the baggage and artillery, and proceeded through the manor of Pelham towards New Rochelle; still with a view to get above Washington's army.

In their march, the British were waylaid and harassed by Colonel Glover of Massachusetts, with his own, Reed's and Shepard's regiments of infantry. Twice the British advance guard were thrown into confusion and driven back with severe loss, by a sharp fire from behind stone fences. A third time they advanced in solid columns. The Americans gave them repeated volleys, and then retreated with the loss of eight killed and thirteen wounded, among whom was Colonel Shepard.

On the 21st, General Howe was encamped about two miles north of New Rochelle, with his outposts extending to Mamaroneck on the Sound. While in this neighborhood, he was reinforced by a second division of Hessians under General Knyphausen, and a regiment of Waldeckers, both of which had recently arrived in New York. He was joined, also, by the whole of the seventeenth light-dragoons, and a part of the sixteenth, which had arrived on the 3d instant from Ireland, with Lieutenant-colonel (afterwards Earl) Harcourt. Some of their horses had been brought with them across the sea, others had been procured since their arrival.

The Americans at first regarded these troopers with great dread. Washington, therefore, took pains to convince them, that in a rough, broken country, like the present, full of stone fences, no troops were so inefficient as cavalry. They could be waylaid and picked off by sharp-shooters from behind walls and thickets, while they could not leave the road to pursue their covert foe. Further to inspirit them against this new enemy, he proclaimed, in general orders, a reward of one hundred dollars for every trooper brought in with his horse and accoutrements, and so on, in proportion to the completeness of the capture.

On the 25th, about two o'clock in the afternoon, intelligence was brought to head-quarters that three or four detachments of the enemy were on the march, within four miles of the camp, and the main army following in columns. The drums beat to arms; the men were ordered to their posts; an attack was expected. The day passed away, however, without any demonstration of the enemy. Howe detached none of his force on lateral expeditions, evidently meditating a general engagement. To prepare for it, Washington drew all his troops from the posts along the Bronx into the fortified camp at White Plains. Here everything remained quiet but expectant, throughout the 26th. In the morning of the 27th, which was Sunday, the heavy booming of cannon was heard from a distance seemingly in the direction of Fort Washington. Scouts galloped off to gain intelligence. We will anticipate their report.

Two of the British frigates, at seven o'clock in the morning, had moved up the Hudson, and come to anchor near Bourdett's Ferry, below the Morris House, Washington's old head-quarters, apparently with the intention of stopping the ferry, and cutting off the communication between Fort Lee and Fort Washington. At the same time, troops made their appearance on Harlem Plains, where Lord Percy held command. Colonel Morgan immediately manned the lines with troops from the garrison of Fort Washington. The ships opened a fire to enfilade and dislodge them. A barbette battery on the cliffs of the Jersey shore, left of the ferry, fired down upon the frigate, but with little effect. Colonel Magaw got down an eighteen-pounder to the lines near the Morris House, and fired fifty or sixty rounds, two balls at a time. Two eighteen-pounders were likewise brought down from Fort Lee, and planted opposite the ships. By the fire from both shores they were hulled repeatedly.

It was the thundering of these cannonades which had reached Washington's camp at White Plains. The ships soon hoisted all sail. The foremost slipped her cable, and appeared to be in the greatest confusion. She could make no way, though towed by two boats. The other ship seeing her distress sent two barges to her assistance, and by the four boats she was dragged out of reach of the American fire, her pumps going all the time. At the time that the fire from the ships began, Lord

Percy brought up his field-pieces and mortars, and made an attack upon the lines. He was resolutely answered by the troops sent down from Fort Washington, and several Hessians were killed. An occasional firing was kept up until evening, when the ships fell down the river, and the troops which had advanced on Harlem Plains drew within their lines again.

While these things were passing at Fort Washington, Lee had struck his tents, and with the rear division, eight thousand strong, the baggage and artillery, and a train of wagons four miles long, laden with stores and ammunition, was lumbering along the rough country roads to join the main army. It was not until Monday morning, after being on the road all night, that he arrived at White Plains.

Washington's camp was situated on high ground, facing the east. The right wing stretched towards the south along a rocky hill, at the foot of which the Bronx, making an elbow, protected it in flank and rear. The left wing rested on a small, deep lake among the hills. The camp was strongly intrenched in front. About a quarter of a mile to the right of the camp, and separated from the height on which it stood by the Bronx and a marshy interval, was a corresponding height called Chatterton's Hill. As this partly commanded the right flank, and as the intervening bend of the Bronx was easily passable, Washington had stationed on its summit a militia regiment.

The whole encampment was a temporary one, to be changed as soon as the military stores collected there could be removed; and now that General Lee was arrived, Washington rode out with him, and other general officers who were off duty, to reconnoitre a height which appeared more eligible. When arrived at it, Lee pointed to another on the north, still more commanding. "Yonder," said he "is the ground we ought to occupy." "Let us go, then, and view it," replied Washington. They were gently riding in that direction, when a trooper came spurring up his panting horse. "The British are in the camp, sir!" cried he. "Then, gentlemen," said Washington, "we have other business to attend to than reconnoitring." Putting spurs to his horse, he set off for the camp at full gallop, the others spurring after him.

Arrived at head-quarters, he was informed by Adjutant-general Reed, that the picket guards had all been driven in, and the enemy were advancing; but that the whole American army was posted in order of battle. Apprehensive that the enemy might attempt to get possession of Chatterton's Hill, he detached Colonel Haslet with his Delaware regiment, to reinforce the militia posted there. To these he soon added General McDougall's brigade, composed of Smallwood's Marylanders, Ritzema's New Yorkers, and two other regiments. General McDougall had command of the whole force upon the hill, which did not exceed 1,600 men.

These dispositions were scarcely made, when the enemy appeared glistening on the high grounds beyond the village of White Plains. They advanced in two columns, the right commanded by Sir Henry Clinton, the left by the Hessian general, De Heister. There was also a troop of horse; so formidable in the inexperienced eyes of the Americans. For a time they halted in a wheat field, behind a rising ground, and the general officers rode up in the centre to hold a consultation.

Washington supposed they were preparing to attack him in front, and such indeed was their intention; but the commanding height of Chatterton's Hill had caught Sir William's eye, and he determined first to get possession of it. Colonel Rahl was accordingly detached with a brigade of Hessians to make a circuit southwardly round a piece of wood, cross the Bronx about a quarter of a mile below, and ascend the south side of the hill; while General Leslie, with a large force, British and Hessian, should advance directly in front, throw a bridge across the stream, and charge up the hill.

A furious cannonade was now opened by the British from fifteen or twenty pieces of artillery, placed on high ground opposite the hill; under cover of which, the troops of General Leslie hastened to construct the bridge. In so doing, they were severely galled by two field-pieces, planted on a ledge of rock on Chatterton's Hill, and in charge of Alexander Hamilton. Smallwood's Maryland battalion also kept up a sharp fire of small arms. As soon as the bridge was finished, the British and Hessians under Leslie rushed over it, formed, and charged up the hill to take Hamilton's two field-pieces. Three times the two field-pieces were discharged, ploughing the ascending columns from hill-top to river, while Smallwood's "blue and buff" Marylanders kept up their volleys of musketry.

In the meantime, Rahl and his Hessian brigade forded the Bronx lower down, pushed up the south side of the hill, and endeavored to turn McDougall's right flank. The militia gave the general but little support. They had been dismayed at the opening of the engagement by a shot from a British cannon, which wounded one of them in the thigh, and nearly put the whole to flight. It was with the utmost difficulty McDougall had rallied them and posted them behind a stone wall. Here they did some service, until a troop of British cavalry, having gained the crest of the hill, came on, brandishing their sabres. At their first charge the militia gave a random, scattering fire, then broke, and fled in complete confusion.

A brave stand was made on the summit of the hill by Haslet, Ritzema, and Smallwood, with their troops. Twice they repulsed horse and foot, British and Hessians, until, cramped for room and greatly outnumbered, they slowly and sullenly retreated down the north side of the hill, where there was a bridge across the Bronx. The loss on both sides, in this short but severe action, was nearly equal. That of the Americans was between three and four hundred men, killed, wounded, and taken prisoners.

The British army now rested with their left wing on the hill they had just taken, and which they were busy intrenching. They were extending their right wing to the left of the American lines, so that their two wings and centre formed nearly a semicircle. It was evidently their design to outflank the American camp, and get in the rear of it. The day, however, being far advanced, was suffered to pass without any further attack; but the morrow was looked forward to for a deadly conflict.

During this anxious night, Washington was assiduously occupied throwing back his right wing to stronger ground; doubling his intrenchments and constructing three redoubts, with a line in front, on the summit of his post. These works were principally intended for defence against small arms, and were thrown up with a rapidity that to the enemy must have savored of magic. They were, in fact, made of the stalks of Indian corn or maize taken from a neighboring corn-field, and pulled up with the earth clinging in masses to the large roots. "The roots of the stalks," says Heath, "and earth on them placed in the face of the works, answered the purpose of sods and fascines. The tops being placed inwards, as the loose earth was thrown upon them, became as so many trees to the work, which was carried up with a despatch scarcely conceivable."

On the morning of the 29th, when Howe beheld how greatly Washington had improved his position and strengthened it, by what appeared to be solidly constructed works, he postponed his meditated assault, ordered up Lord Percy from Harlem with the fourth brigade and two battalions of the sixth, and proceeded to throw up lines and redoubts in front of the American camp, as if preparing to cannonade it. As the enemy were endeavoring to outflank him, especially on his right wing, Washington apprehended one of their objects might be to advance a part of their force and seize on Pine's Bridge over Croton River, which would cut off his communication with the upper country. General Beall, with three Maryland regiments, was sent off with all expedition to secure that pass. It was Washington's idea that, having possession of Croton River and the passes in the Highlands, his army would be safe from further pursuit, and have time to repose after its late excessive fatigue, and would be fresh and ready to harass the enemy should they think fit to winter up the country.

On the night of the 31st, Washington shifted his whole position, set fire to the barns and out-houses containing forage and stores, which there was no time to remove, and leaving a strong rear-guard on the heights, and in the neighboring woods, retired with his main army a distance of five miles, among the high, rocky hills about Northcastle. Here he immediately set to work to intrench and fortify himself. General Howe did not attempt to dislodge him from this fastness. He at one time ordered an attack on the rear-guard, but a violent rain prevented it, and for two or three days he remained seemingly inactive. During the night of the 4th, this quiet was interrupted. A mysterious sound was heard in the direction of the British camp, like the rumbling of wagons and artillery. At daybreak the meaning of it was discovered. The enemy were decamping. Long trains were observed defiling across the hilly country, along the roads leading to Dobbs' Ferry on the Hudson. The movement continued for three successive days, until their whole force, British and Hessians, disappeared from White Plains.

CHAPTER XXXV.

WASHINGTON AT PEEKSKILL.—THE NORTHERN ARMY.

Various were the speculations at head-quarters on the sudden movement of the enemy. Washington writes to General William Livingston (now governor of the Jerseys): "They have gone towards the North River and King's Bridge. Some suppose they are going into winter quarters, and will sit down in New York without doing more than investing Fort Washington. I cannot subscribe wholly to this opinion myself. That they will invest Fort Washington, is a matter of which there can be no doubt; and I think there is a strong probability that General Howe will detach a part of his force to make an incursion into the Jerseys, provided he is going to New York. He must attempt something on account of his reputation, for what has he done as yet with his great army?"

In the same letter he expressed his determination, as soon as it should appear that the present manoeuvre was a real retreat, and not a feint, to throw over a body of troops into the Jerseys to assist in checking Howe's progress. In a letter of the same date, he charged General Greene, should Howe invest Fort Washington with part of his force, to give the garrison all possible assistance. On the following day (Nov. 8), Colonel Tilghman, writes to General Greene from head-quarters: "The enemy are at Dobbs' Ferry with a great number of boats, ready to go into Jersey, *or proceed up the river.*" Greene doubted any intention of the enemy to cross the river; it might only be a feint to mislead; still, as a precaution, he had ordered troops up from the flying camp and was posting them opposite Dobbs' Ferry, and at other passes where a landing might be attempted; the whole being under the command of General Mercer.

Affairs at Fort Washington soon settled the question of the enemy's intention with regard to it. Lord Percy took his station with a body of troops before the lines to the south. Knyphausen advanced on the north. The Americans had previously abandoned Fort Independence, burnt its barracks, and removed the stores and cannon. Crossing King's Bridge, Knyphausen took a position between it and Fort Washington. The approach to the fort, on this side, was exceedingly steep and rocky; as, indeed, were all its approaches excepting that on the south, where the country was more open, and the ascent gradual. The fort could not hold within its walls above one thousand men; the rest of the troops were distributed about the lines and outworks. While the fort was thus menaced, the chevaux-de-frise had again proved inefficient. On the night of the 5th, a frigate and two transports, bound up to Dobbs' Ferry with supplies for Howe's army, had broken through; though, according to Greene's account, not without being considerably shattered by the batteries.

Informed of these facts, Washington wrote to Greene on the 8th: "If we cannot prevent vessels from passing up the river, and the enemy are possessed of all the surrounding country, what valuable purpose can it answer to hold a post from which the expected benefit cannot be had? I am, therefore, inclined to think, that it will not be prudent to hazard the men and stores at Mount Washington; but, as you are on the spot, I leave it to you to give such orders as to evacuating Mount Washington as you may judge best, and so far revoking the orders given to Colonel Magaw, to defend it to the last."

Accounts had been received at head-quarters of a considerable movement on the preceding evening (Nov. 7th) among the enemy's boats at Dobbs' Ferry, with the intention, it was said, of penetrating the Jerseys, and falling down upon Fort Lee. Washington, therefore, in the same letter directed Greene to have all the stores not necessary to the defence removed immediately. Greene, in reply, (Nov. 9th) adhered with tenacity to the policy of maintaining Fort Washington. "The enemy," said he, "must invest it with double the number of men required for its defence. They must keep troops at King's Bridge, to cut off all communication with the country, and in considerable force for fear of an attack."

It is doubtful when or where Washington received this letter, as he left the camp at Northcastle at eleven o'clock on the following morning. There being still considerable uncertainty as to the intentions of the enemy, all his arrangements were made accordingly. All the troops belonging to the States west of the Hudson were to be stationed in the Jerseys, under command of General Putnam. Lord Stirling had already been sent forward with the Maryland and Virginia troops to Peekskill, to cross the river at King's Ferry. Another division, composed of Connecticut and Massachusetts troops, under General Heath, was to co-operate with the brigade of New York militia, under General George Clinton, in securing the Highland posts on both sides of the river. The troops which would remain at Northcastle after the departure of Heath and his division, were to be commanded by Lee.

On the 10th of November, Washington left the camp at Northcastle, at 11 o'clock, and arrived at Peekskill at sunset, whither General Heath with his division had preceded him by a few hours. Lord Stirling was there likewise, having effected the transportation of the Maryland and Virginia troops across the river, and landed them at the ferry south of Stony Point; though a better landing was subsequently found north of the point. His lordship had thrown out a scouting party in the advance, and a hundred men to take possession of a gap in the mountain, through which a road passed toward the Jerseys. Washington was now at the entrance of the Highlands, that grand defile of the Hudson, the object of so much precaution and solicitude. On the following morning, accompanied by Generals Heath, Stirling, James and George Clinton, Mifflin, and others, he made a military visit in boats to the Highland posts. Fort Montgomery was in a considerable state of forwardness, and a work in the vicinity was projected to co-operate with it. Fort Constitution commanded a sudden bend of the river, but Lord Stirling, in his report of inspection, had intimated that the fort itself was commanded by West Point opposite. A glance of the eye, without going on shore, was sufficient to convince Washington of the fact. A fortress subsequently erected on that point, has been considered the Key of the Highlands.

On the morning of the 12th, at an early hour, Washington rode out with General Heath to reconnoitre the east side of the Hudson, at the gorge of the Highlands. Henry Wisner, in a report to the New York Convention, had mentioned a hill to the north of Peekskill, so situated, with the road winding along the side of it, that ten men on the top, by rolling down stones, might prevent ten thousand from passing. Near Robinson's Bridge, in this vicinity, about two miles from Peekskill, Washington chose a place where troops should be stationed to cover the south entrance into the mountains; and here, afterwards, was established an important military depot called Continental Village. Having made all these surveys and arrangements, he placed Heath in the general command of the Highlands, with written instructions to fortify the passes with all possible despatch, and directions how the troops were to be distributed on both sides of the river.

During his brief and busy sojourn at Peekskill, Washington received important intelligence from the Northern army; especially that part of it on Lake Champlain, under the command of General Gates. The preparations for the defence of Ticonderoga, and the nautical service on the lake, had met with difficulties at every step. At length, by the middle of August, a small flotilla was completed, and the command given by Gates to Arnold, in compliance with the advice of Washington.

Sir Guy Carleton, in the meantime, was straining every nerve for the approaching conflict. Vessels were brought from England in pieces and put together at St. Johns, boats of various kinds and sizes were transported over land, or dragged up the rapids of the Sorel. In despite of every exertion, three months elapsed before his armament was completed. By the month of October, between twenty and thirty sail were afloat and ready for action. The flag-ship (the Inflexible) mounted eighteen twelve-pounders; the rest were gunboats, a gondola and a flat-bottomed vessel called a radeau, and named the *Thunderer;* carrying a battery of six twenty-four and twelve six-pounders, besides howitzers. The gunboats mounted brass field-pieces and howitzers. Captain Pringle conducted the armament, but Sir Guy Carleton was too full of zeal, and too anxious for the event, not to head the enterprise; he accordingly took his station on the deck of the flag-ship. They made sail early in October, in quest of the American squadron, which was said to be abroad upon the lake. [Arnold had taken his post under cover of Valcour Island, in the channel between that island and the mainland. The British discovered Arnold's flotilla on the morning of the 11th, and attempted to beat up into the channel. The wind did not permit the largest of them to enter. About twelve o'clock a brisk fire was opened on the American vessels, and the action soon became severe and sanguinary. The enemy landed Indians on the island, who kept up a galling fire upon the Americans. The Congress, on board of which was Arnold, was hulled several times, and many of her crew were killed or wounded. The ardor of Arnold increased with the danger. He cheered on his men by voice and example, often pointing the guns with his own hands. At night the contest was still undecided, and the enemy drew off, anchoring their whole squadron in a line to prevent the escape of the Americans. But Arnold, aware that with his crippled and inferior force further resistance could not be maintained, took advantage of a dark, cloudy night and a strong north wind to slip silently through the enemy's line without being discovered. The next day Arnold's galley, the Congress, the Washington galley and four gondolas, which had suffered severely in the fight, fell astern; and on the following morning, as a fog, which had covered the lake, lifted, the enemy were discerned within a few miles of them in full chase. By noon the Washington was overtaken and captured. Arnold meanwhile maintained a desperate running fight with the advanced vessels of the enemy's fleet, until finding resistance in vain, the crippled vessels were run on shore, fired, and the crews set off through the woods to Crown Point.] Two schooners, two galleys, one sloop and one gondola, the remnant which had escaped of this squadron, were at anchor at the Point, and General Waterbury and most of his men [who had been captured in the Washington galley] arrived there the next day on parole. Seeing that the place must soon fall into the hands of the enemy, they set fire to the houses, destroyed everything they could not carry away, and embarking in the vessels made sail for Ticonderoga. The loss of the Americans in these two actions is said to have been between eighty and ninety men; that of the British about forty. The conduct of Arnold in these naval affairs gained him new laurels.

Sir Guy Carleton took possession of the ruined works at Crown Point, where he was soon joined by the army. He made several movements by land and water, as if meditating an attack upon Ticonderoga. General Gates, in the meantime, strengthened his works with incessant assiduity, and made every preparation for an obstinate defence. A strong easterly wind prevented the enemy's ships from advancing to attack the lines, and gave time for the arrival of reinforcements of militia to the garrison. It also afforded time for Sir Guy Carleton to cool in ardor, and calculate the chances and the value of success. The post, from its strength, could not be taken without great loss of life. If taken, the season was now too far advanced to think of passing Lake George, and exposing the army to the perils of a winter campaign in the inhospitable and impracticable wilds to the southward. Ticonderoga, too, could not be kept during the winter, so that the only result of the capture would be the reduction of the works and the taking of some cannon; all which damage the Americans could remedy before the opening of the summer campaign. If, however, the defence should be obstinate, the British army, even if successful, might sustain a loss sufficient to cripple its operations in the coming year. These, and other prudential reasons, induced Carleton to give up all attempt upon the fortress at present; wherefore, re-embarking his troops, he returned to St. Johns, and cantoned them in Canada for the winter.

CHAPTER XXXVI.

CAPTURE OF FORT WASHINGTON AND GARRISON.—RETREAT THROUGH NEW JERSEY.

On the morning of the 12th of November, Washington crossed the Hudson to the ferry below Stony Point, with the residue of the troops destined for the Jerseys. Far below were to be descried the Phoenix, the Roebuck, and the Tartar, at anchor in the broad waters of Haverstraw Bay and the Tappan Sea, guarding the lower ferries. The army, thus shut out from the nearer passes, was slowly winding its way by a circuitous route through the gap in the mountains, which Lord Stirling had secured. Leaving the troops which had just landed to pursue the same route to the Hackensack, Washington, accompanied by Colonel Reed, struck a direct course for Fort Lee, being anxious about affairs at Fort Washington. He arrived there on the following day, and found, to his disappointment, that General Greene had taken no measures for the evacuation of that fortress; but on the contrary had reinforced it with a part of Colonel Durkee's regiment and the regiment of Colonel Rawlings, so that its garrison now numbered upwards of two thousand men; a great part, however, were militia. Washington's orders for its evacuation had, in fact, been discretionary, leaving the execution of them to Greene's judgment, "as being on the spot." The latter had differed in opinion as to the policy of such a measure; and Colonel Magaw, who had charge of the fortress, was likewise confident it might be maintained. The fort was now invested on all sides but one; and the troops under Howe, which had been encamped at Dobbs' Ferry, were said to be moving down toward it.

Washington was much perplexed. The main object of Howe was still a matter of doubt with him. He could not think that Sir William was moving his whole force upon that fortress, to invest which, a part would be sufficient. He suspected an ulterior object, probably a Southern expedition, as he was told a large number of ships were taking in wood and water at New York. He resolved, therefore, to continue a few days in this neighborhood, during which he trusted the designs of the enemy would be more apparent; in the meantime he would distribute troops at Brunswick, Amboy, Elizabethtown and Fort Lee, so as to be ready at these various points to check any incursions into the Jerseys.

VIEW FROM THE SITE OF FORT WASHINGTON.
VOL. II.

Washington was mistaken in his conjecture as to Sir William Howe's design. The capture of Fort Washington was, at present, his main object; and he was encamped on Fordham Heights, not far from King's Bridge, until preliminary steps should be taken. In the night of the 14th, thirty flat-bottomed boats stole quietly up the Hudson, passed the American forts undiscovered, and made their way through Spyt den Duivel Creek into Harlem River. The means were thus provided for crossing that river and landing before unprotected parts of the American works.

Apprised by Colonel Magaw of his peril, General Greene sent over reinforcements, with an exhortation to him to persist in his defence; and despatched an express to Washington, who was at Hackensack, where the troops which had crossed from Peekskill were encamped. It was nightfall when Washington arrived at Fort Lee. Greene and Putnam were over at the besieged fortress. He threw himself into a boat, and had partly crossed the river, when he met those generals returning. They informed him of the garrison's having been reinforced, and assured him that it was in high spirits and capable of making a good defence. It was with difficulty, however, they could prevail on him to return with them to the Jersey shore, for he was excessively excited.

Early the next morning (16th), Magaw made his dispositions for the expected attack. His forces, with the recent addition, amounted to nearly three thousand men. As the fort could not contain above a third of that number, most of them were stationed about the outworks. Colonel Lambert Cadwalader, with eight hundred Pennsylvanians, was posted in the outer lines, about two miles and a half south of the fort, the side menaced by Lord Percy with sixteen hundred men. Colonel Rawlings, of Maryland, with a body of troops, many of them riflemen, was stationed by a three-gun battery, on a rocky, precipitous hill, north of the fort, and between it and Spyt den Duivel Creek. Colonel Baxter, of Bucks County, Pennsylvania, with his regiment of militia, was posted east of the fort, on rough, woody heights bordering the Harlem River, to watch the motions of the enemy, who had thrown up redoubts on high and commanding ground on the opposite side of the river, apparently to cover the crossing and landing of troops.

Sir William Howe had planned four simultaneous attacks; one on the north by Knyphausen, who was encamped on the York side of King's Bridge, within cannon shot of Fort Washington, but separated from it by high and rough hills, covered with almost impenetrable woods. He was to advance in two columns, formed by detachments made from the Hessians of his corps, the brigade of Rahl, and the regiment of Waldeckers. The second attack was to be by two battalions of light infantry and two battalions of guards, under Brigadier-general Mathew, who was to cross Harlem River in flat-boats, under cover of the redoubts above mentioned, and to land on the right of the fort. This attack was to be supported by the first and second grenadiers, and a regiment of light infantry under command of Lord Cornwallis. The third attack, intended as a feint to distract the attention of the Americans, was to be by Colonel Sterling, with the 42d regiment, who was to drop down the Harlem River in bateaux to the left of the American lines, facing New York. The fourth attack was to be on the south, by Lord Percy, with the English and Hessian troops under his command, on the right flank of the American intrenchments.

About noon, a heavy cannonade thundering along the rocky hills, and sharp volleys of musketry, proclaimed that the action was commenced. Knyphausen's division was pushing on from the north in two columns, as had been arranged. The right was led by Colonel Rahl, the left by himself. Rahl essayed to mount a steep, broken height called Cock Hill, which rises from Spyt den Duivel Creek, and was covered with woods. Knyphausen undertook a hill rising from the King's Bridge road, but soon found himself entangled in a woody defile, difficult to penetrate, and where his Hessians were exposed to the fire of the three-gun battery, and Rawlings' riflemen.

While this was going on at the north of the fort, General Mathew, with his light infantry and guards, crossed the Harlem River in the flat-boats, under cover of a heavy fire from the redoubts. He made good his landing, after being severely handled by Baxter and his men, from behind rocks and trees, and the breastworks thrown up on the steep river bank. A short contest ensued. Baxter, while bravely encouraging his men, was killed by a British officer. His troops, overpowered by numbers, retreated to the fort. General Mathew now pushed on with his guards and light infantry to cut off Cadwalader. That officer had gallantly defended the lines against the attack of Lord Percy, until informed that Colonel Sterling was dropping down Harlem River in bateaux to flank the lines and take him in the rear. He sent off a detachment to oppose his landing. They did it manfully. About ninety of Sterling's men were killed or wounded in their boats, but he persevered, landed, and forced his way up a steep height, which was well defended, gained the summit, forced a redoubt, and took nearly two hundred prisoners. Thus doubly assailed, Cadwalader was obliged to retreat to the fort. He was closely pursued by Percy with his English troops and Hessians, but turned repeatedly on his pursuers. Thus he fought his way to the fort, with the loss of several killed and more taken prisoners; but marking his track by the number of Hessians slain.

The defence on the north side of the fort was equally obstinate and unsuccessful. Rawlings with his Maryland riflemen and the aid of the three-gun battery, had for some time kept the left column of Hessians and Waldeckers under Knyphausen at bay. At length Colonel Rahl, with the right column of the division, having forced his way directly up the north side of the steep hill at Spyt den Duivel Creek, came upon Rawlings' men, whose rifles, from frequent discharges, had become foul and almost useless, drove them from their strong post, and followed them until within a hundred yards of the fort, where he was joined by Knyphausen, who had slowly made his way through dense forest and over felled trees. Here they took post behind a large stone house, and sent in a flag with a summons to surrender.

[Washington had been an anxious spectator of the battle from the opposite side of the Hudson. The action about the lines to the south lay open to him. When he saw Cadwalader assailed in flank, the line broken, and his troops overpowered by numbers, he gave up the game as lost. Seeing the flag from Knyphausen's division go into the fort, he wrote a note to Magaw, telling him that if he could hold out until evening and the place could not be maintained, he would endeavor to bring off the garrison. Captain Gooch offered to be the bearer of the note. He crossed in a small boat, landed on the bank, ran up to the fort and delivered the message. It came too late.] "The fort was so crowded by the garrison and the troops which had retreated into it that it was difficult to move about. The enemy, too, were in possession of the little redoubts around, and could have poured in showers of shells and ricochet balls that would have made dreadful slaughter." It was no longer possible for Magaw to get his troops to man the lines: he was compelled, therefore, to yield himself and his garrison prisoners of war. The only terms granted them were that the men should retain their baggage and the officers their swords.

The sight of the American flag hauled down, and the British flag waving in its place, told Washington of the surrender. His instant care was for the safety of the upper country, now that the lower defences of the Hudson were at an end. Before he knew anything about the terms of capitulation, he wrote to General Lee, informing him of the surrender, and calling his attention to the passes of the Highlands and those which lay east of the river; begging him to have such measures adopted for their defence as his judgment should suggest to be necessary. Lee, in reply, objected to removing from his actual encampment at Northcastle. "It would give us," said he, "the air of being frightened; it would expose a fine, fertile country to their ravages; and I must add, that we are as secure as we could be in any position whatever." After stating that he should deposit his stores, etc., in a place fully as safe, and more central than Peekskill, he adds: "As to ourselves, light as we are, several retreats present themselves. In short, if we keep a good look-out, we are in no danger; but I must entreat your Excellency to enjoin the officers posted at Fort Lee, to give us the quickest intelligence, if they observe any embarkation on the North River." As to the affair of Fort Washington, all that Lee observed on the subject was: "Oh, general, why would you be over-persuaded by men of inferior judgment to your own? It was a cursed affair."[10]

With the capture of Fort Washington, the project of obstructing the navigation of the Hudson, at that point, was at an end. Fort Lee, consequently, became useless, and Washington ordered all the ammunition and stores to be removed, preparatory to its abandonment. This was effected with the whole of the ammunition and a part of the stores, and every exertion was making to hurry off the remainder, when, early in the morning of the 20th, intelligence was brought that the enemy, with two hundred boats, had crossed the river and landed a few miles above. General Greene immediately ordered the garrison under arms, sent out troops to hold the enemy in check, and sent off an express to Washington, at Hackensack.

The enemy had crossed the Hudson, on a very rainy night, in two divisions, one diagonally upward from King's Bridge, landing on the west side, about eight o'clock; the other marched up the east bank, three or four miles, and then crossed to the opposite shore. The whole corps, six thousand strong, and under the command of Lord Cornwallis, were landed, with their cannon, by ten o'clock, at a place called Closter Dock, five or six miles above Fort Lee, and under that line of lofty and perpendicular cliffs known as the Palisades. "The seamen," says Sir William Howe, "distinguished themselves remarkably on this occasion, by their readiness to drag the cannon up a very narrow road for nearly half a mile to the top of a precipice, which bounds the shore for some miles on the west side."

Washington arrived at the fort in three quarters of an hour. Being told that the enemy were extending themselves across the country, he at once saw that they

[10] Colonel Reed, in a letter to General Lee, at this juncture had allowed himself, notwithstanding the devotion he had hitherto manifested for the commander-in-chief, to express himself with great critical freedom on the loss of Fort Lee. After alluding to the fact that Washington's own judgment was averse to the attempt of holding the fort, but that Greene's advice to the contrary had kept his mind in a state of suspense, he exclaims, "Oh, general! an indecisive mind is one of the greatest misfortunes that can befall an army; how often have I lamented it this campaign." Some days later a letter from General Lee came to head-quarters addressed to Colonel Reed, who at the time was absent. Washington supposing it to be on official business, opened it, as he was in the habit of doing on like occasions. To his surprise he discovered it to be a private note, the tenor of which indicated that he was the subject of critical correspondence between a member of his military family and one of his generals. He immediately enclosed the letter to Colonel Reed, explaining how it had been opened, but without further comment. Reed endeavored to explain away the remarks in Lee's letter; but Washington's affectionate confidence in him as a sympathizing friend had received a severe wound. Reed deeply grieved over the error he had committed, and his earnest appeals to Washington at a later date, restored, in a great measure, their relations of friendly confidence.

intended to form a line from the Hudson to the Hackensack, and hem the whole garrison in between the two rivers. Nothing would save it but a prompt retreat to secure the bridge over the Hackensack. No time was to be lost. The troops sent out to check the enemy were recalled. The retreat commenced in all haste. There was a want of horses and wagons; a great quantity of baggage, stores and provisions, therefore, was abandoned. So was all the artillery excepting two twelve-pounders. Even the tents were left standing, and camp-kettles on the fire. With all their speed they did not reach the Hackensack River before the vanguard of the enemy was close upon them. Expecting a brush, the greater part hurried over the bridge, others crossed at the ferry and some higher up. The enemy, however, did not dispute the passage of the river.

From Hackensack, Colonel Grayson, one of Washington's aides-de-camp, wrote instantly, by his orders, to General Lee; informing him that the enemy had crossed into the Jerseys, and, as was reported, *in great numbers*. "His Excellency," adds Grayson, "thinks it would be advisable in you to remove the troops under your command on this side of the North River, and there wait for further commands."

At Hackensack the army did not exceed three thousand men, and they were dispirited by ill success, and the loss of tents and baggage. They were without intrenching tools, in a flat country, where there were no natural fastnesses. Washington resolved, therefore, to avoid any attack from the enemy, though, by so doing, he must leave a fine and fertile region open to their ravages; or a plentiful store-house, from which they would draw voluntary supplies. A second move was necessary, again to avoid the danger of being enclosed between two rivers. Leaving three regiments, therefore, to guard the passes of the Hackensack, and serve as covering parties, he again decamped, and threw himself on the west bank of the Passaic, in the neighborhood of Newark.

His army, small as it was, would soon be less. The term of enlistment of those under General Mercer, from the flying camp, was nearly expired; and it was not probable that, disheartened as they were by defeats and losses, exposed to inclement weather, and unaccustomed to military hardships they would longer forego the comforts of their homes, to drag out the residue of a ruinous campaign. In addition, too, to the superiority of the force that was following him, the rivers gave the enemy facilities, by means of their shipping, to throw troops in his rear. In this extremity he cast about in every direction for assistance. Colonel Reed was despatched to Burlington with a letter to Governor William Livingston, describing his hazardous situation, and entreating him to call out a portion of the New Jersey militia; and General Mifflin was sent to Philadelphia to implore immediate aid from Congress and the local authorities.

His main reliance for prompt assistance, however, was upon Lee. On the 24th came a letter from that general, addressed to Colonel Reed. Washington opened it, as he was accustomed to do, in the absence of that officer, with letters addressed to him on the business of the army. Lee was at his old encampment at Northcastle. He had no means, he said, of crossing at Dobbs' Ferry, and the round by King's Ferry would be so great that he could not get there in time to answer any purpose.

"I have therefore," added he, "ordered General Heath, who is close to the only ferry which can be passed, to detach two thousand men to apprise his Excellency, and await his further orders; a mode which I flatter myself will answer better what I conceive to be the spirit of the orders than should I move the corps from hence. Withdrawing our troops from hence would be attended with some very serious consequences, which at present would be tedious to enumerate; as to myself," adds he, "I hope to set out to-morrow."

On the following day he writes to Washington: "I have received your orders, and shall endeavor to put them in execution, but question whether I shall be able to carry with me any considerable number; not so much from a want of zeal in the men as from their wretched condition, with respect to shoes, stockings, and blankets, which the present bad weather renders more intolerable. I sent Heath orders to transport two thousand men across the river, apprise the general, and wait for further orders; but that great man (as I might have expected) intrenched himself within the letter of his instructions, and refused to part with a single file, though I undertook to replace them with a part of my own."

Scarce had Lee sent this letter when he received one from Washington, informing him that he had mistaken his views in regard to the troops required to cross the Hudson; it was his (Lee's) division that he wanted to have over. The force under Heath must remain to guard the posts and passes through the Highlands, the importance of which was so infinitely great that there should not be the least possible risk of losing them. Lee's reply explained that his idea of detaching troops from Heath's division was merely for expedition's sake, intending to replace them from his own. The want of carriages and other causes had delayed him. From the force of the enemy remaining in Westchester County, he did not conceive the number of them in the Jerseys to be near so great as Washington was taught to believe. He had been making a sweep of the country to clear it of the tories. Part of his army had now moved on, and he would set out on the following day.

The situation of the little army was daily becoming more perilous. In a council of war, several of the members urged a move to Morristown, to form a junction with the troops expected from the Northern army. Washington, however, still cherished the idea of making a stand at Brunswick on the Raritan, or, at all events, of disputing the passage of the Delaware; and in this intrepid resolution he was warmly seconded by Greene. Breaking up his camp once more, therefore, he continued his retreat towards New Brunswick; but so close was Cornwallis upon him that his advance entered one end of Newark just as the American rear-guard had left the other.

From Brunswick, Washington wrote on the 29th to William Livingston, governor of the Jerseys, requesting him to have all boats and river craft, for seventy miles along the Delaware, removed to the western bank out of the reach of the enemy, and put under guard. He was disappointed in his hope of making a stand on the banks of the Raritan. All the force he could muster at Brunswick, including the New Jersey militia, did not exceed four thousand men. Colonel Reed had failed in procuring aid from the New Jersey legislature. That body, shifting from place to place, was on the eve of dissolution. The term of the Maryland and New Jersey troops in the flying camp had expired. General Mercer endeavored to detain them, representing the disgrace of turning their back upon the cause when the enemy was at hand; his remonstrances were fruitless. As to the Pennsylvania levies, they deserted in such numbers that guards were stationed on the roads and ferries to intercept them.

Washington lingered at Brunswick until the 1st of December in the vain hope of being reinforced. The enemy, in the meantime, advanced through the country, impressing wagons and horses, and collecting cattle and sheep, as if for a distant march. At length their vanguard appeared on the opposite side of the Raritan. Washington immediately broke down the end of the bridge next the village, and after nightfall resumed his retreat. At Princeton, Washington left twelve hundred men in two brigades, under Lord Stirling and General Adam Stephen, to cover the country, and watch the motions of the enemy. Stephen was the same officer that had served as a colonel under Washington in the French war, as second in command of the Virginia troops, and had charge of Fort Cumberland.

The harassed army reached Trenton on the 2d of December. Washington immediately proceeded to remove his baggage and stores across the Delaware. In his letters from this place to the President of Congress, he gives his reasons for his continued retreat: "Nothing but necessity obliged me to retire before the enemy, and leave so much of the Jerseys unprotected. Sorry am I to observe that the frequent calls upon the militia of this State, the want of exertion in the principal gentlemen of the country, and a fatal supineness and insensibility of danger, till it is too late to prevent an evil that was not only foreseen but foretold, have been the causes of our late disgraces."

In excuse for the people of New Jersey, it may be observed that they inhabited an open, agricultural country, where the sound of war had never been heard. Many of them looked upon the Revolution as rebellion; others thought it a ruined enterprise; the armies engaged in it had been defeated and broken up. They beheld the commander-in-chief retreating through their country with a handful of men, weary, wayworn, and dispirited; without tents, without clothing, many of them barefooted, exposed to wintry weather, and driven from post to post by a well-clad, well-fed, triumphant force, tricked out in all the glittering bravery of war. Could it be wondered at that peaceful husbandmen, seeing their quiet fields thus suddenly overrun by adverse hosts, and their very hearthstones threatened with outrage, should, instead of flying to arms, seek for the safety of their wives and little ones, and the protection of their humble means, from the desolation which too often marks the course even of friendly armies?

Lord Howe and his brother sought to profit by this dismay and despondency. A proclamation, dated 30th of November, commanded all persons in arms against his majesty's government to disband and return home, and all Congresses to desist from treasonable acts: offering a free pardon to all who should comply within fifty days. Many who had been prominent in the cause, hastened to take advantage of this proclamation. Those who had most property to lose were the first to submit. The middle ranks remained generally steadfast in this time of trial.

In this dark day of peril to the cause, and to himself, Washington remained firm and undaunted. In casting about for some stronghold where he might make a desperate stand for the liberties of his country, his thoughts reverted to the mountain regions of his early campaigns. General Mercer was at hand, who had shared his perils among these mountains, and his presence may have contributed to bring them to his mind. "What think you," said Washington, "if we should retreat to the back parts of Pennsylvania, would the Pennsylvanians support us?" "If the lower counties give up, the back counties will do the same," was the discouraging reply.

"We must then retire to Augusta County in Virginia," said Washington. "Numbers will repair to us for safety, and we will try a predatory war. If overpowered, we must cross the Alleghanies." Such was the indomitable spirit, rising under difficulties, and buoyant in the darkest moment, that kept our tempest-tost cause from foundering.

CHAPTER XXXVII.

RETREAT ACROSS THE DELAWARE.—BATTLE OF TRENTON.

Notwithstanding the repeated and pressing orders and entreaties of the commander-in-chief, Lee did not reach Peekskill until the 30th of November. In a letter of that date to Washington, who had complained of his delay, he simply alleged difficulties which he would explain *when both had leisure*. It was not until the 4th of December that Lee crossed the Hudson and began a laggard march, though aware of the imminent peril of Washington and his army—how different from the celerity of his movements in his expedition to the South! [Lee evidently considered Washington's star in the decline, and his own in the ascendant. The loss of Fort Washington had been made a text by him to comment in his letters about the "indecision of the commander-in-chief." Instead now of heartily co-operating with Washington he was devising side-plans of his own, and meditating, no doubt, on his chances of promotion to the head of the American armies.]

In the meantime, Washington, who was at Trenton, had profited by a delay of the enemy at Brunswick, and removed most of the stores and baggage of the army across the Delaware; and, being reinforced by fifteen hundred of the Pennsylvania militia, procured by Mifflin, prepared to face about, and march back to Princeton with such of his troops as were fit for service, there to be governed by circumstances and the movements of General Lee. Accordingly, on the 5th of December, he sent about twelve hundred men in the advance to reinforce Lord Stirling, and the next day set off himself with the residue. While on the march, Washington received a letter from Greene, who was at Princeton, informing him of a report that Lee was "at the heels of the enemy." "I should think," adds Greene, "he had better keep on the flanks than the rear, unless it were possible to concert an attack at the same instant of time in front and rear.... I think General Lee must be confined within the lines of some general plan, or else his operations will be independent of yours." Lee had no idea of conforming to a general plan; he had an independent plan of his own, and was at that moment at Pompton, indulging speculations on military greatness, and the lamentable want of it in his American contemporaries.

While Lee was thus loitering and speculating, Cornwallis, knowing how far he was in the rear, and how weak was the situation of Washington's army, and being himself strongly reinforced, made a forced march from Brunswick, and was within two miles from Princeton. Stirling, to avoid being surrounded, immediately set out with two brigades for Trenton. Washington, too, receiving intelligence by express of these movements, hastened back to that place, and caused boats to be collected from all quarters, and the stores and troops transported across the Delaware. He himself crossed with the rear-guard on Sunday morning, and took up his quarters about a mile from the river; causing the boats to be destroyed, and troops to be posted opposite the fords.

The rear-guard, says an American account, had barely crossed the river, when Lord Cornwallis "came marching down with all the pomp of war, in great expectation of getting boats, and immediately pursuing." Not one was to be had there or elsewhere; for Washington had caused the boats, for an extent of seventy miles up and down the river, to be secured on the right bank. His lordship was effectually brought to a stand. He made some moves with two columns, as if he would cross the Delaware above and below, either to push on to Philadelphia, or to entrap Washington in the acute angle made by the bend of the river opposite Bordentown. An able disposition of American troops along the upper part of the river, and of a number of galleys below, discouraged any attempt of the kind. Cornwallis, therefore, gave up the pursuit, distributed the German troops in cantonments along the left bank of the river, and stationed his main force at Brunswick, trusting to be able before long to cross the Delaware on the ice.

On the 8th, Washington wrote to the President of Congress: "There is not a moment's time to be lost in assembling such a force as can be collected, as the object of the enemy cannot now be doubted in the smallest degree. Indeed, I shall be out in my conjecture, for it is only conjecture, if the late embarkation at New York is not for Delaware River, to co-operate with the army under General Howe, who, I am informed from good authority, is with the British troops, and his whole force upon this route."

In further letters to Lee, Washington urged the peril of Philadelphia. "Do come on," writes he; "your arrival may be fortunate, and, if it can be effected without delay, it may be the means of preserving a city, whose loss must prove of the most fatal consequence to the cause of America." Putnam was now detached to take command of Philadelphia, and put it in a state of defence, and General Mifflin to have charge of the munitions of war deposited there. By their advice Congress hastily adjourned on the 12th of December, to meet again on the 20th at Baltimore.

Washington's whole force at this time was about five thousand five hundred men. Gates, however, he was informed, was coming on with seven regiments detached by Schuyler from the Northern department; reinforced by these and the troops under Lee, he hoped to be able to attempt a stroke upon the enemy's forces, which lay a good deal scattered, and to all appearances, in a state of security.

While cheering himself with these hopes, and trusting to speedy aid from Lee, that wayward commander, though nearly three weeks had elapsed since he had received Washington's orders and entreaties to join him with all possible despatch, was no farther on his march than Morristown, in the Jerseys; where with militia recruits, his force was about four thousand men. [Lee was secretly planning an independent attack on the enemy. Hearing that three regiments detached under Gates from the Northern army had arrived at Peekskill, he sent orders for them to join him at Morristown. "I am in hopes," he writes, "to reconquer the Jerseys." In the meantime Washington wrote urging his speedy junction with him. Boats were gathered at Tinicum to facilitate his passage across the Delaware. "I have so frequently," wrote Washington, "mentioned our situation and the necessity of your aid, that it is painful for me to add a word on the subject." On the 12th, Lee moved from Morristown, but marched no further than Vealtown, eight miles distant. There he left Sullivan with his troops, while he took up his quarters three miles off, at a tavern at Baskingridge. Intelligence of his exposed and insecure position reached the enemy, a body of dragoons were detached, and guided by a tory, came upon Lee in his quarters without warning. The few guards about the house were soon dispersed, and Lee, bare-headed and in his slippers, was compelled in haste to mount a horse and accompany his captors. This capture gave great exultation to the enemy; for they considered Lee the most scientific and experienced of the rebel generals. General Sullivan now being in command, immediately pressed forward with the troops to join the commander-in-chief.]

The loss of Lee was a severe shock to the Americans, many of whom, as we have shown, looked to him as the man who was to rescue them from their critical and well-nigh desperate situation. General Wilkinson, in his memoirs, [who was at that time brigade-major under General Gates,] points out what he considers the true secret of Lee's conduct. His military reputation, originally very high, had been enhanced of late by its being generally known that he had been opposed to the occupation of Fort Washington; while the fall of that fortress and other misfortunes of the campaign, though beyond the control of the commander-in-chief, had quickened the discontent which, according to Wilkinson, had been generated against him at Cambridge, and raised a party against him in Congress. "It was confidently asserted at the time," adds he, "but is not worthy of credit, that a motion had been made in that body tending to supersede him in the command of the army. In this temper of the times, if General Lee had anticipated General Washington in cutting the cordon of the enemy between New York and the Delaware, the commander-in-chief would probably have been superseded. In this case, Lee would have succeeded him."

What an unfortunate change would it have been for the country! Lee was undoubtedly a man of brilliant talents, shrewd sagacity, and much knowledge and experience in the art of war; but he was wilful and uncertain in his temper, self-indulgent in his habits, and an egoist in warfare; boldly dashing for a soldier's glory rather than warily acting for a country's good. He wanted those great moral qualities which, in addition to military capacity, inspired such universal confidence in the wisdom, rectitude and patriotism of Washington, enabling him to direct and control legislative bodies as well as armies; to harmonize the jarring passions and jealousies of a wide and imperfect confederacy, and to cope with the varied exigencies of the Revolution.

Congress, prior to their adjournment, had resolved that "until they should otherwise order, General Washington should be possessed of all power to order and direct all things relative to the department and to the operations of war." Thus empowered, he proceeded immediately to recruit three battalions of artillery. To those whose terms were expiring he promised an augmentation of twenty-five per cent. upon their pay, and a bounty of ten dollars to the men for six weeks' service. "It was no time," he said, "to stand upon expense; nor in matters of self-evident exigency to refer to Congress at the distance of a hundred and thirty or forty miles. If any good officers will offer to raise men upon continental pay and establishment in this quarter, I shall encourage them to do so, and regiment them when they have done it."

The promise of increased pay and bounties had kept together for a time the dissolving army. The local militia began to turn out freely. Colonel John Cadwalader, a gentleman of gallant spirit, and cultivated mind and manners, brought a large volunteer detachment, well equipped, and composed principally of Philadelphia troops. Washington, who held Cadwalader in high esteem, assigned him an important station at Bristol, with Colonel Reed, who was his intimate friend, as an associate. They had it in charge to keep a watchful eye upon Count Donop's Hessians, who were cantoned along the opposite shore from Bordentown to the Black Horse.

On the 20th of December arrived General Sullivan in camp, with the troops recently commanded by the unlucky Lee. They were in a miserable plight; destitute of almost everything; many of them fit only for the hospital, and those whose terms were nearly out, thinking of nothing but their discharge. On the same day arrived General Gates, with the remnants of four regiments from the Northern army.

The time seemed now propitious for the *coup de main* which Washington had of late been meditating. Everything showed careless confidence on the part of the enemy. Howe was in winter quarters at New York. His troops were loosely cantoned about the Jerseys, from the Delaware to Brunswick, so that they could not readily be brought to act in concert on a sudden alarm. The Hessians were in the advance, stationed along the Delaware, facing the American lines, which were along the west bank. Cornwallis, thinking his work accomplished, had obtained leave of absence, and was likewise at New York, preparing to embark for England. Washington had now between five and six thousand men fit for service; with these he meditated to cross the river at night, at different points, and make simultaneous attacks upon the Hessian advance posts.

He calculated upon the eager support of his troops, who were burning to revenge the outrages on their homes and families, committed by these foreign mercenaries. They considered the Hessians mere hirelings; slaves to a petty despot, fighting for sordid pay, and actuated by no sentiment of patriotism or honor. They had rendered themselves the horror of the Jerseys, by rapine, brutality, and heartlessness. At first, their military discipline had inspired awe, but of late they had become careless and unguarded, knowing the broken and dispirited state of the Americans, and considering them incapable of any offensive enterprise. A brigade of three Hessian regiments, those of Rahl, Lossberg, and Knyphausen, was stationed at Trenton. Colonel Rahl had the command of the post at his own solicitation, and in consequence of the laurels he had gained at White Plains and Fort Washington. We have before us journals of two Hessian lieutenants and a corporal, which give graphic particulars of the colonel and his post. According to their representations, he, with all his bravery, was little fitted for such an important command. He lacked the necessary vigilance and forecast. One of the lieutenants speaks of him in a sarcastic vein, and evidently with some degree of prejudice. According to his account, there was more bustle than business at the post. He was a boon companion; made merry until a late hour in the night, and then lay in bed until nine o'clock in the morning. And then he took no precautions against the possibility of being attacked. A veteran officer, Major Von Dechow, proposed that some works should be thrown up, where the cannon might be placed ready against any assault. The colonel made merry with the very idea. "An assault by the rebels! Let them come! We'll at them with the bayonet."

Such was the posture of affairs at Trenton at the time the *coup de main* was meditated. Whatever was to be done, however, must be done quickly, before the river was frozen. An intercepted letter had convinced Washington of what he had before suspected, that Howe was only waiting for that event to resume active operations, cross the river on the ice, and push on triumphantly to Philadelphia. He communicated his project to Gates, and wished him to go to Bristol, take command there, and co-operate from that quarter. Gates, however, pleaded ill health, and requested leave to proceed to Philadelphia.

The request may have surprised Washington, considering the spirited enterprise that was on foot; but Gates, as has before been observed, had a disinclination to serve immediately under the commander-in-chief; like Lee, he had a disparaging opinion of him, or rather an impatience of his supremacy. He had, moreover, an ulterior object in view. Having been disappointed and chagrined in finding himself subordinate to General Schuyler in the Northern campaign, he was now intent on making interest among the members of Congress for an independent command. Washington urged that on his way to Philadelphia he would at least stop for a day or two at Bristol to concert a plan of operations with Reed and Cadwalader, and adjust any little questions of etiquette and command that might arise between the continental colonels who had gone thither with Lee's troops and the volunteer officers stationed there. He does not appear to have complied even with this request. According to Wilkinson's account, he took quarters at Newtown, and set out thence for Baltimore on the 24th of December, the very day before that of the intended *coup de main*. The projected attack upon the Hessian posts was to be threefold: 1st. Washington was to cross the Delaware with a considerable force, at McKonkey's Ferry (now Taylorsville), about nine miles above Trenton, and march down upon that place, where Rahl's cantonment comprised a brigade of fifteen hundred Hessians, a troop of British light-horse, and a number of chasseurs. 2d. General Ewing, with a body of Pennsylvania militia, was to cross at a ferry about a mile below Trenton; secure the bridge over the Assunpink creek, a stream flowing along the south side of the town, and cut off any retreat of the enemy in that direction. 3d. General Putnam, with the troops occupied in fortifying Philadelphia, and those under General Cadwalader, was to cross below Burlington and attack the lower posts under Count Donop. The several divisions were to cross the Delaware at night, so as to be ready for simultaneous action by five o'clock in the morning.

Seldom is a combined plan carried into full operation. Symptoms of an insurrection in Philadelphia obliged Putnam to remain with some force in that city; but he detached five or six hundred of the Pennsylvania militia under Colonel Griffin, his adjutant-general, who threw himself into the Jerseys, to be at hand to co-operate with Cadwalader.

Early on the eventful evening (Dec. 25th), the troops destined for Washington's part of the attack, about two thousand four hundred strong, with a train of twenty small pieces, were paraded near McKonkey's Ferry, ready to pass as soon as it grew dark, in the hope of being all on the other side by twelve o'clock. Washington repaired to the ground accompanied by Generals Greene, Sullivan, Mercer, Stephen, and Lord Stirling. Greene was full of ardor for the enterprise; eager, no doubt, to wipe out the recollection of Fort Washington. It was, indeed, an anxious moment for all.

Boats being in readiness, the troops began to cross about sunset. The weather was intensely cold, the wind was high, the current strong, and the river full of floating ice. Colonel Glover, with his amphibious regiment of Marblehead fishermen, was in advance. They were men accustomed to battle with the elements, yet with all their skill and experience the crossing was difficult and perilous. The night was dark and tempestuous, the drifting ice drove the boats out of their course, and threatened them with destruction. It was three o'clock before the artillery was landed, and nearly four before the troops took up their line of march. Trenton was nine miles distant; and not to be reached before daylight. To surprise it, therefore, was out of the question. There was no making a retreat without being discovered and harassed in repassing the river. Beside, the troops from the other points might have crossed, and co-operation was essential to their safety. Washington resolved to push forward and trust to Providence. He formed the troops into two columns. The first he led himself, accompanied by Greene, Stirling, Mercer, and Stephen; it was to make a circuit by the upper or Pennington road, to the north of Trenton. The other, led by Sullivan, and including the brigade of St. Clair, was to take the lower river leading to the west end of the town. Sullivan's column was to halt a few moments at a cross-road leading to Howland's Ferry to give Washington's column time to effect its circuit, so that the attack might be simultaneous. On arriving at Trenton they were to force the outer guards and push directly into the town before the enemy had time to form.

It began to hail and snow as the troops commenced their march, and increased in violence as they advanced, the storm driving the sleet in their faces. So bitter was the cold that two of the men were frozen to death that night. The day dawned by the time Sullivan halted at the cross-road. It was discovered that the storm had rendered many of the muskets wet and useless. "What is to be done?" inquired Sullivan of St. Clair. "You have nothing for it but to push on and use the bayonet," was the reply. While some of the soldiers were endeavoring to clear their muskets, and squibbing off priming, Sullivan despatched an officer to apprise the commander-in-chief of the condition of their arms. He came back half dismayed by an indignant burst of Washington, who ordered him to return instantly and tell General Sullivan to "advance and charge."

It was about eight o'clock when Washington's column arrived in the vicinity of the village. The storm which had rendered the march intolerable, had kept every one within doors, and the snow had deadened the tread of the troops and the rumbling of the artillery. As they approached the village, Washington, who was in front, came to a man that was chopping wood by the roadside, and inquired, "Which way is the Hessian picket?" "I don't know," was the surly reply. "You may tell," said Captain Forest of the artillery, "for that is General Washington." The aspect of the man changed in an instant. Raising his hands to heaven, "God bless and prosper you!" cried he. "The picket is in that house, and the sentry stands near that tree."

The advance guard was led by a brave young officer, Captain William A. Washington, seconded by Lieutenant James Monroe (in after years president of the United States). They received orders to dislodge the picket. Here happened to be stationed the very lieutenant whose censures of the negligence of Colonel Rahl we have referred to. By his own account, he was very near being entrapped in the guard-house. His sentries, he says, were not alert enough; and had he not stepped out of the picket-house himself and discovered the enemy, they would have been upon him before his men could scramble to their arms. "Der feind! der feind! heraus! heraus!" (the enemy! the enemy! turn out! turn out!) was now the cry. By this time the American artillery was unlimbered; Washington kept beside it and the column proceeded. The report of fire-arms told that Sullivan was at the lower end of the town. Colonel Stark led his advance guard, and did it in gallant style. The attacks, as concerted, were simultaneous. The outposts were driven in; they retreated, firing from behind houses. The Hessian drums beat to arms; the trumpets of the light-horse sounded the alarm; the whole place was in an uproar. Some of the enemy made a wild and undirected fire from the windows of their quarters; others rushed forth in disorder and attempted to form in the main street, while dragoons, hastily mounted and galloping about, added to the confusion. Washington advanced with his column to the head of King Street, riding beside Captain Forest of the artillery. When Forest's battery of six guns was opened the general kept on the left and advanced with it, giving directions to the fire. His position was an exposed one, and he was repeatedly entreated to fall back; but all such entreaties were useless when once he became heated in action.

The enemy were training a couple of cannon in the main street to form a battery, which might have given the Americans a serious check; but Captain Washington and Lieutenant Monroe, with a part of the advance guard rushed forward, drove the artillerists from their guns, and took the two pieces when on the point of being fired. Both of these officers were wounded; the captain in the wrist, the lieutenant in the shoulder.

While Washington advanced on the north of the town, Sullivan approached on the west, and detached Stark to press on the lower or south end of the town. The British light-horse, and about five hundred Hessians and chasseurs, had been quartered in the lower part of the town. Seeing Washington's column pressing in front, and hearing Stark thundering in their rear, they took headlong flight by the bridge across the Assunpink, and so along the banks of the Delaware towards

Count Donop's encampment at Bordentown. Had Washington's plan been carried into full effect, their retreat would have been cut off by General Ewing; but that officer had been prevented from crossing the river by the ice.

Colonel Rahl, according to the account of the lieutenant who had commanded the picket, completely lost his head in the confusion of the surprise. The latter, when driven in by the American advance, found the colonel on horseback, endeavoring to rally his panic-stricken and disordered men, but himself sorely bewildered. With some difficulty he succeeded in extricating his troops from the town, and leading them into an adjacent orchard. A rapid retreat by the Princeton road was apparently in his thoughts; but he lacked decision. The idea of flying before the rebels was intolerable. Some one, too, exclaimed at the ruinous loss of leaving all their baggage to be plundered by the enemy. Changing his mind he made a rash resolve. "All who are my grenadiers, forward!" cried he, and led his grenadiers bravely but rashly on, when, in the midst of his career, he received a fatal wound from a musket ball and fell from his horse. His men, left without their chief, were struck with dismay; heedless of the orders of the second in command, they retreated by the right up the banks of the Assunpink, intending to escape to Princeton. Washington saw their design, and threw Colonel Hand's corps of Pennsylvania riflemen in their way; while a body of Virginia troops gained their left. Brought to a stand, and perfectly bewildered, they grounded their arms and surrendered at discretion.

The number of prisoners taken in this affair was nearly one thousand, of which thirty-two were officers. Washington's triumph, however, was impaired by the failure of the two simultaneous attacks. General Ewing, who was to have crossed before day at Trenton Ferry, and taken possession of the bridge leading out of the town, over which the light-horse and Hessians retreated, was prevented by the quantity of ice in the river. Cadwalader was hindered by the same obstacle. He got part of his troops over, but found it impossible to embark his cannon, and was obliged, therefore, to return to the Pennsylvania side of the river. Had he and Ewing crossed, Donop's quarters would have been beaten up, and the fugitives from Trenton intercepted.

By the failure of this part of his plan, Washington had been exposed to the most imminent hazard. The force with which he had crossed, twenty-four hundred men, raw troops, was not enough to cope with the veteran garrison, had it been properly on its guard; and then there were the troops under Donop at hand to co-operate with it. Nothing saved him but the utter panic of the enemy, their want of proper alarm places, and their exaggerated idea of his forces. Even now that the place was in his possession he dared not linger in it. There was a superior force under Donop below him, and a strong battalion of infantry at Princeton. His own troops were exhausted by the operations of the night and morning in cold, rain, snow and storm. They had to guard about a thousand prisoners, taken in action or found concealed in houses; there was little prospect of succor, owing to the season and the state of the river. Washington gave up, therefore, all idea of immediately pursuing the enemy or keeping possession of Trenton, and determined to recross the Delaware with his prisoners and captured artillery.

CHAPTER XXXVIII.

WASHINGTON RECROSSES THE DELAWARE.— BATTLE OF PRINCETON.

There was a kind of episode in the affair at Trenton. Colonel Griffin, who had thrown himself previously into the Jerseys with his detachment of Pennsylvania militia, found himself, through indisposition and the scanty number of his troops, unable to render efficient service in the proposed attack. He sent word to Cadwalader, therefore, that he should probably render him more real aid by making a demonstration in front of Donop, and drawing him off so far into the interior as to be out of the way of rendering support to Colonel Rahl. He accordingly presented himself in sight of Donop's cantonment on the 25th of December, and succeeded in drawing him out with nearly his whole force of two thousand men. He then retired slowly before him, skirmishing, but avoiding anything like an action, until he had lured him as far as Mount Holly, when he left him to find his way back to his post at his leisure.

The cannonade of Washington's attack in Trenton on the morning of the 26th was distinctly heard at Cadwalader's camp at Bristol. Imperfect tidings of the result reached there about eleven o'clock, and produced the highest exultation and excitement. Cadwalader made another attempt to cross the river and join Washington, whom he supposed to be still in the Jerseys, following up the blow he had struck. He could not effect the passage of the river with the most of the troops, until mid-day of the 27th, when he received from Washington a detailed account of his success, and of his having recrossed into Pennsylvania.

Cadwalader was now in a dilemma. Donop, he presumed, was still at Mount Holly, whither Griffin had decoyed him; but he might soon march back. His forces were equal if not superior in number to his own, and veterans instead of raw militia. But then there was the glory of rivalling the exploit at Trenton, and the importance of following out the effort for the relief of the Jerseys and the salvation of Philadelphia. Beside, Washington, in all probability, after disposing of his prisoners, had again crossed into the Jerseys and might be acting offensively. Reed relieved Cadwalader from his dilemma by proposing that they should push on to Burlington, and there determine, according to intelligence, whether to proceed to Bordentown or Mount Holly. The plan was adopted, and Cadwalader took up his line of march.

Reed and two companions spurred on to reconnoitre the enemy's outposts, about four miles from Burlington, but pulled up at the place where the picket was usually stationed. There was no smoke, nor any sign of a human being. They rode up and found the place deserted. From the country people in the neighborhood they received an explanation. Count Donop had returned to his post from the pursuit of Griffin, only in time to hear of the disaster at Trenton. He immediately began a retreat in the utmost panic and confusion, calling in his guards and parties as he hurried forward. The troops in the neighborhood of Burlington had decamped precipitately the preceding evening.

Colonel Reed sent back intelligence of this to Cadwalader, and still pushed on with his companions. Arrived at Bordentown not an enemy was to be seen; the fugitives from Trenton had spread a panic on the 26th, and the Hessians and their refugee adherents had fled in confusion, leaving their sick behind them. One of Reed's companions returned to Cadwalader, who had halted at Burlington, and advised him to proceed. Cadwalader wrote in the night to Washington, informing him of his whereabouts, and that he should march for Bordentown in the morning. "If you should think proper to cross over," added he, "it may easily be effected at the place where we passed; a pursuit would keep up the panic. They went off with great precipitation, and pressed all the wagons in their reach; I am told many of them are gone to South Amboy."

Washington needed no prompting of the kind. Bent upon following up his blow, he had barely allowed his troops a day or two to recover from recent exposure and fatigue, that they might have strength and spirit to pursue the retreating enemy, beat up other of their quarters, and entirely reverse affairs in the Jerseys. In this spirit he had written to Generals McDougall and Maxwell at Morristown, to collect as large a body of militia as possible, and harass the enemy in flank and rear. Men of influence also were despatched by him into different parts of the Jerseys, to spirit up the militia to revenge the oppression, the ravage, and insults they had experienced from the enemy, especially from the Hessians.

On the 29th, his troops began to cross the river. It would be a slow and difficult operation, owing to the ice; two parties of light troops therefore were detached in advance, whom Colonel Reed was to send in pursuit of the enemy. They marched into Trenton about two o'clock, and were immediately put on the traces of Donop, to hang on his rear and harass him until other troops should come up. Cadwalader also detached a party of riflemen from Bordentown with like orders. Donop, in retreating, had divided his force, sending one part by a cross road to Princeton, and hurrying on with the remainder to Brunswick. While this was going on, Washington was effecting the passage of his main force to Trenton. He himself had crossed on the 29th of December, but it took two days more to get the troops and artillery over the icy river, and that with great labor and difficulty.

At this critical moment, Washington received a letter from a committee of Congress, transmitting him resolves of that body dated the 27th of December, investing him with military powers quite dictatorial. "Happy is it for this country," write the committee, "that the general of their forces can safely be intrusted with the most unlimited power, and neither personal security, liberty or property, be in the least degree endangered thereby." Washington's acknowledgement of this great mark of confidence was noble and characteristic. "I find Congress have done me the honor to intrust me with powers, in my military capacity, of the highest nature and almost unlimited extent. Instead of thinking myself freed from all *civil* obligations by this mark of their confidence, I shall constantly bear in mind that, as the sword was the last resort for the preservation of our liberties, so it ought to be the first thing laid aside when those liberties are firmly established."

General Howe was taking his ease in winter quarters at New York, waiting for the freezing of the Delaware to pursue his triumphant march to Philadelphia, when tidings were brought him of the surprise and capture of the Hessians at Trenton. He instantly stopped Lord Cornwallis, who was on the point of embarking for England, and sent him back in all haste to resume the command in the Jerseys.

The ice in the Delaware impeded the crossing of the American troops, and gave the British time to draw in their scattered cantonments and assemble their whole force at Princeton. Information was obtained that Lord Cornwallis had joined General Grant with a reinforcement of chosen troops. They had now seven or eight thousand men, and were pressing wagons for a march upon Trenton. Word, too, was brought that General Howe was on the march with a thousand light troops, with which he had landed at Amboy.

The situation of Washington was growing critical. The enemy were beginning to advance their large pickets towards Trenton. Everything indicated an approaching attack. The force with him was small; to retreat across the river would destroy the dawn of hope awakened in the bosoms of the Jersey militia by the late exploit, but to make a stand without reinforcements was impossible. In this emergency he called to his aid General Cadwalader from Crosswicks, and General Mifflin from Bordentown, with their collective forces amounting to about three thousand six hundred men. They promptly answered to his call, and marching in the night, joined him on the 1st of January.

Washington chose a position for his main body on the east side of the Assunpink. There was a narrow stone bridge across it, where the water was very deep; the same bridge over which part of Rahl's brigade had escaped in the recent affair. He planted his artillery so as to command the bridge and the fords. His advance guard was stationed about three miles off in a wood, having in front a stream called Shabbakong Creek. Early on the morning of the 2d, came certain word that Cornwallis was approaching with all his force. Strong parties were sent out under General Greene, who skirmished with the enemy and harassed them in their advance. By twelve o'clock they reached Shabbakong, and halted for a time on its northern bank. Then crossing it, and moving forward with rapidity, they drove the advance guard out of the woods, and pushed on until they reached a high ground near the town. Here Hand's corps of several battalions was drawn up and held them for a time in check. All the parties in advance ultimately retreated to the main body, on the east side of the Assunpink.

From all these checks and delays it was nearly sunset before Cornwallis, with the head of his army, entered Trenton. His rear-guard under General Leslie rested at Maiden Head, about six miles distant, and nearly half way between Trenton and

Princeton. Forming his troops into columns, he now made repeated attempts to cross the Assunpink at the bridge and the fords, but was as often repulsed by the artillery. For a part of the time Washington, mounted on a white horse, stationed himself at the south end of the bridge, issuing his orders. Each time the enemy was repulsed there was a shout along the American lines. At length they drew off, came to a halt, and lighted their camp fires. The Americans did the same, using the neighboring fences for the purpose.

A cannonade was kept up on both sides until dark; but with little damage to the Americans. When night closed in, the two camps lay in sight of each other's fires, ruminating the bloody action of the following day. It was the most gloomy and anxious night that had yet closed in on the American army throughout its series of perils and disasters; for there was no concealing the impending danger. But what must have been the feelings of the commander-in-chief as he anxiously patrolled his camp and considered his desperate position? A small stream, fordable in several places, was all that separated his raw, inexperienced army from an enemy vastly superior in numbers and discipline, and stung to action by the mortification of a late defeat. In this darkest of moments a gleam of hope flashed upon his mind: a bold expedient suggested itself. Almost the whole of the enemy's force must by this time be drawn out of Princeton and advancing by detachments toward Trenton, while their baggage and principal stores must remain weakly guarded at Brunswick. Was it not possible by a rapid night-march along the Quaker road, a different road from that on which General Leslie with the rear-guard was resting, to get past that force undiscovered, come by surprise upon those left at Princeton, capture or destroy what stores were left there, and then push on to Brunswick? This would save the army from being cut off; would avoid the appearance of a defeat; and might draw the enemy away from Trenton, while some fortunate stroke might give additional reputation to the American arms.

Such was the plan which Washington revolved in his mind on the gloomy banks of the Assunpink, and which he laid before his officers in a council of war, held after nightfall, at the quarters of General Mercer. It met with instant concurrence. One formidable difficulty presented itself. The weather was unusually mild; there was a thaw, by which the roads might be rendered deep and miry, and almost impassable. Fortunately, the wind veered to the north in the course of the evening; the weather became intensely cold, and in two hours the roads were once more hard and frost-bound. In the meantime, the baggage of the army was silently removed to Burlington, and every other preparation was made for a rapid march. To deceive the enemy, men were employed to dig trenches near the bridge within hearing of the British sentries, with orders to continue noisily at work until daybreak; others were to go the rounds, relieve guards at the bridge and fords, keep up the camp fires, and maintain all the appearance of a regular encampment. At daybreak they were to hasten after the army.

In the dead of the night the army drew quietly out of the encampment and began its march. General Mercer was in the advance with the remnant of his flying camp, now but about three hundred and fifty men. The Quaker road was a complete roundabout, joining the main road about two miles from Princeton, where

Washington expected to arrive before daybreak. The road, however, was new and rugged; cut through woods, where the stumps of trees broke the wheels of some of the baggage trains and retarded the march of the troops; so that it was near sunrise of a bright, frosty morning when Washington reached the bridge over Stony Brook, about three miles from Princeton. After crossing the bridge he led his troops along the bank of the brook to the edge of a wood, where a by-road led off on the right through low grounds, and was said by the guides to be a short cut to Princeton and less exposed to view. By this road Washington defiled with the main body, ordering Mercer to continue along the brook with his brigade until he should arrive at the main road, where he was to secure, and if possible destroy a bridge over which it passes, so as to intercept any fugitives from Princeton, and check any retrograde movements of the British troops which might have advanced towards Trenton.

Hitherto the movements of the Americans had been undiscovered by the enemy. Three regiments of the latter, the 17th, 40th, and 55th, with three troops of dragoons, had been quartered all night in Princeton, under marching orders to join Lord Cornwallis in the morning. The 17th regiment, under Colonel Mawhood, was already on the march; the 55th regiment was preparing to follow. Mawhood had crossed the bridge by which the old or main road to Trenton passes over Stony Brook, and was proceeding through a wood beyond when, as he attained the summit of a hill about sunrise, the glittering of arms betrayed to him the movement of Mercer's troops to the left, who were filing along the Quaker road to secure the bridge, as they had been ordered. The woods prevented him from seeing their number. He supposed them to be some broken portion of the American army flying before Lord Cornwallis. With this idea, he faced about and made a retrograde movement to intercept them or hold them in check; while messengers spurred off at all speed to hasten forward the regiments still lingering at Princeton, so as completely to surround them.

The woods concealed him until he had recrossed the bridge of Stony Brook, when he came in full sight of the van of Mercer's brigade. Both parties pushed to get possession of a rising ground on the right near the house of a Mr. Clark. The Americans being nearest, reached it first, and formed behind a hedge fence which extended along a slope in front of the house; whence, being chiefly armed with rifles, they opened a destructive fire. It was returned with great spirit by the enemy. At the first discharge Mercer was dismounted. One of his colonels, also, was mortally wounded and carried to the rear. Availing themselves of the confusion thus occasioned, the British charged with the bayonet; the American riflemen having no weapon of the kind were thrown into disorder and retreated. Mercer, who was on foot, endeavored to rally them, when a blow from the butt end of a musket felled him to the ground. He rose and defended himself with his sword, but was surrounded, bayoneted repeatedly, and left for dead. Mawhood pursued the broken and retreating troops to the brow of the rising ground, on which Clark's house was situated, when he beheld a large force emerging from a wood and advancing to the rescue. It was a body of Pennsylvania militia, which Washington, on hearing the firing, had detached to the support of Mercer. Mawhood instantly ceased pursuit, drew up his artillery, and by a heavy discharge brought the militia to a stand.

At this moment Washington himself arrived at the scene of action, having galloped from the by-road in advance of his troops. From a rising ground he beheld Mercer's troops retreating in confusion, and the detachment of militia checked by Mawhood's artillery. Everything was at peril. Putting spurs to his horse he dashed past the hesitating militia, waving his hat and cheering them on. His commanding figure and white horse made him a conspicuous object for the enemy's marksmen; but he heeded it not. Galloping forward under the fire of Mawhood's battery, he called upon Mercer's broken brigade. The Pennsylvanians rallied at the sound of his voice, and caught fire from his example. At the same time the 7th Virginia regiment emerged from the wood, and moved forward with loud cheers, while a fire of grapeshot was opened by Captain Moulder of the American artillery from the brow of a ridge to the south.

Colonel Mawhood, who a moment before had thought his triumph secure, found himself assailed on every side and separated from the other British regiments. He fought, however, with great bravery, and for a short time the action was desperate. Washington was in the midst of it; equally endangered by the random fire of his own men and the artillery and musketry of the enemy. Mawhood by this time had forced his way at the point of the bayonet through gathering foes, though with heavy loss, back to the main road, and was in full retreat towards Trenton to join Cornwallis. Washington detached Major Kelly with a party of Pennsylvania troops to destroy the bridge at Stony Brook, over which Mawhood had retreated, so as to impede the advance of General Leslie from Maiden Head.

In the meantime the 55th regiment, which had been on the left and nearer Princeton, had been encountered by the American advance-guard under General St. Clair, and after some sharp fighting in a ravine had given way and was retreating across fields and along a by-road to Brunswick. The remaining regiment, the 40th, had not been able to come up in time for the action; a part of it fled toward Brunswick; the residue took refuge in the college at Princeton, recently occupied by them as barracks. Artillery was now brought to bear on the college, and a few shot compelled those within to surrender.

In this brief but brilliant action about one hundred of the British were left dead on the field, and nearly three hundred taken prisoners, fourteen of whom were officers. The loss of the Americans was about twenty-five or thirty men and several officers. Among the latter was Colonel Haslet, who had distinguished himself throughout the campaign by being among the foremost in services of danger. A greater loss was that of General Mercer. He was said to be either dead or dying in the house of Mr. Clark, whither he had been conveyed by his aide-de-camp, Major Armstrong. Washington would have ridden back from Princeton to visit him and have him conveyed to a place of greater security, but was assured that, if alive, he was too desperately wounded to bear removal.

Under these circumstances Washington felt compelled to leave his old companion in arms to his fate. Indeed, he was called away by the exigencies of his command, having to pursue the routed regiments which were making a headlong retreat to Brunswick. In this pursuit he took the lead at the head of a detachment of cavalry. At Kingston, however, three miles to the northeast of Princeton, he pulled up, restrained his ardor, and held a council of war on horseback. Should he keep on to Brunswick or not? The capture of the British stores and baggage would make his triumph complete; but, on the other hand, his troops were excessively fatigued by their rapid march all night and hard fight in the morning. All of them had been one night without sleep, and some of them two, and many were half-starved. They were without blankets, thinly clad, some of them barefooted, and this in freezing weather. Cornwallis would be upon them before they could reach Brunswick. His rear-guard, under General Leslie, had been quartered but six miles from Princeton, and the retreating troops must have roused them. Under these considerations, it was determined to discontinue the pursuit and push for Morristown. There they would be in a mountainous country, heavily wooded, in an abundant neighborhood, and on the flank of the enemy, with various defiles by which they might change their position according to his movements. Filing off to the left, therefore, from Kingston, and breaking down the bridges behind him, Washington took the narrow road by Rocky Hill to Pluckamin.

His lordship had retired to rest at Trenton with the sportsman's vaunt that he would "bag the fox in the morning." Nothing could surpass his surprise and chagrin when at daybreak the expiring watchfires and deserted camp of the Americans told him that the prize had once more evaded his grasp; that the general whose military skill he had decried had outgeneralled him. For a time he could not learn whither the army, which had stolen away so silently, had directed its stealthy march. By sunrise, however, there was the booming of cannon, like the rumbling of distant thunder, in the direction of Princeton. The idea flashed upon him that Washington had not merely escaped but was about to make a dash at the British magazines at Brunswick. Alarmed for the safety of his military stores, his lordship forthwith broke up his camp and made a rapid march towards Princeton. As he arrived in sight of the bridge over Stony Brook, he beheld Major Kelly and his party busy in its destruction. A distant discharge of round shot from his field-pieces drove them away, but the bridge was already broken. It would take time to repair it for the passage of the artillery, so Cornwallis in his impatience urged his troops breast-high through the turbulent and icy stream, and again pushed forward.

Without further delay he hurried forward, eager to save his magazines. Crossing the bridge at Kingston, he kept on along the Brunswick road, supposing Washington still before him. The latter had got far in the advance during the delays caused by the broken bridge at Stony Brook, and the alteration of his course at Kingston had carried him completely out of the way of Cornwallis. His lordship reached Brunswick towards evening, and endeavored to console himself by the safety of the military stores for being so completely foiled and out-manoeuvred.

Washington in the meantime was all on the alert; the lion part of his nature was aroused; and while his weary troops were resting at Pluckamin, he was despatching missives and calling out aid to enable him to follow up his successes. In a letter to Putnam, he says: "The enemy appear to be panic-struck. I am in hopes of driving them out of the Jerseys. March the troops under your command to Crosswicks, and keep a strict watch upon the enemy in this quarter." To General Heath, also, who was stationed in the Highlands of the Hudson, he wrote at the same harried moment: "The enemy are in great consternation; and as the panic affords us a favorable opportunity to drive them out of the Jerseys, it has been determined in council that you should move down towards New York with a considerable force, as if you had a design upon the city. That being an object of great importance, the enemy will be reduced to the necessity of withdrawing a considerable part of their force from the Jerseys, if not the whole, to secure the city."

These letters despatched, he continued forward to Morristown, where at length he came to a halt from his incessant and harassing marchings. There he learnt that General Mercer was still alive. He immediately sent his nephew, Major George Lewis, under the protection of a flag to attend upon him. Lewis found him languishing in great pain; he had been treated with respect by the enemy and great tenderness by the benevolent family who had sheltered him. He expired on the 12th of January, in the fifty-sixth year of his age.

From Morristown, Washington again wrote to General Heath, repeating his former orders. To Major-general Lincoln, also, who was just arrived at Peekskill, and had command of the Massachusetts militia, he writes on the 7th: "General Heath will communicate mine of this date to you, by which you will find that the greater part of your troops are to move down towards New York to draw the attention of the enemy to that quarter." Colonel Reed was ordered to send out rangers and bodies of militia to scour the country, waylay foraging parties, cut off supplies and keep the cantonments of the enemy in a state of siege.

The expedition under General Heath towards New York, from which much had been anticipated by Washington, proved a failure. It moved in three divisions, by different routes, but all arriving nearly at the same time at the enemy's outposts at King's Bridge. There was some skirmishing, but the great feature of the expedition was a pompous and peremptory summons of Fort Independence to surrender. "Twenty minutes only can be allowed," said Heath, "for the garrison to give their answer, and, should it be in the negative, they must abide the consequences." The garrison made no answer but an occasional cannonade. Heath failed to follow up his summons by corresponding deeds. He hovered and skirmished for some days about the outposts and Spyt den Duivel Creek, and then retired before a threatened snow-storm and the report of an enemy's fleet from Rhode Island, with troops under Lord Percy, who might land in Westchester and take the besieging force in rear.

But though disappointed in this part of his plan, Washington, having received reinforcements of militia, continued with his scanty army to carry on his system of annoyance. The situation of Cornwallis who but a short time before traversed the Jerseys so triumphantly, became daily more and more irksome. Spies were in his camp to give notice of every movement, and foes without to take advantage of it; so that not a foraging party could sally forth without being waylaid. By degrees he drew in his troops which were posted about the country, and collected them at New Brunswick and Amboy, so as to have a communication by water with New York, whence he was now compelled to draw nearly all his supplies. In fact the recent operations in the Jerseys had suddenly changed the whole aspect of the war, and given a triumphant close to what had been a disastrous campaign. The troops, which for months had been driven from post to post, apparently an undisciplined rabble, had all at once turned upon their pursuers and astounded them by brilliant stratagems and daring exploits. The commander, whose cautious policy had been sneered at by enemies and regarded with impatience by misjudging friends, had all at once shown that he possessed enterprise as well as circumspection, energy as well as endurance, and that beneath his wary coldness lurked a fire to break forth at the proper moment. This year's campaign, the most critical one of the war, and especially the part of it which occurred in the Jerseys, was the ordeal that made his great qualities fully appreciated by his countrymen, and gained for him from the statesmen and generals of Europe the appellation of the AMERICAN FABIUS.

CHAPTER XXXIX.
THE ARMY AT MORRISTOWN.—ATTACK ON PEEKSKILL.

The Howes learned to their mortification that "the mere running through a province is not subduing it." The British commanders had been outgeneralled, attacked and defeated. They had nearly been driven out of the Jerseys, and were now hemmed in and held in check by Washington and his handful of men castled among the heights of Morristown. So far from holding possession of the territory they had so recently overrun, they were fain to ask safe conduct across it for a convoy to their soldiers captured in battle. It must have been a severe trial to the pride of Cornwallis when he had to inquire by letter of Washington whether money and stores could be sent to the Hessians captured at Trenton and a surgeon and medicines to the wounded at Princeton; and Washington's reply must have conveyed a reproof still more mortifying. No molestation, he assured his lordship, would be offered to the convoy by any part of the regular army under his command; but *"he could not answer for the militia, who were resorting to arms in most parts of the State, and were excessively exasperated at the treatment they had met with from both Hessian and British troops."*

In fact, the conduct of the enemy had roused the whole country against them. The proclamations and printed protections of the British commanders, on the faith of which the inhabitants in general had stayed at home and forbore to take up arms, had proved of no avail. The Hessians could not or would not understand them, but plundered friend and foe alike. The British soldiery often followed their example, and the plunderings of both were at times attended by those brutal outrages on the weaker sex which inflame the dullest spirits to revenge. The whole State was thus roused against its invaders. In Washington's retreat of more than a hundred miles through the Jerseys, he had never been joined by more than one hundred of its inhabitants; now sufferers of both parties rose as one man to avenge their personal injuries. The late quiet yeomanry armed themselves and scoured the country in small parties to seize on stragglers, and the militia began to signalize themselves in voluntary skirmishes with regular troops.

Morristown, where the main army was encamped, had not been chosen by Washington as a permanent post, but merely as a halting-place where his troops might repose after their excessive fatigues and their sufferings from the inclement season. Further considerations persuaded him that it was well situated for the system of petty warfare which he meditated, and induced him to remain there. It was protected by forests and rugged heights. It was nearly equidistant from Amboy, Newark, and Brunswick, the principal posts of the enemy; so that any movement made from them could be met by a counter movement on his part, while the forays and skirmishes by which he might harass them would school and season his own troops. He had three faithful generals with him: Greene, Sullivan, and Knox.

Washington's military family at this time was composed of his aides-de-camp, Colonels Meade and Tench Tilghman of Philadelphia; and his secretary, Colonel Robert H. Harrison of Maryland. His head-quarters at first were in what was called the Freemason's Tavern, on the north side of the village green. His troops were encamped about the vicinity of the village, at first in tents, until they could build log huts for shelter against the winter's cold. The main encampment was near Bottle Hill, in a sheltered valley which was thickly wooded and had abundant springs.

The enemy being now concentrated at New Brunswick and Amboy, General Putnam was ordered by Washington to move from Crosswicks to Princeton, with the troops under his command. He was instructed to draw his forage as much as possible from the neighborhood of Brunswick, about eighteen miles off, thereby contributing to distress the enemy; to have good scouting parties continually on the look-out; to keep nothing with him but what could be moved off at a moment's warning, and, if compelled to leave Princeton, to retreat towards the mountains so as to form a junction with the forces at Morristown. Putnam had with him but a few hundred men. "You will give out your strength to be twice as great as it is," writes Washington; a common expedient with him in those times of scanty means.

Cantonments were gradually formed between Princeton and the Highlands of the Hudson, which made the left flank of Washington's position, and where General Heath had command. General Philemon Dickinson, who commanded the New Jersey militia, was stationed on the west side of Millstone River, near Somerset court-house, one of the nearest posts to the enemy's camp at Brunswick. A British foraging party of five or six hundred strong, sent out by Cornwallis, with forty wagons and upward of a hundred draught horses, mostly of the English breed, having collected sheep and cattle about the country, were sacking a mill on the opposite side of the river where a large quantity of flour was deposited. While thus employed, Dickinson set upon them with a force equal in number but composed of raw militia and fifty Philadelphia riflemen. He dashed through the river, waist deep, with his men, and charged the enemy so suddenly and vigorously that, though supported by three field-pieces, they gave way, left their convoy, and retreated so precipitately that he made only nine prisoners. A number of killed and wounded were carried off by the fugitives on light wagons.

To counteract the proclamation of the British commissioners, promising amnesty to all in rebellion who should, in a given time, return to their allegiance, Washington now issued a counter proclamation (Jan. 25th), commanding every person who had subscribed a declaration of fidelity to Great Britain, or taken an oath of allegiance, to repair within thirty days to head-quarters, or the quarters of the nearest general officer of the Continental army or of the militia, and there take the oath of allegiance to the United States of America, and give up any protection, certificate or passport he might have received from the enemy; at the same time granting full liberty to all such as preferred the interest and protection of Great Britain to the freedom and happiness of their country, forthwith to withdraw themselves and families within the enemy's lines. All who should neglect or refuse to comply with this order were to be considered adherents to the crown and treated as common enemies.

COL. MORRIS' HOUSE.
VOL. II.

A cartel for the exchange of prisoners had been a subject of negotiation previous to the affair of Trenton, without being adjusted. The British commanders were slow to recognize the claims to equality of those they considered rebels; Washington was tenacious in holding them up as patriots ennobled by their cause. Among the cases which came up for attention was that of Ethan Allen, the brave but eccentric captor of Ticonderoga. His daring attempts in the "path of renown" had cost him a world of hardships;—thrown into irons as a felon; threatened with a halter; carried to England to be tried for treason; confined in Pendennis Castle; retransported to Halifax, and now a prisoner in New York. Washington had been instructed, considering his long imprisonment, to urge his exchange. This had scarce been urged, when tidings of the capture of General Lee presented a case of still greater importance to be provided for. Lee was reported to be in rigorous confinement in New York, and treated with harshness and indignity. The British professed to consider him a deserter, he having been a lieutenant-colonel in their service, although he alleged that he had resigned his commission before joining the American army.

On the 13th of January, Washington addressed the following letter to Sir William Howe: "I am directed by Congress to propose an exchange of five of the

Hessian field-officers taken at Trenton for Major-general Lee; or, if this proposal should not be accepted, to demand his liberty upon parole, within certain bounds, as has ever been granted to your officers in our custody. I am informed, upon good authority, that your reason for keeping him hitherto in stricter confinement than usual is that you do not look upon him in the light of a common prisoner of war but as a deserter from the British service, as his resignation has never been accepted, and that you intend to try him as such by a court-martial. I will not undertake to determine how far this doctrine may be justifiable among yourselves, but I must give you warning that Major-general Lee is looked upon as an officer belonging to, and under the protection of the United Independent States of America, and that any violence you may commit upon his life and liberty will be severely retaliated upon the lives or liberties of the British officers, or those of their foreign allies in our hands."

In this letter he likewise adverted to the treatment of American prisoners in New York; several who had recently been released having given the most shocking account of the barbarities they had experienced.

Sir William, in reply, proposed to send an officer of rank to Washington to confer upon a mode of exchange and subsistence of prisoners. This proposal led to the appointment of two officers for the purpose, Colonel Walcott by General Howe, and Colonel Harrison, "the old secretary," by Washington.

Lee's actual treatment was not so harsh as had been represented. He was in close confinement it is true, but three rooms had been fitted up for his reception in the Old City Hall of New York, having nothing of the look of a prison excepting that they were secured by bolts and bars. Congress, in the meantime, had resorted to their threatened measure of retaliation. On the 20th of February they had resolved that the Board of War be directed immediately to order the five Hessian field-officers and Lieutenant-colonel Campbell into safe and close custody, "it being the unalterable resolution of Congress to retaliate on them the same punishment as may be inflicted on the person of General Lee."

In a letter to the President of Congress, Washington gives his moderating counsels on the whole subject of retaliation. "Though I sincerely commiserate," writes he, "the misfortunes of General Lee, and feel much for his present unhappy situation, yet with all possible deference to the opinion of Congress, I fear that these resolutions will not have the desired effect, are founded on impolicy, and will, if adhered to, produce consequences of an extensive and melancholy nature.... The balance of prisoners is greatly against us, and a general regard to the happiness of the whole should mark our conduct. Can we imagine that our enemies will not mete the same punishments, the same indignities, the same cruelties, to those belonging to us in their possession that we impose on theirs in our power? Why should we suppose them to possess more humanity than we have ourselves? Or why should an ineffectual attempt to relieve the distresses of one brave, unfortunate man, involve many more in the same calamities?"

Washington was not always successful in instilling his wise moderation into public councils. Congress adhered to their vindictive policy, merely directing that no other hardships should be inflicted on the captive officers than such confinement as was necessary to carry their resolve into effect. There were other circumstances besides the treatment of General Lee to produce this indignant sensibility on the part of Congress. Accounts were rife at this juncture of the cruelties and indignities almost invariably experienced by American prisoners at New York; and an active correspondence on the subject was going on between Washington and the British commanders, at the same time with that regarding General Lee.

The captive Americans who had been in the naval service were said to be confined, officers and men, in prison-ships which, from their loathsome condition and the horrors and sufferings of all kinds experienced on board of them, had acquired the appellation of *floating hells*. Those who had been in the land service were crowded into jails and dungeons like the vilest malefactors; and were represented as pining in cold, in filth, in hunger and nakedness. [In the correspondence between Lord Howe and Washington on this subject, the British commander denied the charges of undue severity in the treatment of prisoners, and pronounced the tales current on the subject as idle and unnatural reports. But the evidence of the truth of that statement is too complete to admit of doubt.] The *Jersey Prison-ship* is proverbial in our revolutionary history; and the bones of the unfortunate patriots who perished on board, form a monument on the Long Island shore. The horrors of the *Sugar House,* converted into a prison, are traditional in New York; and the brutal tyranny of Cunningham, the provost marshal, over men of worth confined in the common jail for the sin of patriotism, has been handed down from generation to generation. That Lord Howe and Sir William were ignorant of the extent of these atrocities we really believe, but it was their duty to be well informed.

The difficulties arising out of the case of General Lee interrupted the operations with regard to the exchange of prisoners; and gallant men, on both sides, suffered prolonged detention in consequence; and among the number the brave, but ill-starred Ethan Allen.

The early part of the year brought the annual embarrassments caused by short enlistments. The brief terms of service for which the Continental soldiery had enlisted, a few months perhaps, at most a year, were expiring, and the men, glad to be released from camp duty, were hastening to their rustic homes. Militia had to be the dependence until a new army could be raised and organized, and Washington called on the council of safety of Pennsylvania speedily to furnish temporary reinforcements of the kind. All his officers that could be spared were ordered away, some to recruit, some to collect the scattered men of the different regiments, who were dispersed, he said, almost over the continent. General Knox was sent off to Massachusetts to expedite the raising of a battalion of artillery. Different States were urged to levy and equip their quotas for the Continental army.

While anxiously exerting himself to strengthen his own precarious army, the security of the northern department was urged upon his attention. Schuyler represented it as in need of reinforcements and supplies of all kinds. He apprehended that Carleton might make an attack upon Ticonderoga as soon as he could cross Lake Champlain on the ice. That important fortress was under the command of a brave officer, Colonel Anthony Wayne, but its garrison had dwindled down to six or seven hundred men, chiefly New England militia. In the present destitute situation of his department as to troops, Schuyler feared that Carleton might not only succeed in an attempt on Ticonderoga, but might push his way to Albany. Although Washington considered a winter attack of the kind specified by Schuyler too difficult and dangerous to be very probable, he urged reinforcements from Massachusetts and New Hampshire, whence they could be furnished most speedily. Massachusetts, in fact, had already determined to send four regiments to Schuyler's aid as soon as possible.

Notwithstanding all Washington's exertions in behalf of the army under his immediate command, it continued to be deplorably in want of reinforcements, and it was necessary to maintain the utmost vigilance at all his posts to prevent his camp from being surprised. The operations of the enemy might be delayed by the bad condition of the roads, and the want of horses to move their artillery, but he anticipated an attack as soon as the roads were passable, and apprehended a disastrous result unless speedily reinforced.

The designs of the enemy being mere matter of conjecture, measures varied accordingly. As the season advanced, Washington was led to believe that Philadelphia would be their first object at the opening of the campaign, and that they would bring round all their troops from Canada by water to aid in the enterprise. Under this persuasion he wrote to General Heath, ordering him to send eight Massachusetts battalions to Peekskill. At Peekskill, he observed, "they would be well placed to give support to any of the Eastern or Middle States; or to oppose the enemy, should they design to penetrate the country up the Hudson; or to cover New England, should they invade it."

On the 18th of March he despatched General Greene to Philadelphia, to lay before Congress such matters as he could not venture to communicate by letter. Greene had scarce departed when the enemy began to give signs of life. The delay in the arrival of artillery, more than his natural indolence, had kept General Howe from formally taking the field; he now made preparations for the next campaign by detaching troops to destroy the American deposits of military stores. One of the chief of these was at Peekskill, the very place whither Washington had directed Heath to send troops from Massachusetts, and which he thought of making a central point of assemblage. Brigadier-general McDougall had the command of it in the absence of General Heath, but his force did not exceed two hundred and fifty men.

As soon as the Hudson was clear of ice, a squadron of vessels of war and transports, with five hundred troops under Colonel Bird ascended the river. McDougall had intelligence of the intended attack, and while the ships were making their way across the Tappan Sea and Haverstraw Bay, exerted himself to remove as much as possible of the provisions and stores to Forts Montgomery and Constitution in the Highlands. On the morning of the 23d the whole squadron came to anchor in Peekskill Bay, and five hundred men landed in Lent's Cove, on the south side of the bay, whence they pushed forward with four light field-pieces drawn by sailors. On their approach, McDougall set fire to the barracks and principal storehouses, and retreated about two miles to a strong post, commanding the entrance to the Highlands and the road to Continental Village, the place of the deposits. It was the post which had been noted by Washington in the preceding year where a small force could make a stand and hurl down masses of rock on their assailants. Hence, McDougall sent an express to Lieutenant-colonel Marinus Willet, who had charge of Fort Constitution, to hasten to his assistance.

The British, finding the wharf in flames where they had intended to embark their spoils, completed the conflagration, besides destroying several small craft laden with provisions. They kept possession of the place until the following day, when a scouting party, which had advanced towards the entrance of the Highlands, was encountered by Colonel Marinus Willet with a detachment from Fort Constitution, and driven back to the main body after a sharp skirmish in which nine of the marauders were killed. Four more were slain on the banks of Canopas Creek as they were setting fire to some boats. The enemy were disappointed in the hope of carrying off a great deal of booty, and finding the country around was getting under arms they contented themselves with the mischief they had done and re-embarked in the evening by moonlight, when the whole squadron swept down the Hudson.

CHAPTER XL.

THE NORTHERN ARMY.—BRITISH EXPEDITION TO CONNECTICUT.

We have now to enter upon a tissue of circumstances connected with the Northern department which will be found materially to influence the course of affairs in that quarter throughout the current year, and ultimately to be fruitful of annoyance to Washington himself. To make these more clear to the reader, it is necessary to revert to events in the preceding year.

The question of command between Schuyler and Gates, when settled as we have shown by Congress, had caused no interruption to the harmony of intercourse between these generals. Schuyler directed the affairs of the department with energy and activity from his head-quarters at Albany, where they had been fixed by Congress, while Gates, subordinate to him, commanded the post of Ticonderoga.

The disappointment of an independent command, however, still rankled in the mind of the latter, and was kept alive by the officious suggestions of meddling friends. In the course of the autumn, his hopes in this respect revived. Schuyler was again disgusted with the service. In the discharge of his various and harassing duties he had been annoyed by sectional jealousies and ill will. His motives and measures had been maligned. The failures in Canada had been attributed to him, and he had repeatedly entreated Congress to order an inquiry into the many charges made against him, "that he might not any longer be insulted."

On the 14th of September he actually offered his resignation of his commission as major-general, and of every other office and appointment; still claiming a court of inquiry on his conduct, and expressing his determination to fulfil the duties of a good citizen and promote the weal of his native country, but in some other capacity. The hopes of Gates, inspired by this proffered resignation, were doomed to be overclouded. Schuyler was informed by President Hancock "that Congress, during the present state of affairs, could not consent to accept of his resignation; ... that they would at an early day appoint a committee to inquire fully into his conduct, which they trusted would establish his reputation in the opinion of all good men."

Schuyler received the resolve of Congress with grim acquiescence, but showed in his reply that he was but half soothed. "At this very critical juncture," writes he, October 16, "I shall continue to act some time longer, but Congress must prepare to put the care of this department into other hands." He had remained at his post, therefore, discharging the various duties of his department with his usual zeal and activity; and Gates, at the end of the campaign, had repaired, as we have shown, to the vicinity of Congress to attend the fluctuation of events.

Circumstances in the course of the winter had put the worthy Schuyler again on points of punctilio with Congress. Among some letters intercepted by the enemy and retaken by the Americans was one from Colonel Joseph Trumbull, the commissary-general, insinuating that General Schuyler had secreted or suppressed a commission sent for his brother, Colonel John Trumbull, as deputy adjutant-general. The purport of the letter was reported to Schuyler. He spurned at the insinuation. "If it be true that he has asserted such a thing," writes he to the president, "I shall expect from Congress that justice which is due to me.... Until Mr. Trumbull and I are upon a footing, I cannot do what the laws of honor and a regard to my own reputation render indispensably necessary. Congress can put us on a par by dismissing one or the other from the service."

Congress failed to comply with the general's request. They added also to his chagrin by dismissing from the service an army physician in whose appointment he had particularly interested himself. Schuyler was a proud-spirited man, and at times somewhat irascible. In a letter to Congress, on the 8th of February, he observed: "As Dr. Stringer had my recommendation to the office he has sustained, perhaps it was a compliment due to me that I should have been advised of the reason of his dismission." And again: "I was in hopes some notice would have been taken of the odious suspicion contained in Mr. Commissary Trumbull's intercepted letter. I really feel myself deeply chagrined on the occasion. I am incapable of the meanness he suspects me of, and I confidently expected that Congress would have done me that justice which it was in their power to give, and which I humbly conceive they ought to have done." This letter gave great umbrage to Congress, but no immediate answer was made to it.

About this time the office of adjutant-general, which had remained vacant ever since the resignation of Colonel Reed, to the great detriment of the service, especially now when a new army was to be formed, was offered to General Gates, who had formerly filled it with ability; and President Hancock informed him, by letter, of the earnest desire of Congress that he should resume it, retaining his present rank and pay. Gates almost resented the proposal. He had a higher object in view. A letter from Schuyler to Congress had informed that body that he should set out for Philadelphia about the 21st of March, and should immediately on his arrival require the promised inquiry into his conduct. Gates, of course, was acquainted with this circumstance. He knew Schuyler had given offence to Congress; he knew that he had been offended on his own part, and had repeatedly talked of resigning. He had active friends in Congress ready to push his interests. On the 15th of March the letter of General Schuyler of the 3d of February, which had given such offence, was brought before the House, and it was resolved that his suggestion concerning the dismission of Dr. Stringer was highly derogatory to the honor of Congress, and that it was expected his letters in future would be written in a style suitable to the dignity of the representative body of these free and independent States and to his own character as their officer. His expressions, too, respecting the intercepted letter, that he had expected Congress would have done him all the justice in their power, were pronounced, "to say the least, ill-advised and highly indecent."

While Schuyler was thus in partial eclipse, the House proceeded to appoint a general officer for the Northern department, of which he had stated it to be in need. On the 25th of March, Gates received the following note from President Hancock: "I have it in charge to direct that you repair to Ticonderoga immediately and take command of the army stationed in that department." Gates obeyed with alacrity. Again the vision of an independent command floated before his mind, and he was on his way to Albany at the time that Schuyler, ignorant of this new arrangement, was journeying to Philadelphia. He arrived in the second week in April, and found himself superseded in effect by General Gates in the Northern department. He enclosed to the committee of Albany the recent resolutions of Congress, passed before his arrival. "By these," writes he, "you will readily perceive that I shall not return a general. Under what influence it has been brought about I am not at liberty now to mention. On my return to Albany I shall give the committee the fullest information."

Taking his seat in Congress as a delegate from New York, he demanded the promised investigation of his conduct during the time he had held a command in the army. It was his intention, when the scrutiny had taken place, to resign his commission and retire from the service. On the 18th a committee of inquiry was appointed, as at his request, composed of a member from each State. In the meantime, as second major-general of the United States (Lee being the first), he held active command at Philadelphia, forming a camp on the western side of the Delaware, completing the works on Fort Island, throwing up works on Red Bank, and accelerating the despatch of troops and provisions to the commander-in-chief. During his sojourn at Philadelphia, also, he contributed essentially to re-organize the commissary department; digesting rules for its regulation, which were mainly adopted by Congress.

The fame of the American struggle for independence was bringing foreign officers as candidates for admission into the patriot army, and causing great embarrassment to the commander-in-chief. Congress determined that no foreign officers should receive commissions who were not well acquainted with the English language and did not bring strong testimonials of their abilities. Still there was embarrassment. Some came with brevet commissions from the French government, and had been assured by Mr. Deane, American commissioner at Paris, that they would have the same rank in the American army. This would put them above American officers of merit and hard service, whose commissions were of more recent date. One Monsieur Ducoudray, on the strength of an agreement with Mr. Deane, expected to have the rank of major-general and to be put at the head of the artillery. Washington deprecated the idea of intrusting a department on which the very salvation of the army might depend to a foreigner, who had no other tie to bind him to the interests of the country than honor.

Among the foreign candidates for appointments was one Colonel Conway, a native of Ireland, but who, according to his own account, had been thirty years in the service of France, and claimed to be a chevalier of the order of St. Louis, of which he wore the decoration. Mr. Deane had recommended him to Washington as an officer of merit, and had written to Congress that he considered him well qualified for the office of adjutant or brigadier-general. Colonel Conway pushed for that of brigadier-general. It had been conferred some time before by Congress on two French officers, De Fermois and Deborre, who, he had observed, had been inferior to him in the French service, and it would be mortifying now to hold rank below them. Conway accordingly received the rank of brigadier-general, of which he subsequently proved himself unworthy. He was boastful and presumptuous, and became noted for his intrigues and for a despicable cabal against the commander-in-chief, which went by his name, and of which we shall have to speak hereafter.

A candidate of a different stamp had presented himself in the preceding year, the gallant, generous-spirited, Thaddeus Kosciuszko. He was a Pole, of an ancient and noble family of Lithuania, and had been educated for the profession of arms at the military school at Warsaw, and subsequently in France. Disappointed in a love affair with a beautiful lady of rank with whom he had attempted to elope, he had emigrated to this country, and came provided with a letter of introduction from Dr. Franklin to Washington.

"What do you seek here?" inquired the commander-in-chief. "To fight for American independence." "What can you do?" "Try me."

Washington was pleased with the curt yet comprehensive reply and with his chivalrous air and spirit, and at once received him into his family as an aide-de-camp. Congress shortly afterwards appointed him an engineer, with the rank of colonel. He proved a valuable officer throughout the Revolution, and won an honorable and lasting name in our country.

Questions of rank among his generals were, as we have repeatedly shown, perpetual sources of perplexity to Washington, and too often caused by what the sarcastic Lee termed "the stumblings of Congress;" such was the case at present. In recent army promotions, Congress had advanced Stirling, Mifflin, St. Clair, Stephen and Lincoln to the rank of major-general, while Arnold, their senior in service, and distinguished by so many brilliant exploits, was passed over and left to remain a brigadier. Washington was surprised at not seeing his name on the list, but supposing it might have been omitted through mistake, he wrote to Arnold, who was at Providence in Rhode Island, advising him not to take any hasty step in consequence, but to allow time for recollection, promising his own endeavors to remedy any error that might have been made. He wrote also to Henry Lee in Congress, inquiring whether the omission was owing to accident or design.

Arnold was, in truth, deeply wounded by the omission, but intimated that he should avoid any hasty step and should remain at his post until he could leave it without any damage to the public interest. The principle upon which Congress had proceeded in their recent promotions was explained to Washington. The number of general officers promoted from each State was proportioned to the number of men furnished by it. Connecticut (Arnold's State) had already two major-generals, which was its full share. An opportunity occurred before long for Arnold again to signalize himself.

The amount of stores destroyed at Peekskill had fallen far short of General Howe's expectations. Something more must be done to cripple the Americans before the opening of the campaign. Accordingly another expedition was set on foot against a still larger deposit at Danbury, within the borders of Connecticut, and between twenty and thirty miles from Peekskill. Ex-governor Tryon, recently commissioned major-general of provincials, conducted it, accompanied by Brigadier-general Agnew and Sir William Erskine. He had a force two thousand strong, and made his appearance on the Sound in the latter part of April with a fleet of twenty-six sail. On the 25th, towards evening, he landed his troops on the beach at the foot of Canepo Hill, near the mouth of the Saugatuck River, and set off for Danbury, about twenty-three miles distant. They were in a patriotic neighborhood. General Silliman, of the Connecticut militia, who resided at Fairfield, a few miles distant, sent out expresses to rouse the country. It so happened that General Arnold was at New Haven, between twenty and thirty miles off, on his way to Philadelphia for the purpose of settling his accounts. At the alarm of a British inroad he forgot his injuries and irritation, mounted his horse, and accompanied by General Wooster hastened to join General Silliman. As they spurred forward every farm house sent out its warrior, until upwards of a hundred were pressing on with them, full of the fighting spirit. Lieutenant Oswald, Arnold's secretary in the Canada campaign, was at this time at New Haven enlisting men for Lamb's regiment of artillery. He, too, heard the note of alarm, and mustering his recruits marched off with three field-pieces for the scene of action.

In the meanwhile the British, marching all night with short haltings, reached Danbury about two o'clock in the afternoon of the 26th. There were but fifty Continental soldiers and one hundred militia in the place. These retreated, as did most of the inhabitants, excepting such as remained to take care of the sick and aged. Four men, intoxicated, as it was said, fired upon the troops from the windows of a large house. The soldiers rushed in, drove them into the cellar, set fire to the house, and left them to perish in the flames. There was a great quantity of stores of all kinds in the village, and no vehicles to convey them to the ships. The work of destruction commenced. The soldiers made free with the liquors found in abundance; and throughout the greater part of the night there was revel, drunkenness, blasphemy, and devastation. Tryon, full of anxiety, and aware that the country was rising, ordered a retreat before daylight, setting fire to the magazines to complete the destruction of the stores. The flames spread to the other edifices, and almost the whole village was soon in a blaze.

While these scenes had been transacted at Danbury, the Connecticut yeomanry had been gathering. Fairfield and the adjacent counties had poured out their minute men. General Silliman had advanced at the head of five hundred. Generals Wooster and Arnold joined him with their chance followers, as did a few more militia. A heavy rain retarded their march; it was near midnight when they reached Bethel, within four miles of Danbury. Here they halted to take a little repose and put their arms in order, rendered almost unserviceable by the rain. They were now about six hundred strong. Wooster took the command, as first major-general of the militia of the State. Though in the sixty-eighth year of his age he was full of ardor, with almost youthful fire and daring. At dawn of day Wooster detached Arnold with four hundred men to push across the country and take post at Ridgefield, by which the British must pass; while he with two hundred remained to hang on and harass them in flank and rear.

The British began their retreat early in the morning, conducting it in regular style with flanking parties and a rear-guard well furnished with artillery. As soon as they had passed his position, Wooster attacked the rear-guard with great spirit and effect; there was sharp skirmishing until within two miles of Ridgefield, when, as the veteran was cheering on his men who began to waver, a musket ball brought him down from his horse and finished his gallant career. On his fall his men retreated in disorder.

The delay which his attack had occasioned to the enemy had given Arnold time to throw up a kind of breastwork or barricade across the road at the north end of Ridgefield, where he took his stand with his little force now increased to about five hundred men. About eleven o'clock the enemy advanced in column, with artillery and flanking parties. They were kept at bay for a time, and received several volleys from the barricade, until it was outflanked and carried. Arnold ordered a retreat, and was bringing off the rear guard when his horse was shot under him and came down upon his knees. Arnold remained seated in the saddle, with one foot entangled in the stirrups. A tory soldier seeing his plight, rushed towards him with fixed bayonet. He had just time to draw a pistol from the holster. "You're my prisoner," cried the tory. "Not yet!" exclaimed Arnold, and shot him dead. Then extricating his foot from the stirrup, he threw himself into the thickets of a neighboring swamp, and escaped unharmed by the bullets that whistled after him and joined his retreating troops.

General Tryon intrenched for the night in Ridgefield, his troops having suffered greatly in their harassed retreat. The next morning, after having set fire to four houses he continued his march for the ships. The militia hung on the rear of the enemy as soon as they were in motion. Arnold was again in the field with his rallied forces, strengthened by Lieutenant-colonel Oswald with two companies of Lamb's artillery regiment and three field-pieces. With these he again posted himself on the enemy's route. Difficulties and annoyances had multiplied upon the latter at every step. When they came in sight of the position where Arnold was waiting for them, they changed their route, wheeled to the left, and made for a ford of Saugatuck River. Arnold hastened to cross the bridge and take them in flank, but they were too quick for him. Colonel Lamb had now reached the scene of action, as had about two hundred volunteers. Leaving to Oswald the charge of the artillery, he put himself at the head of the volunteers and led them up to Arnold's assistance. The enemy finding themselves hard pressed, pushed for Canepo Hill. They reached it in the evening without a round of ammunition in their cartridge-boxes. As they were now within cannon shot of their ships, the Americans ceased the pursuit.

In this inroad the enemy destroyed a considerable amount of military stores, and seventeen hundred tents prepared for the use of Washington's army in the ensuing campaign. The loss of General Wooster was deeply deplored. As to Arnold, his gallantry in this affair gained him fresh laurels, and Congress, to remedy their late error, promoted him to the rank of major-general. Still this promotion did not restore him to his proper position. He was at the bottom of the list of major-generals, with four officers above him, his juniors in service. As an additional balm to his wounded pride, Congress a few days afterwards voted that a horse, properly caparisoned, should be presented to him in their name as a token of their approbation of his gallant conduct in the late action.

The destructive expeditions against the American depots of military stores, were retaliated in kind by Colonel Meigs, a spirited officer who had accompanied Arnold in his expedition through the wilderness against Quebec. Having received intelligence that the British commissaries had collected a great amount of grain, forage, and other supplies at Sag Harbor, a small port in the deep bay which forks the east end of Long Island, he crossed the Sound on the 23d of May from Guilford in Connecticut, with about one hundred and seventy men in whale-boats convoyed by two armed sloops; landed on the island near Southold; carried the boats a distance of fifteen miles across the north fork of the bay, launched them into the latter, crossed it, landed within four miles of Sag Harbor, and before daybreak carried the place, which was guarded by a company of foot. A furious fire of round and grape shot was opened upon the Americans from an armed schooner, anchored about one hundred and fifty yards from shore, and stout defence was made by the crews of a dozen brigs and sloops lying at the wharf to take in freight; but Meigs succeeded in burning these vessels, destroying everything on shore, and carrying off ninety prisoners; among whom were the officers of the company of foot, the commissaries, and the captains of most of the small vessels. Washington was so highly pleased with the spirit and success of this enterprise, that he publicly returned thanks to Colonel Meigs and the officers and men engaged in it.

[The committee of inquiry on General Schuyler's conduct had now made their report to Congress, in which they placed the character of that officer higher than ever as an able and active commander and a zealous and disinterested patriot. Schuyler made a memorial to Congress explaining away or apologizing for the expressions in his letter of the 4th of February which had given offence to the House, which was so far satisfactory that Congress informed him that their sentiments concerning him were now the same as those entertained before the reception of his objectionable letter. Some warm discussions now ensued in Congress relative to the northern command, in which it was stated that General Gates misapprehended his position, and that in sending him to Ticonderoga it was not the intention of Congress to give him the same command formerly held by Schuyler. The friends of Gates, on the other hand, pronounced it an absurdity that an officer holding so important a post as Ticonderoga should be under the order of another a hundred miles distant. The discussion terminated by declaring Ticonderoga, Fort Stanwix, and their defenders to be the Northern department, over which Schuyler was to have supreme command.]

Schuyler was received with open arms at Albany on the 3d of June. "I had the satisfaction," writes he, "to experience the finest feelings which my country

made a joint report to Washington, in which they recommended the completion of the obstructions in the river already commenced. These consisted of a boom, or heavy iron chain, across the river from Fort Montgomery to Anthony's Nose, with cables stretched in front to break the force of any ship under way, before she could strike it. The boom was to be protected by the guns of two ships and two row galleys stationed just above it, and by batteries on shore. This, it was deemed, would be sufficient to prevent the enemy's ships from ascending the river. If these obstructions could be rendered effective, they did not think the enemy would attempt to operate by land; "the passes through the Highlands being so exceedingly difficult."

VIEW FROM FORT MONTGOMERY.
VOL. I.

The general command of the Hudson was offered by Washington to Arnold; intending thus publicly to manifest his opinion of his deserts, and hoping, by giving him so important a post, to appease his irritated feelings. Arnold, however, declined to accept it. In an interview with Washington at Morristown he alleged his anxiety to proceed to Philadelphia and settle his public accounts, which were of considerable amount; especially as reports had been circulated injurious to his character as a man of integrity. He intended, therefore, to wait on Congress and request a committee of inquiry into his conduct. Beside, he did not consider the promotion conferred on him by Congress sufficient to obviate their previous neglect. With these considerations he proceeded to Philadelphia, bearing a letter from Washington to the President of Congress countenancing his complaints and testifying to the excellence of his military character. We may here add that the accusations against him were pronounced false and slanderous by the Board of War.

The important command of the Hudson being declined by Arnold was now given to Putnam, who repaired forthwith to Peekskill. He set about promptly to carry into effect the measures of security which Greene and Knox had recommended; especially the boom and chain at Fort Montgomery, about which General George Clinton had busied himself. A large part of the New York and New England troops were stationed at this post, not merely to guard the Hudson, but to render aid either to the Eastern or Middle States in case of exigency.

About this time, Washington had the satisfaction of drawing near to him his old friend and travelling companion, Dr. James Craik, the same who had served with him in Braddock's campaign and had voyaged with him down the Ohio; for whom he now procured the appointment of assistant director-general of the Hospital department of the middle district, which included the States between the Hudson and the Potomac.

Towards the end of May, Washington broke up his cantonments at Morristown, and shifted his camp to Middlebrook, within ten miles of Brunswick. His whole force fit for duty was now about seven thousand three hundred men, all from the States south of the Hudson. There were forty-three regiments, forming ten brigades, commanded by Brigadiers Muhlenberg, Weedon, Woodford, Scott, Smallwood, Deborre, Wayne, Dehaas, Conway, and Maxwell. These were apportioned into five divisions of two brigades each, under Major-generals Greene, Stephen, Sullivan, Lincoln and Stirling. The artillery was commanded by Knox. Sullivan, with his division, was stationed on the right at Princeton. With the rest of his force, Washington fortified himself in a position naturally strong, among hills, in the rear of the village of Middlebrook. His camp was, on all sides, difficult of approach, and he rendered it still more so by intrenchments. The high grounds about it commanded a wide view of the country around Brunswick, the road to Philadelphia, and the course of the Raritan, so that the enemy could make no important movement on land without his perceiving it.

On the 31st of May, reports were brought to camp that a fleet of a hundred sail had left New York and stood out to sea. Whither bound and how freighted was unknown. If they carried troops, their destination might be Delaware Bay. Eighteen transports also had arrived at New York, with troops in foreign uniforms, which proved to be Anspachers, and other German mercenaries; there were British reinforcements also; and, what was particularly needed, a supply of tents and camp equipage. Sir William Howe had been waiting for the latter, and likewise until the ground should be covered with grass. The country was now in full verdure, affording "green forage" in abundance, and all things seemed to Sir William propitious for the opening of the campaign. Early in June, therefore, he gave up ease and gayety and luxurious life at New York, and crossing into the Jerseys set up his head-quarters at Brunswick.

As soon as Washington ascertained that Sir William's attention was completely turned to this quarter, he determined to strengthen his position with all the force that could be spared from other parts, so as to be able, in case a favorable opportunity presented, to make an attack upon the enemy; in the meantime, he would harass them with his light militia troops, aided by a few Continentals, so as to weaken their numbers by continual skirmishes. With this view he ordered General Putnam to send down most of the Continental troops from Peekskill, leaving only a number sufficient, in conjunction with the militia, to guard that post against surprise.

Arnold, in this critical juncture, had been put in command of Philadelphia, a post which he had been induced to accept, although the question of rank had not been adjusted to his satisfaction. His command embraced the western bank of the Delaware with all its fords and passes, and he took up his station there with a strong body of militia, supported by a few Continentals, to oppose any attempt of the enemy to cross the river. He was instructed by Washington to give him notice by expresses, posted on the road, if any fleet should appear in Delaware Bay; and to endeavor to concert signals with the camp of Sullivan at Princeton, by alarm fires upon the hills.

On the night of the 13th of June, General Howe sallied forth in great force from Brunswick, as if pushing directly for the Delaware, but his advanced guard halted at Somerset court-house, about eight or nine miles distant. Apprised of this movement, Washington at daybreak reconnoitred the enemy from the heights before the camp. He observed their front halting at the court-house, but a few miles distant, while troops and artillery were grouped here and there along the road and the rear-guard was still at Brunswick. It was a question with Washington and his generals, as they reconnoitred the enemy with their glasses, whether this was a real move toward Philadelphia, or merely a lure to tempt them down from their strong position. In this uncertainty, Washington drew out his army in battle array along the heights, but kept quiet. In the present state of his forces it was his plan not to risk a general action, but should the enemy really march toward the Delaware, to hang heavily upon their rear.

The British took up a strong position, having Millstone Creek on their left, the Raritan all along their front, and their right resting on Brunswick, and proceeded to fortify themselves with bastions.

The American and British armies, strongly posted, remained four days grimly regarding each other; both waiting to be attacked. The Jersey militia which now turned out with alacrity, repaired, some to Washington's camp, others to that of Sullivan. The latter had fallen back from Princeton, and taken a position behind the Sourland Hills.

Howe pushed out detachments and made several feints, as if to pass by the American camp and march to the Delaware, but Washington was not to be deceived. Baffled in these attempts to draw his cautious adversary into a general action, Howe, on the 19th, suddenly broke up his camp, and pretended to return with some precipitation to Brunswick, burning as he went several valuable dwelling houses. Washington's light troops hovered round the enemy as far as the Raritan and Millstone, which secured their flanks, would permit; but the main army kept to its stronghold on the heights.

On the next day came warlike news from the North. Amesbury, a British spy, had been seized and examined by Schuyler. Burgoyne was stated as being arrived at Quebec to command the forces in an invasion from Canada. While he advanced with his main force by Lake Champlain, a detachment of British troops, Canadians and Indians, led by Sir John Johnson, was to penetrate by Oswego to the Mohawk River, and place itself between Fort Stanwix and Fort Edward. If this information was correct, Ticonderoga would soon be attacked. The force there might be sufficient for its defence, but Schuyler would have no troops to oppose the inroad of Sir John Johnson, and he urged a reinforcement. Washington forthwith sent orders to Putnam to procure sloops, and hold four Massachusetts regiments in readiness to go up the river at a moment's warning.

On the 22d, Sir William again marched out of Brunswick, but this time proceeded towards Amboy, again burning several houses on the way; hoping, perhaps, that the sight of columns of smoke rising from a ravaged country would irritate the Americans and provoke an attack. Washington sent out three brigades under General Greene to fall upon the rear of the enemy, while Morgan hung upon their skirts with his riflemen. At the same time the army remained paraded on the heights ready to yield support if necessary. Finding that Howe had actually sent his heavy baggage and part of his troops over to Staten Island, Washington, on the 24th, left the heights and descended to Quibbletown (now New Market), six or seven miles on the road to Amboy, to be nearer at hand for the protection of his advanced parties.

General Howe now thought he had gained his point. Recalling those who had crossed, he formed his troops into two columns, the right led by Cornwallis, the left by himself, and marched back rapidly by different routes from Amboy. He had three objects in view: to cut off the principal advanced parties of the Americans; to come up with and bring the main body into an engagement near Quibbletown; or that Lord Cornwallis, making a considerable circuit to the right, should turn the left of Washington's position, get to the heights, take possession of the passes, and oblige him to abandon that stronghold where he had hitherto been so secure. Washington, however, had timely notice of his movements, and penetrating his design, regained his fortified camp at Middlebrook, and secured the passes of the mountains. He then detached a body of light troops under Brigadier-general Scott, together with Morgan's riflemen, to hang on the flank of the enemy and watch their motions.

Cornwallis, in his circuitous march, dispersed the light parties of the advance, but fell in with Lord Stirling's division, strongly posted in a woody country, and well covered by artillery judiciously disposed. A sharp skirmish ensued, when the Americans gave way and retreated to the hills with the loss of a few men and three field-pieces; while the British halted at Westfield, disappointed in the main objects of their enterprise.

Perceiving that every scheme of bringing the Americans to a general action, or at least of withdrawing them from their strongholds, was rendered abortive by the caution and prudence of Washington, and aware of the madness of attempting to march to the Delaware, through a hostile country, with such a force in his rear,

Sir William Howe broke up his head-quarters at Amboy on the last of June and crossed over to Staten Island on the floating bridge, and it was soon apparent that at length the enemy had really evacuated the Jerseys.

The question now was, what would be their next move? A great stir among the shipping seemed to indicate an expedition by water. But whither? Circumstances occurred to perplex the question.

Scarce had the last tent been struck, and the last transport disappeared from before Amboy, when intelligence arrived from General St. Clair announcing the appearance of a hostile fleet on Lake Champlain, and that General Burgoyne with the whole Canada army was approaching Ticonderoga. The judgment and circumspection of Washington were never more severely put to the proof. Was this merely a diversion with a small force of light troops and Indians, intended to occupy the attention of the American forces in that quarter, while the main body of the army in Canada should come round by sea and form a junction with the army under Howe? But General Burgoyne, in Washington's opinion, was a man of too much spirit and enterprise to return from England merely to execute a plan from which no honor was to be derived. Did he really intend to break through by the way of Ticonderoga? In that case it must be Howe's plan to co-operate with him. His next move, in such case, would be to ascend the Hudson, seize on the Highland passes before Washington could form a union with the troops stationed there, and thus open the way for the junction with Burgoyne. Should Washington, however, on such a presumption, hasten with his troops to Peekskill, leaving General Howe on Staten Island, what would prevent the latter from pushing to Philadelphia by South Amboy or any other route?

Such were the perplexities and difficulties presenting themselves under every aspect of the case. In this dilemma Washington sent Generals Parsons and Varnum with a couple of brigades in all haste to Peekskill, and wrote to Generals George Clinton and Putnam—the former to call out the New York militia from Orange and Ulster counties, the latter to summon the militia from Connecticut; and as soon as such reinforcements should be at hand, to despatch four of the strongest Massachusetts regiments to the aid of Ticonderoga. General Sullivan, moreover, was ordered to advance with his division towards the Highlands as far as Pompton, while Washington moved his own camp back to Morristown, to be ready either to push on to the Highlands or fall back upon his recent position at Middlebrook, according to the movements of the enemy.

Deserters from Staten Island and New York soon brought word to the camp that transports were being fitted up with berths for horses, and taking in three weeks' supply of water and provender. All this indicated some other destination than that of the Hudson. Lest an attempt on the Eastern States should be intended, Washington sent a circular to their governors to put them on their guard.

In the midst of his various cares, his yeoman soldiery, the Jersey militia, were not forgotten. It was their harvest time, and the State being evacuated there was no immediate call for their services; he dismissed, therefore, almost the whole of them to their homes.

CHAPTER XLII.
INVASION FROM CANADA.

The armament advancing against Ticonderoga, of which General St. Clair had given intelligence, was not a mere diversion but a regular invasion; the plan of which had been devised by the king, Lord George Germain, and General Burgoyne, the latter having returned to England from Canada in the preceding year. The junction of the two armies, — that in Canada and that under General Howe in New York, — was considered the speediest mode of quelling the rebellion; and as the security and good government of Canada required the presence of Governor Sir Guy Carleton, three thousand men were to remain there with him; the residue of the army was to be employed upon two expeditions — the one under General Burgoyne, who was to force his way to Albany, the other under Lieutenant-colonel St. Leger, who was to make a diversion on the Mohawk River.

The invading army was composed of three thousand seven hundred and twenty-four British rank and file, three thousand sixteen Germans, mostly Brunswickers, two hundred and fifty Canadians, and four hundred Indians; beside these there were four hundred and seventy-three artillery men, in all nearly eight thousand men. The army was admirably appointed. Its brass train of artillery was extolled as perhaps the finest ever allotted to an army of the size. General Phillips, who commanded the artillery, had gained great reputation in the wars in Germany. Brigadiers-general Fraser, Powel, and Hamilton were also officers of distinguished merit. So was Major-general the Baron Riedesel, a Brunswicker, who commanded the German troops.

While Burgoyne with the main force proceeded from St. Johns, Colonel St. Leger, with a detachment of regulars and Canadians about seven hundred strong, was to land at Oswego, and, guided by Sir John Johnson at the head of his loyalist volunteers, tory refugees from his former neighborhood, and a body of Indians, was to enter the Mohawk country, draw the attention of General Schuyler in that direction, attack Fort Stanwix, and, having ravaged the valley of the Mohawk, rejoin Burgoyne at Albany, where it was expected they would make a triumphant junction with the army of Sir William Howe.

Schuyler was uncertain as to the plans and force of the enemy. If information gathered from scouts and a captured spy might be relied on, Ticonderoga would soon be attacked. This information he transmitted to Washington from Fort Edward on the 16th, the very day that Burgoyne embarked at St. Johns. On the following day Schuyler was at Ticonderoga. The works were not in such a state of forwardness as he had anticipated, owing to the tardy arrival of troops and the want of a sufficient number of artificers. The works in question related chiefly to Mount Independence, a high circular hill on the east side of the lake, immediately opposite to the old fort, and considered the most defensible. A star fort with pickets crowned the summit of the hill, which was table land; half way down the side of a hill was a battery, and at its foot were strongly intrenched works well mounted with cannon. Here the French general, De Fermois, who had charge of this fort, was posted.

As this part of Lake Champlain is narrow, a connection was kept up between the two forts by a floating bridge, supported on twenty-two sunken piers in caissons, formed of very strong timber. Between the piers were separate floats, fifty feet long and twelve feet wide, strongly connected by iron chains and rivets. On the north side of the bridge was a boom, composed of large pieces of timber, secured by riveted bolts, and beside this was a double iron chain with links an inch and a half square. The bridge, boom, and chain were four hundred yards in length. This immense work, the labor of months, on which no expense had been spared, was intended, while it afforded a communication between the two forts, to protect the upper part of the lake, presenting, under cover of their guns, a barrier which it was presumed no hostile ship would be able to break through.

RUINS OF FORT TICONDEROGA.
VOL. I.

Having noted the state of affairs and the wants of the garrison, Schuyler hastened to Fort George, whence he sent on provisions for upwards of sixty days; and from the banks of the Hudson, additional carpenters and working cattle. In the meantime, Burgoyne, with his amphibious and semi-barbarous armament, was advancing up the lake. By the 24th, scouts began to bring in word of the approaching foe. Bark canoes had been seen filled with white men and savages. Then three vessels under sail, and one at anchor above Split Rock, and behind it the radeau, Thunderer. Anon came word of encampments sufficient for a large body of troops on both sides of Gilliland's Creek, with bateaux plying about its waters and painted warriors gliding about in canoes. St. Clair wrote word of all this to Schuyler, and that it was supposed the enemy were waiting the arrival of more force. Schuyler urged Washington for reinforcements as soon as possible, and hastened to Albany to bring up the militia.

While there he received word from St. Clair that the enemy's fleet and army were arrived at Crown Point, and had sent off detachments, one up Otter Creek to cut off the communication by Skenesborough, and another on the west side of the lake to cut off Fort George. Claims for assistance came hurrying on from other quarters. A large force (St. Leger's) was said to be arrived at Oswego, and Sir John Johnson with his myrmidons on his way to attack Fort Schuyler, the garrison of which was weak and poorly supplied with cannon.

Schuyler bestirs himself with his usual zeal amid the thickening alarms. He writes urgent letters to the committee of safety of New York, to General Putnam at Peekskill, to the Governor of Connecticut, to the President of Massachusetts, to the committee of Berkshire, and lastly to Washington, stating the impending dangers and imploring reinforcements. He exhorts General Herkimer to keep the militia of Tryon County in readiness to protect the western frontier and to check the inroad of Sir John Johnson, and he assures St. Clair that he will move to his aid with the militia of New York as soon as he can collect them.

Dangers accumulate at Ticonderoga according to advices from St. Clair (28th). Seven of the enemy's vessels are lying at Crown Point; the rest of their fleet is probably but a little lower down. Morning guns are heard distinctly at various places. Some troops have debarked and encamped at Chimney Point. There is no prospect, he says, of being able to defend Ticonderoga unless militia come in, and he has thought of calling in those from Berkshire. "Should the enemy invest and blockade us," writes he, "we are infallibly ruined; we shall be obliged to abandon this side (of the lake), and then they will soon force the other from us, nor do I see that a retreat will in any shape be practicable."

The enemy came advancing up the lake on the 30th, their main body under Burgoyne on the west side, the German reserve under Baron Riedesel on the east; communication being maintained by frigates and gunboats, which, in a manner, kept pace between them. On the 1st of July, Burgoyne encamped four miles north of Ticonderoga, and began to intrench and to throw a boom across the lake. His advanced guard under General Fraser took post at Three Mile Point, and the ships anchored just out of gunshot of the fort.

General St. Clair was a gallant Scotchman who had seen service in the old French war as well as in this, and beheld the force arrayed against him without dismay. It is true his garrison was not numerous, not exceeding three thousand five hundred men, of whom nine hundred were militia. They were badly equipped also, and few had bayonets; yet they were in good heart. Schuyler at this time was at Albany, sending up reinforcements of Continental troops and militia, and awaiting the arrival of further reinforcements, for which sloops had been sent down to Peekskill. He was endeavoring also to provide for the security of the department in other quarters. The savages had been scalping in the neighborhood of Fort Schuyler; a set of renegade Indians were harassing the settlements on the Susquehanna; and the threatenings of Brant, the famous Indian chief, and the prospect of a British inroad by the way of Oswego, had spread terror through Tryon County, the inhabitants of which called upon him for support.

Such was the state of affairs in the north, of which Washington from time to time had been informed. An attack on Ticonderoga appeared to be impending; but as the garrison was in good heart, the commander resolute, and troops were on the way to reinforce him a spirited and perhaps successful resistance was anticipated by Washington. His surprise may therefore be imagined on receiving a letter from Schuyler, dated July 7th, conveying the astounding intelligence that Ticonderoga was evacuated!

Schuyler had just received the news at Stillwater on the Hudson when on his way with reinforcements for the fortress. The first account was so vague that Washington hoped it might prove incorrect. It was confirmed by another letter from Schuyler, dated on the 9th at Fort Edward. A part of the garrison had been pursued by a detachment of the enemy as far as Fort Anne in that neighborhood, where the latter had been repulsed; as to St. Clair himself and the main part of his forces, they had thrown themselves into the forest, and nothing was known what had become of them! "I am here," writes Schuyler, "at the head of a handful of men, not above fifteen hundred, with little ammunition, not above five rounds to a man, having neither balls nor lead to make any. The country is in the deepest consternation; no carriages to remove the stores from Fort George, which I expect every moment to hear is attacked; and what adds to my distress is that a report prevails that I had given orders for the evacuation of Ticonderoga."

Washington's first attention was to supply the wants of General Schuyler. An express was sent to Springfield for musket cartridges, gunpowder, lead, and cartridge papers. Ten pieces of artillery with harness and proper officers were to be forwarded from Peekskill, as well as intrenching tools. Of tents he had none to furnish, neither could heavy cannon be spared from the defence of the Highlands. Six hundred recruits, on their march from Massachusetts to Peekskill, were ordered to repair to his aid—this was all the force that Washington could venture at this moment to send; but this addition to his troops, supposing those under St. Clair should have come in, and any number of militia have turned out, would probably form an army equal, if not superior, to that said to be under Burgoyne. Beside, it was Washington's idea that the latter would suspend his operations until General Howe should make a movement in concert. Supposing that movement would be an immediate attempt against the Highlands, he ordered Sullivan with his division to Peekskill to reinforce General Putnam. At the same time he advanced with his main army to Pompton, and thence to the Clove, a rugged defile through the Highlands on the west side of the Hudson. We will leave Washington at his encampment in the Clove, anxiously watching the movements of the fleet and the lower army, while we turn to the north to explain the mysterious retreat of General St. Clair.

In the accounts given of the approach of Burgoyne to Ticonderoga, it was stated that he had encamped four miles north of the fortress and intrenched himself. On the 2d of July, Indian scouts made their appearance in the vicinity of a blockhouse and some outworks about the strait or channel leading to Lake George. As General St. Clair did not think the garrison sufficient to defend all the outposts, these works with some adjacent saw-mills were set on fire and abandoned. The extreme left of Ticonderoga was weak, and might easily be turned; a post had therefore been established in the preceding year, nearly half a mile in advance of the old French lines, on an eminence to the north of them. General St. Clair, through singular remissness, had neglected to secure it. Burgoyne soon discovered this neglect, and hastened to detach General Phillips and Fraser with a body of infantry and light artillery to take possession of this post. They did so without opposition. Heavy guns were mounted upon it; Fraser's whole corps was stationed there; the post commanded the communication by land and water with Lake George, so as to cut off all supplies from that quarter. In fact, such were the advantages expected from this post, thus neglected by St. Clair, that the British gave it the significant name of Mount Hope.

The enemy now proceeded gradually to invest Ticonderoga. A line of troops was drawn from the western part of Mount Hope round to Three Mile Point, where General Fraser was posted with the advance guard, while General Riedesel encamped with the German reserve in a parallel line on the opposite side of Lake Champlain, at the foot of Mount Independence. For two days the enemy occupied themselves in making their advances and securing these positions, regardless of a cannonade kept up by the American batteries.

With all the pains and expense lavished by the Americans to render these works impregnable, they had strangely neglected the master key by which they were all commanded. This was Sugar Hill, a rugged height, the termination of a mountain ridge which separates Lake Champlain from Lake George. It stood to the south of Ticonderoga, beyond the narrow channel which connected the two lakes, and rose precipitously from the waters of Champlain to the height of six hundred feet. It had been pronounced by the Americans too distant to be dangerous. Colonel Trumbull, some time an aide-de-camp to Washington, had proved the contrary in the preceding year by throwing a shot from a six-pounder in the fort nearly to the summit. It was then pronounced inaccessible to an enemy. This Trumbull had likewise proved to be an error, by clambering with Arnold and Wayne to the top, whence they perceived that a practicable road for artillery might easily and readily be made. Trumbull had insisted that this was the true point for the fort, commanding the neighboring heights, the narrow parts of both lakes, and the communication between. His suggestions were disregarded; their wisdom was now to be proved.

The British general, Phillips, on taking his position, had regarded the hill with a practised eye. He caused it to be reconnoitred by a skilful engineer. The report was that it overlooked and had the entire command of Fort Ticonderoga and Fort Independence—being about fourteen hundred yards from the former, and fifteen hundred from the latter; that the ground could be levelled for cannon, and a road cut up the defiles of the mountain in four and twenty hours. Measures were instantly taken to plant a battery on that height. While the American garrisons were entirely engaged in a different direction, cannonading Mount Hope and the British lines without material effect, and without provoking a reply, the British troops were busy throughout the day and night cutting a road through rocks and trees and up rugged defiles. Guns, ammunition and stores, all were carried up the hill in the night; the cannon were hauled up from tree to tree, and before morning the ground was levelled for the battery on which they were to be mounted. To this work, thus achieved by a *coup de main,* they gave the name of Fort Defiance.

On the 5th of July, to their astonishment and consternation, the garrison beheld a legion of red-coats on the summit of this hill, constructing works which must soon lay the fortress at their mercy. In this appalling emergency, General St. Clair called a council of war. What was to be done? The batteries from this new fort would probably be open the next day: by that time Ticonderoga might be completely invested, and the whole garrison exposed to capture. They had not force sufficient for one half the works, and General Schuyler, supposed to be at Albany, could afford them no relief. The danger was imminent; delay might prove fatal. It was unanimously determined to evacuate both Ticonderoga and Mount Independence that very night, and to retreat to Skenesborough (now Whitehall), at the upper part of the lake, about thirty miles distant, where there was a stockaded fort. The main body of the army, led by General St. Clair, were to cross to Mount Independence and push for Skenesborough by land, taking a circuitous route through the woods on the east side of the lake, by the way of Castleton.

The cannon, stores and provisions, together with the wounded and the women, were to be embarked on board of two hundred bateaux and conducted to the upper extremity of the lake by Colonel Long with six hundred men, two hundred of whom, in five armed galleys, were to form a rear-guard.

It was now three o'clock in the afternoon; yet all the preparations were to be made for the coming night, and that with as little bustle and movement as possible, for they were overlooked by Fort Defiance, and their intentions might be suspected. Everything, therefore, was done quietly, but alertly; in the meantime, to amuse the enemy a cannonade was kept up every half hour toward the new battery on the hill. As soon as the evening closed, and their movements could not be discovered, they began in all haste to load the boats. Such of the cannon as could not be taken were ordered to be spiked. Everything was conducted with such silence and address that, although it was a moonlight night, the flotilla departed undiscovered, and was soon under the shadows of mountains and overhanging forests.

The retreat by land was not conducted with equal discretion and mystery. General St. Clair had crossed over the bridge to the Vermont side of the lake by three o'clock in the morning, and set forward with his advance through the woods toward Hubbardton; but, before the rear-guard under Colonel Francis got in motion, the house at Fort Independence, which had been occupied by the French general, De Fermois, was set on fire—by his orders, it is said, though we are loth to charge him with such indiscretion, such gross and wanton violation of the plan of retreat. The consequences were disastrous. The British sentries at Mount Hope were astonished by a conflagration suddenly lighting up Mount Independence and revealing the American troops in full retreat; for the rear-guard, disconcerted by this sudden exposure, pressed forward for the woods in the utmost haste and confusion.

The drums beat to arms in the British camp. Alarm guns were fired from Mount Hope; General Fraser dashed into Ticonderoga with his pickets, giving orders for his brigade to arm in all haste and follow. By daybreak he had hoisted the British flag over the deserted fortress; before sunrise he had passed the bridge and was in full pursuit of the American rear-guard.

Burgoyne's measures were prompt. General Riedesel was ordered to follow and support Fraser with a part of the German troops; garrisons were thrown into Ticonderoga and Mount Independence; the main part of the army was embarked on board of the frigates and gunboats; the floating bridge with its boom and chain, which had cost months to construct, was broken through by nine o'clock; when Burgoyne set out with his squadron in pursuit of the flotilla.

We left the latter making its retreat on the preceding evening towards Skenesborough. The lake above Ticonderoga becomes so narrow that, in those times, it was frequently called South River. The bateaux, deeply laden, made their way slowly in a lengthened line. The rear-guard of armed galleys followed at wary distance. No immediate pursuit, however, was apprehended. The floating bridge was considered an effectual impediment to the enemy's fleet.

About three o'clock in the afternoon of the succeeding day, the heavily laden bateaux arrived at Skenesborough. The disembarkation had scarcely commenced when the thundering of artillery was heard from below. Could the enemy be at hand? It was even so. The British gunboats, having pushed on in advance of the frigates, had overtaken and were firing upon the galleys. The latter defended themselves for a while, but at length two struck and three were blown up. The fugitives from them brought word that the British ships not being able to come up, troops and Indians were landing from them and scrambling up the hills, intending to get in the rear of the fort and cut off all retreat.

All now was consternation and confusion. The bateaux, the storehouses, the fort, the mill were all set on fire, and a general flight took place toward Fort Anne, about twelve miles distant. Some made their way in boats up Wood Creek, a winding stream. The main body under Colonel Long retreated by a narrow defile cut through the woods, harassed all night by alarms that the Indians were close in pursuit. Both parties reached Fort Anne by daybreak. It was a small picketed fort, near the junction of Wood Creek and East Creek, about sixteen miles from Fort Edward. General Schuyler arrived at the latter place on the following day. The number of troops with him was inconsiderable, but hearing of Colonel Long's situation, he immediately sent him a small reinforcement, with provisions and ammunition, and urged him to maintain his post resolutely. On the same day Colonel Long's scouts brought in word that there were British red-coats approaching. They were in fact a regiment under Lieutenant-colonel Hill, detached from Skenesborough by Burgoyne in pursuit of the fugitives. Long sallied forth to meet them, posting himself at a rocky defile. As the enemy advanced he opened a heavy fire upon them in front; the British took post upon a high hill to their right, where they were warmly besieged for nearly two hours, and would certainly have been forced had not some of their Indian allies arrived. This changed the fortune of the day. The Americans had nearly expended their ammunition, and had not enough left to cope with this new enemy. They retreated, therefore, to Fort Anne, carrying with them a number of prisoners. Supposing the troops under Colonel Hill an advance guard of Burgoyne's army, they set fire to the fort and pushed on to Fort Edward.

St. Clair's retreat through the woods from Mount Independence continued the first day until night, when he arrived at Castleton, thirty miles from Ticonderoga. His rear-guard halted about six miles short, at Hubbardton, to await the arrival of stragglers. It was composed of three regiments, under Colonels Seth Warner, Francis and Hale; in all about thirteen hundred men. Early the next morning, a sultry morning of July, while they were taking their breakfast, they were startled by the report of fire-arms. Their sentries had discharged their muskets, and came running in with word that the enemy were at hand.

It was General Fraser, with his advance of eight hundred and fifty men, who had pressed forward in the latter part of the night, and now attacked the Americans with great spirit, notwithstanding their superiority in numbers; in fact he expected to be promptly reinforced by Riedesel and his Germans. The Americans met the British with great spirit; but at the very commencement of the action, Colonel Hale, with a detachment placed under his command to protect the rear, gave way, leaving Warner and Francis with but seven hundred men to bear the brunt of the battle. These posted themselves behind logs and trees in 'backwood' style, whence they kept up a destructive fire, and were evidently gaining the advantage, when General Riedesel came pressing into the action with his German troops; drums beating and colors flying. There was now an impetuous charge with the bayonet. Colonel Francis was among the first who fell, gallantly fighting at the head of his men. The Americans, thinking the whole German force upon them, gave way and fled, leaving the ground covered with their dead and wounded. Many others who had been wounded perished in the woods, where they had taken refuge. Their whole loss in killed, wounded and taken, was upwards of three hundred; that of the enemy one hundred and eighty-three.

The noise of the firing when the action commenced had reached General St. Clair at Castleton. He immediately sent orders to two militia regiments which were in his rear, and within two miles of the battle-ground to hasten to the assistance of his rear-guard. They refused to obey and hurried forward to Castleton.

At this juncture St. Clair received information of Burgoyne's arrival at Skenesborough, and the destruction of the American works there: fearing to be intercepted at Fort Anne, he immediately changed his route, struck into the woods on his left, and directed his march to Rutland, leaving word for Warner to follow him. The latter overtook him two days afterwards, with his shattered force reduced to ninety men. As to Colonel Hale, who had pressed towards Castleton at the beginning of the action, he and his men were overtaken the same day by the enemy, and the whole party captured without making any fight. It has been alleged in his excuse, with apparent justice, that he and a large portion of his men were in feeble health and unfit for action; for his own part he died while yet a prisoner, and never had the opportunity which he sought to vindicate himself before a court-martial.

On the 12th St. Clair reached Fort Edward, his troops haggard and exhausted by their long retreat through the woods. Such is the story of the catastrophe at Fort Ticonderoga which caused so much surprise and concern to Washington, and of the seven days' mysterious disappearance of St. Clair which kept every one in the most painful suspense. The loss of artillery, ammunition, provisions and stores, in consequence of the evacuation of these northern posts was prodigious, but the worst effect was the consternation spread throughout the country. A panic prevailed at Albany, the people running about as if distracted, sending off their goods and furniture. The great barriers of the North it was said were broken through, and there was nothing to check the triumphant career of the enemy.

CHAPTER XLIII.

EXPLOITS AND MOVEMENTS.—HOWE IN THE CHESAPEAKE.

A spirited exploit to the eastward was performed during the prevalence of adverse news from the North. General Prescott had command of the British forces in Rhode Island. His harsh treatment of Colonel Ethan Allen, and his haughty and arrogant conduct on various occasions had rendered him peculiarly odious to the Americans. Lieutenant-colonel Barton, who was stationed with a force of Rhode Island militia on the mainland, received word that Prescott was quartered at a country house near the western shore of the island, about four miles from Newport, totally unconscious of danger though in a very exposed situation. He determined, if possible, to surprise and capture him. Forty resolute men joined him in the enterprise. Embarking at night in two boats at Warwick Neck, they pulled quietly across the bay with muffled oars, undiscovered by the ships of war and guard-boats; landed in silence; eluded the vigilance of the guard stationed near the house; captured the sentry at the door, and surprised the general in his bed. His aide-de-camp leaped from the window, but was likewise taken. Colonel Barton returned with equal silence and address, and arrived safe at Warwick with his prisoners. A sword was voted to him by Congress and he received a colonel's commission in the regular army.

Washington hailed the capture of Prescott as a peculiarly fortunate circumstance, furnishing him with an equivalent for General Lee. He accordingly wrote to Sir William Howe, proposing the exchange. No immediate reply was received to this letter, Sir William Howe being at sea; in the meantime Prescott remained in durance.

Washington continued his anxious exertions to counteract the operations of the enemy; forwarding artillery and ammunition to Schuyler, with all the camp furniture that could be spared from his own encampment and from Peekskill. A part of Nixon's brigade was all the reinforcement he could afford in his present situation. Schuyler had earnestly desired the assistance of an active officer well acquainted with the country. Washington sent him Arnold. The question of rank about which Arnold was so tenacious was yet unsettled, and though, had his promotion been regular, he would have been superior in command to General St. Clair, he assured Washington that on the present occasion his claim should create no dispute.

Schuyler in the meantime, aided by Kosciuszko the Pole, who was engineer in his department, had selected two positions on Moses Creek, four miles below Fort Edward, where the troops which had retreated from Ticonderoga, and part of the militia were throwing up works. To impede the advance of the enemy he had caused trees to be felled into Wood Creek, so as to render it unnavigable, and the roads between Fort Edward and Fort Anne to be broken up; the cattle in that direction to be brought away, and the forage destroyed. He had drawn off the garrison from Fort George, and left the buildings in flames.

Washington cheered on his faithful coadjutor. His letters to Schuyler were full of that confident hope, founded on sagacious forecast, with which he was prone to animate his generals in times of doubt and difficulty. "Though our affairs for some days past have worn a dark and gloomy aspect, I yet look forward to a fortunate and happy change. I trust General Burgoyne's army will meet sooner or later an effectual check, and, as I suggested before, that the success he has had will precipitate his ruin." [He pointed out that Burgoyne in acting in detachment was pursuing the plan most favorable to the American cause. If some of his detachments could be cut off, it would have, he said, a most inspiriting effect. He also addressed circulars to the brigadier-generals of militia in the western portions of the Eastern States, urging reinforcements for Schuyler. The evacuation of Ticonderoga, he showed them, had opened the door for the invasion of their district, and that Burgoyne, if not vigorously opposed, would be enabled to form a junction with General Howe, and thereby sever the communication between the Eastern and Northern States.]

Washington now ordered that all the vessels and river craft, not required at Albany, should be sent down to New Windsor and Fishkill, and kept in readiness; for he knew not how soon the movements of General Howe might render it suddenly necessary to transport part of his forces up the Hudson.

Further letters from Schuyler urged the increasing exigencies of his situation. It was harvest time. The militia, impatient at being detained from their rural labors, were leaving him in great numbers. In a council of general officers it had been thought advisable to give leave of absence to half, lest the whole should depart. He feared those who remained would do so but a few days. The enemy were steadily employed cutting a road toward him from Skenesborough. In this position of affairs, he urged to be reinforced as speedily as possible. Washington, in reply, informed him that he had ordered a further reinforcement of General Glover's brigade, which was all he could possibly furnish in his own exigencies. He trusted affairs with Schuyler would soon wear a more smiling aspect, that the Eastern States, who were so deeply concerned in the matter, would exert themselves by effectual succors to enable him to check the progress of the enemy and repel a danger by which they were immediately threatened. "I have directed General Lincoln to repair to you as speedily as the state of his health, which is not very perfect, will permit; this gentleman has always supported the character of a judicious, brave, active officer, and he is exceedingly popular in the State of Massachusetts, to which he belongs; he will have a degree of influence over the militia which cannot fail of being highly advantageous."

Washington highly approved of a measure suggested by Schuyler, of stationing a body of troops somewhere about the Hampshire Grants (Vermont,) so as to be in the rear or on the flank of Burgoyne, should he advance. It would make the latter, he said, very circumspect in his advances, if it did not entirely prevent them. It would keep him in continual anxiety for his rear, and oblige him to leave the posts behind him much stronger than he would otherwise do. He advised that General Lincoln should have the command of the corps thus posted, "as no person could be more proper for it."

But now the attention of the commander-in-chief is called to the sea-board. On the 23d of July the fleet, so long the object of watchful solicitude, actually put to sea. Its destination was still a matter of conjecture. Just after it had sailed a young man presented himself at one of General Putnam's outposts. He had been a prisoner in New York, he said, but had received his liberty and a large reward on undertaking to be the bearer of a letter from General Howe to Burgoyne. This letter his feelings of patriotism prompted him to deliver up to General Putnam. The letter was immediately transmitted by the general to Washington. It was in the handwriting of Howe and bore his signature. In it he informed Burgoyne that, instead of any designs up the Hudson, he was bound to the east against Boston. Washington at once pronounced the letter a feint. "No stronger proof could be given," said he, "that Howe is not going to the eastward. The letter was evidently intended to fall into our hands.... I am persuaded more than ever that Philadelphia is the place of destination."

He now set out with his army for the Delaware, ordering Sullivan and Stirling with their divisions to cross the Hudson from Peekskill and proceed towards Philadelphia. On the 30th he writes from Coryell's Ferry, about thirty miles from Philadelphia, to General Gates, who was in that city: "As we are yet uncertain as to the real destination of the enemy, though the Delaware seems the most probable, I have thought it prudent to halt the army at this place, Howell's Ferry, and Trenton, at least till the fleet actually enters the bay and puts the matter beyond a doubt. From hence we can be on the proper ground to oppose them before they can possibly make their arrangements and dispositions for an attack.... As I shall pay no regard to any flying reports of the appearance of the fleet, I shall expect an account of it from you the moment you have ascertained it to your satisfaction."

On the 31st he was informed that the enemy's fleet of two hundred and twenty-eight sail had arrived the day previous at the Capes of Delaware. He instantly wrote to Putnam to hurry on two brigades which had crossed the river, and to let Schuyler and the commanders in the Eastern States know that they had nothing to fear from Howe, and might bend all their forces, continental and militia, against Burgoyne. In the meantime he moved his camp to Germantown, about six miles from Philadelphia, to be at hand for the defence of that city. The very next day came word by express that the fleet had again sailed out of the Capes and apparently shaped its course eastward. "This surprising event gives me the greatest anxiety," writes he to Putnam (Aug. 1). "The probability of his (Howe) going to the eastward is exceedingly small, and the ill effects that might attend such a step inconsiderable in comparison with those that would inevitably attend a successful stroke on the Highlands."

Under this impression Washington sent orders to Sullivan to hasten back with his division and the two brigades which had recently left Peekskill and to recross the Hudson to that post as speedily as possible, intending to forward the rest of the army with all the expedition in his power. He wrote also to General George Clinton, to reinforce Putnam with as many of the New York militia as could be collected. Clinton, be it observed, had just been installed governor of the State of New York; the first person elevated to that office under the Constitution. He still continued in actual command of the militia of the State. Washington, moreover, requested Putnam to send an express to Governor Trumbull, urging assistance from the militia of his State without a moment's loss of time.

We have cited in a preceding page a letter from Washington to Gates at Philadelphia, requiring his vigilant attention to the movements of the enemy's fleet; that ambitious officer, however, was engrossed at the time by matters more important to his individual interests. The command of the Northern department seemed again within his reach. The evacuation of Ticonderoga had been imputed by many either to cowardice or treachery on the part of General St. Clair, and the enemies of Schuyler had for some time past been endeavoring to involve him in the disgrace of the transaction. In the eagerness to excite popular feeling against him, old slanders were revived, and the failure of the invasion of Canada, and all the subsequent disasters in that quarter, were again laid to his charge as commanding-general of the Northern department.

These charges, which for some time existed merely in popular clamor, had recently been taken up in Congress, and a strong demonstration had been made against him by some of the New England delegates. "Your enemies in this quarter," writes his friend, the Hon. William Duer (July 29th), "are leaving no means unessayed to blast your character.... Be not surprised if you should be desired to attend Congress to give an account of the loss of Ticonderoga. With respect to the result of the inquiry I am under no apprehensions. Like gold tried in the fire, I trust that you, my dear friend, will be found more pure and bright than ever."

[Schuyler, in reply, expressed his eagerness to have his conduct subjected to official investigation, but hoped the scrutiny would be postponed until after the engagement with the enemy which was now imminent. Schuyler's enemies were determined, however, that he should be deprived of this chance of distinguishing himself, and pushed the business so urgently in Congress that a resolution was passed summoning both Schuyler and St. Clair to head-quarters to account for the misfortunes in the north. Schuyler's unpopularity with the Eastern troops was used as a powerful argument for this step, it being asserted that the Eastern militia were refusing to serve under him. The nomination of his successor was left to Washington, who excused himself from the duty. The appointment, therefore, was made by Congress, the Eastern influence prevailed, and Gates received the command.]

About this time took effect a measure of Congress, making a complete change in the commissariat. This important and complicated department had hitherto been under the management of one commissary-general, Colonel Joseph Trumbull of Connecticut. By the new arrangement there were to be two commissaries-general, one of purchases, the other of issues; each to be appointed by Congress. They were to have several deputy commissaries under them, but accountable to Congress, and to be appointed and removed by that body. These and many subordinate arrangements had been adopted in opposition to the opinion of Washington, and, most unfortunately, were brought into operation in the midst of this perplexed and critical campaign. Their first effect was to cause the resignation of Colonel Trumbull, who had been nominated commissary of purchases; and the entrance into office of a number of inexperienced men. The ultimate effect was to paralyze the organization of this vital department; to cause delay and confusion in furnishing and forwarding supplies, and to retard and embarrass the operations of the different armies throughout the year. Washington had many dangers and difficulties to harass and perplex him throughout this complicated campaign, and not among the least may be classed the "stumblings of Congress."

For several days Washington remained at Germantown in painful uncertainty about the British fleet; whether gone to the south or to the east. The intense heat of the weather made him unwilling again to move his army, already excessively harassed by marchings and countermarchings. Concluding, at length, that the fleet had actually gone to the east, he was once more on the way to recross the Delaware, when an express overtook him on the 10th of August, with tidings that three days before it had been seen off Sinepuxent Inlet, about sixteen leagues south of the Capes of Delaware.

Again he came to a halt, and waited for further intelligence. Danger suggested itself from a different quarter. Might it not be Howe's plan, by thus appearing with his ships at different places, to lure the army after him, and thereby leave the country open for Sir Henry Clinton with the troops at New York to form a junction with Burgoyne? With this idea Washington wrote forthwith to the veteran Putnam to be on the alert; collect all the force he could to strengthen his post at Peekskill, and send down spies to ascertain whether Sir Henry Clinton was actually at New York, and what troops he had there.

The old general, whose boast it was that he never slept but with one eye, was already on the alert. A circumstance had given him proof positive that Sir Henry was in New York, and had roused his military ire. A spy, sent by that commander, had been detected furtively collecting information of the force and condition of the post at Peekskill, and had undergone a military trial. A vessel of war came up the Hudson in all haste, and landed a flag of truce at Verplanck's Point, by which a message was transmitted to Putnam from Sir Henry Clinton, claiming Edmund Palmer as a lieutenant in the British service. The reply of the old general was brief but emphatic:

"HEAD-QUARTERS, 7th Aug., 1777.

"Edmund Palmer, an officer in the enemy's service, was taken as a spy lurking within our lines; he has been tried as a spy, condemned as a spy, and shall be executed as a spy; and the flag is ordered to depart immediately.

"ISRAEL PUTNAM."

"P. S.—He has, accordingly, been executed."

Governor Clinton, the other guardian of the Highlands, and actually at his post at Fort Montgomery, was equally on the alert. He had faithfully followed Washington's directions in ordering out militia from different counties to reinforce his own garrison and the army under Schuyler.

One measure more was taken by Washington, during this interval, in aid of the Northern department. The Indians who accompanied Burgoyne were objects of great dread to the American troops, especially the militia. As a counterpoise to them, he now sent up Colonel Morgan with five hundred riflemen, to fight them in their own way. "They are all chosen men," said he, "selected from the army at large, and well acquainted with the use of rifles and with that mode of fighting. I expect the most eminent services from them, and I shall be mistaken if their presence does not go far towards producing a general desertion among the savages."

During his encampment in the neighborhood of Philadelphia, Washington was repeatedly at that city, making himself acquainted with the military capabilities of the place and its surrounding country, and directing the construction of fortifications on the river. In one of these visits he became acquainted with the young Marquis de Lafayette, who had recently arrived from France, in company with a number of French, Polish, and German officers, among whom was the Baron de Kalb. The marquis was not quite twenty years of age, yet had already been married nearly three years to a lady of rank and fortune. Full of the romance of liberty, he had torn himself from his youthful bride, turned his back upon the gayeties and splendors of a court, and in defiance of impediments and difficulties multiplied in his path, had made his way to America to join its hazardous fortunes.

It was at a public dinner, where a number of members of Congress were present, that Lafayette first saw Washington. He immediately knew him, he said, from the officers who surrounded him, by his commanding air and person. When the party was breaking up, Washington took him aside, complimented him in a gracious manner on his disinterested zeal and the generosity of his conduct, and invited him to make head-quarters his home.

Many days had now elapsed without further tidings of the fleet, when the tormenting uncertainties concerning it were brought to an end by intelligence that it had actually entered the Chesapeake and anchored at Swan Point, at least two hundred miles within the capes. "By General Howe's coming so far up the Chesapeake," writes Washington, "he must mean to reach Philadelphia by that route, though to be sure it is a strange one." The mystery of these various appearances and vanishings which had caused so much wonder and perplexity is easily explained. Shortly before putting to sea with the ships of war, Howe had sent a number of transports and a ship cut down as a floating battery up the Hudson, which had induced Washington to despatch troops to the Highlands. After putting to sea, the fleet was a week in reaching the Capes of Delaware. When there, the commanders were deterred from entering the river by reports of measures taken to obstruct its navigation. It was then determined to make for Chesapeake Bay, and approach in that way as near as possible to Philadelphia. Contrary winds, however, kept them for a long time from getting into the bay.

Lafayette in his memoirs describes a review of Washington's army which he witnessed about this time. "Eleven thousand men, but tolerably armed and still worse clad, presented," he said, "a singular spectacle; in this parti-colored and often naked state, the best dresses were hunting shirts of brown linen. Their tactics were equally irregular. They were arranged without regard to size, excepting that the smallest men were the front rank: with all this there were good-looking soldiers conducted by zealous officers." The several divisions of the army had been summoned to the immediate neighborhood of Philadelphia, and the militia of Pennsylvania, Delaware, and the northern parts of Virginia were called out. Many of the militia, with Colonel Proctor's corps of artillery, had been ordered to rendezvous at Chester on the Delaware, about twelve miles below Philadelphia; and by Washington's orders General Wayne left his brigade under the next in command and repaired to Chester to arrange the troops assembling there.

As there had been much disaffection to the cause evinced in Philadelphia, Washington, in order to encourage its friends and dishearten its enemies, marched with the whole army through the city, down Front and up Chestnut Street. Great pains were taken to make the display as imposing as possible. All were charged to keep to their ranks, carry their arms well, and step in time to the music of the drums and fifes, collected in the centre of each brigade. Washington rode at the head of the troops attended by his numerous staff, with the Marquis Lafayette by his side. The long column of the army, broken into divisions and brigades, the pioneers with their axes, the squadrons of horse, the extended trains of artillery, the tramp of steed, the bray of trumpet, and the spirit-stirring sound of drum and fife, all had an imposing effect on a peaceful city unused to the sight of marshalled armies. Having marched through Philadelphia, the army continued on to Wilmington at the confluence of Christiana Creek and the Brandywine, where Washington set up his head-quarters, his troops being encamped on the neighboring heights.

CHAPTER XLIV.

ADVANCE OF BURGOYNE.—BATTLE OF ORISKANY.—BATTLE OF BENNINGTON.

In a preceding chapter we left Burgoyne, early in July, at Skenesborough, of which he had just gained possession. He remained there nearly three weeks, awaiting the arrival of the residue of his troops, with tents, baggage and provisions, and preparing for his grand move towards the Hudson River. The progress of the army towards the Hudson was slow and difficult, in consequence of the impediments which Schuyler had multiplied in his way during his long halt at Skenesborough. Bridges broken down had to be rebuilt; great trees to be removed which had been felled across the roads and into Wood Creek, which stream was completely choked. It was not until the latter part of July that Burgoyne reached Fort Anne. At his approach, General Schuyler retired from Fort Edward and took post at Fort Miller, a few miles lower down the Hudson.

The Indian allies who had hitherto accompanied the British army, had been more troublesome than useful. They were of the tribes of Lower Canada, corrupted and debased by intercourse with white men. It had been found difficult to draw them from the plunder of Ticonderoga, or to restrain their murderous propensities. A party had recently arrived of a different stamp—braves of the Ottawa and other tribes from the upper country, painted and decorated with savage magnificence, and bearing trophies of former triumphs. They were under the conduct of two French leaders; one named Langlade, the other named St. Luc, is described by Burgoyne as a Canadian gentleman of honor and abilities, and one of the best partisans of the French in the war of 1756. Burgoyne trusted to his newly-arrived Indians to give a check to the operations of Schuyler, knowing the terror they inspired throughout the country. He was naturally a humane man, and disliked Indian allies, but these had hitherto served in company with civilized troops, and he trusted to the influence possessed over them by St. Luc and Langlade to keep them within the usages of war. A circumstance occurred, however, which showed how little the "wild honor" of these warriors of the tomahawk is to be depended upon.

In General Fraser's division was a young officer, Lieutenant David Jones, an American loyalist. His family had their home in the vicinity of Fort Edward before the Revolution. A mutual attachment had taken place between the youth and a beautiful girl named Jane McCrea, who resided with her brother on the banks of the Hudson, a few miles below Fort Edward. The lovers were engaged to be married, when the breaking out of the war severed families and disturbed all the relations of life. The Joneses were royalists; the brother of Miss McCrea was a stanch whig. The former removed to Canada, where he joined the royal standard, and received a lieutenant's commission. The attachment between the lovers continued, and it is probable that a correspondence was kept up between them. Lieutenant Jones was now in Fraser's camp; in his old neighborhood. Miss McCrea was on a visit to a widow lady, Mrs. O'Niel, residing at Fort Edward. The approach of Burgoyne's army had spread an alarm through the country; the inhabitants were flying from their homes. The brother of Miss McCrea determined to remove to Albany, and sent for his sister to return home and make ready to accompany him. She prepared, reluctantly, to obey, and was to embark in a large bateaux which was to convey several families down the river. The very morning when the embarkation was to take place the neighborhood was a scene of terror. A marauding party of Indians, sent out by Burgoyne to annoy General Schuyler, were harassing the country. Several of them burst into the house of Mrs. O'Niel, sacked and plundered it, and carried off her and Miss McCrea prisoners. In her fright the latter promised the savages a large reward if they would spare her life and take her in safety to the British camp. It was a fatal promise. Halting at a spring, a quarrel arose among the savages, inflamed most probably with drink, as to whose prize she was, and who was entitled to the reward. The dispute became furious, and one, in a paroxysm of rage, killed her on the spot. He completed the savage act by bearing off her scalp as a trophy.

General Burgoyne was struck with horror when he heard of this bloody deed. He summoned a council of the Indian chiefs, in which he insisted that the murderer of Miss McCrea should be given up to receive the reward of his crime. The demand produced a violent agitation. The culprit was a great warrior, a chief, and the "wild honor" of his brother sachems was roused in his behalf. St. Luc took Burgoyne aside and entreated him not to push the matter to extremities, assuring him that from what was passing among the chiefs, he was sure they and their warriors would all abandon the army should the delinquent be executed. Burgoyne was thus reluctantly brought to spare the offender, but thenceforth made it a rule that no party of Indians should be permitted to go forth on a foray unless under the conduct of a British officer, or some other competent person who should be responsible for their behavior.[11]

The mischief to the British cause, however, had been effected. The murder of Miss McCrea resounded throughout the land, counteracting all the benefit anticipated from the terror of Indian hostilities. Those people of the frontiers who had hitherto remained quiet, now flew to arms to defend their families and firesides. In their exasperation they looked beyond the savages to their employers. They abhorred an army which, professing to be civilized, could league itself with such barbarians; and they execrated a government which, pretending to reclaim them as subjects, could let loose such fiends to desolate their homes. The blood of this

[11] These restrictions led to ill-humor among the Indians who soon announced their intention of returning home, unless the restraints imposed by Burgoyne were withdrawn. Burgoyne was greatly embarrassed. The Indian force was valuable and obtained at an immense expense. But to his great credit he refused their demands, and the result was that the greater part of his Indian allies deserted him.

unfortunate girl, therefore, was not shed in vain. Armies sprang up from it. Her name passed as a note of alarm along the banks of the Hudson; it was a rallying word among the Green Mountains of Vermont and brought down all their hardy yeomanry.

As Burgoyne advanced to Fort Edward, Schuyler fell still further back and took post at Saratoga, or rather Stillwater, about thirty miles from Albany. He had been joined by Major-general Lincoln, who, according to Washington's directions, had hastened to his assistance. In pursuance of Washington's plans, Lincoln proceeded to Manchester in Vermont to take command of the militia forces collecting at that point. His presence inspired new confidence in the country people, who were abandoning their homes, leaving their crops ungathered, and taking refuge with their families in the lower towns. He found about five hundred militia assembled at Manchester, under Colonel Seth Warner; others were coming on from New Hampshire and Massachusetts to protect their uncovered frontier.

Burgoyne was now at Fort Edward where new difficulties beset him. The horses which had been contracted for in Canada, for draught, burthen and saddle, arrived slowly and scantily. Artillery and munitions, too, of all kinds, had to be brought from Ticonderoga by the way of Lake George. These, with a vast number of boats for freight, or to form bridges, it was necessary to transport over the carrying places between the lakes, and by land from Fort George to Fort Edward. Unfortunately, the army had not the requisite supply of horses and oxen. So far from being able to bring forward provisions for a march, it was with difficulty enough could be furnished to feed the army from day to day.

While thus situated, Burgoyne received intelligence that the part of his army which he had detached from Canada under Colonel St. Leger, to proceed by Lake Ontario and Oswego and make a diversion on the Mohawk, had penetrated to that river, and were actually investing Fort Stanwix, the stronghold of that part of the country.

To carry out the original plan of his campaign, it now behooved him to make a rapid move down the Hudson, so as to be at hand to co-operate with St. Leger on his approach to Albany. But how was he to do this, deficient as he was in horses and vehicles for transportation? In this dilemma he was informed that at Bennington, about twenty-four miles east of the Hudson, the Americans had a great depot of horses, carriages, and supplies of all kind, intended for their Northern army, which might easily be surprised, being guarded by only a small militia force. An expedition was immediately set on foot, not only to surprise this place, but to scour the country, and bring off all horses fit for the dragoons, or for battalion service, with as many saddles and bridles as could be found.

Before relating the events of this expedition, we will turn to notice those of the detachment under St. Leger, with which it was intended to co-operate, and which was investing Fort Schuyler. This fort, built in 1756, on the site of an old French fortification, and formerly called Fort Stanwix, from a British general of that name, was situated on the right bank of the Mohawk River, at the head of its navigation, and commanded the carrying-place between it and Wood Creek, whence the boats passed to the Oneida Lake, the Oswego River, and Lake Ontario. It was thus a key to the intercourse between Upper Canada and the valley of the Mohawk. The fort was square, with four bastions, and was originally a place of strength—having bombproof magazines, a deep moat and drawbridge, a sally port and covered way. In the long interval of peace subsequent to the French war, it had fallen to decay. Recently it had been repaired by order of General Schuyler, and had received his name. It was garrisoned by seven hundred and fifty Continental troops from New York and Massachusetts, and was under the command of Colonel Gansevoort of the New York line.

It was a motley force which appeared before it; British, Hessian, Royalist, Canadian and Indian, about seventeen hundred in all. Among them were St. Leger's rangers and Sir John Johnson's royalist corps, called his greens. The Indians were led by the famous Brant. On the 3d of August, St. Leger sent in a flag with a summons to surrender. It was disregarded. He now set his troops to work to fortify his camp and clear obstructions from Wood Creek and the roads for the transportation of artillery and provisions, and sent out scouting parties of Indians in all directions, to cut off all communication of the garrison with the surrounding country.

On the 6th of August, three men made their way into the fort through a swamp which the enemy had deemed impassable. They brought the cheering intelligence that General Herkimer, the veteran commander of the militia of Tryon County, was at Oriskany, about eight miles distant, with upwards of eight hundred men. Herkimer requested Colonel Gansevoort, through his two messengers, to fire three signal-guns on receiving word of his vicinage, upon hearing which, he would endeavor to force his way to the fort, depending upon the co-operation of the garrison.

The messengers had been despatched by Herkimer on the evening of the 5th, and he had calculated that they would reach the fort at a very early hour in the morning. Through some delay, they did not reach it until between ten and eleven o'clock. Gansevoort instantly complied with the message. Three signal-guns were fired, and Colonel Willet, of the New York Continentals, with two hundred and fifty men and an iron three-pounder was detached to make a diversion by attacking that part of the enemy's camp occupied by Johnson and his royalists. The delay of the messengers in the night, however, disconcerted the plan of Herkimer. He marshalled his troops by daybreak and waited for the signal-guns. Hour after hour elapsed, but no gun was heard. His officers became impatient of delay, and urged an immediate march. Colonels Cox and Paris were particularly urgent for an advance. Paris was a prominent man in Tryon County, and member of the committee of safety, and in compliance with the wishes of that committee, accompanied Herkimer as his volunteer aide. Losing his temper in the dispute, he accused the latter of being either a tory or a coward. "No," replied the brave old man, "I feel toward you all as a father, and will not lead you into a scrape from which I cannot extricate you." His discretion, however, was overpowered by repeated taunts, and he at length, about nine o'clock, gave the word to march.

The march was rather dogged and irregular. There was ill-humor between the general and his officers. About ten o'clock they came to a place where the road was carried on a causeway of logs across a deep marshy ravine, between high level banks. The main division descended into the ravine, followed by the baggage-wagons. They had scarcely crossed it, when the enemies suddenly sprang up in front and on each side with deadly volleys of musketry and deafening yells and war-whoops. In fact, St. Leger, apprised by his scouts of their intended approach, had sent a force [of Johnson's greens, rangers, and Indians] to waylay them. The rear-guard, which had not entered the ravine, retreated. The main body, though thrown into confusion, defended themselves bravely. One of those severe conflicts ensued, common in Indian warfare, where the combatants take post with their rifles behind rock and tree, or come to deadly struggle with knife and tomahawk.

The veteran Herkimer was wounded early in the action. A musket ball shattered his leg just below the knee, killing his horse at the same time. He made his men place him on his saddle at the foot of a large beech tree, against the trunk of which he leaned, continuing to give his orders. The regulars attempted to charge with the bayonet, but the Americans formed themselves in circles back to back, and repelled them. A heavy storm of thunder and rain caused a temporary lull to the fight, during which the patriots changed their ground. Some of them stationed themselves in pairs behind trees, so that when one had fired the other could cover him until he had reloaded, for the savages were apt to rush up with knife and tomahawk the moment a man had discharged his piece.

A confusion reigns over the accounts of this fight, in which every one saw little but what occurred in his immediate vicinity. The Indians at length, having lost many of their bravest warriors, gave the retreating cry, Oonah! Oonah! and fled to the woods. The greens and rangers, hearing a firing in the direction of the fort, feared an attack upon their camp, and hastened to its defence, carrying off with them many prisoners. The Americans did not pursue them, but placing their wounded on litters made of branches of trees, returned to Oriskany. Both parties have claimed the victory, but it does not appear that either was entitled to it. The Americans had two hundred killed, and a number wounded. Several of these were officers. The loss of the enemy is thought to have been equally great as to numbers. We may add that those who had been most urgent with General Herkimer for this movement, were among the first to suffer from it. Colonel Cox was shot down at the first fire, so was a son of Colonel Paris; the colonel himself was taken prisoner, and fell beneath the tomahawk of the famous Red Jacket. As to General Herkimer, he was conveyed to his residence on the Mohawk River, and died nine days after the battle, not so much from his wound as from bad surgery, sinking gradually through loss of blood from an unskilful amputation.

The sortie of Colonel Willett had been spirited and successful. He attacked the encampments of Sir John Johnson and the Indians which were contiguous, and strong detachments of which were absent on the ambuscade. Sir John and his men were driven to the river; the Indians fled to the woods. Willett sacked their camps; loaded wagons with camp equipage, clothing, blankets, and stores of all kinds, seized the baggage and papers of Sir John and of several of his officers, and retreated safely to the fort, just as St. Leger was up with a powerful reinforcement. Five colors, which he had brought away with him as trophies, were displayed under the flag of the fort, while his men gave three cheers from the ramparts.

St. Leger now endeavored to operate on the fears of the garrison. His prisoners, it is said, were compelled to write a letter, giving dismal accounts of the affair of Oriskany, and of the impossibility of getting any succor to the garrison; of the probability that Burgoyne and his army were then before Albany, and advising surrender to prevent inevitable destruction.

St. Leger accompanied the letter with warnings that, should the garrison persist in resistance, he would not be able to restrain the fury of the savages, who threatened, if further provoked, to revenge the deaths of their warriors and chiefs by slaughtering the garrison, and laying waste the whole valley of the Mohawk. All this failing to shake the resolution of Gansevoort, St. Leger began to lose heart. The fort proved more capable of defence than he had anticipated. His artillery was too light, and the ramparts, being of sod, were not easily battered. He was obliged, reluctantly, to resort to the slow process of sapping and mining, and began to make regular approaches.

Gansevoort, seeing the siege was likely to be protracted, resolved to send to General Schuyler for succor. Colonel Willett volunteered to undertake the perilous errand. He was accompanied by Lieutenant Stockwell, an excellent woodsman, who served as a guide. They left the fort on the 10th after dark, by a sally port, passed by the British sentinels and close by the Indian camp without being discovered, and made their way through bog and morass and pathless forests and all kinds of risks and hardships until they reached the German Flats on the Mohawk. Here Willett procured a couple of horses, and by dint of hoof arrived at the camp of General Schuyler at Stillwater.

Schuyler was in Albany in the early part of August, making stirring appeals in every direction for reinforcements. Burgoyne was advancing upon him; he had received news of the disastrous affair of Oriskany, and the death of General Herkimer, and Tryon County was crying to him for assistance. One of his appeals was to the veteran John Stark. He had his farm in the Hampshire Grants, and his name was a tower of strength among the Green Mountain Boys. But Stark was soured with government and had retired from service, his name having been omitted in the list of promotions. Hearing that he was on a visit to Lincoln's camp at Manchester, Schuyler wrote to that general: "Assure General Stark that I have acquainted Congress of his situation, and that I trust and entreat he will in the present alarming crisis waive his right; the greater the sacrifice he makes to his feelings, the greater will be the honor due to him for not having suffered any consideration whatever to come in competition with the weal of his country."

Schuyler had instant call to practise the very virtue he was inculcating. He was about to mount his horse on the 10th to return to the camp at Stillwater, when a despatch from Congress was put into his hand containing the resolves which recalled him to attend a court of inquiry about the affair of Ticonderoga.

Schuyler felt deeply the indignity of being thus recalled at a time when an engagement was apparently at hand, but endeavored to console himself with the certainty that a thorough investigation of his conduct would prove how much he was entitled to the thanks of his country. He intimated the same in his reply to Congress; in the meantime he considered it his duty to remain at his post until his successor should arrive, or some officer in the department be nominated to the command. His first care was to send relief to Gansevoort and his beleaguered garrison. Eight hundred men were all that he could spare from his army in its present threatened state. A spirited and effective officer was wanted to lead them. Arnold was in camp; recently sent on as an efficient coadjutor by Washington. He stepped promptly forward, and volunteered to lead the enterprise.

After the departure of this detachment, it was unanimously determined in a council of war of Schuyler and his general officers, that the post at Stillwater was altogether untenable with their actual force; part of the army, therefore, retired to the islands at the fords on the mouth of the Mohawk River, where it empties into the Hudson, and a brigade was posted above the Falls of the Mohawk, called the Cohoes, to prevent the enemy from crossing there. It was considered a strong position, where they could not be attacked without great disadvantage to the assailant.

We will now take a view of occurrences on the right and left of Burgoyne, and show the effect of Schuyler's measures, poorly seconded as they were in crippling and straitening the invading army. And first we will treat of the expedition against Bennington. Generals Phillips and Riedesel demurred strongly to the expedition, but their counsels were outweighed by those of Colonel Skene [an influential and worthy royalist, the founder of Skenesborough]. He knew, he said, all the country thereabout. The inhabitants were as five to one in favor of the royal cause, and would be prompt to turn out on the first appearance of a protecting army. He was to accompany the expedition, and much was expected from his personal influence and authority. Lieutenant-colonel Baum was to command the detachment. He had under him, according to Burgoyne, two hundred dismounted dragoons of the regiment of Riedesel, Captain Fraser's marksmen, which were the only British, all the Canadian volunteers, a party of the provincials who perfectly knew the country, one hundred Indians, and two light pieces of cannon. The whole detachment amounted to about five hundred men.

To be nearer at hand in case assistance should be required, Burgoyne encamped on the east side of the Hudson, nearly opposite Saratoga, throwing over a bridge of boats by which General Fraser, with the advanced guard, crossed to that place. Colonel Baum set out from camp at break of day on the 13th of August. He was too slow a man to take a place by surprise. The people of Bennington heard of his approach and were on the alert. The veteran Stark was there with eight or nine hundred troops. During the late alarms the militia of the State had been formed into two brigades, one to be commanded by General William Whipple; Stark had with difficulty been prevailed upon to accept the command of the other, upon the express condition that he should not be obliged to join the main army but should be left to his own discretion to make war in his own partisan style, hovering about the enemy in their march through the country, and accountable to none but the authorities of New Hampshire.

Having heard that Indians had appeared at Cambridge, twelve miles to the north of Bennington, on the 13th, he sent out two hundred men under Colonel Gregg in quest of them. In the course of the night he learnt that they were mere scouts in advance of a force marching upon Bennington. He immediately rallied his brigade, called out the militia of the neighborhood, and sent off for Colonel Seth Warner and his regiment of militia who were with General Lincoln at Manchester. Lincoln instantly detached them, and Warner and his men marched all night through drenching rain, arriving at Stark's camp in the morning, dripping wet.

Stark left them at Bennington to dry and rest themselves and then to follow on; in the meantime he pushed forward with his men to support the party sent out the preceding day under Gregg, in quest of the Indians. He met them about five miles off in full retreat, Baum and his force a mile in their rear. He halted and prepared for action. Baum also halted, posted himself on a high ground at a bend of the little river Walloomscoick and began to intrench himself. Stark fell back a mile to wait for reinforcements and draw down Baum from his strong position. A skirmish took place between the advance guards; thirty of Baum's men were killed and two Indian chiefs. An incessant rain on the 15th prevented an attack on Baum's camp, but there was continual skirmishing. The colonel strengthened his intrenchments, and finding he had a larger force to contend with than he had anticipated, sent off in all haste to Burgoyne for reinforcements. Colonel Breyman marched off immediately with five hundred Hessian grenadiers and infantry and two six-pounders, leaving behind him his tents, baggage, and standards.

In the meantime the Americans had been mustering from all quarters to Stark's assistance, with such weapons as they had at hand. During the night of the 15th, Colonel Symonds arrived with a body of Berkshire militia. On the following morning the sun shone bright, and Stark prepared to attack Baum in his intrenchments; though he had no artillery, and his men, for the most part, had only their ordinary brown firelocks without bayonets. Two hundred of his men, under Colonel Nichols, were detached to the rear of the enemy's left; three hundred under Colonel Herrick, to the rear of his right; they were to join their forces and attack him in the rear, while Colonels Hubbard and Stickney, with two hundred men, diverted his attention in front.

At the first sound of fire-arms, Stark, who had remained with the main body in camp, mounted his horse and gave the word, *forward!* He had promised his men the plunder of the British camp. The homely speech made by him when in sight of the enemy, has often been cited. "Now, my men! There are the red coats! Before night they must be ours, or Molly Stark will be a widow!"

Baum soon found himself assailed on every side, but he defended his works bravely. His two pieces of artillery, advantageously planted, were very effective, and his troops, if slow in march, were steady in action. Stark inspired his men with his own impetuosity. They drove the royalist troops upon the Hessians, and pressing after them stormed the works with irresistible fury. A Hessian eye-witness declares that this time the rebels fought with desperation, pressing within eight paces of the loaded cannon to take surer aim at the artillerists. The latter were slain; the cannon captured. The royalists and Canadians took to flight, and escaped to the woods. The Germans still kept their ground and fought bravely, until there was not a cartridge left. Baum and his dragoons then took to their broadswords, and the infantry to their bayonets, and endeavored to cut their way to a road in the woods, but in vain; many were killed, more wounded, Baum among the number, and all who survived were taken prisoners.

The victors now dispersed, some to collect booty, some to attend to the wounded, some to guard the prisoners, and some to seek refreshment, being exhausted by hunger and fatigue. At this critical juncture, Breyman's tardy reinforcement came, making its way heavily and slowly to the scene of action, joined by many of the enemy who had fled. Attempts were made to rally the militia; but they were in complete confusion. Nothing would have saved them from defeat, had not Colonel Seth Warner's corps fortunately arrived from Bennington, fresh from repose, and advanced to meet the enemy, while the others regained their ranks. It was four o'clock in the afternoon when this second action commenced. It was fought from wood to wood and hill to hill, for several miles, until sunset. The last stand of the enemy was at Van Schaick's mill, where, having expended all their ammunition, of which each man had forty rounds, they gave way, and retreated, under favor of the night, leaving two field-pieces and all their baggage in the hands of the Americans.

Four brass field-pieces, nine hundred dragoon swords, a thousand stand of arms, and four ammunition wagons were the spoils of this victory. Thirty-two officers, five hundred and sixty-four privates, including Canadians and loyalists, were taken prisoners. The number of slain was very considerable, but could not be ascertained; many having fallen in the woods. The brave but unfortunate Baum did not long survive. The Americans had one hundred killed and wounded.

Arnold's march to the relief of Fort Stanwix was slower than suited his ardent and impatient spirit. He was detained in the valley of the Mohawk by bad roads, by the necessity of waiting for baggage and ammunition wagons, and for militia recruits who turned out reluctantly. Conscious of the smallness of his force, he had resorted to stratagem, sending emissaries ahead to spread exaggerated reports of the number of his troops, so as to work on the fears of the enemy's Indian allies and induce them to desert. The most important of these emissaries was one Yan Yost Cuyler, an eccentric, half-witted fellow, known throughout the country as a rank tory. He had been convicted as a spy, and only spared from the halter on the condition that he would go into St. Leger's camp, and spread alarming reports among the Indians, by whom he was well known. To insure a faithful discharge of his mission, Arnold detained his brother as a hostage.

On his way up the Mohawk Valley, Arnold was joined by a New York regiment, under Colonel James Livingston, sent by Gates to reinforce him. On arriving at the German Flats he received an express from Colonel Gansevoort, informing him that he was still besieged, but in high spirits and under no apprehensions.

All this while St. Leger was advancing his parallels and pressing the siege; while provisions and ammunition were rapidly decreasing within the fort. St Leger's Indian allies, however, were growing sullen and intractable. This slow kind of warfare, this war with the spade, they were unaccustomed to, and they by no means relished it. At this juncture, scouts brought word that a force one thousand strong was marching to the relief of the fort. Eager to put his savages in action, St. Leger, in a council of war, offered to their chiefs to place himself at their head, with three hundred of his best troops, and meet the enemy as they advanced. It was agreed, and they sallied forth together to choose a fighting ground. By this time rumors stole into the camp doubling the number of the approaching enemy. Burgoyne's whole army were said to have been defeated. Lastly came Yan Yost Cuyler, with his coat full of bullet-holes, giving out that he had escaped from the hands of the Americans, and had been fired upon by them. His story was believed, for he was known to be a royalist. Mingling among his old acquaintances, the Indians, he assured them that the Americans were close at hand, and "numerous as the leaves on the trees."

Arnold's stratagem succeeded. The Indians, fickle as the winds, began to desert. Sir John Johnson and Colonels Claus and Butler endeavored in vain to reassure and retain them. In a little while two hundred had decamped, and the rest threatened to do so likewise, unless St. Leger retreated. The unfortunate colonel found too late what little reliance was to be placed upon Indian allies. He determined, on the 22d, to send off his sick, his wounded, and his artillery by Wood Creek that very night, and to protect them by the line of march. The Indians, however, goaded on by Arnold's emissaries, insisted on instant retreat. St. Leger still refused to depart before nightfall. The savages now became ungovernable. They seized upon liquor of the officers about to be embarked, and getting intoxicated behaved like very fiends. In a word St. Leger was obliged to decamp about noon in such hurry and confusion that he left his tents standing, and his artillery, with most of his baggage, ammunition and stores, fell into the hands of the Americans.

A detachment from the garrison pursued and harassed him for a time; but his greatest annoyance was from his Indian allies, who plundered the boats which conveyed such baggage as had been brought off; murdered all stragglers who lagged in the rear, and amused themselves by giving false alarms to keep up the panic of the soldiery, who would throw away muskets, knapsacks, and everything that impeded their flight. It was not until he reached Onondaga Falls, that St. Leger discovered by a letter from Burgoyne, and floating reports brought by the bearer, that he had been the dupe of a *ruse de guerre,* and that at the time the advancing foe were reported to be close upon his haunches, they were not within forty miles of him.

Such was the second blow to Burgoyne's invading army; but before the news of it reached that doomed commander, he had already been half paralyzed by the disaster at Bennington.

Means were now augmenting in Schuyler's hands. Colonels Livingston and Pierre van Cortlandt, forwarded by Putnam, were arrived. Governor Clinton was daily expected with New York militia from the Highlands. The arrival of Arnold was anticipated with troops and artillery, and Lincoln with the New England militia. At this propitious moment, when everything was ready for the sickle to be put into the harvest, General Gates arrived in the camp. Schuyler received him with the noble courtesy to which he pledged himself. After acquainting him with all the affairs of the department, the measures he had taken and those he had projected, he informed him of his having signified to Congress his intention to remain in that quarter for the present and render every service in his power, and he entreated Gates to call upon him for council and assistance whenever he thought proper.

Gates was in high spirits. His letters to Washington show how completely he was aware that an easy path of victory had been opened to him. But so far was he from responding to Schuyler's magnanimity, and profiting by his nobly offered counsel and assistance, that he did not even ask him to be present at his first council of war, although he invited up General Ten Broeck of the militia from Albany to attend it.

CHAPTER XLV.

BATTLE OF THE BRANDYWINE.—FALL OF PHILA-DELPHIA.

On the 25th of August the British army under General Howe began to land from the fleet in Elk River, at the bottom of Chesapeake Bay. The place where they landed was about six miles below the Head of Elk (now Elkton), a small town, the capital of Cecil County. This was seventy miles from Philadelphia. Early in the evening Washington received intelligence that the enemy were landing. There was a quantity of public and private stores at the Head of Elk which he feared would fall into their hands if they moved quickly. Every attempt was to be made to check them. The divisions of Generals Greene and Stephen were within a few miles of Wilmington; orders were sent for them to march thither immediately. The two other divisions which had halted at Chester to refresh were to hurry forward. Major-general Armstrong, who now commanded the Pennsylvania militia, was urged to send down in the cool of the night all the men he could muster, properly armed. General Rodney, who commanded the Delaware militia, was ordered to throw out scouts and patrols toward the enemy to watch their motions; and to move near them with his troops as soon as he should be reinforced by the Maryland militia. Light troops were sent out early in the morning to hover about and harass the invaders.

The country was in a great state of alarm. The inhabitants were hurrying off their most valuable effects, so that it was difficult to procure cattle and vehicles to remove the public stores. The want of horses, and the annoyances given by the American light troops, however, kept Howe from advancing promptly, and gave time for the greater part of the stores to be saved. To allay the public alarm, Howe issued a proclamation on the 27th, promising the strictest regularity and order on the part of his army; with security of person and property to all who remained quietly at home, and pardon to those under arms, who should promptly return to their obedience.

The divisions of Generals Greene and Stephen were now stationed several miles in advance of Wilmington, behind White Clay Creek, about ten miles from the Head of Elk. General Smallwood and Colonel Gist had been directed by Congress to take command of the militia of Maryland, who were gathering on the western shore, and Washington sent them orders to co-operate with General Rodney and get in the rear of the enemy.

Washington now felt the want of Morgan and his riflemen, whom he had sent to assist the Northern army; to supply their place, he formed a corps of light troops, by drafting a hundred men from each brigade. The command was given to Major-general Maxwell, who was to hover about the enemy and give them continual annoyance.

The army about this time was increased by the arrival of General Sullivan and his division of three thousand men. He had recently, while encamped at Hanover in Jersey, made a gallant attempt to surprise and capture a corps of one thousand provincials stationed on Staten Island, at a distance from the fortified camp, and opposite the Jersey shore. The attempt was partially successful; a number of the provincials were captured; but the regulars came to the rescue. Sullivan had not brought sufficient boats to secure a retreat. His rear-guard was captured while waiting for the return of the boats, yet not without a sharp resistance. There was loss on both sides, but the Americans suffered most. Congress had directed Washington to appoint a court of inquiry to investigate the matter; in the meantime, Sullivan, whose gallantry remained undoubted, continued in command.

There were now in camp several of those officers and gentlemen from various parts of Europe who had recently pressed into the service, and the suitable employment of whom had been a source of much perplexity to Washington. General Deborre, the French veteran of thirty years' service, commanded a brigade in Sullivan's division. Brigadier-general Conway, the Gallicized Hibernian, was in the division of Lord Stirling. Beside these, there was Louis Fleury, a French gentleman of noble descent, who had been educated as an engineer, and had come out at the opening of the Revolution to offer his services. Washington had obtained for him a captain's commission. Another officer of distinguished merit, was the Count Pulaski, a Pole, recommended by Dr. Franklin as an officer famous throughout Europe for his bravery and conduct in defence of the liberties of his country against Russia, Austria and Prussia.

At this time Henry Lee of Virginia, of military renown, makes his first appearance. He was in the twenty-second year of his age, and in the preceding year had commanded a company of Virginia volunteers. He had recently signalized himself in scouting parties, harassing the enemy's pickets. His adventurous exploits soon won him notoriety and the popular appellation of "Light-horse Harry." He was favorably noticed by Washington throughout the war.

Several days were now passed by the commander-in-chief almost continually in the saddle, reconnoitring the roads and passes, and making himself acquainted with the surrounding country, which was very much intersected by rivers and small streams, running chiefly from northwest to southeast. He had now made up his mind to risk a battle in the open field. It is true his troops were inferior to those of the enemy in number, equipments and discipline. Many of them were militia or raw recruits, yet the divisions of the army had acquired a facility at moving in large masses, and were considerably improved in military tactics. At any rate, it would never do to let Philadelphia, at that time the capital of the States, fall without a blow. Public impatience called for a battle; it was expected even by Europe; his own valiant spirit required it, though hitherto he had been held in check by superior considerations of expediency and by the controlling interference of Congress.

The British army having effected a landing, it was formed into two divisions. One, under Sir William Howe, was stationed at Elkton, with its advanced guard at Gray's Hill, about two miles off. The other division, under General Knyphausen, was on the opposite side of the ferry at Cecil Court House. On the 3d of September the enemy advanced in considerable force, with three field-pieces, moving with great caution, as the country was difficult, woody and not well known to them. About three miles in front of White Clay Creek, their vanguard was encountered by General Maxwell and his light troops, and a severe skirmish took place. The fire of the American sharpshooters and riflemen as usual, was very effective; but being inferior in number and having no artillery, Maxwell was compelled to retreat across White Clay Creek, with the loss of about forty killed and wounded. The loss of the enemy was supposed to be much greater.

The main body of the American army was now encamped on the east side of Red Clay Creek, on the road leading from Elkton to Philadelphia. The light-infantry were in the advance, at White Clay Creek. The armies were from eight to ten miles apart. In this position, Washington determined to await the threatened attack. His numerical force at this time was about fifteen thousand men, but from sickness and other causes the effective force, militia included, did not exceed eleven thousand, and most of these indifferently armed and equipped. The strength of the British was computed at eighteen thousand men, but, it is thought, not more than fifteen thousand were brought into action.

On the 8th, the enemy advanced in two columns—one appeared preparing to attack the Americans in front, while the other extended its left up the west side of the creek, halting at Milltown, somewhat to the right of the American position. Washington now suspected an intention on the part of Sir William Howe to march by his right, suddenly pass the Brandywine, gain the heights north of that stream and cut him off from Philadelphia. He summoned a council of war, therefore, that evening, in which it was determined immediately to change their position, and move to the river in question. By two o'clock in the morning, the army was under march, and by the next evening was encamped on the high grounds in the rear of the Brandywine. The enemy on the same evening moved to Kennet Square, about seven miles from the American position.

The Brandywine Creek, as it is called, commences with two branches, called the East and West branches, which unite in one stream, flowing from west to east about twenty-two miles, and emptying itself into the Delaware about twenty-five miles below Philadelphia. It has several fords; one called Chadd's Ford, was at that time the most practicable, and in the direct route from the enemy's camp to Philadelphia. As the principal attack was expected here, Washington made it the centre of his position, where he stationed the main body of his army, composed of Wayne's, Weedon's, and Muhlenberg's brigades, with the light-infantry under Maxwell. An eminence immediately above the ford had been intrenched in the night, and was occupied by Wayne and Proctor's artillery. Weedon's and Muhlenberg's brigades, which were Virginian troops, and formed General Greene's division, were posted in the rear on the heights as a reserve to aid either wing of the army. With these Washington took his stand. Maxwell's light-infantry were thrown in the advance, south of the Brandywine, and posted on high ground each side of the road leading to the ford.

HEAD-QUARTERS AT BRANDYWINE.
VOL. III.

The right wing of the army commanded by Sullivan, and composed of his division and those of Stephen and Stirling, extended up the Brandywine two miles beyond Washington's position. Its light troops and videttes were distributed quite up to the forks. The left wing, composed of the Pennsylvania militia, under Major-general Armstrong, was stationed about a mile and a half below the main body, to protect the lower fords, where the least danger was apprehended.

Early on the morning of the 11th, a great column of troops was descried advancing on the road leading to Chadd's Ford. A skirt of the woods concealed its force, but it was supposed to be the main body of the enemy; if so, a general conflict was at hand. The Americans were immediately drawn out in order of battle. Washington rode along the front of the ranks, and was everywhere received with acclamations. A sharp firing of small arms soon told that Maxwell's light-infantry

Sullivan on receiving Washington's orders, advanced with his own, Stephen's and Stirling's divisions, and began to form a line in front of an open piece of wood. The time which had been expended in transmitting intelligence, receiving orders, and marching, had enabled Cornwallis to choose his ground and prepare for action. Still more time was given him from the apprehension of the three generals, upon consultation, of being out-flanked upon the right, and that the gap between Sullivan's and Stephen's divisions was too wide, and should be closed up. Orders were accordingly given for the whole line to move to the right; and while in execution, Cornwallis advanced rapidly with his troops in the finest order, and opened a brisk fire of musketry and artillery. The Americans made an obstinate resistance, but being taken at a disadvantage, the right and left wings were broken and driven into the woods. The centre stood firm for a while, but being exposed to the whole fire of the enemy, gave way at length also. The British, in following up their advantage, got entangled in the wood. Lafayette had thrown himself from his horse and was endeavoring to rally the troops, when he was shot through the leg with a musket ball, and had to be assisted into the saddle by his aide-de-camp.

The Americans rallied on a height to the north of Dilworth, and made a still more spirited resistance than at first, but were again dislodged and obliged to retreat with a heavy loss.

While this was occurring with the right wing, Knyphausen, as soon as he learnt from the heavy firing that Cornwallis was engaged, made a push to force his way across Chadd's Ford in earnest. He was vigorously opposed by Wayne with Proctor's artillery, aided by Maxwell and his infantry. Greene was preparing to second him with the reserve, when he was summoned by Washington to the support of the right wing; which the commander-in-chief had found in imminent peril.

Greene advanced to the relief with such celerity, that it is said, on good authority, his division accomplished the march, or rather run, of five miles in less than fifty minutes. He arrived too late to save the battle, but in time to protect the broken masses of the left wing which he met in full flight. Opening his ranks from time to time for the fugitives and closing them the moment they had passed, he covered their retreat by a sharp and well-directed fire from his field-pieces. His grand stand was made at a place about a mile beyond Dilworth, which in reconnoitring the neighborhood Washington had pointed out to him, as well calculated for a second position, should the army be driven out of the first. Weedon's brigade was drawn up in a narrow defile, flanked on both sides by woods, and perfectly commanding the road; while Greene, with Muhlenberg's brigade, passing to the right took his station on the road. The British came on impetuously, expecting but faint opposition. They met with a desperate resistance and were repeatedly driven back. Weedon's brigade on the left maintained its stand also with great obstinacy, and the check given to the enemy by these two brigades allowed time for the broken troops to retreat. Weedon was at length compelled by superior numbers to seek the protection of the other brigade, which he did in good order, and Greene gradually drew off the whole division in face of the enemy, who, checked by this vigorous resistance, and seeing the day far spent, gave up all further pursuit.

The brave stand made by these brigades had likewise been a great protection to Wayne. He had for a long time withstood the attacks of the enemy at Chadd's Ford, until the approach on the right of some of the enemy's troops, who had been entangled in the woods, showed him that the right wing had been routed. He now gave up the defence of his post and retreated by the Chester road. Knyphausen's troops were too fatigued to pursue him, and the others had been kept back, as we have shown, by Greene's division. So ended the varied conflict of the day.

Lafayette gives an animated picture of the general retreat in which he became entangled. All around him was headlong terror and confusion. Chester road, the common retreat of the broken fragments of the army from every quarter, was crowded with fugitives, with cannon, with baggage cars, all hurrying forward pell-mell, and obstructing each other. At Chester, twelve miles from the field of battle, there was a deep stream with a bridge, over which the fugitives would have to pass. Here Lafayette set a guard to prevent their further flight. The commander-in-chief arriving soon after with Greene and his gallant division, some degree of order was restored, and the whole army took its post behind Chester for the night.

The scene of this battle, which decided the fate of Philadelphia, was within six and twenty miles of that city, and each discharge of cannon could be heard there. The two parties of the inhabitants, whig and tory, were to be seen in separate groups in the squares and public places, waiting the event in anxious silence. At length a courier arrived. His tidings spread consternation among the friends of liberty. Many left their homes; entire families abandoned everything in terror and despair, and took refuge in the mountains. Congress, that same evening determined to quit the city and repair to Lancaster, whence they subsequently removed to Yorktown.

Notwithstanding the rout and precipitate retreat of the American army, Sir William Howe did not press the pursuit, but passed the night on the field of battle, and remained the two following days at Dilworth, sending out detachments to take post at Concord and Chester, and seize on Wilmington, whither the sick and wounded were conveyed.

Washington, as usual, profited by the inactivity of Howe; quietly retreating through Derby (on the 12th) across the Schuylkill to Germantown, within a short distance of Philadelphia, where he gave his troops a day's repose. Finding them in good spirits and in nowise disheartened by the recent affair, which they seemed to consider a check rather than a defeat, he resolved to seek the enemy again and give him battle. As preliminary measures, he left some of the Pennsylvania militia in Philadelphia to guard the city; others, under General Armstrong, were posted at the various passes of the Schuylkill, with orders to throw up works; the floating bridge on the lower road was to be unmoored, and the boats collected and taken across the river.

Having taken these precautions against any hostile movement by the lower road, Washington recrossed the Schuylkill on the 14th, and advanced along the Lancaster road, with the intention of turning the left flank of the enemy. Howe, apprised of his intention, made a similar disposition to outflank him. The two armies came in sight of each other near the Warren Tavern, twenty-three miles from Philadelphia, and were on the point of engaging, but were prevented by a violent storm of rain which lasted for four and twenty hours.

This inclement weather was particularly distressing to the Americans, who were scantily clothed, most of them destitute of blankets, and separated from their tents and baggage. The rain penetrated their cartridge-boxes and the ill-fitted locks of their muskets, rendering the latter useless, being deficient in bayonets. In this plight, Washington gave up for the present all thought of attacking the enemy, as their discipline in the use of the bayonet, with which they were universally furnished, would give them a great superiority in action.

The only aim at present was to get to some dry and secure place where the army might repose and refit. All day and for a great part of the night they marched under a cold and pelting rain, and through deep and miry roads to the Yellow Springs, thence to Warwick, on French Creek. At Warwick furnace, ammunition and a few muskets were obtained, to aid in disputing the passage of the Schuylkill, and the advance of the enemy on Philadelphia. From French Creek, Wayne was detached with his division to get in the rear of the enemy, form a junction with General Smallwood and the Maryland militia, and, keeping themselves concealed, watch for an opportunity to cut off Howe's baggage and hospital train; in the meantime Washington crossed the Schuylkill at Parker's Ford and took a position to defend that pass of the river.

Wayne set off in the night, and by a circuitous march got within three miles of the left wing of the British encamped at Trydraffin, and concealing himself in a wood, waited the arrival of Smallwood and his militia. At daybreak he reconnoitred the camp where Howe, checked by the severity of the weather, had contented himself with uniting his columns, and remained under shelter. All day Wayne hovered about the camp; there were no signs of marching; all kept quiet but lay too compact to be attacked with prudence. He sent repeated messages to Washington describing the situation of the enemy. "I believe he knows nothing of my situation, as I have taken every precaution to prevent any intelligence getting to him."

His motions, however, had not been so secret as he imagined. He was in a part of the country full of the disaffected, and Sir William had received accurate information of his force and where he was encamped. General Gray, with a strong detachment, was sent to surprise him at night in his lair. Late in the evening, when Wayne had set his pickets and sentinels and thrown out his patrols, a countryman brought him word of the meditated attack. He doubted the intelligence, but strengthened his pickets and patrols, and ordered his troops to sleep upon their arms. At eleven o'clock the pickets were driven in at the point of the bayonet—the enemy were advancing in column. Wayne instantly took post on the right of his position, to cover the retreat of the left, led by Colonel Hampton, the second in command. The latter was tardy, and incautiously paraded his troops in front of their fires so as to be in full relief. The enemy rushed on without firing a gun; all was the silent but deadly work of the bayonet and cutlass. Nearly three hundred of Hampton's men were killed or wounded, and the rest put to flight. Wayne gave the enemy some well-directed volleys, and then retreating to a small distance, rallied his troops and prepared for further defence. The British, however, contented themselves with the blow they had given and retired with very little loss, taking with them between seventy and eighty prisoners, several of them officers, and eight baggage wagons, heavily laden.

General Smallwood, who was to have co-operated with Wayne, was within a mile of him at the time of his attack, and would have hastened to his assistance with his well-known intrepidity, but he had not the corps under his command with which he had formerly distinguished himself, and his raw militia fled in a panic at the first sight of a return party of the enemy. Wayne was deeply mortified by the result of this affair, and finding it severely criticised in the army, demanded a court-martial, which pronounced his conduct everything that was to be expected from an active, brave, and vigilant officer; whatever blame there was in the matter fell upon his second in command.

On the 21st, Sir William Howe made a rapid march high up the Schuylkill, on the road leading to Reading, as if he intended either to capture the military stores deposited there, or to turn the right of the American army. Washington kept pace with him on the opposite side of the river up to Pott's Grove, about thirty miles from Philadelphia.

The movement on the part of Howe was a mere feint. No sooner had he drawn Washington so far up the river, than by a rapid countermarch on the night of the 22d, he got to the ford below, threw his troops across on the next morning and pushed forward for Philadelphia. By the time Washington was apprised of this counter-movement, Howe was too far on his way to be overtaken by harassed, barefooted troops, worn out by constant marching. Feeling the necessity of immediate reinforcements, he wrote on the same day to Putnam, at Peekskill: "I desire that without a moment's loss of time, you will detach as many effective rank and file, under proper generals and officers, as will make the whole number, including those with General McDougall, amount to twenty-five hundred privates and non-commissioned fit for duty. I must urge you, by every motive, to send this detachment without the least possible delay."

On the next day (24th) he wrote also to General Gates: "I request, if circumstances will admit, that you will order Colonel Morgan to join me again with his corps. I sent him up when I thought you materially wanted him; and if his services can be dispensed with now, you will direct his immediate return."

Having called a council of officers and taken their opinions, which concurred with his own, Washington determined to remain some days at Pott's Grove, to give repose to his troops and await the arrival of reinforcements.

Sir William Howe halted at Germantown, within a short distance of Philadelphia, and encamped the main body of his army in and about that village; detaching Lord Cornwallis with a large force and a number of officers of distinction, to take formal possession of the city. That general marched into Philadelphia on the 26th with a brilliant staff and escort, and followed by splendid legions of British and Hessian grenadiers, long trains of artillery and squadrons of light-dragoons, the finest troops in the army all in their best array.

CHAPTER XLVI.

THE NORTHERN INVASION.—FALL OF THE HIGH-LAND FORTS.—DEFEAT AND SURRENDER OF BURGOYNE.

The checks which Burgoyne had received on right and left, and, in a great measure, through the spontaneous rising of the country, had opened his eyes to the difficulties of his situation, and the errors as to public feeling into which he had been led by his tory counsellors. He declared that had he any latitude in his orders, he would remain where he was, or perhaps fall back to Fort Edward, where his communication with Lake George would be secure, and wait for some event that might assist his movement forward; his orders, however, were positive to force a junction with Sir William Howe. He did not feel at liberty, therefore, to remain inactive longer than would be necessary to receive the reinforcements of the additional companies, the German drafts and recruits actually on Lake Champlain, and to collect provisions enough for twenty-five days. These reinforcements were indispensable, because, from the hour he should pass the Hudson River and proceed towards Albany, all safety of communication would cease.

A feature of peculiar interest is given to this wild and rugged expedition, by the presence of two ladies of rank and refinement, involved in its perils and hardships. One was Lady Harriet Ackland, daughter of the Earl of Ilchester, and wife of Major Ackland of the grenadiers; the other was the Baroness De Riedesel, wife of the Hessian major-general. Both of these ladies had been left behind in Canada. Lady Harriet, however, on hearing that her husband was wounded in the affair at Hubbardton, instantly set out to rejoin him, regardless of danger, and of her being in a condition before long to become a mother. Crossing the whole length of Lake Champlain, she found him in a sick bed at Skenesborough. After his recovery she refused to leave him, but had continued with the army ever since. Her example had been imitated by the Baroness De Riedesel, who had joined the army at Fort Edward, bringing with her her three small children. The friendship and sympathy of these two ladies in all scenes of trial and suffering, and their devoted attachment to their husbands, afford touching episodes in the story of the campaign.

The American army had received various reinforcements. It was now about ten thousand strong. Schuyler, finding himself and his proffered services slighted by Gates, had returned to Albany. His patriotism was superior to personal resentments. He still continued to promote the success of the campaign, exerting his influence over the Indian tribes to win them from the enemy. At Albany he held talks and war feasts with deputations of Oneida, Tuscarora, and Onondaga warriors; and procured scouting parties of them, which he sent to the camp, and which proved of great service.

The dense forests which covered the country between the hostile armies concealed their movements, and as Gates threw out no harassing parties, his information concerning the enemy was vague. Burgoyne, however, was diligently collecting all his forces from Skenesborough, Fort Anne and Fort George, and collecting provisions. So stood matters on the 11th of September, when a report was circulated in the American camp that Burgoyne was in motion, and that he had made a speech to his soldiers, telling them that the fleet had returned to Canada, and their only safety was to fight their way to New York.

As General Gates was to *receive* an attack, it was thought he ought to choose the ground where to receive it. Arnold, therefore, in company with Kosciuszko, the Polish engineer, reconnoitred the neighborhood in quest of a good camping-ground, and at length fixed upon a ridge of hills called Bemis's Heights, which Kosciuszko proceeded to fortify. In the meantime Colonel Colburn was sent off with a small party to ascend the high hills on the east side of the Hudson, and watch the movements of the enemy with glasses from their summits, or from the tops of the trees. For three days he kept thus on the look-out, sending word from time to time to camp of all that he espied.

On the 11th there were the first signs of movement among Burgoyne's troops. On the 13th and 14th they slowly passed over a bridge of boats, which they had thrown across the Hudson, and encamped near Fish Creek. On the 15th, both English and Hessian camps struck their tents, and loaded their baggage wagons. By twelve o'clock both began to march. Colburn neglected to notice the route taken by the Hessians; his attention was absorbed by the British, who made their way slowly and laboriously down the western side of the river, along a wretched road intersected by brooks and rivulets, the bridges over which Schuyler had broken down. The division had with it eighty-five baggage wagons and a great train of artillery; with two unwieldy twenty-four-pounders, acting like drag anchors. Having seen the army advance two miles on its march, Colburn descended from the heights, and hastened to the American camp to make his report. A British prisoner, brought in soon afterwards, stated that Burgoyne had come to a halt about four miles distant.

On the following morning the army was under arms at daylight; the enemy, however, remained encamped, repairing bridges in front, and sending down guard-boats to reconnoitre. The Americans, therefore, went on to fortify their position. The ridge of hills called Bemis's Heights, rises abruptly from the narrow flat bordering the west side of the river. Kosciuszko had fortified the camp with intrenchments three-quarters of a mile in extent, having redoubts and batteries, which commanded the valley and even the hills on the opposite side of the river, for the Hudson, in this upper part, is comparatively a narrow stream. From the foot of the height an intrenchment extended to the river, ending with a battery at the water edge, commanding a floating bridge.

The right wing of the army, under the immediate command of Gates, and composed of Glover's, Nixon's, and Patterson's brigades, occupied the brow of the hill nearest to the river, with the flats below. The left wing, commanded by Arnold, was on the side of the camp farthest from the river, and distant from the latter about three-quarters of a mile. It was composed of the New Hampshire brigade of General Poor, Pierre Van Courtlandt's and James Livingston's regiments of New York militia, the Connecticut militia, Morgan's riflemen, and Dearborn's infantry. The centre was composed of Massachusetts and New York troops.

Burgoyne gradually drew nearer to the camp, throwing out large parties of pioneers and workmen. The Americans disputed every step. A Hessian officer observes: "The enemy bristled up his hair, as we attempted to repair more bridges. At last we had to do him the honor of sending out whole regiments to protect our workmen."

Burgoyne now encamped about two miles from General Gates, disposing his army in two lines; the left on the river, the right extending at right angles to it, about six hundred yards across the low grounds to a range of steep and rocky hills, occupied by the *élite;* a ravine formed by a rivulet from the hills passed in front of the camp. The low ground between the armies was cultivated; the hills were covered with woods, excepting three or four small openings and deserted farms. Beside the ravines which fronted each camp, there was a third one, midway between them, also at right angles to the river.

On the morning of the 19th, General Gates received intelligence that the enemy were advancing in great force on his left. It was in fact their right wing, composed of the British line and led by Burgoyne in person. It was covered by the grenadiers and light-infantry under General Fraser and Colonel Breyman, who kept along the high grounds on the right; while they, in turn, were covered in front and on the flanks by Indians, provincial royalists and Canadians. The left wing and artillery were advancing at the same time, under Major-general Phillips and Riedesel, along the great road and meadows by the river side, but they were retarded by the necessity of repairing broken bridges. It was the plan of Burgoyne that the Canadians and Indians should attack the central outposts of the Americans, and draw their attention in that direction, while he and Fraser, making a circuit through the woods, should join forces and fall upon the rear of the American camp. As the dense forests hid them from each other, signal guns were to regulate their movements. Three, fired in succession, were to denote that all was ready, and be the signal for an attack in front, flank and rear.

The American pickets, stationed along the ravine of Mill Creek, sent repeated accounts to General Gates of the movements of the enemy; but he remained quiet in his camp as if determined to await an attack. The American officers grew impatient. Arnold especially, impetuous by nature, urged repeatedly that a detachment should be sent forth to check the enemy in their advance, and drive the Indians out of the woods. At length he succeeded in getting permission, about noon, to detach Morgan with his riflemen and Dearborn with his infantry from his division. They soon fell in with the Canadians and Indians, which formed the advance guard of the enemy's right, and attacking them with spirit, drove them in, or rather dispersed them. Morgan's riflemen, following up their advantage with too much eagerness, became likewise scattered, and a strong reinforcement of royalists arriving on the scene of action, the Americans, in their turn, were obliged to give way.

Other detachments now arrived from the American camp, led by Arnold, who attacked Fraser on his right, to check his attempt to get in the rear of the camp. Finding the position of Fraser too strong to be forced, he sent to head-quarters for reinforcements, but they were refused by Gates, who declared that no more should go. The reason he gave was that it might be attacked by the enemy's left wing. Arnold now made a rapid countermarch, and his movement being masked by the woods, suddenly attempted to turn Fraser's left. Here he came in full conflict with the British line, and threw himself upon it with a boldness and impetuosity that for a time threatened to break it, and cut the wings of the army asunder. The grenadiers and Breyman's riflemen hastened to its support. General Phillips broke his way through the woods with four pieces of artillery, and Riedesel came on with his heavy dragoons. Reinforcements came likewise to Arnold's assistance; his force, however, never exceeded three thousand men, and with these, for nearly four hours, he kept up a conflict almost hand to hand, with the whole right wing of the British army.

Night alone put an end to the conflict. Both parties claimed the victory. But, though the British remained on the field of battle, where they lay all night upon their arms, they had failed in their object; they had been assailed instead of being the assailants, while the American troops had accomplished the purpose for which they had sallied forth, had checked the advance of the enemy, frustrated their plan of attack, and returned exulting to their camp. Their loss, in killed and wounded, was between three and four hundred, including several officers; that of the enemy upwards of five hundred.

Burgoyne now strengthened his position with intrenchments and batteries, part of them across the meadows which bordered the river, part on the brow of the heights which commanded them. The Americans likewise extended and strengthened their line of breastworks on the left of the camp; the right was already unassailable. The camps were within gunshot, but with ravines and woods between them.

The situation of Burgoyne was growing more and more critical. On the 21st he heard shouts in the American camp, and in a little while their cannon thundered a *feu de joie*. News had been received from General Lincoln, that a detachment of New England troops under Colonel Brown had surprised the carrying-place, mills, and French lines at Ticonderoga, captured an armed sloop, gunboats and bateaux, made three hundred prisoners, beside releasing one hundred American captives, and were laying siege to Fort Independence.

Fortunately for Burgoyne, while affairs were warkening in the North, a ray of hope dawned from the South. While the shouts from the American camp were yet ringing in his ears, came a letter in cipher from Sir Henry Clinton, dated the 12th of September, announcing his intention in about ten days to attack the forts in the Highlands of the Hudson. Burgoyne sent back the messenger the same night, and despatched, moreover, two officers in disguise, by different routes, all bearing messages informing Sir Henry of his perilous situation. [Arnold had been excessively indignant at Gates withholding the reinforcements he had asked for in the recent action, which he attributed to pique or jealousy. Gates, indeed, in the report to Congress made no mention of Arnold. He also withdrew from Arnold's division Morgan's rifle corps and Dearborn's light-infantry, its main reliance. Arnold called on Gates to remonstrate. High words passed between them. Gates in his heat told Arnold that General Lincoln would arrive in a day or two, and then he would have no further occasion for him. Arnold returned to his quarters in a rage, but he determined to remain in camp and abide the anticipated battle.]

Lincoln, in the meantime, arrived in advance of his troops, which soon followed to the amount of two thousand. Part of the troops, detached by him under Colonel Brown, were besieging Ticonderoga and Fort Independence. Colonel Brown himself, with part of his detachment, had embarked on Lake George in an armed schooner and a squadron of captured gunboats and bateaux, and was threatening the enemy's deposit of baggage and heavy artillery at Diamond Island. The toils so skilfully spread were encompassing Burgoyne more and more; the gates of Canada were closing behind him.

We will now cast a look toward New York, and ascertain the cause of Sir Henry's delay in the anxiously expected operations on the Hudson.

The expedition of Sir Henry Clinton had awaited the arrival of reinforcements from Europe, which were slowly crossing the ocean in Dutch bottoms. At length they arrived, after a three months' voyage, and now there was a stir of warlike preparation at New York.

The defences of the Highlands, on which the security of the Hudson depended, were at this time weakly garrisoned; some of the troops having been sent off to reinforce the armies on the Delaware and in the North. Putnam, who had the general command of the Highlands, had but eleven hundred continental and four hundred militia troops with him at Peekskill, his head-quarters. There was a feeble garrison at Fort Independence, in the vicinity of Peekskill, to guard the public stores and workshops at Continental Village. The Highland forts, Clinton, Montgomery and Constitution, situated among the mountains and forming their main defence, were no better garrisoned, and George Clinton, who had the command of them, and who was in a manner the champion of the Highlands, was absent from his post, attending the State Legislature at Kingston (Esopus), in Ulster County, in his capacity of governor.

There were patriot eyes in New York to watch the course of events, and patriot boats on the river to act as swift messengers. [General Putnam in September received intelligence on which he could depend of the arrival of reinforcements in New York, and of preparations by the enemy for a movement. Surmising his object to be the forts of the Highlands, he wrote at once to Governor Clinton, conveying his intelligence and asking for reinforcements of militia.] The governor forthwith hastened to his post in the Highlands with such militia force as he could collect. We have heretofore spoken of his Highland citadel, Fort Montgomery, and of the obstructions of chain, boom, and chevaux-de-frise between it and the opposite promontory of Anthony's Nose, with which it had been hoped to barricade the Hudson. Fort Clinton had subsequently been erected within rifle shot of Fort Montgomery to occupy ground which commanded it. A deep ravine and stream called Peploep's Kill intervened between the two forts, across which there was a bridge. The governor had his head-quarters in Fort Montgomery, which was the northern and largest fort, but its works were unfinished. His brother James had charge of Fort Clinton, which was complete. The whole force to garrison the associate forts did not exceed six hundred men, chiefly militia, but they had the veteran, Colonel Lamb of the artillery, with them, and a company of his artillerists was distributed in the two forts.

The armament of Sir Henry Clinton, which had been waiting for a wind, set sail in the course of a day or two and stood up the Hudson, dogged by American swift-rowing whale-boats. Late at night of the 4th of October came a barge across the river, from Peekskill to Fort Montgomery, bearing a letter from Putnam to the governor. "This morning," writes he, "we had information from our guard-boats that there were two ships of war, three tenders, and a large number of flatbottomed boats coming up the river. They proceeded up as far as Tarrytown where they landed their men. This evening they were followed by one large man-of-war, five topsail vessels, and a large number of small craft."

The landing of troops at Tarrytown was a mere feint on the part of Sir Henry to distract the attention of the Americans; after marching a few miles into the country, they returned and re-embarked; the armament continued across the Tappan Sea and Haverstraw Bay to Verplanck's Point, where, on the 5th, Sir Henry landed with three thousand men, about eight miles below Peekskill. Putnam drew back to the hills in the rear of the village to prepare for the expected attack, and sent off to Governor Clinton for all the troops he could spare. So far the manoeuvres of Sir Henry Clinton had been successful. It was his plan to threaten an attack on Peekskill and Fort Independence, and, when he had drawn the attention of the American commanders to that quarter, to land troops on the western shore of the Hudson, below the Dunderberg (Thunder Hill), make a rapid march through the defiles behind that mountain to the rear of Forts Montgomery and Clinton, come down on them by surprise and carry them by a *coup de main*.

Accordingly at an early hour of the following morning taking advantage of a thick fog, he crossed with two thousand men to Stony Point on the west shore of the river, leaving about a thousand men, chiefly royalists, at Verplanck's Point to keep up a threatening aspect towards Peekskill. Three frigates, also, were to stand up what is called the Devil's Horse Race into Peekskill Bay, and station themselves within cannon shot of Fort Independence. Having accomplished his landing, Sir Henry, conducted by a tory guide, set out on a forced and circuitous march of several miles by rugged defiles, round the western base of the Dunderberg. At the entrance of the pass he left a small force to guard it and keep up his communication with the ships. By eight o'clock in the morning he had effected his march round the Dunderberg, and halted on the northern side in a ravine, between it and a conical mount called Bear Hill. The possibility of an enemy's approach by this pass had been noticed by Washington in reconnoitring the Highlands, and he had mentioned it in his instructions to Generals Greene and Knox, when they were sent to make their military survey, but they considered it impracticable from the extreme difficulty of the mountain passes.

In this ravine Sir Henry divided his forces. One division, nine hundred strong, led by Lieutenant-colonel Campbell, was to make a circuit through the forest round the western side of Bear Hill, so as to gain the rear of Fort Montgomery. After Sir Henry had allowed sufficient time for them to make the circuit, he was to proceed with the other division down the ravine, towards the river, turn to the left along a narrow strip of land between the Hudson and a small lake called Sinipink Pond, which lay at the foot of Bear Hill, and advance upon Fort Clinton. Both forts were to be attacked at the same time.

The detachment under Campbell set off in high spirits; it was composed partly of royalists, led by Colonel Beverly Robinson of New York, partly of Emerick's chasseurs, and partly of grenadiers, under Lord Rawdon. With him went Count Gabrouski, a Polish nobleman, aide-de-camp to Sir Henry Clinton. Everything thus far had been conducted with celerity and apparent secrecy, and complete surprise of both forts was anticipated. Sir Henry had indeed outwitted one of the guardians of the Highlands, but the other was aware of his designs. Governor Clinton, on receiving intelligence of ships of war coming up the Hudson, had sent scouts beyond the Dunderberg to watch their movements. Early on the present morning, word had been brought him that forty boats were landing a large force at Stony Point. He now, in his turn, apprehended an attack, and sent to Putnam for reinforcements, preparing, in the meantime, to make such defence as his scanty means afforded.

A lieutenant was sent out with thirty men from Fort Clinton, to proceed along the river-road and reconnoitre. He fell in with the advance guard of Sir Henry Clinton's division, and retreated skirmishing to the fort. A larger detachment was sent out to check the approach of the enemy on this side; while sixty men, afterwards increased to a hundred, took post with a brass field-piece in the Bear Hill defile, a narrow and rugged pass, bordered by shagged forests. As Campbell and his division came pressing forward, they were checked by the discharge of fire-arms and of the brass field-piece, which swept the steep defile. The British troops then filed off on each side into the woods, to surround the Americans. The latter, finding it impossible to extricate their field-piece in the rugged pass, spiked it, and retreated into the fort.

Sir Henry Clinton had met with equally obstinate opposition in his approach to Fort Clinton; the narrow strip of land between Lake Sinipink and the Hudson, along which he advanced, being fortified by an abatis. By four o'clock the Americans were driven within their works, and both forts were assailed. The defence was desperate; for Governor Clinton was a hard fighter, and he was still in hopes of reinforcements from Putnam; not knowing that the messenger he sent to him had turned traitor, and deserted to the enemy.

About five o'clock, he was summoned to surrender in five minutes, to prevent the effusion of blood: the reply was a refusal. About ten minutes afterwards, there was a general attack upon both forts. It was resisted with obstinate spirit. The action continued until dusk. The ships under Commodore Hotham approached near enough to open an irregular fire upon the forts, and upon the vessels anchored above the chevaux-de-frise. The latter returned the fire, and the flash and roar of their cannonry in the gathering darkness and among the echoes of the mountains increased the terrors of the strife. The works, however, were too extensive to be manned by the scanty garrisons; they were entered by different places and carried at the point of the bayonet; the Americans fought desperately from one redoubt to another—some were slain, some taken prisoners, and some escaped under cover of the night to the river or the mountains. "The garrison," writes Clinton, significantly, "had to fight their way out as many as could, as we determined not to surrender."

His brother James was saved from a deadly thrust of a bayonet by a garrison orderly-book in his pocket; but he received a flesh wound in the thigh. He slid down a precipice, one hundred feet high, into the ravine between the forts, and escaped to the woods. The governor leaped down the rocks to the river side, where a boat was putting off with a number of the fugitives. The boat crossed the Hudson in safety, and before midnight the governor was with Putnam, at Continental Village, concerting further measures.

Putnam had been completely outmanoeuvred by Sir Henry Clinton. He had continued until late in the morning in the belief that Peekskill and Fort Independence were to be the objects of attack. In the course of the morning he sallied forth with Brigadier-general Parsons, to reconnoitre the ground near the enemy. After their return they were alarmed, he says, by "a very heavy and hot firing both of small arms and cannon, at Fort Montgomery." Aware of the real point of danger, he immediately detached five hundred men to reinforce the garrison. They had six miles to march along the eastern shore, and then to cross the river; before they could do so the fate of the forts was decided.

British historians acknowledge that the valor and resolution displayed by the Americans in the defence of these forts were in no instance exceeded during the war; their loss in killed, wounded and missing, was stated at two hundred and fifty, a large proportion of the number engaged. [Colonel Campbell, who commanded the enemy's detachment, Major Grant of the New York volunteers, and Count Gabrouski, Sir Henry's Polish aide-de-camp, were slain in the assault; their fall exasperated the assailants, who revenged their loss with considerable slaughter.]

On the capture of the forts, the American frigates and galleys stationed for the protection of the chevaux-de-frise slipped their cables, made all sail, and endeavored to escape up the river. The wind, however, proved adverse; there was danger of their falling into the hands of the enemy; the crews, therefore, set them on fire and abandoned them. On the following morning, the chevaux-de-frise and other obstructions between Fort Montgomery and Anthony's Nose were cleared away: the Americans evacuated Forts Independence and Constitution, and a free passage up the Hudson was open for the British ships. Sir Henry Clinton proceeded no further in person, but left the rest of the enterprise to be accomplished by Sir

James Wallace and General Vaughan, with a flying squadron of light frigates, and a considerable detachment of troops.

Putnam had retreated to a pass in the mountains, on the east side of the river, near Fishkill, having removed as much of the stores and baggage as possible from the post he had abandoned. In a letter to Washington (Oct. 8th), he writes: "Governor Clinton is exerting himself in collecting the militia of this State. Brigadier-general Parsons I have sent off to forward in the Connecticut militia, which are now arriving in great numbers. I therefore hope and trust, that in the course of a few days, I shall be able to oppose the progress of the enemy."

He had concerted with Governor Clinton that they should move to the northward with their forces along the opposite shores of the Hudson, endeavoring to keep pace with the enemy's ships and cover the country from their attacks. The enemy's light-armed vessels were now making their way up the river; landing marauding parties occasionally to make depredations.

As soon as the governor could collect a little force, he pressed forward to protect Kingston (Esopus), the seat of the State Legislature. The enemy in the meantime landed from their ships, routed about one hundred and fifty militia collected to oppose them, marched to the village, set fire to it in every part, consuming great quantities of stores collected there, and then retreated to their ships. Having laid Kingston in ashes, the enemy proceeded in their ravages, destroying the residences of conspicuous patriots at Rhinebeck, Livingston, Manor, and elsewhere, and among others the mansion of the widow of the brave General Montgomery — trusting to close their desolating career by a triumphant junction with Burgoyne at Albany.

While Sir Henry Clinton had been thundering in the Highlands, Burgoyne and his army had been wearing out hope within their intrenchments, vigilantly watched but unassailed by the Americans. On the 7th of October Burgoyne determined to make a grand movement on the left of the American camp, to discover whether he could force a passage should it be necessary to advance, or dislodge it from its position should he have to retreat. Another object was to cover a forage of the army which was suffering from the great scarcity. For this purpose fifteen hundred of his best troops, with two twelve-pounders, two howitzers and six six-pounders, were to be led by himself, seconded by Major-generals Phillips and Riedesel and Brigadier-general Fraser. On leaving his camp he committed the guard of it on the high grounds to Brigadier-generals Hamilton and Specht, and of the redoubts on the low grounds near the river, to Brigadier-general Gall.

Forming his troops within three-quarters of a mile of the left of the Americans, though covered from their sight by the forest, he sent out a corps of rangers, provincials and Indians to skulk through the woods, get in their rear, and give them an alarm at the time the attack took place in front. The movement, though carried on behind the screen of forests, was discovered. In the afternoon the advanced guard of the American centre beat to arms; the alarm was repeated throughout the line. Gates ordered his officers to their alarm posts, and sent forth Wilkinson, the adjutant-general, to inquire the cause. From a rising ground in an open place he descried the enemy in force. Returning to the camp he reported the position and movements of the enemy; that their front was open, their flanks rested on woods, under cover of which they might be attacked, and their right was skirted by a height; that they were reconnoitring the left, and he thought offered battle.

A plan of attack was soon arranged. Morgan with his riflemen and a body of infantry was sent to make a circuit through the woods and get possession of the heights on the right of the enemy, while General Poor with his brigade of New York and New Hampshire troops, and a part of Leonard's brigade, were to advance against the enemy's left. Morgan was to make an attack on the heights as soon as he should hear the fire opened below.

Burgoyne now drew out his troops in battle array. The grenadiers, under Major Ackland, with the artillery, under Major Williams, formed his left, and were stationed on a rising ground, with a rivulet called Mill Creek in front. Next to them were the Hessians, under Riedesel, and British, under Phillips, forming the centre. The light-infantry, under Lord Balcarras, formed the extreme right; having in the advance a detachment of five hundred picked men, under General Fraser, ready to flank the Americans as soon as they should be attacked in front.

He had scarce made these arrangements, when he was astonished and confounded by a thundering of artillery on his left, and a rattling fire of rifles on the woody heights on his right. The troops under Poor advanced steadily up the ascent where Ackland's grenadiers and Williams' artillery were stationed; received their fire and then rushed forward. Ackland's grenadiers received the first brunt, but it extended along the line as detachment after detachment arrived, and was carried on with inconceivable fury. The artillery was repeatedly taken and retaken, and at length remained in possession of the Americans, who turned it upon its former owners. Major Ackland was wounded in both legs, and taken prisoner. Major Williams of the artillery was also captured. The headlong impetuosity of the attack confounded the regular tacticians. Much of this has been ascribed to the presence and example of Arnold. That daring officer, who had lingered in the camp in expectation of a fight, was exasperated at having no command assigned him. On hearing the din of battle, he could restrain no longer his warlike impulse, but threw himself on his horse and sallied forth. Putting spurs to his horse, he dashed into the scene of action, and was received with acclamation. Being the superior officer in the field his orders were obeyed of course. Putting himself at the head of the troops of Learned's brigade, he attacked the Hessians in the enemy's centre, and broke them with repeated charges. Indeed, for a time his actions seemed to partake of frenzy; riding hither and thither, brandishing his sword, and cheering on the men to acts of desperation.

Morgan, in the meantime, was harassing the enemy's right wing with an incessant fire of small-arms, and preventing it from sending any assistance to the centre. General Fraser with his chosen corps, for some time rendered great protection to this wing. Mounted on an iron-gray charger, his uniform of a field officer made him a conspicuous object for Morgan's sharpshooters. One bullet cut the crupper of his horse, another grazed his mane. A moment afterwards he was shot down by a marksman posted in a tree. Two grenadiers bore him to the camp. His fall was as a deathblow to his corps. The arrival on the field of a large reinforcement of New York troops under General Ten Broeck, completed the confusion. Burgoyne saw that the field was lost, and now only thought of saving his camp. The troops nearest to the lines were ordered to throw themselves within them, while Generals Phillips and Riedesel covered the retreat of the main body, which was in danger of being cut off. The artillery was abandoned, all the horses, and most of the men who had so bravely defended it having been killed. The troops, though hard pressed, retired in good order. Scarcely had they entered the camp when it was stormed with great fury; the Americans, with Arnold at their head, rushing to the lines under a severe discharge of grape-shot and small-arms. Lord Balcarras defended the intrenchments bravely; the action was fierce, and well sustained on both sides. After an ineffectual attempt to make his way into the camp in this quarter at the point of the bayonet, Arnold spurred his horse toward the right flank of the camp occupied by the German reserve, where Lieutenant-colonel Brooks was making a general attack with a Massachusetts regiment. Here, with a part of a platoon, he forced his way into a sallyport, but a shot from the retreating Hessians killed his horse, and wounded him in the same leg which had received a wound before Quebec. He was borne off from the field, but not until the victory was complete; for the Germans retreated from the works, leaving on the field their brave defender, Lieutenant-colonel Breyman, mortally wounded.

The night was now closing in. The victory of the Americans was decisive. They had routed the enemy, killed and wounded a great number, made many prisoners, taken their field-artillery and gained possession of a part of their works which laid open the right and the rear of their camp. They lay all night on their arms, within half a mile of the scene of action, prepared to renew the assault upon the camp in the morning. Affecting scenes had occurred in the enemy's camp during this deadly conflict.

In the morning previous to the battle, the Baroness De Riedesel had breakfasted with her husband in the camp. Generals Burgoyne, Phillips, and Fraser were to dine with her husband and herself in a house in the neighborhood, where she and her children were quartered. She observed much movement in the camp, but was quieted by the assurance that it was to be a mere reconnaissance. On her way home she met a number of Indians, painted and decorated and armed with guns, and shouting war! war! Her fears were awakened, and scarce had she reached home when she heard the rattling of fire-arms and the thundering of artillery. About one o'clock came one of the generals who were to have dined with her—poor General Fraser—brought upon a handbarrow, mortally wounded. The general said to the surgeon: 'Tell me the truth, is there no hope?' There was none. Prayers were read, after which he desired that General Burgoyne should be requested to have him buried on the next day at six o'clock in the evening on a hill where a breastwork had been constructed.

Lady Harriet Ackland was in a tent near by. News came to her that her husband was mortally wounded and taken prisoner. She was in an agony of distress.[12]

[12] Lady Ackland afterward applied to General Burgoyne for permission to pass to the American camp, and obtain General Gates' consent to join her husband. It was granted,

The baroness divided the night between soothing attentions to Lady Harriet, and watchful care of her children who were asleep, but who she feared might disturb the poor dying general. Towards morning, thinking his agony approaching, she wrapped them in blankets and retired with them into the entrance hall. Courteous even in death, the general sent her several messages to beg her pardon for the trouble he thought he was giving her. At eight o'clock in the morning he expired.

Burgoyne had shifted his position during the night to heights about a mile to the north, close to the river, and covered in front by a ravine. Early in the morning the Americans took possession of the camp which he had abandoned. A random fire of artillery and small-arms was kept up on both sides during the day. The British sharpshooters stationed in the ravine did some execution, and General Lincoln was wounded in the leg while reconnoitring. Gates, however, did not think it advisable to force a desperate enemy when in a strong position, at the expense of a prodigal waste of blood. He took all measures to cut off his retreat and insure a surrender. General Fellows, with 1,400 men, had already been sent to occupy the high ground east of the Hudson opposite Saratoga Ford. Other detachments were sent higher up the river in the direction of Lake George.

Burgoyne saw that nothing was left for him but a prompt and rapid retreat to Saratoga, yet in this he was delayed by a melancholy duty of friendship; it was to attend the obsequies of the gallant Fraser, who, according to his dying request, was to be interred at six o'clock in the evening, within a redoubt which had been constructed on a hill. Between sunset and dark, his body was borne to the appointed place by grenadiers of his division, followed by the generals and their staffs. The Americans seeing indistinctly what, in the twilight, appeared to be a movement of troops up the hill and in the redoubt, pointed their artillery in that direction. General Gates protested afterwards that had he known what was going on, he would have stopped the fire immediately.

Preparations had been made to decamp immediately after the funeral, and at nine o'clock at night the retreat commenced. Large fires had been lighted, and many tents were left standing to conceal the movement. It was a dismal retreat. The rain fell in torrents; the roads were deep and broken, and the horses weak and half-starved from want of forage. At daybreak there was a halt to refresh the troops and give time for the bateaux laden with provisions to come abreast. In three hours the march was resumed, but before long there was another halt, to guard against an American reconnoitring party which appeared in sight.

It rained terribly through the residue of the 9th, and in consequence of repeated halts, they did not reach Saratoga until evening. A detachment of Americans had arrived there before them, and were throwing up intrenchments on a commanding height at Fishkill. They abandoned their work, forded the Hudson, and joined a force under General Fellows, posted on the hills east of the river. The bridge over the Fishkill had been destroyed; the artillery could not cross until the ford was examined. Exhausted by fatigue, the men for the most part had not strength nor inclination to cut wood nor make fire, but threw themselves upon the

---

and the American general, according to Burgoyne, received her "with all the humanity and respect that her rank, her merits, and her fortune deserved."

wet ground in their wet clothes, and slept under the continuing rain.

At daylight on the 10th, the artillery and the last of the troops passed the fords of the Fishkill, and took a position upon the heights, and in the redoubts formerly constructed there. To protect the troops from being attacked in passing the ford by the Americans, who were approaching, Burgoyne ordered fire to be set to the farm-houses and other buildings on the south side of the Fishkill. Amongst the rest, the noble mansion of General Schuyler, with store-houses, granaries, mills and the other appurtenances of a great rural establishment, was entirely consumed. The measure was condemned by friend as well as foe, but he justified it on the principles of self-preservation.

The force under General Fellows, posted on the opposite hills of the Hudson, now opened a fire from a battery commanding the ford of that river. Thus prevented from crossing, Burgoyne thought to retreat along the west side as far as Fort George, on the way to Canada, and sent out workmen under a strong escort to repair the bridges, and open the road toward Fort Edward. The escort was soon recalled and the work abandoned, for the Americans under Gates appeared in great force on the heights south of the Fishkill, and seemed preparing to cross and bring on an engagement. The opposite shores of the Hudson were now lined with detachments of Americans. Bateaux laden with provisions, which had attended the movements of the army, were fired upon, many taken, some retaken with loss of life. It was necessary to land the provisions from such as remained, and bring them up the hill into the camp, which was done under a heavy fire from the American artillery.

Burgoyne called now a general council of war, in which it was resolved, since the bridges could not be repaired, to abandon the artillery and baggage, let the troops carry a supply of provisions upon their backs, push forward in the night, and force their way across the fords at or near Fort Edward. Before the plan could be put into execution, scouts brought word that the Americans were intrenched opposite those fords, and encamped in force with cannon on the high ground between Fort Edward and Fort George. In fact by this time the American army, augmented by militia and volunteers from all quarters, had posted itself in strong positions on both sides of the Hudson, so as to extend three-fourths of a circle round the enemy.

Giving up all further attempt at retreat, Burgoyne now fortified his camp on the heights to the north of Fishkill, still hoping that succor might arrive from Sir Henry Clinton, or that an attack upon his trenches might give him some chance of cutting his way through. In this situation his troops lay continually on their arms. His camp was subjected to cannonading from Fellows' batteries on the opposite side of the Hudson, Gates' batteries on the south of Fishkill, and a galling fire from Morgan's riflemen, stationed on heights in the rear.

The Baroness De Riedesel and her helpless little ones were exposed to the dangers and horrors of this long turmoil. On the morning when the attack was opened, General De Riedesel sent them to take refuge in a house in the vicinity. The baroness succeeded in getting to the house. Some women and crippled soldiers had already taken refuge there. It was mistaken for head-quarters and cannonaded. The baroness retreated into the cellar, laid herself in a corner near the door with her children's heads upon her knees, and passed a sleepless night of mental anguish. In the morning the cannonade began anew. Cannon balls passed through the house repeatedly with a tremendous noise. A poor soldier who was about to have a leg amputated, lost the other by one of these balls. The day was passed among such horrors. For six days, she and her children remained in this dismal place of refuge.

Burgoyne was now reduced to despair. His forces were diminished by losses, by the desertion of Canadians and royalists, and the total defection of the Indians; and on inspection it was found that the provisions on hand, even upon short allowance, would not suffice for more than three days. A council of war, therefore, was called of all the generals, field-officers and captains commanding troops. The deliberations were brief. All concurred in the necessity of opening a treaty with General Gates, for a surrender on honorable terms.

Negotiations were accordingly opened on the 13th, under sanction of a flag. Lieutenant Kingston, Burgoyne's adjutant-general, was the bearer of a note, proposing a cessation of hostilities until terms could be adjusted. The first terms offered by Gates were that the enemy should lay down their arms within their intrenchments, and surrender themselves prisoners of war. These were indignantly rejected, with an intimation that, if persisted in, hostilities must recommence.

Counter proposals were then made by General Burgoyne, and finally accepted by General Gates. According to these the British troops were to march out of the camp with artillery and all the honors of war, to a fixed place, where they were to pile their arms at a word of command from their own officers. They were to be allowed a free passage to Europe upon condition of not serving again in America, during the present war. The officers were to be on parole, and to wear their side-arms. All private property to be sacred; no baggage to be searched or molested. The capitulation was signed on the 17th of October.

The British army, at the time of the surrender, was reduced by capture, death and desertion, from nine thousand to five thousand seven hundred and fifty-two men. That of Gates, regulars and militia, amounted to ten thousand five hundred and fifty-four men on duty; between two and three thousand being on the sick list or absent on furlough. By this capitulation, the Americans gained a fine train of artillery, seven thousand stand of arms, and a great quantity of clothing, tents, and military stores of all kinds.

When the British troops marched forth to deposit their arms at the appointed place, Colonel Wilkinson, the adjutant-general, was the only American soldier to be seen. Gates had ordered his troops to keep rigidly within their lines, that they might not add by their presence to the humiliation of a brave enemy. In fact, throughout all his conduct during the campaign, British writers and Burgoyne himself give him credit for acting with great humanity and forbearance.

The surrender of Burgoyne was soon followed by the evacuation of Ticonderoga and Fort Independence, the garrisons retiring to the Isle aux Noix and

St. Johns. As to the armament on the Hudson, the commanders whom Sir Henry Clinton had left in charge of it, received, in the midst of their desolating career the astounding intelligence of the capture of the army with which they had come to co-operate. Nothing remained for them, therefore, but to drop down the river and return to New York. The fortresses in the Highlands could not be maintained, and were evacuated and destroyed.

CHAPTER XLVII.

BATTLE OF GERMANTOWN.—HOSTILITIES ON THE DELAWARE.

Having given the catastrophe of the British invasion from the North, we will revert to that part of the year's campaign which was passing under the immediate eye of Washington. We left him encamped at Pott's Grove towards the end of September, giving his troops a few days' repose after their severe fatigues. Being rejoined by Wayne and Smallwood with their brigades, and other troops being arrived from the Jerseys, his force amounted to about eight thousand Continentals and three thousand militia: with these he advanced on the 30th of September to Skippack Creek, about fourteen miles from Germantown, where the main body of the British army lay encamped; a detachment under Cornwallis occupying Philadelphia.

Immediately after the battle of Brandywine, Admiral Lord Howe with great exertions had succeeded in getting his ships of war and transports round from the Chesapeake into the Delaware, and had anchored them along the western shore from Reedy Island to Newcastle. They were prevented from approaching nearer by obstructions which the Americans had placed in the river. The lowest of these were at Billingsport (Bylling's Point), where chevaux-de-frise in the channel of the river were protected by a strong redoubt on the Jersey shore. Higher up were Fort Mifflin on Mud (or Fort) Island, and Fort Mercer on the Jersey shore; with chevaux-de-frise between them. Washington had exerted himself to throw a garrison into Fort Mifflin, and keep up the obstructions of the river. Sir William Howe had concerted operations with his brother by land and water, to reduce the forts and clear away the obstructions of the river. With this view he detached a part of his force into the Jerseys to proceed, in the first instance, against the fortifications at Billingsport.

Washington had been for some days anxiously on the lookout for some opportunity to strike a blow of consequence, when two intercepted letters gave him intelligence of this movement. He immediately determined to make an attack upon the British camp at Germantown, while weakened by the absence of this detachment. To understand the plan of the attack, some description of the British place of encampment is necessary.

Germantown, at that time, was little more than one continued street, extending two miles north and south. Beyond the village, and about a hundred yards east of the road, stood a spacious stone edifice, the country-seat of Benjamin Chew, chief justice of Pennsylvania previous to the Revolution. Four roads approached the village from above; that is, from the north. The Skippack, which was the main road, led over Chestnut Hill and Mount Airy down to and through the village towards Philadelphia, forming the street of which we have just spoken. On its right and nearly parallel was the Monatawny or Ridge road, passing near the Schuylkill, and entering the main road below the village. On the left of the Skippack or main road was the Limekiln road, running nearly parallel to it for a time, and then turning towards it, almost at right angles, so as to enter the village at the market-place. Still further to the left or east, and outside of all, was the Old York road, falling into the main road some distance below the village.

The main body of the British forces lay encamped across the lower part of the village, divided into almost equal parts by the main street or Skippack road. The right wing commanded by General Grant, was to the east of the road, the left wing to the west. Each wing was covered by strong detachments and guarded by cavalry. General Howe had his head-quarters in the rear. The advance of the army, composed of the 2d battalion of British light-infantry, with a train of artillery, was more than two miles from the main body, on the west of the road, with an outlying picket stationed with two six-pounders at Allen's house on Mount Airy. About three-quarters of a mile in the rear of the light-infantry, lay encamped in a field opposite "Chew's House," the 40th regiment of infantry, under Colonel Musgrave.

According to Washington's plan for the attack, Sullivan was to command the right wing, composed of his own division, principally Maryland troops, and the division of General Wayne. He was to be sustained by a *corps de reserve,* under Lord Stirling, composed of Nash's North Carolina and Maxwell's Virginia brigades, and to be flanked by the brigade of General Conway. He was to march down the Skippack road and attack the left wing; at the same time General Armstrong, with the Pennsylvania militia, was to pass down the Monatawny or Ridge road, and get upon the enemy's left and rear. Greene with the left wing, composed of his own division and the division of General Stephen, and flanked by McDougall's brigade, was to march down the Limekiln road, so as to enter the village at the market-house. The two divisions were to attack the enemy's right wing in front, McDougall with his brigade to attack it in flank, while Smallwood's division of Maryland militia and Forman's Jersey brigade, making a circuit by the Old York road, were to attack it in the rear. Two-thirds of the forces were thus directed against the enemy's right wing, under the idea that, if it could be forced, the whole army must be pushed into the Schuylkill, or compelled to surrender. The attack was to begin on all quarters at daybreak.

About dusk, on the 3d of October, the army left its encampment at Matuchen Hills, by its different routes. Washington accompanied the right wing. It had fifteen miles of weary march to make over rough roads, so that it was after daybreak when the troops emerged from the woods on Chestnut Hill. The morning was dark with a heavy fog. A detachment advanced to attack the enemy's out-picket, stationed at Allen's House. The patrol was led by Captain Allen McLane. He fell in with double sentries, whom he killed with the loss of one man. The alarm, however, was given; the distant roll of a drum and the call to arms resounded through the murky air. The picket guard, after discharging their two six-pounders, were routed, and retreated down the south side of Mount Airy to the battalion of light-infantry who were forming in order of battle. As their pursuers descended into the valley, the sun rose, but was soon obscured. Wayne led the attack upon the light-infantry. They broke at first but soon formed again, when a heavy and well-directed fire took place on both sides. They again gave way, but being supported by the grenadiers, returned to the charge. Sullivan's division and Conway's brigade formed on the west of the road, and joined in the attack; the rest of the troops were too far to the north to render any assistance. The infantry, after fighting bravely for a time, broke and ran, leaving their artillery behind. They were hotly pursued by Wayne. His troops remembered the bloody 20th of September, and the ruthless slaughter of their comrades. It was a terrible melée. The fog, together with the smoke of the cannonry and musketry, made it almost as dark as night; our people mistaking one another for the enemy, frequently exchanged shots before they discovered their error. The whole of the enemy's advance were driven from their camping ground, leaving their tents standing, with all their baggage. Colonel Musgrave, with six companies of the 40th regiment, threw himself into Chew's House, barricaded the doors and lower windows, and took post above stairs; the main torrent of the retreat passed by pursued by Wayne into the village.

As the residue of this division of the army came up to join in the pursuit, Musgrave and his men opened a fire of musketry upon them from the upper windows of his citadel. This brought them to a halt. Some of the officers were for pushing on; but General Knox stoutly objected, insisting on the old military maxim, never to leave a garrisoned castle in the rear. His objection unluckily prevailed. A flag sent with a summons to surrender was fired upon. The house was now cannonaded, but the artillery was too light to have the desired effect. An attempt was made to set fire to the basement. He who attempted it was shot dead from a grated cellar window. At length a regiment was left to keep guard upon the mansion and hold its garrison in check, and the rear division again pressed forward.

This half hour's delay, however, of nearly one-half of the army, disconcerted the action. The divisions and brigades thus separated from each other by the skirmishing attack upon Chew's House, could not be re-united. The fog and smoke rendered all objects indistinct at thirty yards' distance; the different parts of the army knew nothing of the position or movements of each other, and the commander-in-chief could take no view nor gain any information of the situation of the whole. The original plan of attack was only effectively carried into operation in the centre. Still the action, though disconnected, irregular and partial, was animated in various quarters. Sullivan, being reinforced by Nash's North Carolina troops and Conway's brigade, pushed on a mile beyond Chew's House, where the left wing of the enemy gave way before him.

Greene and Stephen, with their divisions, having had to make a circuit, were late in coming into action, and became separated from each other, part of Stephen's division being arrested by a heavy fire from Chew's House and pausing to return it. Greene, however, with his division, pressed rapidly forward, drove an advance regiment of light-infantry before him, took a number of prisoners, and made his way quite to the market-house in the centre of the village, where he encountered the right wing of the British drawn up to receive him. The impetuosity of his attack had an evident effect upon the enemy, who began to waver. Forman and Smallwood, with the Jersey and Maryland militia, were just showing themselves on the right flank of the enemy, and our troops seemed on the point of carrying the whole encampment. At this moment a singular panic seized our army. Various causes are assigned for it. Sullivan alleges that his troops had expended all their cartridges, and were alarmed by seeing the enemy gathering on their left, and by the cry of a light-horseman, that the enemy were getting round them. Wayne's division, which had pushed the enemy nearly three miles, was alarmed by the approach of a large body of American troops on its left flank, which it mistook for foes, and fell back in defiance of every effort of its officers to rally it. In its retreat it came upon Stephen's division and threw it into a panic, being, in its turn, mistaken for the enemy; thus all fell into confusion, and our army fled from their own victory.

In the meantime the enemy, having recovered from the first effects of the surprise, advanced in their turn. General Grey brought up the left wing, and pressed upon the American troops as they receded. Lord Cornwallis, with a squadron of light-horse from Philadelphia, arrived just in time to join in the pursuit. The retreat of the Americans was attended with less loss than might have been expected, and they carried off all their cannon and wounded. The retreat continued through the day to Perkiomen Creek, a distance of twenty miles.

The loss of the enemy in this action is stated by them to be seventy-one killed, four hundred and fifteen wounded, and fourteen missing: among the killed was Brigadier-general Agnew. The American loss was one hundred and fifty killed, five hundred and twenty-one wounded, and about four hundred taken prisoners. Among the killed was General Nash of North Carolina. Among the prisoners was Colonel Mathews of Virginia.

The sudden retreat of the army gave Washington surprise, chagrin and mortification. "Every account," said he subsequently, in a letter to the President of Congress, "confirms the opinion I at first entertained, that our troops retreated at the instant when victory was declaring herself in our favor. The tumult, disorder, and even despair which it seems had taken place in the British army, were scarcely to be paralleled; and it is said, so strongly did the ideas of a retreat prevail, that Chester was fixed on for their rendezvous. I can discover no other cause for not improving this happy opportunity, than the extreme haziness of the weather."

The plan of attack was too widely extended for strict concert, and too complicated for precise co-operation, as it had to be conducted in the night, and with a large proportion of undisciplined militia.

But although the Americans were balked of the victory, which seemed within their grasp, the impression made by the audacity of this attempt upon Germantown was greater we are told than that caused by any single incident of the war after Lexington and Bunker's Hill.

Washington remained a few days at Perkiomen Creek, to give his army time to rest and recover from the disorder incident to a retreat. Having been reinforced by the arrival of twelve hundred Rhode Island troops from Peekskill, under General Varnum, and nearly a thousand Virginia, Maryland and Pennsylvania troops, he gradually drew nearer to Philadelphia, and took a strong position at White Marsh, within fourteen miles of that city. By a resolution of Congress, all persons taken within thirty miles of any place occupied by British troops, in the act of conveying supplies to them, were subjected to martial law. Acting under the resolution, Washington detached large bodies of militia to scour the roads above the city, and between the Schuylkill and Chester, to intercept all supplies going to the enemy.

On the forts and obstructions in the river, Washington mainly counted to complete the harassment of Philadelphia. These defences had been materially impaired. The works at Billingsport had been attacked and destroyed, and some of the enemy's ships had forced their way through the chevaux-de-frise placed there. The American frigate Delaware, stationed in the river between the upper forts and Philadelphia, had run aground before a British battery and been captured.

It was now the great object of the Howes to reduce and destroy, and of Washington to defend and maintain the remaining forts and obstructions. Fort Mifflin, which we have already mentioned, was erected on a low, green, reedy island in the Delaware, a few miles below Philadelphia, and below the mouth of the Schuylkill. It consisted of a strong redoubt with extensive outworks and batteries. There was but a narrow channel between the island and the Pennsylvania shore. The main channel, practicable for ships, was on the other side. In this were sunk strong chevaux-de-frise, difficult either to be weighed or cut through, and dangerous to any ships that might run against them; subjected as they would be to the batteries of Fort Mifflin on one side, and on the other to those of Fort Mercer, a strong work at Red Bank on the Jersey shore.

Fort Mifflin was garrisoned by troops of the Maryland line, under Lieutenant-colonel Samuel Smith of Baltimore; and had kept up a brave defence against batteries erected by the enemy on the Pennsylvania shore. A reinforcement of Virginia troops made the garrison between three and four hundred strong. Floating batteries, galleys, and fire-ships, commanded by Commodore Hazelwood, were stationed under the forts and about the river.

Fort Mercer had hitherto been garrisoned by militia, but Washington now replaced them by four hundred of General Varnum's Rhode Island Continentals. Colonel Christopher Greene was put in command; a brave officer who had accompanied Arnold in his rough expedition to Canada, and fought valiantly under the walls of Quebec. Colonel Greene was accompanied by Captain Mauduit Duplessis, who was to have the direction of the artillery. He was a young French engineer of great merit, who had volunteered in the American cause, and received a commission from Congress. The chevaux-de-frise in the river had been constructed under his superintendence.

Greene, aided by Duplessis, made all haste to put Fort Mercer in a state of defence; but before the outworks were completed, he was surprised (October 22) by the appearance of a large force emerging from a wood within cannon shot of the fort. Their uniforms showed them to be Hessians. They were, in fact, four battalions twelve hundred strong of grenadiers, picked men, beside light-infantry and chasseurs, all commanded by Count Donop, who had figured in the last year's campaign. Colonel Greene, in nowise dismayed by the superiority of the enemy forming in glistening array before the wood, prepared for a stout resistance. In a little while an officer was descried, riding slowly up with a flag, accompanied by a drummer. Greene ordered his men to keep out of sight, that the fort might appear but slightly garrisoned.

When within proper distance the drummer sounded a parley, and the officer summoned the garrison to surrender; with a threat of no quarter in case of resistance. Greene's reply was that the post would be defended to the last extremity. The flag rode back and made a report. Forthwith the Hessians were seen at work throwing up a battery within half a mile of the outworks. It was finished by four o'clock, and opened a heavy cannonade, under cover of which the enemy were preparing to approach.

As the American outworks were but half finished and were too extensive to be manned by the garrison, it was determined by Greene and Duplessis that the troops should make but a short stand there, to gall the enemy in their approach, and then retire within the redoubt, which was defended by a deep intrenchment, boarded and fraised.

Donop led on his troops in gallant style under cover of a heavy fire from his battery. They advanced in two columns to attack the outworks in two places. As they advanced they were excessively galled by a flanking fire from the American galleys and batteries, and by sharp volleys from the outworks. The latter, however, as had been concerted, were quickly abandoned by the garrison. The enemy entered at two places, and imagining the day their own, the two columns pushed on with shouts to storm different parts of the redoubt. As yet no troops were to be seen; but as one of the columns approached the redoubt on the north side, a tremendous discharge of grape-shot and musketry burst forth from the embrasures in front, and a half-masked battery on the left. The slaughter was prodigious; the column was driven back in confusion. Count Donop, with the other column, in attempting the south side of the redoubt, had passed the abatis when a similar tempest of artillery and musketry burst upon them. Some were killed on the spot, many were wounded, and the rest were driven out. Donop himself received a mortal wound; Lieutenant-colonel Mingerode, the second in command, was also dangerously wounded. Several other of the best officers were slain or disabled. The troops retreated in confusion, hotly pursued, and were again cut up in their retreat by the flanking fire from the galleys and floating batteries. The loss of the enemy in killed and wounded, in this brief but severe action, was about four hundred men; that of the Americans, eight killed and twenty-nine wounded.

According to the plan of the enemy, Fort Mifflin, opposite to Fort Mercer, was to have been attacked at the same time by water. The force employed was the Augusta of sixty-four guns, the Roebuck of forty-four, two frigates, the Merlin sloop of eighteen guns, and a galley. They forced their way through the lower line of chevaux-de-frise; but the Augusta and Merlin ran aground below the second line, and every effort to get them off proved fruitless. To divert attention from their situation, the other vessels drew as near to Fort Mifflin as they could, and opened a cannonade. They kept up a fire upon the fort throughout the evening, and recommenced it early in the morning, as did likewise the British batteries on the Pennsylvania shore; hoping that under cover of it the ships might be got off. A strong adverse wind, however, kept the tide from rising sufficiently to float them.

The Americans discovered their situation, and sent down four fire-ships to destroy them, but without effect. A heavy fire was now opened upon them, from the galleys and floating batteries. It was warmly returned. In the course of the action, a red-hot shot set the Augusta on fire. It was impossible to check the flames. She blew up while the second lieutenant, the chaplain, the gunner, and several of the crew were yet on board, most of whom perished. The Merlin was now set on fire and abandoned; the Roebuck and the other vessels dropped down the river, and the attack on Fort Mifflin was given up.

These signal repulses of the enemy had an animating effect on the public mind, and were promptly noticed by Congress. Colonel Greene, who commanded at Fort Mercer, Lieutenant-colonel Smith of Maryland, who commanded at Fort Mifflin, and Commodore Hazelwood, who commanded the galleys, received the thanks of that body; and subsequently, a sword was voted to each, as a testimonial of distinguished merit.

We have heretofore had occasion to advert to the annoyances and perplexities occasioned to Washington by the claims and pretensions of foreign officers who had entered into the service. Among the officers who came out with Lafayette, was the Baron De Kalb, a German by birth, but who had long been employed in the French service, and though a silver-haired veteran, sixty years of age, was yet fresh and active and vigorous. In the month of September, Congress had given him the commission of major-general, to date with that of Lafayette.

This instantly produced a remonstrance from Brigadier-general Conway, who considered himself slighted and forgot, in their giving a superior rank to his own to a person who had not rendered the cause the least service, and who had been his inferior in France. He claimed, therefore, for himself the rank of major-general, and was supported in his pretensions by persons both in and out of Congress; especially by Mifflin, the quartermaster-general.

Washington had already been disgusted by the overweening presumption of Conway, and was surprised to hear that his application was likely to be successful. He wrote on the 17th of October to Richard Henry Lee, then in Congress, warning him that such an appointment would be as unfortunate a measure as ever was adopted. "I would ask," writes he, "why the youngest brigadier in the service should be put over the heads of the oldest, and thereby take rank and command of gentlemen who but yesterday were his seniors?... This truth I am well assured of that they will not serve under him. I leave you to guess, therefore, at the situation this army would be in at so important a crisis, if this event should take place."

This opposition to his presumptuous aspirations at once threw Conway into a faction forming under the auspices of General Mifflin. This gentleman had recently tendered his resignation of the commission of major-general and quartermaster-general on the plea of ill health, but was busily engaged in intrigues against the commander-in-chief, towards whom he had long cherished a secret hostility. Conway now joined with him heart and hand, and soon became so active and prominent a member of the faction that it acquired the name of *Conway's Cabal*. The object was to depreciate the military character of Washington, in comparison with that of Gates, to whom was attributed the whole success of the Northern campaign.

Gates was perfectly ready for such an elevation. In fact, in the excitement of his vanity, he appears to have forgotten that there was a commander-in-chief, to whom he was accountable. He neglected to send him any despatch on the subject of the surrender of Burgoyne, contenting himself with sending one to Congress, then sitting at Yorktown. Washington was left to hear of the important event by casual rumor, until he received a copy of the capitulation in a letter from General Putnam.

Gates was equally neglectful to inform him of the disposition he intended to make of the army under his command. He delayed even to forward Morgan's rifle corps, though their services were no longer needed in his camp, and were so much required in the South. It was determined, therefore, in a council of war, that one of Washington's staff should be sent to Gates to represent the critical state of affairs. Colonel Alexander Hamilton, his youthful but intelligent aide-de-camp, was charged with this mission. He bore a letter from Washington to Gates, dated October 30th, of which the following is an extract: "By this opportunity I do myself the pleasure to congratulate you on the signal success of the army under your command.... At the same time, I cannot but regret that a matter of such magnitude, and so interesting to our general operations, should have reached me by report only; or through the channel of letters not bearing that authenticity which the importance of it required, and which it would have received by a line under your signature stating the simple fact." Such was the calm and dignified notice of an instance of official disrespect, almost amounting to insubordination. It is doubtful whether Gates, in his state of mental effervescence, felt the noble severity of the rebuke.

A fortuitous circumstance, which we shall explain hereafter, apprised Washington about this time that a correspondence, derogatory to his military character and conduct was going on between General Conway and General Gates. Washington conducted himself with dignified forbearance, contenting himself with letting Conway know, by the following brief note, dated November 9th, that his correspondence was detected:

> "Sir—A letter which I received last night contained the following paragraph—'In a letter from General Conway to General Gates, he says: *Heaven has determined to save your country, or a weak general and bad counsellors would have ruined it.*'"

"I am, sir, your humble servant,

«George Washington."

The brevity of this note rendered it the more astounding. It was a hand-grenade thrown into the midst of the cabal. The effect upon other members we shall show hereafter: it seems, at first, to have prostrated Conway. He immediately sent in his resignation. It was not, however, accepted by Congress; on the contrary he was supported by the cabal, and was advanced to further honors, which we shall specify hereafter. In the meantime, the cabal went on to make invidious comparisons between the achievements of the two armies, deeply derogatory to that under Washington. Publicly, he took no notice of them.

The non-arrival of reinforcements from the Northern army continued to embarrass Washington's operations. The enemy were making preparations for further attempts upon Forts Mercer and Mifflin. General Howe was constructing redoubts and batteries on Province Island, on the west side of the Delaware, within five hundred yards of Fort Mifflin, and mounting them with heavy cannon. Washington consulted with his general officers what was to be done. Had the army received the expected reinforcements from the North, it might have detached sufficient force to the west side of the Schuylkill to dislodge the enemy from Province Island; but at present it would require almost the whole of the army for the purpose. This would leave the public stores at Easton, Bethlehem and Allentown, uncovered, as well as several of the hospitals. It would also leave the post at Red Bank unsupported, through which Fort Mifflin was reinforced and supplied. It was determined, therefore, to await the arrival of the expected reinforcements from the North, before making any alteration in the disposition of the army. In the meantime, the garrisons of Forts Mercer and Mifflin were increased, and General Varnum was stationed at Red Bank with his brigade, to be at hand to render reinforcements to either of them as occasion might require.

On the 10th of November, General Howe commenced a heavy fire upon Fort Mifflin from his batteries, which mounted eighteen, twenty-four, and thirty-two pounders. Major Fleury acquitted himself with intelligence and spirit as engineer; but an incessant cannonade and bombardment for several days, defied all repairs. The block-houses were demolished, the palisades beaten down, the guns dismounted, the barracks reduced to ruins. Captain Treat, a young officer of great merit, who commanded the artillery, was killed, as were several non-commissioned officers and privates; and a number were wounded. The survivors, who were not wounded, were exhausted by want of sleep, hard duty, and constant exposure to the rain. Colonel Smith himself was disabled by severe contusions, and obliged to retire to Red Bank.

The fort was in ruins; there was danger of its being carried by storm, but the gallant Fleury thought it might yet be defended with the aid of fresh troops. Such were furnished from Varnum's brigade: Lieutenant-colonel Russell, of the Connecticut line, replaced Colonel Smith. He in his turn was obliged to relinquish the command through fatigue and ill health, and was succeeded by Major Thayer of Rhode Island, aided by Captain (afterwards commodore) Talbot. On the fourth day the enemy brought a large Indiaman, cut down to a floating battery, to bear upon the works; but though it opened a terrible fire, it was silenced before night. The next day several ships-of-war got within gunshot. Two prepared to attack it in front; others brought their guns to bear on Fort Mercer; while two made their way into the narrow channel between Mud Island and the Pennsylvania shore, to operate with the British batteries erected there.

At a concerted signal a cannonade was opened from all quarters. The heroic little garrison stood the fire without flinching; the danger, however, was growing imminent. The batteries on Province Island enfiladed the works. The ships in the inner channel approached so near as to throw hand-grenades into the fort, while marines stationed in the round-tops stood ready to pick off any of the garrison that came in sight. The scene now became awful; incessant firing from ships, forts, gondolas and floating batteries, with clouds of sulphurous smoke, and the deafening thunder of cannon. Before night there was hardly a fortification to defend; palisades were shivered, guns dismounted, the whole parapet levelled. There was terrible slaughter; most of the company of artillery were destroyed; Fleury himself was wounded. Captain Talbot received a wound in the wrist, but continued bravely fighting until disabled by another wound in the hip.

To hold out longer was impossible. Colonel Thayer made preparations to evacuate the fort in the night. Everything was removed in the evening that could be conveyed away without too much exposure to the murderous fire from the round-tops. The wounded were taken over to Red Bank, accompanied by part of the garrison. Thayer remained with forty men until eleven o'clock, when they set fire to what was combustible of the fort they had so nobly defended, and crossed to Red Bank by the light of its flames.

The loss of this fort was deeply regretted by Washington, though he gave high praise to the officers and men of the garrison. Colonel Smith was voted a sword by Congress, and Fleury received the commission of lieutenant-colonel. Washington still hoped to keep possession of Red Bank, and thereby prevent the enemy from weighing the chevaux-de-frise before the frost obliged their ships to quit the river. "I am anxiously waiting the arrival of the troops from the northward," writes he, "who ought, from the time they have had my orders to have been here before this. Colonel Hamilton, one of my aides, is up the North River, doing all he can to push them forward, but he writes me word that he finds many unaccountable delays thrown in his way. The want of these troops has embarrassed all my measures exceedingly."

The delays in question will best be explained by a few particulars concerning the mission of Colonel Hamilton. [Hamilton had expected to find matters in such a train that he would have little to do but hurry on ample reinforcements already on the march; but he soon discovered that it was designed to retain the greater part of the Northern army at Albany and in the Highlands, sparing only about four thousand men to the commander-in-chief. Morgan and his riflemen had been tardily detached, he having met them on the march near New Windsor on the morning of November 2d. Putnam, he found, was busy with the project of an attack on New York; and Gates was full of reasons why more troops should not be despatched southward, claiming that there was no certainty that Sir Henry Clinton had gone to join Howe, and that there was a possibility of his returning up the river. If his army were depleted, Albany would be exposed, New England left open to the ravages of the enemy, and his own contemplated movement against Ticonderoga abandoned. It was with the greatest difficulty that Hamilton induced Gates to detach the brigades of Poor and Patterson to the aid of the commander-in-chief. Washington would not have received a man, he declared, if the whole could have been kept at Albany with any decency. Governor Clinton, Hamilton found, was the only general officer who appreciated Washington's position, and disposed to promote the general good, independent of personal considerations. Putnam who, unlike Gates, was innocent of intrigues against the commander-in-chief, was still so bent upon his favorite scheme of an attack on New York, that only Hamilton's positive orders, as from Washington, to send the Continental troops under him southward, retaining the militia, brought the bellicose veteran to a reluctant compliance. Washington, in a letter to Putnam, reprimanded his tardiness, concluding with, "I could wish that in future my orders may be immediately complied with, without arguing upon the propriety of them." The intrigues in progress around him made it necessary for Washington at this moment to assert his superior command, although he acquitted Putnam of any part in them.]

In the meantime, Sir William Howe was following up the reduction of Fort Mifflin by an expedition against Fort Mercer, which still impeded the navigation of the Delaware. On the 17th of November, Lord Cornwallis was detached with two thousand men to cross from Chester into the Jerseys, where he would be joined by a force advancing from New York. Apprised of this movement, Washington detached General Huntington with a brigade, to join Varnum at Red Bank. General Greene was also ordered to repair thither with his division, and an express was sent off to General Glover who was on his way through the Jerseys with his brigade, directing him to file off to the left towards the same point. These troops, with such militia as could be collected, Washington hoped would be sufficient to save the fort. Before they could form a junction, however, and reach their destination, Cornwallis appeared before it. A defence against such superior force was hopeless. The works were abandoned; they were taken possession of by the enemy who proceeded to destroy them. After the destruction had been accomplished, the reinforcements from the North, so long and so anxiously expected, and so shamefully delayed, made their appearance. "Had they arrived but ten days sooner," writes Washington to his brother, "it would, I think, have put it in my power to save Fort Mifflin, which defended the chevaux-de-frise, and consequently have rendered Philadelphia a very ineligible situation for the enemy this winter."

The evil which Washington had so anxiously striven to prevent had now been effected. The American vessels stationed in the river had lost all protection. Some of the galleys escaped past the batteries of Philadelphia in a fog, and took refuge in the upper part of the Delaware; the rest were set on fire by their crews and abandoned. Washington advised the navy board, now that the enemy had the command of the river, to have all the American frigates scuttled and sunk immediately. The board objected to sinking them, but said they should be ballasted and plugged, ready to be sunk in case of attack. Washington warned them that an attack would be sudden, so as to get possession of them before they could be sunk or destroyed;—his advice and warning were unheeded; the consequence will hereafter be shown.

CHAPTER XLVIII.

THE ARMY ON THE SCHUYLKILL.—AT VALLEY FORGE.—THE CONWAY CABAL.

On the evening of the 24th of November Washington reconnoitred, carefully and thoughtfully, the lines and defences about Philadelphia, from the opposite side of the Schuylkill. His army was now considerably reinforced; the garrison was weakened by the absence of a large body of troops under Lord Cornwallis in the Jerseys. Some of the general officers thought this an advantageous moment for an attack upon the city. Such was the opinion of Lord Stirling, and especially of General Wayne, Mad Anthony, as he was familiarly called, always eager for some daring enterprise. The recent victory at Saratoga had dazzled the public mind and produced a general impatience for something equally striking and effective in this quarter. With an anxious eye Washington scrutinized the enemy's works. They appeared to be exceeding strong. A chain of redoubts extended along the most commanding ground from the Schuylkill to the Delaware. They were framed, planked, and of great thickness, and were surrounded by a deep ditch, enclosed and fraised. The intervals were filled with an abatis, in constructing which all the apple trees of the neighborhood, beside forest trees, had been sacrificed.

The idea of Lord Stirling and those in favor of an attack was, that it should be at different points at daylight; the main body to attack the lines to the north of the city, while Greene, embarking his men in boats at Dunk's Ferry, and passing down the Delaware, and Potter, with a body of Continentals and militia, moving down the west side of the Schuylkill, should attack the eastern and western fronts. Washington saw that there was an opportunity for a brilliant blow, that might satisfy the impatience of the public, but he saw that it must be struck at the expense of a fearful loss of life.

Returning to camp, he held a council of war of his principal officers, in which the matter was debated at great length and with some warmth, but without coming to a decision. At breaking up, Washington requested that each member of the council would give his opinion the next morning in writing, and he sent off a messenger in the night for the written opinion of General Greene.

Only four members of the council, Stirling, Wayne, Scott and Woodford, were in favor of an attack; of which Lord Stirling drew up the plan. Eleven (including Greene) were against it, objecting, among other things, that the enemy's lines were too strong and too well supported, and their force too numerous, well disciplined and experienced, to be assailed without great loss and the hazard of a failure. Had

Washington been actuated by mere personal ambition and a passion for military fame, he might have disregarded the loss and hazarded the failure; but his patriotism was superior to his ambition; he shrank from a glory that must be achieved at such a cost, and the idea of an attack was abandoned.

A letter from General Greene received about this time, gave Washington some gratifying intelligence about his youthful friend, the Marquis de Lafayette. Though not quite recovered from the wound received at the battle of Brandywine, he had accompanied General Greene as a volunteer in his expedition into the Jerseys, and had been indulged by him with an opportunity of gratifying his belligerent humor, in a brush with Cornwallis' outposts. "The marquis," writes Greene, "with about four hundred militia and the rifle corps, attacked the enemy's picket last evening killed about twenty, wounded many more, and took about twenty prisoners. The marquis is charmed with the spirited behavior of the militia and rifle corps.... The marquis is determined to be in the way of danger."

Washington had repeatedly written to Congress in favor of giving the marquis a command equal to his nominal rank. He availed himself of the present occasion to support his former recommendations, by transmitting to Congress an account of Lafayette's youthful exploit. He received, in return, an intimation from that body, that it was their pleasure he should appoint the marquis to the command of a division in the Continental army. The division of General Stephen at this time was vacant; that veteran officer, who had formerly won honor for himself in the French war, having been dismissed for misconduct at the battle of Germantown, the result of intemperate habits, into which he unfortunately had fallen. Lafayette was forthwith appointed to the command of that division.

At this juncture (November 27th), a modification took place in the Board of War, indicative of the influence which was operating in Congress. It was increased from three to five members: General Mifflin, Joseph Trumbull, Richard Peters, Colonel Pickering, and last, though certainly not least, General Gates. Mifflin's resignation of the commission of quartermaster-general had recently been accepted; but that of major-general was continued to him, though without pay. General Gates was appointed president of the board, and the President of Congress was instructed to express to him, in communicating the intelligence, the high sense which that body entertained of his abilities and peculiar fitness to discharge the duties of that important office, upon the right execution of which the success of the American cause so eminently depended; and to inform him it was their intention to continue his rank as major-general, and that he might officiate at the board or in the field, as occasion might require; furthermore, that he should repair to Congress with all convenient despatch to enter upon the duties of his appointment. It was evidently the idea of the cabal that Gates was henceforth to be the master-spirit of the war.

While busy faction was at work, both in and out of Congress, to undermine the fame and authority of Washington, General Howe, according to his own threat, was preparing to "drive him beyond the mountains."

On the 4th of December, Captain Allen McLane, a vigilant officer already mentioned, of the Maryland line, brought word to head-quarters that an attack was to be made that very night on the camp at White Marsh. Washington made his dispositions to receive the meditated assault, and, in the meantime, detached Mc-Lane with one hundred men to reconnoitre. The latter met the van of the enemy about eleven o'clock at night, on the Germantown Road; attacked it at the Three Mile Run, forced it to change its line of march, and hovered about and impeded it throughout the night. About three o'clock in the morning the alarm-gun announced the approach of the enemy. They appeared at daybreak, and encamped on Chestnut Hill, within three miles of Washington's right wing. Brigadier-general James Irvine, with six hundred of the Pennsylvania militia, was sent out to skirmish with their light advanced parties. He encountered them at the foot of the hill, but after a short conflict, in which several were killed and wounded, his troops gave way and fled in all directions, leaving him and four or five of his men wounded on the field, who were taken prisoners.

General Howe passed the day in reconnoitring, and at night changed his ground, and moved to a hill on the left, and within a mile of the American line. It was his wish to have a general action; but to have it on advantageous terms. He had scrutinized Washington's position and pronounced it inaccessible. For three days he manoeuvred to draw him from it, shifting his own position occasionally, but still keeping on advantageous ground. Washington was not to be decoyed. He knew the vast advantages which superior science, discipline and experience gave the enemy in open field fight, and remained within his lines. All his best officers approved of his policy. Several sharp skirmishes occurred at Edge Hill and elsewhere, in which Morgan's riflemen and the Maryland militia were concerned. There was loss on both sides, but the Americans gave way before a great superiority of numbers.

On the 7th there was every appearance that Howe meditated an attack on the left wing. Washington's heart now beat high, and he prepared for a warm and decisive action. In the course of the day he rode through every brigade, giving directions how the attack was to be met, and exhorting his troops to depend mainly on the bayonet. The day wore away with nothing but skirmishes, in which Morgan's riflemen, and the Maryland militia under Colonel Gist, rendered good service. An attack was expected in the night, or early in the morning; but no attack took place. The spirit manifested by the Americans in their recent contests had rendered the British commanders cautious.

The next day in the afternoon, the enemy were again in motion; but instead of advancing, filed off to the left, halted and lit up a long string of fires on the heights; behind which they retreated, silently and precipitately, in the night. By the time Washington received intelligence of their movement they were in full march by two or three routes for Philadelphia. He immediately detached light parties to fall upon their rear, but they were too far on the way for any but light-horse to overtake them.

Here then was another occasion of which the enemies of Washington availed themselves to deride his cautious policy. Yet it was clearly dictated by true wisdom. His heart yearned for a general encounter with the enemy. In his despatch to the President of Congress, he writes, "I sincerely wish that they had made an attack; as the issue, in all probability, from the disposition of our troops and the strong situation of our camp, would have been fortunate and happy. At the same time I must add, that reason, prudence, and every principle of policy forbade us from quitting our post to attack them. Nothing but success would have justified the measure, and this could not be expected from their position."

At this time, one of the earliest measures recommended by the Board of War, and adopted by Congress, showed the increasing influence of the cabal; two inspectors-general were to be appointed for the promotion of discipline and reformation of abuses in the army; and one of the persons chosen for this important office was Conway, with the rank, too, of major-general! This was tacitly in defiance of the opinion so fully expressed by Washington of the demerits of the man, and the ruinous effects to be apprehended from his promotion over the heads of brigadiers of superior claims. Conway, however, was the secret colleague of Gates, and Gates was now the rising sun.

Winter had now set in with all its severity. The troops, worn down by long and hard service, had need of repose. Poorly clad, also, and almost destitute of blankets, they required a warmer shelter than mere tents against the inclemencies of the season. The nearest towns which would afford winter-quarters, were Lancaster, York and Carlisle; but should the army retire to either of these, a large and fertile district would be exposed to be foraged by the foe, and its inhabitants, perhaps, to be dragooned into submission. The plan adopted by Washington, after holding a council of war, and weighing the discordant opinions of his officers, was to hut the army for the winter at Valley Forge, in Chester County, on the west side of the Schuylkill, about twenty miles from Philadelphia. Here he would be able to keep a vigilant eye on that city, and at the same time protect a great extent of country.

Sad and dreary was the march to Valley Forge, uncheered by the recollection of any recent triumph, as was the march to winter-quarters in the preceding year. Hungry and cold were the poor fellows who had so long been keeping the field, for provisions were scant, clothing worn out, and so badly off were they for shoes, that the footsteps of many might be tracked in blood. Yet at this very time we are told, "hogsheads of shoes, stockings and clothing, were lying at different places on the roads and in the woods, perishing for want of teams, or of money to pay the teamsters."

Such were the consequences of the derangement of the commissariat. Washington wrote to the President of Congress on the subject: "I do not know from what cause this alarming deficiency, or rather total failure of supplies arises; but unless more vigorous exertions and better regulations take place in that line (the commissaries' department) immediately, the army must dissolve. I have done all in my power by remonstrating, by writing, by ordering the commissaries on this head, from time to time, but without any good effect, or obtaining more than a present scanty relief."

Scarce had Washington despatched this letter, when he learnt that the Legislature of Pennsylvania had addressed a remonstrance to Congress against his going into winter-quarters, instead of keeping in the open field. This letter, received in his forlorn situation, surrounded by an unhoused, scantily clad, half-starved army, shivering in the midst of December's snow and cold, put an end to his forbearance, and drew from him another letter to the President of Congress, dated on the 23d, which we shall largely quote, not only for its manly and truthful eloquence, but for the exposition it gives of the difficulties of his situation, mainly caused by unwise and intermeddling legislation.

And first as to the commissariat:—

"Though I have been tender, heretofore," writes he, "of giving any opinion, or lodging complaints, as the change in that department took place contrary to my judgment, and the consequences thereof were predicted, yet finding that the inactivity of the army, whether for want of provisions, clothes, or other essentials, is charged to my account, not only by the common vulgar, but by those in power, it is time to speak plain in exculpation of myself. With truth then, I can declare, that no man, in my opinion, ever had his measures more impeded than I have by every department of the army. Since the month of July we have had no assistance from the quartermaster-general; and to want of assistance from this department, the commissary-general charges great part of his deficiency.... As a proof of the little benefit received from a clothier-general, and as a further proof of the inability of an army, under the circumstances of this, to perform the common duties of soldiers (besides a number of men confined to hospitals for want of shoes, and others in farmers' houses on the same account), we have, by a field return this day made, no less than two thousand eight hundred and ninety-eight men now in camp unfit for duty, because they are barefoot, and otherwise naked. By the same return, it appears that our whole strength in Continental troops, including the eastern brigades, which have joined us since the surrender of General Burgoyne, exclusive of the Maryland troops sent to Wilmington, amounts to no more than eight thousand two hundred in camp fit for duty; notwithstanding which, and that since the 4th instant, our numbers fit for duty, from the hardships and exposures they have undergone, particularly on account of blankets, have decreased near two thousand men.

"We find gentlemen, without knowing whether the army was really going into winter-quarters or not (for I am sure no resolution of mine could warrant the remonstrance), reprobating the measure as much as if they thought the soldiers were made of stocks or stones, and equally insensible of frost and snow; and moreover, as if they conceived it easily practicable for an inferior army, under the disadvantages I have described ours to be—which are by no means exaggerated—to confine a superior one, in all respects well appointed and provided for a winter's campaign, within the city of Philadelphia, and to cover from depredation and waste the States of Pennsylvania and Jersey.... I can assure those gentlemen that it is a much easier and less distressing thing to draw remonstrances in a comfortable room by a good fireside, than to occupy a cold, bleak hill, and sleep under frost and snow, without clothes or blankets. However, although they seem to have little feeling for the naked and distressed soldiers, I feel abundantly for them, and, from my soul, I pity those miseries, which it is neither in my power to relieve nor prevent."

In the present exigency to save his camp from desolation and to relieve his starving soldiery, he was compelled to exercise the authority recently given him by Congress, to forage the country round, seize supplies wherever he could find them, and pay for them in money or in certificates redeemable by Congress. He exercised these powers with great reluctance. He was apprehensive of irritating the jealousy of military sway, prevalent throughout the country, and of corrupting the morals of the army.

We here close Washington's operations for 1777; one of the most arduous and eventful years of his military life, and one of the most trying to his character and fortunes. He began it with an empty army chest, and a force dwindled down to four thousand half-disciplined men. Throughout the year he had had to contend, not merely with the enemy, but with the parsimony and meddlesome interference of Congress. In his most critical times that body had left him without funds and without reinforcements. It had made promotions contrary to his advice and contrary to military usage; thereby wronging and disgusting some of his bravest officers. It had changed the commissariat in the very midst of a campaign, and thereby thrown the whole service into confusion.

Among so many cross-purposes and discouragements, it was a difficult task for Washington to "keep the life and soul of the army together." Yet he had done so. Marvellous indeed was the manner in which he had soothed the discontents of his aggrieved officers, and reconciled them to an ill-requiting service; and still more marvellous the manner in which he had breathed his own spirit of patience and perseverance in his yeoman soldiery, during their sultry marchings and countermarchings through the Jerseys, under all kinds of privations, with no visible object of pursuit to stimulate their ardor, hunting, as it were, the rumored apparitions of an unseen fleet.

The same machinations which were so successful in displacing the noble-hearted Schuyler from the head of the Northern department, were now at work to undermine the commander-in-chief, and elevate the putative hero of Saratoga on his ruins. He was painfully aware of them; yet in no part of the war did he more thoroughly evince that magnanimity which was his grand characteristic, than in the last scenes of this campaign, where he rose above the tauntings of the press, the sneerings of the cabal, the murmurs of the public, the suggestions of some of his friends, and the throbbing impulses of his own courageous heart, and adhered to that Fabian policy which he considered essential to the safety of the cause. To dare is often the impulse of selfish ambition or harebrained valor: to forbear is at times the proof of real greatness.

While censure and detraction had dogged Washington throughout his harassing campaign, Gates was the constant theme of popular eulogium, and was held up by the cabal as the only one capable of retrieving the desperate fortunes of the South. Letters from his friends in Congress urged him to hasten on, take his seat at the head of the Board of War, assume the management of military affairs, and *save the country!* Gates was not a strong-minded man. Is it a wonder, then, that his brain should be bewildered by the fumes of incense offered up on every side. In the midst of his triumph, however, while feasting on the sweets of adulation, came the withering handwriting on the wall! It is an epistle from his friend Mifflin. "My dear General," writes he, "an extract from Conway's letter to you has been procured and sent to head-quarters.... General Washington enclosed it to Conway without remarks."

Nothing could surpass the trouble and confusion of mind of Gates on the perusal of this letter. Part of his correspondence with Conway had been sent to head-quarters. But what part? What was the purport and extent of the alleged extracts. How had they been obtained? Who had sent them? Mifflin's letter specified nothing; and this silence as to particulars left an unbounded field for tormenting conjecture. In fact, Mifflin knew nothing in particular when he wrote; nor did any of the cabal. The laconic nature of Washington's note to Conway had thrown them all in confusion. None knew the extent of the correspondence discovered, nor how far they might be individually compromised.

Gates, in his perplexity, suspected that his portfolio had been stealthily opened and his letters copied. But which of them?—and by whom? He wrote to Conway and Mifflin, anxiously inquiring what part of their correspondence had been thus surreptitiously obtained, and made rigid inquiries among the gentlemen of his staff. All disavowed any knowledge of the matter. In this state of mental trepidation, Gates wrote, on the 8th of December, a letter to Washington, [in which, after speaking of his disagreeable situation in discovering his confidential letters exposed to public inspection, he urged Washington to give him his aid in "tracing the author of the infidelity," and asserting that it was in Washington's power to do him and the United States an important service by detecting a wretch "who may betray me, and capitally injure the very operations under your immediate directions." He concluded by announcing his intention of forwarding a copy of his letter to the president, "that the Congress may, in concert with your Excellency, obtain as soon as possible a discovery which so deeply affects the safety of the States."

Washington's reply was characterized with his usual dignity and candor. After expressing his surprise that a copy of Gates' letter should have been sent to Congress, and asserting that he was thereby laid under the necessity of returning his answer through the same body, he proceeds to state that Colonel Wilkinson, in the month of October last, fell in with Major McWilliams, aide-de-camp to Lord Stirling, and informed him, not in confidence, that General Conway had written to Gates as follows: "Heaven has been determined to save your country, or a weak general and bad counsellors would have ruined it." Washington then adds that this circumstance had not been communicated to any officer in the army except Lafayette, to whom it was shown under injunctions of secrecy, so desirous was he of concealing every matter that "could interrupt the tranquillity of the army, or afford a gleam of hope to the enemy by dissensions therein." He concludes by declaring that he considered the information as coming from Gates, given with a view to forewarn and forearm him against a dangerous incendiary, "in which character sooner or later this country will know General Conway."]

Gates was disposed to mark his advent to power by a striking operation. A notable project had been concerted by him and the Board of War for a winter irruption into Canada. An expedition was to proceed from Albany, cross Lake Champlain on the ice, burn the British shipping at St. Johns, and press forward to Montreal. Washington was not consulted in the matter: the project was submitted to Congress, and sanctioned by them without his privity. One object of the scheme was to detach the Marquis de Lafayette from Washington, to whom he was devotedly attached, and bring him into the interests of the cabal. For this purpose he was to have the command of the expedition; an appointment which it was thought would tempt his military ambition. Conway was to be second in command, and it was trusted that his address and superior intelligence would virtually make him the leader.

The first notice that Washington received of the project was in a letter from Gates, enclosing one to Lafayette, informing the latter of his appointment, and requiring his attendance at Yorktown to receive his instructions. Gates, in his letter to Washington, asked his opinion and advice; evidently as a matter of form. The latter expressed himself obliged by the "polite request," but observed that, as he neither knew the extent of the objects in view, nor the means to be employed to effect them, it was not in his power to pass any judgment upon the subject. The cabal overshot their mark. Lafayette, who was aware of their intrigues, was so disgusted by the want of deference and respect to the commander-in-chief evinced in the whole proceeding, that he would at once have declined the appointment had not Washington himself advised him strongly to accept it. [The project was never carried out. Lafayette, still having a favorable opinion of Conway's military talents, was aware of the game he was playing, and succeeded in getting De Kalb appointed to the expedition, whose commission being of older date, would give him the precedence of that officer. When Lafayette arrived at Albany it was soon found that the contemplated irruption was not practicable. Schuyler, Lincoln, and Arnold all opposed it. Instead of twenty-five hundred men which had been promised Lafayette, not twelve hundred in all were found to be fit for duty, and these shrinking from a winter incursion into so cold a country. Stark, who was to have joined the expedition, was disinclined. Enlistments could not be made for want of money, or the means of offering other inducements. The project, in view of the numerous discouragements and difficulties, was at length formally suspended by a resolve of Congress.]

Washington's letter of the 4th of January, on the subject of the Conway correspondence, had not reached General Gates until the 22d of January, after his arrival at Yorktown. No sooner did Gates learn from its context that all Washington's knowledge of that correspondence was confined to a single paragraph of a letter, and that merely as quoted in conversation by Wilkinson, than the whole matter appeared easily to be explained or shuffled off. He accordingly took pen in hand, and addressed Washington as follows, on the 22d of January: "The letter which I had the honor to receive yesterday from your Excellency, has relieved me from unspeakable uneasiness. I now anticipate the pleasure it will give you when you discover that what has been conveyed to you for an extract of General Conway's letter to me, was not an information which friendly motives induced a man of honor to give, that injured virtue might be forearmed against secret enemies. The paragraph which your Excellency has condescended to transcribe, is spurious. It was certainly fabricated to answer the most selfish and wicked purposes." He then goes on to declare that the genuine letter of Conway was perfectly harmless, containing judicious remarks upon the want of discipline in the army, but making no mention of weak generals or bad counsellors.

General Conway, also, in a letter to Washington (dated January 27th), informs him that the letter had been returned to him by Gates, and that he found with great satisfaction that "the paragraph so much spoken of did not exist in the said letter, nor anything like it." He had intended, he adds, to publish the letter, but had been dissuaded by President Laurens and two or three members of Congress, to whom he had shown it, lest it should inform the enemy of a misunderstanding among the American generals. He therefore depended upon the justice, candor, and generosity of General Washington to put a stop to the forgery.

On the 9th of February, Washington wrote Gates a long and searching reply to his letters of the 8th and 23d of January, analyzing them, and showing how, in spirit and import, they contradicted each other; and how sometimes the same letter contradicted itself. How, in the first letter, the reality of the extracts was by implication allowed, and the only solicitude shown was to find out the person who brought them to light; while, in the second letter, the whole was pronounced, "in word as well as in substance, a wicked forgery." "It is not my intention," observes Washington, "to contradict this assertion, but only to intimate some considerations which tend to induce a supposition that, though none of General Conway's letters to you contained the offensive passage mentioned, there might have been something in them too nearly related to it, that could give such an extraordinary alarm. If this were not the case, how easy in the first instance to have declared there was nothing exceptionable in them, and to have produced the letters themselves in support of it?"[13]

---

[13] The Conway letter proved a further source of trouble to the cabal. Wilkinson learning that Gates had denounced him as the betrayer of the letter, and spoken of him in the grossest language, wrote to Gates demanding honorable reparation. They met, however, and the explanations of Gates appeased Wilkinson for the time, who now turned to Lord Stirling as the betrayer of his confidence, asserting that he should "bleed for his conduct." But in this case, as in the other, Wilkinson's irritable honor was easily pacified. Lord Stirling having admitted, according to Wilkinson's request, that the disclosure in question "occurred in a private company during a convivial hour." Subsequently Wilkinson was shown, by Washington, Gates' letter, in which the extract from Conway's letter was pronounced a forgery. Wilkinson, who was secretary of the Board of War, of which Gates was president, now resigned his office, compelled to it, as he said, "by the acts of treachery and falsehood in which he had detected Major-general Gates." Wilkinson, as bearer of the news of the capture of Burgoyne to Congress, had been rewarded by promotion to the rank of brigadier-general. This was protested against by a large number of colonels, whereupon Wilkinson resigned, and withdrew from the army.

CHAPTER XLIX.

EXPLOITS OF LEE AND LAFAYETTE.—BRITISH COMMISSIONERS.

During the winter's encampment at Valley Forge, Washington sedulously applied himself to the formation of a new system for the army. At his earnest solicitation, Congress appointed a committee of five, called the Committee of Arrangement, to repair to the camp and assist him in the task.[14] Before their arrival he had collected the written opinions and suggestions of his officers on the subject, and from these, and his own observations and experience, had prepared a document exhibiting the actual state of the army, the defects of previous systems, and the alterations and reforms that were necessary. The committee remained three months with him in camp, and then made a report to Congress founded on his statement. The reforms therein recommended were generally adopted.

In the meantime, the distresses of the army continued to increase. The surrounding country for a great distance was exhausted, and had the appearance of having been pillaged. The parties sent out to forage too often returned empty-handed. "For some days past there has been little less than a famine in the camp," writes Washington, on one occasion. "A part of the army has been a week without any kind of flesh, and the rest three or four days. Naked and starving as they are, we cannot enough admire the incomparable patience and fidelity of the soldiery, that they have not been, ere this, excited by their suffering to a general mutiny and desertion."

A British historian gives a striking picture of the indolence and luxury which reigned at the same time in the British army in Philadelphia. It is true the investment of the city by the Americans rendered provisions dear and fuel scanty, but the consequent privations were felt by the inhabitants, not by their invaders. The latter revelled as if in a conquered place. Private houses were occupied without rendering compensation; the officers were quartered on the principal inhabitants, many of whom were of the Society of "Friends." The quiet habits of the city were outraged by the dissolute habits of a camp. Gaming prevailed to a shameless degree. A foreign officer kept a faro bank, at which he made a fortune, and some of the young officers ruined themselves. "During the whole of this long winter of riot and dissipation," continues the same writer, "Washington was suffered to remain undisturbed at Valley Forge, with an army not exceeding five thousand effective

---

[14] Names of the committee—General Reed, Nathaniel Folsom, Francis Dana, Charles Carroll, and Gouverneur Morris.

men; and his cannon frozen up and immovable. A nocturnal attack might have forced him to a disadvantageous action or compelled him to a disastrous retreat."

On one occasion there was a flurry at the most advanced post, where Captain Henry Lee (Light-horse Harry) with a few of his troops was stationed. He had made himself formidable to the enemy by harassing their foraging parties. An attempt was made to surprise him. A party of about two hundred dragoons, taking a circuitous route in the night, came upon him by daybreak. He had but a few men with him at the time, and took post in a large store-house. His scanty force did not allow a soldier for each window. The dragoons attempted to force their way into the house. There was a warm contest. The dragoons were bravely repulsed, and sheered off, leaving two killed and four wounded.

Washington, whose heart evidently warmed to this young Virginian officer, not content with noticing his exploit in general orders, not long afterwards strongly recommended him for the command of two troops of horse, with the rank of major, to act as an independent partisan corps. "His genius," observes he, "particularly adapts him to a command of this nature; and it will be the most agreeable to him of any station in which he could be placed." It was a high gratification to Washington when Congress made this appointment; accompanying it with encomiums on Lee as a brave and prudent officer.

In the month of February, Mrs. Washington rejoined the general at Valley Forge, and took up her residence at head-quarters. The arrangements consequent on her arrival bespeak the simplicity of style in this rude encampment. "The general's apartment is very small," writes she to a friend; "he has had a log cabin built to dine in, which has made our quarters much more tolerable than they were at first." Lady Stirling, Mrs. Knox, the wife of the general, and the wives of other of the officers were also in the camp.

The reforms in the commissariat had begun to operate. Provisions arrived in considerable quantities; supplies, on their way to the Philadelphia market to load the British tables were intercepted and diverted into the hungry camp of the patriots; magazines were formed in Valley Forge; the threatened famine was averted; "grim-visaged war" gradually relaxed his features, and affairs in the encampment began to assume a more cheering aspect.

An important arrival in the camp was that of the Baron Steuben, towards the latter part of February. He was a seasoned soldier from the old battle fields of Europe; having served in the seven years' war, been aide-de-camp to the great Frederick, and connected with the quartermaster-general's department. Honors had been heaped upon him in Germany. After leaving the Prussian army he had been grand marshal of the court of the Prince of Hohenzollern-Hechingen, colonel in the circle of Suabia, lieutenant-general under the Prince Margrave of Baden, and knight of the Order of Fidelity; and he had declined liberal offers from the King of Sardinia and the Emperor of Austria. With an income of about three thousand dollars, chiefly arising from various appointments, he was living pleasantly in distinguished society at the German courts, and making occasional visits to Paris, when he was persuaded by the Count de St. Germain, French Minister of War, and others of the French cabinet, to come out to America, and engage in the cause they were preparing to befriend. Their object was to secure for the American armies the services of an officer of experience and a thorough disciplinarian. Through their persuasions he resigned his several offices, and came out at forty-eight years of age, a soldier of fortune, to the rude fighting grounds of America, to aid a half disciplined people in their struggle for liberty.

The baron had brought strong letters from Dr. Franklin and Mr. Deane, our envoys at Paris, and from the Count St. Germain. Landing in Portsmouth in New Hampshire, Dec. 1st, he had forwarded copies of his letters to Washington. By Washington's direction he had proceeded direct to Congress. His letters procured him a distinguished reception from the president. A committee was appointed to confer with him. He offered his services as a volunteer: making no condition for rank or pay, but trusting, should he prove himself worthy and the cause be crowned with success, he would be indemnified for the sacrifices he had made, and receive such further compensation as he might be thought to merit.

The committee having made their report, the baron's proffered services were accepted with a vote of thanks for his disinterestedness, and he was ordered to join the army at Valley Forge. That army, in its ragged condition and squalid quarters, presented a sorry aspect to a strict disciplinarian from Germany, accustomed to the order and appointments of European camps; and the baron often declared, that under such circumstances no army in Europe could be kept together for a single month. The liberal mind of Steuben, however, made every allowance; and Washington soon found in him a consummate soldier, free from pedantry or pretension.

The evils arising from a want of uniformity in discipline and manoeuvres throughout the army, had long caused Washington to desire a well organized inspectorship. He knew that the same desire was felt by Congress. Conway had been appointed to that office, but had never entered upon its duties. The baron appeared to be peculiarly well qualified for such a department; Washington determined, therefore, to set on foot a temporary institution of the kind. Accordingly he proposed to the baron to undertake the office of inspector-general. The latter cheerfully agreed. Two ranks of inspectors were appointed under him; the lowest to inspect brigades, the highest to superintend several of these.

In a little while the whole army was under drill; for a great part, made up of raw militia, scarcely knew the manual exercise. Many of the officers, too, knew little of manoeuvring, and the best of them had much to learn. The baron furnished his sub-inspectors with written instructions relative to their several functions. He took a company of soldiers under his immediate training, and after he had sufficiently schooled it, made it a model for the others, exhibiting the manoeuvres they had to practise. His discipline extended to their comforts. He inquired into their treatment by the officers. He examined the doctors' reports, visited the sick, and saw that they were well lodged and attended.

The strong good sense of the baron was evinced in the manner in which he adapted his tactics to the nature of the army and the situation of the country, instead of adhering with bigotry to the systems of Europe. His instructions were appreciated by all. The officers received them gladly and conformed to them. The men soon became active and adroit. The army gradually acquired a proper organization, and began to operate like a great machine; and Washington found in the baron an intelligent, disinterested, truthful coadjutor, well worthy of the badge he wore as a knight of the Order of *Fidelity*.

Another great satisfaction to Washington was the appointment by Congress (March 3d) of Greene to the office of quartermaster-general; still retaining his rank of major-general in the army. The confusion and derangement of this department during the late campaign, while filled by General Mifflin, had been a source of perpetual embarrassment. That officer, however capable of doing his duty, was hardly ever at hand. The line and the staff were consequently at variance; and the country was plundered in a way sufficient to breed a civil war between the staff and the inhabitants. Greene undertook the office with reluctance, and agreed to perform the military duties of it without compensation for the space of a year.

The spring opened without any material alteration in the dispositions of the armies. Washington at one time expected an attack upon his camp; but Sir William was deficient in the necessary enterprise; he contented himself with sending out parties which foraged the surrounding country for many miles, and scoured part of the Jerseys, bringing in considerable supplies. These forays were in some instances accompanied by wanton excesses and needless bloodshed. A ravaging party ascended the Delaware in flat-bottomed boats and galleys; set fire to public storehouses in Bordentown containing provisions and munitions of war; burnt two frigates, several privateers, and a number of vessels of various classes, some of them laden with military stores. Had the armed vessels been sunk according to the earnest advice of Washington, the greater part of them might have been saved.

A circular letter was sent by Washington on the 20th to all the general officers in camp, requesting their opinions in writing, which of three plans to adopt for the next campaign: to attempt the recovery of Philadelphia; to transfer the war to the north and make an attempt on New York; or to remain quiet in a secure and fortified camp, disciplining and arranging the army until the enemy should begin their operations; then to be governed by circumstances.

Just after the issue of this circular, intelligence received from Congress showed that the ascendency of the cabal was at an end. By a resolution of that body on the 15th, Gates was directed to resume the command of the Northern department, and to proceed forthwith to Fishkill for that purpose. He was invested with powers for completing the works on the Hudson,[15] and authorized to carry on operations against the enemy should any favorable opportunity offer, for which purposes he might call for the artificers and militia of New York and the Eastern States: but he was not to undertake any expedition against New York without previously consulting the commander-in-chief. Washington was requested to assemble a council of major-generals to determine upon a plan of operations, and Gates and Mifflin,

[15] The Highlands had been carefully reconnoitred in the course of the winter by Putnam, Gov. Clinton, James Clinton, and several others, and West Point selected as the most eligible place to be fortified.

by a subsequent resolution, were ordered to attend that council. This arrangement, putting Gates under Washington's order, evinced the determination of Congress to sustain the latter in his proper authority.

And here we may note the downfall of the intriguing individual who had given his name to the now extinguished cabal. Conway, after the departure of Lafayette and De Kalb from Albany, had remained but a short time in the command there, being ordered to join the army under General McDougall, stationed at Fishkill. Thence he was soon ordered back to Albany, whereupon he wrote an impertinent letter to the President of Congress, complaining that he was "boxed about in a most indecent manner," and intimated a wish that the president would make his resignation acceptable to Congress. To his surprise and consternation, his resignation was immediately accepted. He instantly wrote to the president, declaring that his meaning had been misapprehended, and accounting for it by some orthographical or grammatical faults in his letter, being an Irishman, who had learnt his English in France. All his efforts to get reinstated were unavailing, though he went to Yorktown to make them in person.[16]

The capture of Burgoyne and his army was now operating with powerful effect on the cabinets of both England and France. With the former it was coupled with the apprehension that France was about to espouse the American cause. The consequence was Lord North's "Conciliatory Bills," as they were called, submitted by him to Parliament, and passed with but slight opposition. One of these bills regulated taxation in the American colonies, in a manner which, it was trusted, would obviate every objection. The other authorized the appointment of commissioners clothed with powers to negotiate with the existing governments; to proclaim a cessation of hostilities; to grant pardons, and to adopt other measures of a conciliatory nature.

Intelligence that a treaty between France and the United States had actually been concluded at Paris, induced the British minister to hurry off a draft of the bills to America, to forestall the effects of the treaty upon the public mind. General Tryon caused copies of it to be printed in New York and circulated through the country. He sent several of them to General Washington, 15th April, with a request that they should be communicated to the officers and privates of his army. Washington felt the singular impertinence of the request. He transmitted them to Congress, observing that the time to entertain such overtures was past. "Nothing short of independence, it appears to me, can possibly do. A peace on other terms would, if I may be allowed the expression, be a peace of war. The injuries we have received from the British nation were so unprovoked, and have been so great and so many, that they can never be forgotten." These and other objections advanced by him met with the concurrence of Congress, and it was unanimously resolved that no conference could be held, no treaty made with any commissioners on the part of Great Britain, until that power should have withdrawn its fleets and armies, or acknowledged in positive and express terms the independence of the United States.

---

[16] Conway here disappears from this history. He became involved in a duel with Gen. John Cadwalader, in which he was severely wounded. Upon his recovery from his wounds he embarked for France.

On the following day, April 23d, a resolution was passed recommending to the different States to pardon, under such restrictions as might be deemed expedient, such of their citizens as, having levied war against the United States, should return to their allegiance before the 16th of June.

The tidings of the capitulation of Burgoyne had been equally efficacious in quickening the action of the French cabinet. The negotiations, which had gone on so slowly as almost to reduce our commissioners to despair, were brought to a happy termination, and on the 2d of May, ten days after the passing by Congress of the resolves just cited, a messenger arrived express from France with two treaties, one of amity and commerce, the other of defensive alliance, signed in Paris on the 6th of February by M. Girard on the part of France, and by Benjamin Franklin, Silas Deane, and Arthur Lee on the part of the United States. This last treaty stipulated that, should war ensue between France and England, it should be made a common cause by the contracting parties, in which neither should make truce or peace with Great Britain without the consent of the other, nor either lay down their arms until the independence of the United States was established.

These treaties were unanimously ratified by Congress, and their promulgation was celebrated by public rejoicings throughout the country. The 6th of May was set apart for a military fête at the camp at Valley Forge. The army was assembled in best array; there was solemn thanksgiving by the chaplains at the head of each brigade; after which a grand parade, a national discharge of thirteen guns, a general *feu de joie,* and shouts of the whole army, "Long live the King of France—Long live the friendly European Powers—Huzza for the American States." A banquet succeeded, at which Washington dined in public with all the officers of his army, attended by a band of music.

On the 8th, the council of war, ordered by Congress, was convened; at which were present Major-generals Gates, Greene, Stirling, Mifflin, Lafayette, De Kalb, Armstrong and Steuben, and Brigadier-generals Knox and Duportail. After the state of the forces, British and American, their number and distribution, had been laid before the council by the commander-in-chief, and a full discussion had been held, it was unanimously determined to remain on the defensive, and not attempt any offensive operation until some opportunity should occur to strike a successful blow.

The military career of Sir William Howe in the United States was now drawing to a close. His conduct of the war had given much dissatisfaction in England. His enemies observed that everything gained by the troops was lost by the general; that he had suffered an enemy with less than four thousand men to reconquer a province which he had recently reduced, and lay a kind of siege to his army in their winter quarters; and that he had brought a sad reverse upon the British arms by failing to co-operate vigorously and efficiently with Burgoyne. Sir William, on his part, had considered himself slighted by the ministry; his suggestions, he said, were disregarded, and the reinforcements withheld which he considered indispensable for the successful conduct of the war. He had therefore tendered his resignation, which had been promptly accepted, and Sir Henry Clinton ordered to relieve him. Clinton arrived in Philadelphia on the 8th of May, and took command of the army on the 11th.

Soon after he had taken the command, there were symptoms of an intention to evacuate Philadelphia. Whither the enemy would thence direct their course was a matter of mere conjecture. Lafayette was therefore detached by Washington, with twenty-one hundred chosen men and five pieces of cannon, to take a position nearer the city, where he might be at hand to gain information, watch the movements of the enemy, check their predatory excursions, and fall on their rear when in the act of withdrawing.

The marquis crossed the Schuylkill on the 18th of May, and proceeded to Barren Hill, about half way between Washington's camp and Philadelphia, and about eleven miles from both. Here he planted his cannon facing the south, with rocky ridges bordering the Schuylkill on his right; woods and stone houses on his left. Behind him the roads forked, one branch leading to Matson's Ford of the Schuylkill, the other by Swedes' Ford to Valley Forge. In advance of his left wing was McLane's company and about fifty Indians. Pickets and videttes were placed in the woods to the south, through which the roads led to Philadelphia, and a body of six hundred Pennsylvania militia were stationed to keep watch on the roads leading to White Marsh.

In the meantime Sir Henry Clinton having received intelligence through his spies of this movement of Lafayette, concerted a plan to entrap the young French nobleman. Five thousand men were sent out at night under General Grant to make a circuitous march by White Marsh, and get in the rear of the Americans; another force under General Grey was to cross to the west side of the Schuylkill, and take post below Barren Hill, while Sir Henry in person was to lead a third division along the Philadelphia road.

The plan came near being completely successful, through the remissness of the Pennsylvania militia, who had left their post of observation. Early in the morning word was brought that red coats had been descried in the woods near White Marsh. Lafayette was expecting a troop of American dragoons in that quarter who wore scarlet uniforms, and supposed these to be them; to be certain, however, he sent out an officer to reconnoitre. The latter soon came spurring back at full speed. A column of the enemy had pushed forward on the road from White Marsh, were within a mile of the camp, and had possession of the road leading to Valley Forge. Another column was advancing on the Philadelphia road. In fact, the young French general was on the point of being surrounded by a greatly superior force. Lafayette saw his danger, but maintained his presence of mind. Throwing out small parties of troops to show themselves at various points of the intervening wood, as if an attack on Grant was meditated, he brought that general to a halt to prepare for action, while he with his main body pushed forward for Matson's ford on the Schuylkill.

The alarm-guns at sunrise had apprised Washington that the detachment under Lafayette was in danger. The troops at Valley Forge were instantly under arms. Washington, with his aides-de-camp and some of his general officers, galloped to the summit of a hill, and anxiously reconnoitred the scene of action with a glass.

His solicitude for the marquis was soon relieved. The stratagem of the youthful warrior had been crowned with success. He completely gained the march upon General Grant, reached Matson's Ford in safety, crossed it in great order, and took a strong position on high grounds which commanded it. The enemy arrived at the river just in time for a skirmish as the artillery was crossing. Seeing that Lafayette had extricated himself from their hands, and was so strongly posted, they gave over all attack, and returned somewhat disconcerted to Philadelphia; while the youthful marquis rejoined the army at Valley Forge, where he was received with acclamations.

The exchange of General Lee for General Prescott, so long delayed by various impediments, had recently been effected; and Lee was reinstated in his position of second in command. Colonel Ethan Allen, also, had been released from his long captivity in exchange for Colonel Campbell. Allen paid a visit to the camp at Valley Forge, where he had much to tell of his various vicissitudes and hardships. In a few days, a brevet commission of colonel arrived for him; but he had already left camp for his home in Vermont, where he appears to have hung up his sword, for we meet with no further achievements by him on record.

Indications continued to increase of the departure of troops from Philadelphia. New York, it was concluded, would be the place of destination; either as a rendezvous, or a post whence to attempt the occupation of the Hudson. Would they proceed thither by land or water? Supposing the former, Washington would gladly have taken post in Jersey to oppose or harass them on their march through that State. His camp, however, was encumbered by upwards of three thousand sick; and covered a great amount of military stores. He dared not weaken it by detaching a sufficient force; especially as it was said the enemy intended to attack him before their departure. For three weeks affairs remained in this state. Washington held his army ready to march toward the Hudson at a moment's warning, and sent General Maxwell with a brigade of Jersey troops to co-operate with Major-general Dickinson and the militia of that State in breaking down the bridges and harassing the enemy, should they actually attempt to march through it.

In the meantime, the commissioners empowered under the new Conciliatory Bills to negotiate the restoration of peace between Great Britain and her former colonies, arrived in the Delaware in the Trident ship-of-war. These were Frederick Howard, Earl of Carlisle; William Eden (afterwards Lord Auckland), brother of the last colonial governor of Maryland; and George Johnstone, commonly known as Governor Johnstone, having held that office in Florida. The commissioners landed at Philadelphia on the 6th of June, and discovered to their astonishment that they had come out, as it were, in the dark, on a mission in which but a half confidence had been reposed in them by government. Three weeks before their departure from England, orders had been sent out to Sir Henry Clinton to evacuate Philadelphia and concentrate his forces at New York; yet these orders were never imparted to them. Their letters and speeches testify their surprise and indignation at finding their plan of operations so completely disconcerted by their own cabinet.

The orders for evacuation, however, were too peremptory to be evaded, but Johnstone declared that if he had known of them, he never would have gone on the mission. The commissioners had prepared a letter for Congress, merely informing that body of their arrival and powers, and their disposition to promote a reconciliation, intending quietly to await an answer; but the unexpected situation of affairs occasioned by the order for evacuation, obliged them to alter their resolution, and to write one of a different character bringing forward at once all the powers delegated to them. On the 9th of June, Sir Henry Clinton informed Washington of the arrival of the commissioners, and requested a passport for their secretary, Dr. Ferguson, the historian, to proceed to Yorktown bearing a letter to Congress. Washington sent to Congress a copy of Sir Henry's letter, but did not consider himself at liberty to grant the passport until authorized by them.

Without waiting the result, the commissioners forwarded, by the ordinary military post, their letter, accompanied by the "Conciliatory Acts" and other documents. They were received by Congress on the 13th. The reading of the letter was interrupted, and it came near being indignantly rejected, on account of expressions disrespectful to France, charging it with being the insidious enemy of both England and her colonies, and interposing its pretended friendship to the latter "only to prevent reconciliation and prolong this destructive war." In their reply, signed by the president (June 17th), they observed that nothing but an earnest desire to spare further effusion of blood could have induced them to read a paper containing expressions so disrespectful to his most Christian Majesty, or to consider propositions so derogatory to the honor of an independent nation; and in conclusion, they expressed a readiness to treat as soon as the King of Great Britain should demonstrate a sincere disposition for peace, either by an explicit acknowledgment of the independence of the States, or by the withdrawal of his fleets and armies.

We will not follow the commissioners through their various attempts, overtly and covertly, to forward the object of their mission. We cannot, however, pass unnoticed an intimation conveyed from Governor Johnstone to General Joseph Reed, at this time an influential member of Congress, that effectual services on his part to restore the union of the two countries might be rewarded by ten thousand pounds sterling, and any office in the colonies in His Majesty's gift. To this Reed made his brief and memorable reply: "I am not worth purchasing; but such as I am, the King of Great Britain is not rich enough to do it."

The commissioners, disappointed in their hopes of influencing Congress, attempted to operate on the feelings of the public, at one time by conciliatory appeals, at another by threats and denunciations. Their last measure was to publish a manifesto recapitulating their official proceedings; stating the refusal of Congress to treat with them, and offering to treat within forty days with deputies from all or any of the colonies or provincial Assemblies; holding forth, at the same time, the usual offers of conditional amnesty. This measure, like all which had preceded it, proved ineffectual; the commissioners embarked for England, and so terminated this tardy and blundering attempt of the British Government and its agents to effect a reconciliation—the last attempt that was made.

CHAPTER L.

EVACUATION OF PHILADELPHIA.—BATTLE OF MONMOUTH COURT HOUSE.

The delay of the British to evacuate Philadelphia tasked the sagacity of Washington, but he supposed it to have been caused by the arrival of the commissioners from Great Britain. The force in the city in the meantime had been much reduced. Five thousand men had been detached to aid in a sudden descent on the French possessions in the West Indies; three thousand more to Florida. Most of the cavalry with other troops had been shipped with the provision train and heavy baggage to New York. The effective force remaining with Sir Henry was now about nine or ten thousand men; that under Washington was a little more than twelve thousand Continentals, and about thirteen hundred militia. It had already acquired considerable proficiency in tactics and field manoeuvring under the diligent instructions of Steuben.

Early in June it was evident that a total evacuation of the city was on the point of taking place; and circumstances convinced Washington that the march of the main body would be through the Jerseys. Some of his officers thought differently, especially General Lee, who had now the command of a division composed of Poor, Varnum, and Huntington's brigades. In consequence, Washington called a general council of war on the 17th, to consider what measures to adopt; whether to undertake any enterprise against the enemy in their present circumstances—whether the army should remain in its actual position, until the final evacuation had taken place, or move immediately toward the Delaware—whether, should the enemy march through the Jerseys, it would be advisable to attack them while on the way, or to push on directly to the Hudson, and secure that important communication between the Eastern and Southern States? In case an attack while on the march were determined on, should it be a partial or a general one?

Lee was opposed to an attack of any kind. He would make a bridge of gold for the enemy. They were nearly equal in number to the Americans, and far superior in discipline. An attack would endanger the safety of the cause. He advised merely to follow the enemy, observe their motions, and prevent them from committing any excesses. Lee's opinions had still great weight with the army; most of the officers, both foreign and American, concurred with him. Greene, Lafayette, Wayne, and Cadwalader, thought differently. They could not brook that the enemy should evacuate the city, and make a long march through the country unmolested. Washington seeing such want of unanimity among his generals, requested their opinions in writing. Before these were given in, word was brought that the enemy had actually evacuated the city.

Sir Henry had taken his measures with great secrecy and despatch. The army commenced moving at three o'clock on the morning of the 18th, retiring to a point of land below the town formed by the confluence of the Delaware and Schuylkill, and crossing the former river in boats. By ten o'clock in the morning the rear-guard landed on the Jersey shore.

On the first intelligence of this movement, Washington detached General Maxwell with his brigade, to co-operate with General Dickinson and the New Jersey militia in harassing the enemy on their march. He sent General Arnold, also, with a force to take command of Philadelphia, that officer being not yet sufficiently recovered from his wound for field service; then, breaking up his camp at Valley Forge, he pushed forward with his main force in pursuit of the enemy. As the route of the latter lay along the eastern bank of the Delaware as high as Trenton, Washington was obliged to make a considerable circuit, so as to cross the river higher up at Coryell's Ferry, near the place where, eighteen months previously, he had crossed to attack the Hessians.

Heavy rains and sultry summer heat retarded his movements; but the army crossed on the 24th. The British were now at Moorestown and Mount Holly. Thence they might take the road on the left for Brunswick, and so on to Staten Island and New York; or the road to the right through Monmouth, by the Heights of Middletown to Sandy Hook. Uncertain which they might adopt, Washington detached Colonel Morgan with six hundred picked men to reinforce Maxwell, and hang on their rear; while he himself pushed forward with the main body toward Princeton, cautiously keeping along the mountainous country to the left of the most northern road.

The march of Sir Henry was very slow. From his dilatory movements, Washington suspected Sir Henry of a design to draw him down into the level country, and then, by a rapid movement on his right, to gain possession of the strong ground above him, and bring him to a general action on disadvantageous terms. He himself was inclined for a general action whenever it could be made on suitable ground: he halted, therefore, at Hopewell, about five miles from Princeton, and held another council of war. The result of it, writes his aide-de-camp, Colonel Hamilton, "would have done honor to the most honorable society of midwives, and to them only." The purport was to keep at a distance from the enemy, and annoy them by detachments. Lee, according to Hamilton, was the prime mover of this plan, in pursuance of which a detachment of fifteen hundred men was sent off under Brigadier-general Scott, to join the other troops near the enemy's line.

Generals Greene, Wayne, and Lafayette were in the minority in the council, and subsequently gave separately the same opinion in writing, that the rear of the enemy should be attacked by a strong detachment, while the main army should be so disposed as to give a general battle, should circumstances render it advisable. As this opinion coincided with his own, Washington determined to act upon it. Sir Henry Clinton in the meantime had advanced to Allentown, on his way to

Brunswick, to embark on the Raritan. Finding the passage of that river likely to be strongly disputed by the forces under Washington, and others advancing from the north under Gates, he changed his plan, and turned to the right by a road leading through Freehold to Navesink and Sandy Hook; to embark at the latter place.

Washington, no longer in doubt as to the route of the enemy's march, detached Wayne with one thousand men to join the advanced corps, which, thus augmented, was upwards of four thousand strong. The command of the advance properly belonged to Lee as senior major-general; but it was eagerly solicited by Lafayette, as an attack by it was intended, and Lee was strenuously opposed to everything of the kind. Washington willingly gave his consent, provided General Lee were satisfied with the arrangement. The latter ceded the command without hesitation. Scarce, however, had he relinquished the command, when he changed his mind. In a note to Washington he declared that, in assenting to the arrangement, he had considered the command of the detachment one more fitting a young volunteering general than a veteran like himself, second in command in the army. He now viewed it in a different light. Lafayette would be at the head of all the Continental parties already in the line; six thousand men at least; a command next to that of the commander-in-chief. Should the detachment march, therefore, he entreated to have the command of it.

Washington was perplexed how to satisfy Lee's punctilious claims without wounding the feelings of Lafayette. A change in the disposition of the enemy's line of march furnished an expedient. Sir Henry Clinton, finding himself harassed by light troops on the flanks, and in danger of an attack in the rear, placed all his baggage in front under the convoy of Knyphausen, while he threw the main strength of his army in the rear under Lord Cornwallis. This made it necessary for Washington to strengthen his advanced corps; and he took this occasion to detach Lee, with Scott's and Varnum's brigades, to support the force under Lafayette. As Lee was the senior major-general, this gave him the command of the whole advance. Washington explained the matter in a letter to the marquis, who resigned the command to Lee when the latter joined him on the 27th. That evening the enemy encamped on high ground near Monmouth Court House. Lee encamped with the advance at Englishtown, about five miles distant. The main body was three miles in his rear.

About sunset Washington rode forward to the advance, and anxiously reconnoitred Sir Henry's position. It was protected by woods and morasses, and too strong to be attacked with a prospect of success. Should the enemy, however, proceed ten or twelve miles further unmolested, they would gain the heights of Middletown, and be on ground still more difficult. To prevent this, he resolved that an attack should be made on their rear early in the morning, as soon as their front should be in motion. This plan he communicated to General Lee, in presence of his officers, ordering him to make dispositions for the attack keeping his troops lying on their arms, ready for action on the shortest notice; a disposition he intended to observe with his own troops. This done, he rode back to the main body.

Early in the morning, Washington received an express informing him that the enemy were in motion. He instantly sent orders to Lee to push forward and attack them, unless there should be powerful reasons to the contrary, adding that he was coming on to support him. For that purpose he immediately set forward with his own troops, ordering them to throw by their knapsacks and blankets.

Knyphausen, with the British vanguard, had begun about daybreak to descend into the valley between Monmouth Court House and Middletown. To give the long train of wagons and pack horses time to get well on the way, Sir Henry Clinton with his choice troops remained in camp on the heights of Freehold, until eight o'clock, when he likewise resumed the line of march toward Middletown.

In the meantime, Lee had advanced with the brigades of Wayne and Maxwell, to support the light troops engaged in skirmishing. The difficulty of reconnoitring a country cut up by woods and morasses, and the perplexity occasioned by contradictory reports, embarrassed his movements. Being joined by Lafayette with the main body of the advance, he had now about four thousand men at his command, independent of those under Morgan and General Dickinson. Arriving on the heights of Freehold, and riding forward with General Wayne to an open place to reconnoitre, Lee caught sight of a force under march, but partly hidden from view by intervening woods. Supposing it to be a mere covering party of about two thousand men, he detached Wayne with seven hundred men and two pieces of artillery, to skirmish in its rear and hold it in check; while he, with the rest of his force, taking a shorter road through the woods, would get in front of it, and cut it off from the main body. He at the same time sent a message to Washington, apprising him of this movement and of his certainty of success.

Washington in the meantime was on his march with the main body, to support the advance, as he had promised. The booming of cannon at a distance indicated that the attack so much desired had commenced, and caused him to quicken his march. Arrived near Freehold church, where the road forked, he detached Greene with part of his forces to the right, to flank the enemy in the rear of Monmouth Court House, while he, with the rest of the column, would press forward by the other road.

Washington had alighted while giving these directions, and was standing with his arm thrown over his horse, when a countryman rode up and said the Continental troops were retreating. Washington was provoked at what he considered a false alarm. The man pointed, as his authority, to an American fifer who just then came up in breathless affright. The fifer was ordered into custody to prevent his spreading an alarm among the troops who were advancing, and was threatened with a flogging should he repeat the story. Springing on his horse, Washington had moved forward but a short distance when he met other fugitives, one in the garb of a soldier, who all concurred in the report. He now sent forward Colonels Fitzgerald and Harrison to learn the truth, while he himself spurred past Freehold meeting house. Between that edifice and the morass beyond it, he met Grayson's and Patton's regiments in most disorderly retreat, jaded with heat and fatigue. Riding up to the officer at their head, Washington demanded whether the whole advanced corps were retreating. The officer believed they were.

It seemed incredible. There had been scarce any firing—Washington had received no notice of the retreat from Lee. He was still almost inclined to doubt, when the heads of several columns of the advance began to appear. It was too evident—the whole advance was falling back on the main body, and no notice had been given to him. One of the first officers that came up was Colonel Shreve, at the head of his regiment. Washington, greatly surprised and alarmed, asked the meaning of this retreat. The colonel smiled significantly—he did not know—he had retreated by order. There had been no fighting excepting a slight skirmish with the enemy's cavalry, which had been repulsed.

A suspicion flashed across Washington's mind of wrongheaded conduct on the part of Lee, to mar the plan of attack adopted contrary to his counsels. Ordering Colonel Shreve to march his men over the morass, halt them on the hill beyond and refresh them, he galloped forward to stop the retreat of the rest of the advance, his indignation kindling as he rode. At the rear of the regiment he met Major Howard; he, too, could give no reason for the retreat, but seemed provoked at it—declaring that he had never seen the like. Another officer exclaimed with an oath that they were flying from a shadow. Arriving at a rising ground, Washington beheld Lee approaching with the residue of his command in full retreat. By this time he was thoroughly exasperated.

"What is the meaning of all this, sir?" demanded he, in the sternest and even fiercest tone, as Lee rode up to him. Lee for a moment was disconcerted, and hesitated in making a reply, for Washington's aspect, according to Lafayette, was terrible. "I desire to know the meaning of this disorder and confusion," was again demanded still more vehemently.

Lee, stung by the manner more than the words of the demand, made an angry reply, and provoked still sharper expressions, which have been variously reported. "I am very sorry," said Washington, "that you undertook the command, unless you meant to fight the enemy." "I did not think it prudent to bring on a general engagement." "Whatever your opinion may have been," replied Washington, disdainfully, "I expected my orders would have been obeyed." This all passed rapidly, and, as it were, in flashes, for there was no time for parley. The enemy were within a quarter of an hour's march. Washington's appearance had stopped the retreat. The fortunes of the day were to be retrieved, if possible, by instant arrangements. These he proceeded to make with great celerity. The place was favorable for a stand; it was a rising ground, to which the enemy could approach only over a narrow causeway. The rallied troops were hastily formed upon this eminence. Colonels Stewart and Ramsey, with two batteries, were stationed in a covert of woods on their left, to protect them and keep the enemy at bay. Colonel Oswald was posted for the same purpose on a height, with two field-pieces. The promptness with which everything was done showed the effects of the Baron Steuben's discipline.

Washington, having made all his arrangements with great dispatch but admirable clearness and precision, rode back to Lee in calmer mood, and inquired, "Will you retain the command on this height or not? if you will, I will return to the main body, and have it formed on the next height." "It is equal to me where I command," replied Lee. "I expect you will take proper means for checking the enemy," rejoined Washington. "Your orders shall be obeyed; and I shall not be the first to leave the ground," was the reply.

A warm cannonade by Oswald, Stewart and Ramsey had the desired effect. The enemy were brought to a stand, and Washington had time to gallop back and bring on the main body. This he formed on an eminence, with a wood in the rear and the morass in front. The left wing was commanded by Lord Stirling, who had with him a detachment of artillery and several field-pieces. General Greene was on his right.

Lee had maintained his advanced position with great spirit, but was at length obliged to retire. He brought off his troops in good order across a causeway which traversed the morass in front of Lord Stirling. Having formed his men in a line, beyond the morass, he rode up to Washington. "Here, sir, are my troops," said he, "how is it your pleasure I should dispose of them?" Washington saw that the poor fellows were exhausted by marching, countermarching, hard fighting and the intolerable heat of the weather: he ordered Lee, therefore, to repair with them to the rear of Englishtown, and assemble there all the scattered fugitives he might meet with.

The batteries under the direction of Lord Stirling opened a brisk and well-sustained fire upon the enemy; who, finding themselves warmly opposed in front, attempted to turn the left flank of the Americans, but were driven back by detached parties of infantry stationed there. They then attempted the right; but here were met by General Greene, who had planted his artillery, under Knox, on a commanding ground, and not only checked them but enfiladed those who were in front of the left wing. Wayne too, with an advanced party posted in an orchard, and partly sheltered by a barn, kept up a severe and well-directed fire upon the enemy's centre. Repeated attempts were made to dislodge him, but in vain. Colonel Monckton now undertook to drive Wayne from his post at the point of the bayonet. Having made a brief harangue to his men, he led them on in column. Wayne's men reserved their fire, until Colonel Monckton, waving his sword, called out to his grenadiers to charge. At that instant a sheeted volley laid him low, and made great slaughter in his column, which was again repulsed.

The enemy at length gave way, and fell back to the ground which Lee had occupied in the morning. Here their flanks were secured by woods and morasses, and their front could only be approached across a narrow causeway. Notwithstanding the difficulties of the position, Washington prepared to attack it; ordering General Poor with his own and the Carolina brigade, to move round upon their right, and General Woodford on their left; while the artillery should gall them in front. Before these orders could be carried into effect the day was at an end. Many of the soldiers had sunk upon the ground, overcome by fatigue and the heat of the weather; all needed repose. The troops, therefore, which had been in the advance, were ordered to lie on their arms on the ground they occupied, so as to be ready to make the attack by daybreak. The main army did the same, on the field of action, to be at hand to support them. Washington lay on his cloak at the foot of a tree, with Lafayette beside him, talking over the strange conduct of Lee; whose disorderly retreat had come so near being fatal to the army.

It was indeed a matter of general perplexity, to which the wayward character of Lee greatly contributed. Some who recollected his previous opposition to all plan of attack, almost suspected him of wilfully aiming to procure a defeat. It would appear, however, that he had been really surprised and thrown into confusion by a move of Sir Henry Clinton, who, seeing the force under Lee descending on his rear from Freehold heights, had suddenly turned upon it, aided by troops from Knyphausen's division, to oblige it to call to its assistance the flanking parties under Morgan and Dickinson, which were threatening his baggage train. So that Lee, instead of a mere covering party which he had expected to cut off, had found himself front to front with the whole rear division of the British army; and that too, on unfavorable ground, with a deep ravine and a morass in his rear.

At daybreak the drums beat the reveillé. The troops roused themselves from their heavy sleep, and prepared for action. To their surprise, the enemy had disappeared: there was a deserted camp, in which were found four officers and about forty privates, too severely wounded to be conveyed away by the retreating army. Sir Henry Clinton, it appeared, had allowed his wearied troops but short repose on the preceding night. At ten o'clock, when the American forces were buried in their first sleep, he had set forward to join the division under Knyphausen, which, with the baggage train, having pushed on during the action, was far on the road to Middletown. So silent had been his retreat, that it was unheard by General Poor's advance party, which lay near by.

The distance to which the enemy must by this time have attained, the extreme heat of the weather, and the fatigued condition of the troops, deterred Washington from continuing a pursuit through a country where the roads were deep and sandy, and there was great scarcity of water. Besides, persons well acquainted with the country assured him that it would be impossible to annoy the enemy in their embarkation, as he must approach the place by a narrow passage, capable of being defended by a few men against his whole force. Detaching General Maxwell's brigade and Morgan's rifle corps, therefore, to hang on the rear of the enemy, prevent depredation and encourage desertions, he determined to shape his course with his main body by Brunswick toward the Hudson, lest Sir Henry should have any design upon the posts there.

The American loss in the recent battle was eight officers and sixty-one privates killed, and about one hundred and sixty wounded. The officers who had charge of the burying parties reported that they found two hundred and forty-five non-commissioned officers and privates, and four officers, left dead by the enemy on the field of battle.

After giving his troops a day's repose, Washington decamped on the 30th. His march lay through a country destitute of water, with deep, sandy roads wearying to the feet, and reflecting the intolerable heat and glare of a July sun. Many of the troops, harassed by previous fatigue, gave out by the way. Some few died, and a number of horses were likewise lost. Washington, ever considerate of the health and comfort of his men, encamped near Brunswick on open, airy grounds, and gave them time to repose; while Lieutenant-colonel Aaron Burr, at that time a young and enterprising officer, was sent on a reconnoitring expedition, to learn the movements and intentions of the enemy.

Sir Henry Clinton with the royal army had arrived at the Highlands of Navesink, in the neighborhood of Sandy Hook, on the 30th of June. He had lost many men by desertion, Hessians especially, during his march through the Jerseys, which, with his losses by killed, wounded and captured, had diminished his army more than two thousand men. The storms of the preceding winter had cut off the peninsula of Sandy Hook from the mainland, and formed a deep channel between them. Fortunately the squadron of Lord Howe had arrived the day before, and was at anchor within the Hook. A bridge was immediately made across the channel with the boats of the ships, over which the army passed to the Hook on the 5th of July, and thence was distributed.

Having brought the army to a halt, we have time to notice a correspondence between General Lee and Washington, immediately subsequent to the affair of Monmouth. The pride of the general had been deeply wounded by the rebuke he had received on the field of battle. On the following day (June 29th) he addressed a note to Washington on the subject. By mistake it was dated July 1st. "From the knowledge I have of your Excellency's character," writes he, "I must conclude that nothing but the misinformation of some very stupid, or misrepresentation of some very wicked person, could have occasioned your making use of so very singular expressions as you did on my coming up to the ground where you had taken post. They implied that I was guilty either of disobedience of orders, want of conduct, or want of courage. Your Excellency will therefore infinitely oblige me by letting me know on which of these three articles you ground your charge."

Washington, in reply, wrote: "I received your letter (dated through mistake the 1st of July), expressed as I conceive in terms highly improper. I am not conscious of making use of any very singular expressions at the time of meeting you, as you intimate. What I recollect to have said was dictated by duty and warranted by the occasion. As soon as circumstances will permit, you shall have an opportunity of justifying yourself to the army, to Congress, to America, and to the world in general."

To this Lee rejoined, in a note, misdated 28th June: "Sir, you cannot afford me greater pleasure than in giving me the opportunity of showing to America the sufficiency of her respective servants. I trust that temporary power of office, and the tinsel dignity attending it, will not be able, by all the mists they can raise, to obfuscate the bright rays of truth. In the meantime, your Excellency can have no objection to my retiring from the army," etc. Shortly after despatching this note, Lee addressed another to Washington. "I have reflected on both your situation and mine," writes he, "and beg leave to observe, that it will be for our mutual convenience that a court of inquiry should be immediately ordered.... I must entreat, therefore, from your love of justice, that you will immediately exhibit your charge, and that on the first halt I may be brought to a trial."

Washington in reply acknowledged the receipt of the two last notes, and added, "I have sent Colonel Scammel and the adjutant-general to put you under arrest, who will deliver you a copy of the charges on which you will be tried."

A court-martial was accordingly formed on the 4th of July, at Brunswick, the first halting place. It was composed of one major-general, four brigadiers, and eight colonels, with Lord Stirling as president. It moved with the army, and convened subsequently at Paramus, Peekskill, and Northcastle, the trial lasting until the 12th of August. The result of the prolonged and tedious investigation was that he was found guilty of all the charges exhibited against him. [1st. Disobedience of orders. 2d. Misbehavior before the enemy, by making an unnecessary and disorderly retreat. 3d. Disrespect to the commander-in-chief in letters dated July 1st and June 28th.] He was sentenced to be suspended from all command for one year; the sentence to be approved or set aside by Congress.

We must anticipate dates to dispose briefly of the career of General Lee, who is not connected with subsequent events of the Revolution. Congress were more than three months in coming to a decision on the proceedings of the court-martial. At length, on the 5th of December, the sentence was approved in a very thin session of Congress, fifteen members voting in the affirmative and seven in the negative. From that time Lee was unmeasured in his abuse of Washington, and his reprobation of the court-martial, which he termed a "court of inquisition." His aggressive tongue at length involved him in a quarrel with Colonel Laurens, one of Washington's aides, a high-spirited young gentleman who felt himself bound to vindicate the honor of his chief. A duel took place, and Lee was wounded in the side. Towards spring he retired to his estate in Berkley County in Virginia, where he led a kind of hermit life. Dogs and horses were his favorite companions. His house is described as being a mere shell, destitute of comforts and conveniences. For want of partitions the different parts were designated by lines chalked on the floor. In one corner was his bed; in another were his books; his saddles and harness in a third; a fourth served as a kitchen.

The term of his suspension had expired when a rumor reached him that Congress intended to take away his commission. The intelligence "ruffled his temper beyond all bounds." In his hurry and heat, without attempting to ascertain the truth of the report, he scrawled the following note to the President of Congress: "Sir, I understand that it is in contemplation of Congress, on the principle of economy, to strike me out of their service. Congress must know very little of me if they suppose that I would accept of their money, since the confirmation of the wicked and infamous sentence which was passed upon me. I am, sir," etc. This insolent note occasioned his prompt dismissal from the service.

Though bitter in his enmities, Lee had his friendships, and was warm and constant in them as far as his capricious humors would allow. There was nothing crafty or mean in his character, nor do we think he ever engaged in the low intrigues of the cabal; but he was a disappointed and embittered man, and the gall of bitterness overflowed his generous qualities. In such a discordant state of feeling, he was not a man for the sweet solitude of the country. He became weary of his Virginia estate; though in one of the most fertile regions of the Shenandoah Valley. His farm was mismanaged; his agents were unfaithful; he entered into negotiations to dispose of his property, in the course of which he visited Philadelphia. On arriving there he was taken with chills, followed by a fever, which went on increasing in violence, and terminated fatally. A soldier even unto the end, warlike scenes mingled with the delirium of his malady. In his dying moments he fancied himself on the field of battle. The last words he was heard to utter were, "Stand by me, my brave grenadiers!"

CHAPTER LI.

ARRIVAL OF A FRENCH FLEET.—MASSACRE AT WYOMING VALLEY.—CAPTURE OF SAVANNAH.

While encamped at Paramus, Washington, in the night of the 13th of July, received a letter from Congress informing him of the arrival of a French fleet on the coast; instructing him to concert measures with the commander, the Count D'Estaing, for offensive operations by sea and land, and empowering him to call on the States from New Hampshire to New Jersey inclusive, to aid with their militia. The fleet in question was composed of twelve ships of the line and six frigates, with a land force of four thousand men. On board of it came Mons. Gerard, minister from France to the United States, and the Hon. Silas Deane, one of the American ministers who had effected the late treaty of alliance. The fleet had sailed from Toulon on the 13th of April. After struggling against adverse winds for eighty-seven or eighty-eight days, it had made its appearance off the northern extremity of the Virginia coast, and anchored at the mouth of the Delaware on the 8th of July.

Finding the enemy had evacuated both city and river, the count sent up the French minister and Mr. Deane to Philadelphia in a frigate, and then, putting to sea, continued along the coast. A little earlier, and he might have intercepted the squadron of Lord Howe on its way to New York. It had had but a very few days the advantage of him, and when he arrived with his fleet in the road outside of Sandy Hook, he descried the British ships quietly anchored inside of it.

A frank and cordial correspondence took place forthwith between the count and Washington, and a plan of action was concerted between them by the intervention of confidential officers; Washington's aides-de-camp, Laurens and Hamilton, boarding the fleet while off the Hook, and Major Chouin, a French officer of merit, repairing to the American head-quarters.

The first idea of the count was to enter at Sandy Hook, and capture or destroy the British fleet, composed of six ships of the line, four fifty-gun ships, and a number of frigates and smaller vessels; should he succeed in this, which his greatly superior force rendered probable, he was to proceed against the city, with the co-operation of the American forces. To be at hand for such purpose, Washington crossed the Hudson, with his army, at King's Ferry, and encamped at White Plains about the 20th of July. Several experienced American pilots and masters of vessels, however, who had accompanied Colonels Laurens and Hamilton on board of the fleet, declared that there was not sufficient depth of water on the bar to admit the safe passage of the largest ships, one of which carried 80 and another 90 guns; the attempt, therefore, was reluctantly abandoned, and the ships anchored about four miles off, near Shrewsbury on the Jersey coast, taking in provisions and water.

The enterprise which the American and French commanders deemed next worthy of a combined operation, was the recapture of Rhode Island proper, that is to say, the island which gives its name to the State, and which the enemy had made one of their military depots and strongholds. In anticipation of such an enterprise, Washington, on the 17th of July wrote to General Sullivan, who commanded at Providence, ordering him to make the necessary preparations for a descent from the mainland upon the island, and authorizing him to call in reinforcements of New England militia. He subsequently sent to his aid the Marquis Lafayette with two brigades (Varnum's and Glover's). Quartermaster-general Greene also was detached for the service, being a native of the island, well acquainted with its localities, and having great influence among its inhabitants. Sullivan was instructed to form his whole force, Continental, State and militia, into two equal divisions, one to be commanded by Greene, the other by Lafayette.

On the 22d of July, the French fleet, having finished taking in its supplies, stood away to the eastward, and on the 29th arrived off Point Judith, coming to anchor within five miles of Newport.

Rhode Island (proper), the object of this expedition, is about sixteen miles long, running deep into the great Narraganset Bay. Seaconnet Channel separates it on the east from the mainland, and on the west the main channel passes between it and Conanicut Island. The town of Newport is situated near the south end of the island, facing the west, with Conanicut Island in front of it. It was protected by batteries and a small naval force. Here General Sir Robert Pigott, who commanded in the island, had his head-quarters. The force under him was about six thousand strong, variously posted about the island, some in works at the north end, but the greater part within strongly intrenched lines extending across the island, about three miles from the town. General Greene hastened from Providence on hearing of the arrival of the fleet of Count D'Estaing, and went on board of it at the anchorage to concert a plan of operations. It was agreed that the fleet should force its way into the harbor at the same time that the Americans approached by land, and that the landing of the troops from the ships on the west side of the island should take place at the same time that the Americans should cross Seaconnet Channel, and land on the east side near the north end. This combined operation was to have been carried promptly into effect, but was postponed until the 10th of August, to give time for the reinforcements sent by Washington to arrive. The delay was fatal to the enterprise.

On the 8th, the Count D'Estaing entered the harbor and passed up the main channel, exchanging a cannonade with the batteries as he passed, and anchored a little above the town, between Goat and Conanicut Islands. The English, on his approach, burnt or scuttled three frigates and some smaller vessels, which would otherwise have been captured. General Sullivan, to be ready for the concerted attack, had moved down from Providence to the neighborhood of Howland's Ferry, on the east side of Seaconnet passage.

The British troops stationed opposite on the north end of the island, fearful of being cut off, evacuated their works in the night of the 8th, and drew into the lines at Newport. Sullivan, seeing the works thus abandoned, could not resist the temptation to cross the channel in flat-bottomed boats on the morning of the 9th, and take possession of them.

This sudden movement, a day in advance of the concerted time, and without due notice given to the count, surprised and offended him, clashing with his notions of etiquette and punctilio. He, however, prepared to co-operate, and was ordering out his boats for the purpose, when, about two o'clock in the day, his attention was called to a great fleet of ships standing toward Newport. It was, in fact, the fleet of Lord Howe. That gallant nobleman had heard of the danger of Newport, and being reinforced by four stout ships, part of a squadron coming out under Admiral Byron, had hastened to its relief; though still inferior in force to the French admiral. The delay of the concerted attack had enabled him to arrive in time. The wind set directly into the harbor. Had he entered promptly the French would have been placed between two fires, from his ships and the batteries, and cramped up in a confined channel where their largest ships had no room to operate. His lordship, however, came to anchor at Point Judith, some distance from the south-west entrance of the bay.

In the night the wind changed to the north-east. The count hastened to avail himself of the error of the British admiral. Favored by the wind, he stood out of the harbor at eight o'clock in the morning to give the enemy battle where he should have good sea room; previously sending word to General Sullivan that he would land his promised troops and marines, and co-operate with him on his return. The French ships were severely cannonaded as they passed the batteries, but without material damage. Forming in order of battle, they bore down upon the fleet of Lord Howe, confidently anticipating a victory from their superiority of force. The British ships slipt their cables at their approach, and likewise formed in line of battle, but his lordship avoided an encounter while the enemy had the weathergage. To gain this on the one part, and retain it on the other, the two fleets manoeuvred throughout the day standing to the southward, and gradually disappearing from the anxious eyes of the belligerent forces on Rhode Island.

The army of Sullivan, now left to itself before Newport, amounted to ten thousand men, having received the militia reinforcements. Lafayette advised the delay of hostile operations until the return of D'Estaing, but the American commander, piqued and chagrined at the departure of his allies, determined to commence the siege immediately without waiting for his tardy aid. On the 12th, however, came on a tempest of wind and rain which raged for two days and nights with unexampled violence. On the 14th the weather cleared up and the sun shone brightly, but the army was worn down and dispirited. The day was passed in drying their clothes, cleaning their arms, and putting themselves in order for action. By the next morning they were again on the alert. Expecting the prompt return of the French, they now took post on Honeyman's Hill, about two miles from the British lines, and began to construct batteries, form lines of communication, and make regular approaches. The British were equally active in strengthening their defences. There was casual cannonading on each side, but nothing of consequence. Several days elapsed without the re-appearance of the French. The situation of the besiegers was growing critical, when, on the evening of the 19th, they descried the expected fleet standing toward the harbor. All now was exultation in the camp. Should the French with their ships and troops attack the town by sea and land on the one side while the Americans assailed it on the other, the surrender of the place was inevitable.

These sanguine anticipations, however, were shortlived. The French fleet was in a shattered and forlorn condition. After sailing from before Newport on the 20th, it had manoeuvred for two days with the British fleet, each unwilling to enter into action without having the weathergage. While thus manoeuvring, the same furious storm which had raged on shore separated and dispersed them with fearful ravage. Some single encounters of scattered ships subsequently took place, but without definite result. All were too much tempest-tossed and disabled to make good fight. Lord Howe with such of his ships as he could collect bore away to New York to refit, and the French admiral was now before Newport, but in no plight or mood for fighting.

In a letter to General Sullivan, he informed him that pursuant to the orders of his sovereign and the advice of his officers, he was bound for Boston, being instructed to repair to that port should he meet with misfortune, or a superior British force appear upon the coast. Dismayed at this intelligence which threatened ruin and disgrace to the enterprise, Sullivan wrote a letter of remonstrance to the count, and General Greene and the Marquis Lafayette repaired with it on board of the admiral's ship, to enforce it by their personal exertions. They represented to the count the certainty of carrying the place in two days by a combined attack; and the discouragement and reproach that would follow a failure on this their first attempt at co-operation; an attempt, too, for which the Americans had made such great and expensive preparations, and on which they had indulged such sanguine hopes. These and other considerations equally urgent had their weight with the count, and he was inclined to remain and pursue the enterprise, but was overruled by the principal officers of his fleet. The fact is, that he was properly a land officer, and they had been indignant at his having a nautical command over their heads. They were glad, therefore, of any opportunity to thwart and mortify him; and now insisted on his complying with his letter of instructions and sailing for Boston.

At the sailing of the ships there was a feeling of exasperation throughout the camp. Sullivan gave vent to his vexation in a general order on the 24th, wherein he observed: "The general cannot help lamenting the sudden and unexpected departure of the French fleet, as he finds it has a tendency to discourage some who placed great dependence upon the assistance of it; though he can by no means suppose the army or any part of it, endangered by this movement. He yet hopes the event will prove America able to procure that by her own arms which her allies refuse to assist in obtaining." On cooler reflection he thought proper in subsequent orders, to explain away this rash imputation on French loyalty, but a general feeling of irritation against the French continued to prevail in the army.

The departure of the fleet was a death-blow to the enterprise. Between two and three thousand volunteers abandoned the camp in the course of four and twenty hours; others continued to go off; and in a few days the number of besiegers did not exceed that of the besieged. All thoughts of offensive operations were now at an end. The question was how best to extricate the army from its perilous position. On the 28th it was determined, in a council of war, to fall back to the military works at the north end of the island, and fortify there, until it should be known whether the French fleet would soon return to their assistance, the Marquis Lafayette setting off with all speed to have an interview with the Count D'Estaing, and ascertain the fact.

General Sullivan broke up his camp, and commenced his retreat that very night, between nine and ten o'clock. Their retreat was not discovered until daylight, when a pursuit was commenced. The covering parties behaved gallantly, making frequent stands. After a series of skirmishes they were pressed back to the fortified grounds on the north end of the island; but Sullivan had already taken post there, on Batt's Hill, the main body of his army being drawn up in order of battle, with strong works in their rear, and a redoubt in front of the right wing.

The British now took post on an advantageous height called Quaker Hill, a little more than a mile from the American front, whence they commenced a cannonade which was briskly returned. Skirmishing ensued until about ten o'clock, when two British sloops-of-war and some small vessels having gained a favorable position, the enemy's troops, under cover of their fire, advanced in force to turn the right flank of the American army, and capture the redoubt which protected it. This was bravely defended by General Greene; a sharp action ensued, which had nearly become a general one; between two and three hundred men were killed on each side; the British at length drew back to their artillery and works on Quaker Hill, and a mutual cannonade was resumed and kept up until night. On the following day (29th) General Sullivan received intelligence that Lord Howe had again put to sea with the design, no doubt, to attempt the relief of Newport.

Under these circumstances it was determined to abandon Rhode Island. To do so with safety, however, required the utmost caution, as the hostile sentries were within four hundred yards of each other. The position on Batt's Hill favored a deception. Tents were brought forward and pitched in sight of the enemy, and a great part of the troops employed throughout the day in throwing up works, as if the post was to be resolutely maintained; at the same time, the heavy baggage and stores were quietly conveyed away in the rear of the hill, and ferried across the bay. As soon as it was dark the tents were struck, fires were lighted at various points, the troops withdrawn, and in a few hours the whole were transported across the channel to the mainland.

The whole army had crossed by two o'clock in the morning unperceived by the enemy; the very next day Sir Henry Clinton arrived at Newport in a light squadron, with a reinforcement of four thousand men, a naval and land force that might effectually have cut off Sullivan's retreat, had he lingered on the island. Sir Henry, finding he had arrived a day too late, returned to New York, but first detached Major-general Sir Charles Grey with the troops, on a ravaging expedition to the eastward; chiefly against ports which were the haunts of privateers. He destroyed more than seventy vessels in Acushnet River, some of them privateers with their prizes, others peaceful merchant ships. New Bedford and Fair Haven having been made military and naval deposits, were laid waste, wharves demolished, rope-walks, store-houses and mills, with several private dwellings, wrapped in flames. Similar destruction was effected at the Island of Martha's Vineyard. Having thus ravaged the coasts of New England, the squadron returned laden with inglorious spoil to New York.

Lord Howe, also, who had sailed for Boston in the hope of intercepting the Count D'Estaing, and had reached there on the 30th of August, found the French fleet safely sheltered in Nantasket Road, and protected by American batteries erected on commanding points. He also returned to New York, and shortly after-ward, availing himself of a permission granted him some time before by govern-ment, resigned the command of the fleet to Admiral Gambler, to hold it until the arrival of Admiral Byron.

While hostilities were carried on in the customary form along the Atlantic bor-ders, Indian warfare, with all its atrocity, was going on in the interior. The British post at Niagara was its cradle. It was the common rallying place of tories, refugees, savage warriors, and other desperadoes of the frontiers. Hither Brant, the noted Indian chief, had retired after the repulse of St. Leger at Fort Schuyler, to plan fur-ther mischief; and here was concerted the memorable incursion into the Valley of Wyoming, suggested by tory refugees, who had until recently inhabited it.

The Valley of Wyoming is a beautiful region lying along the Susquehanna. Peaceful as was its aspect, it had been the scene of sanguinary feuds prior to the Revolution, between the people of Pennsylvania and Connecticut, who both laid claim to it. Seven rural forts or block-houses, situated on various parts of the val-ley, had been strongholds during these territorial contests, and remained as plac-es of refuge for women and children in times of Indian ravage. The expedition now set on foot against it, in June, was composed of Butler's rangers, Johnson's royal greens, and Brant, with his Indian braves. Their united force, about elev-en hundred strong, was conducted by Colonel John Butler, renowned in Indian warfare. Passing down the Chemung and Susquehanna in canoes, they landed at a place called Three Islands, struck through the wilderness to a gap or "notch" of the mountains, by which they entered the Valley of Wyoming. Butler made his head-quarters at one of the strongholds already mentioned, called Wintermoot's Fort, from a tory family of the same name. Hence he sent out his marauding par-ties to plunder and lay waste the country.

Rumors of this intended invasion had reached the valley some time before the appearance of the enemy, and had spread great consternation. Most of the stur-dy yeomanry were absent in the army. A company of sixty men, enlisted under an act of Congress, and hastily and imperfectly organized, yet styling themselves regulars, took post at one of the strongholds called Forty Fort; where they were joined by about three hundred of the most efficient of the yeomanry, armed and equipped in rude rustic style. In this emergency old men and boys volunteered to meet the common danger, posting themselves in the smaller forts in which women and children had taken refuge. Colonel Zebulon Butler, an officer of the Continental army, took the general command. Several officers arrived from the army, having obtained leave to repair home for the protection of their families. They brought word that a reinforcement, sent by Washington, was on its way.

In the meantime the marauding parties sent out by Butler and Brant were spreading desolation through the valley; farm-houses were wrapped in flames; husbandmen were murdered while at work in the fields; all who had not taken refuge in the fort were threatened with destruction. What was to be done? Wait for the arrival of the promised reinforcement, or attempt to check the ravage? The latter was rashly determined on. Leaving the women and children in Forty Fort, Colonel Zebulon Butler with his men sallied forth on the 3d of July, and made a rapid move upon Wintermoot Fort, hoping to come upon it by surprise. They found the enemy drawn up in front of it, in a line extending from the river to a marsh; Colonel John Butler and his rangers, with Johnson's royal greens, on the left; Indians and tories on the right.

The Americans formed a line of the same extent; the regulars under Colonel Butler on the right flank resting on the river, the militia under Colonel Denison on the left wing on the marsh. A sharp fire was opened from right to left; after a few volleys the enemy in front of Colonel Butler began to give way. The Indians, however, throwing themselves into the marsh, turned the left flank of the Americans and attacked the militia in the rear. Denison, finding himself exposed to a cross fire, sought to change his position, and gave the word to fall back. It was mistaken for an order to retreat. In an instant the left wing turned and fled; all attempts to rally it were vain; the panic extended to the right wing. The savages, throwing down their rifles, rushed on with tomahawk and scalping-knife, and a horrible massacre ensued. Some of the Americans escaped to Forty Fort, some swam the river; others broke their way across the swamp, and climbed the mountain; some few were taken prisoners; but the greater number were slaughtered.

The desolation of the valley was now completed; fields were laid waste, houses burnt, and their inhabitants murdered. According to the British accounts, upwards of four hundred of the yeomanry of Wyoming were slain, and five thousand persons fled in the utmost distress and consternation, seeking refuge in the settlements on the Lehigh and the Delaware. After completing this horrible work of devastation, the enemy retired before the arrival of the troops detached by Washington.

For a great part of the summer, Washington had remained encamped at White Plains, watching the movements of the enemy at New York. Early in September he observed a great stir of preparation; cannon and military stores were embarked, and a fleet of one hundred and forty transports were ready to make sail. What was their destination? There were but two capital objects which they could have in view, beside the defeat and dispersion of his army. One was to get possession of the forts and passes of the Highlands: the other, by a junction of their land and naval forces, to attempt the destruction of the French fleet at Boston, and regain possession of that town. Those points were so far asunder that it was difficult to protect the one without leaving the other exposed. To do the best that the nature of the case would admit, Washington strengthened the works and reinforced the garrison in the Highlands, stationing Putnam with two brigades in the neighborhood of West Point. General Gates was sent with three brigades to Danbury in Connecticut, where he was joined by two brigades under General McDougal, while Washington moved his camp to a rear position at Fredericksburg on the borders of Connecticut, and about thirty miles from West Point, so as to be ready for a movement to the eastward or a speedy junction for the defence of the Hudson.

Scarce had Washington moved from White Plains, when Sir Henry Clinton threw a detachment of five thousand men under Lord Cornwallis into the Jerseys, between the Hackensack and Hudson Rivers, and another of three thousand under Knyphausen into Westchester County, between the Hudson and the Bronx. These detachments held communication with each other, and by the aid of flat-bottomed boats could unite their forces, in twenty-four hours, on either side of the Hudson. Washington considered these mere foraging expeditions, though on a large scale, and detached troops into the Jerseys to co-operate with the militia in checking them; but, as something more might be intended, he ordered General Putnam to cross the river to West Point, for its immediate security; while he himself moved with a division of his army to Fishkill.

Wayne, who was with the detachment in the Jerseys, took post with a body of militia and a regiment of light-horse in front of the division of Lord Cornwallis. The militia were quartered at the village of New Tappan; but Lieutenant-colonel Baylor, who commanded the light-horse, chose to camp apart, to be free, as is supposed, from the control of Wayne. He took up his quarters, therefore, in Old Tappan, where his men lay very negligently and unguardedly in barns. Cornwallis had intelligence of their exposed situation, and laid a plan to cut off the whole detachment. A body of troops from Knyphausen's division was to cross the Hudson in the night, and come by surprise upon the militia in New Tappan: at the same time, Major-general Grey, of marauding renown, was to advance on the left, and attack Baylor and his dragoons in their careless quarters in Old Tappan.

Fortunately Knyphausen's troops, led by Lieutenant-colonel Campbell, were slow in crossing the river, and the militia were apprised by deserters of their danger in time to escape. Not so with Baylor's party. General Grey, having cut off a sergeant's patrol, advanced in silence, and surrounded with his troops three barns in which the dragoons were sleeping. We have seen, in his surprise of Wayne's detachment in the preceding year, how stealthy and effective he was in the work of destruction. To prevent noise he had caused his men to draw the charges and take the flints from their guns, and fix their bayonets. The bayonet was his favorite weapon. With this his men rushed forward, and, deaf for a time to all cries for mercy, made a savage slaughter of naked and defenceless men. Eleven were killed on the spot, and twenty-five mangled with repeated thrusts, some receiving ten, twelve, and even sixteen wounds. Among the wounded were Colonel Baylor and Major Clough, the last of whom soon died.

This whole movement of troops, on both sides of the Hudson, was designed to cover an expedition against Little Egg Harbor, on the east coast of New Jersey, a noted rendezvous of American privateers. Three hundred regular troops, and a body of royalist volunteers from the Jerseys, headed by Captain Patrick Ferguson, embarked at New York on board galleys and transports, and made for Little Egg Harbor under convoy of vessels of war. They were long at sea. The country heard of their coming; four privateers put to sea and escaped; others took refuge up the river. The wind prevented the transports from entering. The troops embarked in row galleys and small craft, and pushed twenty miles up the river to the village of Chestnut Neck. Here were batteries without guns, prize ships which had been hastily scuttled, and storehouses for the reception of prize goods. The batteries and storehouses were demolished, the prize ships burnt, saltworks destroyed, private dwellings sacked and laid in ashes; all, it was pretended, being the property of persons concerned in privateering.

The vessels which brought this detachment being wind-bound for several days, Captain Ferguson had time for another enterprise. Among the forces detached by Washington into the Jerseys to check these ravages, was the Count Pulaski's legionary corps, composed of three companies of foot, and a troop of horse, officered principally by foreigners. A deserter from the corps brought word to the British commander that the legion was cantoned about twelve miles up the river; the infantry in three houses by themselves; Count Pulaski with the cavalry at some distance apart. Informed of these circumstances, Captain Ferguson embarked in boats with two hundred and fifty men, ascended the river in the night, landed at four in the morning, and surrounded the houses in which the infantry were sleeping. "It being a night attack," says the captain in his official report, "little quarter of course could be given, *so there were only five prisoners.*" Fifty of the infantry were butchered on the spot: among whom were two of the foreign officers, the Baron de Bose and Lieutenant de la Broderie. The clattering of hoofs gave note of the approach of Pulaski and his horse, whereupon the British made a rapid retreat to their boats and pulled down the river, and thus ended the marauding expedition of Captain Ferguson, worthy of the times of the buccaneers.

The detachment on the east side of the Hudson likewise made a predatory and disgraceful foray from their lines at King's Bridge, towards the American encampment at White Plains, plundering the inhabitants without discrimination, not only of their provisions and forage, but of the very clothes on their backs. None were more efficient in this ravage than a party of about one hundred of Captain Donop's Hessian yagers, and they were in full maraud between Tarrytown and Dobbs' Ferry, when a detachment of infantry under Colonel Richard Butler, and of cavalry under Major Henry Lee, came upon them by surprise, killed ten of them on the spot, and captured a lieutenant and eighteen privates.

The British detachments having accomplished the main objects of their movements, returned to New York; leaving those parts of the country they had harassed still more determined in their hostility, having achieved nothing but what is least honorable and most detestable in warfare.

About the middle of September Admiral Byron arrived at New York with the residue of the scattered armament, which had sailed from England in June to counteract the designs of the Count D'Estaing. Finding that the count was still repairing his shattered fleet in the harbor of Boston, he put to sea again as soon as his ships were refitted, and set sail for that port to entrap him. Success seemed likely to crown his schemes: he arrived off Boston on the 1st of November; his rival was still in port. Scarce had the admiral entered the bay, however, when another violent storm drove him out to sea, disabled his ships, and compelled him to put into Rhode Island to refit. Meanwhile, the count having his ships in good order, and finding the coast clear, put to sea, and made the best of his way for the West Indies.

The force at New York, which had been an object of watchful solicitude, was gradually dispersed in different directions. Immediately after the departure of Admiral Byron for Boston, another naval expedition had been set on foot by Sir Henry Clinton. All being ready, a fleet of transports with five thousand men, under General Grant, convoyed by Commodore Hotham with a squadron of six ships-of-war, set sail on the 3d of November, with the secret design of an attack on St. Lucia. Towards the end of the same month, another body of troops, under Lieutenant-colonel Campbell, sailed for Georgia in the squadron of Commodore Hyde Parker; the British cabinet having determined to carry the war into the Southern States. At the same time General Prevost, who commanded in Florida, was ordered by Sir Henry Clinton to march to the banks of the Savannah River, and attack Georgia in flank, while the expedition under Campbell should attack it in front on the seaboard.

The squadron of Commodore Hyde Parker anchored in the Savannah River towards the end of December. An American force of about six hundred regulars, and a few militia under General Robert Howe, were encamped near the town. Lieutenant-colonel Campbell landed his troops on the 29th of December. The whole country bordering the river is a deep morass, cut up by creeks, and only to be traversed by causeways. Over one of these, six hundred yards in length, with a ditch on each side, Colonel Campbell advanced, putting to flight a small party stationed to guard it. General Howe had posted his little army on the main road, with the river on his left and a morass in front. A negro gave Campbell information of a path leading through the morass, by which troops might get unobserved to the rear of the Americans. Sir James Baird was detached with the light infantry by this path, while Colonel Campbell advanced in front. The Americans, thus suddenly attacked in front and rear, were completely routed; upwards of one hundred were either killed on the spot or perished in the morass; thirty-eight officers and four hundred and fifteen privates were taken prisoners, the rest retreated up the Savannah River and crossed into South Carolina. Savannah, the capital of Georgia, was taken possession of by the victors, with cannon, military stores and provisions; their loss was only seven killed and nineteen wounded.

While Colonel Campbell had thus invaded Georgia in front, General Prevost, who commanded the British forces in Florida, had received orders from Sir Henry Clinton to take it in flank. He accordingly traversed deserts to its southern frontier, took Sunbury, the only remaining fort of importance, and marched to Savannah, where he assumed the general command, detaching Colonel Campbell against Augusta. By the middle of January (1779) all Georgia was reduced to submission.

A more experienced American general than Howe had by this time arrived to take command of the Southern Department, Major-general Lincoln, who had gained such reputation in the campaign against Burgoyne, and whose appointment to this station had been solicited by the delegates from South Carolina and Georgia. He had received his orders from Washington in the beginning of October. Of his operations at the South we shall have occasion to speak hereafter.

CHAPTER LII.

WASHINGTON IN PHILADELPHIA.—INDIAN WARFARE.—CAPTURE OF STONY POINT.—RAVAGES IN CONNECTICUT.—REPULSE AT SAVANNAH.

About the beginning of December, Washington distributed his troops for the winter in a line of strong cantonments extending from Long Island Sound to the Delaware. General Putnam commanded at Danbury, General McDougall in the Highlands, while the head-quarters of the commander-in-chief were near Middlebrook in the Jerseys. The objects of this arrangement were the protection of the country; the security of the important posts on the Hudson, and the safety, discipline, and easy subsistence of the army.

In the course of this winter he devised a plan of alarm signals, which General Philemon Dickinson was employed to carry into effect. On Bottle Hill, which commanded a vast map of country, sentinels kept watch day and night. Should there be an irruption of the enemy, an eighteen pounder, called the Old Sow, fired every half hour, gave the alarm in the day time or in dark and stormy nights; an immense fire or beacon at other times. On the booming of that heavy gun, lights sprang up from hill to hill along the different ranges of heights; the country was aroused, and the yeomanry, hastily armed, hurried to their gathering places.

Washington was now doomed to experience great loss in the narrow circle of those about him, on whose attachment and devotion he could place implicit reliance. The Marquis Lafayette, seeing no immediate prospect of active employment in the United States, and anticipating a war on the continent of Europe, was disposed to return to France to offer his services to his sovereign; desirous, however, of preserving a relation with America, he merely solicited from Congress the liberty of going home for the next winter; engaging himself not to depart until certain that the campaign was over. Washington backed his application for a furlough, as an arrangement that would still link him with the service; expressing his reluctance to part with an officer who united "to all the military fire of youth an uncommon maturity of judgment." Congress in consequence granted the marquis an unlimited leave of absence, to return to America whenever he should find it convenient.

Much of the winter was passed by Washington in Philadelphia, occupied in devising and discussing plans for the campaign of 1779. It was an anxious moment with him. Circumstances which inspired others with confidence, filled him with solicitude. The alliance with France had produced a baneful feeling of security, which, it appeared to him, was paralyzing the energies of the country. England, it was thought, would now be too much occupied in securing her position in Europe, to increase her force or extend her operations in America. Many, therefore, considered the war as virtually at an end; and were unwilling to make the sacrifices, or supply the means necessary for important military undertakings.

Dissensions, too, and party feuds were breaking out in Congress, owing to the relaxation of that external pressure of a common and imminent danger, which had heretofore produced a unity of sentiment and action. That august body had, in fact, greatly deteriorated since the commencement of the war. Many of those whose names had been as watchwords at the Declaration of Independence, had withdrawn from the national councils; occupied either by their individual affairs, or by the affairs of their individual States. Washington, whose comprehensive patriotism embraced the whole Union, deprecated and deplored the dawning of this sectional spirit. America, he declared, had never stood in more imminent need of the wise, patriotic, and spirited exertions of her sons than at this period.

In discussing the policy to be observed in the next campaign, Washington presumed the enemy would maintain their present posts and conduct the war as heretofore; in which case he was for remaining entirely on the defensive. One single exception was made by him. The horrible ravages and massacres perpetrated by the Indians and their tory allies at Wyoming had been followed by similar atrocities at Cherry Valley, in the State of New York, and called for signal vengeance to prevent a repetition. Washington knew by experience that Indian warfare, to be effective, should never be merely defensive, but must be carried into the enemy's country. The Six Nations, the most civilized of the savage tribes, had proved themselves the most formidable. His idea was to make war upon them in their own style; penetrate their country, lay waste their villages and settlements, and at the same time destroy the British post at Niagara, that nestling-place of tories and refugees.

The policy thus recommended was adopted by Congress. Arrangements were set on foot to carry that part relative to the Indians into execution. The first act was an expedition from Fort Schuyler by Colonel Van Schaick, Lieutenant-colonel Willett, and Major Cochran, with about six hundred men, who, on the 19th of April, surprised the towns of the Onondagas, destroyed the whole settlement, and returned to the fort without the loss of a single man.

The great expedition of the campaign, however, was in revenge of the massacre of Wyoming. Early in the summer three thousand men assembled in that lately desolated region, and, conducted by General Sullivan, moved up the west branch of the Susquehanna into the Seneca country. While on the way they were joined by a part of the western army under General James Clinton, who had come from the valley of the Mohawk by Otsego Lake and the east branch of the Susquehanna. The united forces amounted to about five thousand men, of which Sullivan had the general command.

The Indians, and their allies the tories, had received information of the intended invasion, and appeared in arms to oppose it. They were much inferior in force, however, being about fifteen hundred Indians and two hundred white men, commanded by the two Butlers, Johnson, and Brant. A battle took place at Newtown, on the 29th of August, in which they were easily defeated. Sullivan then pushed forward into the heart of the Indian country, penetrating as far as the Genesee River, laying everything waste, setting fire to deserted dwellings, destroying cornfields, orchards, gardens, everything that could give sustenance to man, the design being to starve the Indians out of the country. The latter retreated before him with their families, and at length took refuge under the protection of the British garrison at Niagara. Having completed his errand, Sullivan returned to Easton in Pennsylvania. The thanks of Congress were voted to him and his army, but he shortly afterward resigned his commission on account of ill health and retired from the service.

A similar expedition was undertaken by Colonel Brodhead, from Pittsburg up the Alleghany, against the Mingo, Muncey, and Seneca tribes, with similar results. The wisdom of Washington's policy of carrying the war against the Indians into their country, and conducting it in their own way, was apparent from the general intimidation produced among the tribes by these expeditions, and the subsequent infrequency of their murderous incursions.

The situation of Sir Henry Clinton must have been mortifying in the extreme to an officer of lofty ambition and generous aims. His force, between sixteen and seventeen thousand strong, was superior in number, discipline, and equipment to that of Washington; yet his instructions confined him to a predatory warfare carried on by attacks and marauds at distant points, harassing, it is true, yet irritating to the country intended to be conciliated, and brutalizing to his own soldiery. Such was the nature of an expedition set on foot against the commerce of the Chesapeake; by which commerce the armies were supplied and the credit of the government sustained. On the 9th of May, a squadron under Sir George Collier, convoying transports and galleys, with twenty-five hundred men, commanded by General Mathews, entered these waters, took possession of Portsmouth without opposition, sent out armed parties against Norfolk, Suffolk, Gosport, Kemp's Landing, and other neighboring places, where were immense quantities of provisions, naval and military stores, and merchandise of all kinds; with numerous vessels, some on the stocks, others richly laden. Wherever they went, a scene of plunder, conflagration, and destruction ensued. A few days sufficed to ravage the whole neighborhood.

While this was going on at the South, Washington received intelligence of movements at New York and in its vicinity, which made him apprehend an expedition against the Highlands of the Hudson. Since the loss of Forts Montgomery and Clinton, the main defences of the Highlands had been established at the sudden bend of the river where it winds between West Point and Constitution Island. Two opposite forts commanded this bend, and an iron chain which was stretched across it.

Washington had projected two works also just below the Highlands, at Stony Point and Verplanck's Point, to serve as outworks of the mountain passes, and to protect King's Ferry, the most direct and convenient communication between the Northern and Middle States. A small but strong fort had been erected on Verplanck's Point, and was garrisoned by seventy men under Captain Armstrong. A more important work was in progress at Stony Point. When completed, these two forts, on opposite promontories, would form as it were the lower gates of the Highlands. To be at hand in case of any real attempt upon the Highlands, Washington drew up with his forces in that direction; moving by the way of Morristown.

An expedition up the Hudson was really the object of Sir Henry Clinton's movements, and for this he was strengthened by the return of Sir George Collier with his marauding ships and forces from Virginia. On the 30th of May, Sir Henry set out on his second grand cruise up the Hudson, with an armament of about seventy sail, great and small, and one hundred and fifty flat-boats. Admiral Sir George Collier commanded the armament, and there was a land force of about five thousand men under General Vaughan.

The first aim of Sir Henry was to get possession of Stony and Verplanck's Points; his former expedition had acquainted him with the importance of this pass of the river. On the morning of the 31st, the forces were landed in two divisions, the largest under General Vaughan, on the east side of the river, about seven or eight miles below Verplanck's Point; the other, commanded by Sir Henry in person, landed in Haverstraw Bay, about three miles below Stony Point. There were but about thirty men in the unfinished fort; they abandoned it on the approach of the enemy, and retreated into the Highlands, having first set fire to the blockhouse. The British took quiet possession of the fort in the evening; dragged up cannon and mortars in the night, and at daybreak opened a furious fire upon Fort Lafayette. It was cannonaded at the same time by the armed vessels, and a demonstration was made on it by the division under General Vaughan. Thus surrounded, the little garrison of seventy men was forced to surrender, with no other stipulation than safety to their persons and to the property they had in the fort. Major André was aide-de-camp to Sir Henry, and signed the articles of capitulation.

Washington presumed that the main object of Sir Henry was to get possession of West Point, the guardian fortress of the river, and that the capture of Stony and Verplanck's Points were preparatory steps. He would fain have dislodged him from these posts, but deferring any attempt on them for the present, he took measures for the protection of West Point. Leaving General Putnam and the main body of the army at Smith's Clove, a mountain pass in the rear of Haverstraw, he removed his head-quarters to New Windsor, to be near West Point in case of need, and to press the completion of its works. General McDougall was transferred to the command of the Point. Three brigades were stationed at different places on the opposite side of the river, under General Heath, from which fatigue parties crossed daily to work on the fortifications.

This strong disposition of the American forces checked Sir Henry's designs against the Highlands. Contenting himself, therefore, for the present, with the acquisition of Stony and Verplanck's Points, he returned to New York, where he soon set on foot a desolating expedition along the seaboard of Connecticut. That State, while it furnished the American armies with provisions and recruits, and infested the sea with privateers, had hitherto experienced nothing of the horrors of war within its borders. Sir Henry, in compliance with his instructions from government, was now about to give it a scourging lesson. General (late Governor) Tryon, was the officer selected by Sir Henry for this inglorious, but apparently congenial service. About the beginning of July he embarked with two thousand six hundred men, in a fleet of transports and tenders, and was convoyed up the Sound by Sir George Collier with two ships-of-war.

On the 5th of July the troops landed near New Haven, in two divisions, one led by Tryon, the other by Brigadier-general Garth, his lieutenant. They came upon the neighborhood by surprise; yet the militia assembled in haste, and made a resolute though ineffectual opposition. The British captured the town, dismantled the fort, and took or destroyed all the vessels in the harbor; with all the artillery, ammunition, and public stores. Several private houses were plundered. They next proceeded to Fairfield; where, meeting with greater resistance, they thought the moment arrived for a wholesome example of severity. Accordingly, they not merely ravaged and destroyed the public stores and the vessels in the harbor, but laid the town itself in ashes. The exact return of this salutary lesson gives the destruction of ninety-seven dwelling-houses, sixty-seven barns and stables, forty-eight store-houses, three places of worship, a court-house, a jail, and two school-houses.

At Norwalk, where they landed on the 11th of July, they burnt one hundred and thirty dwelling-houses, eighty-seven barns, twenty-two store-houses, seventeen shops, four mills, two places of worship, and five vessels which were in the harbor. The loss of the British throughout the whole expedition amounted, according to their own accounts, to twenty killed, ninety-six wounded, and thirty-two missing. It was intended to crown this grand ravage by a descent on New London, a noted rendezvous of privateers; but as greater opposition was expected there than at either of the other places the squadron returned to Huntington Bay, on Long Island, to await reinforcements; and Commodore Collier proceeded to Throg's Neck, to confer with Sir Henry Clinton about further operations.

Washington on hearing of the departure of the expedition to the eastward, and before he was acquainted with its definite object, detached General Heath, with two brigades of Connecticut militia, to counteract the movements of the enemy. This was all that he could spare from the force stationed for the protection of the Highlands. Any weakening of his posts there might bring the enemy suddenly upon him, such was their facility in moving from one place to another by means of their shipping. Indeed, he had divined that a scheme of the kind was at the bottom of the hostile movement to the eastward.

As a kind of counter-check to Sir Henry, Washington had for some days been planning the recapture of Stony Point and Fort Lafayette. He had reconnoitred them in person; spies had been thrown into them, and information collected from deserters. Stony Point having been recently strengthened by the British was now the most important. It was a rocky promontory advancing far into the Hudson, which washed three sides of it. A deep morass, covered at high water, separated it from the mainland, but at low tide might be traversed by a narrow causeway and bridge. The promontory was crowned by strong works, furnished with heavy ordnance, commanding the morass and causeway. Lower down were two rows of abatis, and the shore at the foot of the hill could be swept by vessels of war anchored in the river. The garrison was about six hundred strong, commanded by Lieutenant-colonel Johnson.

To attempt the surprisal of this isolated post, thus strongly fortified, was a perilous enterprise. General Wayne, Mad Anthony as he was called from his daring valor, was the officer to whom Washington proposed it, and he engaged in it with avidity. According to Washington's plan, it was to be attempted by light-infantry only, at night, and with the utmost secrecy, securing every person they met to prevent discovery. Between one and two hundred chosen men and officers were to make the surprise; preceded by a vanguard of prudent, determined men, well commanded, to remove obstructions, secure sentries, and drive in the guards. On getting possession of Stony Point, Wayne was to turn its guns upon Fort Lafayette and the shipping. A detachment was to march down from West Point by Peekskill, to the vicinity of Fort Lafayette, and hold itself ready to join in the attack upon it, as soon as the cannonade began from Stony Point.

On the 15th of July, about mid-day, Wayne set out with his light-infantry from Sandy Beach, fourteen miles distant from Stony Point. About eight in the evening, they arrived within a mile and a half of the forts, without being discovered. About half-past eleven, the whole moved forward, guided by a negro of the neighborhood who had frequently carried in fruit to the garrison, and served the Americans as a spy. He led the way, accompanied by two stout men disguised as farmers. The countersign was given to the first sentinel, posted on high ground west of the morass. While the negro talked with him, the men seized and gagged him. The sentinel posted at the head of the causeway was served in the same manner. The causeway, however, was overflowed, and it was some time after twelve o'clock before the troops could cross; leaving three hundred men under General Muhlenberg, on the western side of the morass, as a reserve.

At the foot of the promontory, the troops were divided into two columns, for simultaneous attacks on opposite sides of the works. One hundred and fifty volunteers, led by Lieutenant-colonel Fleury, seconded by Major Posey, formed the vanguard of the right column; one hundred volunteers under Major Stewart, the vanguard of the left. In the advance of each was a forlorn hope of twenty men, one led by Lieutenant Gibbon, the other by Lieutenant Knox; it was their desperate duty to remove the abatis. So well had the whole affair been conducted, that the Americans were close upon the outworks before they were discovered. There was then severe skirmishing at the pickets. The Americans used the bayonet; the others discharged their muskets. The reports roused the garrison. Stony Point was instantly in an uproar. The drums beat to arms; every one hurried to his alarm post; the works were hastily manned, and a tremendous fire of grape-shot and musketry opened upon the assailants.

The two columns forced their way with the bayonet, at opposite points, surmounting every obstacle. Colonel Fleury was the first to enter the fort and strike the British flag. Major Posey sprang to the ramparts and shouted, "The fort is our own." The two columns arrived nearly at the same time, and met in the centre of the works. The garrison surrendered at discretion. At daybreak, the guns of the fort were turned on Fort Lafayette and the shipping. The latter cut their cables and dropped down the river. Through a series of blunders, the detachment from West Point, which was to have co-operated, did not arrive in time, and came unprovided with suitable ammunition for their battering artillery. This part of the enterprise, therefore, failed; Fort Lafayette held out.

The storming of Stony Point stands out in high relief as one of the most brilliant achievements of the war. The Americans had effected it without firing a musket. On their part it was the silent, deadly work of the bayonet; the fierce resistance they met at the outset may be judged by the havoc made in their forlorn hope; out of twenty-two men, seventeen were either killed or wounded. The whole loss of the Americans was fifteen killed and eighty-three wounded. Of the garrison, sixty-three were slain, including two officers; five hundred and fifty-three were taken prisoners, among whom were a lieutenant-colonel, four captains, and twenty-three subaltern officers.

NEW LONDON, CONN.
VOL. IV.

Tidings of the capture of Stony Point, and the imminent danger of Fort Lafayette, reached Sir Henry Clinton just after his conference with Sir George Collier at Throg's Neck. The expedition against New London was instantly given up; the transports and troops were recalled; a forced march was made to Dobbs' Ferry on the Hudson; a detachment was sent up the river in transports to relieve Fort Lafayette, and Sir Henry followed with a greater force, hoping Washington might quit his fastnesses, and risk a battle for the possession of Stony Point.

Again the Fabian policy of the American commander-in-chief disappointed the British general. Having well examined the post in company with an engineer and several general officers, he found that at least fifteen hundred men would be required to maintain it, a number not to be spared from the army at present. The works, too, were only calculated for defence on the land side, and were open towards the river, where the enemy depended upon protection from their ships. It would be necessary to construct them anew, with great labor. The army, also, would have to be in the vicinity, too distant from West Point to aid in completing or defending its fortifications, and exposed to the risk of a general action on unfavorable terms. For these considerations, in which all his officers concurred, Washington evacuated the post on the 18th, removing the cannon and stores, and destroying the works; after which he drew his forces together in the Highlands, and established his quarters at West Point. Sir Henry retook possession of Stony Point, and fortified and garrisoned it more strongly than ever, but was too wary to risk an attempt upon the strongholds of the Highlands.

The brilliant affair of the storming of Stony Point was somewhat overshadowed by the result of an enterprise at the eastward, undertaken without consulting Washington. A British detachment from Halifax, of seven or eight hundred men, had founded in June a military post on the eastern side of the Bay of Penobscot, nine miles below the river of that name, and were erecting a fort there, intended to protect Nova Scotia, control the frontiers of Massachusetts, and command the vast wooded regions of Maine.

The people of Boston, roused by this movement, which invaded their territory, and touched their pride and interests, undertook, on their own responsibility, a naval and military expedition intended to drive off the invaders. A squadron of armed ships and brigantines under Commodore Saltonstall put to sea, convoying transports, on board of which were near four thousand land troops under General Lovel. Arriving in the Penobscot on the 25th of May, they found Colonel Maclean posted on a peninsula, steep and precipitous toward the bay, and deeply trenched on the land side, with three ships-of-war anchored before it.

Lovel was repulsed, with some little loss, in an attempt to effect a landing on the peninsula; but finally succeeded before daybreak on the 28th. The moment was propitious for a bold and vigorous blow. The fort was but half finished; the guns were not mounted; the three armed vessels could not have offered a formidable resistance; but, unfortunately, the energy of a Wayne was wanting to the enterprise. Lovel proceeded by regular siege. He threw up works at seven hundred and fifty yards distance, and opened a cannonade, which was continued from day to day, for a fortnight. The delay gave time for Admiral Collier at New York to hear of this enterprise, and take measures for its defeat.

On the 13th of August, Lovel was astounded by intelligence that the admiral was arrived before the bay with a superior armament. Thus fairly entrapped, he endeavored to extricate his force with as little loss as possible. Before news of Collier's arrival could reach the fort, he re-embarked his troops in the transports to make their escape up the river. His armed vessels were drawn up in a crescent as if to give battle, but it was merely to hold the enemy in check. They soon gave way; some were captured, others were set on fire or blown up, and abandoned by their crews. The transports being eagerly pursued and in great danger of being taken, disgorged the troops and seamen on the wild shores of the river: whence they had to make the best of their way to Boston, struggling for upwards of a hundred miles through a pathless wilderness, before they reached the settled parts of the country.

If Washington was chagrined by the signal failure of this expedition, he was cheered by the better fortune of one set on foot about the same time, under his own eye, by his young friend, Major Henry Lee of the Virginia dragoons. This active and daring officer had frequently been employed by him in scouring the country on the west side of the Hudson to collect information; keep an eye upon the enemy's posts; cut off their supplies, and check their foraging parties. The *coup de main* at Stony Point had piqued his emulation. In the course of his reconnoitring, and by means of spies, he had discovered that the British post at Paulus Hook, immediately opposite to New York, was very negligently guarded. Paulus Hook is a long low point of the Jersey shore, stretching into the Hudson, and connected to the main land by a sandy isthmus. A fort had been erected on it, and garrisoned with four or five hundred men, under the command of Major Sutherland. It was a strong position. A creek, fordable only in two places, rendered the hook difficult of access. Within this, a deep trench had been cut across the isthmus, traversed by a drawbridge with a barred gate; and still within this was a double row of abatis, extending into the water. Confident in the strength of his position, and its distance from any American force, Major Sutherland had become remiss in his military precautions. All this had been ascertained by Major Lee; and he now proposed the daring project of surprising the fort at night, and thus striking an insulting blow "within cannon shot of New York." Washington was disposed to favor the adventurous schemes of this young officer.

On the 18th of August, Lee set out on the expedition, at the head of three hundred men of Lord Stirling's division, and a troop of dismounted dragoons under Captain McLane. It was between two and three in the morning when he arrived at the creek. It happened, fortunately, that Major Sutherland, the British commander, had the day before detached a foraging party under a Major Buskirk to a part of the country called the English Neighborhood. As Lee and his men approached they were mistaken by the sentinel for this party on its return. The darkness of the night favored the mistake. They passed the creek and ditch, entered the works unmolested, and had made themselves masters of the post before the negligent garrison were well roused from sleep. Major Sutherland and about sixty Hessians threw themselves into a small block-house on the left of the fort and opened an irregular fire. To attempt to dislodge them would have cost too much time. Alarm guns from the ships in the river and the forts at New York threatened speedy reinforcements to the enemy. Having made one hundred and fifty-nine prisoners, among whom were three officers, Lee commenced his retreat, without tarrying to destroy either barracks or artillery. Few of the enemy were slain, for there was but little fighting and no massacre. His own loss was two men killed and three wounded.

The arrival of Admiral Arbuthnot, with a fleet bringing three thousand troops and a supply of provisions and stores, strengthened the hands of Sir Henry Clinton. Still he had not sufficient force to warrant any further attempt up the Hudson, Washington, by his diligence in fortifying West Point, having rendered that fastness of the Highlands apparently impregnable. Sir Henry turned his thoughts, therefore, towards the South, hoping by a successful expedition in that direction to counterbalance ill success in other quarters.

At this juncture news was received of the arrival of the Count D'Estaing with a formidable fleet on the coast of Georgia, having made a successful cruise in the West Indies, in the course of which he had taken St. Vincent's and Granada. A combined attack upon New York was again talked of. In anticipation of it, Washington called upon several of the Middle States for supplies of all kinds, and reinforcements of militia. Sir Henry Clinton also changed his plans; caused Rhode Island to be evacuated; the troops and stores to be brought away; the garrisons brought off from Stony and Verplanck's Points, and all his forces to be concentrated at New York, which he endeavored to put in the strongest posture of defence.

Intelligence recently received, too, that Spain had joined France in hostilities against England, contributed to increase the solicitude and perplexities of the enemy, while it gave fresh confidence to the Americans.

Washington's anticipations of a combined operation with D'Estaing against New York were again disappointed. The French admiral, on arriving on the coast of Georgia, had been persuaded to co-operate with the Southern army, under General Lincoln, in an attempt to recover Savannah. For three weeks a siege was carried on with great vigor, by regular approaches on land, and cannonade and bombardment from the shipping. On the 9th of October, although the approaches were not complete, and no sufficient breach had been effected, Lincoln and D'Estaing, at the head of their choicest troops, advanced before daybreak to storm the works. The assault was gallant but unsuccessful; both Americans and French had planted their standards on the redoubts, but were finally repulsed. After the repulse, both armies retired from before the place, the French having lost in killed and wounded upwards of six hundred men, the Americans about four hundred. D'Estaing himself was among the wounded, and the gallant Count Pulaski among the slain. The loss of the enemy was trifling, being protected by their works.

The tidings of this reverse, which reached Washington late in November, put an end to all prospect of co-operation from the French fleet; a consequent change took place in all his plans. The militia of New York and Massachusetts, recently assembled, were disbanded, and arrangements were made for the winter. The army was thrown into two divisions; one was to be stationed under General Heath in the Highlands, for the protection of West Point and the neighboring posts; the other and principal division was to be hutted near Morristown, where Washington was to have his head-quarters. The cavalry were to be sent to Connecticut.

Understanding that Sir Henry Clinton was making preparations at New York for a large embarkation of troops, and fearing they might be destined against Georgia and Carolina, he resolved to detach the greater part of his Southern troops for the protection of those States; a provident resolution, in which he was confirmed by subsequent instructions from Congress. Accordingly, the North Carolina brigade took up its march for Charleston in November, and the whole of the Virginia line in December.

Notwithstanding the recent preparations at New York, the ships remained in port, and the enemy held themselves in collected force there. Sir Henry was regulating his movements by those the French fleet might make after the repulse at Savannah. Intelligence at length arrived that it had been dispersed by a violent storm. Count D'Estaing, with a part, had shaped his course for France; the rest had proceeded to the West Indies. Sir Henry now lost no time in carrying his plans into operation. Leaving the garrison of New York under the command of Lieutenant-general Knyphausen, he embarked several thousand men on board of transports, to be convoyed by five ships-of-the-line and several frigates under Admiral Arbuthnot, and set sail on the 26th of December, accompanied by Lord Cornwallis, on an expedition intended for the capture of Charleston and the reduction of South Carolina.

CHAPTER LIII.

ARMY AT MORRISTOWN.—ARNOLD IN PHILA-DELPHIA.—CHARLESTON BESIEGED.

The dreary encampment at Valley Forge has become proverbial for its hardships; yet they were scarcely more severe than those suffered by Washington's army during the present winter, while hutted among the heights of Morristown. The winter set in early, and was uncommonly rigorous. The transportation of supplies was obstructed; the magazines were exhausted, and the commissaries had neither money nor credit to enable them to replenish them. For weeks at a time the army was on half allowance; sometimes without meat, sometimes without bread, sometimes without both. There was a scarcity, too, of clothing and blankets, so that the poor soldiers were starving with cold as well as hunger.

HEAD-QUARTERS, MORRISTOWN, N.J.
VOL. III.

A rigorous winter had much to do with the actual distresses of the army, but the root of the evil lay in the derangement of the currency. Congress had commenced the war without adequate funds, and without the power of imposing direct taxes. To meet pressing emergencies, it had emitted paper money, which, for a time, passed currently at par; but sank in value as further emissions succeeded, and that already in circulation remained unredeemed. The several States added to the evil by emitting paper in their separate capacities: thus the country gradually became flooded with a "continental currency," as it was called; irredeemable, and of no intrinsic value. The consequence was a general derangement of trade and finance. The continental currency declined to such a degree, that forty dollars in paper were equivalent to only one in specie. Congress attempted to put a stop to this depreciation, by making paper money a legal tender, at its nominal value, in the discharge of debts, however contracted. This opened the door to knavery, and added a new feature to the evil.

The commissaries now found it difficult to purchase supplies for the immediate wants of the army, and impossible to provide any stores in advance. They were left destitute of funds, and the public credit was prostrated by the accumulating debts suffered to remain uncancelled. The changes which had taken place in the commissary department added to this confusion. The commissary-general, instead of receiving, as heretofore, a commission on expenditures, was to have a fixed salary in paper currency; and his deputies were to be compensated in like manner, without the usual allowance of rations and forage. No competent agents could be procured on such terms; and the derangement produced throughout the department compelled Colonel Wadsworth, the able and upright commissary-general, to resign.

In the present emergency Washington was reluctantly compelled, by the distresses of the army, to call upon the counties of the State for supplies of grain and cattle, proportioned to their respective abilities. These supplies were to be brought into the camp within a certain time; the grain to be measured and the cattle estimated by any two of the magistrates of the county in conjunction with the commissary, and certificates to be given by the latter, specifying the quantity of each and the terms of payment. Wherever a compliance with this call was refused, the articles required were to be impressed: it was a painful alternative, yet nothing else could save the army from dissolution or starving. Washington charged his officers to act with as much tenderness as possible, graduating the exaction according to the stock of each individual, so that no family should be deprived of what was necessary to its subsistence. To the honor of the magistrates and the people of Jersey, Washington testifies that his requisitions were punctually complied with, and in many counties exceeded.

As the winter advanced, the cold increased in severity. It was the most intense ever remembered in the country. The great bay of New York was frozen over. No supplies could come to the city by water. Provisions grew scanty; and there was such lack of firewood that old transports were broken up, and uninhabited wooden houses pulled down for fuel. The safety of the city was endangered. The ships-of-war, immovably ice-bound in its harbor, no longer gave it protection. The insular security of the place was at an end. An army with its heaviest artillery and baggage might cross the Hudson on the ice.

Washington was aware of the opportunity which offered itself for a signal *coup de main*, but was not in a condition to profit by it. His troops, hutted among the heights of Morristown, were half fed, half clothed, and inferior in number to the garrison of New York. He was destitute of funds necessary to fit them for the enterprise, and the quartermaster could not furnish means of transportation.

Still, in the frozen condition of the bay and rivers, some minor blow might be attempted, sufficient to rouse and cheer the spirits of the people. With this view, having ascertained that the ice formed a bridge across the strait between the Jersey shore and Staten Island, he projected a descent upon the latter by Lord Stirling with twenty-five hundred men, to surprise and capture a British force of ten or twelve hundred. His lordship crossed on the night of the 14th of January, from De Hart's Point to the island. His approach was discovered; the troops took refuge in the works, which were too strongly situated to be attacked; a channel remaining open through the ice across the bay, a boat was despatched to New York for reinforcements. The projected surprise having thus proved a complete failure, and his own situation becoming hazardous, Lord Stirling recrossed to the Jersey shore with a number of prisoners whom he had captured.

By way of retort, Knyphausen, on the 25th of January, sent out two detachments to harass the American outposts. One crossed to Paulus Hook, and being joined by part of the garrison of that post, pushed on to Newark, surprised and captured a company stationed there, set fire to the academy, and returned without loss. The other detachment, consisting of one hundred dragoons and between three and four hundred infantry, under Lieutenant-colonel Boskirk, crossed from Staten Island to Trembly's Point, surprised the picket-guard at Elizabethtown, and captured two majors, two captains, and forty-two privates. This, likewise, was effected without loss. The disgraceful part of the expedition was the burning of the town house, a church, and a private residence, and the plundering of the inhabitants. The church destroyed was a Presbyterian place of worship, and its pastor, the Rev. James Caldwell, had rendered himself an especial object of hostility to both Briton and tory. His church had at times served as hospital to the American soldier; or shelter to the hastily assembled militia. Its bell was the tocsin of alarm; from its pulpit he had many a time stirred up the patriotism of his countrymen by his ardent, eloquent, and pathetic appeals. His popularity in the army, and among the Jersey people, was unbounded.

Another noted maraud during Knyphausen's military sway, was in the lower part of Westchester County, in a hilly region lying between the British and American lines, which had been the scene of part of the past year's campaign. In this region, about twenty miles from the British outposts, and not far from White Plains, the Americans had established a post of three hundred men at a stone building commonly known as Young's house, from the name of its owner. It commanded a road which passed from north to south down along the narrow but fertile valley of the Sawmill River. On this road the garrison of Young's house kept a vigilant eye, to intercept the convoys of cattle and provisions which had been collected or plundered by the enemy, and which passed down this valley toward New York. This post had long been an annoyance to the enemy, but its distance from the British lines had hitherto saved it from attack. The country now was covered with snow; troops could be rapidly transported on sleighs; and it was determined that Young's house should be surprised, and this rebel nest broken up.

On the evening of the 2d of February, an expedition set out for the purpose from King's Bridge, led by Lieutenant-colonel Norton, and consisting of four flank companies of guards, two companies of Hessians, and a party of Yagers, all in sleighs; beside a body of Yager cavalry, and a number of mounted Westchester refugees, with two three-pounders. The snow being newly fallen, was deep; the sleighs broke their way through it with difficulty. The troops at length abandoned them and pushed forward on foot. The cannon were left behind for the same reason. It was a weary tramp. The sun rose while they were yet seven miles from Young's house. To surprise the post was out of the question; still they kept on. Before they could reach the house the country had taken the alarm, and the Westchester yeomanry had armed themselves, and were hastening to aid the garrison. The British light infantry and grenadiers invested the mansion; the cavalry posted themselves on a neighboring eminence, to prevent retreat or reinforcement, and the house was assailed. It made a brave resistance, and was aided by some of the yeomanry stationed in an adjacent orchard. The garrison, however, was overpowered; numbers were killed, and ninety taken prisoners. The house was sacked and set in flames.

The most irksome duty that Washington had to perform during this winter's encampment at Morristown, regarded General Arnold and his military government of Philadelphia in 1778. To explain it requires a glance back to that period.

At the time of entering upon this command, Arnold's accounts with government were yet unsettled; the committee appointed by Congress at his own request to examine them having considered some of his charges dubious and others exorbitant. The command of Philadelphia at this time was a delicate and difficult one, and required to be exercised with extreme circumspection. The boundaries between the powers vested in the military commander and those inherent in the State government were ill defined. Disaffection to the American cause prevailed both among the permanent and casual residents, and required to be held in check with firmness but toleration. By a resolve of Congress, no goods, wares, or merchandise were to be removed, transferred, or sold, until the ownership of them could be ascertained by a joint committee of Congress and of the Council of Pennsylvania; any public stores belonging to the enemy were to be seized and converted to the use of the army. Washington, in his letter of instructions left it to Arnold's discretion to adopt such measures as should appear to him most effectual and least offensive in executing this resolve of Congress; in which he was to be aided by an assistant quartermaster-general, subject to his directions.

One of Arnold's first measures was to issue a proclamation enforcing the resolve of Congress. In so doing, he was countenanced by leading personages of Philadelphia, and the proclamation was drafted by General Joseph Reed. The measure excited great dissatisfaction, and circumstances attending the enforcement of it gave rise to scandal. Former instances of a mercenary spirit made Arnold liable to suspicions, and it was alleged that, while by the proclamation he shut up the stores and shops so that even the officers of the army could not procure necessary articles of merchandise, he was privately making large purchases for his own enrichment.

His style of living gave point to this scandal. He occupied one of the finest houses in the city; set up a splendid establishment; had his carriage and four horses and a train of domestics; gave expensive entertainments, and indulged in a luxury and parade which were condemned as little befitting a republican general. Ostentatious prodigality, in fact, was Arnold's besetting sin. In the exercise of his military functions he had become involved in disputes with the president (Wharton) and executive council of Pennsylvania, and by his conduct, which was deemed arbitrary and arrogant, had drawn upon himself the hostility of that body, which became stern and unsparing censors of his conduct.

He had not been many weeks in Philadelphia before he became attached to one of its reigning belles, Miss Margaret Shippen, daughter of Mr. Edward Shippen, in after years chief justice of Pennsylvania. Her family were not considered well affected to the American cause; the young lady herself, during the occupation of the city by the enemy, had been a "toast" among the British officers. Party feeling at that time ran high in Philadelphia on local subjects connected with the charge of the State government. Arnold's connection with the Shippen family increased his disfavor with the president and executive council, who were whigs to a man.

In the beginning of December, General Reed became president of the executive council of Pennsylvania, and under his administration the ripening hostility to Arnold was brought to a crisis. His public conduct [during Arnold's absence at Washington's camp on the Raritan] was discussed in the executive council of Pennsylvania, and it was resolved unanimously, that the course of his military command in the city had been in many respects oppressive, unworthy of his rank and station, and highly discouraging to the liberties and interests of America, and disrespectful to the supreme executive authority of the State. As he was an officer of the United States, the complaints and grievances of Pennsylvania were set forth by the executive council in eight charges, and forwarded to Congress, accompanied by documents, and a letter from President Reed.

Information of these facts, with a printed copy of the charges, reached Arnold at Washington's camp. On the following day he issued an address to the public, recalling his faithful services of nearly four years, and inveighing against the proceedings of the president and council; who, not content with injuring him in a cruel and unprecedented manner with Congress, had ordered copies of their charges to be printed and dispersed throughout the several States, for the purpose of prejudicing the public mind against him, while the matter was yet in suspense. In conclusion, Arnold informed the public that he had requested Congress to direct a court-martial to inquire into his conduct, and trusted his countrymen would suspend their judgment in the matter, until he should have an opportunity of being heard.

On the 16th of February, Arnold's appeal to Congress was referred to the committee which had under consideration the letter of President Reed and its accompanying documents, and it was charged to make a report with all convenient despatch. Arnold, in the course of January, had obtained permission from Washington to resign the command of Philadelphia, but deferred to act upon it, until the charges against him should be examined. About the middle of March, the committee brought in a report exculpating him from all criminality in the matters charged against him. As soon as the report was brought in, he considered his name vindicated, and resigned.

Whatever exultation he may have felt was short-lived. Congress did not call up and act upon the report, as, in justice to him, they should have done, whether to sanction it or not; but referred the subject anew to a joint committee of their body and the assembly and council of Pennsylvania. The report of the joint committee brought up animated discussions in Congress. Several resolutions recommended by the committee were merely of a formal nature, and intended to soothe the wounded sensibilities of Pennsylvania; these were passed without dissent; but it was contended that certain charges advanced by the executive council of that State were only cognizable by a court-martial, and, after a warm debate, it was resolved (April 3d,) by a large majority, that the commander-in-chief should appoint such a court for the consideration of them.

Arnold inveighed bitterly against the injustice of subjecting him to a trial before a military tribunal for alleged offences of which he had been acquitted by the committee of Congress. He was sacrificed, he said, to avoid a breach with Pennsylvania. In a letter to Washington, he charged it all to the hostility of President Reed, who, he affirmed, had by his address kept the affair in suspense for two months, and at last obtained the resolution of Congress directing the court-martial. He urged Washington to appoint a speedy day for the trial, that he might not linger under the odium of an unjust public accusation.

It was doubtless soothing to his irritated pride, that the woman on whom he had placed his affections remained true to him; for his marriage with Miss Shippen took place just five days after the mortifying vote of Congress.

Washington sympathized with Arnold's impatience, and appointed the 1st of May for the trial, but it was repeatedly postponed; first, at the request of the Pennsylvania council, to allow time for the arrival of witnesses from the South; afterwards, in consequence of threatening movements of the enemy, which obliged every officer to be at his post. Arnold, in the meantime, continued to reside at Philadelphia, holding his commission in the army, but filling no public office; getting deeper and deeper in debt, and becoming more and more unpopular. For months, he remained in this anxious and irritated state. At length, when the campaign was over, and the army had gone into winter-quarters, the long-delayed court-martial was assembled at Morristown. Of the eight charges originally advanced against Arnold by the Pennsylvania council, four only came under cognizance of the court. Of two of these he was entirely acquitted. The remaining two were:

First. That while in the camp at Valley Forge, he, without the knowledge of the commander-in-chief, or the sanction of the State government, had granted a written permission for a vessel belonging to disaffected persons to proceed from the port of Philadelphia, then in possession of the enemy, to any port of the United States.

Second. That, availing himself of his official authority, he had appropriated the public wagons of Pennsylvania, when called forth on a special emergency, to the transportation of private property, and that of persons who voluntarily remained with the enemy, and were deemed disaffected to the interests and independence of America.

In regard to the first of these charges, Arnold alleged that the person who applied for the protection of the vessel, had taken the oath of allegiance to the State of Pennsylvania required by the laws; and that the intentions of that person and his associates with regard to the vessel and cargo appeared to be upright. In regard to the second charge, while it was proved that under his authority public wagons had been so used, it was allowed in extenuation that they had been employed at private expense, and without any design to defraud the public or impede the military service. In regard to both charges, nothing fraudulent on the part of Arnold was proved, but the transactions involved in the first were pronounced irregular, and contrary to one of the articles of war; and in the second, imprudent and reprehensible, considering the high station occupied by the general at the time, and the court sentenced him to be reprimanded by the commander-in-chief. The sentence was confirmed by Congress on the 12th of February (1780).

The reprimand adjudged by the court-martial was administered by Washington with consummate delicacy. The following were his words: "Our profession is the chastest of all; even the shadow of a fault tarnishes the lustre of our finest achievements. The least inadvertence may rob us of the public favor, so hard to be acquired. I reprehend you for having forgotten, that, in proportion as you had rendered yourself formidable to our enemies, you should have been guarded and temperate in your deportment towards your fellow-citizens. Exhibit anew those noble qualities which have placed you on the list of our most valued commanders. I will myself furnish you, as far as it may be in my power, with opportunities of regaining the esteem of your country."

A reprimand so mild and considerate accompanied by such high eulogiums and generous promises, might have had a favorable effect upon Arnold, had he been in a different frame of mind; but he had persuaded himself that the court would incline in his favor and acquit him altogether; and he resented deeply a sentence, which he protested against as unmerited. His resentment was aggravated by delays in the settlement of his accounts, as he depended upon the sums he claimed as due to him for the payment of debts by which he was harassed.

In the month of March we find him intent on a new and adventurous project. He had proposed to the Board of Admiralty an expedition requiring several ships-of-war and three or four hundred land troops, offering to take command of it should it be carried into effect, as his wounds still disabled him from duty on land. Washington, who knew his abilities in either service was disposed to favor his proposition, but the scheme fell through from the impossibility of sparing the requisite number of men from the army. On the failure of the project, he requested and obtained from Washington leave of absence from the army for the summer, there being, he said, little prospect of an active campaign, and his wounds unfitting him for the field.

The return of spring brought little alleviation to the sufferings of the army at Morristown. All means of supplying its wants or recruiting its ranks were paralyzed by the continued depreciation of the currency. While Washington saw his forces gradually diminishing, his solicitude was intensely excited for the safety of the Southern States. The reader will recall the departure from New York, in the latter part of December, of the fleet of Admiral Arbuthnot with the army of Sir Henry Clinton, destined for the subjugation of South Carolina.

The voyage proved long and tempestuous. The ships were dispersed. Several fell into the hands of the Americans. One ordnance vessel foundered. Most of the artillery horses, and all those of the cavalry perished. The scattered ships rejoined each other about the end of January, at Tybee Bay on Savannah River; where those that had sustained damage were repaired as speedily as possible. The loss of the cavalry horses was especially felt by Sir Henry. There was a corps of two hundred and fifty dragoons, on which he depended greatly in the kind of guerilla warfare he was likely to pursue in a country of forests and morasses. Lieutenant-colonel Banastre Tarleton, who commanded them, was one of those dogs of war which Sir Henry was prepared to let slip on emergencies, to scour and maraud the country. This "bold dragoon," so noted in Southern warfare, was about twenty-six years of age, of a swarthy complexion, with small, black, piercing eyes. He is described as being rather below the middle size, square-built and strong, "with large muscular legs." Landing from the fleet, perfectly dismounted, he repaired with his dragoons, in some of the quartermasters' boats to Port Royal Island, on the seaboard of South Carolina, "to collect at that place, from friends or enemies, by money or by force, all the horses belonging to the islands in the neighborhood."

In the meantime, the transports having on board a great part of the army, sailed under convoy on the 10th of February from Savannah to North Edisto Sound, where the troops disembarked on the 11th, on St. John's Island, about thirty miles below Charleston. Thence, Sir Henry Clinton set out for the banks of Ashley River opposite to the city, while a part of the fleet proceeded round by sea, for the purpose of blockading the harbor. The advance of Sir Henry was slow and cautious. Much time was consumed by him in fortifying intermediate ports, to keep up a secure communication with the fleet. He ordered from Savannah all the troops that could be spared, and wrote to Knyphausen, at New York, for reinforcements from that place.

General Lincoln [now in command at Charleston] took advantage of this slowness on the part of his assailant, to extend and strengthen the works. Charleston stands at the end of an isthmus formed by the Ashley and Cooper Rivers. Beyond the main works on the land side he cut a canal, from one to the other of the swamps which border these rivers. In advance of the canal were two rows of abatis and a double picketed ditch. Within the canal, and between it and the main works, were strong redoubts and batteries, to open a flanking fire on any approaching column, while an inclosed hornwork of masonry formed a kind of citadel. A squadron commanded by Commodore Whipple, and composed of nine vessels of war of various sizes, the largest mounting forty-four guns, was to co-operate with Forts Moultrie and Johnston, and the various batteries in defence of the harbor. They were to lie before the bar so as to command the entrance of it. Great reliance also was placed on the bar itself, which it was thought no ship-of-the-line could pass.

Governor Rutledge, a man eminent for talents, patriotism, firmness and decision, was clothed with dictatorial powers during the present crisis; he called out the militia of the State, and it was supposed they would duly obey the call. Large reinforcements of troops also were expected from the North. Under all these circumstances, General Lincoln yielded to the entreaties of the inhabitants, and, instead of remaining with his army in the open country, as he had intended, shut himself up with them in the place for its defence, leaving merely his cavalry and two hundred light troops outside, who were to hover about the enemy and prevent small parties from marauding.

It was not until the 12th of March that Sir Henry Clinton effected his tardy approach, and took up a position on Charleston Neck, a few miles above the town. Admiral Arbuthnot soon showed an intention of introducing his ships into the harbor; barricading their waists, anchoring them in a situation where they might take advantage of the first favorable spring-tide, and fixing buoys on the bar for their guidance. Commodore Whipple had by this time ascertained by sounding, that a wrong idea had prevailed of the depth of water in the harbor, and that his ships could not anchor nearer than within three miles of the bar, so that it would be impossible for him to defend the passage of it. He quitted his station within it, therefore, after having destroyed a part of the enemy's buoys, and took a position where his ships might be abreast, and form a cross-fire with the batteries of Fort Moultrie, where Colonel Pinckney commanded.

Washington was informed of these facts, by letters from his former aide-de-camp, Colonel Laurens, who was in Charleston at the time. The information caused anxious forebodings. "The impracticability of defending the bar, I fear, amounts to the loss of the town and garrison," writes he in reply. His solicitude for the safety of the South was increased, by heaving of the embarkation at New York of two thousand five hundred British and Hessian troops, under Lord Rawdon, reinforcements for Sir Henry Clinton. It seemed evident the enemy intended to push their operations with vigor at the South; perhaps, to make it the principal theatre of the war.

Gladly would Washington have hastened to the South in person, but at this moment his utmost vigilance was required to keep watch upon New York and maintain the security of the Hudson, the vital part of the confederacy. The weak state of the American means of warfare in both quarters, presented a choice of difficulties. The South needed support. Could the North give it without exposing itself to ruin, since the enemy, by means of their ships, could suddenly unite their forces, and fall upon any point that they might consider weak? Such were the perplexities to which he was continually subjected, in having with scanty means to provide for the security of a vast extent of country, and with land forces merely, to contend with an amphibious enemy.

Looking, however, as usual, to the good of the whole Union, he determined to leave something at hazard in the Middle States, where the country was internally so strong, and yield further succor to the Southern States, which had not equal military advantages. With the consent of Congress, therefore, he put the Maryland line under marching orders, together with the Delaware regiment, which acted with it, and the first regiment of artillery. The Baron De Kalb, now at the head of the Maryland division, was instructed to conduct this detachment with all haste to the aid of General Lincoln. He might not arrive in time to prevent the fall of Charleston, but he might assist to arrest the progress of the enemy and save the Carolinas.

CHAPTER LIV.

DISCONTENTS IN THE ARMY.—FALL OF CHARLESTON.

We have cited the depreciation of the currency as a main cause of the difficulties and distresses of the army. The troops were paid in paper money at its nominal value. A memorial of the officers of the Jersey line to the legislature of their State, represented the depreciation to be so great, that four months' pay of a private soldier would not procure for his family a single bushel of wheat; the pay of a colonel would not purchase oats for his horse, and a common laborer or express rider could earn four times the pay in paper of an American officer.

Congress, too, in its exigencies, being destitute of the power of levying taxes, which vested in the State governments, devolved upon those governments, in their separate capacities, the business of supporting the army. This produced a great inequality in the condition of the troops; according to the means and the degree of liberality of their respective States. Some States furnished their troops amply not only with clothing, but with many comforts and conveniencies; others were more contracted in their supplies; while others left their troops almost destitute. Some of the States, too, undertook to make good to their troops the loss in their pay caused by the depreciation of the currency. As this was not general it increased the inequality of condition.

These, and other defects in the military system, were pressed by Washington upon the attention of Congress in a letter to the President. In consequence it was proposed in Congress to send a committee of three of its members to head-quarters to consult with the commander-in-chief, and, in conjunction with him, to effect such reforms and changes in the various departments of the army as might be deemed necessary. After a prolonged debate, a committee of three was chosen by ballot; it consisted of General Schuyler and Messrs. John Mathews, and Nathaniel Peabody. It was a great satisfaction to Washington to have his old friend and coadjutor, Schuyler, near him in this capacity, in which, he declared, no man could be more useful.

The committee, on arriving at the camp, found the disastrous state of affairs had not been exaggerated. For five months the army had been unpaid. Every department was destitute of money or credit; there were rarely provisions for six days in advance; on some occasions the troops had been for several successive days without meat; there was no forage; the medical department had neither tea, chocolate, wine, nor spirituous liquors of any kind.

To soothe the discontents of the army, and counteract the alarming effects of the depreciation of the currency, Congress now adopted the measure already observed by some of the States, and engaged to make good to the Continental and the independent troops the difference in the value of their pay caused by this depreciation; and that all moneys or other articles heretofore received by them, should be considered as advanced on account, and comprehended at their just value in the final settlement.

At this gloomy crisis came a letter from the Marquis de Lafayette, dated April 27th, announcing his arrival at Boston. Washington's eyes, we are told, were suffused with tears as he read this most welcome epistle. He would immediately have sent a troop of horse to escort the marquis through the tory settlements between Morristown and the Hudson, had he known the route he intended to take; the latter, however, arrived safe at head-quarters on the 12th of May, where he was welcomed with acclamations, for he was popular with both officers and soldiers. Washington folded him in his arms in a truly paternal embrace, and they were soon closeted together to talk over the state of affairs, when Lafayette made known the result of his visit to France. His generous efforts at court had been crowned with success, and he brought the animating intelligence that a French fleet, under the Chevalier de Ternay, was to put to sea early in April, bringing a body of troops under the Count de Rochambeau, and might soon be expected on the coast to co-operate with the American forces; this, however, he was at liberty to make known only to Washington and Congress. Remaining but a single day at head-quarters, he hastened on to the seat of government, where he met the reception which his generous enthusiasm in the cause of American independence had so fully merited.

Within three days after the departure of the marquis from Morristown, Washington in a letter to him, gave his idea of the plan which it would be proper for the French fleet and army to pursue on their arrival upon the coast. The reduction of New York he considered the first enterprise to be attempted by the co-operating forces. The whole effective land force of the enemy he estimated at about eight thousand regulars and four thousand refugees, with some militia on which no great dependence could be placed. Their naval force consisted of one seventy-four gun ship, and three or four small frigates. In this situation of affairs the French fleet might enter the harbor and gain possession of it without difficulty, cut off its communications, and, with the co-operation of the American army, oblige the city to capitulate. He advised Lafayette, therefore, to write to the French commanders, urging them on their arrival on the coast to proceed with their land and naval forces with all expedition to Sandy Hook, and there await further advices; should they learn, however, that the expedition under Sir Henry Clinton had returned from the South to New York, they were to proceed to Rhode Island.

General Arnold was at this time in Philadelphia, and his connection with subsequent events requires a few words concerning his career, daily becoming more perplexed. He had again petitioned Congress on the subject of his accounts. The Board of Treasury had made a report far short of his wishes. He had appealed, and his appeal, together with all the documents connected with the case, was referred to a committee of three. Old doubts and difficulties continued; there was no prospect of a speedy settlement; he was in extremity. [In his extremity he applied to the French minister, M. de Luzerne, a generous-spirited man, representing the hardships of his case, the ingratitude of his country, the hostility he had experienced from Pennsylvania, his urgent private necessities, and implored a loan equal to the amount of his debts, intimating that the attachment and gratitude of an American general of his rank and influence would be of vast importance to France in the transactions likely to arise between the two countries. M. de Luzerne, in reply, said that the league between France and America had for its basis a reciprocal interest and good will, and that it could be fulfilled without intrigue or secret practices. Arnold retired from the interview a mortified and desperate man; and writing to General Schuyler, who was about to visit the camp as one of the committee, expressed a wish to rejoin the army, and intimated that as his wounds made it painful for him to ride or walk, the command of West Point would best suit his present condition.]

In the meantime, the army with which Washington was to co-operate in the projected attack upon New York, was so reduced by the departure of troops whose term had expired and the tardiness in furnishing recruits, that it did not amount quite to four thousand rank and file, fit for duty. Among these was a prevalent discontent. Their pay was five months in arrear; if now paid it would be in Continental currency, without allowance for depreciation, consequently, almost worthless for present purposes.

A long interval of scarcity and several days of actual famine, brought matters to a crisis. On the 25th of May, in the dusk of the evening, two regiments of the Connecticut line assembled on their parade by beat of drum, and declared their intention to march home bag and baggage, "or, at best, to gain subsistence at the point of the bayonet." Every argument and expostulation was used with the mutineers. They were reminded of their past good conduct, of the noble objects for which they were contending, and of the future indemnifications promised by Congress. Their answer was, that their sufferings were too great to be allayed by promises, in which they had little faith; they wanted present relief. It was with difficulty they could be prevailed upon to return to their huts. Indeed, a few turned out a second time, with their packs, and were not to be pacified. These were arrested and confined.

In this alarming state of destitution, Washington looked round anxiously for bread for his famishing troops. New York, Jersey, Pennsylvania, and Maryland were what he termed his "flour country." Virginia was sufficiently tasked to supply the South. New York, by legislative coercion, had already given all that she could spare from the subsistence of her inhabitants. Jersey was exhausted by the long residence of the army. Maryland had made great exertions, and might still do something more, and Delaware might contribute handsomely, in proportion to her extent: but Pennsylvania was now the chief dependence, for that State was represented to be full of flour. Washington's letter of the 16th of December to President Reed, had obtained temporary relief from that quarter; he now wrote to him a second time, and still more earnestly, and sought to rouse President Reed to extraordinary exertions. "This is a time," writes he, "to hazard and to take a tone of energy and decision. All parties but the disaffected will acquiesce in the necessity and give it their support." He urges Reed to press upon the legislature of Pennsylvania the policy of investing its executive with plenipotentiary powers. His letter procured relief for the army from the legislature, and a resolve empowering the president and council, during its recess, to declare martial law, should circumstances render it expedient.

In like manner, he endeavored to rouse the dormant fire of Congress, and impart to it his own indomitable energy. "Certain I am," writes he to a member of that body, "unless Congress speak in a more decisive tone, unless they are vested with powers by the several States, competent to the purposes of war, or assume them as matters of right, and they and the States respectively act with more energy than they have hitherto done, that our cause is lost. We can no longer drudge on in the old way. By ill-timing the adoption of measures, by delays in the execution of them, or by unwarrantable jealousies, we incur enormous expenses and derive no benefit from them. One State will comply with a requisition of Congress; another neglects to do it; a third executes it by halves; and all differ, either in the manner, the matter, or so much in point of time, that we are always working up-hill; and, while such a system as the present one, or rather want of one, prevails, we shall ever be unable to apply our strength or resources to any advantage."

At this juncture came official intelligence from the South to connect which with the general course of events, requires a brief notice of the operations of Sir Henry Clinton in that quarter.

In the preceding chapter we left the British fleet under Admiral Arbuthnot, preparing to force its way into the harbor of Charleston. Several days elapsed before the ships were able, by taking out their guns, provisions, and water, and availing themselves of wind and tide to pass the bar. They did so on the 20th of March, with but slight opposition from several galleys. Commodore Whipple, then, seeing the vast superiority of their force, made a second retrograde move, stationing some of his ships in Cooper River, and sinking the rest at its mouth so as to prevent the enemy from running up that river, and cutting off communication with the country on the east: the crews and heavy cannon were landed to aid in the defence of the town. The reinforcements expected from the North were not yet arrived; the militia of the State did not appear at Governor Rutledge's command, and other reliances were failing.

At this time the reinforcements which Sir Henry Clinton had ordered from Savannah were marching toward the Cambayee under Brigadier-general Patterson. On his flanks moved Major Ferguson with a corps of riflemen, and Major Cochrane with the infantry of the British legion; two brave and enterprising officers. It was a toilsome march, through swamps and difficult passes. Being arrived in the neighborhood of Port Royal, where Tarleton had succeeded, though indifferently, in remounting his dragoons, Patterson sent orders to that officer to join him. Tarleton hastened to obey the order. His arrival was timely. The Carolina militia having heard that all the British horses had perished at sea, made an attack on the front of General Patterson's force, supposing it to be without cavalry. To their surprise, Tarleton charged them with his dragoons, routed them, took several prisoners, and, what was more acceptable, a number of horses.

Tarleton had soon afterwards to encounter a worthy antagonist in Colonel William Washington, the same cavalry officer who had distinguished himself at Trenton, and was destined to distinguish himself still more in this Southern campaign. He is described as being six feet in height, broad, stout and corpulent. Bold in the field, careless in the camp; kind to his soldiers; harassing to his enemies; gay and good-humored; with an upright heart and a generous hand, a universal favorite. He was now at the head of a body of Continental cavalry, consisting of his own and Bland's light-horse, and Pulaski's hussars. A brush took place in the neighborhood of Rantoul's Bridge. Colonel Washington had the advantage, took several prisoners, and drove back the dragoons of the British legion, but durst not pursue them for want of infantry.

On the 7th of April, Brigadier-general Woodford with seven hundred Virginia troops, after a forced march of five hundred miles in thirty days, crossed from the east side of Cooper River, by the only passage now open, and threw himself into Charleston. It was a timely reinforcement, and joyfully welcomed; for the garrison, when in greatest force, amounted to little more than two thousand regulars and one thousand North Carolina militia.

About the same time Admiral Arbuthnot, in the Roebuck, passed Sullivan's Island, with a fresh southerly breeze, at the head of a squadron of seven armed vessels and two transports. Colonel Pinckney opened a heavy cannonade from the batteries of Fort Moultrie. The ships thundered in reply, and clouds of smoke were raised, under the cover of which they slipped by, with no greater loss than twenty-seven men killed and wounded. A store-ship which followed the squadron ran aground, was set on fire and abandoned, and subsequently blew up. The ships took a position near Fort Johnston, just without the range of the shot from the American batteries. After the passage of the ships, Colonel Pinckney and a part of the garrison withdrew from Fort Moultrie.

The enemy had by this time completed his first parallel, and the town being almost entirely invested by sea and land, received a joint summons from the British general and admiral to surrender. "Sixty days have passed," writes Lincoln in reply, "since it has been known that your intentions against this town were hostile, in which, time has been afforded to abandon it, but duty and inclination point to the propriety of supporting it to the last extremity."

The British batteries were now opened. The siege was carried on deliberately by regular parallels, and on a scale of magnitude scarcely warranted by the moderate strength of the place. A great object with the besieged was to keep open the channel of communication with the country by the Cooper River, the last that remained by which they could receive reinforcements and supplies, or could retreat if necessary. For this purpose, Governor Rutledge, leaving the town in the care of Lieutenant-governor Gadsden, and one half of the executive council, set off with the other half, and endeavored to rouse the militia between the Cooper and Santee Rivers. His success was extremely limited. Two militia posts were established by him; one between these rivers, the other at a ferry on the Santee; some regular troops, also, had been detached by Lincoln to throw up works about nine miles above the town, on the Wando, a branch of Cooper River, and at Lempriere's Point; and Brigadier-general Huger,[17] with a force of militia and Continental cavalry, including those of Colonel William Washington, was stationed at Monk's Corner, about thirty miles above Charleston, to guard the passes at the head waters of Cooper River.

Sir Henry Clinton, when proceeding with his second parallel, detached Lieutenant-colonel Webster with fourteen hundred men to break up these posts. The most distant one was that of Huger's cavalry at Monk's Corner. The surprisal of this was entrusted to Tarleton, who, with his dragoons was in Webster's advanced guard. He was to be seconded by Major Patrick Ferguson with his riflemen. Ferguson was a fit associate for Tarleton, in hardy, scrambling, partisan enterprise: equally intrepid and determined, but cooler and more open to impulses of humanity.

On the evening of the 13th of April, Tarleton moved with the van towards Monk's Corner. A night march had been judged the most advisable. It was made in profound silence and by unfrequented roads. A few dollars gained the services of a negro as a guide. The surprisal of General Huger's camp was complete. Several officers and men who attempted to defend themselves were killed or wounded. General Huger, Colonel Washington, with many others, officers and men, escaped in the darkness to the neighboring swamps. One hundred officers, dragoons and hussars were taken, with about four hundred horses and near fifty wagons, laden with arms, clothing, and ammunition. Biggins Bridge on Cooper River was likewise secured, and the way opened for Colonel Webster to advance nearly to the head of the passes, in such a manner as to shut up Charleston entirely.

The American cavalry had gradually re-assembled on the north of the Santee, under Colonel White of New Jersey, where they were joined by some militia infantry, and by Colonel William Washington, with such of his dragoons as had escaped at Monk's Corner. Cornwallis had committed the country between Cooper and Wando Rivers to Tarleton's charge, with orders to be continually on the move with the cavalry and infantry of the legion; to watch over the landing-places; obtain intelligence from the town, the Santee River and the back country, and to burn such stores as might fall into his hands rather than risk their being retaken by the enemy. Hearing of the fortuitous assemblage of American troops, Tarleton came suddenly upon them by surprise at Laneau's Ferry. It was one of his bloody exploits. Five officers and thirty-six men were killed and wounded, and seven officers and six dragoons taken, with horses, arms and equipments. Colonels White, Washington and Jamieson, with other officers and men, threw themselves in the river and escaped by swimming; while some who followed their example, perished.

The arrival of a reinforcement of three thousand men from New York enabled Sir Henry Clinton to throw a powerful detachment under Lord Cornwallis, to the east of Cooper River, to complete the investment of the town and cut off all retreat.

[17] Pronounced Hugee — of French Huguenot descent.

Fort Moultrie surrendered. The batteries of the third parallel were opened upon the town. This fire was kept up for two days. The besiegers crossed the canal; pushed a double sap to the inside of the abatis, and prepared to make an assault by sea and land. All hopes of successful defence were at an end. The works were in ruins; the guns almost all dismounted; the garrison exhausted with fatigue, the provisions nearly consumed. The inhabitants, dreading the horrors of an assault, joined in a petition to General Lincoln and prevailed upon him to offer a surrender on terms which had already been offered and rejected. These terms were still granted, and the capitulation was signed on the 12th of May. The garrison were allowed some of the honors of war.

The loss of the British in the siege was seventy-six killed and one hundred and eighty-nine wounded; that of the Americans nearly the same. The prisoners taken by the enemy, exclusive of the sailors, amounted to five thousand, six hundred and eighteen men; comprising every male adult in the city. The Continental troops did not exceed two thousand, five hundred of whom were in the hospital; the rest were citizens and militia.

Sir Henry Clinton considered the fall of Charleston decisive of the fate of South Carolina. To complete the subjugation of the country, he planned three expeditions into the interior; one, under Lieutenant-colonel Brown, was to move up the Savannah River to Augusta, on the borders of Georgia; another, under Lieutenant-colonel Cruger, was to proceed up the southwest side of the Santee River to the district of Ninety-Six,[18] a fertile and salubrious region, between the Savannah and the Saluda rivers: while a third, under Cornwallis, was to cross the Santee, march up the northeast bank, and strike at a corps of troops under Colonel Buford, which were retreating to North Carolina with artillery and a number of wagons, laden with arms, ammunition and clothing.

Colonel Buford, in fact, had arrived too late for the relief of Charleston, and was now making a retrograde move; he had come on with three hundred and eighty troops of the Virginia line, and two field pieces, and had been joined by Colonel Washington with a few of his cavalry that had survived the surprisal by Tarleton. As Buford was moving with celerity, and had the advantage of distance, Cornwallis detached Tarleton in pursuit of him, with one hundred and seventy dragoons, a hundred mounted infantry, and a three-pounder. The bold partisan pushed forward with his usual ardor and rapidity, and coming upon Buford's rear-guard captured a sergeant and four dragoons. Buford hastily drew up his men in order of battle, in an open wood, on the right of the road. His artillery and wagons, which were in the advance escorted by part of his infantry, were ordered to continue on their march.

There appears to have been some confusion on the part of the Americans, and they had an impetuous foe to deal with. Before they were well prepared for action they were attacked in front and on both flanks by cavalry and mounted infantry. The American battalion was broken; most of the men threw down their arms and begged for quarter, but were cut down without mercy. One hundred and thirteen

[18] So called in early times from being ninety-six miles from the principal town of the Cherokee nation.

were slain on the spot, and one hundred and fifty so mangled and maimed that they could not be removed. Colonel Buford and a few of the cavalry escaped, as did about a hundred of the infantry, who were with the baggage in the advance. Fifty prisoners were all that were in a condition to be carried off by Tarleton as trophies of this butchery.

The two other detachments which had been sent out by Clinton, met with nothing but submission. The people in general, considering resistance hopeless, accepted the proffered protection, and conformed to its humiliating terms. Sir Henry now persuaded himself that South Carolina was subdued, and proceeded to station garrisons in various parts to maintain it in subjection. In the fullness of his confidence, he issued a proclamation on the 3d of June, discharging all the military prisoners from their paroles after the 20th of the month, excepting those captured in Fort Moultrie and Charleston. All thus released from their parole were reinstated in the rights and duties of British subjects. All were to be ready to take up arms at a moment's notice. Those who had families were to form a militia for home defence. Those who had none were to serve with the royal forces. All who should neglect to return to their allegiance, or should refuse to take up arms against the independence of their country, were to be considered as rebels and treated accordingly.

Having struck a blow, which, as he conceived, was to insure the subjugation of the South, Sir Henry embarked for New York on the 5th of June with a part of his forces, leaving the residue under the command of Lord Cornwallis who was to carry the war into North Carolina and thence into Virginia.

CHAPTER LV.

MARAUDS IN THE JERSEYS.—THE FRENCH FLEET AT NEWPORT.

A handbill published by the British authorities in New York reached Washington's camp on the 1st of June, and made known the surrender of Charleston. [With this intelligence came reports of a large fleet entering Sandy Hook, which was supposed to be the return of Sir Henry with the whole or part of his force.] The report proved to be erroneous, but on the 6th of June came a new alarm. The enemy, it was said, were actually landing in force at Elizabethtown Point, to carry fire and sword into the Jerseys! It was even so. Knyphausen, through spies and emissaries, had received exaggerated accounts of the recent outbreak in Washington's camp and of the general discontent among the people of New Jersey, and was persuaded that a sudden show of military protection, following up the news of the capture of Charleston, would produce a general desertion among Washington's troops, and rally back the inhabitants of the Jerseys to their allegiance to the crown.

In this belief he projected a descent into the Jerseys with about five thousand men, and some light artillery, who were to cross in divisions in the night of the 5th of June from Staten Island to Elizabethtown Point. The first division, led by Brigadier-general Sterling, actually landed before dawn of the 6th, and advanced as silently as possible. The heavy and measured tramp of the troops, however, caught the ear of an American sentinel stationed at a fork where the roads from the old and new point joined. He challenged the dimly descried mass as it approached, and receiving no answer, fired into it. That shot wounded General Sterling in the thigh, and ultimately proved mortal. The wounded general was carried back, and Knyphausen took his place.

This delayed the march until sunrise, and gave time for the troops of the Jersey line, under Colonel Elias Dayton, stationed in Elizabethtown, to assemble. They were too weak in numbers, however, to withstand the enemy, but retreated in good order, skirmishing occasionally. Signal guns and signal fires were rousing the country. The militia and yeomanry armed themselves with such weapons as were at hand, and hastened to their alarm posts. The enemy took the old road, by what was called Galloping Hill, towards the village of Connecticut Farms; fired upon from behind walls and thickets by the hasty levies of the country.

At Connecticut Farms, the retreating troops under Dayton fell in with the Jersey brigade, under General Maxwell, and a few militia joining them, the Americans were enabled to make some stand, and even to hold the enemy in check. The latter, however, brought up several field pieces, and being reinforced by a second division which had crossed from Staten Island some time after the first, compelled the Americans again to retreat. Some of the enemy, exasperated at the unexpected opposition they had met with throughout their march, and pretending that the inhabitants of this village had fired upon them from their windows, began to pillage and set fire to the houses.[19]

In the meantime Knyphausen was pressing on with his main force towards Morristown. The booming of alarm guns had roused the country; every valley was pouring out its yeomanry. Two thousand were said to be already in arms below the mountains. Within half a mile of Springfield, Knyphausen halted to reconnoitre. That village, through which passes the road to Springfield, had been made the American rallying-point. It stands at the foot of what are called the Short Hills, on the west side of Rahway River, which runs in front of it. On the bank of the river, General Maxwell's Jersey brigade and the militia of the neighborhood were drawn up to dispute the passage. Washington had arrived and taken his position that afternoon, prepared to withstand an encounter though not to seek one. All night his camp fires lighted up the Short Hills, and he remained on the alert expecting to be assailed in the morning; but in the morning no enemy was to be seen. Knyphausen had experienced enough to convince him that he had been completely misinformed as to the disposition of the Jersey people and of the army. Disappointed as to the main objects of his enterprise, he had retreated under cover of the night.

On the 17th of June the fleet from the South actually arrived in the bay of New York, and Sir Henry Clinton landed his troops on Staten Island, but almost immediately re-embarked them; as if meditating an expedition up the river. Fearing for the safety of West Point, Washington set off on the 21st June, with the main body of his troops, towards Pompton; while General Greene, with Maxwell and Stark's brigades, Lee's dragoons and the militia of the neighborhood, remained encamped on the Short Hills, to cover the country and protect the stores at Morristown.

Washington's movements were slow and wary, unwilling to be far from Greene until better informed of the designs of the enemy. At Rockaway Bridge, about eleven miles beyond Morristown, he received word on the 23d that the enemy were advancing from Elizabethtown against Springfield. Supposing the military depot at Morristown to be their ultimate object, he detached a brigade to the assistance of Greene, and fell back five or six miles, so as to be in supporting distance of him.

The re-embarkation of the troops at Staten Island had, in fact, been a stratagem of Sir Henry Clinton to divert the attention of Washington, and enable Knyphausen to carry out the enterprise which had hitherto hung fire. No sooner did the latter ascertain that the American commander-in-chief had moved off with his main force towards the Highlands, than he sallied from Elizabethtown, five thousand strong, with a large body of cavalry, and fifteen or twenty pieces of artillery; hoping not merely to destroy the public stores at Morristown, but to get possession of those difficult hills and defiles among which Washington's army had been so

[19] The wife of the Rev. James Caldwell, already alluded to, was in the village at the time, and while sitting on the side of a bed, holding a child by the hand, a musket was discharged in at the window, and the ball striking her in the breast, she fell dead on the floor.

securely posted, and which constituted the strength of that part of the country.

It was early on the morning of the 23d that Knyphausen pushed forward toward Springfield. Beside the main road which passes directly through the village toward Morristown, there is another north of it, called the Vauxhall road, crossing several small streams, the confluence of which forms the Rahway. These two roads unite beyond the village in the principal pass of the Short Hills. The enemy's troops advanced rapidly in two compact columns, the right one by the Vauxhall road, the other by the main or direct road. General Greene was stationed among the Short Hills, about a mile above the town. His troops were distributed at various posts, for there were many passes to guard.

At five o'clock in the morning, signal-guns gave notice of the approach of the enemy. The drums beat to arms throughout the camp. The troops were hastily called in from their posts among the mountain passes, and preparations were made to defend the village. Major Lee, with his dragoons and a picket-guard, was posted on the Vauxhall road to check the right column of the enemy in its advance. Colonel Dayton, with his regiment of New Jersey militia, was to check the left column on the main road. Colonel Angel of Rhode Island, with about two hundred picked men, and a piece of artillery, was to defend a bridge over the Rahway, a little west of the town. Colonel Shreve, stationed with his regiment at a second bridge over a branch of the Rahway, east of the town, was to cover, if necessary, the retreat of Colonel Angel. Those parts of Maxwell and Stark's brigades which were not thus detached were drawn up on high grounds in the rear of the town, having the militia on their flanks.

There was some sharp fighting at a bridge on the Vauxhall road, where Major Lee with his dragoons and picket-guard held the right column at bay; a part of the column, however, forded the stream above the bridge, gained a commanding position, and obliged Lee to retire. The left column met with similar opposition from Dayton and his Jersey regiment. The severest fighting of the day was at the bridge over the Rahway. For upwards of half an hour Colonel Angel defended it with his handful of men against a vastly superior force. One-fourth of his men were either killed or disabled: the loss of the enemy was still more severe. Angel was at length compelled to retire. He did so in good order, carrying off his wounded, and making his way through the village to the bridge beyond it. Here his retreat was bravely covered by Colonel Shreve, but he too was obliged to give way before the overwhelming force of the enemy, and join the brigades of Maxwell and Stark upon the hill.

General Greene, finding his front too much extended for his small force, and that he was in danger of being outflanked on the left by the column pressing forward on the Vauxhall road, took post with his main body on the first range of hills, where the roads were brought near to a point and passed between him and the height occupied by Stark and Maxwell. He then threw out a detachment which checked the further advance of the right column of the enemy along the Vauxhall road, and secured that pass through the Short Hills. Feeling himself now strongly posted, he awaited with confidence the expected attempt of the enemy to gain the height. No such attempt was made. The resistance already experienced, especially at the bridge, and the sight of militia gathering from various points, dampened the ardor of the hostile commander. He saw that, should he persist in pushing for Morristown, he would have to fight his way through a country abounding with difficult passes, every one of which would be obstinately disputed; and that the enterprise, even if successful, might cost too much, beside taking him too far from New York, at a time when a French armament might be expected.

Before the brigade detached by Washington arrived at the scene of action, therefore, the enemy had retreated. Previous to their retreat they wreaked upon Springfield the same vengeance they had inflicted on Connecticut Farms. The whole village, excepting four houses, was reduced to ashes. Their second retreat was equally ignoble with their first. They were pursued and harassed the whole way to Elizabethtown by light scouting parties and by the militia and yeomanry of the country, exasperated by the sight of the burning village. Lee, too, came upon their rear-guard with his dragoons; captured a quantity of stores abandoned by them in the hurry of retreat, and made prisoners of several refugees. It was sunset when the enemy reached Elizabethtown. During the night they passed over to Staten Island by their bridge of boats. By six o'clock in the morning all had crossed, and the bridge had been removed — and the State of New Jersey, so long harassed by the campaignings of either army was finally evacuated by the enemy.

Apprehensive that the next move of the enemy would be up the Hudson, Washington resumed his measures for the security of West Point; moving towards the Highlands in the latter part of June. Circumstances soon convinced him that the enemy had no present intention of attacking that fortress, but merely menaced him at various points to retard his operations, and oblige him to call out the militia; thereby interrupting agriculture, distressing the country, and rendering his cause unpopular. Having, therefore, caused the military stores in the Jerseys to be removed to more remote and secure places, he countermanded by letter the militia which were marching to camp from Connecticut and Massachusetts.

He now exerted himself to the utmost to procure from the different State Legislatures their quotas and supplies for the regular army. The desired relief, however, had to be effected through the ramifications of general and State governments and their committees. The operations were tardy and unproductive. Liberal contributions were made by individuals; a bank was established by the inhabitants of Philadelphia to facilitate the supplies of the army, and an association of ladies of that city raised by subscription between seven and eight thousand dollars which were put at the disposition of Washington.

The capture of General Lincoln at Charleston had left the Southern department without a commander-in-chief. As there were likely to be important military operations in that quarter, Washington had intended to recommend General Greene for the appointment. He was an officer on whose abilities, discretion, and disinterested patriotism he had the fullest reliance, and whom he had always found thoroughly disposed to act in unison with him in his general plan of carrying on the war. Congress, however, with unbecoming precipitancy, gave that important command to General Gates (June 13th), without waiting to consult Washington's views or wishes.

On the 10th of July a French fleet, under the Chevalier de Ternay, arrived at Newport, in Rhode Island. It was composed of seven ships-of-the-line, two frigates and two bombs, and convoyed transports on board of which were upwards of five thousand troops. This was the first division of the forces promised by France, of which Lafayette had spoken. The second division had been detained at Brest for want of transports, but might soon be expected. The Count de Rochambeau, Lieutenant-general of the royal armies, was commander-in-chief of this auxiliary force. He was a veteran, fifty-five years of age, who had early distinguished himself, when colonel of the regiment of Auvergne, and had gained laurels in various battles. Another officer of rank and distinction in this force, was Major-general the Marquis de Chastellux, a friend and relative of Lafayette, but much his senior, being now forty-six years of age. He was not only a soldier, but a man of letters, and one familiar with courts as well as camps.

The instructions of the French ministry to the Count de Rochambeau placed him entirely under the command of General Washington. The French troops were to be considered as auxiliaries, and as such were to take the left of the American troops, and, in all cases of ceremony, to yield them the preference. This considerate arrangement was intended to prevent the recurrence of those questions of rank and etiquette which had heretofore disturbed the combined service.

Washington, in general orders, congratulated the army on the arrival of this timely and generous succor, which he hailed as a new tie between France and America; anticipating that the only contention between the two armies would be to excel each other in good offices, and in the display of every military virtue. The American cockade had hitherto been black, that of the French was white; he recommended to his officers a cockade of black and white intermingled in compliment to their allies, and as a symbol of friendship and union.

His joy at this important reinforcement was dashed by the mortifying reflection that he was still unprovided with the troops and military means requisite for the combined operations meditated. Still he took upon himself the responsibility of immediate action, and forthwith despatched Lafayette to have an interview with the French commanders, explain the circumstances of the case, and concert plans for the proposed attack upon New York. The arrival, however, of the British Admiral, Graves, at New York, on the 13th of July, with six ships-of-the-line, gave the enemy such a superiority of naval force that the design on New York was postponed until the second French division should make its appearance, or a squadron under the Count de Guichen, which was expected from the West Indies.

In the meantime, Sir Henry Clinton, who had information of all the plans and movements of the allies, determined to forestall the meditated attack upon New York, by beating up the French quarters on Rhode Island. This he was to do in person at the head of six thousand men, aided by Admiral Arbuthnot with his fleet. Sir Henry accordingly proceeded with his troops to Throg's Neck on the Sound; there to embark on board of transports which Arbuthnot was to provide. No sooner did Washington learn that so large a force had left New York, than he crossed the Hudson to Peekskill, and prepared to move towards King's Bridge, with the main body of his troops, which had recently been reinforced. His intention was, either to oblige Sir Henry to abandon his project against Rhode Island, or to strike a blow at New York during his absence.

The expedition of Sir Henry was delayed by the tardy arrival of transports. In the meantime he heard of the sudden move of Washington, and learned, moreover, that the position of the French at Newport had been strengthened by the militia from the neighboring country. These tidings disconcerted his plans. He left Admiral Arbuthnot to proceed with his squadron to Newport, blockade the French fleet, and endeavor to intercept the second division, supposed to be on its way, while he with his troops hastened back to New York. In consequence of their return, Washington again withdrew his forces to the west side of the Hudson; first establishing a post and throwing up small works at Dobbs' Ferry, about ten miles above King's Bridge.

Arnold now received the important command which he had so earnestly coveted. It included the fortress at West Point and the posts from Fishkill to King's Ferry, together with the corps of infantry and cavalry advanced toward the enemy's line on the east side of the river. Washington took post at Orangetown or Tappan, on the borders of the Jerseys, and opposite to Dobbs' Ferry, to be at hand for any attempt upon New York. The execution of this cherished design, however, was again postponed by intelligence that the second division of the French reinforcements was blockaded in the harbor of Brest by the British: Washington still had hopes that it might be carried into effect by the aid of the squadron of the Count de Guichen from the West Indies; or of a fleet from Cadiz.

At this juncture, a derangement took place in the quartermaster-general's department, of which General Greene was the head. The reorganization of this department had long been in agitation. A system had been digested by Washington, Schuyler and Greene, adapted, as they thought, to the actual situation of the country. Greene had offered, should it be adopted, to continue in the discharge of the duties of the department, without any extra emolument other than would cover the expenses of his family. Congress devised a different scheme. He considered it incapable of execution, and likely to be attended with calamitous and disgraceful results; he, therefore, tendered his resignation. The tone and manner assumed by General Greene in offering his resignation, were deeply offensive to Congress. His resignation was promptly accepted, and Colonel Pickering appointed to succeed him. The commissariat was equally in a state of derangement. "At this very juncture," writes Washington (Aug. 20th), "I am reduced to the painful alternative, either of dismissing a part of the militia now assembling, or of letting them come forward to starve; which it will be extremely difficult for the troops already in the field to avoid.... Every day's experience proves more and more that the present mode of supplies is the most uncertain, expensive and injurious that could be devised. It is impossible for us to form any calculations of what we are to expect, and consequently to concert any plans for future execution." The anxiety of Washington at this moment of embarrassment was heightened by the receipt of disastrous intelligence from the South.

CHAPTER LVI.

BATTLE OF CAMDEN.

Lord Cornwallis, when left in military command at the South by Sir Henry Clinton, was charged, it will be recollected, with the invasion of North Carolina. It was an enterprise in which much difficulty was to be apprehended, both from the character of the people and the country. The original settlers were from various parts, most of them men who had experienced political or religious oppression, and had brought with them a quick sensibility to wrong, a stern appreciation of their rights, and an indomitable spirit of freedom and independence. It was this spirit which gave rise to the confederacy, called the Regulation, formed to withstand the abuses of power; and the first blood shed in our country, in resistance to arbitrary taxation, was at Almance in this province, in a conflict between the regulators and Governor Tryon. Above all, it should never be forgotten, that at Mecklenburg, in the heart of North Carolina, was fulminated the first declaration of independence of the British crown, upwards of a year before like declaration by Congress.

The physical difficulties arising from the nature of the country consisted in its mountain fastnesses in the northwestern part, its vast forests, its sterile tracts, its long rivers, destitute of bridges, and which, though fordable in fair weather, were liable to be swollen by sudden storms and freshets, and rendered deep, turbulent and impassable. These rivers, in fact, which rushed down from the mountain, but wound sluggishly through the plains, were the military strength of the country, as we shall have frequent occasion to show in the course of our narrative.

Lord Cornwallis forbore to attempt the invasion of North Carolina until the summer heats should be over and the harvests gathered in. In the meantime he disposed of his troops in cantonments, to cover the frontiers of South Carolina and Georgia, and maintain their internal quiet. The command of the frontiers was given by him to Lord Rawdon, who made Camden his principal post. This town, the capital of Kershaw District, a fertile, fruitful country, was situated on the east bank of the Wateree River, on the road leading to North Carolina. It was to be the grand military depot for the projected campaign.

The proclamation of Sir Henry Clinton, putting an end to all neutrality, and the rigorous penalties and persecutions with which all infractions of its terms were punished, had for a time quelled the spirit of the country. By degrees, however, the dread of British power gave way to impatience of British exactions. Symptoms of revolt manifested themselves in various parts. They were encouraged by intelligence that De Kalb, sent by Washington, was advancing through North Carolina at the head of two thousand men, and that the militia of that State and of Virginia were joining his standard. This was soon followed by tidings that Gates, the conqueror of Burgoyne, was on his way to take command of the Southern forces.

The prospect of such aid from the North reanimated the Southern patriots. One of the most eminent of these was Thomas Sumter, whom the Carolinians had surnamed the Game Cock. [He was now between forty and fifty years of age, brave, hardy and vigorous. He had seen service against the Indians, and in the French war, and had held the rank of lieutenant-colonel in the Continental line. After the fall of Charleston he had sought refuge with his family in one of the open savannahs that lie concealed amid the swamps with which the lower part of South Carolina abounds. In one of his temporary absences his retreat had been invaded, his house burnt to the ground, and his wife and children driven forth without shelter.] Private injury had thus been added to the incentives of patriotism. Emerging from his hiding-place, he had thrown himself among a handful of his fellow-sufferers who had taken refuge in North Carolina. They chose him at once as a leader, and resolved on a desperate struggle for the deliverance of their native State. Destitute of regular weapons, they forged rude substitutes out of the implements of husbandry. Old mill-saws were converted into broad-swords; knives at the ends of poles served for lances; while the country housewives gladly gave up their pewter dishes and other utensils, to be melted down and cast into bullets for such as had fire-arms.

When Sumter led this gallant band of exiles over the border, they did not amount in number to two hundred; yet with these he attacked and routed a well-armed body of British troops and tories, the terror of the frontier. His followers supplied themselves with weapons from the slain. In a little while his band was augmented by recruits. Parties of militia, also, recently embodied under the compelling measures of Cornwallis, deserted to the patriot standard. Thus reinforced to the amount of six hundred men, he made, on the 30th of July, a spirited attack on the British post at Rocky Mount, near the Catawba, but was repulsed. A more successful attack was made by him, eight days afterwards, on another post at Hanging Rock.

The advance of De Kalb with reinforcements from the North, had been retarded by various difficulties, the most important of which was want of provisions. This had been especially the case, he said, since his arrival in North Carolina. The legislative or executive power, he complained, gave him no assistance, nor could he obtain supplies from the people but by military force. There was no flour in the camp, nor were dispositions made to furnish any. His troops were reduced for a time to short allowance, and at length, on the 6th of July, brought to a positive halt at Deep River. The North Carolina militia, under General Caswell, were already in the field, on the road to Camden, beyond the Pedee River. He was anxious to form a junction with them, but a wide and sterile region lay between him and them, difficult to be traversed, unless magazines were established in advance, or he were supplied with provisions to take with him. For three weeks he remained in this encampment, foraging an exhausted country for a meagre subsistence, and was thinking of deviating to the right, and seeking the fertile counties of Mecklenburg and Rowan, when on the 25th of July, General Gates arrived at the camp.

Gates approved of De Kalb's standing orders, but at the first review of the troops, to the great astonishment of the baron, gave orders for them to hold themselves in readiness to march at a *moment's warning*. It was evident he meant to signalize himself by celerity of movement in contrast with protracted delays. It was in vain the destitute situation of the troops was represented to him, and that they had not a day's provision in advance. His reply was, that wagons laden with supplies were coming on, and would overtake them in two days.

On the 27th he actually put the army in motion over the Buffalo Ford, on the direct road to Camden. Colonel Williams, the adjutant-general of De Kalb, warned him of the sterile nature of that route, and recommended a more circuitous one further north, which passed through the abundant county of Mecklenburg. Gates persisted in taking the direct route, which proved all that had been represented. It led through a region of pine barrens, sand hills and swamps, with few human habitations, and those mostly deserted. The supplies of which he had spoken never overtook him. His army had to subsist itself on lean cattle roaming almost wild in the woods; and to supply the want of bread with green Indian corn, unripe apples and peaches. The consequence was a distressing prevalence of dysentery.

Having crossed the Pedee River on the 3d of August, the army was joined by a handful of brave Virginia regulars under Lieutenant-colonel Porterfield, who had been wandering about the country since the disaster of Charleston; and on the 7th, the much-desired junction took place with the North Carolina militia. On the 13th they encamped at Rugeley's Mills, otherwise called Clermont, about twelve miles from Camden, and on the following day were reinforced by a brigade of seven hundred Virginia militia under General Stephens.

On the approach of Gates, Lord Rawdon had concentrated his forces at Camden. The post was flanked by the Wateree River and Pine-tree Creek, and strengthened with redoubts. Lord Cornwallis had hastened hither from Charleston on learning that affairs in this quarter were drawing to a crisis, and had arrived here on the 13th. The British effective force thus collected was something more than two thousand, including officers. About five hundred were militia and tory refugees from North Carolina. The forces under Gates according to the return of his adjutant-general, were three thousand and fifty-two fit for duty; more than two-thirds of them, however, were militia.

On the 14th he received an express from General Sumter, who, with his partisan corps, after harassing the enemy at various points, was now endeavoring to cut off their supplies from Charleston. The object of the express was to ask a reinforcement of regulars to aid him in capturing a large convoy of clothing, ammunition and stores, on its way to the garrison, and which would pass Wateree Ferry, about a mile from Camden. Gates accordingly detached Colonel Woolford of the Maryland line with one hundred regulars, a party of artillery, and two brass field-pieces. On the same evening he moved with his main force to take post at a deep stream about seven miles from Camden, intending to attack Lord Rawdon or his redoubts should he march out in force to repel Sumter.

By a singular coincidence, Lord Cornwallis on the very same evening sallied forth from Camden to attack the American camp at Clermont. About two o'clock at night the two forces blundered, as it were, on each other about half way. A skirmish took place between their advanced guards, in which Porterfield of the Virginia regulars was mortally wounded. Some prisoners were taken on either side. Gates was astounded at being told that the enemy at hand was Cornwallis with three thousand men. Calling a council of war he demanded what was best to be done. For a moment or two there was blank silence. It was broken by General Stevens of the Virginia militia, with the significant question, "Gentlemen, is it not too late *now* to do anything but fight?" No other advice was asked or offered, and all were required to repair to their respective commands. In forming the line, the first Maryland division, including the Delawares, was on the right, commanded by De Kalb. The Virginia militia under Stevens, were on the left. Caswell with the North Carolinians formed the centre. The artillery was in battery on the road. Each flank was covered by a marsh. The second Maryland brigade formed a reserve, a few hundred yards in rear of the first.

At daybreak (Aug. 16th), the enemy were dimly descried advancing in column; they appeared to be displaying to the right. Gates ordered that Stevens should advance briskly with his brigade of Virginia militia and attack them while in the act of displaying. No sooner did Stevens receive the order than he put his brigade in motion, but discovered that the right wing of the enemy was already in line. A few sharp-shooters were detached to run forward, post themselves behind trees within forty or fifty yards of the enemy to extort their fire while at a distance, and render it less terrible to the militia. The expedient failed. The British rushed on shouting and firing. The inexperienced militia, dismayed and confounded by this impetuous assault, threw down their loaded muskets and fled. The panic spread to the North Carolina militia. Part of them made a temporary stand, but soon joined with the rest in flight, rendered headlong and disastrous by the charge and pursuit of Tarleton and his cavalry.

Gates, seconded by his officers, made several attempts to rally the militia, but was borne along with them. The day was hazy; there was no wind to carry off the smoke, which hung over the field of battle like a thick cloud. Nothing could be seen distinctly. Supposing that the regular troops were dispersed like the militia, Gates gave up all for lost, and retreated from the field.

The regulars, however, had not given away. The Maryland brigades and the Delaware regiment, unconscious that they were deserted by the militia, stood their ground, and bore the brunt of the battle. Though repeatedly broken, they as often rallied, and braved even the deadly push of the bayonet. At length a charge of Tarleton's cavalry on their flank threw them into confusion, and drove them into the woods and swamps. None showed more gallantry on this disastrous day than the Baron De Kalb; he fought on foot with the second Maryland brigade, and fell exhausted after receiving eleven wounds. His aide-de-camp, De Buysson, supported him in his arms and was repeatedly wounded in protecting him. He announced the rank and nation of his general, and both were taken prisoners. De Kalb died in the course of a few days.

General Gates in retreating had hoped to rally a sufficient force at Clermont to cover the retreat of the regulars, but the further they fled, the more the militia were dispersed, until the generals were abandoned by all but their aides. To add to the mortification of Gates, he learned in the course of his retreat that Sumter had been completely successful, and having reduced the enemy's redoubt on the Wateree, and captured one hundred prisoners and forty loaded wagons, was marching off with his booty on the opposite side of the river; apprehending danger from the quarter in which he had heard firing in the morning.

Cornwallis was apprehensive that Sumter's corps might form a rallying point to the routed army. On the morning of the 17th of August, therefore, he detached Tarleton in pursuit with a body of cavalry and light infantry, about three hundred and fifty strong. Sumter was retreating up the western side of the Wateree, much encumbered by his spoils and prisoners. Tarleton pushed up by forced and concealed marches on the eastern side. At dusk Tarleton descried the fires of the American camp about a mile from the opposite shore. In the morning his sentries gave word that the Americans were quitting their encampment. It was evident they knew nothing of a British force being in pursuit of them. Tarleton now crossed the Wateree. The delay in crossing, and the diligence of Sumter's march, increased the distance between the pursuers and the pursued. About noon a part of Tarleton's force gave out through heat and fatigue. Leaving them to repose on the bank of Fishing Creek, he pushed on with about one hundred dragoons, the freshest and most able; still marching with great circumspection. A sergeant and five dragoons rode up to the summit of a neighboring hill to reconnoitre. Crouching on their horses they made signs to Tarleton. He cautiously approached the crest of the hill, and looking over, beheld the American camp on a neighboring height in a most negligent condition. The troops, having for the last four days been almost without food or sleep, were indulged in complete relaxation. Their arms were stacked, and they were scattered about, some strolling, some lying on the grass under the trees, some bathing in the river. Sumter himself had thrown off part of his clothes on account of the heat of the weather.

Tarleton prepared for instant attack. His cavalry and infantry formed into one line, dashed forward with a general shout, and, before the Americans could recover from their surprise, got between them and the parade ground on which the muskets were stacked. All was confusion and consternation in the American camp. Some opposition was made from behind baggage wagons, and there was skirmishing in various quarters, but in a little while there was a universal flight to the river and the woods. Between three and four hundred were killed and wounded; all their arms and baggage with two brass field-pieces fell into the hands of the enemy, who also recaptured the prisoners and booty taken at Camden. Sumter with about three hundred and fifty of his men effected a retreat; he galloped off, it is said, without saddle, hat or coat.

It was not until the beginning of September that Washington received word of the disastrous reverse at Camden. The shock was the greater as previous reports from that quarter had represented the operations a few days preceding the action as much in our favor. It was evident to Washington that the course of war must ultimately tend to the Southern States, yet the situation of affairs in the North did not permit him to detach any sufficient force for their relief. All that he could do for the present was to endeavor to hold the enemy in check in that quarter. For this purpose he gave orders that some regular troops, enlisted in Maryland for the war, and intended for the main army, should be sent to the southward. He wrote to Governor Rutledge of South Carolina (12th September), to raise a permanent, compact, well-organized body of troops, instead of depending upon a numerous army of militia, always "inconceivably expensive, and too fluctuating and undisciplined" to oppose a regular force. He was still more urgent and explicit on this head in his letters to the President of Congress (September 15th). "Regular troops alone," said he, "are equal to the exigencies of modern war, as well for defence as offence; and whenever a substitute is attempted, it must prove illusory and ruinous. No militia will ever acquire the habits necessary to resist a regular force."

He had scarce written the foregoing, when he received a letter from the now unfortunate Gates, dated at Hillsborough, August 30th and September 3d, giving particulars of his discomfiture. No longer vaunting and vainglorious, he pleads nothing but his patriotism, and deprecates the fall which he apprehends awaits him. The appeal which he makes to Washington's magnanimity to support him in this day of his reverse, is the highest testimonial he could give to the exalted character of the man whom he once affected to underrate and aspired to supplant.

Washington still cherished the idea of a combined attack upon New York as soon as a French naval force should arrive. The destruction of the enemy here would relieve this part of the Union from an internal war, and enable its troops and resources to be united with those of France in vigorous efforts against the common enemy elsewhere. Hearing, therefore, that the Count de Guichen with his West India squadron was approaching the coast, Washington prepared to proceed to Hartford, in Connecticut, there to hold a conference with the Count de Rochambeau and the Chevalier de Ternay, and concert a plan for future operations, of which the attack on New York was to form the principal feature.

CHAPTER LVII.

THE TREASON OF ARNOLD.—TRIAL AND EXECUTION OF ANDRÉ.

We have now to enter upon a sad episode of our revolutionary history—the treason of Arnold. Of the military skill, daring enterprise, and indomitable courage of this man, ample evidence has been given in the foregoing pages. Of the implicit confidence reposed in his patriotism by Washington, sufficient proof is manifested in the command with which he was actually entrusted. But Arnold was false at heart, and at the very time of seeking that command had been for many months in traitorous correspondence with the enemy.

The first idea of proving recreant to the cause he had vindicated so bravely, appears to have entered his mind when the charges preferred against him by the council of Pennsylvania were referred by Congress to a court-martial. Before that time he had been incensed against Pennsylvania; but now his wrath was excited against his country, which appeared so insensible to his services. Disappointment in regard to the settlement of his accounts added to his irritation, and mingled sordid motives with his resentment; and he began to think how, while he wreaked his vengeance on his country, he might do it with advantage to his fortunes. With this view he commenced a correspondence with Sir Henry Clinton in a disguised handwriting, and under the signature of *Gustavus*, representing himself as a person of importance in the American service, who, being dissatisfied with the late proceedings of Congress, particularly the alliance with France, was desirous of joining the cause of Great Britain, could he be certain of personal security and indemnification for whatever loss of property he might sustain. His letters occasionally communicated articles of intelligence of some moment which proved to be true, and induced Sir Henry to keep up the correspondence; which was conducted on his part by his aide-de-camp, Major John André,[20] likewise in a disguised hand, and under the signature of John Anderson. Months elapsed before Sir Henry discovered who was his secret correspondent. Even after discovering it

---

[20] Major André was born in London in 1751, but his parents were of Geneva, Switzerland, where he was educated. He was designed for mercantile life, and entered a London counting-house, the sober routine of which, however, was so distasteful to him that he soon abandoned it for the army. An engagement in his eighteenth year to a beautiful girl, Miss Honora Sneyd, which the father of the young lady broke off, is said to have been one cause of this step. He came to America in 1774 as lieutenant of the Royal Fusiliers. His temper was light and festive, and his varied, graceful talents, and his engaging manners rendered him generally popular.

he did not see fit to hold out very strong inducements to Arnold for desertion. The latter was out of command and had nothing to offer but his services; which in his actual situation were scarcely worth buying.

In the meantime the circumstances of Arnold were daily becoming more desperate. Debts were accumulating, and creditors becoming more and more importunate as his means to satisfy them decreased. The public reprimand he had received was rankling in his mind, and filling his heart with bitterness. Still he hesitated on the brink of absolute infamy, and attempted a half-way leap. Such was his proposition to M. de Luzerne to make himself subservient to the policy of the French government, on condition of receiving a loan equal to the amount of his debts. It was his last card before resorting to utter treachery. Failing in it, his desperate alternative was to get some important command, the betrayal of which to the enemy might obtain for him a munificent reward. Such was the secret of his eagerness to obtain the command of West Point, the great object of British and American solicitude, on the possession of which were supposed by many to hinge the fortunes of the war.

He took command of the post and its dependencies about the beginning of August, fixing his head-quarters at Beverley, a country-seat a little below West Point, on the opposite or eastern side of the river. It was commonly called the Robinson House, having formerly belonged to Colonel Beverley Robinson. Colonel Robinson was a royalist; had entered into the British service, and was now residing in New York, and Beverley with its surrounding lands had been confiscated.

From this place Arnold carried on a secret correspondence with Major André. Their letters still in disguised hands, and under the names of Gustavus and John Anderson, purported to treat merely of commercial operations, but the real matter in negotiation was the betrayal of West Point and the Highlands to Sir Henry Clinton. This stupendous piece of treachery was to be consummated at the time when Washington, with the main body of his army, would be drawn down towards King's Bridge, and the French troops landed on Long Island, in the projected co-operation against New York. At such time, a flotilla under Rodney, having on board a large land force, was to ascend the Hudson to the Highlands, which would be surrendered by Arnold almost without opposition, under pretext of insufficient force to make resistance. The immediate result of this surrender, it was anticipated, would be the defeat of the combined attempt upon New York; and its ultimate effect might be the dismemberment of the Union and the dislocation of the whole American scheme of warfare.

Correspondence had now done its part in the business; for the completion of the plan and the adjustment of the traitor's recompense, a personal meeting was necessary between Arnold and André. The former proposed that it should take place at his own quarters, where André should come in disguise as a bearer of intelligence, and under the feigned name of John Anderson. André positively objected to entering the American lines; it was arranged, therefore, that the meeting should take place on neutral ground, near the American out-posts at Dobbs' Ferry, on the 11th of September, at twelve o'clock. André attended at the appointed place and time, accompanied by Colonel Beverley Robinson, who was acquainted with the plot. An application of the latter for the restoration of his confiscated property in the Highlands seemed to have been used occasionally as a blind in these proceedings.

Arnold had passed the preceding night at what was called the White House, the residence of Mr. Joshua Hett Smith, situated on the west side of the Hudson, in Haverstraw Bay, about two miles below Stony Point. He set off thence in his barge for the place of rendezvous; but not being protected by a flag, was fired upon and pursued by the British guard-boats stationed near Dobbs' Ferry. He took refuge at an American post on the western shore, whence he returned in the night to his quarters. New arrangements were made for an interview, but it was postponed until after Washington should depart for Hartford to hold the proposed conference with Count Rochambeau and the other French officers. In the meantime the British sloop-of-war, Vulture, anchored a few miles below Teller's Point, to be at hand in aid of the negotiation. On board was Colonel Robinson, who, pretending to believe that General Putnam still commanded in the Highlands, addressed a note to him requesting an interview on the subject of his confiscated property. This letter he sent by a flag, enclosed in one addressed to Arnold; soliciting of him the same boon should General Putnam be absent.

On the 18th September, Washington with his suite crossed the Hudson to Verplanck's Point, in Arnold's barge, on his way to Hartford. Arnold accompanied him as far as Peekskill, and on the way, laid before him, with affected frankness, the letter of Colonel Robinson, and asked his advice. Washington disapproved of any such interview, observing that the civil authorities alone had cognizance of these questions of confiscated property. Arnold now openly sent a flag on board of the Vulture, as if bearing a reply to the letter he had communicated to the commander-in-chief. By this occasion he informed Colonel Robinson that a person with a boat and flag would be alongside of the Vulture on the night of the 20th; and that any matter he might wish to communicate, would be laid before General Washington on the following Saturday, when he might be expected back from Newport.

On the faith of the information thus covertly conveyed, André proceeded up the Hudson on the 20th, and went on board of the Vulture, where he found Colonel Robinson, and expected to meet Arnold. The latter, however, had made other arrangements, probably with a view to his personal security. About half-past eleven of a still and starlight night (the 21st), a boat was descried from on board, gliding silently along, rowed by two men with muffled oars. She was hailed by an officer on watch, and called to account. A man seated in the stern gave out that they were from King's Ferry, bound to Dobbs' Ferry. He was ordered alongside and soon made his way on board. He proved to be Mr. Joshua Hett Smith, already mentioned, whom Arnold had prevailed upon to go on board of the Vulture, and bring a person on shore who was coming from New York with important intelligence. He had given him passes to protect him and those with him, in case he should be stopped, either in going or returning, by the American water guard, which patrolled the river in whale-boats. He had made him the bearer of a letter addressed to Colonel Beverley Robinson, which was to the following purport:

"This will be delivered to you by Mr. Smith, who will conduct you to a place of safety. Neither Mr. Smith nor any other person shall be made acquainted with your proposals: if they (which I doubt not) are of such a nature that I can officially take notice of them, I shall do it with pleasure. I take it for granted Colonel Robinson will not propose anything that is not for the interest of the United States as well as of himself." All this use of Colonel Robinson's name was intended as a blind, should the letter be intercepted.

Robinson introduced André to Smith by the name of John Anderson, who was to go on shore in his place (he being unwell), to have an interview with General Arnold. André wore a blue great coat which covered his uniform, and Smith always declared that at the time he was totally ignorant of his name and military character. André, embarking in the boat with Smith, was silently rowed to the western side of the river, about six miles below Stony Point. Here they landed a little after midnight, at the foot of a shadowy mountain called the Long Clove. Arnold was in waiting, but standing aloof among thickets. The midnight negotiation between André and Arnold was carried on in darkness among the trees. One hour after another passed away when Smith approached the place of conference, and gave warning that it was near daybreak, and if they lingered much longer the boat would be discovered.

The nefarious bargain was not yet completed, and Arnold feared the sight of a boat going to the Vulture might cause suspicion. He prevailed therefore upon André to remain on shore until the following night. The boat was accordingly sent to a creek higher up the river, and André set off with Arnold for Smith's house. The road passed through the village of Haverstraw. As they rode along in the dark, the voice of a sentinel demanding the countersign startled André with the fearful conviction that he was within the American lines, but it was too late to recede. It was daybreak when they arrived at Smith's house. They had scarcely entered when the booming of cannon was heard from down the river. It gave André uneasiness, and with reason. Colonel Livingston, who commanded above at Verplanck's Point, learning that the Vulture lay within shot of Teller's Point, which divides Haverstraw Bay from the Tappan Sea, had sent a party with cannon to that point in the night, and they were now firing upon the sloop-of-war. André watched the cannonade with an anxious eye from an upper window of Smith's house. He was relieved from painful solicitude when he saw the vessel weigh anchor, and drop down the river out of reach of cannon shot.

After breakfast, the plot for the betrayal of West Point and its dependent posts was adjusted, and the sum agreed upon that Arnold was to receive, should it be successful. André was furnished with plans of the works, and explanatory papers, which, at Arnold's request, he placed between his stockings and his feet; promising in case of accident, to destroy them.

All matters being thus arranged, Arnold prepared to return in his own barge to his head-quarters at the Robinson House. As the Vulture had shifted her ground, he suggested to André a return to New York by land, as most safe and expeditious; the latter, however, insisted upon being put on board of the sloop-of-war on the ensuing night. Arnold consented; but, before his departure, to provide against the possible necessity of a return by land, he gave André the following pass, dated from the Robinson House:

> "Permit Mr. John Anderson to pass the guards to the White Plains, or below, if he chooses; he being on public business by my direction.
>
> B. Arnold, M. Gen'l."

Smith also, who was to accompany him, was furnished with passports to proceed either by water or by land. Arnold departed about ten o'clock. André passed a lonely day, casting many a wistful look toward the Vulture. As evening approached he grew impatient, and spoke to Smith about departure. To his surprise he found the latter had made no preparation for it; he had discharged his boatmen, who had gone home: in short, he refused to take him on board the Vulture. The cannonade of the morning had probably made him fear for his personal safety, should he attempt to go on board, the Vulture having resumed her exposed position. He offered, however, to cross the river with André at King's Ferry, put him in the way of returning to New York by land, and accompany him some distance on horseback.

André was in an agony at finding himself, notwithstanding all his stipulations, forced within the American lines; but there seemed to be no alternative, and he prepared for the hazardous journey. He wore, as we have noted, a military coat under a long blue surtout; he was now persuaded to lay it aside, and put on a citizen's coat of Smith's; thus adding disguise to the other humiliating and hazardous circumstances of the case.

It was about sunset when André and Smith crossed from King's Ferry to Verplanck's Point. After proceeding about eight miles on the road toward White Plains, they were stopped between eight and nine o'clock, near Crompond, by a patrolling party. The captain of it was uncommonly inquisitive and suspicious. The passports with Arnold's signature satisfied him. He warned them, however, against the danger of proceeding further in the night. Cow Boys from the British lines were scouring the country, and had recently marauded the neighborhood. Smith's fears were again excited, and André was obliged to yield to them. A bed was furnished them in a neighboring house, where André passed an anxious and restless night. At daybreak he awoke Smith, and hurried their departure.

They were now approaching that noted part of the country heretofore mentioned as the Neutral Ground, extending north and south about thirty miles, between the British and American lines. A beautiful region of forest-clad hills, fertile valleys, and abundant streams, but now almost desolated by the scourings of Skinners and Cow Boys; the former professing allegiance to the American cause, the latter to the British, but both arrant marauders. About two and a half miles from Pine's Bridge, on the Croton River, André and his companion partook of a scanty meal at a farm-house. Here they parted, Smith to return home, André to pursue his journey alone to New York.

He had not proceeded far, when coming to a place where a small stream crossed the road and ran into a woody dell, a man stepped out from the trees, levelled a musket and brought him to a stand, while two other men, similarly armed, showed themselves prepared to second their comrade. The man who had first stepped out wore a refugee uniform. At sight of it, André's heart leapt, and he felt himself secure. Losing all caution, he exclaimed, eagerly: "Gentlemen, I hope you belong to our party?" "What party?" was asked. "The lower party," said André. "We do," was the reply. All reserve was now at an end. André declared himself to be a British officer; that he had been up the country on particular business, and must not be detained a single moment. To his consternation, the supposed refugee now avowed himself and his companions to be Americans, and told André he was their prisoner![21]

André was astounded at finding into what hands he had fallen; and how he had betrayed himself by his heedless avowal. Promptly, however, recovering his self possession he endeavored to pass off his previous account of himself as a mere subterfuge. "A man must do anything," said he laughingly, "to get along." He now declared himself to be a Continental officer, going down to Dobbs' Ferry to get information from below; so saying, he drew forth and showed them the pass of General Arnold.

This, in the first instance, would have been sufficient; but his unwary tongue had ruined him. The suspicions of his captors were completely roused. Paulding asked whether he had any letters about him. He answered, no. They proceeded to search him. They obliged him to take off his coat and vest, and found on him eighty dollars in Continental money, but nothing to warrant suspicion of anything sinister, and were disposed to let him proceed, when Paulding exclaimed: "Boys, I am not satisfied—his boots must come off!" At this André changed color. His boots, he said, came off with difficulty, and he begged he might not be subjected to the inconvenience and delay. His remonstrances were in vain. He was obliged to sit down; his boots were drawn off, and the concealed papers discovered. Hastily scanning them, Paulding exclaimed, "My God! He is a spy!" He demanded of André where he had gotten these papers. "Of a man at Pine's Bridge, a stranger to me," was the reply.

While dressing himself, André endeavored to ransom himself from his captors; rising from one offer to another. He would give any reward they might name either in goods or money, and would remain with two of their party while one went to New York to get it. Here Paulding broke in and declared with an oath that if he would give ten thousand guineas he should not stir one step.

The unfortunate André now submitted to his fate, and the captors set off with their prisoner for North Castle, the nearest American post, distant ten or twelve miles. Arrived at North Castle, Lieutenant-colonel Jameson, who was in command there, recognized the handwriting of Arnold in the papers found upon André, and, perceiving that they were of a dangerous nature, sent them off by express to General Washington, at Hartford.

André, still adhering to his assumed name, begged that the commander at West Point might be informed that John Anderson, though bearing his passport, was

---

[21] The names of the captors were John Paulding, Isaac Van Wart, and David Williams.

detained. Jameson appears completely to have lost his head on the occasion. He wrote to Arnold, stating the circumstances of the arrest, and that the papers found upon the prisoner had been despatched by express to the commander-in-chief, and at the same time he sent the prisoner himself, under a strong guard, to accompany the letter.

Shortly afterwards, Major Tallmadge, next in command to Jameson, but of a much clearer head, arrived at North Castle, having been absent on duty to White Plains. When the circumstances of the case were related to him, he at once suspected treachery on the part of Arnold. At his earnest entreaties, an express was sent after the officer who had André in charge, ordering him to bring the latter back to North Castle; but by singular perversity or obtuseness in judgment, Jameson neglected to countermand the letter which he had written to Arnold. When André was brought back, and was pacing up and down the room, Tallmadge saw at once by his air and movements, and the mode of turning on his heel, that he was a military man. By his advice, and under his escort, the prisoner was conducted to Colonel Sheldon's post at Lower Salem, as more secure than North Castle.

Here André, being told that the papers found upon his person had been forwarded to Washington, addressed to him immediately the following lines: "I beg your Excellency will be persuaded that no alteration in the temper of my mind or apprehensions for my safety induces me to take the step of addressing you; but that it is to secure myself from the imputation of having assumed a mean character for treacherous purposes or self-interest.... It is to vindicate my fame that I speak, and not to solicit security. The person in your possession is Major John André, adjutant-general of the British army. The influence of one commander in the army of his adversary is an advantage taken in war. A correspondence for this purpose I held; as confidential (in the present instance) with his Excellency, Sir Henry Clinton. To favor it, I agreed to meet upon ground not within the posts of either army, a person who was to give me intelligence. I came up in the Vulture man-of-war for this effect, and was fetched from the shore to the beach. Being there, I was told that the approach of day would prevent my return, and that I must be concealed until the next night. I was in my regimentals, and had fairly risked my person. Against my stipulation, my intention, and without my knowledge beforehand, I was conducted within one of your posts. Thus was I betrayed into the vile condition of an enemy within your posts...."

This letter he submitted to the perusal of Major Tallmadge, who was surprised and agitated at finding the rank and importance of the prisoner he had in charge. The letter being despatched, and André's pride relieved on a sensitive point, he resumed his serenity, apparently unconscious of the awful responsibility of his situation.

On the very day that the treasonable conference between Arnold and André took place, on the banks of Haverstraw Bay, Washington had his interview with the French officers at Hartford. It led to no important result. Intelligence was received that the squadron of the Count de Guichen, on which they had relied to give them superiority by sea, had sailed for Europe. This disconcerted their plans, and Washington, in consequence, set out two or three days sooner than had been

anticipated on his return to his head-quarters on the Hudson. He was accompanied by Lafayette and General Knox with their suites; also, part of the way, by
Count Matthew Dumas, aide-de-camp to Rochambeau.

On approaching the Hudson, Washington took a more circuitous route than
the one he had originally intended, striking the river at Fishkill, just above the
Highlands, that he might visit West Point, and show the marquis the works which
had been erected there during his absence in France. Circumstances detained them
a night at Fishkill. Their baggage was sent on to Arnold's quarters in the Robinson
House, with a message apprising the general that they would breakfast there the
next day. In the morning (Sept. 24th) they were in the saddle before break of day,
having a ride to make of eighteen miles through the mountains. When within a
mile of the Robinson House, Washington turned down a cross road leading to the
banks of the Hudson. Lafayette apprised him that he was going out of the way,
and hinted that Mrs. Arnold must be waiting breakfast for him. "Ah, marquis!"
replied he good-humoredly, "you young men are all in love with Mrs. Arnold. Go
you and breakfast with her, and tell her not to wait for me. I must ride down and
examine the redoubts on this side of the river, but will be with her shortly." The
marquis and General Knox, however, turned off and accompanied him down to
the redoubts, while Colonel Hamilton and Lafayette's aide-de-camp, Major James
McHenry, continued along the main road to the Robinson House, bearing Washington's apology, and request that the breakfast might not be retarded.

The family with the two aides-de-camp sat down to breakfast. Mrs. Arnold
had arrived but four or five days previously from Philadelphia, with her infant
child, then about six months old. She was bright and amiable as usual. Arnold
was silent and gloomy. It was an anxious moment with him. In the midst of the
repast a horseman alighted at the gate. It was the messenger bearing Jameson's
letter to Arnold, stating the capture of André, and that dangerous papers found on
him had been forwarded to Washington. The mine had exploded beneath Arnold's
feet. Controlling the dismay that must have smitten him to the heart, he beckoned
Mrs. Arnold from the breakfast table, signifying a wish to speak with her in private. When alone with her in her room up-stairs, he announced in hurried words
that he was a ruined man, and must instantly fly for his life! Overcome by the
shock, she fell senseless on the floor. Without pausing to aid her, he hurried down
stairs, informed his guests that he must haste to West Point to prepare for the
reception of the commander-in-chief; and mounting the horse of the messenger,
which stood saddled at the door, galloped down to the landing-place, where his
six-oared barge was moored. Throwing himself into it, he ordered his men to pull
out into the middle of the river, and then made down with all speed for Teller's
Point.

Washington arrived at the Robinson House shortly after the flight of the traitor. Being informed that Mrs. Arnold was in her room, unwell, and that Arnold
had gone to West Point to receive him, he took a hasty breakfast, and repaired to
the fortress, leaving word that he and his suite would return to dinner.

He remained at the Point throughout the morning inspecting the fortifications. In the meantime, the messenger whom Jameson had despatched to Hartford

with a letter covering the papers taken on André, arrived at the Robinson House. He had learnt, while on the way to Hartford, that Washington had left that place, whereupon he turned bridle to overtake him, but missed him in consequence of the general's change of route. Coming by the lower road, the messenger had passed through Salem, where André was confined, and brought with him the letter written by that unfortunate officer to the commander-in-chief, the purport of which has already been given. These letters being represented as of the utmost moment, were opened and read by Colonel Hamilton, as Washington's aide-de-camp and confidential officer. He maintained silence as to their contents; met Washington, as he and his companions were coming up from the river, on their return from West Point, spoke to him a few words in a low voice, and they retired together into the house. Whatever agitation Washington may have felt when these documents of deep-laid treachery were put before him, he wore his usual air of equanimity when he rejoined his companions. Taking Knox and Lafayette aside, he communicated to them the intelligence, and placed the papers in their hands.

His first idea was to arrest the traitor. Conjecturing the direction of his flight, he despatched Colonel Hamilton on horseback to spur with all speed to Verplanck's Point, with orders to the commander to intercept Arnold should he not already have passed that post. In the meantime, Arnold, panic-stricken, had sped his caitiff flight through the Highlands; infamy howling in his rear; arrest threatening him in the advance; a fugitive past the posts which he had recently commanded; shrinking at the sight of that flag which hitherto it had been his glory to defend!

He had passed through the Highlands in safety, but there were the batteries at Verplanck's Point yet to fear. Fortunately for him, Hamilton, with the order for his arrest had not arrived there. His barge was known by the garrison. A white handkerchief displayed gave it the sanction of a flag of truce: it was suffered to pass without question, and the traitor effected his escape to the Vulture sloop-of-war, anchored a few miles below. As if to consummate his degradation by a despicable act of treachery and meanness, he gave up to the commander his coxswain and six bargemen as prisoners of war. We are happy to add that this perfidy excited the scorn of the British officers; and, when it was found that the men had supposed they were acting under the protection of a flag, they were released by order of Sir Henry Clinton.

Colonel Hamilton returned to the Robinson House and reported the escape of the traitor. He brought two letters also to Washington, which had been sent on shore from the Vulture, under a flag of truce. One was from Arnold, in which he wrote: "I ask no favor for myself. I have too often experienced the ingratitude of my country to attempt it; but, from the known humanity of your Excellency, I am induced to ask your protection for Mrs. Arnold from every insult and injury that a mistaken vengeance of my country may expose her to.... I beg she may be permitted to return to her friends in Philadelphia, or to come to me as she may choose." The other letter was from Colonel Beverley Robinson, interceding for the release of André, on the plea that he was on shore under the sanction of a flag of truce, at the request of Arnold.

Notwithstanding Washington's apparent tranquillity and real self-possession, it was a time of appalling distrust. How far the treason had extended, who else might be implicated in it, was unknown. Arnold had escaped, and was actually on board of the Vulture; he knew everything about the condition of the posts: might he not persuade the enemy in the present weak state of the garrisons to attempt a *coup de main?* Washington instantly, therefore, despatched a letter to Colonel Wade, who was in temporary command at West Point. "General Arnold is gone to the enemy," writes he. "I request that you will be as vigilant as possible, and as the enemy may have it in contemplation to attempt some enterprise, *even to-night*, against these posts, I wish you to make, immediately after the receipt of this, the best disposition you can of your force, so as to have a proportion of men in each work on the west side of the river." A regiment stationed in the Highlands was ordered to the same duty, as well as a body of the Massachusetts militia from Fishkill. At half-past seven in the evening, Washington wrote to General Greene, who, in his absence, commanded the army at Tappan; urging him to put the left division in motion as soon as possible, with orders to proceed to King's Ferry, where, or before they should arrive there, they would be met with further orders.

In the meantime, Mrs. Arnold remained in her room in a state bordering on frenzy. Arnold might well confide in the humanity and delicacy of Washington in respect to her. He regarded her with the sincerest commiseration, acquitting her of all previous knowledge of her husband's guilt. During the brief time she remained at the Robinson House, she was treated with the utmost deference and delicacy, but soon set off under a passport of Washington, for her father's house in Philadelphia.

On the 26th of September, the day after the treason of Arnold had been revealed to Washington, André arrived at the Robinson House, having been brought on in the night, under escort and in charge of Major Tallmadge. Washington made many inquiries of the major, but declined to have the prisoner brought into his presence, apparently entertaining a strong idea of his moral obliquity, from the nature of the scheme in which he had been engaged, and the circumstances under which he had been arrested. The same evening he transmitted him to West Point, and shortly afterwards, Joshua H. Smith, who had likewise been arrested. Still, not considering them secure even there, he determined on the following day to send them on to the camp.

Major Tallmadge continued to have the charge of André. Not regarding him from the same anxious point with the commander-in-chief, and having had opportunities of acquiring a personal knowledge of him, he had become fascinated by his engaging qualities. "The ease and affability of his manners," writes he, "polished by the refinement of good society and a finished education, made him a most delightful companion. It often drew tears from my eyes to find him so agreeable in conversation on different subjects, when I reflected on his future fate, and that too, as I feared, so near at hand."

Early on the morning of the 28th, the prisoners were embarked in a barge, to be conveyed from West Point to King's Ferry. After disembarking at King's Ferry, near Stony Point, they set off for Tappan under the escort of a body of horse. As they approached the Clove, a deep defile in the rear of the Highlands, André, who rode beside Tallmadge, became solicitous to know the opinion of the latter as to what would be the result of his capture, and in what light he would be regarded by General Washington and by a military tribunal, should one be ordered. Tallmadge evaded the question as long as possible, but being urged to a full and explicit reply, gave it, he says, in the following words: "I had a much-loved classmate in Yale College, by the name of Nathan Hale, who entered the army in 1775. Immediately after the battle of Long Island, General Washington wanted information respecting the strength, position, and probable movements of the enemy. Captain Hale tendered his services, went over to Brooklyn, and was taken, just as he was passing the outposts of the enemy on his return; said I with emphasis—'Do you remember the sequel of the story?' 'Yes,' said André. 'He was hanged as a spy! But you surely do not consider his case and mine alike?' 'Yes, precisely similar.'"[22]

The capture of André caused a great sensation at New York. He was universally popular with the army, and an especial favorite of Sir Henry Clinton. The latter addressed a letter to Washington on the 29th, claiming the release of André on similar ground to that urged by Colonel Robinson—his having visited Arnold at the particular request of that general officer, and under the sanction of a flag of truce; and his having been stopped while travelling under Arnold's passports. The same letter inclosed one addressed by Arnold to Sir Henry, and intended as a kind of certificate of the innocence of André. "I commanded at the time at West Point,"

---

[22] The fate of the heroic youth here alluded to, deserves a more ample notice. Born in Coventry, Connecticut, June 6th, 1755, he entered Yale College in 1770, and graduated with some distinction in September, 1773. On quitting college he engaged as a teacher, as is common with young men in New England, while studying for a profession. His half-formed purpose was to devote himself to the ministry. He was teaching at New London, when an express arrived, bringing tidings of the outbreak at Lexington. A town meeting was called, and Hale was among the most ardent of the speakers, proposing an instant march to the scene of hostilities, and offering to volunteer.

He served in the army before Boston as a lieutenant; prevailed on his company to extend their term of service by offering them his own pay, and for his good conduct received from Congress the commission of captain. He commanded a company in Colonel Knowlton's regiment in the following year. After the disastrous battle of Long Island, Washington applied to that officer for a competent person to penetrate the enemy's camp, and procure intelligence of their designs. Hale, in the ardor of patriotism, volunteered for the unenviable enterprise, though fully aware of its peril, and the consequences of capture. Assuming his old character as schoolmaster, he crossed the Sound at night from Norwalk to Huntington on Long Island, visited the British encampments unsuspected, made drawings of the enemy's works, and noted down memoranda in Latin of the information he gathered, and then retraced his steps to Huntington, where a boat was to meet him and convey him back to the Connecticut shore. Unfortunately a British guard ship was at that time anchored out of view in the Sound, and had sent a boat on shore for water. Hale mistook it for the expected boat, and did not discover his mistake until he found himself in the hands of enemies. He was stripped and searched, the plans and memoranda were found concealed in the soles of his shoes, and proved him to be a spy. He was conveyed to the guard ship, and thence to New York, where he was landed on the 21st of September, the day of the great fire. He was taken to General Howe's head-quarters, and after brief parley with his judge, ordered for execution the next morning at daybreak. His patriot spirit shone forth in his dying words— "I only regret that I have but one life to lose for my country."

writes the renegade, "had an undoubted right to send my flag of truce to Major André, who came to me under that protection, and, having held conversation with him, I delivered him confidential papers in my own hand-writing to deliver to your Excellency."

Neither the official demand of Sir Henry Clinton, nor the impudent certificate of Arnold, had any effect on the steady mind of Washington. He considered the circumstances under which André had been taken such as would have justified the most summary proceedings, but he determined to refer the case to the examination and decision of a board of general officers, which he convened on the 29th of September, the day after his arrival at Tappan. It was composed of six major-generals—Greene, Stirling, St. Clair, Lafayette, R. Howe, and Steuben; and eight brigadiers—Parsons, Jas. Clinton, Knox, Glover, Paterson, Hand, Huntingdon, and Stark. General Greene, who was well versed in military law, and was a man of sound head and kind heart, was president, and Colonel John Lawrence, judge advocate-general.

Colonel Alexander Hamilton gives, in letters to his friends, many interesting particulars concerning the conduct of the prisoner. "When brought before the board of officers," writes he, "he met with every mark of indulgence, and was required to answer no interrogatory which would even embarrass his feelings. On his part, while he carefully concealed everything that might implicate others, he frankly confessed all the facts relating to himself, and upon his confession, without the trouble of examining a witness, the board made up their report." It briefly stated the circumstances of the case, and concluded with the opinion of the court, that Major André, adjutant-general of the British army, ought to be considered a spy from the enemy, and, agreeably to the law and usage of nations, ought to suffer death.

André met the result with manly firmness. Even in this situation of gathering horrors, he thought of others more than of himself. "There is only one thing that disturbs my tranquillity," said he to Hamilton. "Sir Henry Clinton has been too good to me; he has been lavish of his kindness. I am bound to him by too many obligations, and love him too well, to bear the thought that he should reproach himself, or others should reproach him, on the supposition of my having conceived myself obliged, by his instructions, to run the risk I did. I would not for the world leave a sting in his mind that should embitter his future days." He could scarce finish the sentence; bursting into tears, in spite of his efforts to suppress them, and with difficulty collected himself enough afterwards to add, "I wish to be permitted to assure him that I did not act under this impression, but submitted to a necessity imposed upon me, as contrary to my own inclination as to his wishes." His request was complied with, and he wrote a letter to Sir Henry Clinton to the above purport. He made mention also of his mother and three sisters, to whom the value of his commission would be an object. "It is needless," said he, "to be more explicit on this subject; I am persuaded of your Excellency's goodness."

This letter accompanied one from Washington to Sir Henry Clinton, stating the report of the board of inquiry, omitting the sentence. Captain Aaron Ogden, a worthy officer of the New Jersey line, was selected by Washington to bear these despatches to the enemy's post at Paulus Hook, thence to be conveyed across the Hudson to New York. Before his departure, he called by Washington's request on the Marquis Lafayette, who gave him instructions to sound the officer commanding at that post whether Sir Henry Clinton might not be willing to deliver up Arnold in exchange for André. Ogden arrived at Paulus Hook in the evening, and made the suggestion, as if incidentally, in the course of conversation. The officer crossed the river before morning, and communicated the matter to Sir Henry Clinton, but the latter instantly rejected the expedient as incompatible with honor and military principle.

The execution was to have taken place on the 1st of October, at five o'clock in the afternoon; but in the interim Washington received a second letter from Sir Henry Clinton, dated September 30th, expressing an opinion that the board of inquiry had not been rightly informed of all the circumstances on which a judgment ought to be formed, and that, in order that he might be perfectly apprised of the state of the matter before he proceeded to put that judgment in execution, he should send a commission on the following day, composed of Lieutenant-governor Elliot, William Smith, chief justice of the province, and Lieutenant-general Robertson, to wait near Dobbs' Ferry for permission and safe conduct to meet Washington, or such persons as he should appoint to converse with them on the subject. This letter caused a postponement of the execution, and General Greene was sent to meet the commissioners at Dobbs' Ferry. They came up in the morning of the 1st of October, in a schooner, with a flag of truce, and were accompanied by Colonel Beverley Robinson. General Robertson, however, was the only commissioner permitted to land, the others not being military officers. A long conference took place between him and General Greene, without any agreement of opinion upon the question at issue. Greene returned to camp promising to report faithfully to Washington the arguments urged by Robertson, and to inform the latter of the result.

Greene, in a brief letter to General Robertson, informed him that he had as full a report of their conference to the commander-in-chief as his memory would serve, but that it had made no alteration in Washington's opinion and determination. Robertson was piqued at the brevity of the note, and professed to doubt whether Greene's memory had served him with sufficient fulness and exactness; he addressed therefore to Washington his own statement of his reasoning on the subject; after despatching which, he and the other commissioners returned in the schooner to New York.

During this day of respite André had conducted himself with his usual tranquillity. A likeness of himself, seated at a table in his guard-room, which he sketched with a pen and gave to the officer on guard, is still extant. It being announced to him that one o'clock on the following day was fixed on for his execution, he remarked, that since it was his lot to die, there was still a choice in the mode; he therefore addressed a note to Washington, concluding as follows: "Let me hope, sir, that if aught in my character impresses you with esteem towards me; if aught in my misfortunes marks me as the victim of policy and not of resentment, I shall experience the operation of these feelings in your breast by being informed that I am not to die on a gibbet."

MAJOR JOHN ANDRÉ.
VOL. IV.

Had Washington consulted his feelings merely, this affecting appeal might not have been in vain, for, though not impulsive, he was eminently benevolent. He had no popular censure to apprehend should he exercise indulgence, for the popular feeling was with the prisoner. But he had a high and tenacious sense of the duties and responsibilities of his position, and never more than in this trying moment, when he had to elevate himself above the contagious sympathies of those around him, dismiss all personal considerations, and regard the peculiar circumstances of the case. The long course of insidious operations which had been pursued to undermine the loyalty of one of his most trusted officers; the greatness of the evil which the treason would have effected, if successful; the uncertainty how far the enemy had carried, or might still be carrying, their scheme of corruption, for anonymous intimations spoke of treachery in other quarters; all these considerations pointed this out as a case in which a signal example was required. He took counsel with some of his general officers. Their opinions coincided with his own—that under present circumstances, it was important to give a signal warning to the enemy, by a rigorous observance of the rules of war and the usages of nations in like cases.

But although André's request as to the mode of his death was not to be granted, it was thought best to let him remain in uncertainty on the subject; no answer, therefore, was returned to his note. On the morning of the 2d, he maintained a calm demeanor, though all around him were gloomy and silent. He even rebuked his servant for shedding tears. Having breakfasted, he dressed himself with care in the full uniform of a British officer, which he had sent for to New York, placed his hat upon the table, and accosting the officers on guard—"I am ready," said he, "at any moment gentlemen to wait upon you."

He walked to the place of execution between two subaltern officers, arm in arm, with a serene countenance, bowing to several gentlemen whom he knew. Colonel Tallmadge accompanied him, and we quote his words: "When he came within sight of the gibbet, he appeared to be startled, and inquired with some emotion whether he was not to be shot. Being informed that the mode first appointed for his death could not consistently be altered, he exclaimed, 'How hard is my fate!' but immediately added, 'it will soon be over.' I then shook hands with him under the gallows, and retired." All things being ready, he stepped into the wagon; appeared to shrink for an instant, but recovering himself, exclaimed: "It will be but a momentary pang!"

Taking off his hat and stock, and opening his shirt collar, he deliberately adjusted the noose to his neck, after which he took out a handkerchief, and tied it over his eyes. Being told by the officer in command that his arms must be bound, he drew out a second handkerchief, with which they were pinioned. Colonel Scammel now told him that he had an opportunity to speak, if he desired it. His only reply was, "I pray you to bear witness that I meet my fate like a brave man." The wagon moved from under him, and left him suspended. He died almost without a struggle. His remains were interred within a few yards of the place of his execution; whence they were transferred to England in 1821, by the British consul, then resident in New York, and were buried in Westminster Abbey, near a mural monument which had been erected to his memory.

Washington, in a letter to the President of Congress, passed a high eulogium on the captors of André, and recommended them for a handsome gratuity. Congress accordingly expressed, in a formal vote, a high sense of their virtuous and patriotic conduct; awarded to each of them a farm, a pension for life of two hundred dollars, and a silver medal, bearing on one side an escutcheon on which was engraved the word FIDELITY, and on the other side the motto, *Vincit amor Patriæ*. These medals were delivered to them by General Washington at head-quarters, with impressive ceremony.

Joshua H. Smith, who aided in bringing André and Arnold together, was tried by a court-martial, on a charge of participating in the treason, but was acquitted, no proof appearing of his having had any knowledge of Arnold's plot, though it was thought he must have been conscious of something wrong in an interview so mysteriously conducted.

Arnold was now made brigadier-general in the British service, and put on an official level with honorable men who scorned to associate with the traitor. What golden reward he was to have received had his treason been successful, is not known; but six thousand three hundred and fifteen pounds sterling were paid to him, as a compensation for losses which he pretended to have suffered in going over to the enemies of his country.

The vilest culprit, however, shrinks from sustaining the obloquy of his crimes. Shortly after his arrival in New York, Arnold published an address to the Inhabitants of America, in which he endeavored to vindicate his conduct. He alleged that he had originally taken up arms merely to aid in obtaining a redress of grievances. He had considered the Declaration of Independence precipitate, and the reasons for it obviated, by the subsequent proffers of the British government; and he inveighed against Congress for rejecting those offers, without submitting them to the people. Finally, the treaty with France, a proud, ancient and crafty foe, the enemy of the Protestant faith and of real liberty, had completed, he said, the measure of his indignation, and determined him to abandon a cause sustained by iniquity and controlled by usurpers.

Besides this address, he issued a proclamation inviting the officers and soldiers of the American army, who had the real interest of their country at heart, and who were determined to be no longer the tools and dupes of Congress, and of France, to rally under the royal standard, and fight for true American liberty; holding out promises of large bounties and liberal subsistence, with compensation for all the implements and accoutrements of war they might bring with them. Both the address and the proclamation were regarded by Americans with the contempt they merited. None rallied to the standard of the renegade but a few deserters and refugees, who were already within the British lines, and prepared for any desperate or despicable service.

Mrs. Arnold, on arriving at her father's house in Philadelphia, had decided on a separation from her husband, to whom she could not endure the thoughts of returning after his dishonor. This course, however, was not allowed her. The executive council, wrongfully suspecting her of having aided in the correspondence between her husband and André, knowing its treasonable tendency, ordered her to leave the State within fourteen days, and not to return during the continuance of the war. "We tried every means," writes one of her connections, "to prevail on the council to permit her to stay among us." It was all in vain, and, strongly against her will, she rejoined her husband in New York. She returned home but once, about five years after her exile, and was treated with such coldness and neglect that she declared she never could come again. In England her charms and virtues, it is said, procured her sympathy and friendship, and helped to sustain the social position of her husband, who, however, was "generally slighted, and sometimes insulted." She died in London, in the winter of 1796.

CHAPTER LVIII.

PLAN TO ENTRAP ARNOLD.—PROJECTS AGAINST NEW YORK.

At this time a plan was formed at Washington's suggestion to get possession of the person of Arnold. The agent pitched upon by Lee for the purpose, was the sergeant-major of cavalry in his legion, John Champe by name, a young Virginian about twenty-four years of age. By many promises and much persuasion, Lee brought him to engage in the attempt. Champe was to make a pretended desertion to the enemy at New York. There he was to enlist in a corps which Arnold was raising, insinuate himself into some menial or military situation about his person, and watching for a favorable moment, was, with the aid of a confederate from Newark, to seize him in the night, gag him, and bring him across the Hudson into Bergen woods, in the Jerseys. Washington, in approving the plan, enjoined and stipulated that Arnold should be brought to him alive.

The pretended desertion of the sergeant took place on the night of October 20th, and was attended with difficulties. He had to evade patrols of horse and foot, beside stationary guards and irregular scouting parties. Major Lee could render him no assistance other than to delay pursuit, should his departure be discovered. About eleven o'clock the sergeant took his cloak, valise, and orderly book, drew his horse from the picket, and mounting, set out on his hazardous course, while the major retired to rest. He had not been in bed half an hour, when Captain Carnes, officer of the day, hurrying into his quarters, gave word that one of the patrols had fallen in with a dragoon, who, on being challenged, put spurs to his horse, and escaped. Lee pretended to be annoyed by the intrusion, and to believe that the pretended dragoon was some countryman of the neighborhood. The captain was piqued; made a muster of the dragoons, and returned with word that the sergeant-major was missing, who had gone off with horse, baggage, arms, and orderly book.

Lee was now compelled to order out a party in pursuit under Cornet Middleton, but in so doing, he contrived so many delays, that, by the time they were in the saddle, Champe had an hour's start. His pursuers, too, were obliged in the course of the night, to halt occasionally, dismount and examine the road, to guide themselves by the horse's tracks. At daybreak they pressed forward more rapidly, and from the summit of a hill descried Champe not more than half a mile in front. The sergeant at the same moment caught sight of his pursuers, and now the chase became desperate. Champe had originally intended to make for Paulus Hook but changed his course, threw his pursuers at fault, and succeeded in getting abreast of two British galleys at anchor near the shore beyond Bergen. He had no time to lose. Cornet Middleton was but two or three hundred yards behind him. Throwing himself off his horse, and running through a marsh, he plunged into the river, and called to the galleys for help. A boat was sent to his assistance, and he was conveyed on board of one of those vessels.

For a time the whole plan promised to be successful. Champe enlisted in Arnold's corps; was employed about his person; and every arrangement was made to surprise him at night in a garden in the rear of his quarters, convey him to a boat, and ferry him across the Hudson. On the appointed night, Lee, with three dragoons and three led horses, was in the woods of Hoboken, on the Jersey shore, waiting to receive the captive. Hour after hour passed away—no boat approached—day broke; and the major with his dragoons and his led horses, returned perplexed and disappointed to the camp. It subsequently proved that on the day preceding the night fixed on for the capture, Arnold had removed his quarters to another part of the town, and that the American legion, consisting chiefly of American deserters, had been transferred from their barracks to one of the transports. Among the troops thus transferred was John Champe: nor was he able for a long time to effect his escape, and resume his real character of a loyal and patriotic soldier. He was rewarded when he did so, by the munificence of the commander-in-chief, and the admiration of his old comrades in arms.

We have here to note the altered fortunes of the once prosperous General Gates. The sudden annihilation of an army from which so much had been expected, and the retreat of the general before the field was absolutely lost, appeared to demand a strict investigation. Congress therefore passed a resolution (October 5th), requiring Washington to order a court of inquiry into the conduct of Gates as commander of the Southern army, and to appoint some other officer to the command until the inquiry should be made. Washington at once selected Greene for the important trust. His choice was in concurrence with the expressed wishes of the delegates of the three Southern States, conveyed to him by one of their number.

With regard to the court of inquiry, Baron Steuben, who was to accompany Greene to the South was to preside, and the members of the court were to be such general and field-officers of the Continental troops as were not present at the battle of Camden, or having been present, were not wanted as witnesses, or were persons to whom General Gates had no objection. The affair was to be conducted with the greatest impartiality, and with as much despatch as circumstances would permit.

Ravaging incursions from Canada had harassed the northern parts of the State of New York of late, and laid desolate some parts of the country from which Washington had hoped to receive great supplies of flour for the armies. Major Carleton, a nephew of Sir Guy, at the head of a motley force, European, Tory, and Indian, had captured Forts Anne and George. Sir John Johnson also, with Joseph Brant, and a mongrel half-savage crew, had laid waste the fertile region of the Mohawk River, and burned the villages of Schoharie and Caughnawaga. The greatest alarm prevailed throughout the neighboring country. Governor Clinton himself took the field at the head of the militia, but before he arrived at the scene of mischief, the marauders had been encountered and driven back by General Van Rensselaer and the militia of those parts; not, however, until they had nearly destroyed the settlements on the Mohawk. Washington now put Brigadier-general James Clinton (the governor's brother) in command of the Northern department.

The state of the army was growing more and more a subject of solicitude to the commander-in-chief. He felt weary of struggling on with such scanty means, and such vast responsibility. The campaign, which at its commencement had seemed pregnant with favorable events, had proved sterile and inactive, and was drawing to a close. The short terms for which most of the troops were enlisted must soon expire, and then the present army would be reduced to a mere shadow. "To suppose," writes he, "that this great Revolution can be accomplished by a temporary army, that this army will be subsisted by State supplies, and that taxation alone is adequate to our wants, is in my opinion absurd, and as unreasonable as to expect an inversion in the order of nature to accommodate itself to our views. If it was necessary, it could be proved to any person of a moderate understanding, that an annual army, raised on the spur of the occasion, besides being unqualified for the end designed, is, in various ways which could be enumerated, ten times more expensive than a permanent body of men under good organization and military discipline, which never was nor ever will be the case with new troops."

We will here add that the repeated and elaborate reasonings of Washington, backed by dear bought experience, slowly brought Congress to adopt a system suggested by him for the organization and support of the army, according to which, troops were to be enlisted to serve throughout the war, and all officers who continued in service until the return of peace were to receive half pay during life.

The Marquis Lafayette at this time commanded the advance guard of Washington's army, composed of six battalions of light infantry. They were better clad than the other soldiery; in trim uniforms, leathern helmets, with crests of horsehair. The officers were armed with spontoons, the non-commissioned officers with fusees; both with short sabres which the marquis had brought from France, and presented to them. He was proud of his troops, and had a young man's ardor for active service. The inactivity which had prevailed for some time past was intolerable to him. The marquis saw with repining the campaign drawing to a close, and nothing done that would rouse the people in America, and be spoken of at the Court of Versailles. He was urgent with Washington that the campaign should be terminated by some brilliant stroke. Complaints, he hinted, had been made in France of the prevailing inactivity. The brilliant stroke, suggested with some detail by the marquis, was a general attack upon Fort Washington, and the other posts at the north end of the island of New York, and, under certain circumstances, which he specified, *make a push for the city.*

Washington regarded the project of his young and ardent friend with a more sober and cautious eye. "It is impossible, my dear marquis," replies he, "to desire more ardently than I do to terminate the campaign by some happy stroke; but we must consult our means rather than our wishes, and not endeavor to better our affairs by attempting things, which for want of success may make them worse.... It would, in my opinion, be imprudent to throw an army of ten thousand men upon an island, against nine thousand, exclusive of seamen and militia. This, from the accounts we have, appears to be the enemy's force. All we can do at present, therefore, is to endeavor to gain a more certain knowledge of their situation, and act accordingly."

The British posts in question were accordingly reconnoitred from the opposite banks of the Hudson, by Colonel Gouvion, an able French engineer. Preparations were made to carry the scheme into effect, should it be determined upon, when news was received of the unexpected and accidental appearance of several British armed vessels in the Hudson; the effect was to disconcert the plan and finally to cause it to be abandoned.

Some parts of the scheme were attended with success. The veteran Stark, with a detachment of twenty-five hundred men, made an extensive forage in Westchester County, and Major Tallmadge with eighty men, chiefly dismounted dragoons of Sheldon's regiment, crossed in boats from the Connecticut shore to Long Island, where the Sound was twenty miles wide; traversed the island on the night of the 22d of November, surprised Fort George at Coram, captured the garrison of fifty-two men, demolished the fort, set fire to magazines of forage, and recrossed the Sound to Fairfield, without the loss of a man: an achievement which drew forth a high eulogium from Congress.

At the end of November the army went into winter-quarters; the Pennsylvania line in the neighborhood of Morristown, the Jersey line about Pompton, the New England troops at West Point, and the other posts of the Highlands; and the New York line was stationed at Albany, to guard against any invasion from Canada. The French army remained stationed at Newport, excepting the Duke of Lauzun's legion, which was cantoned at Lebanon in Connecticut. Washington's head-quarters were established at New Windsor, on the Hudson.

We will now turn to the South to note the course of affairs in that quarter during the last few months.

CHAPTER LIX.

THE WAR IN THE SOUTH.—BATTLE OF KING'S MOUNTAIN.

Cornwallis having, as he supposed, entirely crushed the "rebel cause" in South Carolina, by the defeats of Gates and Sumter, remained for some time at Camden, detained by the excessive heat of the weather and the sickness of part of his troops, broken down by the hardships of campaigning under a southern sun. He awaited also supplies and reinforcements.

Immediately after the victory at Camden, he had ordered the friends to royalty in North Carolina "to arm and intercept the beaten army of General Gates," promising that he would march directly to the borders of that province in their support: he now detached Major Patrick Ferguson to its western confines, to keep the war alive in that quarter. This resolute partisan had with him his own corps of light infantry, and a body of royalist militia of his own training. His whole force was between eleven and twelve hundred men, noted for activity and alertness, and unincumbered with baggage or artillery. His orders were to skirr the mountain country between the Catawba and the Yadkin, harass the whigs, inspirit the tories, and embody the militia under the royal banner. This done, he was to repair to Charlotte, the capital of Mecklenburg County, where he would find Lord Cornwallis, who intended to make it his rendezvous. Should he, however, in the course of his tour, be threatened by a superior force, he was immediately to return to the main army.

During the suspense of his active operations in the field, Cornwallis instituted rigorous measures against Americans who continued under arms. Among these were included many who had taken refuge in North Carolina. A commissioner was appointed to take possession of their estates and property; of the annual product of which a part was to be allowed for the support of their families, the residue to be applied to the maintenance of the war. Letters from several of the principal inhabitants of Charleston having been found in the baggage of the captured American generals, the former were accused of breaking their parole, and holding a treasonable correspondence with the armed enemies of England; they were in consequence confined on board of prison ships, and afterwards transported to St. Augustine in Florida. Among the prisoners taken in the late combats, many, it was discovered, had British protections in their pockets; these were deemed amenable to the penalties of the proclamation issued by Sir Henry Clinton on the 3d of June; they were therefore led forth from the provost and hanged almost without the form of an inquiry. These measures certainly were not in keeping with the character for moderation and benevolence usually given to Lord Cornwallis; but they accorded with the rancorous spirit manifested toward each other both by whigs and tories in Southern warfare.

Cornwallis decamped from Camden, and set out for North Carolina. In the subjugation of that province, he counted on the co-operation of the troops which Sir Henry Clinton was to send to the lower part of Virginia, which, after reducing the Virginians to obedience, were to join his lordship's standard on the confines of North Carolina. Advancing into the latter province, he took post at Charlotte, where he had given rendezvous to Ferguson. The surrounding country was wild and rugged, covered with close and thick woods, and crossed in every direction by narrow roads. The inhabitants were stanch whigs, with the pugnacious spirit of the old Covenanters. Instead of remaining at home and receiving the king's money in exchange for their produce, they turned out with their rifles, stationed themselves in covert places, and fired upon the foraging parties; convoys of provisions from Camden had to fight their way, and expresses were shot down and their despatches seized.

The capture of his expresses was a sore annoyance to Cornwallis, depriving him of all intelligence concerning the movements of Colonel Ferguson, whose arrival he was anxiously awaiting. The expedition of that doughty partisan officer here calls for especial notice. He had been chosen for this military tour as being calculated to gain friends by his conciliating disposition and manners. He however, had a loyal hatred of whigs, and to his standard flocked many rancorous tories, besides outlaws and desperadoes, so that his progress through the country was attended by many exasperating excesses.

He was on his way to join Cornwallis when a chance for a signal exploit presented itself. An American force under Colonel Elijah Clarke, of Georgia, was retreating to the mountain districts of North Carolina, after an unsuccessful attack upon the British post at Augusta. Ferguson resolved to cut off their retreat. Turning towards the mountains, he made his way through a rugged wilderness and took post at Gilbert-town, a small frontier village of log-houses. "All of a sudden," say the British chroniclers just cited, "a numerous, fierce and unexpected enemy sprung up in the depths of the desert. The scattered inhabitants of the mountains assembled without noise or warning, under the conduct of six or seven of their militia colonels, to the number of six hundred strong, daring, well-mounted and excellent horsemen."

These were the people of the mountains which form the frontiers of the Carolinas and Georgia, "mountain men," as they were commonly called, a hardy race, half huntsmen, half herdsmen. Beside these, there were other elements of war suddenly gathering in Ferguson's vicinity. A band of what were termed "the wild and fierce" inhabitants of Kentucky, with men from other settlements west of the Alleghanies, had crossed the mountains, led by Colonels Campbell and Boone, to pounce upon a quantity of Indian goods at Augusta; but had pulled up on hearing of the repulse of Clarke. The stout yeomen, also, of the district of Ninety-Six, roused by the marauds of Ferguson, had taken the field, under the conduct of

Colonel James Williams, of Granville County. Here, too, were hard-riders and sharp-shooters, from Holston River, Powel's Valley, Botetourt, Fincastle, and other parts of Virginia, commanded by Colonels Campbell, Cleveland, Shelby and Sevier. Such were the different bodies of mountaineers and backwoodsmen, suddenly drawing together from various parts to the number of three thousand.

In this exigency, Ferguson remembered the instructions of Cornwallis, that he should rejoin him should he find himself threatened by a superior force; breaking up his quarters, therefore, he pushed for the British army, sending messengers ahead to apprise his lordship of his danger. Unfortunately for him, his missives were intercepted. Gilbert-town had not long been vacated by Ferguson and his troops, when the motley host we have described thronged in. Some were on foot, but the greater part on horseback. Some were in homespun garb; but the most part in hunting-shirts. Each man had his long rifle and hunting-knife, his wallet, or knapsack and blanket, and either a buck's tail or sprig of evergreen in his hat. There was neither tent nor tent equipage, neither baggage nor baggage-wagon to encumber the movements of that extemporaneous host. Being told that Ferguson had retreated by the Cherokee road toward North Carolina, about nine hundred of the hardiest and best mounted set out in urgent pursuit; leaving those who were on foot, or weakly mounted, to follow on as fast as possible. Colonel William Campbell, of Virginia, having come from the greatest distance was allowed to have command of the whole party; but there was not much order nor subordination. Each colonel led his own men in his own way.

A rapid and irregular march was kept up all night in murky darkness and through a heavy rain. About daybreak they crossed Broad River, where an attack was apprehended. Not finding the enemy, they halted, lit their fires, made their morning's meal, and took a brief repose. By nine o'clock they were again on the march. The rainy night had been succeeded by a bright October morning, and all were in high spirits. Ferguson, they learnt, had taken the road toward King's Mountain, about twelve miles distant. When within three miles of it their scouts brought in word that he had taken post on its summit. The officers now held a short consultation on horseback, and then proceeded. The position taken by Ferguson was a strong one. King's Mountain rises out of a broken country, and is detached, on the north, from inferior heights by a deep valley, so as to resemble an insulated promontory about half a mile in length, with sloping sides, excepting on the north. The mountain was covered for the most part with lofty forest trees, free from underwood, interspersed with boulders and masses of gray rock. The forest was sufficiently open to give free passage to horsemen.

Dismounting at a small stream which runs through a ravine, the Americans picketed their horses or tied them to the branches of the trees, and gave them in charge of a small guard. They then formed themselves into three divisions of nearly equal size, and prepared to storm the heights on three sides. Campbell, seconded by Shelby, was to lead the centre division; Sevier with McDowell the right, and Cleveland and Williams the left. The divisions were to scale the mountain as nearly as possible at the same time. The fighting directions were in frontier style;— when once in action, everyone must act for himself. The men were not to wait for the word of command, but to take good aim and fire as fast as possible. When they could no longer hold their ground, they were to get behind trees, or retreat a little, and return to the fight, but never to go quite off.

Campbell allowed time for the flanking divisions to move to the right and left along the base of the mountain, and take their proper distances; he then pushed up in front with the centre division, he and Shelby each at the head of his men. The first firing was about four o'clock, when a picket was driven in by Cleveland and Williams on the left, and pursued up the mountain. Campbell soon arrived within rifle distance of the crest of the mountain, whence a sheeted fire of musketry was opened upon him. He instantly deployed his men, posted them behind trees, and returned the fire with deadly effect. Ferguson, rushed out with his regulars, made an impetuous charge with the bayonet, and dislodging his assailants from their coverts, began to drive them down the mountain, they not having a bayonet among them. He had not proceeded far, when a flanking fire was opened by one of the other divisions; facing about and attacking this he was again successful, when a third fire was opened from another quarter. Thus, as fast as one division gave way before the bayonet, another came to its relief; while those who had given way rallied and returned to the charge. Ferguson found that he was completely in the hunter's toils, beset on every side; but he stood bravely at bay, until the ground around him was strewed with the killed and wounded, picked off by the fatal rifle. His men were at length broken, and retreated in confusion along the ridge. He galloped from place to place endeavoring to rally them, when a rifle ball brought him to the ground, and his white horse was seen careering down the mountain without a rider.

This closed the bloody fight; for Ferguson's second in command, seeing all further resistance hopeless, hoisted a white flag, beat a parley and sued for quarters. One hundred and fifty of the enemy had fallen, and as many been wounded; while of the Americans, but twenty were killed, though a considerable number were wounded. Among those slain was Colonel James Williams, who had commanded the troops of Ninety-Six, and proved himself one of the most daring of the partisan leaders. Eight hundred and ten men were taken prisoners, one hundred of whom were regulars, the rest royalists. The rancor awakened by civil war was shown in the treatment of some of the prisoners. A court-martial was held the day after the battle, and a number of tory prisoners who had been bitter in their hostility to the American cause, and flagitious in their persecution of their countrymen, were hanged. This was to revenge the death of American prisoners hanged at Camden and elsewhere.

The army of mountaineers and frontier men, thus fortuitously congregated, did not attempt to follow up their signal blow. They had no general scheme, no plan of campaign; it was the spontaneous rising of the sons of the soil, to revenge it on its invaders, and, having effected their purpose, they returned in triumph to their homes. They were little aware of the importance of their achievement. The battle of King's Mountain, inconsiderable as it was in the numbers engaged, turned the tide of Southern warfare. The destruction of Ferguson and his corps gave a complete check to the expedition of Cornwallis. He began to fear for the safety of South Carolina, liable to such sudden irruptions from the mountains; lest, while he was facing to the north, these hordes of stark-riding warriors might throw themselves behind him, and produce a popular combustion in the province he had left. He resolved, therefore, to return with all speed to that province and provide for its security.

On the 14th of October he commenced his retrograde and mortifying march, conducting it in the night, and with such hurry and confusion, that nearly twenty wagons, laden with baggage and supplies, were lost. As he proceeded, the rainy season set in; the brooks and rivers became swollen, and almost impassable; the roads deep and miry; provisions and forage scanty; the troops generally sickly, having no tents. At length the army arrived at Winnsborough, in South Carolina. Hence, by order of Cornwallis, Lord Rawdon wrote on the 24th October to Brigadier-general Leslie, who was at that time in the Chesapeake, with the force detached by Sir Henry Clinton for a descent upon Virginia, suggesting the expediency of his advancing to North Carolina, for the purpose of co-operation with Cornwallis, who feared to proceed far from South Carolina, lest it should be again in insurrection.

The victory at King's Mountain had set the partisan spirit throughout the country in a blaze. Francis Marion was soon in the field. He had been made a brigadier-general by Governor Rutledge, but his brigade, as it was called, was formed of neighbors and friends, and was continually fluctuating in numbers. He was nearly fifty years of age, and small of stature, but hardy, healthy and vigorous. He had his haunts and strongholds in the morasses of the Pedee and Black River. His men were hardy and abstemious as himself; they ate their meat without salt, often subsisted on potatoes, were scantily clad, and almost destitute of blankets. Marion was full of stratagems and expedients. Sallying forth from his morasses, he would overrun the lower districts, pass the Santee, beat up the small posts in the vicinity of Charleston, cut up the communication between that city and Camden; and having struck some signal blow, so as to rouse the vengeance of the enemy, would retreat again into his fenny fastnesses. Hence the British gave him the bye-name of the *Swamp Fox,* but those of his countrymen who knew his courage, his loftiness of spirit and spotless integrity, considered him the *Bayard of the South.*

Tarleton, who was on duty in that part of the country, undertook, as he said, to draw the swamp fox from his cover. He accordingly marched cautiously down the east bank of the Wateree with a body of dragoons and infantry, in compact order. The fox, however, kept close; he saw that the enemy was too strong for him. Tarleton now changed his plan. By day he broke up his force into small detachments or patrols, giving them orders to keep near enough to each other to render mutual support if attacked, and to gather together at night. The artifice had its effect. Marion sallied forth from his covert just before daybreak to make an attack upon one of these detachments, when, to his surprise, he found himself close upon the British camp. Perceiving the snare that had been spread for him, he made a rapid retreat. A close pursuit took place. For seven hours Marion was hunted from one swamp and fastness to another; several stragglers of his band were captured, and Tarleton was in strong hope of bringing him into action, when an express came spurring from Cornwallis, calling for the immediate services of himself and his dragoons in another quarter.

Sumter was again in the field! That indefatigable partisan having recruited a strong party in the mountainous country, to which he retreated after his defeat on the Wateree, had re-appeared on the west side of the Santee, repulsed a British party sent against him, killing its leader; then, crossing Broad River, had effected a junction with Colonels Clark and Brannan, and now menaced the British posts in the district of Ninety-Six.

It was to disperse this head of partisan war that Tarleton was called off from beleaguering Marion. Advancing with his accustomed celerity, he thought to surprise Sumter on the Enoree River. A deserter apprised the latter of his danger. He pushed across the river, but was hotly pursued, and his rear-guard roughly handled. He now made for the Tyger River, noted for turbulence and rapidity; once beyond this, he might disband his followers in the woods. Tarleton, to prevent his passing it unmolested, spurred forward in advance of his main body with one hundred and seventy dragoons and eighty mounted men of the infantry. Before five o'clock (Nov. 20th) his advanced guard overtook and charged the rear of the Americans, who retreated to the main body. Sumter finding it impossible to cross Tyger River in safety, took post on Black Stock Hill with a rivulet and rail fence in front, the Tyger River in the rear and on the right flank, and a large log barn on the left. The barn was turned into a fortress, and a part of the force stationed in it to fire through the apertures between the logs.

Tarleton halted on an opposite height to await the arrival of his infantry, and part of his men dismounted to ease their horses. Sumter seized this moment for an attack. He was driven back after some sharp fighting. The enemy pursued, but were severely galled by the fire from the log barn. Enraged at seeing his men shot down, Tarleton charged with his cavalry but found it impossible to dislodge the Americans from their rustic fortress. At the approach of night he fell back to join his infantry, leaving the ground strewed with his killed and wounded. The loss of the Americans was only three killed and four wounded. Sumter who had received a severe wound in the breast, remained several hours on the field of action; but understanding the enemy would be powerfully reinforced in the morning, he crossed the Tyger River in the night. He was then placed on a litter between two horses, and thus conducted across the country by a few faithful adherents. The rest of his little army dispersed themselves through the woods.

While the attention of the enemy was thus engaged by the enterprises of Sumter and Marion and their swamp warriors, General Gates was gathering together the scattered fragments of his army at Hillsborough. The vanity of Gates was completely cut down by his late reverses. To add to his depression of spirits, he received the melancholy intelligence of the death of an only son, and, while he was yet writhing under the blow, came official despatches informing him of his being superseded in command. A letter from Washington, we are told, accompanied them, sympathizing with him in his domestic misfortunes, adverting with peculiar delicacy to his reverses in battle, assuring him of his undiminished confidence in his zeal and capacity. The effect of this letter was overpowering. Gates was found walking about his room in the greatest agitation, pressing the letter to his lips, breaking forth into ejaculations of gratitude and admiration, and when he could find utterance to his thoughts, declared that its tender sympathy and considerate delicacy had conveyed more consolation and delight to his heart than he had believed it possible ever to have felt again.

General Greene arrived at Charlotte, on the 2d of December. On his way from the North he had made arrangements for supplies from the different States; and had left the Baron Steuben in Virginia to defend that State and procure and send on reinforcements and stores for the Southern army. On the day following his arrival, Greene took formal command. The delicacy with which he conducted himself towards his unfortunate predecessor is said to have been "edifying to the army." Consulting with his officers as to the court of inquiry on the conduct of General Gates, ordered by Congress, it was determined that there was not a sufficient number of general officers in camp to sit upon it; that the state of General Gates' feelings, in consequence of the death of his son, disqualified him from entering upon the task of his defence; and that it would be indelicate in the extreme to press on him an investigation, which his honor would not permit him to defer. Gates, in fact, when informed in the most delicate manner of the order of Congress, was urgent that a court of inquiry should be immediately convened: he acknowledged there was some important evidence that could not at present be procured; but he relied on the honor and justice of the court to make allowance for the deficiency. He was ultimately brought to acquiesce in the decision of the council of war for the postponement, but declared that he could not think of serving until the matter should have been properly investigated. He determined to pass the interim on his estate in Virginia.

The whole force at Charlotte, when Greene took command, did not much exceed twenty-three hundred men, and more than half of them were militia. It had been broken in spirit by the recent defeat. The officers had fallen into habits of negligence; the soldiers were loose and disorderly, without tents and camp equipage; badly clothed and fed, and prone to relieve their necessities by depredating upon the inhabitants.

A recent exploit had given some animation to the troops. Lieutenant-colonel Washington, detached with a troop of light-horse to check a foraging party of the enemy, scoured the country within thirteen miles of Camden. Here he found a body of loyalist militia strongly posted at Clermont, the seat of Colonel Rugeley, their tory commander. They had ensconced themselves in a large barn, built of logs, and had fortified it by a slight intrenchment and a line of abatis. To attack it with cavalry was useless. Colonel Washington dismounted part of his troops to appear like infantry; placed on two wagon-wheels the trunk of a pine-tree, shaped and painted to look like a field-piece, brought it to bear upon the enemy, and, displaying his cavalry, sent in a flag summoning the garrison to surrender instantly, on pain of having their log castle battered about their ears. The garrison, to the number of one hundred and twelve men, with Colonel Rugeley at their head, gave themselves up prisoners of war.

The first care of General Greene was to reorganize his army. He went to work quietly but resolutely; called no councils of war; communicated his plans and intentions to few, and such only as were able and willing to aid in executing them. Finding the country round Charlotte exhausted by repeated foragings, he separated the army into two divisions. One, about one thousand strong, was commanded by Brigadier-general Morgan, of rifle renown, and was composed of four hundred Continental infantry, under Lieutenant-colonel Howard of the Maryland line, two companies of Virginia militia under Captains Tripplet and Tate, and one hundred dragoons under Lieutenant-colonel Washington. With these Morgan was detached towards the district of Ninety-Six, in South Carolina, with orders to take a position near the confluence of the Pacolet and Broad Rivers, and assemble the militia of the country. With the other division, Greene made a march of toilful difficulty through a barren country, to Hicks' Creek, in Chesterfield district, on the east side of the Pedee River, opposite the Cheraw Hills. There he posted himself, on the 26th, partly to discourage the enemy from attempting to possess themselves of Cross Creek, which would give them command of the greatest part of the provisions of the lower country—partly to form a camp of repose.

CHAPTER LX.

HOSTILITIES IN THE SOUTH.—MUTINY.

The occurrences recorded in the last few pages made Washington apprehend a design on the part of the enemy to carry the stress of war into the Southern States. Conscious that he was the man to whom all looked in time of emergency, and who was, in a manner, responsible for the general course of military affairs, he deeply felt the actual impotency of his position. In a letter to Franklin, who was minister-plenipotentiary at the court of Versailles, he strongly expresses his chagrin: "Latterly, we have been obliged to become spectators of a succession of detachments from the army at New York in aid of Lord Cornwallis, while our naval weakness, and the political dissolution of a great part of our army, put it out of our power to counteract them at the southward, or to take advantage of them here."

The last of these detachments to the South took place on the 20th of December, but was not destined, as Washington had supposed, for Carolina. Sir Henry Clinton had received information that the troops already mentioned as being under General Leslie in the Chesapeake, had, by orders from Cornwallis, sailed for Charleston, to reinforce his lordship; and this detachment was to take their place in Virginia. It was composed of British, German, and refugee troops, about seventeen hundred strong, and was commanded by Benedict Arnold, now a brigadier-general in his majesty's service. Sir Henry Clinton, who distrusted the fidelity of the man he had corrupted, sent with him Colonels Dundas and Simcoe, experienced officers, by whose advice he was to be guided in every important measure. He was to make an incursion into Virginia, destroy the public magazines, assemble and arm the loyalists, and hold himself ready to co-operate with Lord Cornwallis.

As Washington beheld one hostile armament after another winging its way to the South, and received applications from that quarter for assistance, which he had not the means to furnish, it became painfully apparent to him, that the efforts to carry on the war had exceeded the natural capabilities of the country. Its widely diffused population, and the composition and temper of some of its people, rendered it difficult to draw together its resources. Commerce was almost extinct; there was not sufficient natural wealth on which to found a revenue; paper currency had depreciated through want of funds for its redemption until it was nearly worthless. The mode of supplying the army by assessing a proportion of the productions of the earth, had proved ineffectual, oppressive, and productive of an alarming opposition. Domestic loans yielded but trifling assistance. These considerations Washington was continually urging upon the attention of Congress in his full and perspicuous manner; the end of which was to enforce his opinion that a foreign loan was indispensably necessary to a continuance of the war. His earnest counsels and entreaties were at length successful in determining Congress to seek aid both in men and money from abroad. Accordingly, on the 28th of December they commissioned Lieutenant-colonel John Laurens, special minister at the court of Versailles, to apply for such aid. The situation he had held, as aide-de-camp to the commander-in-chief, had given him an opportunity of observing the course of affairs, and acquainting himself with the wants and resources of the country; and he was instructed to confer with Washington, previous to his departure, as to the objects of his mission. Scarce had Colonel Laurens been appointed when a painful occurrence proved the urgent necessity of the required aid.

In the arrangement for winter-quarters, the Pennsylvania line, consisting of six regiments, was hutted near Morristown. These troops had experienced the hardships and privations common to the whole army, but had an additional grievance peculiar to themselves. Many of them had enlisted to serve "for three years, or during war," that is to say, for less than three years should the war cease in less time. When, however, having served for three years, they sought their discharge, the officers, loth to lose such experienced soldiers, interpreted the terms of enlistment to mean three years, or to the end of the war, should it continue for a longer time. This chicanery naturally produced great exasperation.

The first day of the New Year arrived. The men were excited by an extra allowance of ardent spirits. In the evening, at a preconcerted signal, a great part of the Pennsylvania line, non-commissioned officers included, turned out under arms, declaring their intention to march to Philadelphia and demand redress from Congress. Wayne endeavored to pacify them; they were no longer to be pacified by words. Three regiments which had taken no part in the mutiny were paraded under their officers. The mutineers compelled them to join their ranks. Their number being increased to about thirteen hundred, they seized upon six field-pieces, and set out in the night for Philadelphia under command of their sergeants.

Fearing the enemy might take advantage of this outbreak, Wayne detached a Jersey brigade to Chatham, and ordered the militia to be called out there. Alarm fires were kindled upon the hills; alarm guns boomed from post to post; the country was soon on the alert. Wayne was not "Mad Anthony" on the present occasion. All his measures were taken with judgment and forecast. He sent provisions after the mutineers, lest they should supply their wants from the country people by force. Two officers of rank spurred to Philadelphia, to apprise Congress of the approach of the insurgents, and put it upon its guard. Wayne sent a despatch with news of the outbreak to Washington; he then mounted his horse, and accompanied by Colonels Butler and Stewart, two officers popular with the troops, set off after the mutineers, either to bring them to a halt, or to keep with them, and seek every occasion to exert a favorable influence over them.

In the meantime, Sir Henry Clinton received intelligence at New York of the mutiny, and hastened to profit by it. Emissaries were despatched to the camp of the mutineers, holding out offers of pardon, protection, and ample pay, if they would return to their allegiance to the crown.

General Wayne and his companions, Colonels Butler and Stewart, had overtaken the insurgent troops on the 3d of January, at Middlebrook. They were proceeding in military form, under the control of a self-constituted board of sergeants, whose orders were implicitly obeyed. Conferences were held by Wayne with sergeants delegated from each regiment. They appeared to be satisfied with the mode and promises of redress held out to them; but the main body of the mutineers persisted in revolt, and proceeded on the next day to Princeton. Their proceedings continued to be orderly; military forms were still observed; they obeyed their leaders, behaved well to the people of the country, and committed no excesses. General Wayne and Colonels Butler and Stewart remained with them in an equivocal position; popular, but without authority, and almost in durance. The insurgents professed themselves still ready to march under them against the enemy, but would permit none other of their former officers to come among them. The Marquis de Lafayette, General St. Clair and Colonel Laurens, the newly-appointed minister to France, arrived at the camp and were admitted; but afterwards were ordered away at a short notice.

The news of the revolt caused great consternation in Philadelphia. A committee of Congress set off to meet the insurgents, accompanied by Reed, the president of Pennsylvania, and one or two other officers, and escorted by a city troop of horse. The committee halted at Trenton, whence President Reed wrote to Wayne, requesting a personal interview at four o'clock in the afternoon, at four miles' distance from Princeton. Wayne was moreover told to inform the troops, that he (Reed) would be there to receive any propositions from them, and redress any injuries they might have sustained; but that, after the indignities they had offered to the marquis and General St. Clair, he could not venture to put himself in their power. Wayne, knowing that the letter was intended for his troops more than for himself, read it publicly on the parade. It had a good effect upon the sergeants and many of the men. Still it was not thought prudent for President Reed to trust himself within their camp. Wayne promised to meet him on the following day (7th), though it seemed uncertain whether he was master of himself, or whether he was not a kind of prisoner.

At this critical juncture, two of Sir Henry's emissaries arrived in the camp, and delivered to the leaders of the malcontents a paper containing his seductive proposals and promises. The mutineers, though openly arrayed in arms against their government, spurned at the idea of turning "Arnolds," as they termed it. The emissaries were seized and conducted to General Wayne, who placed them in confinement, promising that they should be liberated should the pending negotiation fail. This incident had a great effect in inspiring hope of the ultimate loyalty of the troops; and the favorable representations of the temper of the men, made by General Wayne in a personal interview, determined President Reed to venture among them.

The propositions now offered to the troops were:—To discharge all those who had enlisted indefinitely for three years or during the war; the fact to be inquired into by three commissioners appointed by the executive. To give immediate certificates for the deficit in their pay caused by the depreciation of the currency, and the arrearages to be settled as soon as circumstances would permit. To furnish them immediately with certain specified articles of clothing which were most wanted.

These propositions proving satisfactory, the troops set out for Trenton, where the negotiation was concluded. The two spies who had tampered with the fidelity of the troops, were tried by a court-martial, found guilty, and hanged at the cross-roads near Trenton.

The accommodation entered into with the mutineers of the Pennsylvania line appeared to Washington of doubtful policy, and likely to have a pernicious effect on the whole army. His apprehensions were soon justified by events. On the night of the 20th of January, a part of the Jersey troops, stationed at Pompton, rose in arms, claiming the same terms just yielded to the Pennsylvanians. For a time it was feared the revolt would spread throughout the line. In this instance, Washington adopted a more rigorous course than in the other. The present insurgents were not so formidable in point of numbers as the Pennsylvanians; the greater part of them, also, were foreigners, for whom he felt less sympathy than for native troops. A detachment from the Massachusetts line was sent under Major-general Howe, who was instructed to compel the mutineers to unconditional submission; to grant them no terms while in arms, or in a state of resistance; and on their surrender, instantly to execute a few of the most active and incendiary leaders.

His orders were punctually obeyed, and were crowned with complete success. Howe had the good fortune, after a tedious night march, to surprise the mutineers napping in their huts just at daybreak. Five minutes only were allowed them to parade without their arms and give up their ringleaders. This was instantly complied with, and two of them were executed on the spot. Thus the mutiny was quelled, the officers resumed their command, and all things were restored to order.

A great cause of satisfaction to Washington was the ratification of the articles of confederation between the States, which took place not long after this agitating juncture. A set of articles had been submitted to Congress by Dr. Franklin, as far back as 1775. A form had been prepared and digested by a committee in 1776, and agreed upon, with some modifications in 1777, but had ever since remained in abeyance, in consequence of objections made by individual States. The confederation was now complete, and Washington, in a letter to the President of Congress, congratulated him and the body over which he presided, on an event long wished for, and which he hoped would have the happiest effects upon the politics of this country, and be of essential service to our cause in Europe.

The armament under command of Arnold met with that boisterous weather which often rages along our coast in the winter. His ships were tempest tost and scattered, and half of his cavalry horses and several of his guns had to be thrown overboard. It was the close of the year when he anchored in the Chesapeake.

Virginia, at the time, was almost in a defenceless state. Baron Steuben, who had the general command there, had recently detached such of his regular troops as were clothed and equipped to the South, to reinforce General Greene. Governor Jefferson, on hearing of the arrival of the fleet, called out the militia from the neighboring counties; but few could be collected on the spur of the moment, for the whole country was terror-stricken and in confusion. Having land and sea forces at his command, Arnold opened the new year with a buccaneering ravage. Ascending James River with some small vessels which he had captured, he landed on the 4th of January with nine hundred men at Westover, about twenty-five miles below Richmond, and pushed for the latter place, at that time little more than a village, though the metropolis of Virginia.

It was Arnold's hope to capture the governor; but the latter, after providing for the security of as much as possible of the public stores, had left Richmond the evening before on horseback to join his family at Tuckahoe, whence, on the following day, he conveyed them to a place of safety. Governor Jefferson got back by noon to Manchester, on the opposite side of James River, in time to see Arnold's marauders march into the town. Arnold sent some of the citizens to the governor, offering to spare the town, provided his ships might come up James River to be laden with tobacco from the warehouses. His offer was indignantly rejected, whereupon fire was set to the public edifices, stores, and workshops; private houses were pillaged, and a great quantity of tobacco consumed.

While this was going on, Colonel Simcoe had been detached to Westham, six miles up the river, where he destroyed a cannon foundry and sacked a public magazine; and after effecting a complete devastation, rejoined Arnold at Richmond. Having completed his ravage, Arnold re-embarked at Westover and fell slowly down the river, landing occasionally to burn, plunder, and destroy; pursued by Steuben with a few Continental troops and all the militia that he could muster. General Nelson, also, with similar levies opposed him. Lower down the river some skirmishing took place, a few of Arnold's troops were killed and a number wounded, but he made his way to Portsmouth, opposite Norfolk, where he took post on the 20th of January, and proceeded to fortify. Steuben would have attempted to drive him from this position, but his means were totally inadequate. Collecting from various parts of the country all the force that could be mustered, he so disposed it at different points as to hem the traitor in, and prevent his making further incursions.

About this time an important resolution was adopted in Congress. Washington had repeatedly, in his communications to that body, attributed much of the distresses and disasters of the war to the congressional mode of conducting business through committees and "boards," thus causing irregularity and delay, preventing secrecy and augmenting expense. He was greatly rejoiced, therefore, when Congress decided to appoint heads of departments; secretaries of foreign affairs, of war and of marine, and a superintendent of finance. "I am happy, thrice happy, on private as well as public account," writes he, "to find that these are in train. For it will ease my shoulders of an immense burthen, which the deranged and perplexed situation of our affairs, and the distresses of every department of the army, had placed upon them."

[Colonel Hamilton was suggested to take charge of the department of finance, and Washington in reply to General Sullivan, who had sounded him on the subject, spoke in warm terms of his fitness for the post. A few days after Washington had penned this eulogium, a scene occurred between him and Colonel Hamilton that gave him deep chagrin. Washington, in passing Hamilton on the stairs, informed him that he wished to speak to him. Hamilton allowed some circumstances to delay his compliance with this request; and Washington, when they met, accosted him with warmth. "Colonel Hamilton," said he, "you have kept me waiting at the head of the stairs these ten minutes. I must tell you, sir, you treat me with disrespect." Hamilton promptly replied: "I am not conscious of it, sir; but since you have thought it necessary to tell me so, we part," and they separated. Washington soon after sent to Hamilton stating his desire, in a candid conversation, to heal a difference which could not have happened but in a moment of passion. But Hamilton had long determined, according to his own statement, that if a breach should occur between them not to consent to an accommodation. He was ambitious of an independent position, and declared that he had always disliked the office of an aide-de-camp. But although a coolness ensued between Washington and his favorite aide, it proved but temporary.] The friendship between these illustrious men was destined to survive the Revolution, and to signalize itself through many eventful years.

CHAPTER LXI.

BATTLE OF THE COWPENS.—BATTLE OF GUIL-FORD COURT-HOUSE.

The stress of war, as Washington apprehended, was at present shifted to the South. In a former chapter we left General Greene, in the latter part of December, posted with one division of his army on the east side of the Pedee River in North Carolina, having detached General Morgan with the other division, one thousand strong, to take post near the confluence of the Pacolet and Broad Rivers in South Carolina.

Cornwallis lay encamped about seventy miles to the southwest of Greene, at Winnsborough, in Fairfield district. General Leslie had recently arrived at Charleston from Virginia, and was advancing to reinforce him with fifteen hundred men. This would give Cornwallis such a superiority of force, that he prepared for a second invasion of North Carolina. His plan was to leave Lord Rawdon at the central post of Camden with a considerable body of troops to keep all quiet, while his lordship by rapid marches would throw himself between Greene and Virginia, cut him off from all reinforcements in that quarter, and oblige him either to make battle with his present force, or retreat precipitately from North Carolina. By recent information, he learnt that Morgan had passed both the Catawba and Broad Rivers, and was about seventy miles to the northwest of him, on his way to the district of Ninety-Six. As he might prove extremely formidable if left in his rear, Tarleton was sent in quest of him, with about three hundred and fifty of his famous cavalry, a corps of legion and light infantry, and a number of the royal artillery with two field-pieces; about eleven hundred choice troops in all.

Cornwallis moved with his main force on the 12th of December, in a northwest direction between the Broad River and the Catawba, leading toward the back country. This was for the purpose of crossing the great rivers at their fords near their sources; for they are fed by innumerable petty streams which drain the mountains, and are apt in the winter time, when storms of rain prevail, to swell and become impassable below their forks. He took this route also, to cut off Morgan's retreat, or prevent his junction with Greene, should Tarleton's expedition fail of its object.

Tarleton, after several days' hard marching, came upon the traces of Morgan, who was posted on the north bank of the Pacolet, to guard the passes of that river. He sent word to Cornwallis of his intention to force a passage across the river, and compel Morgan either to fight or retreat, and suggested that his lordship should proceed up the eastern bank of Broad River, so as to be at hand to co-operate. His lordship, in consequence, took up a position at Turkey Creek, on Broad River.

Morgan had been recruited by North Carolina and Georgia militia, so that his force was nearly equal in number to that of Tarleton, but, in point of cavalry and discipline, vastly inferior. Cornwallis, too, was on his left, and might get in his rear; checking his impulse, therefore, to dispute the passage of the Pacolet, he crossed that stream and retreated towards the upper fords of Broad River. Tarleton reached the Pacolet on the evening of the 15th, and pressed on in pursuit. At ten o'clock at night he reached an encampment which Morgan had abandoned a few hours previously, apparently in great haste, for the camp fires were still smoking, and provisions had been left behind half-cooked. Eager to come upon his enemy while in the confusion of a hurried flight, Tarleton allowed his exhausted troops but a brief repose, and, leaving his baggage under a guard, resumed his dogged march about two o'clock in the night. A little before daylight of the 17th, he captured two videttes, from whom he learnt, to his surprise, that Morgan, instead of a headlong retreat, had taken a night's repose, and was actually preparing to give him battle.

Morgan, in fact, had been urged by his officers to retreat across Broad River, which was near by, and make for the mountainous country; but, closely pressed as he was, he feared to be overtaken while fording the river, and while his troops were fatigued and in confusion; beside, being now nearly equal in number to the enemy, military pride would not suffer him to avoid a combat. The place where he came to halt was known in the early grants by the name of Hannah's Cowpens, being part of a grazing establishment of a man named Hannah. It was in an open wood, favorable to the action of cavalry. There were two eminences of unequal height, and separated from each other by an interval about eighty yards wide. To the first eminence, which was the highest, there was an easy ascent of about three hundred yards. On these heights Morgan had posted himself.

In arranging his troops for action, he drew out his infantry in two lines. The first was composed of the North and South Carolina militia, under Colonel Pickens, having an advanced corps of North Carolina and Georgia volunteer riflemen. This line, on which he had the least dependence, was charged to wait until the enemy were within dead shot; then to take good aim, fire two volleys and fall back. The second line, drawn up a moderate distance in the rear of the first, and near the brow of the main eminence, was composed of Colonel Howard's light infantry and the Virginia riflemen; all Continental troops. They were informed of the orders which had been given to the first line, lest they should mistake their falling back for a retreat. Colonel Howard had the command of this line, on which the greatest reliance was placed. About a hundred and fifty yards in the rear of the second line, and on the slope of the lesser eminence, was Colonel Washington's troop of cavalry, about eighty strong; with about fifty mounted Carolinian volunteers, under Major McCall, armed with sabres and pistols.

It was about eight o'clock in the morning (Jan. 17th), when Tarleton came up. The position of the Americans seemed to him to give great advantage to his cavalry, and he made hasty preparation for immediate attack, anticipating an easy victory. Part of his infantry he formed into a line, with dragoons on each flank. The rest of the infantry and cavalry were to be a reserve, and to wait for orders. Impetuous at all times, he did not even wait until the reserve could be placed, but led on his first line, which rushed shouting to the attack. The North Carolina and Georgia riflemen in the advance, delivered their fire with effect, and fell back to the flanks of Picken's militia. These, as they had been instructed, waited until the enemy were within fifty yards, and then made a destructive volley, but soon gave way before the push of the bayonet. The British infantry pressed up to the second line, while forty of their cavalry attacked it on the right, seeking to turn its flank. Colonel Howard seeing himself in danger of being outflanked, endeavored to change his front to the right. His orders were misunderstood, and his troops were falling into confusion, when Morgan rode up and ordered them to retreat over the hill, where Colonel Washington's cavalry were hurried forward for their protection.

The British, seeing the troops retiring over the hill, rushed forward irregularly in pursuit of what they deemed a routed foe. To their astonishment they were met by Colonel Washington's dragoons, who spurred on them impetuously, while Howard's infantry, facing about, gave them an effective volley of musketry, and then charged with the bayonet. The enemy now fell into complete confusion. Some few artillerymen attempted to defend their guns, but were cut down or taken prisoners, and the cannon and colors captured. A panic seized upon the British troops. Tarleton endeavored to bring his legion cavalry into action to retrieve the day. They had stood aloof as a reserve, and now, infected by the panic, turned their backs upon their commander, and galloped off through the woods, riding over the flying infantry. Fourteen of his officers, however, and forty of his dragoons, remained true to him; with these he attempted to withstand the attack of Washington's cavalry, and a fierce melée took place; but on the approach of Howard's infantry, Tarleton gave up all for lost, and spurred off with his few but faithful adherents, trusting to the speed of their horses for safety.

The loss of the British in this action was ten officers and above one hundred men killed, two hundred wounded, and between five and six hundred rank and file made prisoners; while the Americans had but twelve men killed and sixty wounded. The spoils taken by Morgan, according to his own account, were two field-pieces, two standards, eight hundred muskets, one traveling forge, thirty-five wagons, seventy negroes, upwards of one hundred dragoon-horses, and all the music. The enemy, however, had destroyed most of their baggage, which was immense.

Morgan did not linger on the field of battle. Leaving Colonel Pickens with a body of militia under the protection of a flag, to bury the dead and provide for the wounded of both armies, he set out the same day about noon with his prisoners and spoils. Lord Cornwallis, with his main force, was at Turkey Creek, only twenty-five miles distant, and must soon hear of the late battle. His object was to get to the Catawba before he could be intercepted by his lordship, who lay nearer than he did to the fords of that river. Before nightfall he crossed Broad river at the Cherokee ford, and halted for a few hours on its northern bank. Before daylight of the 18th he was again on the march. Colonel Washington, who had been in pursuit of the enemy, rejoined him in the course of the day, as also did Colonel Pickens, who had left such of the wounded as could not be moved, under the protection of the flag of truce.

Cornwallis, on the eventful day of the 17th, was at his camp on Turkey Creek, confidently waiting for tidings from Tarleton of a new triumph, when, towards evening, some of his routed dragoons came straggling into camp, haggard and forlorn, to tell the tale of his defeat. It was a thunder-stroke. Tarleton defeated! and by the rude soldier he had been so sure of entrapping! It seemed incredible. It was confirmed, however, the next morning, by the arrival of Tarleton himself, discomfited and crest-fallen. In his account of the recent battle, he represented the force under Morgan to be two thousand. This exaggerated estimate, together with the idea that the militia would now be out in great force, rendered his lordship cautious. He remained a day or two at Turkey Creek to collect the scattered remains of Tarleton's forces, and to await the arrival of General Leslie.

On the 19th, having been rejoined by Leslie, his lordship moved towards King's Creek, and thence in the direction of King's Mountain, until informed of Morgan's retreat toward the Catawba. Cornwallis now altered his course in that direction, and, trusting that Morgan, encumbered, as he supposed him to be, by prisoners and spoils, might be overtaken before he could cross that river, detached a part of his force, without baggage, in pursuit of him, while he followed on with the remainder.

Nothing, say the British chroniclers, could exceed the exertions of the detachment; but Morgan succeeded in reaching the Catawba and crossing it in the evening, just two hours before those in pursuit of him arrived on its banks. A heavy rain came on and fell all night, and by daybreak the river was so swollen as to be impassable. It continued for several days, and gave Morgan time to send off his prisoners who had crossed several miles above, and to call out the militia of Mecklenburg and Rowan Counties to guard the fords of the river.

Lord Cornwallis had moved slowly with his main body. He was encumbered by an immense train of baggage; the roads were through deep red clay, and the country was cut up by streams and morasses. It was not until the 25th that he assembled his whole force at Ramsour's Mills, on the Little Catawba, as the south fork of that river is called, and learnt that Morgan had crossed the main stream. Now he felt the loss he had sustained in the late defeat of Tarleton, of a great part of his light troops. In this crippled condition, he determined to relieve his army of everything that could impede rapid movement in his future operations. Two days, therefore, were spent by him at Ramsour's Mills, in destroying all such baggage and stores as could possibly be spared.

General Greene was gladdened by a letter from Morgan, written shortly after his defeat of Tarleton, and transmitted the news to Washington with his own generous comments. He had recently received intelligence of the landing of troops at Wilmington, from a British squadron, supposed to be a force under Arnold, destined to push up Cape Fear River, and co-operate with Cornwallis; he had to prepare, therefore, not only to succor Morgan, but to prevent this co-operation. He accordingly detached General Stevens with his Virginia militia (whose term of service was nearly expired) to take charge of Morgan's prisoners, and conduct them to Charlottesville in Virginia. At the same time he wrote to the governors of North Carolina and Virginia for all the aid they could furnish; to Steuben to hasten forward his recruits, and to Shelby, Campbell and others to take arms once more and rival their achievements at King's Mountain.

This done, he left General Huger in command of the division on the Pedee, with orders to hasten on by forced marches to Salisbury, to join the other division; in the meantime he set off on horseback for Morgan's camp, attended merely by a guide, an aide-de-camp, and a sergeant's guard of dragoons. His object was to aid Morgan in assembling militia and checking the enemy until the junction of his forces could be effected. It was a hard ride of upwards of a hundred miles through a rough country. On the last day of January he reached Morgan's camp at Sherrard's ford on the east side of the Catawba. The British army lay on the opposite side of the river, but a few miles distant from it, and appeared to be making preparations to force a passage across, as it was subsiding, and would soon be fordable. Greene supposed Cornwallis had in view a junction with Arnold at Cape Fear; he wrote, therefore, to General Huger to hurry on, so that with their united forces they could give his lordship a defeat before he could effect the junction.

More correct information relieved him from the apprehension of a co-operation of Arnold and Cornwallis. The British troops which had landed at Wilmington, were merely a small detachment sent from Charleston to establish a military depot for the use of Cornwallis in his southern campaign. They had taken possession of Wilmington without opposition. Greene now changed his plans. He was aware of the ill-provided state of the British army, from the voluntary destruction of their wagons, tents and baggage. His plan now was to tempt the enemy continually with the prospect of a battle, but continually to elude one; to harass them by a long pursuit, draw them higher into the country, and gain time for the division advancing under Huger to join him. It was the Fabian policy that he had learnt under Washington, of whom he prided himself on being a disciple.

As the subsiding of the Catawba would enable Cornwallis to cross, Greene ordered Morgan to move off silently with his division on the evening of the 31st, and to press his march all night, so as to gain a good start in advance, while he (Greene) would remain to bring on the militia, who were employed to check the enemy. These militia, assembled from the neighboring counties, did not exceed five hundred. Two hundred of them were distributed at different fords: the remaining three hundred, forming a corps of mounted riflemen under General Davidson, were to watch the movements of the enemy, and attack him wherever he should make his main attempt to cross. When the enemy should have actually crossed, the different bodies of militia were to make the best of their way to a rendezvous, sixteen miles distant, on the road to Salisbury. While these dispositions were being made by the American commander, Cornwallis was preparing to cross the river. The night of the 31st was chosen for the attempt. To divert the attention of the Americans, he detached Colonels Webster and Tarleton with a part of the army to a public ford called Beattie's ford, where he supposed Davidson to be stationed. There they were to make a feint of forcing a passage. The main attempt, however, was to be made six miles lower down, where little, if any, opposition was anticipated.

Cornwallis set out with the main body of his army at one o'clock in the morning. The night was dark and rainy. It was near daybreak by the time the head of the column reached the ford. To their surprise, they beheld numerous camp fires on the opposite bank. Word was hastily carried to Cornwallis that the ford was guarded. It was so indeed: Davidson was there with his riflemen. At that place the Catawba was nearly five hundred yards wide, about three feet deep, very rapid, and full of large stones. The troops entered the river in platoons, to support each other against the current, and were ordered not to fire until they should gain the opposite bank. Colonel Hall, of the light infantry of the guards, led the way; the grenadiers followed. The noise of the water and the darkness covered their movements until they were nearly half-way across, when they were descried by an American sentinel. He challenged them three times, and receiving no answer, fired. Terrified by the report, the man who was guiding the British turned and fled. Colonel Hall, thus abandoned, led the way directly across the river; whereas the true ford inclined diagonally further down. Hall had to pass through deeper water, but he reached a part of the bank where it was unguarded. The American pickets, too, which had turned out at the alarm given by the sentinel, had to deliver a distant and slanting fire. Still it had its effect. Three of the British were killed, and thirty-six wounded. Colonel Hall pushed on gallantly, but was shot down as he ascended the bank.

General Davidson hastened with his men towards the place where the British were landing. The latter formed as soon as they found themselves on firm ground, charged Davidson's men before he had time to get them in order, killed and wounded about forty, and put the rest to flight. General Davidson was the last to leave the ground, and was killed just as he was mounting his horse.

General Greene, informed that the enemy had crossed the Catawba at daybreak, awaited anxiously at the rendezvous the arrival of the militia. It was not until after midnight that he heard of their utter dispersion, and of the death of Davidson. Apprehending the rapid advance of Cornwallis, he hastened to rejoin Morgan, who with his division was pushing forward for the Yadkin, first sending orders to General Huger to conduct the other division by the most direct route to Guilford Court-house, where the forces were to be united. Greene spurred forward through heavy rain and deep miry roads. It was a dreary ride and a lonely one, for he had detached his aides-de-camp in different directions to collect the scattered militia.

Cornwallis did not advance so rapidly as had been apprehended. After crossing the Catawba, he had to wait for his wagons and artillery, which had remained on the other side in the woods; so that by nightfall of the 1st of February he was not more than five miles on the road to Salisbury. Eager to come up with the Americans, he mounted some of the infantry upon the baggage horses, joined them to the cavalry, and sent the whole forward under General O'Hara. They arrived on the banks of the Yadkin at night, between the 2d and 3d of February, just in time to capture a few wagons lingering in the rear of the American army, which had passed. The riflemen who guarded them retreated after a short skirmish. There were no boats with which to cross; the Americans had secured them on the other side. The rain which had fallen throughout the day had overflooded the ford by which the American cavalry had passed. The pursuers were again brought to a stand. After some doubt and delay, Cornwallis took his course up the south side of the Yadkin, and crossed by what is still called the Shallow ford, while Greene continued on unmolested to Guilford Court-house, where he was joined by General Huger and his division on the 9th. Cornwallis was now encamped about twenty-five miles above them, at the old Moravian town of Salem.

The great object of Greene now was to get across the river Dan, and throw himself into Virginia. With the reinforcements and assistance he might there expect to find, he hoped to effect the salvation of the South, and prevent the dismemberment of the Union. The object of Cornwallis was to get between him and Virginia, force him to a combat before he could receive those reinforcements, or enclose him in between the great rivers on the west, the sea on the east, and the two divisions of the British army under himself and Lord Rawdon on the north and south. His lordship had been informed that the lower part of the Dan, at present, could only be crossed in boats, and that the country could not afford a sufficient number for the passage of Greene's army; he trusted, therefore, to cut him off from the upper part of the river, where alone it was fordable. Greene, however, had provided against such a contingency. Boats had been secured at various places by his agents, and could be collected at a few hours' notice at the lower ferries. Instead, therefore, of striving with his lordship for the upper fords, Greene shaped his course for Boyd's and Irwin's fords, just above the confluence of the Dan and Staunton rivers which forms the Roanoke, and about seventy miles from Guilford Court-house. This would give him twenty-five miles advantage of Lord Cornwallis at the outset. General Kosciuszko was sent with a party in advance to collect the boats and throw up breastworks at the ferries.

In ordering his march, General Greene took the lead with the main body, the baggage, and stores. General Morgan would have had the command of the rear-guard, but being disabled by a violent attack of ague and rheumatism, it was given to Colonel Otho H. Williams (formerly adjutant-general), who had with him Colonels Howard, Washington and Lee. This corps, detached some distance in the rear, did infinite service. Being lightly equipped, it could manoeuvre in front of the British line of march, break down bridges, sweep off provisions, and impede its progress, in a variety of ways, while the main body moved forward unmolested. It was now that Cornwallis most felt the severity of the blow he had received at the battle of the Cowpens in the loss of his light troops, having so few to cope with the élite corps under Williams.

We forbear to enter into the details of this masterly retreat, the many stratagems and manoeuvres of the covering party to delay and hoodwink the enemy. Tarleton himself bears witness, in his narrative, that every measure of the Americans was judiciously designed and vigorously executed. So much had Cornwallis been misinformed at the outset as to the means below of passing the river, that he pushed on in the firm conviction that he was driving the American army into a trap, and would give it a signal blow before it could cross the Dan.

In the meantime, Greene, with the main body, reached the banks of the river, and succeeded in crossing over with ease in the course of a single day at Boyd's and Irwin's ferries, sending back word to Williams, who with his covering party was far in the rear. That intelligent officer encamped, as usual, in the evening, at a wary distance in front of the enemy, but stole a march upon them after dark, leaving his camp fires burning. He pushed on all night, arrived at the ferry in the morning of the 15th, having marched forty miles within the last four and twenty hours; and made such despatch in crossing, that his last troops had landed on the Virginia shore by the time the astonished enemy arrived on the opposite bank.

For a day the two armies lay panting within sight of each other on the opposite banks of the river, which had put an end to the race. On the 16th, the river began to subside; the enemy might soon be able to cross. Greene prepared for a further retreat by sending forward his baggage on the road to Halifax, and securing the passage of the Staunton. At Halifax he was resolved to make a stand, rather than suffer the enemy to take possession of it without a struggle. Its situation on the Roanoke would make it a strong position for their army, supported by a fleet, and would favor their designs both on Virginia and the Carolinas. With a view to its defence, intrenchments had already been thrown up, under the direction of Kosciuszko.

Lord Cornwallis, however, did not deem it prudent, under present circumstances, to venture into Virginia, where Greene would be sure of powerful reinforcements. North Carolina was in a state of the utmost disorder and confusion; he thought it better to remain in it for a time, and profit by having compelled Greene to abandon it. After giving his troops a day's repose, therefore, he put them once more in motion on the 18th, along the road by which he had pursued Greene. This changed the game. Lee, with his legion, strengthened by two veteran Maryland companies, and Pickens, with a corps of South Carolina militia, all light troops, were transported across the Dan in the boats, with orders to gain the front of Cornwallis, hover as near as safety would permit, cut off his intercourse with the disaffected parts of the country, and check the rising of the royalists. Greene, in the meanwhile, remained with his main force on the northern bank of the Dan; waiting to ascertain his lordship's real designs, and ready to cross at a moment's warning.

The movements of Cornwallis, for a day or two, were of a dubious nature, designed to perplex his opponents; or the 20th, however, he took post at Hillsborough. Here he issued a proclamation, inviting all loyal subjects to assist in suppressing the remains of rebellion, and re-establishing good order and constitutional government. By another instrument, all who could raise independent companies were called upon to give in their names at head-quarters, and a bounty in money and lands was promised to those who should enlist under them. Tarleton was detached with the cavalry and a small body of infantry to a region of country lying between the Haw and Deep Rivers, to bring on a considerable number of loyalists who were said to be assembling there.

Rumor, in the meantime, had magnified the effect of his lordship's proclamations. Word was brought to Greene, that the tories were flocking from all quarters to the royal standard. Seven companies, it was said, had been raised in a single day. At this time the reinforcements to the American camp had been little more than six hundred Virginia militia, under General Stevens. Greene saw that at this rate, if Cornwallis was allowed to remain undisturbed, he would soon have complete command of North Carolina; he boldly determined, therefore, to recross the Dan at all hazards with the scanty force at his command, and give his lordship check. In this spirit he broke up his camp and crossed the river on the 23d.

In the meantime, Lee and Pickens, who were scouring the country about Hillsborough, received information of Tarleton's recruiting expedition. There was no foe they were more eager to cope with; and they resolved to give him a surprise. Having forded the Haw one day about noon, they learned that he was encamped about three miles off, that his horses were unsaddled, and that everything indicated confident security. They now pushed on under covert of the woods, prepared to give the bold partisan a blow after his own fashion. Before they reached the place, Tarleton had marched on. Being informed that he was to halt for the night at the distance of six miles, they still trusted to surprise him. On the way, however, they had an encounter with a body of three or four hundred mounted royalists, armed with rifles, and commanded by a Colonel Pyle, marching in quest of Tarleton. As Lee with his cavalry was in the advance, he was mistaken for Tarleton, and hailed with loyal acclamations. He favored the mistake, and was taking measures to capture the royalists, when some of them, seeing the infantry under Pickens, discovered their error and fired upon the rear-guard. The cavalry instantly charged upon them; ninety were cut down and slain, and a great number wounded; among the latter was Colonel Pyle himself, who took refuge among the thickets on the borders of a piece of water which still bears his name.

After all, Lee and Pickens missed the object of their enterprise. The approach of night and the fatigue of their troops, made them defer their attack upon Tarleton until morning. In the meantime, the latter had received an express from Cornwallis, informing him that Greene had passed the Dan, and ordering him to return to Hillsborough as soon as possible. He hastened to obey. Lee with his legion was in the saddle before daybreak; but Tarleton's troops were already on the march. Before sunrise, he had forded the Haw, and "Light-horse Harry" gave over the pursuit.

The re-appearance of Greene and his army in North Carolina, heralded by the scourings of Lee and Pickens, disconcerted the schemes of Lord Cornwallis. The recruiting service was interrupted. Many royalists, who were on the way to his camp, returned home. Forage and provisions became scarce in the neighborhood. He found himself, he said, "amongst timid friends and adjoining to inveterate rebels." On the 26th, therefore, he abandoned Hillsborough, threw himself across the Haw, and encamped near Alamance Creek, one of its principal tributaries, in a country favorable to supplies and with a tory population. His position was commanding, at the point of concurrence of roads from Salisbury, Guilford, High Rockford, Cross Creek, and Hillsborough. It covered also the communication with Wilmington, where a dépôt of military stores, so important to his half-destitute army, had recently been established.

Greene with his main army took post about fifteen miles above him, on the heights between Troublesome Creek and Reedy Fork, one of the tributaries of the Haw. His plan was to cut the enemy off from the upper counties; to harass him by skirmishes, but to avoid a general battle; thus gaining time for the arrival of reinforcements daily expected.

On the 6th of March, Cornwallis, learning that the light troops under Williams were very carelessly posted, put his army suddenly in motion, and crossed the Alamance in a thick fog; with the design to beat up their quarters, drive them in upon the main army, and bring Greene to action should he come to their assistance. His movement was discovered by the American patrols, and the alarm given. Williams hastily called in his detachments, and retreated with his light troops across Reedy Fork, while Lee with his legion manoeuvred in front of the enemy. A stand was made by the Americans at Wetzell's Mill, but they were obliged to retire with the loss of fifty killed and wounded. Cornwallis did not pursue; evening was approaching, and he had failed in his main object; that of bringing Greene to action. The latter, fixed in his resolve of avoiding a conflict, had retreated across the Haw.

Greene's long-expected reinforcements now arrived, having been hurried on by forced marches. They consisted of a brigade of Virginia militia, under General Lawson, two brigades of North Carolina militia, under Generals Butler and Eaton, and four hundred regulars, enlisted for eighteen months. His whole effective force, according to official returns, amounted to four thousand two hundred and forty-three foot, and one hundred and sixty-one cavalry. Of his infantry, not quite two thousand were regulars, and of these, three-fourths were new levies. His force nearly doubled in number that of Cornwallis, which did not exceed two thousand four hundred men; but many of Greene's troops were raw and inexperienced, and had never been in battle; those of the enemy were veterans, schooled in warfare. Greene knew the inferiority of his troops in this respect; his reinforcements, too, fell far short of what he had been led to expect, yet he determined to accept the battle which had so long been offered. All detachments were ordered to assemble at Guilford, within eight miles of the enemy, where he encamped on the 14th, sending his wagons and heavy baggage to the Iron Works at Troublesome Creek, ten miles in his rear.

Cornwallis sent his carriages and baggage to Bell's Mills, on Deep River, and set out at daybreak on the 15th for Guilford. Within four miles of that place, near the New Garden Meeting-house, Tarleton with the advanced guard came upon the American advance-guard, composed of Lee's partisan legion, and some mountaineers and Virginia militia. Tarleton and Lee were well matched in military prowess, and the skirmish between them was severe. Lee's horses, being from Virginia and Pennsylvania, were superior in weight and strength to those of his opponent, which had been chiefly taken from plantations in South Carolina. The latter were borne down by a charge in close column. Tarleton, seeing that his weakly-mounted men fought to a disadvantage, sounded a retreat; Lee endeavored to cut him off. A general conflict of the vanguards, horse and foot, ensued, when the appearance of the main body of the enemy obliged Lee, in his turn, to retire with precipitation.

During this time, Greene was preparing for action on a woody eminence, a little more than a mile south of Guilford Court-house. The neighboring country was covered with forest, excepting some cultivated fields about the court-house, and along the Salisbury road, which passed through the centre of the place, from south to north. He had drawn out his troops in three lines. The first, composed of North Carolina militia, volunteers and riflemen, under Generals Butler and Eaton, was posted behind a fence, with an open field in front, and woods on the flanks and in the rear. About three hundred yards behind this, was the second line, composed of Virginia militia, under Generals Stevens and Lawson, drawn up across the road, and covered by a wood. The third line, about four hundred yards in the rear of the second, was composed of Continental troops or regulars; those of Virginia under General Huger on the right, those of Maryland under Colonel Williams on the left. Colonel Washington with a body of dragoons, Kirkwood's Delaware infantry, and a battalion of Virginia militia covered the right flank; Lee's legion, with the Virginia riflemen under Colonel Campbell, covered the left. Two six-pounders were in the road, in advance of the first line; two field-pieces with the rear-line near the court-house, where General Greene took his station.

About noon the head of the British army was descried advancing spiritedly from the south along the Salisbury road, and defiling into the fields. A cannonade was opened from the two six-pounders, in front of the first American line. It was answered by the British artillery. Neither produced much effect. The enemy now advanced coolly and steadily in three columns; the Hessians and Highlanders under General Leslie on the right, the Royal artillery and guards in the centre, and Webster's brigade on the left. The North Carolinians, who formed the first line, waited until the enemy were within one hundred and fifty yards, when, agitated by their martial array and undaunted movement, they began to fall into confusion; some fired off their pieces without taking aim; others threw them down, and took to flight. A volley from the foe, a shout, and a charge of the bayonet, completed their discomfiture. Some fled to the woods, others fell back upon the Virginians, who formed the second line. General Stevens, who commanded the latter, ordered his men to open and let the fugitives pass, pretending that they had orders to retire. Under his spirited command and example, the Virginians kept their ground and fought bravely.

The action became much broken up and diversified by the extent of the ground. The thickness of the woods impeded the movements of the cavalry. The reserves on both sides were called up. The British bayonet again succeeded; the second line gave way, and General Stevens, who had kept the field for some time, after being wounded in the thigh by a musket-ball, ordered a retreat. The enemy pressed with increasing ardor against the third line, composed of Continental troops, and supported by Colonel Washington's dragoons and Kirkwood's Delawares. Greene counted on these to retrieve the day. They were regulars; they were fresh, and in perfect order. He rode along the line, calling on them to stand firm, and give the enemy a warm reception.

The first Maryland regiment which was on the right wing, was attacked by Colonel Webster, with the British left. It stood the shock bravely, and being seconded by some Virginia troops, and Kirkwood's Delawares, drove Webster across a ravine. The second Maryland regiment was not so successful. Impetuously attacked by Colonel Stewart, with a battalion of the guards and a company of grenadiers, it faltered, gave way and fled, abandoning two field-pieces, which were seized by the enemy. Stewart was pursuing, when the first regiment which had driven Webster across the ravine, came to the rescue with fixed bayonets, while Colonel Washington spurred up with his cavalry. The fight now was fierce and bloody. Stewart was slain; the two field-pieces were retaken, and the enemy in their turn gave way and were pursued with slaughter; a destructive fire of grape-shot from the enemy's artillery checked the pursuit. Two regiments approached on the right and left; Webster recrossed the ravine and fell upon Kirkwood's Delawares. There was intrepid fighting in different parts of the field; but Greene saw that the day was lost; there was no retrieving the effect produced by the first flight of the North Carolinians. Unwilling to risk the utter destruction of his army, he directed a retreat, which was made in good order, but they had to leave their artillery on the field, most of the horses having been killed. About three miles from the field of action he made a halt to collect stragglers, and then continued on to the place of rendezvous at Speedwell's Iron Works on Troublesome Creek. The British were too much cut up and fatigued to follow up their victory. Two regiments, with Tarleton's cavalry, attempted a pursuit, but were called back.

The loss of the Americans in this hard-fought affair was never fully ascertained. Their official returns, made immediately after the action, give little more than four hundred killed and wounded, and between eight and nine hundred missing; but Lord Cornwallis states in his despatches, that between two and three hundred of the Americans were found dead on the field of battle. The loss sustained by his lordship, even if numerically less, was far more fatal; for, in the circumstances in which he was placed, it was not to be supplied, and it completely maimed him. Of his small army, ninety-three had fallen, four hundred and thirteen were wounded, and twenty-six missing. Among the killed and wounded were several officers of note. Thus, one-fourth of his army was either killed or disabled; his troops were exhausted by fatigue and hunger; his camp was encumbered by the wounded. His victory, in fact, was almost as ruinous as a defeat.

Greene lay for two days within ten miles of him, near the Iron Works on Troublesome Creek, gathering up his scattered troops. He had imbibed the spirit of Washington, and remained undismayed by hardships or reverses. Cornwallis, so far from being able to advance in the career of victory, could not even hold the ground he had so bravely won, but was obliged to retreat from the scene of triumph to some secure position where he might obtain supplies for his famished army.

Leaving, therefore, about seventy of his officers and men, who were too severely wounded to bear travelling, together with a number of wounded Americans, under the protection of a flag of truce, he set out, on the third day after the action, by easy marches, for Cross Creek, an eastern branch of Cape Fear River, where was a settlement of Scottish Highlanders, stout adherents, as he was led to believe, to the royal cause. Here he expected to be plentifully supplied with provisions, and to have his sick and wounded well taken care of. Hence, too, he could open a communication by Cape Fear River, with Wilmington.

No sooner did Greene learn that Cornwallis was retreating, than he set out to follow him, determined to bring him again to action; and presenting the singular spectacle of the vanquished pursuing the victor. His troops, however, suffered greatly in this pursuit from wintry weather, deep, wet, clayey roads, and scarcity of provisions. On the 28th, Greene arrived at Ramsey's Mills, on Deep River, hard on the traces of Cornwallis, who had left the place a few hours previously with such precipitation, that several of his wounded, who had died while on the march, were left behind unburied. At Deep River, Greene was brought to a stand. Cornwallis had broken down the bridge by which he had crossed; and further pursuit for the present was impossible. The constancy of the militia now gave way. They had been continually on the march with little to eat, less to drink, and obliged to sleep in the woods in the midst of smoke. Every step had led them from their homes and increased their privations. They were now in want of everything, for the retreating enemy left a famished country behind him. The term for which most of them had enlisted was expired, and they now demanded their discharge. The demand was just and reasonable, and, after striving in vain to shake their determination, Greene felt compelled to comply with it. His force thus reduced, it would be impossible to pursue the enemy further.

In this situation, remote from reinforcements, inferior to the enemy in numbers, and without hope of support, what was to be done? "If the enemy falls down toward Wilmington," said he, "they will be in a position where it would be impossible for us to injure them if we had a force." Suddenly he determined to change his course, and carry the war into South Carolina. This would oblige the enemy either to follow him, and thus abandon North Carolina, or to sacrifice all his posts in the upper part of North Carolina and Georgia. To Washington, to whom he considered himself accountable for his policy, and from whose council he derived confidence and strength, he writes on the present occasion: "All things considered, I think the movement is warranted by the soundest reasons, both political and military...."

He apprised Sumter, Pickens, and Marion, by letter, of his intentions, and called upon them to be ready to co-operate. On the 30th of March he discharged all his militia, with many thanks for the courage and fortitude with which they had followed him through so many scenes of peril and hardship. Then, after giving his army a short taste of the repose they needed, and having collected a few days' provisions, he set forward on the 5th of April toward Camden, where Lord Rawdon had his head-quarters.

Cornwallis, in the meantime, was grievously disappointed in the hopes he had formed of obtaining ample provisions and forage at Cross Creek, and strong reinforcements from the royalists in the neighborhood. Neither could he open a communication by Cape Fear River for the conveyance of his troops to Wilmington. The distance by water was upwards of a hundred miles, the breadth of the river seldom above one hundred yards, the banks high, and the inhabitants on each side generally hostile. He was compelled, therefore, to continue his retreat by land, quite to Wilmington, where he arrived on the 7th of April.

It was his lordship's intention, as soon as he should have equipped his own corps and received a part of the expected reinforcements from Ireland, to return to the upper country, in hopes of giving protection to the royal interests in South Carolina, and of preserving the health of his troops until he should concert new measures with Sir Henry Clinton. His plans were all disconcerted, however, by intelligence of Greene's rapid march toward Camden. All thoughts of offensive operations against North Carolina were at an end. Sickness, desertion, and the loss sustained at Guilford Court-house, had reduced his little army to fourteen hundred and thirty-five men. In this sad predicament, after remaining several days in a painful state of irresolution he determined to take advantage of Greene's having left the back part of Virginia open, to march directly into that province, and attempt a junction with the force acting there under General Phillips.

By this move, he might draw Greene back to the northward, and by the reduction of Virginia, he might promote the subjugation of the South. The move, however, he felt to be perilous. His troops were worn down by upwards of eight hundred miles of marching and countermarching, through an inhospitable and impracticable country; they had now three hundred more before them; under still worse circumstances than those in which they first set out. There was no time for hesitation or delay; Greene might return and render the junction with Phillips impracticable; having sent an express to the latter, therefore, informing him of his coming, and appointing a meeting at Petersburg, his lordship set off on the 25th of April, on his fated march into Virginia.

We must now step back in dates to bring up events in the more northern parts of the Union.

CHAPTER LXII.

THE WAR IN VIRGINIA.—DEMONSTRATIONS AGAINST NEW YORK.

In a former chapter we left Benedict Arnold fortifying himself at Portsmouth, after his ravaging incursion. At the solicitation of Governor Jefferson, backed by Congress, the Chevalier de la Luzerne had requested the French commander at the eastward to send a ship-of-the-line and some frigates to Chesapeake Bay to oppose the traitor. Fortunately, at this juncture a severe snowstorm (Jan. 22d) scattered Arbuthnot's blockading squadron, wrecking one ship-of-the-line and dismasting others, and enabled the French fleet at Newport to look abroad; and Rochambeau wrote to Washington that the Chevalier Destouches, who commanded the fleet, proposed to send three or four ships to the Chesapeake.

Washington feared the position of Arnold and his well-known address might enable him to withstand a mere attack by sea; anxious to ensure his capture, he advised that Destouches should send his whole fleet, and that De Rochambeau should embark about a thousand men on board of it, with artillery and apparatus for a siege; engaging, on his own part, to send off immediately a detachment of twelve hundred men to co-operate.

Before the receipt of this letter, the French commanders, acting on their first impulse, had, about the 9th of February, detached M. de Tilly, with a sixty-gun ship and two frigates, to make a dash into the Chesapeake. Washington was apprised of their sailing just as he was preparing to send off the twelve hundred men spoken of in his letter to De Rochambeau. He gave the command of this detachment to Lafayette, instructing him to act in conjunction with the militia and the ships sent by Destouches against the enemy's corps actually in Virginia. As the case was urgent, he was to suffer no delay, when on the march, for want either of provisions, forage, or wagons, but where ordinary means did not suffice, he was to resort to military impress.

Lafayette set out on his march on the 22d of February, and Washington was indulging the hope that, scanty as was the naval force sent to the Chesapeake, the combined enterprise might be successful, when on the 27th he received a letter from the Count de Rochambeau announcing its failure. De Tilly had made his dash into Chesapeake Bay, but Arnold had been apprised by the British Admiral Arbuthnot of his approach, and had drawn his ships high up Elizabeth River. The water was too shallow for the largest French ships to get within four leagues of him. One of De Tilly's frigates ran aground, and was got off with difficulty, and that commander, seeing that Arnold was out of his reach, and fearing to be himself blockaded should he linger, put to sea and returned to Newport; having captured during his cruise a British frigate of forty-four guns, and two privateers with their prizes.

The French commanders now determined to follow the plan suggested by Washington, and operate in the Chesapeake with their whole fleet and a detachment of land troops, being, as they said, disposed to risk everything to hinder Arnold from establishing himself at Portsmouth. Washington set out for Newport to concert operations with the French commanders, where he arrived on the 6th of March, and found the French fleet ready for sea, the troops eleven hundred strong, commanded by General the Baron de Viomenil, being already embarked. He went immediately on board of the admiral's ship, where he had an interview with the Count de Rochambeau, and arranged the plan of the campaign. On the 8th of March, at ten o'clock at night, he writes to Lafayette: "I have the pleasure to inform you that the whole fleet went out with a fair wind this evening about sunset." The British fleet made sail in pursuit, on the morning of the 10th; as the French had so much the start, it was hoped they would reach Chesapeake Bay before them.

In the meantime, Lafayette with his detachment was pressing forward by forced marches for Virginia. Arriving at the Head of Elk on the 3d of March, he halted until he should receive tidings respecting the French fleet. On the 7th he received Washington's letter of the 1st, apprising him of the approaching departure of the whole fleet with land forces. Lafayette now conducted his troops by water to Annapolis, and concluding, from the time the ships were to sail, and the winds which had since prevailed, the French fleet must be already in the Chesapeake, he crossed the bay in an open boat to Virginia, and pushed on to confer with the American and French commanders: get a convoy for his troops, and concert matters for a vigorous co-operation. Arriving at York on the 14th, he found the Baron Steuben in the bustle of military preparations, and confident of having five thousand militia ready to co-operate. These, with Lafayette's detachment, would be sufficient for the attack by land; nothing was wanting but a co-operation by sea; and the French fleet had not yet appeared, though double the time necessary for the voyage had elapsed.

On the 20th, word was brought that a fleet had come to anchor within the capes. It was supposed of course to be the French, and now the capture of the traitor was certain. He himself from certain signs appeared to be in great confusion; none of his ships ventured down the bay. An officer of the French navy bore down to visit the fleet, but returned with the astounding intelligence that it was British!

Admiral Arbuthnot had in fact overtaken Destouches on the 16th of March, off the capes of Virginia. Their forces were nearly equal; eight ships-of-the-line, and four frigates on each side, the French having more men, the English more guns. An engagement took place which lasted about an hour. The British van at first took the brunt of the action, and was severely handled; the centre came up to its relief. The French line was broken and gave way, but rallied, and formed again at some distance. The crippled state of some of his ships prevented the British admiral from bringing on a second encounter; nor did the French seek one, but shaped their course the next day back to Newport. Both sides claimed a victory. The British certainly effected the main objects they had in view; the French were cut off from the Chesapeake; the combined enterprise against Portsmouth was disconcerted, and Arnold was saved.

A detachment [of two thousand troops] from New York, under General Phillips, arrived at Portsmouth on the 26th of March. That officer immediately took command, greatly to the satisfaction of the British officers, who had been acting under Arnold. The force now collected there amounted to three thousand five hundred men. The disparity in force was now so great, that the Baron Steuben had to withdraw his troops, and remove the military stores into the interior. Many of the militia, too, their term of three months being expired, stacked their arms, and set off for their homes, and most of the residue had to be discharged.

General Phillips had hitherto remained quiet in Portsmouth, completing the fortifications, but evidently making preparations for an expedition. On the 16th of April he left one thousand men in garrison, and embarking the rest in small vessels of light draught, proceeded up James River, destroying armed vessels, public magazines, and a ship-yard belonging to the State. Landing at City Point, he advanced against Petersburg, a place of deposit of military stores and tobacco. He was met about a mile below the town by about one thousand militia, under General Muhlenburg, who, after disputing the ground inch by inch for nearly two hours, with considerable loss on both sides, retreated across the Appomattox, breaking down the bridge behind them.

Phillips entered the town, set fire to the tobacco warehouses, and destroyed all the vessels lying in the river. Repairing and crossing the bridge over the Appomattox, he proceeded to Chesterfield Court-house, where he destroyed barracks and public stores; while Arnold, with a detachment, laid waste the magazines of tobacco in the direction of Warwick. A fire was opened by the latter from a few field-pieces on the river bank, upon a squadron of small, armed vessels, which had been intended to co-operate with the French fleet against Portsmouth. The crews scuttled or set fire to them, and escaped to the north side of the river.

This destructive course was pursued until they arrived at Manchester, a small place opposite Richmond, where the tobacco warehouses were immediately in a blaze. Richmond was a leading object of this desolating enterprise, for there a great part of the military stores of the State had been collected. Fortunately, Lafayette, with his detachment of two thousand men, had arrived there, by forced marches, the evening before, and being joined by about two thousand militia and sixty dragoons (the latter, principally young Virginians of family), had posted himself strongly on the high banks on the north side of the river. There being no bridge across the river at that time, General Phillips did not think it prudent to attempt a passage in face of such a force so posted. Returning down the south bank of the river, to the place where his vessels awaited him, he re-embarked on the 2d of May, and dropped slowly down the river below the confluence of the Chickahomony. He was followed cautiously, and his movements watched by Lafayette, who posted himself behind the last-named river.

Despatches from Cornwallis now informed Phillips that his lordship was advancing with all speed from the South to effect a junction with him. The general immediately made a rapid move to regain possession of Petersburg, where the junction was to take place. Lafayette attempted by forced marches to get there before him, but was too late. Falling back, therefore, he recrossed James River and stationed himself some miles below Richmond, to be at hand for the protection of the public stores collected there.

During this main expedition of Phillips, some of his smaller vessels had carried on the plan of plunder and devastation in other of the rivers emptying into the Chesapeake Bay; setting fire to the houses where they met with resistance.

In the meantime the desolating career of General Phillips was brought to a close. He had been ill for some days previous to his arrival at Petersburg, and by the time he reached there, was no longer capable of giving orders. He died four days afterwards; honored and deeply regretted by his brothers in arms, as a meritorious and well-tried soldier.

Lord Cornwallis arrived at Petersburg on the 20th of May, after nearly a month's weary marching from Wilmington. His lordship, on taking command, found his force augmented by a considerable detachment of royal artillery, two battalions of light infantry, the 76th and 80th British regiments, a Hessian regiment, Lieutenant-colonel Simcoe's corps of Queen's rangers, cavalry and infantry, one hundred yagers, Arnold's legion of royalists, and the garrison of Portsmouth. His mind, we are told, was now set at ease with regard to Southern affairs; his spirits, so long jaded by his harassing tramps about the Carolinas, were again lifted up by his augmented strength.

While affairs were approaching a crisis in Virginia, troubles were threatening from the North. There were rumors of invasion from Canada; of war councils and leagues among the savage tribes; of a revival of the territorial feuds between New York and Vermont. Such, however, was the deplorable inefficiency of the military system, that though, according to the resolves of Congress, there were to have been thirty-seven thousand men under arms at the beginning of the year, Washington's whole force on the Hudson in the month of May did not amount to seven thousand men, of whom little more than four thousand were effective.

He still had his head-quarters at New Windsor, just above the Highlands, and within a few miles of West Point. Here he received intelligence that the enemy were in force on the opposite side of the Hudson, marauding the country on the north side of Croton River, and he ordered a hasty advance of Connecticut troops in that direction. The Croton River flows from east to west across Westchester County, and formed as it were the barrier of the American lines. The advanced posts of Washington's army guarded it, and by its aid, protected the upper country from the incursions of those foraging parties and marauders which had desolated the neutral ground below it. The incursions most to be guarded against were those of Colonel Delancey's loyalists, a horde of tories and refugees which had their stronghold in Morrisania.

The object of their present incursion was to surprise an outpost of the American army stationed near a fordable part of the Croton River, not far from Pine's Bridge. The post was commanded by Colonel Christopher Greene, of Rhode Island, the same who had successfully defended Fort Mercer on the Delaware, when assailed by Count Donop. He was a valuable officer, highly prized by Washington. Colonel Delancey, who led this foray, was successor to the unfortunate André as adjutant-general of the British army. He conducted it secretly, and in the night, at the head of a hundred horse and two hundred foot. The Croton was forded at daybreak, just as the night-guard had been withdrawn, and the farm-houses were surprised and assailed in which the Americans were quartered. That occupied by Colonel Greene and a brother officer, Major Flagg, was first surrounded. The major started from his bed, and discharged his pistols from a window, but was shot through the head, and afterwards despatched by cuts and thrusts of the sabre.

The door of Greene's room was burst open. He defended himself vigorously and effectively with his sword, for he had great strength, but he was overpowered by numbers, cut down, and barbarously mangled. A massacre was going on in other quarters. Besides these two officers, there were between thirty and forty killed and wounded, and several made prisoners. It is said that Colonel Delancey was not present at the carnage, but remained on the south side of the Croton to secure the retreat of his party. Before the troops ordered out by Washington arrived at the post, the marauders had made a precipitate retreat. They had attempted to carry off Greene a prisoner, but he died within three-quarters of a mile of the house. The commander-in-chief, we are told, heard with anguish and indignation the tragical fate of this, his faithful friend and soldier.

At this juncture Washington's attention was called in another direction. A frigate had arrived at Boston, bringing the Count de Barras, to take command of the French naval force. He was a veteran about sixty years of age, and had commanded D'Estaing's vanguard, when he forced the entrance of Newport harbor. The count brought the cheering intelligence, that an armament of twenty ships-of-the-line, with land forces, was to sail, or had sailed, from France, under the Count de Grasse for the West Indies, and that twelve of these ships were to relieve the squadron at Newport, and might be expected on the coast of the United States in July or August.

The Count de Rochambeau, having received despatches from the court of France, now requested an interview with Washington. The latter appointed Weathersfield in Connecticut for the purpose; and met the count there on the 22d of May, hoping to settle a definite plan of the campaign. Both as yet were ignorant of the arrival of Cornwallis in Virginia. The policy of a joint expedition to relieve the Carolinas was discussed. As the French ships in Newport were still blockaded by a superior force, such an expedition would have to be made by land. A march to the Southern States was long and harassing, and always attended with a great waste of life. On the other hand, an effective blow might be struck at New York, the garrison having been reduced one-half by detachments to the South. It was determined, therefore, that the French troops should march from Newport as soon as possible, and form a junction with the American army on the Hudson, and that both should move down to the vicinity of New York to make a combined attack, in which the Count de Grasse should be invited to co-operate with his fleet and a body of land troops.

A vessel was despatched by De Rochambeau, to inform the Count de Grasse of this arrangement; and letters were addressed by Washington to the executive authorities of New Jersey and the New England States, urging them to fill up their battalions and furnish their quotas of provisions. Notwithstanding all his exertions, however, when he mustered his forces at Peekskill, he was mortified to find not more than five thousand effective men. Notwithstanding, too, all the resolutions passed in the legislatures of the various States for supplying the army, it would, at this critical moment, have been destitute of provisions, especially bread, had it not been for the zeal, talents, and activity of Mr. Robert Morris, now a delegate to Congress, from the State of Pennsylvania, and recently appointed superintendent of finance. This patriotic and energetic man, when public means failed, pledged his own credit in transporting military stores and feeding the army.

The Count de Rochambeau and the Duke de Lauzun being arrived with their troops in Connecticut, on their way to join the American army, Washington prepared for spirited operations; quickened by the intelligence that a part of the garrison of New York had been detached to forage the Jerseys. Two objects were contemplated by him: one, the surprisal of the British works at the north end of New York Island; the other the capture or destruction of Delancey's corps of refugees in Morrisania. The attack upon the posts was to be conducted by General Lincoln, with a detachment from the main army, which he was to bring down by water—that on Delancey's corps by the Duke de Lauzun with his legion, aided by Sheldon's dragoons, and a body of Connecticut troops. Both operations were to be carried into effect on the 3d of July. The duke was to march down from Ridgebury in Connecticut, for the purpose. Everything was to be conducted with secrecy and by the way of surprisal. Should anything occur to prevent Lincoln from attempting the works on New York Island, he was to land his men above Spyt den Duivel Creek, march to the high grounds in front of King's Bridge, lie concealed there until the duke's attack on Delancey's corps should be announced by firing or other means; then to dispose of his force in such a manner as to make the enemy think it larger than it really was; thereby deterring troops from coming over the bridge to turn Lauzun's right, while he prevented the escape over the bridge of Delancey's refugees when routed from Morrisania.

In pursuance of the plan, Lincoln left the camp near Peekskill on the 1st, with eight hundred men, and artillery, and proceeded to Teller's Point, where they were embarked in boats with muffled oars, and rowed silently at night down the Tappan Sea. At daylight they kept concealed under the land. The Duke de Lauzun was supposed, at the same time, to be on the way from Connecticut. Washington, at three o'clock on the morning of the 2d, left his tents standing at Peekskill, and commenced his march with his main force, to Valentine's Hill, four miles above King's Bridge. There he posted himself to cover the detached troops, and improve any advantages that might be gained them.

Lincoln, on the morning of the 2d, had left his flotilla concealed under the eastern shore, and crossed to Fort Lee to reconnoitre Fort Washington from the cliffs on the opposite side of the Hudson. To his surprise and chagrin, he discovered a British force encamped on the north end of New York Island, and a ship-of-war anchored in the river. In fact, the troops which had been detached into the Jerseys, had returned, and the enemy were on the alert; the surprisal of the forts, therefore, was out of the question. His thoughts now were to aid the Duke de Lauzun's part of the scheme, as he had been instructed. Before daylight on the 3d, he landed his troops above Spyt den Duivel Creek, and took possession of the high ground on the north of Harlem River, where Fort Independence once stood. Here he was discovered by a foraging party of the enemy, fifteen hundred strong, who had sallied out at daybreak to scour the country. An irregular skirmish ensued. The firing was heard by the Duke de Lauzun, who was just arrived with his troops at Eastchester, fatigued by a long and forced march in sultry weather. Finding the country alarmed, and all hope of surprising Delancey's corps at an end, he hastened to the support of Lincoln. Washington also advanced with his troops from Valentine's Hill. The British, perceiving their danger, retreated to their boats on the east side of Harlem River, and crossed over to New York Island. A trifling loss in killed and wounded had been sustained on each side, and Lincoln had made a few prisoners.

Being disappointed in both objects, Washington did not care to fatigue his troops any more, but suffered them to remain on their arms, and spent a good part of the day reconnoitring the enemy's works. In the afternoon he retired to Valentine's Hill, and the next day marched to Dobbs' Ferry, where he was joined by the Count de Rochambeau on the 6th July. The two armies now encamped—the American in two lines, resting on the Hudson at Dobbs' Ferry, where it was covered by batteries, and extending eastward toward the Neperan or Sawmill River; the French in a single line on the hills further east, reaching to the Bronx River.

The two armies lay thus encamped for three or four weeks. In the meantime letters urged Washington's presence in Virginia. Richard Henry Lee advised that he should come with two or three thousand good troops, and be clothed with dictatorial powers. "I am fully persuaded, and upon good military principles," writes Washington in reply, "that the measures I have adopted will give more effectual and speedy relief to the State of Virginia than my marching thither, with dictatorial powers, at the head of every man I could draw from hence, without leaving the important posts on the North River quite defenceless, and these States open to devastation and ruin. My present plan of operation, which I have been preparing with all the zeal and activity in my power, will, I am morally certain, with proper support produce one of two things, either the fall of New York, or a withdrawal of the troops from Virginia, excepting a garrison at Portsmouth, at which place I have no doubt of the enemy's intention of establishing a permanent post."

Within two or three days after this letter was written, Washington crossed the river at Dobbs' Ferry, accompanied by the Count de Rochambeau, General de Beville, and General Duportail, to reconnoitre the British posts on the north end of New York Island. They were escorted by one hundred and fifty of the New Jersey troops, and spent the day on the Jersey heights ascertaining the exact position of the enemy on the opposite shore. Their next movement was to reconnoitre the enemy's posts at King's Bridge and on the east side of New York Island, and to cut off, if possible, such of Delancey's corps as should be found without the British lines. Five thousand troops, French and American, led by the Count de Chastellux and General Lincoln, were to protect this reconnoissance, and menace the enemy's posts. Everything was prepared in secrecy. On the 21st of July, at eight o'clock in the evening, the troops began their march. The detachment arrived at King's Bridge about daylight, and formed on the height back of Fort Independence. The enemy's forts on New York Island did not appear to have the least intelligence of what was going on, nor to be aware that hostile troops were upon the heights opposite, until the latter displayed themselves in full array, their arms flashing in the morning sunshine, and their banners, American and French, unfolded to the breeze.

While the enemy was thus held in check, Washington and De Rochambeau, accompanied by engineers and by their staffs, set out under the escort of a troop of dragoons to reconnoitre the enemy's position and works from every point of view. It was a wide reconnoissance, extending across the country outside of the British lines from the Hudson to the Sound. The whole was done slowly and scientifically, exact notes and diagrams being made of everything that might be of importance in future operations. While the enemy's works had been thoroughly reconnoitred, light troops and lancers had performed their duty in scouring the neighborhood. The refugee posts which had desolated the country were broken up. Most of the refugees, Washington says, had fled and hid themselves in secret places; some got over by stealth to the adjacent islands and to the enemy's shipping, and a few were caught.

CHAPTER LXIII.

RAVAGES IN VIRGINIA.—OPERATIONS IN CAROLINA.—ATTACK ON NEW LONDON.

The first object of Lord Cornwallis on the junction of his forces at Petersburg in May, was to strike a blow at Lafayette. The marquis was encamped on the north side of James River, between Wilton and Richmond, with about one thousand regulars, two thousand militia, and fifty dragoons. He was waiting for reinforcements of militia, and for the arrival of General Wayne, with the Pennsylvania line. His lordship hoped to draw him into an action before thus reinforced, and with that view, marched, on the 24th of May, from Petersburg to James River, which he crossed at Westover, about thirty miles below Richmond. Here he was joined on the 26th by a reinforcement just arrived from New York, part of which he sent under General Leslie to strengthen the garrison at Portsmouth. He was relieved also from military companionship with the infamous Arnold, who obtained leave of absence to return to New York, where business of importance was said to demand his attention.

Being now strongly reinforced, Cornwallis moved to dislodge Lafayette from Richmond. This latter, conscious of the inferiority of his forces, decamped as soon as he heard his lordship had crossed James River, and directed his march toward the upper country, inclining to the north, to favor a junction with Wayne. Cornwallis followed him as far as the upper part of Hanover County, destroying public stores wherever found. He soon found it impossible either to overtake Lafayette, or prevent his junction with Wayne; he turned his attention, therefore, to other objects.

Greene, in his passage through Virginia, had urged the importance of removing horses out of the way of the enemy; his caution had been neglected; the consequences were now felt. The great number of fine horses in the stables of Virginia gentlemen, who are noted for their love of the noble animal, had enabled Cornwallis to mount many of his troops in first-rate style. These he employed in scouring the country, and destroying public stores. Tarleton and his legion, it is said, were mounted on race-horses.

The State Legislature had been removed for safety to Charlottesville, where it was assembled for the purpose of levying taxes, and drafting militia. Tarleton, with one hundred and eighty cavalry and seventy mounted infantry, was ordered by Cornwallis to make a dash there, break up the legislature, and carry off members. On his way thither, on the 4th of June, he captured and destroyed a convoy of arms and clothing destined for Greene's army in North Carolina. At another place he surprised several persons of note at the house of a Dr. Walker, but lingered so long breakfasting, that a person mounted on a fleet horse had time to reach Charlottesville before him, and spread the alarm. Tarleton crossed the Rivanna, which washes the hill on which Charlottesville is situated; dispersed a small force collected on the bank, and galloped into the town thinking to capture the whole assembly. Seven alone fell into his hands; the rest had made their escape. No better success attended a party of horse under Captain McLeod, detached to surprise the Governor (Thomas Jefferson), at his residence in Monticello.

Having set fire to all the public stores at Charlottesville, Tarleton pushed for the point of Fork at the confluence of the Rivanna and Fluvanna; to aid, if necessary, a detachment sent under Colonel Simcoe to destroy a great quantity of military stores collected at that post. The Baron Steuben, who was stationed there with five hundred Virginia regulars and a few militia, and had heard of the march of Tarleton, had succeeded in transporting the greater part of the stores, as well as his troops, across the river, and as the water was deep and the boats were all on his side, he might have felt himself secure. The unexpected appearance of Simcoe's infantry, however, designedly spread out on the opposite heights, deceived him into the idea that it was the van of the British army. In his alarm he made a night retreat of thirty miles, leaving the greater part of the stores scattered along the river bank; which were destroyed the next morning by a small detachment of the enemy sent across in canoes.

On the 10th of June, Lafayette was at length gladdened by the arrival of Wayne with about nine hundred of the Pennsylvania line. Thus reinforced, he changed his whole plan, and ventured on the aggressive. Cornwallis had gotten between him and a large deposit of military stores at Albemarle Old Court-house. The marquis, by a rapid march at night, through a road long disused, threw himself between the British army and the stores, and, being joined by a numerous body of mountain militia, took a strong position to dispute the advance of the enemy.

Cornwallis did not think it advisable to pursue this enterprise, especially as he heard Lafayette would soon be joined by forces under Baron Steuben. He turned his face, therefore, toward the lower part of Virginia, and made a retrograde march, first to Richmond, and afterwards to Williamsburg. Lafayette, being joined by Steuben and his forces, had about four thousand men under him, one half of whom were regulars. He now followed the British army at the distance of eighteen or twenty miles, throwing forward his light troops to harass their rear, which was covered by Tarleton and Simcoe with their cavalry and infantry.

Cornwallis arrived at Williamsburg on the 25th, and sent out Simcoe to destroy some boats and stores on the Chickahominy River, and to sweep off the cattle of the neighborhood. Lafayette heard of the ravage, and detached Lieutenant-colonel Butler, of the Pennsylvania line, with a corps of light troops, and a body of horse under Major McPherson, to intercept the marauders. As the infantry could not push on fast enough for the emergency, McPherson took up fifty of them behind fifty of his dragoons, and dashed on. He overtook a company of Simcoe's rangers under Captain Shank about six miles from Williamsburg, foraging at a farm; a sharp encounter took place; McPherson at the outset was unhorsed and severely hurt. The action continued. Simcoe with his infantry, who had been in the advance convoying a drove of cattle, now engaged in the fight. Butler's riflemen began to arrive, and supported the dragoons. Neither knew the strength of the force they were contending with; but supposed it the advance guard of the opposite army. An alarm gun was fired by the British on a neighboring hill. It was answered by alarm guns at Williamsburg. The Americans supposed the whole British force coming out to assail them, and began to retire. Simcoe, imagining Lafayette to be at hand, likewise drew off, and pursued his march to Williamsburg. The loss in killed and wounded on both sides was severe for the number engaged; but the statements vary, and were never reconciled.

An express was received by Cornwallis at Williamsburg which obliged him to change his plans. The movements of Washington in the neighborhood of New York, menacing an attack, had produced the desired effect. Sir Henry Clinton, alarmed for the safety of the place, had written to Cornwallis requiring a part of his troops for its protection. His lordship prepared to comply with this requisition, but as it would leave him too weak to continue at Williamsburg, he set out on the 4th of July for Portsmouth.

Lafayette followed him on the ensuing day, and took post within nine miles of his camp; intending, when the main body of the enemy should have crossed the ford to the island of Jamestown, to fall upon the rear guard. Cornwallis suspected his design, and prepared to take advantage of it. The wheel carriages, bat horses and baggage, were passed over to the island under the escort of the Queen's rangers; making a great display, as if the main body had crossed; his lordship, however, with the greater part of his forces, remained on the mainland, his right covered by ponds, the centre and left by morasses over which a few narrow causeways of logs connected his position with the country, and James Island lay in the rear. His camp was concealed by a skirt of woods, and covered by an outpost.

In the morning of the 6th, as the Americans were advancing, a negro and a dragoon, employed by Tarleton, threw themselves in their way, pretending to be deserters, and informed them that the body of the king's troops had passed James River in the night, leaving nothing behind but the rear guard, composed of the British legion and a detachment of infantry. Persuaded of the fact, Lafayette with his troops crossed the morass on the left of the enemy by a narrow causeway of logs, and halted beyond about sunset. Wayne was detached with a body of riflemen, dragoons and Continental infantry, to make the attack, while the marquis with nine hundred Continentals and some militia stood ready to support him.

Wayne easily routed a patrol of cavalry and drove in the pickets, who had been ordered to give way readily. The outpost which covered the camp defended itself more obstinately; though exceedingly galled by the riflemen. Wayne pushed forward with the Pennsylvania line, eight hundred strong, and three field-pieces, to attack it; at the first discharge of a cannon more than two thousand of the enemy emerged from their concealment, and he found too late that the whole British line was in battle array before him. To retreat was more dangerous than to go on. So thinking, with that impetuous valor which had gained him the name of "Mad

Anthony," he ordered a charge to be sounded, and threw himself, horse and foot, with shouts upon the enemy. It was a sanguinary conflict and a desperate one, for the enemy were outflanking him right and left. Fortunately, the heaviness of the fire had awakened the suspicions of Lafayette;—it was too strong for the outpost of a rear-guard. Spurring to a point of land which commanded a view of the British camp, he discovered the actual force of the enemy, and the peril of Wayne. Galloping back, he sent word to Wayne to fall back to General Muhlenburg's brigade, which had just arrived, and was forming within half a mile of the scene of conflict. Wayne did so in good order, leaving behind him his three cannon; the horses which drew them having been killed. The whole army then retired across the morass.

The loss of the Americans in this brief but severe conflict is stated by Lafayette to have been one hundred and eighteen killed, wounded and prisoners, including ten officers. The British loss was said to be five officers wounded, and seventy-five privates killed and wounded. Lafayette retreated to Green Springs, where he rallied and reposed his troops. Cornwallis crossed over to Jamestown Island after dark, and three days afterwards, passing the James River with his main force, proceeded to Portsmouth.

We will now turn to resume the course of General Greene's campaigning in the Carolinas. It will be recollected that he, on the 5th of April, set out from Deep River on a retrograde march to carry the war again into South Carolina, beginning by an attack on Lord Rawdon's post at Camden. Sumter and Marion had been keeping alive the revolutionary fire in that State. On the re-appearance of Greene, they stood ready to aid with heart and hand.

On his way to Camden, Greene detached Lee to join Marion with his legion, and make an attack upon Fort Watson by way of diversion. For himself, he appeared before Camden, but finding it too strong and too well garrisoned, fell back about two miles, and took post at Hobkirk's Hill, hoping to draw his lordship out. He succeeded but too well. His lordship attacked him on the 25th of April, coming upon him partly by surprise. There was a hard-fought battle, but through some false move among part of his troops, Greene was obliged to retreat. His lordship did not pursue, but shut himself up in Camden, waiting to be rejoined by part of his garrison which was absent. Greene posted himself near Camden ferry on the Wateree, to intercept these reinforcements. Lee and Marion, who had succeeded in capturing Fort Watson, also took a position on the high hills of Santee for the same purpose. Their efforts were unavailing. Lord Rawdon was rejoined by the other part of his troops. His superior force now threatened to give him the mastery. Greene felt the hazardous nature of his situation. His troops were fatigued by their long marchings; he was disappointed of promised aid and reinforcements from Virginia; still he was undismayed, and prepared for another of his long and stubborn retreats. The next morning there was a joyful reverse. Rawdon was preparing to evacuate Camden. His lordship had heard of the march of Cornwallis into Virginia, and that all hope of aid from him was at an end. His garrison was out of provisions. All supplies were cut off by the Americans; he had no choice but to evacuate. He left Camden in flames.

Rapid successes now attended the American arms. Fort Motte, the middle post between Camden and Ninety-Six, was taken by Marion and Lee. Lee next captured Granby, and marched to aid Pickens in the siege of Augusta; while Greene, having acquired a supply of arms, ammunition and provisions from the captured forts, sat down before the fortress of Ninety-Six, on the 22d of May. It was the great mart and stronghold of the royalists, and was principally garrisoned by royalists from New Jersey and New York, commanded by Colonel Cruger, a native of New York. The siege lasted for nearly a month. The place was valiantly defended. Lee arrived with his legion, having failed before Augusta, and invested a stockaded fort which formed part of the works.

Word was brought that Lord Rawdon was pressing forward with reinforcements, and but a few miles distant on the Saluda. Greene endeavored to get up Sumter, Marion and Pickens to his assistance, but they were too far on the right of Lord Rawdon to form a junction. The troops were eager to storm the works before his lordship should arrive. A partial assault was made on the 18th of June. It was a bloody contest. The stockaded fort was taken, but the troops were repulsed from the main works.

Greene retreated across the Saluda, and halted at Bush River, at twenty miles distance, to observe the motion of the enemy. Lord Rawdon entered Ninety-Six on the 21st, but sallied forth again on the 24th, taking with him all the troops capable of fatigue, two thousand in number, without wheel carriage of any kind, or even knapsacks, hoping by a rapid move to overtake Greene. Want of provisions soon obliged him to give up the pursuit, and return to Ninety-Six. Leaving about one half of his force there, under Colonel Cruger, he sallied a second time from Ninety-Six, at the head of eleven hundred infantry, with cavalry, artillery, and field-pieces, marching by the south side of the Saluda for the Congaree.

He was now pursued in his turn by Greene and Lee. In this march more than fifty of his lordship's soldiers fell dead from heat, fatigue and privation. At Orangeburg, where he arrived on the 8th of July, his lordship was joined by a large detachment under Colonel Stuart. Greene had followed him closely, and having collected all his detachments, and being joined by Sumter, appeared within four miles of Orangeburg, on the 10th of July, and offered battle. The offer was not accepted, and the position of Lord Rawdon was too strong to be attacked. Greene remained there two or three days; when, learning that Colonel Cruger was advancing with the residue of the forces from Ninety-Six, which would again give his lordship a superiority of force, he moved off with his infantry on the night of the 13th of July, crossed the Saluda, and posted himself on the east side of the Wateree, at the high hills of Santee.

He now detached Sumter with about a thousand light troops to scour the lower country, and attack the British posts in the vicinity of Charleston, now left uncovered by the concentration of their forces at Orangeburg. Under Sumter acted Marion, Lee, the Hamptons, and other enterprising partisans. They were to act separately in breaking up the minor posts at and about Dorchester, but to unite at Monk's Corner, where Lieutenant-colonel Coates was stationed with the 9th Regiment. This post carried, they were to re-unite with Greene's army on the high hills of Santee.

Scarce was Sumter on his march, when he received a letter from Greene, dated July 14th, stating that Cruger had formed a junction with Lord Rawdon the preceding night; no time, therefore, was to be lost. "Push your operations night and day: station a party to watch the enemy's motions at Orangeburg. Keep Colonel Lee and General Marion advised of all matters from above, and tell Colonel Lee to thunder even at the gates of Charleston." Conformably to these orders, Colonel Henry Hampton with a party was posted to keep an eye on Orangeburg. Lee with his legion, accompanied by Lieutenant-colonel Wade Hampton, and a detachment of cavalry, was sent to carry Dorchester, and then press forward to the gates of Charleston; while Sumter with the main body, took up his line of march along the road on the south side of the Congaree, towards Monk's Corner.

As Lee approached Dorchester, Colonel Wade Hampton, with his cavalry, passed to the east of that place, to a bridge on Goose Creek, to cut off all communication between the garrison and Monk's Corner. His sudden appearance gave the alarm, the garrison abandoned its post, and when Lee arrived there he found it deserted. He proceeded to secure a number of horses and wagons, and some fixed ammunition, which the garrison had left behind, and to send them off to Hampton. Hampton, kept in suspense by this delay, lost patience. He feared that the alarm would spread through the country, and the dash into the vicinity of Charleston be prevented. Abandoning the bridge at Goose Creek, therefore, he set off with his cavalry, clattered down to the neighborhood of the lines, and threw the city into confusion. The bells rang, alarm guns were fired, the citizens turned out under arms. Hampton captured a patrol of dragoons and a guard, at the Quarter-house; and then retired, carrying off fifty prisoners, several of them officers.

Lee arrived in the neighborhood on the following day, but Hampton had been beforehand with him, made the dash, and "thundered at the gate." Both now hastened to rejoin Sumter on the evening of the 16th, who was only waiting to collect his detachments, before he made an attack on Colonel Coates at Monk's Corner. The assault was to be made on the following morning. During the night Coates decamped. A pursuit was commenced; Lee with his legion, and Hampton with the State cavalry, took the lead; Sumter followed with the infantry. The rear-guard of the British, about one hundred strong, was overtaken with the baggage, at the distance of eighteen miles. They were new troops recently arrived from Ireland, and had not seen service. On being charged by the cavalry, sword in hand, they threw down their arms without firing a shot, and cried for quarter, which was granted. While Lee was securing them, Captain Armstrong with the first section of cavalry pushed on in pursuit of Coates and the main body. That officer had crossed a wooden bridge over Quimby Creek, loosened the planks, and was only waiting to be rejoined by his rear-guard, to throw them off, and cut off all pursuit. His troops were partly on a causeway beyond the bridge, partly crowded in a lane. He knew nothing of an enemy being at hand, until he saw Armstrong spurring up with his section. Coates gave orders for his troops to halt, form, and march up; a howitzer was brought to bear upon the bridge, and a fatigue party rushed forward to throw off the planks. Armstrong saw the danger, dashed across the bridge, with his section, drove off the artillerists, and captured the howitzer before it could be discharged. The fatigue men, who had been at work on the bridge, snatched up their guns, gave a volley and fled. Armstrong's party, in crossing the bridge, had displaced some of the planks, and formed a chasm. Lieutenant Carrington with the second section of dragoons leaped over it; the chasm being thus enlarged, the horses of the third section refused. A pell-mell fight took place between the handful of dragoons who had crossed, and some of the enemy. Armstrong, seeing the foe too strong in front, and no reinforcement coming on in rear, wheeled off with some of his men to the left, galloped into the woods, and pushed up along the stream to ford it, and seek the main body.

During the melée, Lee had come up and endeavored with the dragoons of the third section to replace the planks of the bridge. Their efforts were vain; the water was deep, the mud deeper; there was no foothold, nor was there any firm spot where to swim the horses across. While they were thus occupied, Colonel Coates, with his men, opened a fire upon them from the other end of the bridge; having no fire-arms to reply with, they were obliged to retire. The remainder of the planks were then thrown off from the bridge, after which Colonel Coates took post on an adjacent plantation.

It was not until three o'clock in the afternoon, that Sumter with his forces appeared upon the ground, having had to make a considerable circuit on account of the destruction of the bridge. By four o'clock the attack commenced. Sumter, with part of the troops, advanced in front under cover of a line of negro huts, which he wished to secure. Marion, with his brigade, much reduced in number, approached on the right of the enemy, where there was no shelter but fences; the cavalry, not being able to act, remained at a distance as a reserve, and, if necessary, to cover a retreat. Sumter's brigade soon got possession of the huts, where they used their rifles with sure effect. Marion and his men rushed up through a galling fire to the fences on the right. The enemy retired within the house and garden, and kept up a sharp fire from doors and windows and picketed fence. Unfortunately, the Americans had neglected to bring on their artillery. Having repaired the bridge, they sent off for the artillery and a supply of powder, which accompanied it. The evening was at hand; their ammunition was exhausted, and they retired in good order, intending to renew the combat with artillery in the morning. When they came to compare notes, it was found that the loss in killed and wounded had chiefly fallen on Marion's corps. His men, from their exposed situation, had borne the brunt of the battle; while Sumter's had suffered but little, being mostly sheltered in the huts. Jealousy and distrust were awakened, and discord reigned in the camp. Partisan and volunteer troops readily fall asunder under such circumstances. Many moved off in the night. Lee, accustomed to act independently, and unwilling, perhaps, to acknowledge Sumter as his superior officer, took up his line of march for head-quarters without consulting him. Sumter still had force enough, now that he was joined by the artillery, to have held the enemy in a state of siege; but he was short of ammunition, and he apprehended the approach of Lord Rawdon, who, it was said, was moving down from Orangeburg. He therefore retired across the Santee, and rejoined Greene at his encampment.

So ended this foray, which fell far short of the expectations formed from the spirit and activity of the leaders and their men. One of the best effects of the incursion was the drawing down Lord Rawdon from Orangeburg, with five hundred of his troops. He returned no more to the upper country, but sailed not long after from Charleston for Europe. Colonel Stuart, who was left in command at Orangeburg, moved forward from that place, and encamped on the south side of the Congaree River, near its junction with the Wateree, and within sixteen miles of Greene's position on the high hills of Santee. The two armies lay in sight of each other's fires, but two large rivers intervened, to secure each party from sudden attack. Both armies, however, needed repose, and military operations were suspended, as if by mutual consent, during the sultry summer heat.

After the grand reconnoissance of the posts on New York Island, related in a former page, the confederate armies remained encamped about Dobbs' Ferry and the Greenburg hills, awaiting an augmentation of force for their meditated attack. Letters now came from Lafayette, dated 26th and 30th of July, speaking of the embarkation of the greatest part of Cornwallis' army at Portsmouth. He supposed their destination to be New York, yet, though wind and weather were favorable, they did not sail. "Should a French fleet now come into Hampton Roads," adds the sanguine marquis, "the British army would, I think be ours." At this juncture arrived the French frigate Concorde at Newport, bringing despatches from Admiral the Count de Grasse. He was to leave St. Domingo on the 3d of August, with between twenty-five and thirty ships-of-the-line, and a considerable body of land forces, and to steer immediately for the Chesapeake.

This changed the face of affairs, and called for a change in the game. All attempt upon New York was postponed; the whole of the French army, and as large a part of the Americans as could be spared, were to move to Virginia, and co-operate with the Count de Grasse for the redemption of the Southern States. Washington apprised the count by letter of this intention. He wrote also to Lafayette on the 15th of August: "By the time this reaches you the Count de Grasse will either be in the Chesapeake, or may be looked for every moment. Under these circumstances, whether the enemy remain in full force, or whether they have only a detachment left, you will immediately take such a position as will best enable you to prevent their sudden retreat through North Carolina, which I presume they will attempt the instant they perceive so formidable an armament."

Washington's "soul was now in arms." At length, after being baffled and disappointed so often by the incompetency of his means, and above all, thwarted by the enemy's naval potency, he had the possibility of coping with them both on land and sea. The contemplated expedition was likely to consummate his plans and wind up the fortunes of the war, and he determined to lead it in person. He would take with him something more than two thousand of the American army; the rest, chiefly Northern troops, were to remain with General Heath, who was to hold command of the posts of the Hudson. Perfect secrecy was maintained as to this change of plan. Preparations were still carried on, as if for an attack upon New York. An extensive encampment was marked out in the Jerseys, and ovens erected and fuel provided for the baking of bread; as if a part of the besieging force was to be stationed there, thence to make a descent upon the enemy's garrison on Staten Island, in aid of the operations against the city. The American troops, themselves, were kept in ignorance of their destination.

Previous to his decampment, Washington sent forward a party of pioneers to clear the roads towards King's Bridge, as if the posts recently reconnoitred were about to be attempted. On the 19th of August, his troops were paraded with their faces in that direction. When all were ready, however, they were ordered to face about, and were marched up along the Hudson River towards King's Ferry. De Rochambeau, in like manner, broke up his encampment, and took the road by White Plains, North Castle, Pine's Bridge, and Crompond, toward the same point.

On the 20th, Washington arrived at King's Ferry, and his troops began to cross the Hudson with their baggage, stores and cannon, and encamp at Haverstraw. He himself crossed in the evening, and took up his quarters at Colonel Hay's, at the White House. Thence he wrote to the Count de Grasse, (presuming that the letter would find him in the Chesapeake,) urging him to send up all his frigates and transports to the Head of Elk, by the 8th of September, for the transportation of the combined army, which would be there by that time. He informed him also that the Count de Barras had resolved to join him in the Chesapeake with his squadron.

On the 22d the French troops arrived by their circuitous route, and began to cross to Stony Point with their artillery, baggage and stores. The two armies having safely crossed the Hudson, commenced, on the 25th, their several lines of march toward the Jerseys. Both armies were still kept in the dark, as to the ultimate object of their movement. An intelligent observer, who accompanied the army, writes: "Our situation reminds me of some theatrical exhibition, where the interest and expectations of the spectators are continually increasing, and where curiosity is wrought to the highest point." The mystery was at length solved. "We have now passed all the enemy's posts," continues the foregoing writer, "and are pursuing our route, with increased rapidity, toward Philadelphia."

Washington reached the Delaware with his troops before Sir Henry Clinton was aware of their destination. It was too late to oppose their march, even had his forces been adequate. As a kind of counterplot, therefore, and in the hope of distracting the attention of the American commander, and drawing off a part of his troops, he hurried off an expedition to the eastward, to insult the State of Connecticut, and attack her seaport of New London. The command of this expedition, which was to be one of ravage and destruction, was given to Arnold, as if it was necessary to complete the measure of his infamy, that he should carry fire and sword into his native State, and desecrate the very cradle of his infancy.

On the 6th of September he appeared off the harbor of New London with a fleet of ships and transports and a force of two thousand infantry and three hundred cavalry. New London stands on the west bank of the river Thames. The approach to it was defended by two forts on opposite sides of the river, and about a mile below the town; Fort Trumbull on the west and Fort Griswold on the east side, on a height called Groton Hill. The troops landed in two divisions of about eight hundred men each; one under Lieutenant-colonel Eyre on the east side, the other under Arnold on the west, on the same side with New London, and about three miles below it. Arnold met with but little opposition. The few militia who manned an advance battery and Fort Trumbull, abandoned their posts, and crossed the river to Fort Griswold. He pushed on and took possession of the town.

Colonel Eyre had a harder task. The militia, about one hundred and fifty-seven strong, had collected in Fort Griswold, hastily and imperfectly armed it is true, but they were brave men, and had a brave commander, Colonel William Ledyard, brother of the celebrated traveller. The fort was square and regularly built. Arnold, unaware of its strength, had ordered Colonel Eyre to take it by a *coup de main*. He discovered his mistake, and sent counter orders, but too late. Colonel Eyre forced the pickets; made his way into the fosse, and attacked the force on three sides; it was bravely defended; the enemy were repeatedly repulsed; they returned to the assault, scrambled up on each other's shoulders, effected a lodgment on the fraise, and made their way with fixed bayonets through the embrasures. Colonel Eyre received a mortal wound near the works; Major Montgomery took his place; a negro thrust him through with a spear as he mounted the parapet; Major Bromfield succeeded to the command, and carried the fort at the point of the bayonet. In fact, after the enemy were within the walls, the fighting was at an end and the slaughter commenced. Colonel Ledyard had ordered his men to lay down their arms; but the enemy, exasperated by the resistance they had experienced, and by the death of their officers, continued the deadly work of the musket and the bayonet. Colonel Ledyard, it is said, was thrust through with his own sword after yielding it up to Major Bromfield. Seventy of the garrison were slain, and thirty-five desperately wounded; and most of them after the fort had been taken. The loss of the enemy was two officers and forty-six soldiers killed, and eight officers and one hundred and thirty-five soldiers wounded.

Arnold, in the meantime, had carried on the work of destruction at New London. Some of the American shipping had effected their escape up the river, but a number were burnt. Fire, too, was set to the public stores; it communicated to the dwelling-houses, and, in a little while, the whole place was wrapped in flames. Having completed his ravage, Arnold retreated to his boats, leaving the town still burning. So ended his career of infamy in his native land; a land which had once delighted to honor him, but in which his name was never thenceforth to be pronounced without a malediction.

On the 30th of August, Washington, with his suite, had arrived at Philadelphia. During his sojourn in the city he was hospitably entertained at the house of Mr. Morris, the patriotic financier. The greatest difficulty with which he had to contend in his present enterprise was the want of funds, part of his troops not having received any pay for a long time, and having occasionally given evidence of great discontent. In this emergency he was accommodated by the Count de Rochambeau, with a loan of twenty thousand hard dollars, which Mr. Robert Morris engaged to repay by the 1st of October. This pecuniary pressure was relieved by the arrival in Boston, on the 25th of August, of Colonel John Laurens from his mission to France, bringing with him two and a half millions of livres in cash, being part of a subsidy of six millions of livres granted by the French king. On the 2d of

September the American troops passed through Philadelphia. The French troops entered on the following day.

At Philadelphia, Washington received despatches from Lafayette, dated the 21st and 24th of August, from his camp at the Forks of York River in Virginia. The embarkation at Portsmouth, which the marquis had supposed might be intended for New York, was merely for Yorktown, where Cornwallis had determined to establish the permanent post ordered in his instructions. Yorktown was a small place situated on a projecting bank on the south side of York River, opposite a promontory called Gloucester Point. The river between was not more than a mile wide, but deep enough to admit ships of a large size and burthen. Here concentrating his forces, he had proceeded to fortify the opposite points, calculating to have the works finished by the beginning of October. Believing that he had no present enemy but Lafayette to guard against, Cornwallis felt so secure in his position that he wrote to Sir Henry on the 22d of August, offering to detach a thousand or twelve hundred men to strengthen New York against the apprehended attack of the combined armies.

Washington left Philadelphia on the 5th of September, on his way to the Head of Elk. About three miles below Chester, he was met by an express bearing tidings of the arrival of the Count de Grasse in the Chesapeake with twenty-eight ships-of-the-line. Washington instantly rode back to Chester to rejoice with the Count de Rochambeau, who was coming down to that place from Philadelphia by water.

Washington reached the Head of Elk on the 6th. The troops and a great part of the stores were already arrived, and beginning to embark. Thence he wrote to the Count de Grasse, felicitating him on his arrival; and informing him that the van of the two armies were about to embark and fall down the Chesapeake, form a junction with the troops under the Count de St. Simon and the Marquis de La-fayette, and co-operate in blocking up Cornwallis in York River, so as to prevent his retreat by land or his getting any supplies from the country. Everything had thus far gone on well, but there were not vessels enough at the Head of Elk for the immediate transportation of all the troops, ordnance and stores; a part of the troops would have to proceed to Baltimore by land. Leaving General Heath to bring on the American forces, and the Baron de Viomenil the French, Washington, accompanied by De Rochambeau, crossed the Susquehanna early on the 8th, and pushed forward for Baltimore.

On the 9th he left Baltimore a little after daybreak, accompanied only by Colonel Humphreys; the rest of his suite were to follow at their ease; for himself, he was determined to reach Mount Vernon that evening. Six years had elapsed since last he was under its roof; six wearing years of toil, of danger, and of constant anxiety. During all that time, and amid all his military cares, he had kept up a regular weekly correspondence with his steward or agent, regulating all the affairs of his rural establishment with as much exactness as he did those of the army. It was a late hour when he arrived. He was joined by his suite at dinner-time on the following day, and by the Count de Rochambeau in the evening. General Chastel-lux and his aides-de-camp arrived there on the 11th, and Mount Vernon was now crowded with guests, who were all entertained in the ample style of old Virginian hospitality. On the 12th, tearing himself away once more from the home of his heart, Washington with his military associates continued onward to join Lafayette at Williamsburg.

CHAPTER LXIV.

OPERATIONS BEFORE YORKTOWN.—GREENE IN THE SOUTH.

Lord Cornwallis had been completely roused from his dream of security by the appearance, on the 28th of August, of the fleet of Count de Grasse within the capes of the Delaware. Three French ships-of-the-line and a frigate soon anchored at the mouth of York River. The boats of the fleet were immediately busy conveying three thousand three hundred land forces, under the Marquis de St. Simon, up James River to form the preconcerted junction with those under Lafayette. Awakened to his danger, Cornwallis, as Washington had foreseen, meditated a retreat to the Carolinas. It was too late. York River was blocked up by French ships; James River was filled with armed vessels covering the transportation of the troops. His lordship reconnoitred Williamsburg; it was too strong to be forced, and Wayne had crossed James River to join his troops to those under the marquis. Seeing his retreat cut off in every direction, Cornwallis proceeded to strengthen his works; sending off repeated expresses to apprise Sir Henry Clinton of his perilous situation.

The Count de Grasse had been but a few days anchored within the Chesapeake, and fifteen hundred of his seamen were absent, conveying the troops up James River, when Admiral Graves, who then commanded the British naval force on the American coast, appeared with twenty sail off the capes of Virginia. De Grasse, anxious to protect the squadron of the Count de Barras, which was expected from Rhode Island, and which it was the object of Graves to intercept, immediately slipped his cables and put to sea with twenty-four ships, leaving the rest to blockade York and James Rivers.

Admiral Graves, immediately prepared for action, although he had five ships less than De Grasse. The latter, however, was not disposed to accept the challenge, his force being weakened by the absence of so many of his seamen, employed in transporting troops. His plan was to occupy the enemy by partial actions and skilful manoeuvres, so as to retain his possession of the Chesapeake, and cover the arrival of De Barras.

The vans of the two fleets, and some ships of the centre, engaged about four o'clock in the afternoon of the 7th of September. The conflict soon became animated. Several ships were damaged, and many men killed and wounded on both sides. De Grasse, who had the advantage of the wind, drew off after sunset; satisfied with the damage done and sustained, and not disposed for a general action.

For four days the fleets remained in sight of each other, repairing damages and manoeuvring; but the French having still the advantage of the wind, maintained their prudent policy of avoiding a general engagement. At length De Grasse, learning that De Barras was arrived within the capes, formed a junction with him, and returned with him to his former anchoring ground, with two English frigates which he had captured. Admiral Graves, disappointed in his hope of interrupting De Barras, and finding the Chesapeake guarded by a superior force with which he could not prudently contend, left the coast and bore away for New York. Under convoy of the squadron of De Barras came a fleet of transports, conveying land forces under M. de Choisy, with siege artillery and military stores.

From Williamsburg, Washington sent forward Count Fersen, one of the aides-de-camp of De Rochambeau, to hurry on the French troops with all possible despatch. He wrote to the same purport to General Lincoln: "Every day we now lose," said he, "is comparatively an age; as soon as it is in our power with safety, we ought to take our position near the enemy. Hurry on, then, my dear sir, with your troops, on the wings of speed."

It was with great satisfaction Washington learned that Admiral de Barras had anticipated his wishes, in sending transports and prize vessels up the bay to assist in bringing on the French troops. In the meantime, he with Count de Rochambeau was desirous of having an interview with the admiral on board of his ship, provided he could send some fast-sailing cutter to receive them. A small ship, the Queen Charlotte, was furnished by the admiral for the purpose. It had been captured on its voyage from Charleston to New York, having Lord Rawdon on board, and had been commodiously fitted up for his lordship's reception.

On board of this vessel Washington and De Rochambeau, with the Chevalier de Chastellux and Generals Knox and Duportail, embarked on the 18th, and proceeding down James River, came the next morning in sight of the French fleet riding at anchor in Lynn Haven Bay, just under the point of Cape Henry. About noon they got alongside of the admiral's ship, the Ville de Paris, and were received on board with great ceremony, and naval and military parade. Admiral de Grasse was a tall, fine-looking man, plain in his address and prompt in the discharge of business. A plan of co-operation was soon arranged, to be carried into effect on the arrival of the American and French armies from the North, which were actually on their way down the Chesapeake from the Head of Elk. Business being despatched, dinner was served, after which they were conducted throughout the ship, and received the officers of the fleet, almost all of whom came on board.

By the 25th the American and French troops were mostly arrived and encamped near Williamsburg, and preparations were made for the decisive blow.

Yorktown, as has already been noted, is situated on the south side of York River, immediately opposite Gloucester Point. Cornwallis had fortified the town by seven redoubts and six batteries on the land side, connected by intrenchments; and there was a line of batteries along the river. The town was flanked on each side by deep ravines and creeks emptying into York River; their heads, in front of the town, being not more than half a mile apart. The enemy had availed themselves of these natural defences, in the arrangement of extensive outworks, with redoubts strengthened by abatis; field-works mounted with cannon, and trees cut down and left with the branches pointed outward. Gloucester Point had likewise been fortified. Its batteries, with those of Yorktown, commanded the intervening river. Ships of war were likewise stationed on it, protected by the guns of the forts, and the channel was obstructed by sunken vessels. The defence of Gloucester Point was confided to Lieutenant-colonel Dundas, with six or seven hundred men.

That evening Cornwallis received despatches from Sir Henry Clinton, informing him of the arrival of Admiral Digby, and that a fleet of twenty-three ships-of-the-line, with about five thousand troops, would sail to his assistance probably on the 5th of October. Cornwallis immediately wrote in reply: "I have ventured these last two days to look General Washington's whole force in the face in the position on the outside of my works, and have the pleasure to assure your Excellency that there is but one wish throughout the army, which is that the enemy would advance.... I shall retire this night within the works, and have no doubt, if relief arrives in any reasonable time, York and Gloucester will be both in the possession of his Majesty's troops." That night his lordship accordingly abandoned his outworks, and drew his troops within the town. The outworks thus abandoned were seized upon the next morning by detachments of American light infantry and French troops, and served to cover the troops employed in throwing up breastworks.

The combined French and American forces were now twelve thousand strong, exclusive of the Virginia militia which General Thomas Nelson [now governor of Virginia], had brought into the field. On the morning of the 28th of September, the combined armies marched from Williamsburg toward Yorktown, about twelve miles distant, and encamped at night within two miles of it, driving in the pickets and some patrols of cavalry. General de Choisy was sent across York River, with Lauzun's legion and General Weedon's brigade of militia, to watch the enemy on the side of Gloucester Point. By the 1st of October the line of the besiegers, nearly two miles from the works, formed a semicircle, each end resting on the river, so that the investment by land was complete; while the Count de Grasse, with the main fleet, remained in Lynn Haven Bay, to keep off assistance by sea.

The besieged army began now to be greatly distressed for want of forage, and had to kill many of their horses, the carcasses of which were continually floating down the river. In the evening of the 2d of October, Tarleton with his legion and the mounted infantry were passed over the river to Gloucester Point, to assist in foraging. At daybreak Lieutenant-colonel Dundas led out part of his garrison to forage the neighboring country. About ten o'clock the wagons and bat horses laden with Indian corn were returning, covered by Tarleton and his dragoons as a rear-guard, when word was brought that an enemy was advancing in force. The report was confirmed by a cloud of dust from which emerged Lauzun and the Frence hussars and lancers.

Tarleton, with part of his legion, advanced to meet them; the rest, with Simcoe's dragoons, remained as a rear-guard in a skirt of woods. A skirmish ensued, gallantly sustained on each side, but the superiority of Tarleton's horses gave him the advantage. General Choisy hastened up with a corps of cavalry and infantry to support the hussars. In the medley fight, a dragoon's horse, wounded by a lance, plunged, and overthrew both Tarleton and his steed. The rear-guard rushed from their covert to rescue their commander. They came galloping up in such disorder, that they were roughly received by Lauzun's hussars, who were drawn up on the plain. In the meantime Tarleton scrambled out of the melée, mounted another horse, and ordered a retreat, to enable his men to recover from their confusion. Dismounting forty infantry, he placed them in a thicket. Their fire checked the hussars in their pursuit. The British dragoons rallied, and were about to charge, when the hussars retired behind their infantry, and a fire was opened upon the British by some militia from behind a fence. Tarleton again ordered a retreat to be sounded, and the conflict came to an end. This was the last affair of Tarleton and his legion in the revolutionary war. The next day General Choisy, being reinforced by a detachment of marines from the fleet of De Grasse, cut off all communication by land between Gloucester and the country.

At this momentous time, when the first parallel before the besieged city was about to be opened, Washington received dispatches from his faithful coadjutor, General Greene, giving him important intelligence of his co-operations in the South; to consider which we will suspend for a moment our narrative of affairs before Yorktown.

For some weeks in the months of July and August, General Greene had remained encamped with his main force on the high hills of Santee, refreshing and disciplining his men, and awaiting the arrival of promised reinforcements. In the meantime, Marion with his light troops, aided by Colonel Washington with his dragoons, held control over the lower Santee. Lee was detached to operate with Sumter's brigade on the Congaree, and Colonel Harden with his mounted militia was scouring the country about the Edisto.

Greene was disappointed as to reinforcements. All that he had received were two hundred North Carolina levies and five hundred South Carolina militia; still he prepared for a bold effort to drive the enemy from their remaining posts. For that purpose, on the 22d of August he broke up his encampment to march against Colonel Stuart. The latter still lay encamped about sixteen miles distant, in a straight line; but the Congaree and Wateree lay between, bordered by swamps overflowed by recent rains; to cross them and reach the hostile camp, it was necessary to make a circuit of seventy miles. While Greene was making it, Stuart abandoned his position, and moved down forty miles to the vicinity of Eutaw Springs, where he was reinforced by a detachment from Charleston with provisions.

Greene followed on by easy marches. He had been joined by General Pickens with a party of the Ninety-Six militia, and by the State troops under Lieutenant-colonel Henderson; and now moved slowly to give time for Marion, who was scouring the country about the Edisto, to rejoin him. This was done on the 5th of September at Laurens' place, within seventeen miles of Stuart's camp. Here baggage, tents, everything that could impede motion was left behind, and on the afternoon of the 7th the army was pushed on within seven miles of the Eutaws, where it bivouacked for the night. At four o'clock in the morning this little army was in motion. Greene's whole force at that time did not exceed two thousand men; that of the enemy he was seeking, about twenty-three hundred. The Americans, however, were superior in cavalry. His army advanced in two columns, which were to form the two lines of battle. Within four miles of Eutaw they met with a British detachment of one hundred and fifty infantry and fifty cavalry under Major Coffin, sent forward to reconnoitre; it was put to flight after a severe skirmish. Supposing this to be the van of the enemy, Greene halted his columns and formed. The South Carolinians in equal divisions formed the right and left of the first line, the North Carolinians the centre. General Marion commanded the right; General Pickens the left; Colonel Malmedy the centre. Colonel Henderson with the State troops covered the left of the line; Colonel Lee with his legion the right.

Of the second line, composed of regulars, the North Carolinians, under General Sumner, were on the right; the Marylanders, under Colonel Williams, on the left; the Virginians, under Colonel Campbell, in the centre. Colonel Washington with his cavalry followed in the rear as a corps de reserve. Two three-pounders moved on the road in the centre of the first line; two six-pounders in a like position in the second line. In this order the troops moved forward, keeping their lines as well as they could through open woods, which covered the country on each side of the road.

Within a mile of the camp they encountered a body of infantry thrown forward by Colonel Stuart, to check their advance while he had time to form his troops in order of battle. These were drawn up in line in a wood two hundred yards west of Eutaw Springs. The right rested on Eutaw Creek, and was covered by a battalion of grenadiers and infantry under Major Majoribanks, partly concealed among thickets on the margin of the stream. The left of the line extended across the Charleston road, with a reserve corps in a commanding situation covering the road. About fifty yards in the rear of the British line was a cleared field, in which was their encampment, with the tents all standing. Adjoining it was a brick house with a palisadoed garden, which Colonel Stuart intended as a protection, if too much pressed by cavalry. The advanced party of infantry, which had retired firing before the Americans, formed on the flanks of Colonel Stuart's line. The Carolinian militia had pressed after them. About nine o'clock the action was commenced by the left of the American line, and soon became general. The militia fought until they had expended seventeen rounds, when they gave way, covered by Lee and Henderson, who fought bravely on the flanks of the line.

Sumner, with the regulars who formed the second line, advanced in fine style to take the place of the first. The enemy likewise brought their reserve into action; the conflict continued to be bloody and severe. Sumner's brigade, formed partly of recruits, gave way under the superior fire of the enemy. The British rushed forward to secure their fancied victory. Greene, seeing their line disordered, instantly ordered Williams with his Marylanders to "sweep the field with the bayonet." Williams was seconded by Colonel Campbell with the Virginians. The order was gallantly obeyed. They delivered a deadly volley at forty yards' distance, and then advanced at a brisk rate, with loud shouts and trailed arms. The British recoiled. While the Marylanders and Virginians attacked them in front, Lee with his legion turned their left flank and charged them in rear. Colonel Hampton with the State cavalry made a great number of prisoners, and Colonel Washington, coming up with his reserve of horse and foot, completed their defeat. They were driven back through their camp; many were captured; many fled along the Charleston road, and others threw themselves into the brick house.

Major Majoribanks and his troops could still enfilade the left flank of the Americans from their covert among the thickets on the border of the stream. Greene ordered Colonel Washington with his dragoons and Kirkwood's Delaware infantry to dislodge them, and Colonel Wade Hampton to assist with the State troops. Colonel Washington, without waiting for the infantry, dashed forward with his dragoons. It was a rash move. The thickets were impervious to cavalry. The dragoons separated into small squads, and endeavored to force their way in. Horses and riders were shot down or bayoneted; most of the officers were either killed or wounded. Colonel Washington had his horse shot under him; he himself was bayoneted, and would have been slain, had not a British officer interposed, who took him prisoner. By the time Hampton and Kirkwood came up, the cavalry were routed. While Hampton rallied them, Kirkwood with his Delawares charged with bayonet upon the enemy in the thickets. Majoribanks fell back with his troops, and made a stand in the palisadoed garden of the brick house.

Victory now seemed certain on the side of the Americans. Unfortunately, the soldiers, thinking the day their own, fell to plundering the tents, devouring the food and carousing on the liquors found there. Many of them became intoxicated and unmanageable—the officers interfered in vain; all was riot and disorder.

The enemy in the meantime recovered from their confusion, and opened a fire from every window of the house and from the palisadoed garden. There was a scattering fire also from the woods and thickets on the right and left. Colonel Stuart was by this time rallying his left wing, and advancing to support the right; when Greene, finding his ammunition nearly exhausted, determined to give up the attempt to dislodge the enemy from their places of refuge, since he could not do it without severe loss. He remained on the ground long enough to collect his wounded, excepting those who were too much under the fire of the house, and then, leaving Colonel Hampton with a strong picket on the field, he returned to the position seven miles off, which he had left in the morning.

The enemy decamped in the night after destroying a large quantity of provisions, and breaking upwards of a thousand stand of arms; they left behind also seventy of their wounded. Their loss in killed, wounded and captured, in this action, was six hundred and thirty-three, of whom five hundred were prisoners; the loss sustained by the Americans in killed, wounded and missing, was five hundred and thirty-five. One of the slain most deplored was Colonel Campbell, who had so bravely led on the Virginians.

Stuart met with reinforcements about fourteen miles from Eutaw, but continued his retreat to Monk's Corner, within twenty-five miles of Charleston. Greene followed with his main force almost to Monk's Corner: finding the number and position of the enemy too strong to be attacked with prudence, he fell back to Eutaw, where he remained a day or two to rest his troops, and then returned by easy marches to his old position near the heights of Santee.

CHAPTER LXV.
SIEGE AND SURRENDER OF YORKTOWN.

General Lincoln had the honor, on the night of the 6th of October, of opening the first parallel before Yorktown. It was within six hundred yards of the enemy; nearly two miles in extent, and the foundations were laid for two redoubts. He had under him a large detachment of French and American troops, and the work was conducted with such silence and secrecy in a night of extreme darkness, that the enemy were not aware of it until daylight. A severe cannonade was then opened from the fortifications; but the men were under cover and continued working. By the afternoon of the 9th the parallel was completed, and two or three batteries were ready to fire upon the town. "General Washington put the match to the first gun," says an observer who was present; "a furious discharge of cannon and mortars immediately followed, and Earl Cornwallis received his first salutation."

The cannonade was kept up almost incessantly for three or four days from the batteries above mentioned, and from three others managed by the French. The half-finished works of the enemy suffered severely, the guns were dismounted or silenced, and many men killed. The red-hot shot from the French batteries northwest of the town reached the English shipping. The Charon, a forty-four gun ship, and three large transports, were set on fire by them. The flames ran up the rigging to the tops of the masts. The conflagration, seen in the darkness of the night, with the accompanying flash and thundering of cannon, and soaring and bursting of shells, and the tremendous explosions of the ships, all presented a scene of mingled magnificence and horror.

On the night of the 11th the second parallel was opened by the Baron Steuben's division, within three hundred yards of the works. The British now made new embrasures, and for two or three days kept up a galling fire upon those at work. The latter were still more annoyed by the flanking fire of two redoubts three hundred yards in front of the British works. As they enfiladed the intrenchments, and were supposed also to command the communication between Yorktown and Gloucester, it was resolved to storm them both on the night of the 14th; the one nearest the river by a detachment of Americans commanded by Lafayette, the other by a French detachment led by the Baron de Viomenil. In the arrangements for the assault, Lafayette had given the honor of leading the advance to his own aide-de-camp, Lieutenant-colonel Gimat. This instantly touched the military pride of Hamilton, who exclaimed against it as an unjust preference, it being his tour of duty. It was therefore arranged that Colonel Gimat's battalion should lead the van, and be followed by that of Hamilton, and that the latter should command the whole advanced corps.

About eight o'clock in the evening rockets were sent up as signals for the simultaneous attack. Hamilton, to his great joy, led the advance of the Americans. The men, without waiting for the sappers to demolish the abatis in regular style, pushed them aside or pulled them down with their hands, and scrambled over, like rough bush-fighters. Hamilton was the first to mount the parapet, placing one foot on the shoulder of a soldier, who knelt on one knee for the purpose. The men mounted after him. Not a musket was fired. The redoubt was carried at the point of the bayonet. The loss of the Americans was one sergeant and eight privates killed, seven officers and twenty-five non-commissioned officers and privates wounded. The loss of the enemy was eight killed and seventeen taken prisoners. Among the latter was Major Campbell, who had commanded the redoubt.

The French stormed the other redoubt, which was more strongly garrisoned, with equal gallantry, but less precipitation. They proceeded according to rule. The soldiers paused while the sappers removed the abatis, during which time they were exposed to a destructive fire, and lost more men than did the Americans in their headlong attack. The abatis being removed, the troops rushed to the assault. The Chevalier de Lameth, Lafayette's adjutant-general, was the first to mount the parapet of the redoubt, and received a volley at arms' length from the Hessians who manned it. Shot through both knees, he fell back into the ditch, and was conveyed away under care of his friend, the Count de Dumas. The Count de Deux-ponts, leading on the royal grenadiers of the same name, was likewise wounded. The grenadiers of the Gatinais regiment fought with true Gallic fire. One third of them were slain, and among them Captain de Sireuil, a valiant officer of chasseurs.

The redoubts thus taken were included the same night in the second parallel, and howitzers were mounted upon them the following day. The capture of them reduced Lord Cornwallis almost to despair. Writing that same day to Sir Henry Clinton, he observes, "My situation now becomes very critical; we dare not show a gun to their old batteries, and I expect that their new ones will open to-morrow morning.... The safety of the place is, therefore, so precarious, that I cannot recommend that the fleet and army should run great risk in endeavoring to save us," a generous abnegation of self on the part of the beleaguered commander. Had the fleet and army sailed, as he had been given to expect, about the 5th of October, they might have arrived in time to save his lordship; but at the date of the above letter they were still lingering in port. Delay of naval succor was fatal to British operations in this war.

The second parallel was now nearly ready to open. Cornwallis dreaded the effect of its batteries on his almost dismantled works. To retard the danger as much as possible, he ordered an attack on two of the batteries that were in the greatest state of forwardness, their guns to be spiked. It was made a little before daybreak of the 16th, by about three hundred and fifty men, under the direction of Lieutenant-colonel Abercrombie. The redoubts which covered the batteries were forced in gallant style, and several pieces of artillery hastily spiked. By this time the supporting troops from the trenches came up, and the enemy were obliged to retreat. The mischief had been done too hastily. The spikes were easily extracted, and before evening all the batteries and the parallel were nearly complete.

At this time the garrison could not show a gun on the side of the works exposed to attack, and the shells were nearly expended; the place was no longer tenable. Rather than surrender, Cornwallis determined to attempt an escape. His plan was to leave his sick and wounded and his baggage behind, cross over in the night to Gloucester Point, attack Choisy's camp before daybreak, mount his infantry on the captured cavalry horses, and on such other as could be collected on the road, push for the upper country by rapid marches until opposite the fords of the great rivers, then turn suddenly northward, force his way through Maryland, Pennsylvania and the Jerseys, and join Sir Henry Clinton in New York. It was a wild and daring scheme, but his situation was desperate, and the idea of surrender intolerable.

In pursuance of this design, sixteen large boats were secretly prepared; a detachment was appointed to remain and capitulate for the townspeople, the sick and the wounded; a large part of the troops were transported to the Gloucester side of the river before midnight, and the second division had actually embarked, when a violent storm of wind and rain scattered the boats, and drove them a considerable distance down the river. They were collected with difficulty. It was now too late to effect the passage of the second division before daybreak, and an effort was made to get back the division which had already crossed. It was not done until the morning was far advanced, and the troops in recrossing were exposed to the fire of the American batteries.

The hopes of Lord Cornwallis were now at an end. His works were tumbling in ruins about him, under an incessant cannonade; his garrison was reduced in number by sickness and death, and exhausted by constant watching and severe duty. Unwilling to expose the residue of the brave troops which had stood by him so faithfully, to the dangers and horrors of an assault, which could not fail to be successful, he ordered a parley to be beaten about ten o'clock on the morning of the 17th, and despatched a flag with a letter to Washington proposing a cessation of hostilities for twenty-four hours, and that two officers might be appointed by each side to meet and settle terms for the surrender of the posts of York and Gloucester. Washington felt unwilling to grant such delay, when reinforcements might be on the way for Cornwallis from New York. In reply, therefore, he requested that, previous to the meeting of commissioners, his lordship's proposals might be sent in writing to the American lines, for which purpose a suspension of hostilities during two hours from the delivery of the letter, would be granted. This was complied with; but as the proposals offered by Cornwallis were not all admissible, Washington drew up a schedule of such terms as he would grant, and transmitted it to his lordship.

The armistice was prolonged. Commissioners met, the Viscount de Noailles and Lieutenant-colonel Laurens on the part of the allies; Colonel Dundas and Major Ross on the part of the British. After much discussion, a rough draft was made of the terms of capitulation to be submitted to the British general. These Washington caused to be promptly transcribed, and sent to Lord Cornwallis early in the morning of the 19th, with a note expressing his expectation that they would be signed by eleven o'clock, and that the garrison would be ready to march out by two o'clock in the afternoon. Lord Cornwallis was fain to comply, and, accordingly, on the same day, the posts of Yorktown and Gloucester were surrendered to General Washington as commander-in-chief of the combined army; and the ships of war, transports and other vessels, to the Count de Grasse, as commander of the French fleet. The garrison of Yorktown and Gloucester, including the officers of the navy and seamen of every denomination, were to surrender as prisoners of war to the combined army; the land force to remain prisoners to the United States, the seamen to the King of France.[23] The garrison was to be allowed the same honors granted to the garrison of Charleston when it surrendered to Sir Henry Clinton. The officers were to retain their side arms; both officers and soldiers their private property, and no part of their baggage or papers was to be subject to search or inspection. The soldiers were to be kept in Virginia, Maryland, or Pennsylvania, as much by regiments as possible, and supplied with the same rations of provisions as the American soldiers. The officers were to be permitted to proceed, upon parole, to Europe or to any maritime port on the continent of America in possession of British troops.

On the following morning, Washington in general orders congratulated the allied armies on the recent victory, awarding high praise to the officers and troops both French and American, for their conduct during the siege, and specifying by name several of the generals and other officers who had especially distinguished themselves. All those of his army who were under arrest were pardoned and set at liberty.

Cornwallis felt deeply the humiliation of this close to all his wide and wild campaigning, and was made the more sensitive on the subject by circumstances of which he soon became apprised. On the very day that he had been compelled to lay down his arms before Yorktown, the lingering armament intended for his relief sailed from New York. It consisted of twenty-five ships-of-the-line, two fifty-gun ships, and eight frigates; with Sir Henry Clinton and seven thousand of his best troops. Sir Henry arrived off the capes of Virginia on the 24th, and gathered information which led him to apprehend that Lord Cornwallis had capitulated. He hovered off the mouth of the Chesapeake until the 29th, when, having fully ascertained that he had come too late, he turned his tardy prows toward New York.

In the meantime rejoicings spread throughout the Union. "Cornwallis is taken!" was the universal acclaim. It was considered a death-blow to the war. Congress gave way to transports of joy. Thanks were voted to the commander-in-chief, to the Counts De Rochambeau and De Grasse, to the officers of the allied armies generally, and to the corps of artillery and engineers especially. Two stands of colors, trophies of the capitulation, were voted to Washington, two pieces of field

[23] The number of prisoners amounted to 7,073, of whom 5,950 were rank and file, six commissioned, and twenty-eight non-commissioned officers and privates, had previously been captured in the two redoubts, or in the sortie of the garrison. The loss sustained by the garrison during the siege, in killed, wounded, and missing, amounted to 552. That of the combined army in killed was about 300. The combined army to which Cornwallis surrendered, was estimated at 16,000, of whom 7,000 were French, 5,500 continentals, and 3,500 militia.—*Holmes' Annals.*

ordnance to De Rochambeau and De Grasse; and it was decreed that a marble column, commemorative of the alliance between France and the United States, and of the victory achieved by their associated arms, should be erected in Yorktown. Finally, Congress issued a proclamation, appointing a day for general thanksgiving and prayer, in acknowledgment of this signal interposition of Divine Providence.

Far different was the feeling of the British ministry when news of the event reached the other side of the Atlantic. Lord George Germain was the first to announce it to Lord North at his office in Downing street. "And how did he take it?" was the inquiry. "As he would have taken a ball in the breast," replied Lord George, "for he opened his arms, exclaiming wildly as he paced up and down the apartment, 'Oh God! it is all over!'"

CHAPTER LXVI.

DISSOLUTION OF THE COMBINED ARMIES.—DIS-CONTENTS IN THE ARMY.

Washington would have followed up the reduction of Yorktown by a combined operation against Charleston, and addressed a letter to the Count de Grasse on the subject, but the count alleged in reply that the orders of his court, ulterior projects, and his engagements with the Spaniards, rendered it impossible to remain the necessary time for the operation.

The prosecution of the Southern war, therefore, upon the broad scale which Washington had contemplated, had to be relinquished; for, without shipping and a convoy, the troops and everything necessary for a siege would have to be transported by land with immense trouble, expense and delay; while the enemy, by means of their fleets, could reinforce or withdraw the garrison at pleasure. Under these circumstances, Washington had to content himself, for the present, with detaching two thousand Pennsylvania, Maryland, and Virginia Continental troops, under General St. Clair, for the support of General Greene, trusting that, with this aid, he would be able to command the interior of South Carolina, and confine the enemy to the town of Charleston.

A dissolution of the combined forces now took place. The Marquis St. Simon embarked his troops on the last of October, and the Count de Grasse made sail on the 4th of November, taking with him two beautiful horses which Washington had presented to him in token of cordial regard. Lafayette, seeing there was no probability of further active service in the present year, resolved to return to France on a visit to his family, and, with Washington's approbation, set out for Philadelphia to obtain leave of absence from Congress.

The British prisoners were marched to Winchester in Virginia, and Frederickstown in Maryland, and Lord Cornwallis and his principal officers sailed for New York on parole. The main part of the American army embarked for the Head of Elk, and returned northward under the command of General Lincoln, to be cantoned for the winter in the Jerseys and on the Hudson, so as to be ready for operations against New York, or elsewhere, in the next year's campaign. The French army were to remain for the winter in Virginia, and the Count de Rochambeau established his head-quarters at Williamsburg.

Having attended in person to the distribution of ordnance and stores, the departure of prisoners, and the embarkation of the troops under Lincoln, Washington left Yorktown on the 5th of November, and arrived the same day at Eltham, the seat of his friend Colonel Bassett. He arrived just in time to receive the last breath of John Parke Custis, the son of Mrs. Washington. The deceased had been an object of Washington's care from childhood, and had been cherished by him with paternal affection. Formed under his guidance and instructions, he had been fitted to take a part in the public concerns of his country, and had acquitted himself with credit as a member of the Virginia Legislature. He was but twenty-eight years old at the time of his death, and left a widow and four young children. It was an unexpected event, and the dying scene was rendered peculiarly affecting from the presence of the mother and wife of the deceased. As a consolation to Mrs. Washington in her bereavement, Washington adopted the two youngest children of the deceased, a boy and girl, who thenceforth formed a part of his immediate family.

From Eltham, Washington proceeded to Mount Vernon; but public cares gave him little leisure to attend to his private concerns. We have seen how repeatedly his steady mind had been exercised in the darkest times of the revolutionary struggle, in buoying up the public heart when sinking into despondency. He had now an opposite task to perform, to guard against an overweening confidence inspired by the recent triumph. In a letter to General Greene, he writes: "I shall remain but a few days here, and shall proceed to Philadelphia, when I shall attempt to stimulate Congress to the best improvement of our late success, by taking the most vigorous and effectual measures to be ready for an early and decisive campaign the next year. My greatest fear is, that Congress, viewing this stroke in too important a point of light, may think our work too nearly closed, and will fall into a state of languor and relaxation."

Towards the end of November, Washington was in Philadelphia, where Congress received him with distinguished honors. He lost no time in enforcing the policy respecting the ensuing campaign, which he had set forth in his letter to General Greene. His views were met by the military committee of Congress, with which he was in frequent consultation, and by the secretaries of war, finance, and public affairs, who attended their conferences. Under his impulse and personal supervision, the military arrangements for 1782 were made with unusual despatch. On the 10th of December resolutions were passed in Congress for requisitions of men and money from the several States; and Washington backed those requisitions by letters to the respective governors, urging prompt compliance. The persuasion that peace was at hand was, however, too prevalent for the public to be roused to new sacrifices and toils to maintain what was considered the mere shadow of a war. The States were slow in furnishing a small part of their respective quotas of troops, and still slower in answering to the requisitions for money. After remaining four months in Philadelphia, Washington set out in March to rejoin the army at Newburg on the Hudson.

In a recent letter to General Greene, Washington had expressed himself strongly on the subject of retaliation. "Of all laws it is the most difficult to execute, where you have not the transgressor himself in your possession. Humanity will ever interfere, and plead strongly against the sacrifice of an innocent person for the guilt of another." His judgment and feelings were soon put to the proof in this respect. A New York refugee, by the name of Philip White, had been captured by the Jersey people, and killed in attempting to escape. His partisans in New York determined on a signal revenge. Captain Joseph Huddy, who had been captured when bravely defending a blockhouse in Monmouth County, was now drawn forth from prison, conducted into the Jerseys by a party of refugees, headed by a Captain Lippencott, and hanged on the heights of Middletown. The neighboring country cried out for retaliation. Washington submitted the matter to a board of general and field-officers. It was unanimously determined that the offender should be demanded for execution, and, if not given up, that retaliation should be exercised on a British prisoner of equal rank. Washington accordingly sent proofs to Sir Henry Clinton of what he stigmatized as a murder, and demanded that the officer who commanded the execution of Captain Huddy should be given up. Sir Henry declined a compliance, but stated that he had ordered a strict inquiry into the circumstances of Captain Huddy's death, and would bring the perpetrators of it to immediate trial.

Washington about the same time received the copy of a resolution of Congress approving of his firm and judicious conduct, and promising to support him "in his fixed purpose of exemplary retaliation." He accordingly ordered a selection to be made by lot, for the above purpose, from among the British officers, prisoners at Lancaster, in Pennsylvania. The lot fell upon Captain Charles Asgill, of the guards, a youth only nineteen years of age, of an amiable character, and only son and heir of Sir Charles Asgill, a wealthy baronet. The youth bore his lot with firmness, but his fellow prisoners were incensed at Sir Henry Clinton for exposing him to such a fate by refusing to deliver up the culprit. One of their number, a son of the Earl of Ludlow, solicited permission from Washington to proceed to New York and lay the case before Sir Guy Carleton, who had succeeded in command to Sir Henry Clinton. The matter remained for some time in suspense.

Lippencott was at length tried by a court-martial, but acquitted, it appearing that he had acted under the verbal orders of Governor Franklin, president of the Board of Associated Loyalists. The British commander reprobated the death of Captain Huddy, and broke up the board.

These circumstances changed in some degree the ground upon which Washington was proceeding. He laid the whole matter before Congress, admitted Captain Asgill on parole at Morristown, and subsequently intimated to the secretary of war his private opinion in favor of his release, with permission to go to his friends in Europe. In the meantime Lady Asgill, the mother of the youth, had written a pathetic letter to the Count de Vergennes, the French minister of State, imploring his intercession in behalf of her son. The letter was shown to the king and queen, and by their direction the count wrote to Washington, soliciting the liberation of Asgill. Washington referred to Congress the communication from the count, and urged a favorable decision. To his great relief, he received their directions to set Captain Asgill at liberty.

The solicitude felt by Washington on account of the universal relaxation of the sinews of war, was not allayed by reports of pacific speeches, and motions made in the British parliament, which might be delusive. "Even if the nation and parliament," said he, "are really in earnest to obtain peace with America, it will, undoubtedly, be wisdom in us to meet them with great caution and circumspection, and by all means to keep our arms firm in our hands; and instead of relaxing one iota in our exertions, rather to spring forward with redoubled vigor, that we may take the advantage of every favorable opportunity, until our wishes are fully obtained. No nation ever yet suffered in treaty by preparing, even in the moment of negotiation, most vigorously for the field."

Sir Guy Carleton arrived in New York early in May to take the place of Sir Henry Clinton, who had solicited his recall. In a letter dated May 7th, Sir Guy informed Washington of his being joined with Admiral Digby in the commission of peace; he transmitted at the same time printed copies of the proceedings in the House of Commons on the 4th of March, respecting an address to the king in favor of peace; and of a bill reported in consequence thereof, authorizing the king to conclude a peace or truce with the revolted provinces of North America. As this bill, however, had not passed into a law when Sir Guy left England, it presented no basis for a negotiation; and was only cited by him to show the pacific disposition of the British nation, with which he professed the most zealous concurrence. Still, though multiplied circumstances gradually persuaded Washington of a real disposition on the part of Great Britain to terminate the war, he did not think fit to relax his preparations for hostilities.

On the 2d of August, Sir Guy Carleton and Admiral Digby wrote a joint letter to Washington, informing him that they were acquainted, by authority, that negotiations for a general peace had already been commenced at Paris, and that the independence of the United States would be proposed in the first instance by the British commissioner, instead of being made a condition of a general treaty. Even yet, Washington was wary. No offers had been made on the part of Great Britain for a general cessation of hostilities, and, although the British commanders were in a manner tied down by the resolves of the House of Commons, to a defensive war, only in the United States, they might be at liberty to transport part of their force to the West Indies, to act against the French possessions in that quarter. With these considerations he wrote to the Count de Rochambeau, then at Baltimore, advising him, for the good of the common cause, to march his troops to the banks of the Hudson, and form a junction with the American army. The junction took place about the middle of September. The French army crossed the Hudson at King's Ferry to Verplanck's Point, where the American forces were paraded under arms to welcome them.

[Great discontents prevailed at this time in the army, both among officers and men. The army was almost destitute, and there were days when the troops were absolutely in want of provisions. The pay of the officers, too, was greatly in arrear; many doubted whether they would ever receive the half-pay decreed to them by Congress for a term of years after the war, and fears began to be expressed that, in the event of peace, they would all be disbanded with their claims unliquidated and themselves cast upon the community penniless, and unfitted, by long military habitudes for the gainful pursuits of peace.]

[The army went into winter-quarters at Newburg, and in the leisure and idleness of a winter camp, the discontents among the officers had time to ferment. The arrearages of pay became a topic of constant and angry comment, and a memorial was addressed to Congress representing the hardships of the case, and proposing that a specific sum should be granted them for the money actually due, and as a commutation for half-pay. The memorial gave rise to prolonged discussions, and the winter passed without any definite measures on the subject. Meanwhile anonymous papers of a dangerous and incendiary character began to be circulated in the camp, and meetings were summoned having in view ulterior measures of redress. This Washington anticipated by summoning a meeting of the officers in his own name, which he addressed in a forcible and feeling manner, dwelling upon their services, the good intentions of Congress, and urging them in the most eloquent terms to turn a deaf ear to the specious arguments of those who were attempting "to open the flood-gates of civil discord, and deluge our rising empire in blood." His earnest appeal was of effect; resolutions were passed, declaring that no circumstances of distress or danger should induce them to sully the reputation and glory acquired at the price of their blood and eight years' faithful services. Washington now urged the subject upon the attention of Congress, and a resolution was concurred in commuting the half-pay into a sum equal to five years' whole pay.]

CHAPTER LXVII.

NEWS OF PEACE.—WASHINGTON'S FAREWELL TO THE ARMY, AND RESIGNATION OF HIS COMMISSION.

At length arrived the wished-for news of peace. A general treaty had been signed at Paris on the 20th of January. An armed vessel, the Triumph, belonging to the Count d'Estaing's squadron, arrived at Philadelphia from Cadiz, on the 23d of March, bringing a letter from the Marquis de Lafayette, to the President of Congress, communicating the intelligence. In a few days Sir Guy Carleton informed Washington, by letter, that he was ordered to proclaim a cessation of hostilities by sea and land.

A similar proclamation issued by Congress, was received by Washington on the 17th of April. Being unaccompanied by any instructions respecting the discharge of the part of the army with him, should the measure be deemed necessary, he found himself in a perplexing situation.

The accounts of peace received at different times had raised an expectation in the minds of those of his troops that had engaged "for the war," that a speedy discharge must be the consequence of the proclamation. Most of them could not distinguish between a proclamation of a cessation of hostilities and a definitive declaration of peace, and might consider any further claim on their military services an act of injustice. It was becoming difficult to enforce the discipline necessary to the coherence of an army. Washington represented these circumstances in a letter to the president, and earnestly entreated a prompt determination on the part of Congress, as to what was to be the period of the services of these men, and how he was to act respecting their discharge. He urged that, in discharging those who had been engaged "for the war," the non-commissioned officers and soldiers should be allowed to take with them, as their own property, and as a gratuity, their arms and accoutrements.

His letter produced a resolution in Congress, that the services of the men engaged in the war did not expire until the ratification of the definitive articles of peace; but that the commander-in-chief might grant furloughs to such as he thought proper, and that they should be allowed to take their arms with them. Washington availed himself freely of this permission: furloughs were granted without stint; the men set out singly or in small parties for their rustic homes, and the danger and inconvenience were avoided of disbanding large masses, at a time, of unpaid soldiery.

In the meantime Sir Guy Carleton was making preparations for the evacuation of the city of New York. On the 6th of May a personal conference took place between Washington and Sir Guy at Orangetown, about the transfer of posts in the United States held by the British troops, and the delivery of all property stipulated by the treaty to be given up to the Americans. On the 8th of May, Egbert Benson, William S. Smith, and Daniel Parker, were commissioned by Congress to inspect and superintend at New York the embarkation of persons and property in fulfilment of the seventh article of the provisional treaty.

The officers in the patriot camp on the Hudson were not without gloomy feelings at the thought of their approaching separation from each other. Eight years of dangers and hardships, shared in common and nobly sustained, had welded their hearts together, and made it hard to rend them asunder. Prompted by such feelings, General Knox suggested, as a mode of perpetuating the friendships thus formed, and keeping alive the brotherhood of the camp, the formation of a society composed of the officers of the army. The suggestion met with universal concurrence, and the hearty approbation of Washington. Meetings were held, at which the Baron Steuben, as senior officer, presided. A plan was drafted, and the society was organized.

In memory of the illustrious Roman, Lucius Quintius Cincinnatus, who retired from war to the peaceful duties of the citizen, it was to be called "The Society of the Cincinnati." The objects proposed by it were to preserve inviolate the rights and liberties for which they had contended; to promote and cherish national honor and union between the States; to maintain brotherly kindness toward each other, and extend relief to such officers and their families as might stand in need of it. The general society, for the sake of frequent communications, was to be divided into State societies, and these again into districts. Washington was chosen unanimously to officiate as president of it, until the first general meeting, to be held in May, 1784.

On the 8th of June, Washington addressed a letter to the governors of the several States on the subject of the dissolution of the army. The opening of it breathes that aspiration after the serene quiet of private life, which had been his dream of happiness throughout the storms and trials of his anxious career, but the full fruition of which he was never to realize. His letter then described the enviable condition of the citizens of America, and proceeded ably and eloquently to discuss what he considered the four things essential to the well-being, and even the existence of the United States as an independent power.

First. An indissoluble union of the States under one federal head, and a perfect acquiescence of the several States, in the full exercise of the prerogative vested in such a head by the constitution.

Second. A sacred regard to public justice in discharging debts and fulfilling contracts made by Congress, for the purpose of carrying on the war.

Third. The adoption of a proper peace establishment; in which care should be taken to place the militia throughout the Union on a regular, uniform and efficient footing.

And Fourth. A disposition among the people of the United States to forget local prejudices and policies; to make mutual concessions, and to sacrifice individual advantages to the interests of the community.

These four things Washington pronounced the pillars on which the glorious character must be supported. "Liberty is the basis; and whoever would dare to sap the foundation, or overturn the structure, under whatever specious pretext he may attempt it, will merit the bitterest execration and the severest punishment which can be inflicted by his injured country." We forbear to go into the ample and admirable reasoning with which he expatiates on these heads, and above all, enforces the sacred inviolability of the Union; they have become familiar with every American mind, and ought to govern every American heart.

Washington resolved to while away part of the time that must intervene before the arrival of the definitive treaty, by making a tour to the northern and western parts of the State, and visiting the places which had been the theatre of important military transactions. He had another object in view; he desired to facilitate as far as in his power the operations which would be necessary for occupying, as soon as evacuated by British troops, the posts ceded by the treaty of peace.

Governor Clinton accompanied him on the expedition. They set out by water from Newburg, ascended the Hudson to Albany, visited Saratoga and the scene of Burgoyne's surrender, embarked on Lake George, where light boats had been provided for them, traversed that beautiful lake so full of historic interest, proceeded to Ticonderoga and Crown Point; and after reconnoitring those eventful posts, returned to Schenectady, whence they proceeded up the valley of the Mohawk River. Having reached Fort Schuyler, formerly Fort Stanwix, they crossed over to Wood Creek, which empties into Oneida Lake, and affords the water communication with Ontario. They then traversed the country to the head of the eastern branch of the Susquehanna, and viewed Lake Otsego and the portage between that lake and the Mohawk River. Washington returned to head-quarters at Newburg on the 5th of August, after a tour of at least seven hundred and fifty miles, performed in nineteen days, and for the most part on horseback.

By a proclamation of Congress, dated 18th of October, all officers and soldiers absent on furlough were discharged from further service; and all others who had engaged to serve during the war, were to be discharged from and after the 3d of November. A small force only, composed of those who had enlisted for a definite time, were to be retained in service until the peace establishment should be organized. In general orders of November 2d, Washington, after adverting to this proclamation, adds: "It only remains for the commander-in-chief to address himself once more, and that for the last time, to the armies of the United States, however widely dispersed the individuals who compose them may be, and to bid them an affectionate and a long farewell."

He then goes on to make them one of those paternal addresses which so eminently characterize his relationship with his army, so different from that of any other commander. He takes a brief view of the glorious struggle from which they had just emerged; the unpromising circumstances under which they had undertaken it, and the signal interposition of Providence in behalf of their feeble condition; the unparalleled perseverance of the American armies for eight long years, through almost every possible suffering and discouragement; a perseverance which he justly pronounces to be little short of *a standing miracle*. Adverting then to the enlarged prospects of happiness opened by the confirmation of national independence and sovereignty, and the ample and profitable employments held out in a Republic so happily circumstanced, he exhorts them to maintain the strongest attachment to THE UNION, and to carry with them into civil society the most conciliatory dispositions; proving themselves not less virtuous and useful as citizens, than they had been victorious as soldiers.

Notwithstanding every exertion had been made for the evacuation of New York, such was the number of persons and the quantity of effects of all kinds to be conveyed away, that the month of November was far advanced before it could be completed. Sir Guy Carleton had given notice to Washington of the time he supposed the different posts would be vacated, that the Americans might be prepared to take possession of them. On the 21st the British troops were drawn in from the oft-disputed post of King's Bridge and from M'Gowan's Pass, also from the various posts on the eastern part of Long Island. Paulus Hook was relinquished on the following day, and the afternoon of the 25th of November was appointed by Sir Guy for the evacuation of the city and the opposite village of Brooklyn.

Washington, in the meantime, had taken his station at Harlem, accompanied by Governor Clinton, who, in virtue of his office, was to take charge of the city. They found there General Knox with the detachment from West Point. Sir Guy Carleton had intimated a wish that Washington would be at hand to take immediate possession of the city, and prevent all outrage, as he had been informed of a plot to plunder the place whenever the king's troops should be withdrawn. He had engaged, also, that the guards of the redoubts on the East River, covering the upper part of the town, should be the first to be withdrawn, and that an officer should be sent to give Washington's advanced guard information of their retiring.

Although Washington doubted the existence of any such plot as that which had been reported to the British commander, yet he took precautions accordingly. On the morning of the 25th the American troops, composed of dragoons, light infantry and artillery, moved from Harlem to the Bowery at the upper part of the city. There they remained until the troops in that quarter were withdrawn, when they marched into the city and took possession, the British embarking from the lower parts. A formal entry then took place of the military and civil authorities.

In the course of a few days Washington prepared to depart for Annapolis, where Congress was assembling, with the intention of asking leave to resign his command. A barge was in waiting about noon on the 4th of December at Whitehall ferry to convey him across the Hudson to Paulus Hook. The principal officers of the army assembled at Fraunces' Tavern, in the neighborhood of the ferry, to take a final leave of him. On entering the room, and finding himself surrounded by his old companions in arms, who shared with him so many scenes of hardship, difficulty, and danger, his agitated feelings overcame his usual self-command. Filling a glass of wine, and turning upon them his benignant but saddened countenance,

"With a heart full of love and gratitude," said he, "I now take leave of you, most devoutly wishing that your latter days may be as prosperous and happy as your former ones have been glorious and honorable." Having drunk his farewell benediction, he added with emotion, "I cannot come to each of you to take my leave, but shall be obliged if each of you will come and take me by the hand."

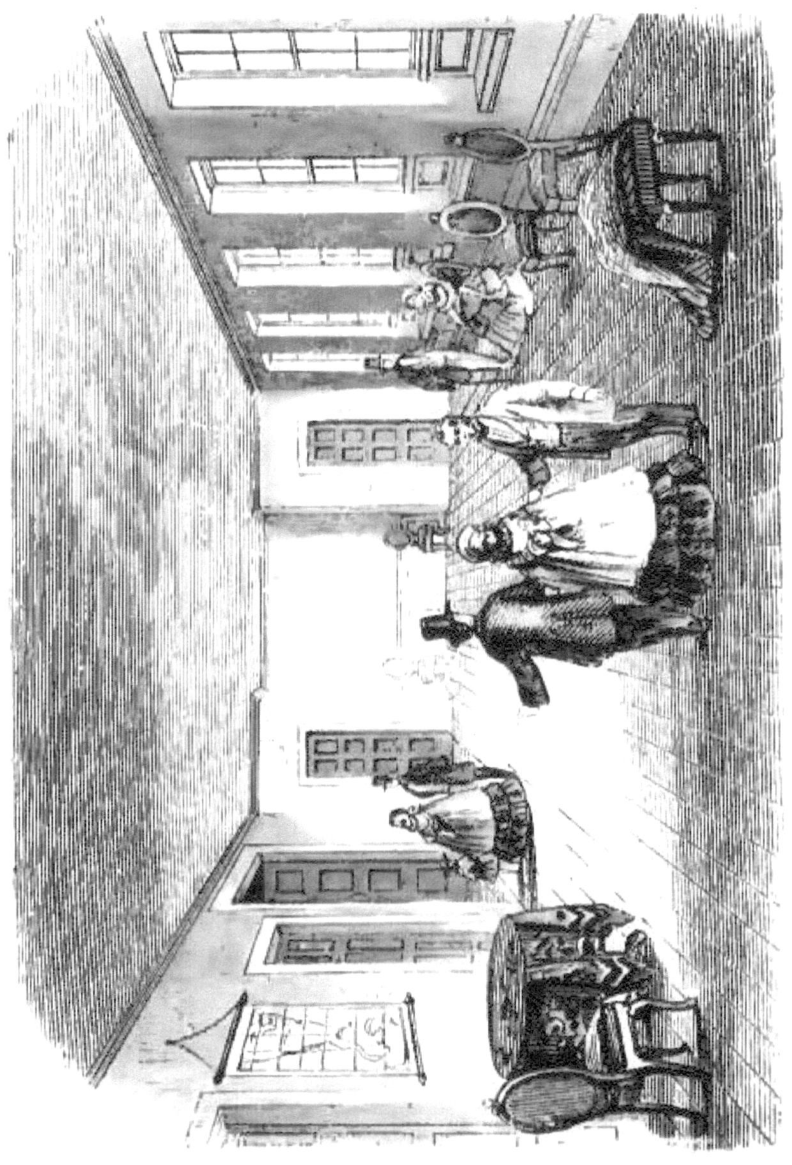

ROOM IN FRAUNCES' TAVERN.
VOL. IV.

General Knox, who was nearest, was the first to advance. Washington, affected even to tears, grasped his hand and gave him a brother's embrace. In the same affectionate manner he took leave severally of the rest. Not a word was spoken. The deep feeling and manly tenderness of these veterans in the parting moment could find no utterance in words. Silent and solemn they followed their loved commander as he left the room, passed through a corps of light infantry, and proceeded on foot to Whitehall ferry. Having entered the barge, he turned to them, took off his hat and waved a silent adieu. They replied in the same manner, and having watched the barge until the intervening point of the Battery shut it from sight, returned, still solemn and silent, to the place where they had assembled.

On his way to Annapolis, Washington stopped for a few days at Philadelphia, where with his usual exactness in matters of business, he adjusted with the Comptroller of the Treasury his accounts from the commencement of the war down to the 13th of the actual month of December. These were all in his own handwriting, and kept in the cleanest and most accurate manner, each entry being accompanied by a statement of the occasion and object of the charge. The gross amount was about fourteen thousand five hundred pounds sterling; in which were included moneys expended for secret intelligence and service, and in various incidental charges. All this, it must be noted, was an account of money actually expended in the progress of the war; not for arrearage of pay; for it will be recollected Washington accepted no pay.

In passing through New Jersey, Pennsylvania, and Maryland, the scenes of his anxious and precarious campaigns, Washington was everywhere hailed with enthusiasm by the people, and greeted with addresses by legislative assemblies, and learned and religious institutions. Being arrived at Annapolis, he addressed a letter to the President of Congress, on the 20th of December, requesting to know in what manner it would be most proper to offer his resignation; whether in writing or at an audience. The latter mode was adopted, and the Hall of Congress appointed for the ceremonial.

At twelve o'clock [the 23d,] the gallery, and a great part of the floor of the Hall of Congress, were filled with ladies, with public functionaries of the State, and with general officers. Washington entered, conducted by the secretary of Congress, and took his seat in a chair appointed for him. After a brief pause, the president (General Mifflin) informed him, that "the United States in Congress assembled, were prepared to receive his communication." Washington then rose, and delivered a short address.

"The great events," said he, "on which my resignation depended, having at length taken place, I now have the honor of offering my sincere congratulations to Congress, and of presenting myself before them, to surrender into their hands the trust committed to me, and to claim the indulgence of retiring from the service of my country."

After expressing his obligations to the army in general, and acknowledging the peculiar services and distinguished merits of the confidential officers who had been attached to his person, and composed his family during the war, and whom he especially recommended to the favor of Congress, he continued — "Having now finished the work assigned me, I retire from the great theatre of action; and, bidding an affectionate farewell to this august body, under whose orders I have long acted, I here offer my commission, and take my leave of all the employments of public life."

Having delivered his commission into the hands of the president, the latter, in reply to his address, bore testimony to the patriotism with which he had answered to the call of his country, and defended its invaded rights before it had formed alliances, and while it was without funds or a government to support him; to the wisdom and fortitude with which he had conducted the great military contest, invariably regarding the rights of the civil power, through all disasters and changes. "You retire," added he, "from the theatre of action with the blessings of your fellow-citizens; but the glory of your virtues will not terminate with your military command; it will continue to animate remotest ages."

The very next morning Washington left Annapolis, and hastened to his beloved Mount Vernon, where he arrived the same day, on Christmas-eve, in a frame of mind suited to enjoy the sacred and genial festival. "The scene is at last closed," said he in a letter to Governor Clinton; "I feel myself eased of a load of public care. I hope to spend the remainder of my days in cultivating the affections of good men, and in the practice of the domestic virtues."

CHAPTER LXVIII.
WASHINGTON AT MOUNT VERNON.

For some time after his return to Mount Vernon, Washington was in a manner locked up by the ice and snow of an uncommonly rigorous winter, so that social intercourse was interrupted, and he could not even pay a visit of duty and affection to his aged mother at Fredericksburg. But it was enough for him at present that he was at length at home at Mount Vernon. Yet the habitudes of the camp still haunted him; he could hardly realize that he was free from military duties; on waking in the morning he almost expected to hear the drum going its stirring rounds and beating the reveillé.

During the winter storms he anticipates the time when the return of the sun will enable him to welcome his friends and companions in arms to partake of his hospitality; and lays down his unpretending plan of receiving the curious visitors who are likely to throng in upon him. "My manner of living," writes he to a friend, "is plain, and I do not mean to be put out of it. A glass of wine and a bit of mutton are always ready; and such as will be content to partake of them, are always welcome. Those who expect more will be disappointed." Some degree of economy was necessary, for his financial concerns had suffered during the war, and the products of his estate had fallen off during his long absence.

In the meantime the supreme council of Pennsylvania, properly appreciating the disinterestedness of his conduct, aware that popular love and popular curiosity would attract crowds of visitors to Mount Vernon, and subject him to extraordinary expenses, had instructed their delegates in Congress to call the attention of that body to these circumstances, with a view to produce some national reward for his eminent services. Before acting upon these instructions, the delegates were directed to send a copy of them to Washington for his approbation.

He received the document while buried in accounts and calculations, and when, had he been of a mercenary disposition, the offered intervention in his favor would have seemed most seasonable; but he at once most gratefully and respectfully declined it, jealously maintaining the satisfaction of having served his country at the sacrifice of his private interests.

As spring advanced, Mount Vernon, as had been anticipated, began to attract numerous visitors. They were received in the frank, unpretending style Washington had determined upon. It was truly edifying to behold how easily and contentedly he subsided from the authoritative commander-in-chief of armies into the quiet country gentleman. There was nothing awkward or violent in the transition.

He seemed to be in his natural element. Mrs. Washington, too, who presided with quiet dignity at head-quarters, and cheered the wintry gloom of Valley Forge with her presence, presided with equal amenity and grace at the simple board of Mount Vernon. She had a cheerful good sense that always made her an agreeable companion, and was an excellent manager.

In entering upon the out-door management of his estate, Washington was but doing in person what he had long been doing through others. He had never virtually ceased to be the agriculturist. Throughout all his campaigns he had kept himself informed of the course of rural affairs at Mount Vernon. By means of maps on which every field was laid down and numbered, he was enabled to give directions for their several cultivation, and receive accounts of their several crops. No hurry of affairs prevented a correspondence with his overseer or agent, and he exacted weekly reports. Thus his rural were interwoven with his military cares; the agriculturist was mingled with the soldier.

The Fairfaxes, the kind friends of his boyhood, and social companions of his riper years, were no longer at hand to share his pleasures and lighten his cares. There were no more hunting dinners at Belvoir. George William Fairfax, its former possessor, was in England; his political principles had detained him there during the war, and part of his property had been sequestered. Old Lord Fairfax, the Nimrod of Greenway Court, Washington's early friend and patron, with whom he had first learned to follow the hounds, had lived on in a green old age at his sylvan retreat in the beautiful valley of the Shenandoah; popular with his neighbors and unmolested by the Whigs, although frank and open in his adherence to Great Britain. He had attained his ninety-second year, when tidings of the surrender of Yorktown wounded the national pride of the old cavalier to the quick, and snapped the attenuated thread of his existence.

On the 17th of August, Washington was gladdened by having the Marquis de Lafayette under his roof, who had recently arrived from France. The marquis passed a fortnight with him, a loved and cherished guest, at the end of which he departed for a time, to be present at the ceremony of a treaty with the Indians.

Washington now prepared for a tour to the west of the Appalachian Mountains, to visit his lands on the Ohio and Kanawha Rivers. Dr. Craik, the companion of his various campaigns, and who had accompanied him in 1770 on a similar tour, was to be his fellow-traveller. His original intention had been to survey and inspect his lands on the Monongahela River; then to descend the Ohio to the great Kanawha, where also he had large tracts of wild land. On arriving on the Monongahela, however, he heard such accounts of discontent and irritation among the Indian tribes, that he did not consider it prudent to venture among them. Some of his land on the Monongahela was settled; the rest was in the wilderness, and of little value in the present unquiet state of the country. He abridged his tour, therefore; proceeded no further west than the Monongahela; ascended that river, and then struck southward through the wild, unsettled regions of the Alleghanies, until he came out into the Shenandoah Valley near Staunton. He returned to Mount Vernon on the 4th of October.

During all this tour he had carefully observed the course and character of the streams flowing from the west into the Ohio, and the distance of their navigable parts from the head navigation of the rivers east of the mountains, with the nearest and best portage between them. For many years he had been convinced of the practicability of an easy and short communication between the Potomac and James Rivers, and the waters of the Ohio, and thence on to the great chain of lakes; and of the vast advantages that would result therefrom to the States of Virginia and Maryland. He had even attempted to set a company on foot to undertake at their own expense the opening of such a communication, but the breaking out of the Revolution had put a stop to the enterprise. One object of his recent tour was to make observations and collect information on the subject; and all that he had seen and heard quickened his solicitude to carry the scheme into effect. [He set forth his views upon the subject to Benjamin Harrison, governor of Virginia, urging its importance to the State, and predicting that New York would lose no time in forming communication by water with the western lakes. The governor laid the letter before the State legislature, and Washington was induced to go to Richmond to give the measure his personal support.]

In a letter to Richard Henry Lee, recently chosen President of Congress, he urged it upon his attention; suggesting that the western waters should be explored, their navigable capabilities ascertained, and that a complete map should be made of the country. In the latter part of December he was at Annapolis, at the request of the Assembly of Virginia, to arrange matters with the Assembly of Maryland respecting it. Through his indefatigable exertions two companies were formed under the patronage of the governments of these States, for opening the navigation of the Potomac and James Rivers, and he was appointed president of both. By a unanimous vote of the Assembly of Virginia, fifty shares in the Potomac, and one hundred in the James River Company, were appropriated for his benefit.

Washington was exceedingly embarrassed by the appropriation. To decline so noble and unequivocal a testimonial of the good opinion and good will of his countrymen might be construed into disrespect, yet he wished to be perfectly free to exercise his judgment and express his opinions in the matter, without being liable to the least suspicion of interested motives. While, however, he declined to receive the proffered shares for his own benefit, he intimated a disposition to receive them in trust, to be applied to the use of some object or institution of a public nature. His wishes were complied with, and the shares were ultimately appropriated by him to institutions devoted to public education. Yet, though the love for his country would thus interfere with his love for his home, the dream of rural retirement at Mount Vernon still went on.

At the opening of the year (1785) the entries in his diary show him diligently employed in preparations to improve his groves and shrubbery. On the 10th of January he notes that the white thorn is full in berry. On the 20th he begins to clear the pine groves of undergrowth. In February he transplants ivy under the walls of the garden to which it still clings. In March he is planting hemlock trees, that most beautiful species of American evergreen, numbers of which had been brought hither from Occoquan. In April he is sowing holly berries in drills, some adjoining a green-briar hedge on the north side of the garden gate; others in a semicircle on the lawn. Many of the holly bushes thus produced, are still flourishing about the place in full vigor.

We find in his diary noted down with curious exactness each day's labor and the share he took in it; his frequent rides to the Mill Swamp, the Dogue Creek, the "Plantation of the Neck," and other places along the Potomac in quest of young elms, ash trees, white thorn, crab-apples, maples, mulberries, willows and lilacs; the winding walks which he lays out, and the trees and shrubs which he plants along them. Now he sows acorns and buck-eye nuts brought by himself from the Monongahela; now he opens vistas through the Pine Grove, commanding distant views through the woodlands; and now he twines round his columns scarlet honeysuckles, which his gardener tells him will blow all the summer.

The ornamental cultivation of which we have spoken was confined to the grounds appertaining to what was called the mansion-house farm; but his estate included four other farms, all lying contiguous, and containing three thousand two hundred and sixty acres; each farm having its bailiff or overseer, with a house for his accommodation, barns and out-houses for the produce, and cabins for the negroes. On a general map of the estate, drawn out by Washington himself, these farms were all laid down accurately and their several fields numbered; he knew the soil and local qualities of each, and regulated the culture of them accordingly. In addition to these five farms there were several hundred acres of fine woodland, so that the estate presented a beautiful diversity of land and water. In the stables near the mansion-house were the carriage and saddle horses, of which he was very choice; on the four farms there were 54 draught horses, 12 mules, 317 head of black cattle, 360 sheep, and a great number of swine, which last ran at large in the woods.

In the management of his estate he was remarkably exact. No negligence on the part of the overseers or those under them was passed over unnoticed. He seldom used many words on the subject of his plans; rarely asked advice; but, when once determined, carried them directly and silently into execution; and was not easily dissuaded from a project when once commenced.

While Washington was thus calmly employed, came a letter from Henry Lee, who was now in Congress, conveying a mournful piece of intelligence: "Your friend and second, the patriot and noble Greene, is no more. Universal grief reigns here." Greene died on the 18th of June, at his estate of Mulberry Grove, on Savannah River, presented to him by the State of Georgia. His last illness was brief; caused by a stroke of the sun; he was but forty-four years of age. The news of his death struck heavily on Washington's heart, to whom, in the most arduous trials of the Revolution, he had been a second self. He had taken Washington as his model, and possessed naturally many of his great qualities. Like him, he was sound in judgment; persevering in the midst of discouragements; calm and self-possessed in time of danger; heedful of the safety of others; heedless of his own. Like him, he was modest and unpretending, and like him he had a perfect command of temper.

Other deaths pressed upon Washington's sensibility about the same time. That of General McDougall, who had served his country faithfully through the war, and since with equal fidelity in Congress. That, too, of Colonel Tench Tilghman, for a long time one of Washington's aides-de-camp, and "who left," writes he, "as fair a reputation as ever belonged to a human character." "Thus," adds he, "some of the pillars of the Revolution fall. Others are mouldering by insensible degrees. May our country never want props to support the glorious fabric!"

CHAPTER LXIX.

THE CONSTITUTIONAL CONVENTION.—WASH-INGTON ELECTED PRESIDENT.

From his quiet retreat of Mount Vernon, Washington, though ostensibly withdrawn from public affairs, was watching with intense solicitude the working together of the several parts in the great political confederacy; anxious to know whether the thirteen distinct States, under the present organization, could form a sufficiently efficient general government. He was daily becoming more and more doubtful of the solidity of the fabric he had assisted to raise. The form of confederation which had bound the States together and met the public exigencies during the Revolution, when there was a pressure of external danger, was daily proving more and more incompetent to the purposes of a national government. Congress had devised a system of credit to provide for the national expenditure and the extinction of the national debts, which amounted to something more than forty millions of dollars. The system experienced neglect from some States and opposition from others; each consulting its local interests and prejudices, instead of the interests and obligations of the whole. In like manner treaty stipulations, which bound the good faith of the whole, were slighted, if not violated by individual States, apparently unconscious that they must each share in the discredit thus brought upon the national name.

In letters to his correspondents Washington writes: "The confederation appears to me to be little more than a shadow without the substance, and Congress a nugatory body; their ordinances being little attended to.... The wheels of government are clogged, and our brightest prospects, and that high expectation which was entertained of us by the wondering world, are turned into astonishment; and from the high ground on which we stood, we are descending into the vale of confusion and darkness." ... "I have ever been a friend to adequate powers in Congress, without which it is evident to me we never shall establish a national character, or be considered as on a respectable footing by the powers of Europe. We are either a united people under one head and for federal purposes, or we are thirteen independent sovereignties, eternally counteracting each other." ... "We have probably had too good an opinion of human nature in forming our confederation. Experience has taught us that men will not adopt and carry into execution measures the best calculated for their own good, without the intervention of coercive power. I do not conceive we can exist long as a nation, without lodging, somewhere, a power which will pervade the whole Union in as energetic a manner as the authority of the State governments extends over the several States.... We are apt to run from one extreme to another. I am told that even respectable characters speak of a monarchial form of government without horror. From thinking proceeds speaking, thence acting is often but a single step. But how irrevocable and tremendous! What a triumph for our enemies to verify their predictions! What a triumph for the advocates of despotism to find that we are incapable of governing ourselves, and that systems, founded on the basis of equal liberty, are merely ideal and fallacious! Would to God that wise measures may be taken in time to avert the consequences we have but too much reason to apprehend."

His anxiety on the subject was quickened by accounts of discontents and commotions in the Eastern States produced by the pressure of the times, the public and private indebtedness, and the imposition of heavy taxes, at a moment of financial embarrassment. General Knox, now Secretary at War, who had been sent by Congress to Massachusetts to inquire into these troubles, thus writes about the insurgents: "Their creed is, that the property of the United States has been protected from the confiscation of Britain by the joint exertions of *all*, and therefore ought to be *the common property of all*, and he that attempts opposition to this creed is an enemy to equity and justice, and ought to be swept from off the face of the earth." Again: "They are determined to annihilate all debts, public and private, and have agrarian laws, which are easily effected by the means of unfunded paper, which shall be a tender in all cases whatever."

In reply to Colonel Henry Lee in Congress, who had addressed several letters to him on the subject, Washington writes: "You talk, my good sir, of employing influence to appease the present tumults in Massachusetts. I know not where that influence is to be found, or, if attainable, that it would be a proper remedy for the disorders. *Influence* is not *government*. Let us have a government by which our lives, liberties and properties will be secured, or let us know the worst at once. There is a call for decision. Know precisely what the insurgents aim at. If they have *real* grievances, redress them, if possible; or acknowledge the justice of them, and your inability to do it at the moment. If they have not, employ the force of government against them at once.... Let the reins of government, then, be braced and held with a steady hand, and every violation of the constitution be reprehended. If defective, let it be amended; but not suffered to be trampled upon whilst it has an existence."

A letter to him from his former aide-de-camp, Colonel Humphreys, dated New Haven, November 1st, says: "The troubles in Massachusetts still continue. Government is prostrated in the dust, and it is much to be feared that there is not energy enough in that State to re-establish the civil powers. The leaders of the mob, whose fortunes and measures are desperate, are strengthening themselves daily; and it is expected that they will soon take possession of the Continental magazine at Springfield, in which there are from ten to fifteen thousand stand of arms in excellent order. A general want of compliance with the requisitions of Congress for money seems to prognosticate that we are rapidly advancing to a crisis. Congress, I am told, are seriously alarmed, and hardly know which way to turn or what to expect. Indeed, my dear General, nothing but a good Providence can extricate us from the present convulsion."

"What, gracious God! is man," writes Washington, "that there should be such inconsistency and perfidiousness in his conduct. It was but the other day that we were shedding our blood to obtain the constitutions under which we now live; constitutions of our own choice and making; and now we are unsheathing the sword to overturn them.... How melancholy is the reflection, that in so short a time we should have made such large strides towards fulfilling the predictions of our transatlantic foes! 'Leave them to themselves, and their government will soon dissolve.' Will not the wise and good strive hard to avert this evil? Or will their supineness suffer ignorance and the arts of self-interested and designing, disaffected and desperate characters, to involve this great country in wretchedness and contempt? What stronger evidence can be given of the want of energy in our government than these disorders? If there is not power in it to check them, what security has a man for life, liberty, or property?"

Thus Washington, even though in retirement, was almost unconsciously exercising a powerful influence on national affairs; no longer the soldier, he was now becoming the statesman. The opinions and counsels given in his letters were widely effective. The expedient for federate organization, had extended and ripened in legislative Assemblies, and ended in a plan of a convention composed of delegates from all the States, to meet in Philadelphia for the sole and express purpose of revising the federal system, and correcting its defects; the proceedings of the convention to be subsequently reported to Congress, and the several Legislatures, for approval and confirmation.

Washington was unanimously put at the head of the Virginia delegation, but for some time objected to accept the nomination. He feared to be charged with inconsistency in again appearing in a public situation, after his declared resolution to the contrary. These considerations were strenuously combated, for the weight and influence of his name and counsel were felt to be all-important in giving dignity to the delegation. Two things contributed to bring him to a favorable decision: First, an insinuation that the opponents of the convention were monarchists, who wished the distractions of the country should continue, until a monarchial government might be resorted to as an ark of safety. The other was the insurrection in Massachusetts. Before the time arrived for the meeting of the convention, which was the second Monday in May, his mind was relieved from poignant solicitude, by learning that the insurrection in Massachusetts had been suppressed with but little bloodshed, and that the principals had fled to Canada.

On the 9th of May, Washington set out from Mount Vernon to attend the convention. It was not until the 25th of May that a sufficient number of delegates were assembled to form a quorum, when they proceeded to organize the body, and by a unanimous vote Washington was called up to the chair as President.

We forbear to go into the voluminous proceedings of this memorable convention, which occupied from four to seven hours each day for four months; and in which every point was the subject of able and scrupulous discussion by the best talent and noblest spirits of the country. Washington felt restrained by his situation as President from taking a part in the debates, but his well-known opinions influenced the whole. The result was the formation of the constitution of the United States, which (with some amendments made in after years) still exists.

The constitution thus formed was forwarded to Congress, and thence transmitted to the State Legislatures, each of which submitted it to a State convention composed of delegates chosen for that express purpose by the people. The ratification of the instrument by nine States was necessary to carry it into effect; and as the several State conventions would assemble at different times, nearly a year must elapse before the decisions of the requisite number could be obtained. During this time, Washington resumed his retired life at Mount Vernon, seldom riding, as he says, beyond the limits of his own farms, but kept informed by his numerous correspondents, such as James Madison, John Jay, and Generals Knox, Lincoln and Armstrong, of the progress of the constitution through its various ordeals, and of the strenuous opposition which it met with in different quarters, both in debate and through the press.

The testimonials of ratification having been received by Congress from a sufficient number of States, an act was passed by that body on the 13th of September, appointing the first Wednesday in January, 1789, for the people of the United States to choose electors of a President according to the constitution, and the first Wednesday in the month of February following for the electors to meet and make a choice. The meeting of the government was to be on the first Wednesday in March, and in the city of New York.

Before the official forms of an election could be carried into operation, a unanimous sentiment throughout the Union pronounced Washington the nation's choice to fill the presidential chair. He looked forward to the possibility of his election with characteristic modesty and unfeigned reluctance; as his letters to his confidential friends bear witness. "It has no fascinating allurements for me," writes he to Lafayette. "At my time of life and under my circumstances, the increasing infirmities of nature and the growing love of retirement do not permit me to entertain a wish beyond that of living and dying an honest man on my own farm. Let those follow the pursuits of ambition and fame who have a keener relish for them, or who may have more years in store for the enjoyment."

The election took place at the appointed time, and it was soon ascertained that Washington was chosen President for the term of four years from the 4th of March. By this time the arguments and entreaties of his friends, and his own convictions of public expediency, had determined him to accept; and he made preparations to depart for the seat of government as soon as he should receive official notice of his election. Among other duties he paid a visit to his mother at Fredericksburg; it was a painful, because likely to be a final one, for she was afflicted with a malady which, it was evident, must soon terminate her life. Their parting was affectionate, but solemn; she had always been reserved and moderate in expressing herself in regard to the successes of her son; but it must have been a serene satisfaction at the close of her life to see him elevated by his virtues to the highest honor of his country.

From a delay in forming a quorum of Congress the votes of the electoral college were not counted until early in April, when they were found to be unanimous in favor of Washington. On the 14th of April, he received a letter from the president of Congress, duly notifying him of his election; and he prepared to set out immediately for New York, the seat of government.

His progress was a continued ovation. The ringing of bells and roaring of cannonry proclaimed his course through the country. The old and young, women and children, thronged the highways to bless and welcome him. Deputations of the most respectable inhabitants from the principal places came forth to meet and escort him. At Baltimore, on his arrival and departure, his carriage was attended by a numerous cavalcade of citizens, and he was saluted by the thunder of artillery. At the frontier of Pennsylvania he was met by his former companion-in-arms, Mifflin, now governor of the State, who with Judge Peters and a civil and military escort, was waiting to receive him. Washington had hoped to be spared all military parade, but found it was not to be evaded. At Chester, where he stopped to breakfast, there were preparations for a public entrance into Philadelphia. Cavalry had assembled from the surrounding country; a superb white horse was led out for Washington to mount, and a grand procession set forward, with General St. Clair, of revolutionary notoriety, at its head. It gathered numbers as it advanced; passed under triumphal arches entwined with laurel, and entered Philadelphia amid the shouts of the multitude.

We question whether any of these testimonials of a nation's gratitude affected Washington more sensibly than those he received at Trenton. It was on a sunny afternoon when he arrived on the banks of the Delaware, where, twelve years before, he had crossed in darkness and storm, through clouds of snow and drifts of floating ice, on his daring attempt to strike a blow at a triumphant enemy. On the bridge crossing that eventful stream, the ladies of Trenton had caused a triumphal arch to be erected. It was entwined with evergreens and laurels, and bore the inscription, "The defender of the mothers will be the protector of the daughters." At this bridge the matrons of the city were assembled to pay him reverence; and as he passed under the arch, a number of young girls, dressed in white and crowned with garlands, strewed flowers before him, singing an ode expressive of their love and gratitude. Never was ovation more graceful, touching and sincere; and Washington, tenderly affected, declared that the impression of it on his heart could never be effaced.

In respect to his reception at New York, Washington had signified in a letter to Governor Clinton, that none could be so congenial to his feelings as a quiet entry devoid of ceremony; but his modest wishes were not complied with. At Elizabethtown Point, a committee of both Houses of Congress, with various civic functionaries, waited by appointment to receive him. He embarked on board of a splendid barge, constructed for the occasion. It was manned by thirteen branch pilots, masters of vessels, in white uniforms, and commanded by Commodore Nicholson. Other barges fancifully decorated followed, having on board the heads of departments and other public officers, and several distinguished citizens. As they passed through the strait between the Jerseys and Staten Island, called the Kills, other boats decorated with flags fell in their wake, until the whole, forming a nautical procession, swept up the broad and beautiful bay of New York to the sound of instrumental music.

He approached the landing-place of Murray's Wharf amid the ringing of bells, the roaring of cannonry, and the shouting of multitudes collected on every pier-head. On landing he was received by Governor Clinton. General Knox, too, who had taken such affectionate leave of him on his retirement from military life, was there to welcome him in his civil capacity. Other of his fellow-soldiers of the Revolution were likewise there, mingled with the civic dignitaries.

Carpets had been spread to a carriage prepared to convey him to his destined residence, but he preferred to walk. He was attended by a long civil and military train. In the streets through which he passed the houses were decorated with flags, silken banners, garlands of flowers and evergreens, and bore his name in every form of ornament. The streets were crowded with people, so that it was with difficulty a passage could be made by the city officers.

The inauguration was delayed for several days, in which a question arose as to the form or title by which the President elect was to be addressed, and a committee in both Houses was appointed to report upon the subject. It was finally resolved that the address should be simply "the President of the United States," without any addition of title; a judicious form which has remained to the present day.

The inauguration took place on the 30th of April. At nine o'clock in the morning there were religious services in all the churches. At twelve o'clock the city troops paraded before Washington's door, and soon after the committees of Congress and heads of departments came in their carriages. At half-past twelve the procession moved forward, preceded by the troops; next came the committees and heads of departments in their carriages; then Washington in a coach of state, his aide-de-camp, Colonel Humphreys, and his secretary, Mr. Lear, in his own carriage. The foreign ministers and a long train of citizens brought up the rear.

About two hundred yards before reaching the hall, Washington and his suite alighted from their carriages, and passed through the troops, who were drawn up on each side, into the hall and senate chamber, where the vice-president, the Senate and House of Representatives were assembled. The vice-president, John Adams, recently inaugurated, advanced and conducted Washington to a chair of state at the upper end of the room. A solemn silence prevailed, when the vice-president rose, and informed him that all things were prepared for him to take the oath of office required by the constitution.

The oath was to be administered by the Chancellor of the State of New York, in a balcony in front of the senate chamber, and in full view of an immense multitude occupying the street, the windows, and even roofs of the adjacent houses. The balcony formed a kind of open recess, with lofty columns supporting the roof. In the centre was a table with a covering of crimson velvet, upon which lay a superbly bound Bible on a crimson velvet cushion. This was all the paraphernalia for the august scene.

All eyes were fixed upon the balcony, when, at the appointed hour, Washington made his appearance, accompanied by various public functionaries, and members of the Senate and House of Representatives. He was clad in a full suit of dark-brown cloth, of American manufacture, with a steel-hilted dress sword, white silk stockings, and silver shoe-buckles. His hair was dressed and powdered in the fashion of the day, and worn in a bag and solitaire. His entrance on the balcony was hailed by universal shouts. He was evidently moved by this demonstration of public affection. Advancing to the front of the balcony, he laid his hand upon his heart, bowed several times, and then retreated to an arm-chair near the table. The populace appeared to understand that the scene had overcome him, and were hushed at once into profound silence.

After a few moments Washington rose and again came forward. John Adams, the vice-president, stood on his right; on his left the Chancellor of the State, Robert R. Livingston; somewhat in the rear were Roger Sherman, Alexander Hamilton, Generals Knox, St. Clair, the Baron Steuben and others. The chancellor advanced to administer the oath prescribed by the constitution, and Mr. Otis, the secretary of the Senate, held up the Bible on its crimson cushion. The oath was read slowly and distinctly; Washington at the same time laying his hand on the open Bible. When it was concluded, he replied solemnly, "I swear—so help me God!" The chancellor now stepped forward, waved his hand and exclaimed, "Long live George Washington, President of the United States!" At this moment a flag was displayed on the cupola of the hall; on which signal there was a general discharge of artillery on the battery. All the bells in the city rang out a joyful peal, and the multitude rent the air with acclamations.

Washington again bowed to the people and returned into the senate chamber, where he delivered, to both Houses of Congress, his inaugural address. After this he proceeded with the whole assemblage on foot to St. Paul's church, where prayers suited to the occasion were read by Dr. Prevost, Bishop of the Protestant Episcopal Church in New York, who had been appointed by the Senate one of the chaplains of Congress. So closed the ceremonies of the inauguration.

We have been accustomed to look to Washington's private letters for the sentiments of his heart. Those written to several of his friends immediately after his inauguration show how little he was excited by his official elevation. "I greatly fear," writes he, "that my countrymen will expect too much from me. I fear, if the issue of public measures should not correspond with their sanguine expectations, they will turn the extravagant, and I might almost say undue praises, which they are heaping upon me at this moment, into equally extravagant, though I will fondly hope unmerited censures." Little was his modest spirit aware that the praises so dubiously received were but the opening notes of a theme that was to increase from age to age, to pervade all lands and endure throughout all generations.

CHAPTER LXX.
ORGANIZATION OF THE NEW GOVERNMENT.

The eyes of the world were upon Washington at the commencement of his administration. He had won laurels in the field; would they continue to flourish in the cabinet? His position was surrounded by difficulties. Inexperienced in the duties of civil administration, he was to inaugurate a new and untried system of government, composed of States and people, as yet a mere experiment, to which some looked forward with buoyant confidence, many with doubt and apprehension. The constitution had met with vehement opposition, when under discussion in the General and State governments. Only three States, New Jersey, Delaware and Georgia, had accepted it unanimously. Several of the most important States had adopted it by a mere majority; five of them under an expressed expectation of specified amendments or modifications; while two States, Rhode Island and North Carolina, still stood aloof.

The very extent of the country he was called upon to govern, ten times larger than that of any previous republic, must have pressed with weight upon Washington's mind. It presented to the Atlantic a front of fifteen hundred miles, divided into individual States, differing in the forms of their local governments, differing from each other in interests, in territorial magnitudes, in amount of population, in manners, soils, climates and productions, and the characteristics of their several peoples. Beyond the Alleghanies extended regions almost boundless, as yet for the most part wild and uncultivated. Vast tracts, however, were rapidly being peopled, and would soon be portioned into sections requiring local governments. The great natural outlet for the exportation of the products of this region of inexhaustible fertility, was the Mississippi; but Spain opposed a barrier to the free navigation of this river. Here was peculiar cause of solicitude. Before leaving Mount Vernon, Washington had heard that the hardy yeomanry of the far West were becoming impatient of this barrier, and indignant at the apparent indifference of Congress to their prayers for its removal. He had heard, moreover, that British emissaries were fostering these discontents, sowing the seed of disaffection, and offering assistance to the Western people to seize on the city of New Orleans and fortify the mouth of the Mississippi; while, on the other hand, the Spanish authorities at New Orleans were represented as intriguing to effect a separation of the Western territory from the Union, with a view or hope of attaching it to the dominion of Spain.

Great Britain, too, was giving grounds for territorial solicitude in these distant quarters by retaining possession of the Western posts, the surrender of which had been stipulated by treaty. Her plea was, that debts due to British subjects, for which by the same treaty the Union States were bound, remained unpaid. This the Americans alleged was a mere pretext; the real object of their retention being the monopoly of the fur trade; and to the mischievous influence exercised by these posts over the Indian tribes, was attributed much of the hostile disposition manifested by the latter along the Western frontier.

While these brooding causes of anxiety existed at home, the foreign commerce of the Union was on a most unsatisfactory footing, and required prompt and thorough attention. It was subject to maraud, even by the corsairs of Algiers, Tunis and Tripoli, who captured American merchant vessels and carried their crews into slavery; no treaty having yet been made with any of the Barbary powers excepting Morocco.

To complete the perplexities which beset the new government, the finances of the country were in a lamentable state. There was no money in the treasury. The efforts of the former government to pay or fund its debts, had failed; there was a universal state of indebtedness, foreign and domestic, and public credit was prostrate.

Such was the condition of affairs when Washington entered upon his new field of action. As yet he was without the support of constitutional advisers, the departments under the new government not being organized; he could turn with confidence, however, for counsel in an emergency to John Jay, who still remained at the head of affairs, where he had been placed in 1784. He was sure of sympathy also in his old comrade, General Knox, who continued to officiate as secretary of war; while the affairs of the treasury were managed by a board, consisting of Samuel Osgood, Walter Livingston, and Arthur Lee. Among the personal friends not in office, to whom Washington felt that he could safely have recourse for aid in initiating the new government, was Alexander Hamilton. It was also a great satisfaction to Washington, on looking round for reliable advisers at this moment, to see James Madison among the members of Congress: Madison, who had been with him in the convention, who had labored in "The Federalist," and whose talents as a speaker, and calm, dispassionate reasoner; whose extensive information and legislative experience destined him to be a leader in the House. Highly appreciating his intellectual and moral worth, Washington would often turn to him for counsel.

The moment the inauguration was over, Washington was made to perceive that he was no longer master of himself or of his home. "By the time I had done breakfast," writes he, "and thence till dinner, and afterwards till bedtime, I could not get rid of the ceremony of one visit before I had to attend to another. In a word, I had no leisure to read or to answer the despatches that were pouring in upon me from all quarters."

How was he to be protected from these intrusions? What, too, were to be the forms and ceremonials to be adopted in the presidential mansion that would maintain the dignity of his station, allow him time for the performance of its official duties, and yet be in harmony with the temper and feelings of the people, and the prevalent notions of equality and republican simplicity? Looking round upon the able men at hand, such as Adams, Hamilton, Jay, Madison, he propounded to them a series of questions as to a line of conduct proper for him to observe.

In regard to visitors, for instance, would not one day in the week be sufficient for visits of compliment, and one hour every morning (at eight o'clock for example) for visits on business? Might he make social visits to acquaintances and public characters, not as President, but as private individual? And then as to his table—under the preceding form of government, the Presidents of Congress had been accustomed to give dinners twice a week to large parties of both sexes, and invitations had been so indiscriminate, that every one who could get introduced to the President conceived he had a right to be invited to his board. Washington was resolved not to give general entertainments of this kind, but in his series of questions he asked whether he might not invite, informally or otherwise, six, eight, or ten official characters, including in rotation the members of both Houses of Congress, to dine with him on the days fixed for receiving company, without exciting clamors in the rest of the community.

Adams in his reply talked of chamberlains, aides-de-camp, masters of ceremony, and evinced a high idea of the presidential office and the state with which it ought to be maintained. Two days in a week would be required for the receipt of visits of compliment. Persons desiring an interview with the President should make application through the minister of State. In every case the name, quality or business of the visitor should be communicated to a chamberlain or gentleman in waiting, who should judge whom to admit, and whom to exclude. The time for receiving visits ought to be limited, as for example, from eight to nine or ten o'clock, lest the whole morning be taken up. The President might invite what official character, members of Congress, strangers, or citizens of distinction he pleased, in small parties without exciting clamors; but this should always be done without formality. His private life should be at his own discretion, as to giving or receiving informal visits among friends and acquaintances; but in his official character, he should have no intercourse with society but upon public business, or at his levees.

Hamilton, in his reply, while he considered it a primary object for the public good that the dignity of the presidential office should be supported, advised that care should be taken to avoid so high a tone in the demeanor of the occupant, as to shock the prevalent notions of equality. The President, he thought, should hold a levee at a fixed time once a week, remain half an hour, converse cursorily on indifferent subjects with such persons as invited his attention, and then retire. He should accept no invitations, give formal entertainments twice, or at most, four times in the year; on levee days to give informal invitations to family dinners; not more than six or eight to be asked at a time, and the civility to be confined essentially to members of the legislature, and other official characters—the President never to remain long at table. The heads of departments should, of course, have access to the President on business. Foreign ministers of some descriptions should also be entitled to it. Members of the Senate should also have a right of *individual* access on matters relative to the *public administration*. The reason alleged by Hamilton for giving the Senate this privilege, and not the Representatives, was, that in the constitution "the Senate are coupled with the President in certain executive functions, treaties, and appointments. This makes them in a degree his constitutional counsellors, and give them a peculiar claim to the right of access."

These are the only written replies that we have before us of Washington's advisers on this subject. Colonel Humphreys, formerly one of Washington's aides-de-camp, and recently secretary of Jefferson's legation at Paris, was at present an inmate in the presidential mansion. General Knox was frequently there; to these Jefferson assures us, on Washington's authority, was assigned the task of considering and prescribing the minor forms and ceremonies, the etiquette, in fact, to be observed on public occasions. Some of the forms proposed by them, he adds, were adopted. Others were so highly strained that Washington absolutely rejected them.

On the 17th of May, Mrs. Washington, accompanied by her grandchildren, Eleanor Custis and George Washington Parke Custis set out from Mount Vernon in her travelling carriage with a small escort of horse, to join her husband at the seat of government: as she had been accustomed to join him at head-quarters, in the intervals of his revolutionary campaigns. Throughout the journey she was greeted with public testimonials of respect and affection.

On the following day [after her arrival in New York] Washington gave a demi-official dinner, of which Mr. Wingate, a senator from New Hampshire, who was present, writes as follows: "The guests consisted of the Vice-President, the foreign ministers, the heads of departments, the Speaker of the house of Representatives, and the Senators from New Hampshire and Georgia, the then most Northern and Southern States. It was the least showy dinner that I ever saw at the President's table, and the company was not large."

On the evening of the following day, (Friday, May 29th,) Mrs. Washington had a general reception, which was attended by all that were distinguished in official and fashionable society. Henceforward there were similar receptions every Friday evening, from eight to ten o'clock, to which the families of all persons of respectability, native or foreign, had access, without special invitation; and at which the President was always present. These assemblages were as free from ostentation and restraint as the ordinary receptions of polite society; yet the reader will find they were soon subject to invidious misrepresentation; and cavilled at as "court-like levees" and "queenly drawing-rooms."

In regard to the deportment of Washington at this juncture, we have been informed by one who had opportunities of seeing him, that he still retained a military air of command which had become habitual to him. At levees and drawing-rooms he sometimes appeared cold and distant, but this was attributed by those who best knew him to the novelty of his position and his innate diffidence, which seemed to increase with the light which his renown shed about him. Though reserved at times, his reserve had nothing repulsive in it, and in social intercourse, where he was no longer under the eye of critical supervision, soon gave way to soldier-like frankness and cordiality. At all times his courtesy was genuine and benignant, and totally free from that stately condescension sometimes mistaken for politeness. Nothing we are told could surpass the noble grace with which he presided at a ceremonial dinner; kindly attentive to all his guests, but particularly attentive to put those at their ease and in a favorable light who appeared to be most diffident.

Much has been said of Washington's equipages, when at New York, and of his having four and sometimes six horses before his carriage, with servants and outriders in rich livery. Such style we would premise was usual at the time both in England and the colonies, and had been occasionally maintained by the continental dignitaries, and by the Governors of the several States, prior to the adoption of the new constitution. It was still prevalent, we are told, among the wealthy planters of the South, and sometimes adopted by 'merchant princes' and rich individuals at the North.

As soon as Washington could command sufficient leisure to inspect papers and documents, he called unofficially upon the heads of departments to furnish him with such reports in writing as would aid him in gaining a distinct idea of the state of public affairs. For this purpose also he had recourse to the public archives, and proceeded to make notes of the foreign official correspondence from the close of the war until his inauguration. He was interrupted in his task by a virulent attack of anthrax, which for several days threatened mortification. The knowledge of his perilous condition spread alarm through the community; he, however, remained unagitated. His sufferings were intense, and his recovery was slow. For six weeks he was obliged to lie on his right side; but after a time he had his carriage so contrived that he could extend himself at full length in it, and take exercise in the open air.

While yet in a state of convalescence, Washington received intelligence of the death of his mother. The event, which took place at Fredericksburg in Virginia, on the 25th of August, was not unexpected; she was eighty-two years of age, and had for some time been sinking under an incurable malady, so that when he last parted with her he had apprehended that it was a final separation.

Hitherto the new government had not been properly organized, but its several duties had been performed by the officers who had them in charge at the time of Washington's inauguration. It was not until the 10th of September that laws were passed instituting a department of Foreign Affairs (afterwards termed Department of State,) a Treasury department, and a department of War, and fixing their respective salaries. On the following day, Washington nominated General Knox to the department of War, the duties of which that officer had hitherto discharged.

The post of Secretary of the Treasury was one of far greater importance at the present moment. It was a time of financial exigency. As yet no statistical account of the country had been attempted; its fiscal resources were wholly unknown; its credit was almost annihilated, for it was obliged to borrow money even to pay the interest of its debts. Under these circumstances Washington needed an able and zealous coadjutor in the treasury department. Such a person he considered Alexander Hamilton, whom he nominated as Secretary of the Treasury, and whose qualifications for the office were so well understood by the Senate that his nomination was confirmed on the same day on which it was made.

Within a few days after Hamilton's appointment, the House of Representatives (Sept. 21), acting upon the policy so ardently desired by Washington, passed a resolution, declaring their opinion of the high importance to the honor and prosperity of the United States, that an adequate provision should be made for the support of public credit; and instructing the Secretary of the Treasury to prepare a plan for the purpose, and report it at their next session.

The arrangement of the Judicial department was one of Washington's earliest cares. On the 27th of September he wrote unofficially to Edmund Randolph, of Virginia, informing him that he had nominated him Attorney-General of the United States, and would be highly gratified with his acceptance of that office. Randolph promptly accepted the nomination, but did not take his seat in the cabinet until some months after Knox and Hamilton.

By the judicial system established for the Federal Government, the Supreme Court of the United States was to be composed of a chief justice and five associate judges. There were to be district courts with a judge in each State, and circuit courts held by an associate judge and a district judge. John Jay, of New York, received the appointment of chief justice. Jay's associate judges were, John Rutledge of South Carolina, James Wilson of Pennsylvania, William Cushing of Massachusetts, John Blair of Virginia, and James Iredell of North Carolina.

On the 29th of September, Congress adjourned to the first Monday in January, after an arduous session, in which many important questions had been discussed, and powers organized and distributed.

The cabinet was still incomplete; the department of foreign affairs, or rather of State, as it was now called, was yet to be supplied with a head. John Jay would have received the nomination had he not preferred the bench. Washington next thought of Thomas Jefferson, who had so long filled the post of Minister Plenipotentiary at the Court of Versailles, but had recently solicited and obtained permission to return, for a few months, to the United States for the purpose of placing his children among their friends in their native country, and of arranging his private affairs, which had suffered from his protracted absence.

At the time of writing to Jefferson, offering him the department of State, Washington was on the eve of a journey through the Eastern States, with a view, as he said, to observe the situation of the country, and with a hope of perfectly re-establishing his health, which a series of indispositions had much impaired. Having made all his arrangements and left the papers appertaining to the office of Foreign Affairs under the temporary superintendence of Mr. Jay, he set out from New York on the 15th of October, travelling in his carriage with four horses, and accompanied by his official secretary, Major Jackson, and his private secretary, Mr. Lear. Though averse from public parade, he could not but be deeply affected and gratified at every step by the manifestations of a people's love. Wherever he came, all labor was suspended; business neglected. The bells were rung, the guns were fired; there were civic processions and military parades and triumphal arches, and all classes poured forth to testify, in every possible manner, their gratitude and affection for the man whom they hailed as the Father of his country; and well did his noble stature, his dignified demeanor, his matured years, and his benevolent aspect, suit that venerable appellation.

His journey eastward terminated at Portsmouth, whence he turned his face homeward by a middle route through the interior of the country to Hartford, and thence to New York, where he arrived between two and three o'clock on the 13th of November.

CHAPTER LXXI.

FINANCIAL DIFFICULTIES.—PARTY JEALOU-SIES.—OPERATIONS AGAINST THE INDIANS.

Congress re-assembled on the 4th of January (1790), but a quorum of the two Houses was not present until the 8th, when the session was opened by Washington in form, with an address delivered before them in the Senate chamber. Among the most important objects suggested in the address for the deliberation of Congress, were provisions for national defence; provisions for facilitating intercourse with foreign nations, and defraying the expenses of diplomatic agents; laws for the naturalization of foreigners; uniformity in the currency, weights, and measures of the United States; facilities for the advancement of commerce, agriculture, and manufactures; attention to the post-office and post-roads; measures for the promotion of science and literature, and for the support of public credit.

This last object was the one which Washington had more immediately at heart. The government was now organized, apparently, to the satisfaction of all parties; but its efficiency would essentially depend on the success of a measure which Washington had pledged himself to institute, and which was yet to be tried; namely, a system of finance adapted to revive the national credit, and place the public debt in a condition to be paid off. At the close of the war the debt amounted to forty-two millions of dollars; but so little had the country been able to fulfil its engagements, owing to the want of a sovereign legislature having the sole and exclusive power of laying duties upon imports, and thus providing adequate resources, that the debt had swollen, through arrears of interest, to upwards of fifty-four millions. Of this amount nearly eight millions were due to France, between three and four millions to private lenders in Holland, and about two hundred and fifty thousand in Spain; making altogether, nearly twelve millions due abroad. The debt contracted at home amounted to upwards of forty-two millions, and was due, originally, to officers and soldiers of the revolutionary war, who had risked their lives for the cause; farmers who had furnished supplies for the public service, or whose property had been assumed for it; capitalists who, in critical periods of the war, had adventured their fortunes in support of their country's independence. The domestic debt, therefore, could not have had a more sacred and patriotic origin; but in the long delay of national justice, the paper which represented these outstanding claims, had sunk to less than a sixth of its nominal value, and the larger portion of it had been parted with at that depreciated rate, either in the course of trade, or to speculative purchasers.

The debt, when thus transferred, lost its commanding appeal to patriotic sympathy, but remained as obligatory in the eye of justice. In public newspapers, however, and in private circles, the propriety of a discrimination between the assignees and the original holders of the public securities, was freely discussed. Beside the foreign and domestic debt of the federal government, the States, individually, were involved in liabilities contracted for the common cause, to an aggregate amount of about twenty-five millions of dollars; of which, more than one-half was due from three of them; Massachusetts and South Carolina each owing more than five millions, and Virginia more than three and a half. The reputation and the well-being of the government were, therefore, at stake upon the issue of some plan to retrieve the national credit, and establish it upon a firm and secure foundation.

The Secretary of the Treasury (Mr. Hamilton), it will be remembered, had been directed by Congress to prepare such a plan during its recess. In the one thus prepared, he asserted, what none were disposed to question, the propriety of paying the foreign debt according to its terms. He asserted, also, the equal validity of the original claims of the American creditors of the government; whether those creditors were the original holders of its certificates or subsequent purchasers of them at a depreciated value. The idea of any distinction between them, which some were inclined to advance, he repudiated as alike unjust, impolitic, and impracticable. He urged, moreover, the assumption, by the general government, of the separate debts of the States, contracted for the common cause, and that a like provision should be made for their payment as for the payment of those of the Union. They were all contracted in the struggle for national independence, not for the independence of any particular part. No more money would be required for their discharge as federal, than as State debts. He recommended, therefore, that the entire mass of debt be funded; the Union made responsible for it, and taxes imposed for its liquidation.

The plan was reported to the House by Mr. Hamilton, the 14th of January, but did not undergo consideration until the 8th of February, when it was opposed with great earnestness, especially the point of assuming the State debts, as tending to consolidation, as giving an undue influence to the general government, and as being of doubtful constitutionality. This financial union of the States was reprobated not only on the floor of Congress, but in different parts of the Union, as fraught with political evil. The Northern and Eastern States generally favored the plan, as did also South Carolina, but Virginia manifested a determined opposition. The measure, however, passed, in Committee of the Whole, on the 9th of March, by a vote of 31 to 26.

The funding of the State debts was supposed to benefit materially the Northern States, in which was the entire capital of the country; yet, South Carolina voted for the assumption. The fact is, opinions were honestly divided on the subject. The great majority were aiming to do their duty—to do what was right; but their disagreement was the result of real difficulties incident to the intricate and complicated problem with which they had to deal.

At this juncture (March 21st), when Virginian discontents were daily gaining strength, Mr. Jefferson arrived in New York to undertake the duties of the Department of State. He had just been in Virginia, where the forms and ceremonials adopted at the seat of our government were subjects of cavil and sneer; where it was reported that Washington affected a monarchial style in his official intercourse, that he held court-like levees, and Mrs. Washington "queenly drawing-rooms," at which none but the aristocracy were admitted, that the manners of both were haughty, and their personal habits reserved and exclusive.

The impressions thus made on Jefferson's mind, received a deeper stamp on his arrival in New York, from conversations with his friend Madison, in the course of which the latter observed, that "the satellites and sycophants which surrounded Washington, had wound up the ceremonials of the government to a pitch of stateliness which nothing but his personal character could have supported, and which no character after him could ever maintain."

Thus prepossessed and premonished, Jefferson looked round him with an apprehensive eye, and appears to have seen something to startle him at every turn. We give, from his private correspondence, his own account of his impressions. "Being fresh from the French revolution, while in its first and pure stage, and, consequently, somewhat whetted up in my own republican principles, I found a state of things in the general society of the place, which I could not have supposed possible. The revolution I had left, and that we had just gone through in the recent change of our own government, being the common topics of conversation, I was astonished to find the general prevalence of monarchial sentiments, insomuch, that in maintaining those of republicanism, I had always the whole company on my hands, never scarcely finding among them a single co-advocate in that argument, unless some old member of Congress happened to be present. The furthest that any one would go in support of the republican features of our new government, would be to say, 'the present constitution is well as a beginning, and may be allowed a fair trial, but it is, in fact, only a stepping stone to something better.'"

Alexander Hamilton, though pledged and sincerely disposed to support the republican form, with regard to our country, preferred *theoretically,* a monarchial form; and, being frank of speech, and, as Gouverneur Morris writes, "prone to mount his hobby," may have spoken openly in favor of that form as suitable to France; and as his admirers took their creed from him, opinions of the kind may have been uttered pretty freely at dinner-tables. These, however, which so much surprised and shocked Mr. Jefferson, were probably merely speculative opinions, broached in unguarded hours, with no sinister design, by men who had no thought of paving the way for a monarchy. They made, however, a deep impression on his apprehensive mind, which sank deeper and deeper until it became a fixed opinion with him, that there was the desire and aim of a large party, of which Hamilton was the leader, to give a regal form to the government.

The question of the assumption of the State debts was resumed in Congress on the 29th of March, on a motion to commit, which was carried by a majority of two; the five members from North Carolina (now a State of the Union) who were strongly opposed to assumption, having taken their seats and reversed the position of parties on the question. An angry and intemperate discussion was revived, much to the chagrin of Washington, who was concerned for the dignity of

Congress; and who considered the assumption of the State debts, under proper restrictions and scrutiny into accounts, to be just and reasonable. On the 12th of April, when the question to commit was taken, there was a majority of two against the assumption.

On the 26th the House was discharged, for the present, from proceeding on so much of the report as related to the assumption. Jefferson, who had arrived in New York in the midst of what he terms "this bitter and angry contest," had taken no concern in it; being, as he says, "a stranger to the ground, a stranger to the actors in it, so long absent as to have lost all familiarity with the subject, and to be unaware of its object." We give his own account of an earnest effort made by Hamilton, who, he says, was "in despair," to resuscitate, through his influence, his almost hopeless project. "As I was going to the President's one day, I met him [Hamilton] in the street. He walked me backwards and forwards before the President's door for half an hour. He painted pathetically the temper into which the legislature had been wrought; the disgust of those who were called the creditor States; the danger of the *secession* of their members, and the separation of the States. He observed that the members of the administration ought to act in concert; that though this question was not of my department, yet a common duty should make it a common concern; that the President was the centre on which all administrative questions ultimately rested, and that all of us should rally around him, and support, with joint efforts, measures approved by him.... I proposed to him to dine with me the next day, and I would invite another friend or two, bring them into conference together, and I thought it impossible that reasonable men, consulting together, coolly, could fail, by some mutual sacrifices of opinion, to form a compromise which was to save the Union. The discussion took place. I could take no part in it but an exhortatory one, because I was a stranger to the circumstances which should govern it. But it was finally agreed, that whatever importance had been attached to the rejection of this proposition, the preservation of the Union and of concord among the States, was more important, and that, therefore, it would be better that the vote of rejection should be rescinded, to effect which some members should change their votes. But it was observed that this pill would be peculiarly bitter to the Southern States, and that some concomitant measure should be adopted to sweeten it a little to them. There had before been projects to fix the seat of government either at Philadelphia or at Georgetown on the Potomac; and it was thought that, by giving it to Philadelphia for ten years, and to Georgetown permanently afterwards, this might, as an anodyne, calm in some degree the ferment which might be excited by the other measure alone. So two of the Potomac members (White and Lee, but White with a revulsion of stomach almost convulsive) agreed to change their votes, and Hamilton undertook to carry the other point. In doing this, the influence he had established over the eastern members, with the agency of Robert Morris with those of the Middle States, effected his side of the engagement."

The decision of Congress was ultimately in favor of assumption, though the form in which it finally passed differed somewhat from the proposition of Hamilton. A specific sum was assumed ($21,500,000), and this was distributed among the States in specific portions. Thus modified, it passed the Senate, July 22d, by the close vote of fourteen to twelve; and the House, July 24th, by thirty-four to twenty-eight.

The question about the permanent seat of government, which, from the variety of contending interests, had been equally a subject of violent contest, was now compromised. It was agreed that Congress should continue for ten years to hold its sessions at Philadelphia; during which time the public buildings should be erected at some place on the Potomac, to which the government should remove at the expiration of the above term. A territory, ten miles square, selected for the purpose on the confines of Maryland and Virginia, was ceded by those States to the United States, and subsequently designated as the District of Columbia.

One of the last acts of the Executive during this session was the conclusion of a treaty of peace and friendship with the Creek nation of Indians, represented at New York by Mr. M'Gillivray, and thirty of the chiefs and head men. By this treaty (signed August 7th), an extensive territory, claimed by Georgia, was relinquished, greatly to the discontent of that State; being considered by it an unjustifiable abandonment of its rights and interests.

Congress adjourned on the 12th of August. Jefferson, commenting on the discord that had prevailed for a time among the members, observes, that in the latter part of the session, they had reacquired the harmony which had always distinguished their proceedings before the introduction of the two disagreeable subjects of the Assumption and the Residence: "these," said he, "really threatened, at one time, a separation of the legislature *sine die.*"

Washington, too, however grieved and disappointed he may have been by the dissensions which had prevailed in Congress, consoled himself by the fancied harmony of his cabinet. Singularly free himself from all jealousy of the talents and popularity of others, and solely actuated by zeal for the public good, he had sought the ablest men to assist him in his arduous task, and supposed them influenced by the same unselfish spirit. Yet, at this very moment, a lurking spirit of rivalry between Jefferson and Hamilton was already existing and daily gaining strength. Jefferson, who, as we have intimated, already considered Hamilton a monarchist in his principles, regarded all his financial schemes with suspicion, as intended to strengthen the influence of the treasury and make its chief the master of every vote in the legislature, "which might give to the government the direction suited to his political views." Under these impressions, Jefferson looked back with an angry and resentful eye, to the manner in which Hamilton had procured his aid in effecting the measure of assumption. He now regarded it as a finesse by which he had been entrapped, and stigmatized the measure itself as a "fiscal manoeuvre, to which he had most ignorantly and innocently been made to hold the candle."

Frequent depredations had of late been made on our frontier settlements by what Washington termed "certain banditti of Indians" from the north-west side of the Ohio. Some of our people had been massacred and others carried into deplorable captivity. The Indians of the Wabash and the Miami rivers, who were the present aggressors, were numerous, warlike, and not deficient in discipline.

Washington had deprecated a war with these savages, but finding all pacific overtures unavailing, and rather productive of more daring atrocities, he felt compelled to resort to it, alike by motives of policy, humanity and justice. An act had been provided for emergencies, by which the President was empowered to call out the militia for the protection of the frontier; this act he put in force in the interval of Congress; and under it an expedition was set on foot, which began its march on the 30th of September from Fort Washington (which stood on the site of the present city of Cincinnati). Brigadier-General Harmer, a veteran of the revolution, led the expedition, having under him three hundred and twenty regulars, with militia detachments from Pennsylvania and Virginia (or Kentucky), making in all fourteen hundred and fifty-three men. After a march of seventeen days, they approached the principal village of the Miamis. The Indians did not await an attack, but set fire to the village and fled to the woods. The destruction of the place, with that of large quantities of provisions, was completed.

An Indian trail being discovered, Colonel Hardin, a continental officer who commanded the Kentucky militia, was detached to follow it, at the head of one hundred and fifty of his men, and about thirty regulars, under Captain Armstrong and Ensign Hartshorn. They followed the trail for about six miles, and were crossing a plain covered by thickets, when suddenly there were volleys of rifles on each side, from unseen marksmen, accompanied by the horrid war-whoop. The trail had, in fact, decoyed them into an ambush of seven hundred savages, under the famous warrior Little Turtle. The militia fled, without firing a musket. The savages now turned upon the little handful of regulars, who stood their ground, and made a brave resistance with the bayonet until all were slain, excepting Captain Armstrong, Ensign Hartshorn, and five privates.

The army, notwithstanding, effected the main purpose of the expedition in laying waste the Indian villages and destroying their winter's stock of provisions, after which it commenced its march back to Fort Washington. On the 21st of October, when it was halted about ten miles to the west of Chillicothe, an opportunity was given Colonel Hardin to wipe out the late disgrace of his arms. He was detached with a larger body of militia than before, and sixty regulars, under Major Willys, to seek and bring the savages to action. The accounts of these Indian wars are very confused. It appears, however, that he had another encounter with Little Turtle and his braves. It was a bloody battle, fought well on both sides. The militia behaved bravely, and lost many men and officers, as did the regulars; Major Willys fell at the commencement of the action. Colonel Hardin was at length compelled to retreat, leaving the dead and wounded in the hands of the enemy. After he had rejoined the main force, the whole exhibition made its way back to Fort Washington, on the banks of the Ohio.

Congress reassembled, according to adjournment, on the first Monday in December, at Philadelphia, which was now, for a time, the seat of government.

Congress, at its opening, was chiefly occupied in financial arrangements, intended to establish the public credit and provide for the expenses of government. According to the statement of the Secretary of the Treasury, an additional annual revenue of eight hundred and twenty-six thousand dollars would be required, principally to meet the additional charges arising from the assumption of the State debts. He proposed to raise it by an increase of the impost on foreign distilled spirits, and a tax by way of excise on spirits distilled at home. An Impost and Excise bill was accordingly introduced into Congress, and met with violent opposition. An attempt was made to strike out the excise, but failed, and the whole bill was finally carried through the House.

Mr. Hamilton, in his former Treasury report, had recommended the establishment of a National Bank; he now, in a special report, urged the policy of the measure. A bill, introduced in conformity with his views, was passed in the Senate, but vehemently opposed in the House; partly on considerations of policy, but chiefly on the ground of constitutionality. On one side it was denied that the constitution had given to Congress the power of incorporation; on the other side it was insisted that such power was incident to the power vested in Congress for raising money.

The question was argued at length, and with great ardor, and after passing the House of Representatives by a majority of nineteen votes, came before the executive for his approval. Washington was fully alive to the magnitude of the question and the interest felt in it by the opposing parties. The cabinet was divided on it. Jefferson and Randolph denied its constitutionality; Hamilton and Knox maintained it. Washington required of each minister the reasons of his opinion in writing; and, after maturely weighing them, gave his sanction to the act, and the bill was carried into effect.

The objection of Jefferson to a bank was not merely on constitutional grounds. In his subsequent writings he avows himself opposed to banks, as introducing a paper instead of a cash system—raising up a moneyed aristocracy, and abandoning the public to the discretion of avarice and swindlers. Paper money might have some advantages, but its abuses were inevitable, and by breaking up the measure of value, it made a lottery of all private property. These objections he maintained to his dying day; but he had others, which may have been more cogent with him in the present instance. He considered the bank as a powerful engine intended by Hamilton to complete the machinery by which the whole action of the legislature was to be placed under the direction of the treasury, and shaped to further a monarchial system of government.

[The opposite policy of these rival statesmen brought them into incessant collision. "Hamilton and myself," writes Jefferson, "were daily pitted in the cabinet like two cocks." In the meantime two political parties were forming under their adverse standards.] Both had the good of the country at heart, but differed as to the policy by which it was to be secured. The Federalists, who looked up to Hamilton as their model, were in favor of strengthening the general government so as to give it weight and dignity abroad and efficiency at home; to guard it against the encroachments of the individual States and a general tendency to anarchy. The other party, known as republicans or democrats, and taking Mr. Jefferson's view of affairs, saw in all the measures advocated by the Federalists, an intention to convert the Federal into a great central or consolidated government, preparatory to a change from a republic to a monarchy.

The particulars of General Harmer's expedition against the Indians, when reported to Congress, gave great dissatisfaction. The conduct of the troops, in suffering themselves to be surprised, was for some time stigmatized as disgraceful. Further troubles in that quarter were apprehended, for the Miamis were said to be less disheartened by the ravage of their villages than exultant at the successful ambuscades of Little Turtle. Three Seneca chiefs, Cornplanter, Half Town and Great Tree, being at the seat of government on business of their own nation, offered to visit these belligerent tribes, and persuade them to bury the hatchet. Washington, in a set speech, encouraged them in the undertaking.

In the course of the present session, Congress received and granted the applications of Kentucky and Vermont for admission into the Union, the former after August, 1792; the latter immediately. On the 3d of March the term of this first Congress expired.

As the Indians on the north-west side of the Ohio still continued their hostilities, one of the last measures of Congress had been an act to augment the military establishments, and to place in the hands of the executive more ample means for the protection of the frontiers. A new expedition against the belligerent tribes had, in consequence, been projected. General St. Clair, actually governor of the territory west of the Ohio, was appointed commander-in-chief of the forces to be employed.

Washington had been deeply chagrined by the mortifying disasters of General Harmer's expedition to the Wabash, resulting from Indian ambushes. In taking leave of his old military comrade, St. Clair, he wished him success and honor, but gave him a solemn warning. "You have your instructions from the Secretary of War. I had a strict eye to them, and will add but one word—Beware of a surprise! You know how the Indians fight. I repeat it—*beware of a surprise!*" With these warning words sounding in his ear, St. Clair departed.

CHAPTER LXXII.

TOUR SOUTHWARD.—DEFEAT OF ST. CLAIR.— DISSENSIONS IN THE CABINET.

In the month of March, Washington set out on a tour through the Southern States; travelling with one set of horses and making occasional halts. The route projected, and of which he had marked off the halting places, was by Fredericksburg, Richmond, Wilmington (N. C.), and Charleston to Savannah; thence to Augusta, Columbia, and the interior towns of North Carolina and Virginia comprising a journey of eighteen hundred and eighty-seven miles; all which he accomplished without any interruption from sickness, bad weather, or any untoward accident.

He returned to Philadelphia on the 6th of July, much pleased with his tour. It had enabled him, he said, to see, with his own eyes, the situation of the country, and to learn more accurately the disposition of the people, than he could have done from any verbal information. He had looked around him, in fact, with a paternal eye, been cheered as usual by continual demonstrations of a nation's love, and his heart had warmed with the reflection how much of this national happiness had been won by his own patriotic exertions.

A few weeks of autumn were passed by Washington at Mount Vernon, with his family in rural enjoyment, and in instructing a new agent, Mr. Robert Lewis, in the management of his estate; his nephew, Major George A. Washington, who ordinarily attended to his landed concerns being absent among the mountains in quest of health.

The second Congress assembled at Philadelphia on the 24th of October, and on the 25th Washington delivered his opening speech. After remarking upon the prosperous situation of the country, and the success which had attended its financial measures, he adverted to the offensive operations against the Indians, which government had been compelled to adopt for the protection of the Western frontier. Some of these operations, he observed, had been successful. Others were still depending. A brief statement will be sufficient for the successful operations alluded to.

Two expeditions had been organized in Kentucky against the villages on the Wabash. The first in May, was led by General Charles Scott, having General Wilkinson as second in command. The second, a volunteer enterprise, in August was led by Wilkinson alone. Very little good was effected, or glory gained by either of these expeditions. Indian villages and wigwams were burned, and fields laid waste; some few warriors were killed and prisoners taken, and an immense expense incurred.

Of the events of a third enterprise, led by General St. Clair himself, no tidings had been received at the time of Washington's opening speech; but we will anticipate the official despatches, and proceed to show how it fared with that veteran soldier, and how far he profited by the impressive warning which he had received from the President at parting.

The troops for his expedition assembled early in September, in the vicinity of Fort Washington (now Cincinnati). There were about two thousand regulars, and one thousand militia. The regulars included a corps of artillery and several squadrons of horse. An arduous task was before them. Roads were to be opened through a wilderness; bridges constructed for the conveyance of artillery and stores, and forts to be built so as to keep up a line of communication between the Wabash and the Ohio, the base of operations. The troops commenced their march directly north, on the 6th or 7th of September, cutting their way through the woods, and slowly constructing the line of forts.

After placing garrisons in the forts, the general continued his march. It was a forced one with him, for he was so afflicted with the gout that he could not walk, and had to be helped on and off his horse; but his only chance to keep his little army together was to move on. The army had proceeded six days after leaving Fort Jefferson, and were drawing near a part of the country where they were likely to meet with Indians, when, on the 30th of October, sixty of the militia deserted in a body; intending to supply themselves by plundering the convoys of provisions which were coming forward in the rear. The 1st United States regiment, under Major Hamtranck, was detached to march back beyond Fort Jefferson, apprehend these deserters, if possible, and, at all events, prevent the provisions that might be on the way, from being rifled. The force thus detached, consisted of three hundred of the best disciplined men in the service, with experienced officers.

Thus reduced to 1,400 effective rank and file, the army continued its march to a point about twenty-nine miles from Fort Jefferson, and ninety-seven from Fort Washington, and fifteen miles south of the Miami villages, where it encamped, November 3d, on a rising ground with a stream forty feet wide in front, running westerly. The militia were encamped beyond the stream about a quarter of a mile in the advance, on a high flat.

It was the intention of St. Clair to throw up a slight work on the following day, [Nov. 4th] and to move on to the attack of the Indian villages as soon as he should be rejoined by Major Hamtranck and the first United States regiment. But about half an hour before sunrise, just after the troops had been dismissed on parade, a horrible sound burst forth from the woods around the militia camp, resembling, says an officer, the jangling of an infinitude of horse-bells. It was the direful Indian yell, followed by the sharp reports of the deadly rifle. The militia returned a feeble fire and then took to flight, dashing helter-skelter into the other camp. The first line of the continental troops, which was hastily forming, was thrown into disorder. The Indians were close upon the heels of the flying militia, and would have entered the camp with them, but the sight of troops drawn up with fixed bayonets to receive them, checked their ardor, and they threw themselves behind logs and bushes at the distance of seventy yards; and immediately commenced an attack upon the first line, which was soon extended to the second. The great weight of the attack was upon the centre of each line where the artillery was placed. The artillery, if not well served, was bravely fought; a quantity of canister and some round shot were thrown in the direction whence the Indians fired; but, concealed as they were, and only seen occasionally as they sprang from one covert to another, it was impossible to direct the pieces to advantage.

St. Clair, who, unable to mount his horse, was borne about on a litter, preserved his coolness in the midst of the peril and disaster, giving his orders with judgment and self-possession. Seeing to what disadvantage his troops fought with a concealed enemy, he ordered Colonel Darke, with his regiment of regulars, to rouse the Indians from their covert with the bayonet, and turn their left flank. This was executed with great spirit: the enemy were driven three or four hundred yards; but, for want of cavalry or riflemen, the pursuit slackened, and the troops were forced to give back in turn. The savages had now got into the camp by the left flank; again several charges were made, but in vain. The contest had now endured for more than two hours and a half. Half the army was killed, and the situation of the remainder was desperate. There appeared to be no alternative but a retreat.

At half-past nine, General St. Clair ordered Colonel Darke, with the second regiment, to make another charge, as if to turn the right wing of the enemy, but, in fact, to regain the road from which the army was cut off. This object was effected. "Having collected in one body the greatest part of the troops," writes one of the officers, "and such of the wounded as could possibly hobble along with us, we pushed out from the left of the rear line, sacrificing our artillery and baggage." It was a disorderly flight. The troops threw away arms, ammunition, and accoutrements; even the officers, in some instances, divested themselves of their fusees. Fortunately, the enemy did not pursue above a mile or two, returning, most probably, to plunder the camp.

By seven in the evening, the fugitives reached Fort Jefferson, a distance of twenty-nine miles. Here they met Major Hamtranck with the first regiment; but, as this force was far from sufficient to make up for the losses of the morning, the retreat was continued to Fort Washington, where the army arrived on the 8th, at noon, shattered and broken-spirited. In this disastrous battle the whole loss amounted to six hundred and seventy-seven killed, including thirty women, and two hundred and seventy-one wounded.

[Washington was at dinner with company when the news of the disaster reached him. An officer had dismounted at the President's door, bearing despatches which he insisted should be placed in the President's hands immediately. Washington, with an apology to his guests, left the table to receive them, and presently returned, resuming his seat without allusion to the incident. Mrs. Washington held her drawing-room that evening, and Washington appeared in the assembly with his usual serenity. At ten o'clock he and his secretary, Mr. Lear, were alone.] The general walked slowly backward and forward for some minutes in silence. As yet there had been no change in his manner. Taking a seat on a sofa by the fire he told Mr. Lear to sit down; the latter had scarce time to notice that he was extremely agitated, when he broke out suddenly: "It's all over!—St. Clair's defeated!—routed: the officers nearly all killed, the men by wholesale; the rout complete; too shocking to think of, and a surprise into the bargain!" All this was uttered with great vehemence. Then pausing and rising from the sofa, he walked up and down the room in silence, violently agitated, but saying nothing. When near the door he stopped short; stood still for a few moments, when there was another terrible explosion of wrath.

"Yes," exclaimed he, "HERE, on this very spot, I took leave of him; I wished him success and honor. 'You have your instructions from the Secretary of War,' said I, 'I had a strict eye to them, and will add but one word, BEWARE OF A SURPRISE! You know how the Indians fight us. I repeat it, BEWARE OF A SURPRISE.' He went off with that, my last warning, thrown into his ears. And yet! To suffer that army to be cut to pieces, hacked, butchered, tomahawked, by a surprise—the very thing I guarded him against—O God! O God!" exclaimed he, throwing up his hands, and while his very frame shook with emotion, "he's worse than a murderer! How can he answer it to his country! The blood of the slain is upon him—the curse of widows and orphans—the curse of heaven!"

Mr. Lear remained speechless; awed into breathless silence by the appalling tones in which this torrent of invective was poured forth. The paroxysm passed by. Washington again sat down on the sofa—he was silent—apparently uncomfortable, as if conscious of the ungovernable burst of passion which had overcome him. "This must not go beyond this room," said he, at length, in a subdued and altered tone—there was another and a longer pause; then, in a tone quite low: "General St. Clair shall have justice," said he. "I looked hastily through the despatches; saw the whole disaster, but not all the particulars. I will receive him without displeasure; I will hear him without prejudice; he shall have full justice."

In the course of the present session of Congress a bill was introduced for apportioning representatives among the people of the several States, according to the first enumeration. The constitution had provided that the number of representatives should not exceed one for every thirty thousand persons, and the House of Representatives passed a bill allotting to each State one member for this amount of population. This ratio would leave a fraction, greater or less, in each State. Its operation was unequal, as in some States a large surplus would be unrepresented, and hence, in one branch of the legislature, the relative power of the State be affected. That, too, was the popular branch, which those who feared a strong executive, desired to provide with the counterpoise of as full a representation as possible.

To obviate this difficulty the Senate adopted a new principle of apportionment. They assumed the total population of the United States, and not the population of each State, as the basis on which the whole number of representatives should be ascertained. This aggregate they divided by thirty thousand: the quotient gave one hundred and twenty as the number of representatives; and this number they apportioned upon the several States according to their population; allotting to each one member for every thirty thousand, and distributing the residuary members (to make up the one hundred and twenty) among the States having the largest fractions.

After an earnest debate, the House concurred, and the bill came before the President for his decision. The sole question was as to its constitutionality; that being admitted, it was unexceptionable. Washington took the opinion of his cabinet. Jefferson and Randolph considered the act at variance with the constitution. Knox was undecided. Hamilton thought the clause of the constitution relating to the subject somewhat vague, and was in favor of the construction given to it by the legislature. After weighing the arguments on both sides, and maturely deliberating, the president made up his mind that the act was unconstitutional. He accordingly returned the bill with his objections, being the first exercise of the veto power. A new bill was substituted, and passed into a law; giving a representative for every thirty-three thousand to each State.

Great heat and asperity were manifested in the discussions of Congress throughout the present session. Washington had observed with pain the political divisions which were growing up in the country; and was deeply concerned at finding that they were pervading the halls of legislation. The press, too, was contributing its powerful aid to keep up and increase the irritation. Two rival papers existed at the seat of government; one was Fenno's Gazette, of the United States, the other was the National Gazette, edited by Philip Freneau. Freneau had been editor of the New York Daily Advertiser, but had come to Philadelphia in the autumn of 1791 to occupy the post of translating clerk in Mr. Jefferson's office, and had almost immediately (Oct. 31) published the first number of his Gazette. Notwithstanding his situation in the office of the Secretary of State, Freneau became and continued to be throughout the session, a virulent assailant of most of the measures of government; excepting such as originated with Mr. Jefferson, or were approved by him.

Heart-weary by the political strifes and disagreements which were disturbing the country and marring the harmony of his cabinet, the charge of government was becoming intolerably irksome to Washington; and he longed to be released from it, and to be once more master of himself, free to indulge those rural and agricultural tastes which were to give verdure and freshness to his future existence. He had some time before this expressed a determination to retire from public life at the end of his presidential term. But one more year of that term remained to be endured, and he congratulated himself with the thought. He had confidential conversations with Mr. Madison on the subject, and asked him to think what would be the proper time and mode of announcing his intention to the public; and intimating a wish that Mr. Madison would prepare for him the announcement. Mr. Madison remonstrated in the most earnest manner against such a resolution, setting forth, in urgent language, the importance to the country of his continuing in the presidency. Washington listened to his reasoning with profound attention, but still clung to his resolution.

In consequence of St. Clair's disastrous defeat and the increasing pressure of the Indian war, bills had been passed in Congress for increasing the army, by adding three regiments of infantry and a squadron of cavalry (which additional force was to serve for three years, unless sooner discharged), also for establishing a uniform militia system. St. Clair resigned his commission, and was succeeded in his western command by General Wayne, the mad Anthony of the revolution, still in the vigor of his days, being forty-seven years of age.

Washington's first thought was that a decisive expedition conducted by this energetic man of the sword, might retrieve the recent frontier disgrace, and put an end to the persevering hostility of the Indians. In deference, however, to the clamors which had been raised against the war and its expenses, and to meet what appeared to be the prevalent wish of the nation, he reluctantly relinquished his more energetic policy, and gave in to that which advised further negotiations for peace; though he was far from anticipating a beneficial result.

In regard to St. Clair, we will here add that a committee of the house of Representatives ultimately inquired into the cause of the failure of his expedition, and rendered a report, in which he was explicitly exculpated. His adjutant general also (Winthrop Sargent), in his private diary, testifies to St. Clair's coolness and bravery, though debilitated by illness. Public sentiment, however, remained for a long time adverse to him; but Washington, satisfied with the explanations which had been given, continued to honor him with his confidence and friendship.

Congress adjourned on the 8th of May, and soon afterward Washington set off on a short visit to Mount Vernon. The season was in all its beauty, and never had this rallying place of his affections appeared to him more attractive. How could he give up the prospect of a speedy return to its genial pursuits and pleasures from the harassing cares and janglings of public life. On the 20th of May, he wrote to Mr. Madison on the subject of their late conversation. He now renewed the request he had made him, for advice as to the proper time and mode for announcing his intention of retiring, and for assistance in preparing the announcement. "In revolving this subject myself," writes he, "my judgment has always been embarrassed. On the one hand, a previous declaration to retire, not only carries with it the appearance of vanity and self-importance, but it may be construed into a manoeuvre to be invited to remain; and, on the other hand, to say nothing, implies consent, or, at any rate, would leave the matter in doubt; and to decline afterwards, might be deemed as bad and uncandid."

"I would fain carry my request to you further," adds he. "As the recess [of Congress] may afford you leisure, and, I flatter myself, you have dispositions to oblige me, I will, without apology, desire, if the measure in itself should strike you as proper, or likely to produce public good, or private honor, that you would turn your thoughts to a valedictory address from me to the public." He then went on to suggest a number of the topics and ideas which the address was to contain; all to be expressed in "plain and modest terms." But, in the main, he left it to Mr. Madison to determine whether, in the first place, such an address would be proper; if so, what matters it ought to contain and when it ought to appear; whether at the same time with his [Washington's] declaration of his intention to retire, or at the close of his career.

Madison, in reply, approved of the measure, and advised that the notification and address should appear together, and be promulgated through the press in time to pervade every part of the Union by the beginning of November. With the letter he sent a draft of the address. "You will readily observe," writes he, "that in executing it I have aimed at that plainness and modesty of language, which you had in view, and which, indeed, are so peculiarly becoming the character and the occasion; and that I had little more to do as to the matter than to follow the just and comprehensive outline which you had sketched. I flatter myself, however, that in everything which has depended on me, much improvement will be made, before so interesting a paper shall have taken its last form." Before concluding his letter, Madison expressed a hope that Washington would reconsider his idea of retiring from office, and that the country might not, at so important a conjuncture, be deprived of the inestimable advantage of having him at the head of its councils.

On the 23d of May, Jefferson also addressed a long letter to Washington on the same subject, [stating that, when Washington first mentioned to him his purpose of retiring, he was silent, although he felt all the magnitude of the event; because he reflected that, as the nation would some day have to walk alone, if the essay should be made while he were alive and looking on, they would derive confidence from that circumstance, and resource if it failed. The public mind, moreover, was then calm and confident, and in a favorable state for making the experiment. This was now changed; the public mind had become disturbed and excited. There was a determined purpose in many, by the funding system, and other plans, "to prepare the way for a change from the present Republican form of government to that of a monarchy, of which the English constitution is to be the model." He concluded by declaring the continuance of Washington at the head of affairs to be of the last importance. The confidence of the whole Union was centred in him. North and South would hang together if they had him to hang on; and his being at the helm would be an answer to every argument which might be used from any quarter, to lead the people into violence or secession.]

The letter of Jefferson was not received by Washington until after his return to Philadelphia, and the purport of it was so painful to him, that he deferred from day to day having any conversation with that statesman on the subject. In regard to the suspicions and apprehensions which were haunting Jefferson's mind, Hamilton expressed himself roundly in one of his cabinet papers: "The idea of introducing a monarchy or aristocracy into this country, by employing the influence and force of a government continually changing hands, towards it, is one of those visionary things that none but madmen could meditate, and that no wise man will believe. If it could be done at all, which is utterly incredible, it would require a long series of time, certainly beyond the life of any individual, to effect it—who, then, would enter into such a plot? for what purpose of interest or ambition?"

On the 10th of July, Washington had a conversation with Jefferson on the subject of the letter; and endeavored with his usual supervising and moderating assiduity to allay the jealousies and suspicions which were disturbing the mind of that ardent politician. These, he intimated, had been carried a great deal too far. There might be *desires,* he said, among a few in the higher walks of life, particularly in the great cities, to change the form of government into a monarchy, but he did not believe there were any *designs;* and he believed the main body of the people in the

Eastern States were as steadily for republicanism as in the Southern.

Hamilton was equally strenuous with Jefferson in urging upon Washington the policy of a re-election, as it regarded the public good, and wrote to him fully on the subject. It was the opinion of every one, he alleged, with whom he had conversed, that the affairs of the national government were not yet firmly established; that its enemies, generally speaking, were as inveterate as ever; that their enmity had been sharpened by its success and all the resentments which flow from disappointed predictions and mortified vanity; that a general and strenuous effort was making in every State to place the administration of it in the hands of its enemies, as if they were its safest guardians; that the period of the next House of Representatives was likely to prove the crisis of its national character; that if Washington continued in office, nothing materially mischievous was to be apprehended; but, if he should quit, much was to be dreaded.

Mr. Edmund Randolph also, after a long letter on the "jeopardy of the Union," which seemed to him "at the eve of a crisis," adds: "The fuel which has been already gathered for combustion wants no addition. But how awfully might it be increased, were the violence, which is now suspended by a universal submission to your pretensions, let loose by your resignation." Not the cabinet, merely, divided as it was in its political opinions, but all parties, however discordant in other points, concurred in a desire that Washington should continue in office—so truly was he regarded as the choice of the nation.

But though the cabinet was united in feeling on this one subject, in other respects its dissensions were increasing in virulence. Washington had noticed this growing feud with excessive pain, and at length found it necessary to interfere and attempt a reconciliation between the warring parties. In the course of a letter to Jefferson (Aug. 23d), on the subject of Indian hostilities, and the possibility of their being furnished by foreign agents to check, as far as possible, the rapid increase, extension, and consequence of the United States, "How unfortunate then," observes he, "and how much to be regretted that, while we are encompassed on all sides with armed enemies and insidious friends, internal dissensions should be harrowing and tearing our vitals. The latter, to me, is the most serious, the most alarming and the most afflicting of the two; and without more charity for the opinions and acts of one another in governmental matters, or some more infallible criterion by which the truth of speculative opinions, before they have undergone the test of experience, are to be prejudged, than has yet fallen to the lot of fallibility, I believe it will be difficult, if not impracticable, to manage the reins of government, or to keep the parts of it together; for if, instead of laying our shoulders to the machine after measures are decided on, one pulls this way and another that, before the utility of the thing is fairly tried, it must inevitably be torn asunder; and, in my opinion, the fairest prospect of happiness and prosperity that ever was presented to man, will be lost perhaps forever."

Admonitions to the same purport were addressed by him to Hamilton. "Having premised these things," adds he, "I would fain hope that liberal allowances will be made for the political opinions of each other; and, instead of those wounding suspicions and irritating charges, with which some of our gazettes are so strongly impregnated, and which cannot fail, if persevered in, of pushing matters to extremity, and thereby tearing the machine asunder, that there may be mutual forbearance and temporizing yielding *on all sides*. Without these I do not see how the reins of government are to be managed, or how the Union of the States can be much longer preserved."

Washington's solicitude for harmony in his cabinet had been rendered more anxious by public disturbances in some parts of the country. The excise law on ardent spirits distilled within the United States, had, from the time of its enactment by Congress in 1791, met with opposition from the inhabitants of the Western counties of Pennsylvania. It had been modified and rendered less offensive within the present year; but the hostility to it had continued. Combinations were formed to defeat the execution of it, and the revenue officers were riotously opposed in the execution of their duties. Determined to exert all the legal powers with which he was invested to check so daring and unwarrantable a spirit, Washington, on the 15th of September, issued a proclamation, warning all persons to desist from such unlawful combinations and proceedings, and requiring all courts, magistrates, and officers to bring the infractors of the law to justice; copies of which proclamation were sent to the governors of Pennsylvania and of North and South Carolina.

CHAPTER LXXIII.

WASHINGTON'S SECOND TERM.—DIFFICULTIES WITH THE FRENCH AMBASSADOR.

It was after a long and painful conflict of feelings that Washington consented to be a candidate for a re-election. There was no opposition on the part of the public, and the vote for him in the Electoral College was unanimous. In a letter to a friend, he declared himself gratefully impressed by so distinguished and honorable a testimony of public approbation and confidence. George Clinton, of New York, was held up for the vice-presidency, in opposition to John Adams; but the latter was re-elected by a majority of twenty-seven electoral votes.

The session of Congress opened on the 5th of November. The continuance of the Indian war formed a painful topic in the President's address. Efforts at pacification had as yet been unsuccessful; two brave officers, Colonel Hardin and Major Trueman, who had been sent to negotiate with the savages, had been severally murdered. Vigorous preparations were therefore making for an active prosecution of hostilities, in which Wayne was to take the field. The factious and turbulent opposition which had been made in some parts of the country to the collection of duties on spirituous liquors distilled in the United States, was likewise adverted to by the President, and a determination expressed to assert and maintain the just authority of the laws. In a part of the speech addressed to the House of Representatives, he expressed a strong hope that the state of the national finances was now sufficiently matured to admit of an arrangement for the redemption and discharge of the public debt.

The address was well received by both houses, and a disposition expressed to concur with the President's views and wishes. The discussion of the subjects to which he had called their attention, soon produced vehement conflicts of opinion in the House, marking the growing virulence of parties. The Secretary of the Treasury, in reporting, at the request of the House, a plan for the annual reduction of so much of the national debt as the United States had a right to redeem, spoke of the expenses of the Indian war, and the necessity of additional internal taxes. The consideration of the report was parried or evaded, and a motion made to reduce the military establishment. This gave an opportunity for sternly criticising the mode in which the Indian war had been conducted; for discussing the comparative merits and cost of regular and militia forces, and for inveighing against standing armies, as dangerous to liberty. These discussions, while they elicited much heat, led to no present result, and gave way to an inquiry into the conduct of the Secretary of the

Treasury in regard to certain loans, which the President in conformity to acts of Congress, had authorized him to make; but concerning the management of which he had not furnished detailed reports to the legislature. The subject was opened by Mr. Giles, of Virginia, who moved in the House of Representatives a series of resolutions seeking information in the matter, and who followed his resolutions by a speech, charging the Secretary of the Treasury with official misconduct, and intimating that a large balance of public money had not been accounted for. A report of the Secretary gave all the information desired; but the charges against him continued to be urged with great acrimony to the close of the session, when they were signally rejected, not more than sixteen members voting for any one of them.

Washington, though he never courted popularity, was attentive to the signs of public opinion, and disposed to be guided by them when right. The time for entering upon his second term of Presidency was at hand. There had been much cavilling at the parade attending his first installation. To guide him on the coming occasion, Washington called the heads of departments together, and desired they would consult with one another, and agree on any changes they might consider for the better, assuring them he would willingly conform to whatever they should advise.

They held such consultation, and ultimately gave their individual opinions in writing, with regard to the time, manner, and place of the President's taking the oath of office. As they were divided in opinion, and gave no positive advice as to any change, no change was made. On the 4th of March, the oath was publicly administered to Washington by Mr. Justice Cushing, in the Senate Chamber, in presence of the heads of departments, foreign ministers, such members of the House of Representatives as were in town, and as many other spectators as could be accommodated.

It was under gloomy auspices, a divided cabinet, an increasing exasperation of parties, a suspicion of monarchial tendencies, and a threatened abatement of popularity, that Washington entered upon his second term of presidency. It was a portentous period in the history of the world, for in a little while came news of that tragical event, the beheading of Louis XVI. An event followed hard upon it to shake the quiet of the world. Early in April intelligence was received that France had declared war against England. Popular excitement was now wound up to the highest pitch. What, it was asked, were Americans to do in such a juncture? Could they remain unconcerned spectators of a conflict between their ancient enemy and republican France? Should they fold their arms and look coldly on a war, begun, it is true, by France, but threatening the subversion of the republic, and the re-establishment of a monarchial government?

Many, in the wild enthusiasm of the moment, would at once have precipitated the country into a war. Fortunately this belligerent impulse was not general, and was checked by the calm, controlling wisdom of Washington. He was at Mount Vernon when he received news of the war, and understood that American vessels were already designated, and some even fitting out to serve in it as privateers. Hastening back to Philadelphia, he held a cabinet council on the 19th of April to deliberate on the measures proper to be observed by the United States in the present crisis; and to determine upon a general plan of conduct for the Executive.

In this council it was unanimously determined that a proclamation should be issued by the President, "forbidding the citizens of the United States to take part in any hostilities on the seas, and warning them against carrying to the belligerents any articles deemed contraband according to the modern usages of nations, and forbidding all acts and proceedings inconsistent with the duties of a friendly nation towards those at war." It was unanimously agreed also, that should the republic of France send a minister to the United States, he should be received.

No one at the present day questions the wisdom of Washington's proclamation of neutrality. It was our true policy to keep aloof from European war, in which our power would be inefficient, our loss certain. The measure, however, was at variance with the enthusiastic feelings and excited passions of a large portion of the citizens. They treated it for a time with some forbearance, out of long-cherished reverence for Washington's name; but his popularity, hitherto unlimited, was no proof against the inflamed state of public feeling. The proclamation was stigmatized as a royal edict; a daring assumption of power; an open manifestation of partiality for England and hostility to France. Washington saw that a deadly blow was aimed at his influence and his administration, and that both were at hazard; but he was convinced that neutrality was the true national policy, and he resolved to maintain it, whatever might be his immediate loss of popular favor. His resolution was soon put to the test.

The French republic had recently appointed Edmond Charles Genet, or 'Citizen Genet,' as he was styled, minister to the United States. He was represented as a young man of good parts, very well educated, and of an ardent temper. A letter from Gouverneur Morris [at that time minister to France] apprised Mr. Jefferson that the Executive Council had furnished Genet with three hundred blank commissions for privateers, to be given clandestinely to such persons as he might find in America inclined to take them.

Genet's conduct proved the correctness of this information. He had landed at Charleston, South Carolina, from the French frigate, the Ambuscade, on the 8th of April, a short time before the proclamation of neutrality, and was received with great rejoicing and extravagant demonstrations of respect. His landing at a port several hundred miles from the seat of government was a singular move for a diplomat; but his object in so doing was soon evident. It is usual for a foreign minister to present his credentials to the government to which he comes, and be received by it in form before he presumes to enter upon the exercise of his functions. Citizen Genet, however, did not stop for these formalities. Confident in his nature, heated in his zeal, and flushed with the popular warmth of his reception, he could not pause to consider the proprieties of his mission and the delicate responsibilities involved in diplomacy. The contiguity of Charleston to the West Indies made it a favorable port for fitting out privateers against the trade of these islands; and during Genet's short sojourn there he issued commissions for arming and equipping vessels of war for that purpose, and manning them with Americans.

In the latter part of April, Genet set out for the north by land. As he proceeded on his journey, the newspapers teemed with accounts of the processions and addresses with which he was greeted, and the festivities which celebrated his arrival at each place. On the 16th of May he arrived at Philadelphia. His belligerent operations at Charleston had already been made a subject of complaint to the government by Mr. Hammond, the British minister; but they produced no abatement in the public enthusiasm.

On the following day, various societies and a large body of citizens waited upon him with addresses, recalling with gratitude the aid given by France in the achievement of American independence, and extolling and rejoicing in the success of the arms of the French republic. On the same day, before Genet had presented his credentials and been acknowledged by the President, he was invited to a grand republican dinner, "at which," we are told, "the company united in singing the Marseilles Hymn." On the 18th of May, Genet presented his letter of credence to the President: by whom, notwithstanding his late unwarrantable proceedings at Charleston, he was well received. Washington taking the occasion to express his sincere regard for the French nation.

The acts of this diplomatic personage at Charleston had not been the sole ground of the complaint preferred by the British minister. The capture of the British vessel, the Grange, by the frigate Ambuscade, formed a graver one. Occurring within our waters, it was a clear usurpation of national sovereignty, and a violation of neutral rights. The British minister demanded a restitution of the prize, and the cabinet were unanimously of opinion that restitution should be made; nor was there any difficulty with the French minister on this head; but restitution was likewise claimed of other vessels captured on the high seas and brought into port by the privateers authorized by Genet. In regard to these there was a difference of sentiment in the cabinet. Hamilton and Knox were of opinion that the government should interpose to restore the prizes; it being the duty of a neutral nation to remedy any injury sustained by armaments fitted out in its ports. Jefferson and Randolph contended that the case should be left to the decision of the courts of justice. If the courts adjudged the commissions issued by Genet to be invalid, they would, of course, decide the captures made under them to be void, and the property to remain in the original owners; if, on the other hand, the legal right to the property had been transferred to the captors, they would so decide.

Seeing this difference of opinion in the cabinet, Washington reserved the point for further deliberation; but directed the Secretary of State to communicate to the ministers of France and Britain the principles in which they concurred; these being considered as settled. Circular letters, also, were addressed to the governors of several States, requiring their co-operation, with force, if necessary, to carry out the rules agreed upon.

Genet took umbrage at these decisions of the government, and expressed his dissatisfaction in a letter, complaining of them as violations of natural right, and subversive of the existing treaties between the two nations. His letter, though somewhat wanting in strict decorum of language, induced a review of the subject in the cabinet; and he was informed that no reason appeared for changing the system adopted. He was further informed that, in the opinion of the executive, the vessels which had been illegally equipped should depart from the ports of the United States.

Genet was not disposed to acquiesce in these decisions. He was aware of the grateful feelings of the nation to France; of the popular disposition to go all lengths, short of war, in her favor; of the popular idea that republican interests were identical on both sides of the Atlantic; that a royal triumph over republicanism in Europe would be followed by a combination to destroy it in this country. The people, he thought, were with him, if Washington was not, and he believed the latter would not dare to risk his popularity in thwarting their enthusiasm. He persisted, therefore, in disregarding the decisions of the government, and spoke of them as a departure from the obligations it owed to France; a cowardly abandonment of friends when danger menaced.

Another event added to the irritation of Genet. Two American citizens, whom he had engaged at Charleston to cruise in the service of France, were arrested on board of the privateer, conducted to prison, and prosecutions commenced against them. The indignant feelings of Genet were vented in an extraordinary letter to the Secretary of State. When speaking of their arrest, "The crime laid to their charge," writes he—"the crime which my mind cannot conceive, and which my pen almost refuses to state—is the serving of France, and defending with her children the common glorious cause of liberty." The lofty and indignant tone of this letter had no effect in shaking the determination of government, or obtaining the release of the prisoners. Washington confesses, however, that he was very much hurried and perplexed by the "disputes, memorials, and what not," with which he was pestered, by one or other of the powers at war. It was a sore trial of his equanimity, his impartiality and his discrimination, and wore upon his spirits and his health.

In the latter part of July, Washington was suddenly called to Mount Vernon by the death of Mr. Whiting, the manager of his estates. During his brief absence from the seat of government, occurred the case of the Little Sarah. This was a British merchant vessel which had been captured by a French privateer, and brought into Philadelphia, where she had been armed and equipped for privateering; manned with one hundred and twenty men, many of them Americans, and her name changed into that of *Le Petit Democrat*. This, of course, was in violation of Washington's decision, which had been communicated to Genet.

General Mifflin, now Governor of Pennsylvania, being informed, on the 6th of July, that the vessel was to sail the next day, sent his secretary, Mr. Dallas, at midnight to Genet, to persuade him to detain her until the President should arrive, intimating that otherwise force would be used to prevent her departure. Genet flew into one of the transports of passion to which he was prone; contrasted the treatment experienced by him from the officers of government, with the attachment to his nation professed by the people at large; declared that the President was not the sovereign of the country, and had no right, without consulting Congress, to give such instructions as he had issued to the State Governors; threatened to appeal from his decision to the people, and to repel force by force, should an attempt be made to seize the privateer.

Apprised of this menace, Governor Mifflin forthwith ordered out one hundred and twenty of the militia to take possession of the privateer, and communicated the circumstances of the case to the cabinet.

Mr. Jefferson now took the matter in hand, and, on the 7th of July, in an interview with Genet, repeated the request that the privateer be detained until the arrival of the President. Genet, he writes, instantly took up the subject in a very high tone, and went into an immense field of declamation and complaint. Jefferson made a few efforts to be heard, but, finding them ineffectual, suffered the torrent of vituperation to pour on. When Genet had subsided into coolness, Jefferson pressed the detention of the Little Sarah until the President's return; intimating that her previous departure would be considered a very serious offence. Genet made no promise, but expressed himself very happy to be able to inform Mr. Jefferson that the vessel was not in a state of readiness; she had to change her position that day, he said, and fall down the river, somewhere about the lower end of the town, for the convenience of taking some things on board, and would not depart yet. Jefferson was accordingly impressed with the belief that the privateer would remain in the river until the President should decide on her case, and, on communicating this conviction to the governor, the latter ordered the militia to be dismissed.

Washington arrived at Philadelphia on the 11th of July, when papers requiring "instant attention" were put into his hands. They related to the case of the Little Sarah, and were from Jefferson, who, being ill with fever, had retired to his seat in the country. Nothing could exceed the displeasure of Washington when he examined these papers. In a cabinet council held the next day, it was determined to detain in port all privateers which had been equipped within the United States by any of the belligerent powers. No time was lost in communicating this determination to Genet; but, in defiance of it, the vessel sailed on her cruise. It must have been a severe trial of Washington's spirit to see his authority thus braved and insulted, and to find that the people, notwithstanding the indignity thus offered to their chief magistrate, sided with the aggressors, and exulted in their open defiance of his neutral policy.

Fresh mortifications awaited him, from the distempered state of public sentiment. The trial came on of Gideon Henfield, an American citizen, prosecuted under the advice of the Attorney-General, for having enlisted, at Charleston, on board of a French privateer which had brought prizes into the port of Philadelphia. The populace took part with Henfield. He had enlisted before the proclamation of neutrality had been published, and even if he had enlisted at a later date, was he to be punished for engaging with their ancient ally, France, in the cause of liberty against the royal despots of Europe? His acquittal exposed Washington to the obloquy of having attempted a measure which the laws would not justify. It showed him, moreover, the futility of attempts at punishment for infractions of the rules proclaimed for the preservation of neutrality; while the clamorous rejoicing by which the acquittal of Henfield had been celebrated, evinced the popular disposition to thwart that line of policy which he considered most calculated to promote the public good. Nothing, however, could induce him to swerve from that policy.

Hitherto Washington had exercised great forbearance toward the French minister, notwithstanding the little respect shown by the latter to the rights of the United States; but the official communications of Genet were becoming too offensive and insulting to be longer tolerated. Meetings of the heads of departments and the Attorney-General were held at the President's on the 1st and 2d of August, in which the whole of the official correspondence and conduct of Genet was passed in review; and it was agreed that his recall should be desired. It was proposed that a publication of the whole correspondence, and a statement of the proceedings, should be made by way of appeal to the people. This produced animated debates. Hamilton spoke with great warmth in favor of an appeal. Jefferson opposed it. "Genet," said he, "will appeal also; it will become a contest between the President and Genet."

Washington, already weary and impatient under the incessant dissensions of his cabinet, was stung by the suggestion that he might be held up as in conflict with Genet, and subjected, as he had been, to the ribaldry of the press. At this unlucky moment Knox blundered forth with a specimen of the scandalous libels already in circulation; a pasquinade lately printed, called the Funeral of George Washington, wherein the President was represented as placed upon a guillotine, a horrible parody on the late decapitation of the French King. "The President," writes Jefferson, "now burst forth into one of those transports of passion beyond his control; inveighed against the personal abuse which had been bestowed upon him, and defied any man on earth to produce a single act of his since he had been in the government that had not been done on the purest motives. He had never repented but once the having slipped the moment of resigning his office, and that was every moment since. In the agony of his heart he declared that he had rather be in his grave than in his present situation; that he had rather be on his farm than to be made emperor of the world—and yet, said he, indignantly, they are charging me with wanting to be a king!

"All were silent during this burst of feeling—a pause ensued—it was difficult to resume the question. Washington, however, who had recovered his equanimity, put an end to the difficulty. There was no necessity, he said, for deciding the matter at present; perhaps events would show whether the appeal would be necessary or not."

Washington had hitherto been annoyed and perplexed by having to manage a divided cabinet; he was now threatened with that cabinet's dissolution. Mr. Hamilton had informed him by letter, that private as well as public reasons had determined him to retire from office towards the close of the next session; probably with a view to give Congress an opportunity to examine into his conduct. Now came a letter from Mr. Jefferson, dated July 31st, in which he announced his intention to withdraw; "at the close of the ensuing month of September, I shall beg leave to retire to scenes of greater tranquillity, from those for which I am every day more and more convinced that neither my talents, tone of mind, nor time of life fit me."

Washington was both grieved and embarrassed by this notification. Full of concern, he called upon Jefferson at his country residence near Philadelphia; pictured his deep distress at finding himself, in the present perplexing juncture of affairs, about to be deserted by those of his cabinet on whose counsel he had counted, and whose places he knew not where to find persons competent to supply; and, in his chagrin, again expressed his repentance that he himself had not resigned as he had once meditated. The public mind, he went on to observe, was in an alarming state of ferment; political combinations of various kinds were forming; where all this would end he knew not. A new Congress was to assemble, more numerous than the last, perhaps of a different spirit; the first expressions of its sentiments would be important, and it would relieve him considerably if Jefferson would remain in office, if it were only until the end of the session.

Washington had the highest opinion of Jefferson's abilities, his knowledge of foreign affairs, his thorough patriotism; and it was his earnest desire to retain him in his cabinet through the whole of the ensuing session of Congress; before the close of which he trusted the affairs of the country relating to foreign powers, Indian disturbances, and internal policy, would have taken a more decisive, and it was to be hoped agreeable form than they then had. A compromise was eventually made, according to which Jefferson was to be allowed a temporary absence in the autumn, and on his return was to continue in office until January.

In the meantime Genet had proceeded to New York, which was just then in a great agitation. The frigate Ambuscade, while anchored in the harbor, had been challenged to single combat by the British frigate Boston, Captain Courtney, which was cruising off the Hook. The challenge was accepted; a severe action ensued; Courtney was killed; and the Boston, much damaged, was obliged to stand for Halifax. The Ambuscade returned triumphant to New York, and entered the port amid the enthusiastic cheers of the populace. On the same day, a French fleet of fifteen sail arrived from the Chesapeake and anchored in the Hudson river. The officers and crews were objects of unbounded favor with all who inclined to the French cause. In the midst of this excitement, the ringing of bells and the firing of cannon announced that Citizen Genet was arrived at Powles Hook Ferry, directly opposite the city. There was an immediate assemblage of the republican party in the fields now called the Park. A committee was appointed to escort Genet into the city. He entered it amid the almost frantic cheerings of the populace. Addresses were made to him, expressing devoted attachment to the French republic, and abjuring all neutrality in regard to its heroic struggle.

In the midst of his self-gratulation and complacency, however, he received a letter from Mr. Jefferson (Sept. 15), acquainting him with the measures taken to procure his recall, and inclosing a copy of the letter written for that purpose to the American minister at Paris. It was added, that, out of anxious regard lest the interests of France might suffer, the Executive would, in the meantime, receive his (M. Genet's) communications in writing, and admit the continuance of his functions so long as they should be restrained within the law as theretofore announced to him, and should be of the tenor usually observed towards independent nations, by the representative of a friendly power residing with them.

The letter of the Secretary of State threw Genet into a violent passion, and produced a reply (Sept. 18), written while he was still in a great heat. Unfortunately for Genet's ephemeral popularity, a rumor got abroad that he had expressed a determination to appeal from the President to the people. The spirit of audacity thus manifested by a foreign minister shocked the national pride. Meetings were held in every part of the Union to express the public feeling in the matter. In these meetings the proclamation of neutrality and the system of measures flowing from it, were sustained, partly from a conviction of their wisdom and justice, but more from an undiminished affection for the person and character of Washington; for many who did not espouse his views, were ready to support him in the exercise of his constitutional functions.

CHAPTER LXXIV.

NEUTRALITY.—WHISKEY INSURRECTION.— WAYNE'S SUCCESS AGAINST THE INDIANS.

While the neutrality of the United States, so jealously guarded by Washington, was endangered by the intrigues of the French minister, it was put to imminent hazard by ill-advised measures of the British cabinet. There was such a scarcity in France, in consequence of the failure of the crops, that a famine was apprehended. England, availing herself of her naval ascendency, determined to increase the distress of her rival by cutting off all her supplies from abroad. In June, 1793, therefore, her cruisers were instructed to detain all vessels bound to France with cargoes of corn, flour, or meal, take them into port, unload them, purchase the cargoes, make a proper allowance for the freight, and then release the vessels; or to allow the masters of them, on a stipulated security, to dispose of their cargoes in a port in amity with England. This measure gave umbrage to all parties in the United States, and brought out an earnest remonstrance from the government, as being a violation of the law of neutrals, and indefensible on any proper construction of the law of nations.

Another grievance which helped to swell the tide of resentment against Great Britain, was the frequent impressment of American seamen, a wrong to which they were particularly exposed from national similarity. To these may be added the persistence of Great Britain in holding the posts to the south of the lakes, which, according to treaty stipulations, ought to have been given up. Washington did not feel himself in a position to press our rights under the treaty, with the vigorous hand that some would urge; questions having risen in some of the State courts, to obstruct the fulfilment of our part of it, which regarded the payment of British debts contracted before the war.

The hostilities of the Indians north of the Ohio, by many attributed to British wiles, still continued. The attempts at an amicable negotiation had proved as fruitless as Washington had anticipated. The troops under Wayne had, therefore, taken the field to act offensively; but from the lateness of the season, had formed a winter camp near the site of the present city of Cincinnati, whence Wayne was to open his campaign in the ensuing spring.

Congress assembled on the 2d of December (1793), with various causes of exasperation at work; the intrigues of Genet and the aggressions of England, uniting to aggravate to a degree of infatuation the partiality for France, and render imminent the chance of a foreign war. Washington, in his opening speech, after expressing his deep and respectful sense of the renewed testimony of public approbation manifested in his re-election, proceeded to state the measures he had taken, in consequence of the war in Europe, to protect the rights and interests of the United States, and maintain peaceful relations with the belligerent parties. Still he pressed upon Congress the necessity of placing the country in a condition of complete defence. One part of his speech conveyed an impressive admonition to the House of Representatives: "No pecuniary consideration is more urgent than the regular redemption and discharge of the public debt; in none can delay be more injurious, or an economy of time more valuable." The necessity of augmenting the public revenue in a degree commensurate with the objects suggested, was likewise touched upon.

The choice of speaker showed that there was a majority of ten against the administration, in the House of Representatives; yet it was manifest, from the affectionate answer on the 6th, of the two Houses, to Washington's speech, and the satisfaction expressed at his re-election, that he was not included in the opposition which, from this act, appeared to await his political system. Notwithstanding the popular ferment in favor of France, both Houses seem to have approved the course pursued by Washington in regard to that country; and as to his proclamation of neutrality, while the House approved of it in guarded terms, the Senate pronounced it a "measure well-timed and wise; manifesting a watchful solicitude for the welfare of the nation, and calculated to promote it."

Early in the session, Mr. Jefferson, in compliance with a requisition which the House of Representatives had made, Feb. 23, 1791, furnished an able and comprehensive report of the state of trade of the United States with different countries; the nature and extent of exports and imports, and the amount of tonnage of the American shipping: specifying, also, the various restrictions and prohibitions by which our commerce was embarrassed, and in some instances, almost ruined. "Two methods," he said, "presented themselves, by which these impediments might be removed, modified, or counteracted; friendly arrangement or countervailing legislation. Friendly arrangements were preferable with all who would come into them, and we should carry into such arrangements all the liberality and spirit of accommodation which the nature of the case would admit. But," he adds, "should any nation continue its system of prohibitive duties and regulations, it behooves us to protect our citizens, their commerce, and navigation, by counter prohibitions, duties, and regulations."

With this able and elaborate report, Jefferson closed his labors as Secretary of State. Washington had been especially sensible of the talents and integrity displayed by Jefferson during the closing year of his secretaryship, and particularly throughout this French perplexity, and had recently made a last attempt, but an unsuccessful one, to persuade him to remain in the cabinet. The place thus made vacant was filled by Mr. Edmond Randolph, whose office of Attorney-General was conferred on Mr. William Bradford, of Pennsylvania.

The report of Mr. Jefferson on commercial intercourse, was soon taken up in the House in a committee of the whole. A series of resolutions based on it, and relating to the privileges and restrictions of the commerce of the United States, were introduced by Mr. Madison, and became the subject of a warm and acrimonious debate. The report upheld the policy of turning the course of trade from England to France, by discriminations in favor of the latter; and the resolutions were to the same purport. The idea was to oppose commercial resistance to commercial injury; to enforce a perfect commercial equality by retaliating impositions, assuming that the commercial system of Great Britain was hostile to the United States—a position strongly denied by some of the debaters.

Though the subject was, or might seem to be, of a purely commercial nature, it was inevitably mixed up with political considerations, according as a favorable inclination to England or France was apprehended. The debate, which had commenced on the 13th of January, (1794,) was protracted to the 3d of February, when the question being taken on the first resolution, it was carried by a majority of only five, so nearly were parties divided. The further consideration of the remaining resolutions was postponed to March, when it was resumed, but, in consequence of the new complexion of affairs, was suspended without a decision.

The next legislative movement was also productive of a warm debate, though connected with a subject which appealed to the sympathies of the whole nation. Algerine corsairs had captured eleven American merchant vessels, and upwards of one hundred prisoners, and the regency manifested a disposition for further outrages. A bill was introduced into Congress proposing a force of six frigates, to protect the commerce of the United States against the cruisers of this piratical power. The bill met with strenuous opposition, but was eventually passed by both Houses.

In the course of this session, fresh instances had come before the government of the mischievous activity and audacity of Genet; showing that, not content with compromising the neutrality of the United States at sea, he was attempting to endanger it by land. From documents received, it appeared that in November he had sent emissaries to Kentucky, to enroll American citizens in an expedition against New Orleans, and the Spanish possessions; furnishing them with blank commissions for the purpose. It was an enterprise in which the adventurous people of that State were ready enough to embark, through enthusiasm for the French nation and impatience at the delay of Spain to open the navigation of the Mississippi. Another expedition was to proceed against the Floridas; men for the purpose to be enlisted at the South, to rendezvous in Georgia, and to be aided by a body of Indians and by a French fleet, should one arrive on the coast. A proclamation from Governor Moultrie checked all such enlistments in South Carolina.

Documents relating to these transactions were communicated to Congress by Washington early in January. But, though the expedition set on foot in South Carolina had been checked, it was subsequently reported that the one in Kentucky against Louisiana, was still in progress and about to descend the Ohio. These schemes showed such determined purpose, on the part of Genet, to undermine the peace of the United States, that Washington, without waiting a reply to the demand for his recall, resolved to keep no further terms with that headlong diplomat. In a cabinet council it was determined to supersede his diplomatic functions, deprive him of the consequent privileges, and arrest his person; a message to

Congress, avowing such determination, was prepared, but at this critical juncture came despatches from Gouverneur Morris announcing his recall. Mr. Fauchet, secretary of the executive council, was appointed to succeed him.

About this time vigilance was required to guard against wrongs from an opposite quarter. We have noticed the orders issued by Great Britain to her cruisers in June, 1793, and the resentment thereby excited in the United States. On the 6th of the following month of November, she had given them additional instructions to detain all vessels laden with the produce of any colony belonging to France, or carrying supplies to any such colony, and to bring them, with their cargoes, to British ports, for adjudication in the British courts of admiralty. Captures of American vessels were taking place in consequence of these orders, and heightening public irritation. They were considered indicative of determined hostility on the part of Great Britain, and they produced measures in Congress preparatory to an apprehended state of war. An embargo was laid, prohibiting all trade from the United States to any foreign place for the space of thirty days, and vigorous preparations for defence were adopted with but little opposition.

On the 27th of March, resolutions were moved that all debts due to British subjects be sequestered and paid into the treasury, as a fund to indemnify citizens of the United States for depredations sustained from British cruisers, and that all intercourse with Great Britain be interdicted until she had made compensation for these injuries, and until she should make surrender of the Western posts.

The popular excitement was intense. Meetings were held on the subject of British spoliations. 'Peace or war' was the absorbing question. While the public mind was in this inflammable state, Washington received advices from Mr. Pinckney, the American minister in London, informing him that the British ministry had issued instructions to the commanders of armed vessels, revoking those of the 6th of November, 1793. Lord Grenville also, in conversation with Mr. Pinckney, had explained the real motives for that order, showing that, however oppressive in its execution, it had not been intended for the special vexation of American commerce. Washington laid Pinckney's letter before Congress on the 4th of April. It had its effect on both parties; Federalists saw in it a chance of accommodating difficulties, and, therefore, opposed all measures calculated to irritate; the other party did not press their belligerent propositions to any immediate decision, but showed no solicitude to avoid a rupture.

The war cry, however, is too obvious a means of popular excitement to be readily given up. Busy partisans saw that the feeling of the populace was belligerent, and every means were taken by the press and the democratic societies to exasperate this feeling; according to them the crisis called, not for moderation, but for decision, for energy. Still to adhere to a neutral position would argue tameness—cowardice! Washington, however, was too morally brave to be clamored out of his wise moderation by such taunts. He resolved to prevent a war, if possible, by an appeal to British justice, to be made through a special envoy, who should represent to the British government the injuries we had sustained from it in various ways, and should urge indemnification.

The measure was decried by the party favorable to France, as an undue advance to the British government; but they were still more hostile to it when it was rumored that Hamilton was to be chosen for the mission. A member of the House of Representatives addressed a strong letter to the President, deprecating the mission, but especially the reputed choice of the envoy. Hamilton, aware of the "collateral obstacles" which existed with respect to himself, had resolved to advise Washington to drop him from the consideration and to fix upon another character, and recommended John Jay, the chief justice of the United States, as the man whom it would be advisable to send.

Mr. Jay was the person ultimately chosen. Washington, in his message, thus nominating an additional envoy to Great Britain, expressed undiminished confidence in the minister actually in London. "But a mission like this," observes he, "while it corresponds with the solemnity of the occasion, will announce to the world a solicitude for a friendly adjustment of our complaints and a reluctance to hostility." The nomination was approved by a majority of ten Senators.

The French government having so promptly complied with the wishes of the American government in recalling citizen Genet, requested, as an act of reciprocity, the recall of Gouverneur Morris, whose political sympathies were considered highly aristocratical. The request was granted accordingly, but Washington, in a letter to Morris, notifying him of his being superseded, assured him of his own undiminished confidence and friendship. James Munroe was appointed in his place.

[The discontents in the western part of Pennsylvania excited by the excise law, now broke out into open insurrection.] We have already mentioned the riotous opposition this law had experienced. Bills of indictment had been found against some of the rioters. The marshal, when on the way to serve the processes issued by the court, was fired upon by armed men, and narrowly escaped with his life. He was subsequently seized and compelled to renounce the exercise of his official duties. The house of General Nevil, inspector of the revenue, was assailed, but the assailants were repulsed. They assembled in greater numbers; the magistrates and militia officers shrank from interfering, lest it should provoke a general insurrection; a few regular soldiers were obtained from the garrison at Fort Pitt. There was a parley. The insurgents demanded that the inspector and his papers should be given up; and the soldiers march out of the house and ground their arms. The demand being refused, the house was attacked, the out-houses set on fire, and the garrison was compelled to surrender. The marshal and inspector finally escaped out of the country; descended the Ohio, and, by a circuitous route, found their way to the seat of government; bringing a lamentable tale of their misadventures.

It was intimated that the insurgent district could bring seven thousand men into the field. Delay would only swell the growing disaffection. On the 7th of August, Washington issued a proclamation, warning the insurgents to disperse, and declaring that if tranquillity were not restored before the 1st of September, force would be employed to compel submission to the laws. To show that this was not an empty threat, he, on the same day, made a requisition on the governors of New Jersey, Pennsylvania, Maryland, and Virginia, for militia to compose an army of twelve thousand men.

The insurgents manifesting a disposition to persevere in their rebellious conduct, the President issued a second proclamation on the 25th of September, describing in forcible terms, the perverse and obstinate spirit with which the lenient propositions of government had been met, and declaring his fixed purpose to reduce the refractory to obedience. Shortly after this he left Philadelphia for Carlisle, to join the army, then on its march to suppress the insurrection in the western part of Pennsylvania. On the 10th, the Pennsylvania troops set out from Carlisle for their rendezvous at Bedford, and Washington proceeded to Williamsport, thence to go on to Fort Cumberland, the rendezvous of the Virginia and Maryland troops. He arrived at the latter place on the 16th of October, and found a respectable force assembled from those States, and learnt that fifteen hundred more from Virginia were at hand. All accounts agreed that the insurgents were greatly alarmed at the serious appearance of things. At Bedford, Washington arranged matters and settled a plan of military operations. The governors of Virginia, Maryland and Pennsylvania, were at the head of the troops of their respective States, but Governor Lee was to have the general command. This done, Washington prepared to shape his course for Philadelphia.

Washington pushed on for Philadelphia, through deep roads and a three days' rain, and arrived there about the last of October. Governor Lee marched with the troops in two divisions, amounting to fifteen thousand men, into the western counties of Pennsylvania. This great military array extinguished at once the kindling elements of a civil war, "by making resistance desperate." At the approach of so overwhelming a force the insurgents laid down their arms, and gave assurance of submission, and craved the clemency of government. It was extended to them. A few were tried for treason, but were not convicted; but as some spirit of discontent was still manifest, Major-general Morgan was stationed with a detachment for the winter, in the disaffected region.

It was with great satisfaction that Washington had been able to announce [in his speech at the opening of Congress, Nov. 9th] favorable intelligence of the campaign of General Wayne against the hostile Indians west of the Ohio. That brave commander had conducted it with a judgment and prudence little compatible with the hare-brained appellation he had acquired by his rash exploits during the Revolution. Leaving his winter encampment on the Ohio, in the spring (of 1794), he had advanced cautiously into the wild country west of it; skirmishing with bands of lurking savages as he advanced, and establishing posts to keep up communication and secure the transmission of supplies. It was not until the 8th of August that he arrived at the junction of the rivers Au Glaize and Miami, in a fertile and populous region, where the Western Indians had their most important villages. Here he threw up some works, which he named Fort Defiance. Being strengthened by eleven hundred mounted volunteers from Kentucky, his force exceeded that of the savage warriors who had collected to oppose him, which scarcely amounted to two thousand men. These, however, were strongly encamped in the vicinity of Fort Miami, a British post, about thirty miles distant, and far within the limits of the United States, and seemed prepared to give battle, expecting, possibly, to be aided by the British garrison.

On the 20th, being arrived near the enemy's position, his advanced guard was fired upon by an ambush of the enemy concealed in a thicket, and was compelled to retreat. The general now ordered an attack of horse and foot upon the enemy's position; the Indians were roused from their lair with the point of the bayonet; driven, fighting for more than two miles, through thick woods, and pursued with great slaughter, until within gunshot of the British fort.

In his official address to Congress, Washington had urged the adoption of some definite plan for the redemption of the public debt. A plan was reported by Mr. Hamilton, 20th January, 1795, which he had digested and prepared on the basis of the actual revenues, for the further support of public credit. The report embraced a comprehensive view of the system which he had pursued, and made some recommendations, which after much debate were adopted.

So closed Mr. Hamilton's labors as Secretary of the Treasury. He had long meditated a retirement from his post, the pay of which was inadequate to the support of his family, but had postponed it, first, on account of the accusations brought against him in the second Congress, and of which he awaited the investigation; secondly, in consequence of events which rendered the prospect of a continuance of peace precarious. But these reasons no longer operating, he gave notice, that on the last day of the ensuing month of January he should give in his resignation.

Hamilton was succeeded in office by Oliver Wolcott, of Connecticut, a man of judgment and ability, who had served as comptroller, and was familiar with the duties of the office. Knox likewise had given in his resignation at the close of the month of December. "After having served my country nearly twenty years," writes he to Washington, "the greatest portion of which under your immediate auspices, it is with extreme reluctance that I find myself constrained to withdraw from so honorable a station. But the natural and powerful claims of a numerous family will no longer permit me to neglect their essential interests." Knox was succeeded in the war department by Colonel Timothy Pickering, at that time Postmaster-General.

CHAPTER LXXV.

JAY'S TREATY.—PARTY CLAIMS.—DIFFICULTIES WITH FRANCE.—FAREWELL ADDRESS.

Washington had watched the progress of the mission of Mr. Jay to England with an anxious eye. He was aware that he had exposed his popularity to imminent hazard, by making an advance toward a negotiation with that power; but what was of still greater moment with him, he was aware that the peace and happiness of his country were at stake on the result of that mission. It was, moreover, a mission of great delicacy, from the many intricate and difficult points to be discussed, and the various and mutual grounds of complaint to be adjusted. Mr. Jay, in a letter dated August 5th, 1794, had informed him confidentially, that the ministry were prepared to settle the matters in dispute upon just and liberal terms; still, what those terms, which they conceived to be just and liberal, might prove when they came to be closely discussed, no one could prognosticate.

At length, on the 7th of March, 1795, four days after the close of the session of Congress, a treaty arrived which had been negotiated by Mr. Jay, and signed by the ministers of the two nations on the 19th of November, and was sent out for ratification. Washington immediately made the treaty a close study; some of the provisions were perfectly satisfactory; of others, he did not approve; on the whole, believing the advantages to outweigh the objections, and that it was the best treaty attainable, he made up his mind to ratify it, should it be approved by the Senate.

As a system of predetermined hostility to the treaty, however, was already manifested, and efforts were made to awaken popular jealousy concerning it, Washington kept its provisions secret, that the public mind might not be preoccupied on the subject. In the course of a few days, however, enough leaked out to be seized upon by the opposition press to excite public distrust, though not enough to convey a distinct idea of the merits of the instrument.

In the course of this month arrived Mr. Adet, who had been appointed by the French government to succeed Mr. Fauchet as minister to the United States.

The Senate was convened by Washington on the 8th of June, and the treaty of Mr. Jay was laid before it, with its accompanying documents. The session was with closed doors, discussions were long and arduous, and the treaty underwent a scrutinizing examination. The twelfth article met with especial objections.

FROM HOUDON'S BUST.
VOL. IV.

This article provided for a direct trade between the United States and the British West India Islands, in American vessels not exceeding seventy tons burden, conveying the produce of the States or of the Islands; but it prohibited the exportation of molasses, sugar, coffee, cocoa, or cotton, in American vessels, either from the United States or the Islands, to any part of the world. Under this article it was a restricted intercourse, but Mr. Jay considered the admission even of small vessels, to the trade of these islands, an important advantage to the commerce of the United States. He had not sufficiently adverted to the fact that, among the prohibited articles, cotton was also a product of the Southern States. Its cultivation had been but recently introduced there; so that when he sailed for Europe hardly sufficient had been raised for domestic consumption, and at the time of signing the treaty very little, if any, had been exported. Still it was now becoming an important staple of the South, and hence the objection of the Senate to this article of the treaty. On the 24th of June two-thirds of the Senate, the constitutional majority, voted for the ratification of the treaty, stipulating, however, that an article be added suspending so much of the twelfth article as respected the West India trade, and that the President be requested to open, without delay, further negotiation on this head.

In the meantime the popular discontent which had been excited concerning the treaty was daily increasing. The secrecy which had been maintained with regard to its provisions was wrested into a cause of offence. Such was the irritable condition of the public mind when, on the 29th of June, a Senator of the United States (Mr. Mason of Virginia) sent an abstract of the treaty to be published in a leading opposition paper in Philadelphia. The whole country was immediately in a blaze. Beside the opposition party, a portion of the Cabinet was against the ratification. Of course it received but a faltering support, while the attack upon it was vehement and sustained. The assailants seemed determined to carry their point by storm. Meetings to oppose the ratification were held in Boston, New York, Philadelphia, Baltimore, and Charleston. The smaller towns throughout the Union followed their example. In New York a copy of the treaty was burnt before the governor's house. In Philadelphia it was suspended on a pole carried about the streets, and finally burnt in front of the British minister's house, amid the shoutings of the populace. The whole country seemed determined, by prompt and clamorous manifestations of dissatisfaction, to make Washington give way.

He saw their purpose; he was aware of the odious points of view on which the treaty might justly be placed; his own opinion was not particularly favorable to it; but he was convinced that it was better to ratify it, in the manner the Senate had advised, and with the reservation already mentioned, than to suffer matters to remain in their present unsettled and precarious state. Before he could act upon this conviction a new difficulty arose to suspend his resolution. News came that the order of the British government of the 8th of June, 1793, for the seizure of provisions in vessels going to French ports, was renewed. Washington instantly directed that a strong memorial should be drawn up against this order; as it seemed to favor a construction of the treaty which he was determined to resist. While this memorial was in course of preparation, he was called off to Mount Vernon.

The opposition made to the treaty from meetings in different parts of the Union gave him the most serious uneasiness, from the effect it might have on the relations with France and England. His reply (July 28th) to an address from the selectmen of Boston, contains the spirit of his replies to other addresses of the kind: "Without a predilection for my own judgment I have weighed with attention every argument which has at any time been brought into view. But the constitution is the guide which I never can abandon. It has assigned to the President the power of making treaties with the advice and consent of the Senate. It was, doubtless, supposed that these two branches of government would combine, without passion, and with the best means of information, those facts and principles upon which the success of our foreign relations will always depend; that they ought not to substitute for their own conviction the opinions of others, or to seek truth through any channel but that of a temperate and well-informed investigation. Under this persuasion, I have resolved on the manner of executing the duty before me. To the high responsibility of it, I freely submit, and you, gentlemen, are at liberty to make these sentiments known as the grounds of my procedure. While I feel the most lively gratitude for the many instances of approbation from my country, I can no otherwise deserve it than by obeying the dictates of my conscience." Never, during his administration, had he seen a crisis, in his judgment, so pregnant with interesting events, nor one from which, whether viewed on one side or the other, more was to be apprehended. It was a crisis, he said, that most eminently called upon the administration to be wise and temperate, as well as firm. The public clamor continued, and induced a reiterated examination of the subject; but did not shake his purpose.

The difficult and intricate questions pressing upon the attention of government left Washington little mood to enjoy the retirement of Mount Vernon, being constantly in doubt whether his presence in Philadelphia were not necessary. In his letters to Randolph, he requested to be kept continually advised on this head. "I do not require more than a day's notice to repair to the seat of government." His promptness was soon put to the test. Early in August came a mysterious letter, dated July 31, from Mr. Pickering, the secretary of war. "On the subject of the treaty," writes Pickering, "I confess I feel extreme solicitude, and for a *special reason*, which can be communicated to you only in person. I entreat, therefore, that you will return with all convenient speed to the seat of government. In the meanwhile, for the reason above referred to, I pray you to decide on no important political measure, in whatever form it may be presented to you."

The receipt of this enigmatical letter induced Washington to cut short his sojourn at Mount Vernon, and hasten to Philadelphia. He arrived there on the 11th of August; and on the same day received a solution of the mystery. A despatch written by Fauchet, the French minister, to his government in the preceding month of November, was placed in Washington's hands with a translation of it made by Mr. Pickering. The despatch had been found on board of a French privateer, captured by a British frigate, and had been transmitted to the ministry. Lord Grenville, finding it contained passages relating to the intercourse of Mr. Randolph, the American secretary of State, with Mr. Fauchet, had sent it to Mr. Hammond, the British minister in Philadelphia. He had put it into the hands of Mr. Wolcott, the secretary of the treasury, who had shown it to the secretary of war and the attorney-general; and the contents had been considered so extraordinary as to call forth the mysterious letter entreating the prompt return of Washington.

The following passages in Fauchet's intercepted despatch related to the Western insurrection and the proclamation of Washington: "Two or three days before the proclamation was published, and of course before the cabinet had resolved on its measures, the secretary of State came to my house. All his countenance was grief. He requested of me a private conversation. It is all over, he said to me; a civil war is about to ravage our unhappy country. Four men, by their talents, their influence, and their energy, may save it. But debtors of English merchants, they will be deprived of their liberty if they take the smallest step. Could you lend them instantaneously funds to shelter them from English prosecution? This inquiry astonished me much. It was impossible for me to make a satisfactory answer. You know my want of power and deficiency in pecuniary means.... Thus, with some thousands of dollars, the Republic could have decided on civil war or peace. Thus *the consciences of the pretended patriots of America have already their price."*

The perusal of the letter gave Washington deep perplexity and concern. He revolved the matter in his mind in silence. The predominant object of his thoughts recently had been to put a stop to the public agitation on the subject of the treaty; and he postponed any new question of difficulty until decided measures had laid the other at rest. On the next day, therefore, (12th,) he brought before the cabinet the question of immediate ratification. It was finally agreed to ratify the treaty immediately; but to accompany the ratification with a strong memorial against the provision order. The ratification was signed by Washington on the 18th of August.

His conduct towards Randolph, in the interim, had been as usual, but now that the despatch of public business no longer demanded the entire attention of the cabinet, he proceeded to clear up the doubts occasioned by the intercepted despatch. Accordingly, on the following day, as Randolph entered the cabinet, Washington, who was conversing with Pickering and Wolcott, rose and handed to him the letter of Fauchet, asking an explanation of the questionable parts. Randolph appears to have been less agitated by the production of the letter, than hurt that the inquiry concerning it had not first been made of him in private. He postponed making any specific reply until he should have time to examine the letter at his leisure; and observed on retiring, that, after the treatment he had experienced he could not think of remaining in office a moment longer.

In a letter to the President the same day he writes: "Your confidence in me, sir, has been unlimited, and I can truly affirm unabused. My sensations, then, cannot be concealed, when I find that confidence so suddenly withdrawn, without a word or distant hint being previously dropped to me. This, sir, as I mentioned in your room, is a situation in which I cannot hold my present office, and therefore I hereby resign it. It will not, however, be concluded from hence that I mean to relinquish the inquiry. No, sir; very far from it. I will also meet any inquiry; and to prepare for it, if I learn there is a chance of overtaking Mr. Fauchet before he sails, I will go to him immediately. I have to beg the favor of you to permit me to be furnished with a copy of the letter, and I will prepare an answer to it; which I perceive that I cannot do as I wish, merely upon the few hasty memoranda which I took with my pencil....

"I here most solemnly deny that any overture came from me, which was to produce money to me or any others for me; and that in any manner, directly or indirectly, was a shilling ever received by me; nor was it ever contemplated by me, that one shilling should be applied by Mr. Fauchet to any purpose relative to the insurrection."

Washington, in reply, observes: "Whilst you are in pursuit of means to remove the strong suspicions arising from this letter, no disclosure of its contents will be made by me; and I will enjoin the same on the public officers who are acquainted with the purport of it.... No man would rejoice more than I to find that the suspicions which have resulted from the intercepted letter were unequivocally and honorably removed."

Mr. Fauchet, in the meantime, having learnt previous to embarkation, that his despatch had been intercepted, wrote a declaration, denying that Mr. Randolph had ever indicated a willingness to receive money for personal objects, and affirming that he had had no intention to say anything in his letter to his government to the disadvantage of Mr. Randolph's character.

Mr. Randolph now set to work to prepare a pamphlet in explanation of his conduct. While thus occupied he addressed several notes to Washington, requiring information on various points, and received concise answers to all his queries. On one occasion, where he had required a particular paper, he published in the Gazette an extract from his note to Washington; as if fearing the request might be denied, lest the paper in question should lay open many confidential and delicate matters.

In reply, Washington writes: "That you may have no cause to complain of the withholding of any paper, however private and confidential, which you shall think necessary in a case of so serious a nature ... you are at full liberty to publish, without reserve, *any* and *every* private and confidential letter I ever wrote to you; nay more, every word I ever uttered to you or in your hearing, from whence you can derive any advantage in your vindication."

The vindication which Mr. Randolph had been preparing appeared in December. In this, he gave a narrative of the principal events relating to the case, his correspondence with the President, and the whole of the French minister's letter. He endeavored to explain those parts of the letter which had brought the purity of his conduct in question; but, as has been observed, "he had a difficult task to perform, as he was obliged to prove a negative, and to explain vague expressions and insinuations connected with his name in Fauchet's letter."

Fauchet himself furnished the best vindication in his certificate above mentioned; but it is difficult to reconcile his certificate with the language of his official letter to his government. We are rather inclined to attribute to misconceptions and hasty inferences of the French minister, the construction put by him in his letter on the conversation he had held with Mr. Randolph. The latter injured his cause by the embittered feelings manifested in his vindication, and the asperity with which he spoke of Washington there and elsewhere. He deeply regretted it in after life.

After a considerable interval from the resignation of Randolph, Colonel Pickering was transferred to the department of State, and Mr. James McHenry was appointed Secretary of War. The office of attorney-general becoming vacant by the death of Mr. Bradford, was offered to Mr. Charles Lee of Virginia, and accepted by him on the last day of November.

During the late agitations, George Washington Lafayette, the son of the general, had arrived at Boston under the name of Motier, accompanied by his tutor, M. Frestel, and had written to Washington apprising him of his arrival. It was an embarrassing moment to Washington. The letter excited his deepest sensibility, bringing with it recollections of Lafayette's merits, services, and sufferings, and of their past friendship, and he resolved to become "father, friend, protector, and supporter" to his son. But he must proceed with caution; on account of his own official character as Executive of the United States, and of the position of Lafayette in regard to the French government. Caution, also, was necessary, not to endanger the situation of the young man himself, and of his mother and friends whom he had left behind. Philadelphia would not be an advisable residence for him at present, until it was seen what opinions would be excited by his arrival; as Washington would for some time be absent from the seat of government, while all the foreign functionaries were residing there, particularly those of his own nation. Washington suggested, therefore, that he should enter for the present as a student at the University in Cambridge, Massachusetts, and engaged to pay all the expenses for the residence there of himself and his tutor. It was subsequently thought best that young Lafayette should proceed to New York, and remain in retirement, at the country house of a friend in its vicinity, pursuing his studies with his tutor, until Washington should direct otherwise.

In his speech at the opening of the session of Congress in December, Washington presented a cheerful summary of the events of the year. First he announced that a treaty had been concluded provisionally by General Wayne, with the Indians north-west of the Ohio, by which the termination of the long, expensive, and distressing war with those tribes was placed at the option of the United States.

A letter from the Emperor of Morocco, recognizing a treaty which had been made with his deceased father, insured the continuance of peace with that power.

The terms of a treaty with the Dey and regency of Algiers had been adjusted in a manner to authorize the expectation of a speedy peace in that quarter, and the liberation of a number of American citizens from a long and grievous captivity.

A speedy and satisfactory conclusion was anticipated of a negotiation with the court of Madrid, "which would lay the foundation of lasting harmony with a power whose friendship," said Washington, "we have uniformly and sincerely desired to cherish."

Adverting to the treaty with Great Britain and its conditional ratification, the result on the part of his Britannic Majesty was yet unknown, but when ascertained, would immediately be placed before Congress.

"In regard to internal affairs, every part of the Union gave indications of rapid and various improvement. With burthens so light as scarcely to be perceived; with resources fully adequate to present exigencies; with governments founded on the genuine principles of rational liberty; and with mild and wholesome laws, was it too much to say that our country exhibited a spectacle of national happiness never surpassed, if ever before equalled?"

There was, as usual, a cordial answer from the Senate; but, in the present House of Representatives, as in the last one, the opposition were in the majority. In the response reported by a committee, one clause expressing undiminished confidence in the chief magistrate was demurred to; some members affirmed that, with them, it had been considerably diminished by a late transaction. After a warm altercation, to avoid a direct vote, the response was recommitted, and the clause objected to modified. The following is the form adopted: "In contemplating that spectacle of national happiness which our country exhibits, and of which you, sir, have been pleased to make an interesting summary, permit us to acknowledge and declare the very great share which your zealous and faithful services have contributed to it, and to express the affectionate attachment which we feel for your character."

In February the treaty with Great Britain, as modified by the advice of the Senate, came back ratified by the king of Great Britain, and on the last of the month a proclamation was issued by the President, declaring it to be the supreme law of the land.

The opposition in the House of Representatives were offended that Washington should issue this proclamation before the sense of that body had been taken on the subject, and denied the power of the President and Senate to complete a treaty without its sanction. They were bent on defeating it by refusing to pass the laws necessary to carry it into effect; and, as a preliminary, passed a resolution requesting the President to lay before the House the instruction to Mr. Jay, and the correspondence and other documents relative to the treaty.

Washington, believing that these papers could not be constitutionally demanded, resolved, he said, from the first moment, and from the fullest conviction of his mind, to *resist the principle,* which was evidently intended to be established by the call of the House; he only deliberated on the manner in which this could be done with the least bad consequences. After mature deliberation and with the assistance of the heads of departments and the Attorney-General, he prepared and sent in to the House an answer to their request. In this he dwelt upon the necessity of caution and secrecy in foreign negotiations, as one cogent reason for vesting the power of making treaties in the President, with the advice and consent of the Senate, the principle on which that body was formed, confining it to a small number of members. To admit a right in the House of Representatives to demand and have all the papers respecting a foreign negotiation would, he observed, be to establish a dangerous precedent.

After various further remarks, he concludes: "As, therefore, it is perfectly clear to my understanding that the assent of the House of Representatives is not necessary to the validity of a treaty; as the treaty with Great Britain exhibits itself in all the objects requiring legislative provision; and on these, the papers called for can throw no light; and as it is essential to the due administration of the government that the boundaries fixed by the constitution between the different departments should be observed, a just regard to the constitution and to the duty of my office, under all the circumstances of this case, forbid a compliance with your request."

A resolution to make provision for carrying the treaty into effect, gave rise to an animated and protracted debate. Meanwhile, the whole country became agitated on the subject; meetings were held throughout the United States, and it soon became apparent that the popular feeling was with the minority in the House of Representatives, who favored the making of the necessary appropriations. The public will prevailed, and, on the last day of April, the resolution was passed, though by a close vote of fifty-one to forty-eight.

For some months past, Mr. Thomas Pinckney had been solicitous to be relieved from his post of minister-plenipotentiary at London, but the doubtful issue of the above dispute, and the difficulty of finding a fit substitute for him, had caused delay in the matter. Such a man at length presented in Mr. Rufus King, of New York. Mr. King was nominated to the Senate on the 19th of May, and his nomination was confirmed. On the 1st of June this session of Congress terminated.

Shortly after the recess of Congress another change was made in the foreign diplomacy. Mr. Monroe, when sent envoy to France, had been especially instructed to explain the views and conduct of the United States in forming the treaty with England; and had been amply furnished with documents for the purpose. From his own letters, however, it appeared that he had omitted to use them. Whether this rose from undue attachment to France, from mistaken notions of American interests, or from real dislike to the treaty, the result was the very evil he had been instructed to prevent. The French government misconceived the views and conduct of the United States, suspected their policy in regard to Great Britain, and when aware that the House of Representatives would execute the treaty made by Jay, became bitter in their resentment. Symptoms of this appeared in the capture of an American merchantman by a French privateer. Under these circumstances it was deemed expedient by Washington and his cabinet to recall Mr. Monroe, and appoint another American citizen in his stead. The person chosen was Charles Cotesworth Pinckney of South Carolina, elder brother of the late minister to London.

The period for the presidential election was drawing near, and great anxiety began to be felt that Washington would consent to stand for a third term. No one, it was agreed, had greater claim to the enjoyment of retirement, in consideration of public services rendered; but it was thought the affairs of the country would be in a very precarious condition should he retire before the wars of Europe were brought to a close.

Washington, however, had made up his mind irrevocably on the subject, and resolved to announce, in a farewell address, his intention of retiring. Such an instrument, it will be recollected, had been prepared for him from his own notes, by Mr. Madison, when he had thought of retiring at the end of his first term. As he was no longer in confidential intimacy with Mr. Madison, he turned to Mr. Hamilton as his adviser and coadjutor, and appears to have consulted him on the subject early in the present year.

We forbear to go into the vexed question concerning this address; how much of it is founded on Washington's original "notes and heads of topics;" how much was elaborated by Madison, and how much is due to Hamilton's recasting and revision. The whole came under the supervision of Washington; and the instrument, as submitted to the press, was in his handwriting, with many ultimate corrections and alterations. Washington had no pride of authorship; his object always was to effect the purpose in hand, and for that he occasionally invoked assistance, to ensure a plain and clear exposition of his thoughts and intentions. The address certainly breathes his spirit throughout, is in perfect accordance with his words and actions. It was published in September, in a Philadelphia paper called the Daily Advertiser.

Congress formed a quorum on the 5th day of December, the first day of the session which succeeded the publication of the Farewell Address. On the 7th, Washington met the two Houses of Congress for the last time. In his speech he recommended an institution for the improvement of agriculture, a military academy, a national university, and a gradual increase of the navy. The disputes with France were made the subject of the following remarks: "While in our external relations some serious inconveniences and embarrassments have been overcome and others lessened, it is with much pain and deep regret I mention that circumstances of a very unwelcome nature have lately occurred. Our trade has suffered and is suffering extensive injuries in the West Indies from the cruisers and agents of the French Republic; and communications have been received from its minister here, which indicate the danger of a further disturbance of our commerce by its authority, and which are in other respects far from agreeable. It has been my constant, sincere, and earnest wish, in conformity with that of our nation, to maintain cordial harmony and a perfectly friendly understanding with that Republic."

In concluding his address he observes: "The situation in which I now stand for the last time in the midst of the representatives of the people of the United States, naturally recalls the period when the administration of the present form of government commenced, and I cannot omit the occasion to congratulate you and my country on the success of the experiment, nor to repeat my fervent supplications to the Supreme Ruler of the universe and Sovereign Arbiter of nations, that his providential care may be still extended to the United States; that the virtue and happiness of the people may be preserved, and that the government which they have instituted for the protection of their liberties may be perpetual."

The Senate, in their reply to the address, after concurring in its views of the national prosperity, as resulting from the excellence of the constitutional system and the wisdom of the legislative provisions, added, that they would be deficient in gratitude and justice did they not attribute a great portion of these advantages to the virtue, firmness and talents of his administration, conspicuously displayed in the most trying times, and on the most critical occasions. The reply of the House, after premising attention to the various subjects recommended to their consideration in the address, concluded by a warm expression of gratitude and admiration, inspired by the virtues and services of the President, by his wisdom, firmness, moderation and magnanimity; and testifying to the deep regret with which they contemplated his intended retirement from office.

The reverence and affection expressed for him in both Houses of Congress, and their regret at his intended retirement, were in unison with testimonials from various State legislatures and other public bodies, which were continually arriving since the publication of his Farewell Address.

During the actual session of Congress, Washington endeavored to prevent the misunderstandings, which were in danger of being augmented, between the United States and the French Government. In the preceding month of November, Mr. Adet, the French minister, had addressed a letter to the Secretary of State, recapitulating the complaints against the government of the United States made by his predecessors and himself, denouncing the *insidious* proclamation of neutrality and the wrongs growing out of it, and using language calculated to inflame the partisans of France; a copy of which letter had been sent to the press for publication. One of the immediate objects he had in view in timing the publication was supposed by Washington to be to produce an effect on the presidential election; his ultimate object, to establish such an influence in the country as to sway the government and control its measures. Early in January, 1797, therefore, Washington requested Mr. Pickering, the Secretary of State, to address a letter to Mr. Pinckney, United States minister to France, stating all the complaints alleged by the French minister against the government, examining and reviewing the same, and accompanying the statement with a collection of letters and papers relating to the transaction therein adverted to. The letter to Mr. Pinckney, with its accompanying documents, was laid before Congress on the 19th of January, (1797), to be transmitted to that minister.

In the month of February the votes taken at the recent election were opened and counted in Congress; when Mr. Adams, having the highest number, was declared President, and Mr. Jefferson, having the next number, Vice-President; their term of four years to commence on the 4th of March next ensuing.

Washington now began to count the days and hours that intervened between him and his retirement. On the day preceding it, he writes to his old fellow-soldier and political coadjutor, Henry Knox: "To the wearied traveller, who sees a resting place, and is bending his body to lean thereon, I now compare myself.... The remainder of my life, which in the course of nature cannot be long, will be occupied in rural amusements; and though I shall seclude myself as much as possible from the noisy and bustling world, none would, more than myself, be regaled by the company of those I esteem, at Mount Vernon, more than twenty miles from which, after I arrive there, it is not likely that I shall ever be."

On the 3d of March, he gave a kind of farewell dinner to the foreign ministers and their wives, Mr. and Mrs. Adams, Mr. Jefferson, and other conspicuous personages of both sexes. "During the dinner much hilarity prevailed," says Bishop White, who was present. When the cloth was removed Washington filled his glass: "Ladies and gentlemen," said he, "this is the last time I shall drink your health as a public man; I do it with sincerity, wishing you all possible happiness." The gayety of the company was checked in an instant; all felt the importance of this leave-taking.

On the 4th of March, an immense crowd had gathered about Congress Hall. At eleven o'clock, Mr. Jefferson took the oath as Vice-President in the presence of the Senate; and proceeded with that body to the Chamber of the House of Representatives, which was densely crowded, many ladies occupying chairs ceded to them by members. After a time, Washington entered amidst enthusiastic cheers and acclamations, and the waving of handkerchiefs.

At the close of the ceremony, as Washington moved toward the door to retire, there was a rush from the gallery to the corridor that threatened the loss of life or limb, so eager were the throng to catch a last look of one who had so long been the object of public veneration. When Washington was in the street he waved his hat in return for the cheers of the multitude, his countenance radiant with benignity, his gray hairs streaming in the wind. The crowd followed him to his door; there, turning round, his countenance assumed a grave and almost melancholy expression, his eyes were bathed in tears, his emotions were too great for utterance, and only by gestures could he indicate his thanks and convey his farewell blessing.

In the evening a splendid banquet was given to him by the principal inhabitants of Philadelphia in the Amphitheatre, which was decorated with emblematical paintings. All the heads of departments, the foreign ministers, several officers of the late army, and various persons of note, were present. Among the paintings, one represented the home of his heart, the home to which he was about to hasten—Mount Vernon.

CHAPTER LXXVI.

WASHINGTON'S RETIREMENT AND DEATH.

[The limitations of this volume render it necessary to condense the remaining portions of Washington's biography into as few sentences as possible.

Washington's official career being terminated, he set off for Mount Vernon accompanied by Mrs. Washington, her grand-daughter, Miss Nelly Custis, and George Washington Lafayette, with his preceptor. Once more at Mount Vernon, that haven of repose to which he had so often turned a wistful eye, he surrendered himself to those agricultural and rural pursuits for which he had a fondness. He was beset with many visitors, and as a relief from some of the duties of hospitality he persuaded his nephew, Lawrence Lewis, to become an inmate of Mount Vernon. An attachment grew up between young Lewis and Miss Nelly Custis, which eventuated in their union.

The fate of Lafayette, who had been thrown into prison at Olmutz, had awakened the earnest solicitude of Washington, but in the autumn of this year (1797), letters were received by young Lafayette that his father had been released and was on his way to Paris. George Lafayette, anxious to join his father's family, immediately sailed from New York with his tutor, on the 26th of October.

The differences between France and America were now assuming an alarming aspect. The French government, in the recall of Mr. Monroe, had refused to receive his successor. In view of this fact, and of the capture of American vessels by French cruisers, President Adams convened an extra session of Congress on the 15th of May. Three special envoys to France were appointed by Mr. Adams, who, it was hoped, would be able to adjust all differences by a treaty between the two powers. Their mission was unsuccessful. The Directory now believing that the PEOPLE of America would not sustain their government in a war against France, enacted a law subjecting to capture and condemnation neutral vessels and their cargoes, if any portion of the latter was of British production, although the entire property belonged to neutrals. As the United States were at this time the great neutral carriers, this decree struck at a vital point in their maritime power. When this act became known the spirit of the nation was aroused, and war with France seemed inevitable. The government resolved on vigorous measures; the President was authorized to enlist ten thousand men, and the Senate nominated Washington commander-in-chief of all the armies raised or to be raised. The Secretary of War bore the commission to Washington in person, who accepted the commission with great reluctance, with the condition that he should not be called into the field until the army was in a situation to require his presence. Hamilton, Pinckney, and Knox were appointed major-generals. Knox, indignant at being placed below those who were his juniors in the war of the Revolution, refused to serve.

These military measures soon had their effect on French policy. President Adams received intimations that whatever plenipotentiary the United States might send to France to put an end to the existing differences between the two countries, would be received with the respect due to the representative of a free, independent, and powerful nation. Mr. Adams, glad to escape from his belligerent difficulties, laid these facts before the Senate on the 18th of February, (1799), and nominated Mr. Murray as envoy. Oliver Ellsworth and Mr. Davie were ultimately associated with him in the mission. They sailed on the 3d of the following November.]

Washington continued to superintend from a distance the concerns of the army, as his ample and minute correspondence manifests; and he was at the same time earnestly endeavoring to bring the affairs of his rural domain into order. It was a period of incessant activity and toil, therefore, both mental and bodily. He was for hours in his study occupied with his pen, and for hours on horseback, riding the rounds of his extensive estate, visiting the various farms, and superintending the works in operation. All this he did with unfailing vigor, though now in his sixty-seventh year.

Winter had now set in, with occasional wind and rain and frost, yet Washington still kept up his active round of in-door and out-door avocations, as his diary records. He was in full health and vigor, dined out occasionally, and had frequent guests at Mount Vernon. For some time past he had been occupied in digesting a complete system on which his estate was to be managed for several succeeding years; specifying the cultivation of the several farms, with tables designating the rotations of the crops. It occupied thirty folio pages, and was executed with that clearness and method which characterized all his business papers. This was finished on the 10th of December, and was accompanied by a letter of that date to his manager or steward.

According to his diary, the morning on which these voluminous instructions to his steward were dated was clear and calm, but the afternoon was lowering. The next day (11th), he notes that there was wind and rain, and "at night *a large circle round the moon.*" The morning of the 12th was overcast. About ten o'clock he mounted his horse, and rode out as usual to make the rounds of the estate. The ominous ring round the moon, which he had observed on the preceding night, proved a fatal portent. "About one o'clock," he notes, "it began to snow, soon after to hail, and then turned to a settled cold rain." Having on an overcoat, he continued his ride without regarding the weather, and did not return to the house until after three. His secretary approached him with letters to be franked, that they might be taken to the post-office in the evening. Washington franked the letters, but observed that the weather was too bad to send a servant out with them. Mr. Lear perceived that snow was hanging from his hair, and expressed fears that he had got wet; but he replied, "No, his great coat had kept him dry." As dinner had been waiting for him he sat down to table without changing his dress. "In the evening," writes his secretary, "he appeared as well as usual."

On the following morning the snow was three inches deep and still falling, which prevented him from taking his usual ride. He complained of a sore throat, and had evidently taken cold the day before. In the afternoon the weather cleared up, and he went out on the grounds between the house and the river, to mark some trees which were to be cut down. A hoarseness which had hung about him through the day grew worse towards night, but he made light of it. He was very cheerful in the evening, as he sat in the parlor with Mrs. Washington and Mr. Lear, amusing himself with the papers which had been brought from the post-office.

On retiring to bed, Mr. Lear suggested that he should take something to relieve the cold. "No," replied he, "you know I never take anything for a cold. Let it go as it came." In the night he was taken extremely ill with ague and difficulty of breathing. Between two and three o'clock in the morning he awoke Mrs. Washington, who would have risen to call a servant; but he would not permit her, lest she should take cold. At daybreak, when the servant woman entered to make a fire, she was sent to call Mr. Lear. He found the general breathing with difficulty, and hardly able to utter a word intelligibly. Washington desired that Dr. Craik, who lived in Alexandria, should be sent for, and that in the meantime, Rawlins, one of the overseers, should be summoned to bleed him before the doctor could arrive.

A gargle was prepared for his throat, but whenever he attempted to swallow any of it, he was convulsed and almost suffocated. Rawlins made his appearance soon after sunrise, but when the general's arm was ready for the operation became agitated. "Don't be afraid," said the general, as well as he could speak. Rawlins made an incision. "The orifice is not large enough," said Washington. The blood, however, ran pretty freely, and Mrs. Washington, uncertain whether the treatment was proper, and fearful that too much blood might be taken, begged Mr. Lear to stop it. When he was about to untie the string the general put up his hand to prevent him, and as soon as he could speak, murmured, "more—more;" but Mrs. Washington's doubts prevailed, and the bleeding was stopped, after about half a pint of blood had been taken. External applications were now made to the throat, and his feet were bathed in warm water, but without affording any relief. His old friend, Dr. Craik, arrived between eight and nine, and two other physicians, Drs. Dick and Brown, were called in. Various remedies were tried, and additional bleeding, but all of no avail.

"About half-past four o'clock," writes Mr. Lear, "he desired me to call Mrs. Washington to his bedside, when he requested her to go down into his room and take from his desk two wills, which she would find there, and bring them to him, which she did. Upon looking at them, he gave her one, which he observed was useless, as being superseded by the other, and desired her to burn it, which she did, and took the other and put it into her closet."

In the course of the afternoon he appeared to be in great pain and distress from the difficulty of breathing, and frequently changed his posture in the bed. About five o'clock his old friend, Dr. Craik, came again into the room, and approached the bedside. "Doctor," said the general, "I die hard, but I am not afraid to go. I believed, from my first attack, that I should not survive it—my breath cannot last long." The doctor pressed his hand in silence, retired from the bedside, and sat by the fire absorbed in grief.

Between five and six the other physicians came in, and he was assisted to sit up in his bed. "I feel I am going," said he; "I thank you for your attentions, but I pray you to take no more trouble about me; let me go off quietly; I cannot last long." He lay down again; all retired excepting Dr. Craik. The general continued uneasy and restless, but without complaining, frequently asking what hour it was. Further remedies were tried without avail in the evening. He took whatever was offered him, did as he was desired by the physicians, and never uttered sigh or complaint.

"About ten minutes before he expired (which was between ten and eleven o'clock)," Mr. Lear further writes, "his breathing became easier. He lay quietly; he withdrew his hand from mine and felt his own pulse. I saw his countenance change. I spoke to Dr. Craik, who sat by the fire. He came to the bedside. The general's hand fell from his wrist. I took it in mine and pressed it to my bosom. Dr. Craik put his hands over his eyes, and he expired without a struggle or a sigh."

We add from Mr. Lear's account a few particulars concerning the funeral. The old family vault on the estate had been opened, the rubbish cleared away, and a door made to close the entrance, which before had been closed with brick. The funeral took place on the 18th of December. About eleven o'clock the people of the neighborhood began to assemble. The corporation of Alexandria, with the militia and Freemasons of the place, and eleven pieces of cannon, arrived at a later hour. A schooner was stationed off Mount Vernon to fire minute guns. About three o'clock the procession began to move, passing out through the gate at the left wing of the house, proceeding round in front of the lawn and down to the vault, on the right wing of the house; minute guns being fired at the time. The troops, horse and foot, formed the escort; then came four of the clergy; then the general's horse, with his saddle, holsters, and pistols, led by two grooms in black. The body was borne by the Freemasons and officers; several members of the family and old friends, among the number Dr. Craik, and some of the Fairfaxes, followed as chief mourners. The corporation of Alexandria and numerous private persons closed the procession. The Rev. Mr. Davis read the funeral service at the vault, and pronounced a short address; after which the Masons performed their ceremonies, and the body was deposited in the vault.

On opening the will which he had handed to Mrs. Washington shortly before his death, it was found to have been carefully drawn up by himself in the preceding July; and by an act in conformity with his whole career, one of its first provisions directed the emancipation of his slaves on the decease of his wife. It had long been his earnest wish that the slaves held by him *in his own right* should receive their freedom during his life, but he had found that it would be attended with insuperable difficulties on account of their intermixture by marriage with the "dower negroes," whom it was not in his power to manumit under the tenure by which they were held. With provident benignity he also made provision in his will for such as were to receive their freedom under this devise, but who, from age, bodily infirmities, or infancy, might be unable to support themselves, and he expressly forbade, under any pretence whatsoever, the sale or transportation out of Virginia of any slave of whom he might die possessed.

A deep sorrow spread over the nation on hearing that Washington was no more. Congress, which was in session, immediately adjourned for the day. The next morning it was resolved that the Speaker's chair be shrouded with black: that the members and officers of the House wear black during the session, and that a joint committee of both Houses be appointed to consider on the most suitable manner of doing honor to the memory of the man, "first in war, first in peace, and first in the hearts of his fellow-citizens."

Public testimonials of grief and reverence were displayed in every part of the Union. Nor were these sentiments confined to the United States. When the news of Washington's death reached England, Lord Bridport, who had command of a British fleet of nearly sixty sail of the line, lying at Torbay, lowered his flag half-mast, every ship following the example; and Bonaparte, First Consul of France, on announcing his death to the army, ordered that black crape should be suspended from all the standards and flags throughout the public service for ten days.

The character of Washington may want some of those poetical elements which dazzle and delight the multitude, but it possessed fewer inequalities, and a rarer union of virtues than perhaps ever fell to the lot of one man. Prudence, firmness, sagacity, moderation, an overruling judgment, an immovable justice, courage that never faltered, patience that never wearied, truth that disdained all artifice, magnanimity without alloy. It seems as if Providence had endowed him in a preëminent degree with the qualities requisite to fit him for the high destiny he was called upon to fulfil—to conduct a momentous revolution which was to form an era in the history of the world, and to inaugurate a new and untried government, which, to use his own words, was to lay the foundation "for the enjoyment of much purer civil liberty, and greater public happiness, than have hitherto been the portion of mankind."

The fame of Washington stands apart from every other in history; shining with a truer lustre and a more benignant glory. With us his memory remains a national property, where all sympathies throughout our widely-extended and diversified empire meet in unison. Under all dissensions and amid all the storms of party, his precepts and example speak to us from the grave with a paternal appeal; and his name—by all revered—forms a universal tie of brotherhood—a watchword of our Union.

THE END.

Lector House believes that a society develops through a two-fold approach of continuous learning and adaptation, which is derived from the study of classic literary works spread across the historic timeline of literature records. Therefore, we aim at reviving, repairing and redeveloping all those inaccessible or damaged but historically as well as culturally important literature across subjects so that the future generations may have an opportunity to study and learn from past works to embark upon a journey of creating a better future.

This book is a result of an effort made by Lector House towards making a contribution to the preservation and repair of original ancient works which might hold historical significance to the approach of continuous learning across subjects.

HAPPY READING & LEARNING!

LECTOR HOUSE LLP
E-MAIL: lectorpublishing@gmail.com

www.ingramcontent.com/pod-product-compliance
Lightning Source LLC
LaVergne TN
LVHW091520170726
843492LV00004B/1000